GERMAN U-BOAT
COMMANDERS
OF WORLD WAR II

GERMAN U-BOAT COMMANDERS OF WORLD WAR II

A Biographical Dictionary

Rainer Busch & Hans-Joachim Röll

Translated by Geoffrey Brooks

GREENHILL BOOKS, LONDON
NAVAL INSTITUTE PRESS, ANNAPOLIS, MARYLAND

This edition of
German U-Boat Commanders of World War II
first published 1999 by Greenhill Books, Lionel Leventhal Limited,
Park House, 1 Russell Gardens, London NW11 9NN

Published and distributed in the United States of America by
the Naval Institute Press, 118 Maryland Avenue, Annapolis,
Maryland 21402-5035

The first edition of this work was published by Verlag E. S. Mittler & Sohn
GmbH, 32052 Herford, Germany, under the title
Die Deutschen U-Boot-Kommandanten (1996)
Copyright © Verlag E. S. Mittler & Sohn GmbH, Hamburg, Berlin, Bonn

English-language edition copyright © Lionel Leventhal Limited, 1999

All rights reserved. No part of this publication may be reproduced, stored in a
retrieval system or transmitted in any form or by any means, electronic,
mechanical or otherwise, without the written permission of the Publisher.

British Library Cataloguing-in-Publication Data
Busch, Rainer
German U-boat Commanders of World War II: a biographical dictionary
1.Submarine captains – German – Biography 2.World War, 1939–1945 –
Naval operations, German
I.Title II.Röll, Hans-Joachim
359.9'33'092243

Greenhill ISBN 1-85367-366-8

Library of Congress Cataloging-in-Publication Data available

Naval Institute Press ISBN 1-55750-186-6

Edited and designed by Roger Chesneau

Printed and bound in Singapore

Contents

Foreword *by Jürgen Rohwer*	7
Preface	9
Translator's Note	11
German Naval Ranks	17
German U-Boat Commanders	**19**
Index	283

Foreword

For many years, at his *Traditionsarchiv U-boote* in Cuxhaven-Altenbruch, Horst Bredow has dedicated himself to the work of collating and scientifically analysing every imaginable scrap of information about the Second World War German U-boat arm. Countless domestic and overseas visitors have made use of the Archive, and many books about the U-boat war in a variety of languages could not have been written had the Archive not existed.

Two of his young assistants, the authors of the present work, have now addressed the task of making the archive material available to a much wider readership by means of books which will effectively update many earlier publications.

As the Archive has always placed special emphasis on determining the composition of U-boat crews, it is fitting that this volume should deal with personnel, being the potted career biographies of the 1,411 known German U-boat commanders of the period 1935–1945.

We are indebted to the U-Boat Archive and the two authors for this unique work of reference, which will undoubtedly be the stimulus for continuing research.

More than 50 years after the end of the Second World War, the U-Boat Archive continues to receive fresh information almost every day. Exchange of information regarding U-boats and the support of the U-Boat Archive is the objective of the FTU e.V (*Freundeskreis Traditionsarchiv Unterseeboote*). Readers interested in becoming members of the Society are invited to apply to: FTU e.V., Bahnhofstrasse 57, 27478 Cuxhaven-Altenbruch, Germany.

Professor Dr Jürgen Rohwer
Committee Member
International Commission for Military History

Preface

Although members of the younger generation, we have long been involved in the compilation of the history of the Second World War German U-boat arm, and it gives us pleasure to present in this volume the results of our endeavours. The book is not merely a list of people, for every military commander's biography also involves those with whom he served as well as his former wartime enemies.

Our work is based on various publications such as *Die Deutsche Kriegsmarine, 1939–45: Gliederung-Einsatz-Stellenbesetzung* (Walter Lohmann and Hans H. Hildebrand, 1956), while we also had unrestricted access to all the sources at the U-Boat Archive at Cuxhaven-Altenbruch. For his support and commitment to our task we wish to place on record our heartfelt thanks to the Archive's founder and director, Herr Horst Bredow.

Many missing details were filled in as a result of enquiries made of surviving commanders and crew members: for their efforts and patience, which we much appreciate, our thanks are due. We are also indebted to Professor Jürgen Rohwer, who gave us the benefit of his advice throughout the compilation of this work. Furthermore, the information could not have been put together without the help of workers at *Die Deutsche Dienststelle für die Benachrichtigung der nächsten Angehörigen von Gefallenen der ehemaligen Wehrmacht* (German Office for the Notification to the Next of Kin of Wehrmacht War Dead, or WASt).

Despite all our efforts, however, there will always be a number of gaps in a research topic of this nature, and some matters of detail may still yet come to light. An example of this problem was the difficulty we experienced in verifying the commanders of U-boats in commission prior to the outbreak of war. The boats involved were the Type IIA and IIB submarines numbered *U 1* to *U 24* inclusive, which were divided into four groups. In 1937 *U 1* to *U 6* inclusive formed the U-boat School Flotilla and the Training Group of the U-boat school. The 1st U-Flotilla, *Weddigen*, was composed of seven boats, namely *U 9* and the six odd-numbered vessels *U 13* to *U 23* inclusive. The 3rd U-Flotilla, *Lohs*, consisted of the seven even-numbered boats *U 10* to *U 22* inclusive. The remaining four submarines were in reserve, *U 7* and *U 11* for *Weddigen* and *U 8* and *U 24* for *Lohs*. These had no assigned commanders, for during the scheduled shipyard lay-up of a flotilla boat, the commander concerned would take command of a reserve boat for a special purpose, usually the sea trials for a new technical development. This resulted in such a rapid turnover of commanders on the reserve boats that it has proved impossible to put together anything like a full list.

To any reader who wishes to assist, we are grateful for further information. Finally, we express our thanks to the staff of the German publishers Koehler/Mittler for their friendly cooperation and understanding.

Rainer Busch and Hans-Joachim Röll

Translator's Note

This is a biographical dictionary of the 1,411 officers of the German Kriegsmarine known to have commanded a U-boat between 28 June 1935, when *U 1* was commissioned with due ceremony at Kiel by Klaus Ewerth [262], and August 1945, when Heinz Schäffer [1062] finally decided to surrender *U 977* to Argentina.

Sources of Information

The basis for the biographies is described by the authors in their Preface, as amended by reference to each individual officer's personal service file, indicated '(per P/F)' where appropriate in the text. Two other primary documents exist which may tend to confirm or contradict the information contained in the personal file: '(per WASt)', indicating the source as the file maintained by WASt (*Deutsche Dienststelle für die Benachrichtigung der nächsten Angehörigen von Gefallenen der ehemaligen Wehrmacht*); and '(per U— WD)', indicating an entry made by a commander in the *Kriegstagebuch* (War Diary) of the particular U-boat of which he had command at that time. Sources of secondary information are statements made to the U-Boat Archive, Cuxhaven, or appearing in published material by former U-boat commanders or personnel.

The Biographies

Heading: Each biography is headed by the subject's full name, with titles (if any), followed by an identification number for ease of reference. German alphabetical order has been retained in the translation (i.e., the modified vowels ä, ö and ü assume the position that would be occupied by ae, oe and ue respectively).

First two lines: The first line contains (i) the date and place of birth; the second line contains (i) the date of full entry into naval service and (ii) the highest rank attained by the officer during the period covered in this book, together with the date when conferred with retroactivity (if any).

In the second line, the designation 'Class' (the German term is *Crew* or *Jahrgang*) signifies original entry into the German Navy as an officer cadet of the Seaman Branch. Outside the emergency period, there was one intake each year on 1 April. However, once the political situation dictated the accelerated recruitment of officers, the number of courses each year proliferated, so that IX/1939 (for example) means Course IX of 1939, and not September. An officer commencing his career in the Seaman Branch could of course transfer into another branch of the Navy later, but initial entry into an ancillary branch, such as Coastal Artillery, Ordnance or Medical, is classified in the biography as an 'Entry'.

A surprising number of U-boat commanders had come through the ranks. An entry into the German Navy has been treated as an enlistment between 1919 and 1939 but as a conscription in 1939 and subsequently. The original work is not always clear on the point, and long before 1939 any fit young man would have done at least compulsory RAD service, which was basically pre-military training followed by periods of training with one of the armed forces. A rating in the German mercantile marine or fishing fleet conscripted into the Kriegsmarine would usually commence his service in an equivalent rank.

'(R)' following the rank indicates a reservist, and the date is that of his induction into full naval service.

'(zV)'—*zur Verwendung*—following the rank indicates a voluntary element in the contract of service, e.g. an officer serving beyond the normal retirement age.

TRANSLATOR'S NOTE

'(S)'—*Sonderführer*—following the rank indicates a temporary or honorary assimilation into the Kriegsmarine for special purposes. This would include mercantile marine officers requisitioned aboard warships in the role of Prize Officers; officers, including sea personnel, of the *Trossschiffsverband*, the organisation controlling fleet oilers and supply ships; and scientists, including meteorologists, aboard naval vessels. These personnel wore a naval uniform with silver braid, buttons and trimmings instead of the normal gold and because of this were known as *Silberlinge*.

German naval ranks, together with the abbreviations employed in this dictionary, are shown in the accompanying table. They were not precisely equivalent to the ranks in the Royal Navy or US Navy.

Career Details

Officer training for the sea cadet began with a three-month period of basic infantry training on the island of Dänholm near Stralsund. This shore establishment was known as *S.St.ABt* (*Schiffsstammabteilung* = Basic Training Establishment for Sea Personnel). Recruits to the Coastal Artillery branch underwent basic training at *Mar.St.Abt* (*Marinestammabteilung* = Basic Training Establishment for Navy Personnel), their depot being the Army Induction Centre at Munsterlager.

Before the war the sea cadet spent a considerable period afloat aboard one of the three auxiliary sail training barques, *Albert Leo Schlageter*, *Horst Wessel* or *Gorch Fock*, or the two former pre-dreadnought battleships *Schlesien* and *Schleswig-Holstein*, all of which made distant cruises 'showing the flag'. (During the war, sea experience was gained from a wider range of fighting vessels. Fifty sea cadets were aboard the heavy cruiser *Admiral Scheer* on her six-month raiding voyage to the South Atlantic and Indian Ocean in 1940–41 but the practice of sea training aboard operational U-boats was discontinued once losses began to increase dramatically in 1943.) The midshipman then returned to shore and completed his training at the Naval College, Flensburg-Mürwik, after which he would receive his commission and first appointment. In wartime, the period between entry and the award of the commission was necessarily more brief.

Kriegsmarine Basic Command Structure

OKM (*Oberkommando der Marine*) was the Naval High Command.

SKL (*Seekriegsleitung*) was the Directorate of the Naval War.

BdU (*Befehlshaber der U-boote*), personified by Admiral Dönitz, was the C-in-C of the U-boat arm in the Second World War.

FdU (*Führer der U-boote*) had been the C-in-C U-boats in the First World War and until 1939, when the title was reduced to that of a Regional Commander.

Appointment to the Luftwaffe (See)

Some idea of the infrastructure and varied deployment of naval air arm personnel can be gauged from Paul Just's [569] book *Vom Seeflieger zum U-bootfahrer*. Following his basic military training at Dänholm, Just was compulsorily listed for the *Seeluftwaffe*. After a long training voyage to South America aboard the *Schlesien*, he completed his period as midshipman at Mürwik and was posted to the Aircraft Weapons School at Rügen in October 1938. At the outbreak of war he made a number light bombing raids against Polish positions on the Hela peninsula as navigator/bomb-aimer with a coastal reconnaissance group, *Küstenaufklärungsgruppe 1./306*, flying He 60 floatplanes. In October 1939 he spent a period in He 59 floatplanes on anti-contraband operations against neutral shipping in the Baltic, and the following month on anti-submarine patrols from Rügen with the He 60. In December 1939 the group was based at Kiel-Holtenau and made long-range reconnaissance flights over the North Sea in antiquated He 111J bombers from airfields at Hamburg-Uetersen and Oldenburg-Jever/Varrelbusch, and later from Stavanger, Norway.

After several months' conversion training to the Ju 88 bomber, in July 1940 Just was transferred to a coastal group at Nantes, *Küstenfliegergruppe 806*, which flew anti-shipping patrols alongside *Stukageschwader 3*. They came under the umbrella of *Luftflotte 3*, and because Kriegsmarine personnel remained on an associated basis with the Luftwaffe, this meant that they were the only troops in the Wehrmacht responsible to two commanders-in-chief. Luftwaffe uniform was worn except when walking out, when naval dress was required. Naval ranks were always retained. From Nantes the group made four or five anti-shipping flights weekly to St George's Channel, Bristol Docks and the Irish Sea. This was known as 'armed reconnaissance', the purpose of being to disrupt seaborne traffic by dive-bombing freighters and ports.

In August 1940 the Group was absorbed further under Luftwaffe direction when it received orders to begin high-level night bombing raids against British inland cities, continuing to use the Ju 88. By day, formation flying was practised for Operation 'Sealion'. After a shift of airfield to Caen in the wake of the setback in September 1940, single-bomber night-time nuisance raids on London were instituted. On 15 November 1940 nearly all bomber aircraft in Luftflotte 3, including the naval air group, were committed to the attack on Coventry. Other cities bombed by the Group were Liverpool, Birmingham, Bristol and Southampton. On 31 December 1940, when Just was ordered to report to the U-boat arm, he had flown 162 operational missions and held the German Cross in Gold.

In the biographies, Luftwaffe designations have generally been retained as the reader is more likely to recognise them in the original German. Shipboard aircraft crews were drawn from *Bordfliegerstaffeln*. The *Fliegerführer Atlantik* was the Biscay-based Luftwaffe AOC Atlantic flying anti-shipping and reconnaissance mainly with the FW 200 four-engine bomber and less commonly with other aircraft types. There were Fliegerführer for other sea areas.

Sea-going Appointments (non U-boat)

Prior to 1942, the majority of naval officers emerging from the training schools were appointed to the surface navy.

Larger units of torpedo-boat size and above need no explanation except, by way of observation, that the three cruisers of the *Deutschland* class were originally designated *Panzerschiffe* (armoured ships), for which there is no British equivalent. Under the 1922 Washington Agreement they were battleships according to their armament and cruisers according to their displacement, and were later assigned *Schwerer Kreuzer* (heavy cruiser) status by the Kriegsmarine. They have been classed in this dictionary as heavy cruisers throughout. The popular British term 'pocket battleship' has not been employed.

A 'raider' here means a requisitioned merchant ship fitted out with a heavy concealed armament and sent out on long oceanic voyages masquerading as a freighter.

An 'E-boat' means a motor torpedo boat (*Schnellboot*). These very fast, diesel-powered craft were deployed throughout hostilities in the mine-laying and anti-shipping roles in the North Sea, Baltic, English Channel and Mediterranean.

Escort Flotillas (*Sicherungsflotillen*) were to be found at every U-boat base. They comprised mainly *Sperrbrecher*, M-boats and R-boats. The role of the minesweeper was a very important factor in U-boat operations since enemy aircraft and submarines regularly laid mines at the port approaches. *Sperrbrecher* were requisitioned merchant ships packed with barrels and cork to make them virtually unsinkable, bristling with a heavy flak armament and equipped with asdic and remote mine detonation equipment.

R-boats (*Räumboote*) were small motor minesweepers.

M-boats (*Minensuchboote*) were large, purpose-built, often coal-fired minesweepers.

VP-boats (*Vorpostenboote*) were usually converted distant-water steam trawlers or patrol vessels constructed to a fishing vessel design and labelled KFK (*Küstenfischkutter*). They were employed in coastal escort work of all kinds and had anti-submarine and minesweeping gear fitted.

UJ-boats (*U-bootjäger*) were usually steam trawlers specially equipped for anti-submarine operations.

Minesweeping and minelaying techniques were taught at the Mine Warfare School (*Sperrschule*) situated at Kiel-Wik, adjacent to the first lock of the Kiel Canal.

The *K-Verband* (*Kleinkampfverband*) was a specialist independent arm of the Kriegsmarine. One and two-man submarines, manned torpedoes and frogmen (*Kampfschwimmer*) came under its umbrella.

A WO (*Wachoffizier*) was a person of any rank, including a rating, qualified to lead a watch.

Appointment to the U-boat Arm

All persons passed fit for U-boats were required to volunteer for them, and accordingly the U-boat arm was not strictly speaking composed entirely of volunteers. At the beginning of the war Dönitz set up a number of *U-Stamm Kompanien* (U-Holding Companies), which were personnel reserves of trained U-boat men without a boat and volunteers to the U-boat arm from other branches of the Kriegsmarine. The idea was to establish a clear separation of control and prevent 'poaching' and other forms of interference by the surface navy.

A U-boat WO (*Wachoffizier*) was a person of any rank qualified to lead one of the three shipboard watches. 1WO and 2WO indicate the watchkeeping officers of a U-boat in seniority: 3WO, at least on Type VII and Type IX boats, was normally the coxswain, the most senior NCO aboard, who also did the chartwork.

When a U-boat officer was selected for training as a commander, he was required to go through a training course which lasted in the order of three months. First he learned submarine handling at a UAA (*U-Fahrausbildungslehrgang*) establishment or ULD (*U-Lehrdivision* = U-boat Training Division), and at some time during this period he would receive training in the techniques of torpedo attack on a *Kommandanten-Schiesslehrgang* (U-Commanders' Torpedo Course). After the officer had qualified, a period of sea training usually ensued aboard an operational U-boat. KKpt Fritz Wentzel said of this in his book *Single or Return?* (William Kimber, 1954): 'When they had finished their special training, would-be U-boat commanders like myself were sent out as "apprentices" with an experienced U-boat commander in order to get to know the ropes and perhaps see a bit of action before being entrusted with their own boats . . . on such cruises we weren't "real U-boat men" to the crews and they didn't take us very seriously.'

The next step was usually the award of a boat about to be built, and for this the officer was known as the *Baubelehrung* Commander. *Baubelehrung* can be broadly translated as 'boat familiarisation', but the term embraced a grander philosophy. The concept was that all crew-members from the commander to the most junior rating should be present at the construction of the boat from the keel-laying onwards, so that each man knew not only every nook and cranny and the source and destination of every piece of wiring and piping but was also familiar with the tasks of all other crewmen. In this way crew and boat were welded together into a homogeneous unit greater than the sum of all its parts, mechanical and human. A KLA (*Kriegsschiffbaulehrabteilung*) was a warship construction training division under the auspices of which a *Baubelehrung* was supervised.

Once completed, the U-boat was commissioned into the German Navy by the commander, with due ceremony, and if not already in the Baltic proceeded there for handling trials under the supervision of the Technische Ausbildungsgruppe für Front U-boote (AGRU-Front, or Technical Training Group for Front-Line U-boats). Tactical convoy-attack exercises followed, and once these had been successfully concluded the boat would be declared *frontreif*—fit to sail on her first operational mission.

I am indebted to Herr Wolfgang Hirschfeld, former Oberfunkmeister of *U 234*, for his kind advice and assistance with regard to much of the foregoing.

Decorations

Decorations at the level of the Knight's Cross of the Iron Cross and above are listed, giving the date of the award and its position chronologically *vis-à-vis* previous Kriegsmarine (KM) and U-boat arm recipients. In the case of the Oak Leaves, Swords and Diamonds, an additional indication is made as regards Wehrmacht (WM) recipients as a whole.

Captivity

A distinction has been made between the status of Prisoner-of-War (POW), where the officer was captured by the enemy under the normal rules of warfare prior to 9 May 45, and Detention, i.e. arbitrary arrest and custody for political investigation subsequent to the capitulation, although there was no difference in the treatment. According to KKpt Wentzel, after the cessation of hostilities German officers were interrogated and placed in four categories. Group A contained known anti-Nazis such as Topp [1280] and those who had succeeded in deceiving the interrogators in the matter. Group B contained 'hopefuls' (from the standpoint of their mentors) and Group C the 'not altogether hopeless' cases. The men in Group C+ were, at least outwardly, the really determined Nazis who gave the Hitler salute on entering and leaving the interrogation office and regarding whom all hope for reform had been abandoned. However, as Wentzel recorded, there were quite a number of those classified 'C+' who were not fanatical Nazis in the least but chose this method of demonstrating their resentment of the re-education process.

Some Allied educational officers referred to the U-boat arm as the 'blue SS' and put all U-boat men into Group C or C+ on principle. Wentzel was aggrieved to be categorised as Group C when Kretschmer [663] and most of his friends were classified as C+, because this stigmatised him as a 'namby-pamby'. Thus the process tended to be counter-productive: some officers might be more interested in being downgraded for the sake of face. The rescreening process took place regularly, normally at six-month intervals. The 'carrot and stick' system was employed, since an officer's Group determined the privileges to which he was entitled. On the whole, however, the length of time spent in detention is not necessarily an indication of what the officer's political loyalties were at any particular time.

Curiosities

Kiesewetter [603], at age 62, was the oldest and von Friedeburg [321], at age 20, the youngest officer to command a Second World War U-boat in commission. Radermacher [963] served aboard *U 5* in all grades from seaman to commander. Peters [916] was in command of a U-boat in commission on every day of the war from first to last. And within the same fortnight of 1944, Ballert [34] and Ballert [35] had their commands, *U 1196* and *U 1166* respectively, seriously damaged and decommissioned as the result of a defective torpedo exploding. From recent Argentinian publications it would seem that the officers of *Admiral Graf Spee* were given the option of returning to Germany to resume naval service or continuing the war as 'militant internees' in South America, a term of rather wide implications. Half returned within a year and a large number of these eventually gravitated to the U-boat arm.

Geoffrey Brooks

German Naval Ranks

The following abbreviations of rank have been employed:

Non-Commissioned Officers

ObBtsMt	Oberbootsmannsmaat (Boatswain's Mate)
StrmMt	Steuermannsmaat (Helmsman's Mate)
ObBtsm	Oberbootsmann (Boatswain)
Strm	Steuermann (Helmsman)
ObStrm	Obersteuermann (Warrant Officer II Coxswain)
StabsObStrm	Stabsobersteuermann (Warrant Officer I Coxswain)

Midshipmen

FzS	Fähnrich zur See (Midshipman)
OFzS	Oberfähnrich zur See (Senior Midshipman)

Commissioned Officers

LtzS	Leutnant zur See
ObltzS	Oberleutnant zur See
Kplt	Kapitänleutnant
KKpt	Korvettenkapitän
FKpt	Fregattenkapitän
KptzS	Kapitän zur See (full Captain)
KAdm	Konteradmiral (Rear-Admiral)
VAdm	Vizeadmiral (Vice-Admiral)
Adm	Admiral
GenAdm	Generaladmiral
GrAdm	Grossadmiral (Grand Admiral)

Note: German naval ranks were not precisely equivalent to those of either the Royal Navy or US Navy.

A

ABEL, ULRICH, DR (LAW) [1]
b. 3.3.1912, Leipzig
Entry 1939; ObltzS (R) date not known
WO 17th Minesweeping Flotilla 7/39–9/40; M/S-Cdr 15th Minesweeping Flotilla 9/40–7/42; U-boat trg 8/42–1/43; 1WO *U 154* 1/43–1/44; U-Cdr's Course, 23rd and 27th U-Flotillas 1/44–3/44
Cdr *U 193* 1.4.44–28.4.44
Lost 28.4.1944 Biscay, west of Nantes

ACHILLES, ALBRECHT [2]
b. 25.1.1914, Karlsruhe
Class 1934; KKapt 1.10.1943 posthumously
Signals Officer battleship *Gneisenau* 2/39–3/39; Midshipmen's Trg Officer battleship *Gneisenau* 4/39–4/40; U-boat trg 4/40–11/40; *Baubelehrung*, U-Boats North Sea, 11/40–1/41; 1WO *U 66* 1/41–11/41; U-Cdr's Course, 24th U-Flotilla 11/41–12/41; 2nd U-Flotilla 21.12.41–31.12.41
Cdr *U 161* 1.1.42 (per P/F) to 27.9.43
Lost 12.9.43 off Bahia, Brazil
Knight's Cross 16.1.43 (144th KM, 76th U-boat holder)

ACKERMANN, PAUL [3]
b. 16.9.1920, Mustamaki, Viborg, Denmark
Class XII/1939; ObltzS 1.12.43
Officer and U-boat trg 12/39–2/42; *Baubelehrung* KLA for U-Boats North 2/42–3/42; 2WO *U 177* 3/42–11/43; Course 3.ULD 12/43–1/44 (U-Cdr's Torpedo Course 61)
Cdr *U 1221* 20.1.44–3.4.45
Personnel Reserve 33rd U-Flotilla 4/45 to capitulation

ACKERMANN, WOLF [4]
b. 8.3.1921, Heideck, Bavaria
Class 1939a; ObltzS 1.10.43
Officer and U-boat trg 9/39–9/41; *Baubelehrung* 10/41–11/41; 2WO *U 509* 11/41–12/42; 1WO *U 509* 12/42–5/43; U-Cdr's Course, 2UAA and 24th U-Flotilla 5/43–7/43 (U-Cdr's Torpedo Course 49); *Baubelehrung* 8th KLA 7/43–9/43
Cdr *U 994* 2.9.43–31.3.44
5th U-Flotilla 4/44–7/44; Personnel Officer, Flag Lt and II. Situational Reporting Officer, Staff, Commanding Adm. U-Boats 7/44–capitulation
Detained; freed 25.7.45

ADY, GERHARD [5]
b. 5.9.1923, Reideberg, Halle
Class X/1940; ObltzS 1.10.44
Officer and U-boat trg, inc. WO sea trg *U 652* 10/40–12/42; WO 24th U-Flotilla 12/42–3/43; *Baubelehrung* 8.KLA 3/43–4/43; 2WO *U 672* 4/43–2/44; U-Cdr's Course, 23rd U-Flotilla 3/44–4/44
Cdr *U 704* 4/44–7/44
Cdr *U 677* 17.07.44–5.4.45
31st U-Flotilla 4/45–capitulation

VON AHLEFELD, HUNOLD [6]
b. 2.4.1923, Linz, Rhineland
Class X/1940; ObltzS 1.10.44
Officer and U-boat trg 10/40–8/41; WO sea trg *U 455* 8/41–4/42; (supernumerary) WO *U 94*, 5/42–6/42; trg and courses 7/42–1/43; *Baubelehrung* 1/43–3/43; 1WO *U 967* 3/43–3/44; U-Cdr's Trg Course, 3.ULD and 23rd U-Flotilla 3/44–5/44; tactical trg 27th U-Flotilla 5/44–7/44

Cdr *U 150* 16.7.44–21.12.44

Baubelehrung Cdr Type XXIII boat *U 4714* from 12/44 (never commissioned; scuttled by the commander at Kiel 3.5.45)

AHLERS, KURT [7]

b. 31.7.1922, Lüneburg

Class XII/1939; ObltzS 1.12.43

Officer and U-boat trg and *Baubelehrung* 12/39–5/42, inc. WO sea trg *U 562* 1941; (supernumerary) WO *U 301* 5/42–9/42; 1WO *U 301* 10/42–12/42; 2WO *U 566* 12/42–3/43; 1WO *U 566* 4/43–10/43; 1st U-Flotilla 10/43–11/43; U-Cdr's Course, 3.ULD and 24th U-Flotilla 12/43–1/44 (U-Cdr's Torpedo Course 61)

Cdr *U 10* 2/44–1.7.44

Cdr *U 1201* 2.7.44–13.10.44

Details not available for 10/44–3/45 but probably under instruction for Type XXI boat

Additional Cdr *U 3512* 24.3.45–8.4.45 under Hornkohl [515]

Additional Cdr *U 3041* 27.4.45–capitulation under Hornkohl

ALBRECHT, FRITZ [8]

b. 10.5.1920, Magdeburg

Class 1937b; ObltzS 1.4.42

Light cruiser *Königsberg* 12/39–4/40; VP-Cdr, Coastal Defence Group, Norwegian West Coast, 4/40–12/41; U-boat trg 1/42–8/42; 1WO *U 43* 9/42–3/43; U-Cdr's Course and *Baubelehrung* 3/43–5/43 (U-Cdr's Torpedo Course 45)

Cdr *U 386* 10.6.43–19.2.44

POW 19.2.44

ALBRECHT, KARL [9]

b. 21.4.1904, Essen

Enlisted 1923; ObltzS 1.4.43

Strm *U 19* from 1/36; Strm *U 62* 12/39–1/40; Obstrm *U 9* 1/40–3/40; Obstrm U-depot ship *Weichsel* 4/40–6/40; UAA, Plön, 6/40–7/40; Platoon Cdr 1.ULD 7/40–10/41; *Baubelehrung* 10/41–11/41; Obstrm *U 214* 11/41–8/42; courses and *Baubelehrung* 9/42–6/43 (U-Cdr's Torpedo Course 46)

Cdr *U 1062* 19.6.43–30.9.44

Lost 30.9.44 Central Atlantic, SW Cape Verde Is

ALDEGARMANN, WOLFGANG [10]

b. 24.6.1916, Hamelin

Class 1939; ObltzS 1.9.43

Courses and trg 9/39–4/40; WO 18th Minesweeping Flotilla 4/40–11/42; 1WO 28th Minesweeping Flotilla 11/42–1/43; U-boat trg 1/43–7/43; U-Cdr's Course, 27th and 24th U-Flotillas and *Baubelehrung* 7/43–11/43 (U-Cdr's Torpedo Course 54)

Cdr *U 297* 17.11.43–6.12.44

Lost 6.12.44 Pentland Firth

ALTMEIER, FRIEDRICH [11]

b. 16.7.1920, Mettlach, Saar

Class 1938; ObltzS 1.4.43

Officer trg, trg ship *Schlesien* 6/39–10/39; light cruiser *Nürnberg* 5/40–10/40; U-boat trg 10/40–3/41; *Baubelehrung* 3/41–4/41; 2WO *U 80* 4/41–12/41; 2WO *U 508* 12/41–1/43; 1WO *U 508* 2/43–9/43; U-Cdr's Course and *Baubelehrung* 10/43–12/43 (U-Cdr's Torpedo Course 57)

Cdr *U 1227* 8.12.43–10.4.45

Cdr *U 155* 21.4.45–capitulation

Detained; freed 3.3.47

AMBROSIUS, WILHELM [12]

b. 14.6.1903, Tuchel, West Prussia

Class 1926; FKpt 1.6.44

U-Cdr's Course, U-Boat School Kiel, completed 30.4.36; U-Cdr, U-Flotilla *Saltzwedel* from 1.5.36, inc. Cdr *U 28* 12.9.36–1.11.38 and Cdr *U 21* (1937); attached U-Flotilla *Hundius*, later U-Cdr U-Flotilla *Hundius* until 3.1.39 (per rank

listings 1.11.38), also acting CO U-Flotilla *Hundius* 6.8.38–31.7.39; *Baubelehrung* 1.8.39–25.8.39
Cdr *U 43* 26.8.39–20.10.40
Cdr 1. Section/2.ULD 10/40–6/43, inc. CO 22nd U-Flotilla 1/41–1/44 and acting (caretaker) Cdr 2.ULD 12/43–2/44; CO 2nd Minesweeping Flotilla 2/44–8/44; Cdr at Mine Warfare School 10/44–2/45; Leader 11th Escort Division 3/45–capitulation
Detained; freed 8.12.48

ANDERSEN, KLAUS [13]
b. 19.10.1918, Wilhelmshaven
Class 1937b; Kplt 1.1.45
Destroyer *Z 2 Georg Thiele* 12/39–4/40; Comp. Cdr Naval Regiment *Berger* 4/40–7/40; Naval Planning Staff, Operation 'Sealion' 7/40–11/40; Flag Lt, Staff 2/Adm. of the Fleet, 12/40–5/41; Flag Lt, Staff, Fleet Command, 6/41–1/42; U-boat trg 1/42–7/42; 1WO *U 81* 7/42–4/43; U-Cdr's Trg Course 4/43–6/43 (U-Cdr's Torpedo Course 46)
Cdr *U 708* 6/43–29.2.44
Cdr *U 481* 1.3.44–capitulation (1WO Herbert Bischoff was acting Cdr *U 481*, voyage Danzig–Königsberg, 28.12.44)
Detained; freed 11/47

ANGERMANN, WALTER [14]
b. 22.1.1923, Gelnhausen, Hesse
Class X/1940; ObltzS 1.10.44
Officer trg, U-boat trg and *Baubelehrung* 10/40–10/42; 2WO *U 272* 10/42–11/42; 2WO *U 618* 2/43–9/43; 1WO *U 618* 9/43–1/44; U-Cdr's Trg Course 1/44–3/44; *Baubelehrung* Type XXIII 4/44–7/44
Cdr *U 2323* 18.7.44–26.7.44
Cdr *U 2334* 21.9.44–capitulation
Detained; freed 1.4.47

ANSCHÜTZ, HANS-HELMUT [15]
b. 27.6.1923, Erfurt
Class 1941; ObltzS 1.1.45
U-boat trg 10/42–6/43; WO sea trg *U 427* 6/43–7/43; 2WO *U 586* 8/43–2/44; 29th U-Flotilla 3/44–8/44; course 8/44–11/44; Cdr U-Holding Company 24 11/44–12/44
Cdr *U 150*, 22.12.44–31.3.45
Duties to capitulation not known

VON ARCO, GRAF FERDINAND [16]
b. 6.6.1921, Gotschdorf, Jägerndorf, Sudetenland
Class 1/1941; ObltzS 1.1.45
Officer trg, U-boat trg and *Baubelehrung* 1/41–6/43; WO *U 346* 6/43–7/43; 2WO *U 617* 7/43–9/43; interned Africa 9/43–4/44; repatriated 4/44
Cdr *U 151* 1.9.44–2.5.45

VON UND ZU ARCO-ZINNEBERG, GRAF ULRICH-PHILIPP [17]
b. 12.12.1917, Schloss Maxlrain, Bad Aibling, Bavaria
Class X/1939; ObltzS 1.10.43
Light cruiser *Emden* 7/39–10/39; duties not recorded 11/39–8/40 and 12/40–1/41; torpedo-boat *T 12*, 9/40–11/40; U-boat trg, WO sea trg and WO 2/41–3/42; WO *U 117* 3/42–5/43; U-Cdr's Trg Course 6/43–7/43 (U-Cdr's Torpedo Course 49); *Baubelehrung* 7/43
Cdr *U 922* 1.8.43–2.11.43
Cdr *U 29* 3.11.43–17.4.44
Cdr *U A* 18.4.44–15.3.45
Comp. Cdr 1.UAA 3/45–capitulation

ARENDT, RUDOLF [18]
b. 25.1.1923, Ballenstedt, Thüringen
Class 1940; ObltzS 1.5.44
U-boat trg 1/42–8/42; Platoon Cdr 1.UAA 8/42–1/43; 1WO *U 18* 1/43–12/43; U-Cdr's Course 11/43–3/44; 1WO *U 18*, 3/44–5/44

Acting Cdr *U 18*, 25.5.44–7.6.44
Cdr *U 23* 20.6.44–10.9.44
Interned in Turkey 10.9.44

ATZINGER, SIEGFRIED [19]

b. 22.10.1916, Amberg, Bavaria
Class 1936; Kplt 1.7.43
Heavy cruiser *Admiral Scheer* 12/38–2/40; sail trg ship *Albert Leo Schlageter* 2/40–4/40; U-boat trg 4/40–9/40; 1WO *U 61* 9/40–10/40; UAA, Plön and *Baubelehrung* 10/40–1/41; 1WO *U 72* 1/41–4/41; 2WO *U 48* 4/41–7/41; 1WO *U 48* 7/41–8/41
Cdr *U 48* 8/41–9/42
A former crew member informed the U-Boat Archive that on 12 September 1942 the commander of *U 262*, Schiebusch [1082], was admitted to sick-bay and relieved by Atzinger. The boat then set out on patrol from Bergen on 24 September, allegedly under Atzinger's command, but put back into Bergen on the 28th having been bombed and damaged by Hudson aircraft 'A' and 'D' of No 48 Squadron RAF on the 26th. However, the *U 262* War Diary makes no mention of Atzinger and only records a substitution for Schiebusch on 26 October 1942 by Franke [308]. This appears to be supported by WASt and Franke's personal file, which both show him in command for two days, 19 and 20 October 1942. Probably Atzinger was acting commander for only a brief period
U-Cdr 3rd and 5th U-Flotillas 9/42–1/43; Group Trg Officer 2.UAA 1/43–7/43; Kplt, Staff (21st U-Flotilla), 8/43–3/45 (25th U-Flotilla), 3/45–capitulation

AUFFERMANN, HANS-JÜRGEN [20]

b. 1.10.1914, Göttingen
Class 1934; Kplt 1.9.41
U-boat trg 1/41–3/41; 1WO *U 69* 4/41–10/41, also acting Cdr *U 69* 24.8.41–28.8.41 (assumed temporary command on 24.8.41 when Metzler [816] fell ill; the mission was abandoned and the boat put into St Nazaire on 27.8.41); U-Cdr's Course and *Baubelehrung* 6.KLA 11/41–1/42
Cdr *U 514* 24.1.42–8.7.43
Lost 8.7.43 Bay of Biscay, NE Cape Finisterre

AUFFHAMMER, LEONHARD [21]

b. 9.6.1917 Kulmbach, Bavaria
Class 1936; ObltzS 1.10.40
Light cruiser *Nürnberg* 2/39–3/40; 1/NCO Trg Div 3/40–1/41; U-boat trg 1/41–5/41; *Baubelehrung* 5/41–7/41; 1WO *U 86* 7/41–4/42; U-Cdr's Course and *Baubelehrung* 4/42–6/42
Cdr *U 265* 6.6.42–3.2.43
Lost 3.2.43 North Atlantic, S of Iceland

AUGUSTIN, HANS-ECKART [22]

b. 7.1.24 Vluyn, Rhine Valley
Class V/1941; ObltzS 1.4.45
2WO *U 255* 10/43–7/44; 1WO *U 255*, 7/44–8/44; UAA 8/44–9/44; U-Cdr's Course, 23rd U-Flotilla 9/44–10/44
Cdr *U 62* 1.11.44–20.3.45
UAA 3/45–capitulation

AUST, EDUARD [23]

b. 11.8.1920, Stolp, Pomerania
Class 1939; ObltzS 1.10.43
1WO *U 613* 3/42–4/43; U-Cdr's Course, 24th U-Flotilla 4/43–6/43
Cdr *U 34* 12.6.43–5.8.43
Cdr *U 29* 21.8.43–2.11.43
Cdr *U 922* 3.11.43–20.10.44
Cdr *U 679* 21.10.44–9.1.45
Missing 9.1.45 Baltic Sea, off Baltisch Port

B

BABERG, KURT [24]
b. 23.2.1917, Duisburg-Ruhrort
Class 1936; Kplt 1.9.43
Platoon Officer and sailing instructor, 10/Basic Trg Est. Stralsund, 4/39–8/39; U-Flotilla *Weddigen* 9/39–11/39; 2WO *U A* 11/39–3/41; U-Cdr's Torpedo Course, 24th U-Flotilla 3/41–4/41
Cdr *U 30* 23.4.41–9.3.42
Baubelehrung 8.KLA 3/42–4/42
Cdr *U 618* 16.4.42–15.4.44 (U-Boat Archive per Baberg)
Torpedo attack and tactical instructor 25th and 26th U-Flotillas 5/44–4/45
Cdr *U 827* 26.4.45–5.5.45
Detained; freed 3.12.45

BACH, HELMUT [25]
b. 5.12.1906, Helfda, Mansfelder Seekreis, Saxony-Anhalt
Entry IX/39; Kplt (R) 1.4.45
Merchant raider *Pinguin* 2/40–5/41; VP-Cdr 16th VP-Boat Flotilla 6/41–3/43; U-boat trg 3/43–10/43; U-Cdr's Course and *Baubelehrung* 8.KLA 10/43–2/44
Cdr *U 681* from 3.2.44 until either 2.8.44 (per WD *U 681*, and see Gebauer [341]) or 7.8.44 (per WASt)
Staff Officer FdU/Trg 8/44–capitulation

BACH, JOACHIM-WERNER [26]
b. 7.8.1918, Dresden
Class 1937b; ObltzS 1.6.43
WO 1st Torpedo-Boat Flotilla 12/39–3/41; WO 2nd Torpedo-Boat Flotilla 4/41–8/41; Platoon Leader 1/NCO Trg Div 8/41–4/42; WO heavy cruiser *Admiral Scheer* 4/42–7/42; WO destroyer *Z 15 Erich Steinbrinck* 7/42–5/43; U-boat trg 5/43–1/44; U-Cdr under instrn 2/44–6/44 (U-Cdr's Torpedo Course 65); 1.UAA 6/44–8/44; *Baubelehrung* 8/44–9/44
Cdr *U 1110* 24.9.44–capitulation

BADE, HANS-BOTHO [27]
b. 15.11.1909, Hamburg-Blankenese
Entry X/1939; LtzS (R) 1.7.41
2WO *U 69* 1/41–2/42; courses and *Baubelehrung* 2/42–6/42
Cdr *U 626* 11.6.42–15.12.42
Lost 15.12.42 central North Atlantic

BADEN, HANS-HEINRICH [28]
b. 30.4.1915, Bremen
Entry 1938; ObltzS (R) 1.4.43
2WO *U 558* 4/41–3/42; courses and 1st U-Flotilla 3/42–6/42; 1WO *U 558* 6/42–10/42; U-Cdr's Course and *Baubelehrung* 8.KLA 11/42–12/42
Cdr *U 955* 31.12.42–7.6.44
Lost 7.6.44 Bay of Biscay N of Cape Ortegal

BAHN, ROLF [29]
b. 6.3.1918, Rüstringen
Class 1936; Kplt 1.8.43
Light cruiser *Emden* 11/39–10/40; U-boat trg 10/40–3/41; *Baubelehrung* 4/41–5/41; 2WO *U 128* 5/41–9/42; Instructor 2.ULD 9/42–10/43; Course, Naval Warfare Academy, 11/43–3/44; *Baubelehrung* Cdr *U 1235* 3/44–4/44 and *U 876* 4/44–5/44
Cdr *U 876* 24.5.44–5.5.45

BAHR, RUDOLF [30]
b. 1.4.1916, Landsberg, Warthe, Mark Brandenburg
Class 1935; Kplt 1.10.42
Heavy cruiser *Prinz Eugen* 8/40–6/41; U-boat trg 7/41–10/41; 1WO *U 69* 10/41–6/42; U-Cdr's Course, 24th U-Flotilla and *Baubelehrung* 3.KLA 7/42–9/42
Cdr *U 305* 17.9.42–17.1.44
Lost 17.1.44 SW of Ireland

BALDUHN, ERNST-LUDWIG [31]
b. 27.10.1919, Rodmannshöfen, East Prussia
Class 1938; ObltzS 1.4.43
Heavy cruiser *Prinz Eugen* 11/40–7/42; U-boat trg 7/42–12/42; 1WO *U 211* 12/42–8/43; U-Cdr's Course, 24th U-Flotilla 8/43–10/43 (U-Cdr's Torpedo Course 54)
Cdr *U 1163* 6.10.43–capitulation

BALDUS, HUGO [32]
b. 12.4.1921, Hohenbudberg, Lower Rhine
Class 1939a; ObltzS 1.10.43
2WO and 1WO torpedo-boat *Löwe* 6/41–6/43; U-boat trg 6/43–1/44; U-Cdr sea trg *U 618* 2/44–4/44
Cdr *U 773* 18.4.44–capitulation
Detained; freed 3/47

BALKE, DIETHELM [33]
b. 22.9.1919, place not recorded
Class 1937b; Kplt 1.1.45
Light cruiser *Leipzig* 11/39–1/40; Torpedo Trg Flotilla 1/40–3/40; trg and courses 4/40–10/40; bomber pilot *Kampfgruppe 606 (See)* 11/40–3/41; long-range reconaissance pilot *3./Fernaufklärergruppe 123* 4/41–7/41; Trg Officer *KG 6* 7/41–3/42; U-boat trg 3/42–9/42; 2WO *U 134* 9/42–2/43; 1WO *U 134* 2/43–5/43; U-Cdr's Course and *Baubelehrung* 8.KLA 5/43–7/43 (U-Cdr's Torpedo Course 48)
Cdr *U 991* 29.7.43–capitulation

BALLERT, RENÉ [34]
b. 3.3.1920, Tilsit
Class XII/1939; ObltzS 1.12.43
Officer and U-boat trg 2/40–2/42; *Baubelehrung* 3/42–4/42; 2WO *U 518* 4/42–5/43; 1WO *U 518* 5/43–12/43; 3.ULD 12/43–1/44; U-Cdr's Course 24th U-Flotilla 1/44–2/44 (U-Cdr's Torpedo Course 63)
Cdr *U 1196* 2/44–3.5.45 (*U 1196* was decommissioned following a torpedo explosion in August 1944)

BALLERT, SARTO [35]
b. 21.4.1917, St Petersburg, Russia
Class X/1937; Kplt 1.1.45
Officer trg and courses 3/39–5/40; WO 13th Minesweeping Flotilla 5/40–6/41; 1WO 8th Minesweeping Flotilla 6/41–1/43; U-boat trg 1/43–11/43 (U-Cdr's Torpedo Course 57); (supplementary) WO *U 198* 11/43–12/43; WO *U 758* 12/43–4/44
Cdr *U 1166* 4/44–28.8.44 (*U 1166* was seriously damaged by a torpedo explosion at Eckernförde on 28.7.44, towed to Kiel and decommissioned there 28.8.44)
Courses and *Baubelehrung* Type XXI, 7.KLA, 8/44–1/45
Cdr *U 3520* from 12.1.45 (commissioning date of *U 3520* per U-Boat Archive, Aschmoneit List) to 31.1.45
Lost 31.1.45 Baltic Sea NE of Bülk

BALTZ, RUDOLF [36]
b. 2.7.1920, Berlin-Charlottenburg
Class 1938; ObltzS 1.4.43
Officer trg and courses 7/39–10/40; U-boat trg 11/40–3/41; Divisional Officer 24th U-Flotilla 3/41–11/41; *Baubelehrung* 11/41–1/42; 1WO

U 603 1/42–3/43; U-Cdr's Course, 24th U-Flotilla 4/43–5/43 (U-Cdr's Torpedo Course 45)
Cdr *U 603* 3.5.43–28.1.44
Platoon Officer 1.ULD 3/44–4/45; ULD Neustadt 2/45–4/45; U-boat base Bergen 4/45–capitulation; detained, freed 5.8.45

BARBER, BRUNO [37]
b. 6.3.1904, Deichhausen, Delmenhors
Rating (R) entry 1922; ObltzS (R) 1.2.42
Obstrm WO *U 57* 12/38–5/40; *Baubelehrung* 6/40–7/40; Obstrm WO *U 93* 7/40–10/41
Cdr *U 58* 10/41–31.8.42
Seconded BdU and *Baubelehrung* 9/42–3/43
Cdr *U 220* 27.3.43–28.10.43
Lost 28.10.43 central North Atlantic

BARGSTEN, KLAUS [38]
b. 31.10.1911, Bad Oldesloe
Class 1936; Kplt 1.8.42
U-boat trg 4/39–8/39; WO *U 6* 8/39–10/39; Platoon Leader, U-Boat School, Neustadt, 10/39–11/39; ADC U-School Flotilla 11/39–1/40; ADC U-Boat School, Neustadt, 1/40–3/40; *Baubelehrung* U-Boats East 3/40–4/40; 1WO *U 99* 4/40–1/41; U-Cdr's Torpedo Course, 24th U-Flotilla 1/41–2/41; *Baubelehrung U 563* 2/41–3/41
Cdr *U 563* 27.3.41 until either 31.3.42 (per P/F) or 15.3.42 (per *U 563* WD; see von Hartmann [426])
Baubelehrung 8.KLA 4/42–6/42
Cdr *U 521* 3.6.42–2.6.43
POW 2.6.43–30.11.46
Knight's Cross 30.4.43 (164th KM, 93rd U-boat holder)

BARLEBEN, CURT [39]
b. 28.3.1909, Oldenburg
Entry 1935; Kplt (R) date not known
VP-Cdr 12th VP-Boat Flotilla 9/39–4/40; VP-Cdr 11th VP-Boat Flotilla 4/40–9/41; VP-Cdr 12th VP-Boat Flotilla 9/41; U-boat trg 9/41–3/42; 1WO *U 553* 3/42–7/42; U-Cdr's Course, 24th U-Flotilla and *Baubelehrung* 7/42–9/42
Cdr *U 271* 23.9.42–28.1.44
Lost 28.1.44 W of Limerick, Ireland

BARSCH, FRANZ [40]
b. 30.11.1911, Berlin
Enlisted 1930; Kplt 1.12.44
Obstrm heavy cruiser *Admiral Scheer* 2/39–5/41; trg, courses and *Baubelehrung* 5/41–8/41; variously Div. Officer 26th U-Flotilla and Cdr Torpedo Retrieval Boat No 1 8/41–7/43; U-boat trg and U-Cdr's Course 7/43–3/44 (U-Cdr's Torpedo Course 65); *Baubelehrung* 4/44–5/44
Cdr *U 1235* 17.5.44–15.4.45
Lost 15.4.45 central North Atlantic

BARSCHKIS, HANS-HEINRICH [41]
b. 8.4.1920, Lübeck
Class XII/1939; ObltzS 1.12.43
Officer trg and WO sea trg *U 46* 12/39–3/42; 1WO *U 72* 3/42–12/42; *Baubelehrung* 12/42–1/43; 1WO *U 421* 1/43–1/44; U-Cdr's Course 1/44–3/44 (U-Cdr's Torpedo Course 65); *Baubelehrung* Type XXIII 3/44–6/44
Cdr *U 2321* 12.6.44–capitulation
Detained; freed 26.10.47

BART, FRITZ [42]
b. 29.3.1909, Gera, Thüringen
Entry 1929/1937a; Kplt 1.12.44
ADC 24th U-Flotilla 10/40–11/42; U-boat trg and courses 12/42–7/43; 1WO *U 96* 8/43–3/44; 1WO *U 107* 4/44–8/44; U-Cdr's Course 8/44–10/44 (U-Cdr's Torpedo Course 77)
Cdr *UD 4* 23.11.44–19.3.45
1WO *U 3501* 20.3.45–5.5.45 (Bart was awarded command of *U 3060* but the boat was destroyed

on the slipway by bombing before launching; he was then appointed 1WO of *U 3501* instead)

BARTELS, ROBERT [43]
b. 28.4.1911, Kiel-Pries
Class 1935; KKpt 1.8.43
WO *U 21* 1937 (per rankings list of 1.11.37) and until 6/40; U-Cdr under instrn and *Baubelehrung* 7/40
Cdr *U 139* 24.7.40–20.12.40
1st U-Flotilla and *Baubelehrung* 12/40–3/41
Cdr *U 561* 13.3.41–5.9.42 (dates per *U 561* WD)
Baubelehrung 6.KLA 9/42–10/42
Cdr *U 197* 10.10.42–20.8.43
Lost 20.8.43 Indian Ocean, S of Madagascar

BARTEN, WOLFGANG [44]
b. 18.8.1909, Minden, Westphalia
Class 1931; KKpt 1.10.39
WO *U 29* 1936 (per rankings list of 1.11.36) and 1937 (per rankings list of 1.11.37); subsequent activities until 2/39 not recorded
Cdr *U 52* 4.2.39–17.9.39
Cdr *U 40* 21.9.39–13.10.39
Lost 13.10.39 English Channel

BARTKE, ERWIN [45]
b. 28.4.1909, Königsberg
Entry 1940; ObltzS (R) 1.6.43
2WO *U 403* 6/41–11/42; U-Cdr's Course, 24th U-Flotilla and *Baubelehrung* 12/42–1/43
Cdr *U 488* 1.2.43–2/44
Course and *Baubelehrung* 3/44–7/44
Cdr *U 1106* 5.7.44–29.3.45
Lost 29.3.45 NE of Faroes

BARTSCH, HANS-JÜRGEN [46]
b. 31.3.1921, Hannover
Class XII/1939; ObltzS 1.12.43
Platoon Officer 1.UAA until 12/42; *Baubelehrung* 12/42–1/43; 2WO *U 57* 1/43–3/43; 1WO *U 957* 3/43–1/44; 11th U-Flotilla 1/44–3/44; U-Cdr under instrn, 23rd U-Flotilla, 3/44–5/44
Acting Cdr *U 18* 2.5.44–25.5.44 (Per Gerd Enders, *Auch kleine Igel haben Stacheln*, Fleige [294] was commander of *U 18* until 25.5.44; Arendt [18] took over as acting commander until 7.6.44, on which date Fleige resumed command until 25.8.44. If the book is correct, Bartsch could not have been acting commander of *U 18* in the period.)
Cdr *U 17* 26.5.44–21.12.44
11th U-Flotilla 12/44–2/45
WO *U 1023* 1.3.45–capitulation

BASSE, GEORG-WILHELM [47]
b. 27.8.1917, Berlin-Charlottenburg
Class 1936; Kplt 1.4.43
3./Kampfgruppe 606 (See) 10/39–3/41; *III./KG40* 3/41–8/41; U-boat trg 8/41–1/42; 7th U-Flotilla 1/42–2/42; 1WO *U 751* 2/42–3/42; 1WO *U 575* 3/42–5/42; U-Cdr's Course, 24th U-Flotilla 6/42–7/42; *Baubelehrung* 7/42–8/42
Cdr *U 339* 25.8.42–17.5.43
Baubelehrung 5/43–6/43
Cdr *U 314* 10.6.43–30.1.44
Lost 30.1.44 Arctic Ocean, SE of Bear I

BAUER, ERNST [48]
b. 3.2.1914, Fürth, Bavaria
Class 1933; KKpt 1.4.45
U-boat trg 1/38–5/38; WO *U 10* 5/38–7/38; *Baubelehrung* Deschimag U-boat yard, Bremen, 7/38–8/38; 1WO *U 37* 8/38–11/39; U-Cdr's Course, U-Trg Flotilla 11/39–1/40; *Baubelehrung* U-Boats East (Flender Werke Lübeck) 1/40–4/40
Cdr *U 120*, 20.4.40–25.11.40
21st U-Flotilla 11/40–2/41; *Baubelehrung* Deschimag U-boat yard, Bremen, 2/41–3/41

Cdr *U 126* 22.3.41–28.2.43
Trg Officer 27th U-Flotilla 3/43–10/44; CO 27th U-Flotilla 8/44 and 10/44–4/45; CO 26th U-Flotilla 4/45–capitulation
Held in detention Mürwik Military Hospital until 10/45, freed 31.12.45
Knight's Cross 16.3.42 (104th KM, 47th U-boat holder)

BAUER, HERMANN [49]
b. 14.8.1917, Koblenz
Class 1936; ObltzS 1.10.40, posthumously Kplt seniority 1.4.43
1WO 1st Minesweeping Flotilla 4/39–4/40; Group Officer, Naval College Flensburg-Mürwik, 4/4–8/40; Cdr and Group Leader 36th Minesweeping Flotilla 8/40–1/41; 1WO *U 67* 6/41–1/42; U-Cdr's Course, 24th U-Flotilla 1/42–2/42
Cdr *U 30* 10.3.42–4.10.42
Baubelehrung 10/42–11/42
Cdr *U 169* 16.11.42–27.3.43
Lost 27.3.43 S of Iceland

BAUER, MAX-HERMANN [50]
b. 24.7.1912, Rüstringen (son of Hermann Bauer, FdU, First World War)
Class 1930; Kplt 1.4.39, posthumously KKpt seniority 1.5.40
Cdr *U 18* 30.9.37 or 1.11.37 to 24.11.39 (see Beduhn [64])
Baubelehrung 11/39–12/39
Cdr *U 50* 12.12.39–10.4.40
Lost 10.4.40 NW of Shetland Is

BAUM, HEINZ [51]
b. 5.11.1912, Heilbronn
Conscripted 1940; ObltzS (R) 1.2.44
Strm *Sperrbrecher 1* 7/40–6/42; courses and 6th Sperrbrecher Flotilla 7/42–1/43; U-boat trg and U-Cdr's Course 1/43–10/43 (U-Cdr's Torpedo Course 53); *Baubelehrung* 10/43–12/43
Cdr *U 1197* 2.12.43–19.3.44
Cdr *U 1303* 5.4.44–4/45
Cdr *U 290* 4/45–4.5.45

BAUMANN, AREND [52]
b. 30.3.1903, place not recorded
Class 1922; FKpt 1.7.42
Navigation Officer light cruiser *Köln* 10/38–10/40; U-boat trg, U-Cdr's Course and *Baubelehrung* 11/40–6/41
Cdr *U 131* 1.7.41–17.12.41
POW 17.12.41–31.12.47

BAUMANN, HEINZ [53]
b. 6.3.1922, Hamburg
Entry 1940; ObltzS (R) 1.6.44
U-boat trg completed 3/43; *Baubelehrung* 3/43–4/43; 1WO *U 672* 4/43 6/44; course 3.ULD and *Baubelehrung* 8.KLA 6/44–12/44
Cdr *U 2333* 18.12.44–5.5.45

LA BAUME, GÜNTER [54]
b. 29.4.1911, Danzig
Class 1929; Kplt 1.8.38, posthumously KKpt seniority 1.4.44
Comp. Cdr 1/NCO Trg Div 3/38–9/39; Specialist, OKW Abwehr (Foreign), 9/39–4/41; U-boat trg 4/41–8/41; U-Cdr's Course, 24th U-Flotilla and *Baubelehrung* 9/41–10/41
Cdr *U 355* 29.10.41–1.4.44
Lost 1.4.44 Barents Sea, SW of Bear I

BAUMGÄRTEL, FRIEDRICH [55]
b. 24.3.1923, Allenstein, East Prussia
Class 1940; ObltzS 1.10.44
Officer trg (cadet aboard destroyer *Z 27*), courses and U-boat trg 10/40–2/43, inc. WO sea trg *U 592* 1942; *Baubelehrung* 8.KLA 2/43–3/43;

2WO *U 969* 3/43–5/44; 1WO *U 969* 5/44–8/44;
29th U-Flotilla 8/44–9/44; courses 9/44–12/44
Cdr *U 17* 22.12.44–6.2.45
Cdr *U 142* 7.2.45–2.5.45
Detained; freed 10.8.45

BAUR, GÖTZ [56]
b. 1.8.1917, Shanghai, China
Class 1935; Kplt 1.11.42
Secretarial Officer and WO destroyer *Z 10 Hans Lody* 9/38–10/40; U-boat trg 11/40–5/41; 1WO *U 552* 5/41–10/41; U-Cdr's Course, 24th U-Flotilla and *Baubelehrung* 11/41–1/42
Cdr *U 660* 8.1.42–12.11.42
POW 12.11.42

BECK, DIETER [57]
b. 7.5.1915, Ravensburg, Württemberg
Class 1934; Kplt 1.11.41
Light cruiser *Nürnberg* 3/40–10/41; heavy cruiser *Prinz Eugen* 10/41–8/43; U-boat trg 8/43–2/44; U-Cdr under instrn, 19th and 23rd U-Flotillas 2/44–8/44; Cdr (supernumerary) 8th U-Flotilla 9/44–2/45; *Baubelehrung* Cdr 6.KLA 2/45–capitulation (The Lohmann-Hildebrand almanac has Beck as *Baubelehrung* Cdr *U 3051* 5.2.45 until the capitulation, whereas WASt shows Müller-Koelbl [851].)

BECKER, KLAUS [58]
b. 17.3.1918, Göttingen
Class 1936; Kplt 1.7.43
Light cruiser *Köln* 12/38–4/40; 1WO 1st Minesweeping Flotilla 4/40–6/40; M/S-Cdr and Group Leader 36th Minesweeping Flotilla 6/40–11/40; Liaison Officer 4th Escort Div 11/40–3/41; M/S-Cdr 2nd Minesweeping Flotilla 3/41–10/41; U-boat trg 10/41–4/42; 1WO *U 586* 5/42–12/42; U-Cdr's Course, 24th U-Flotilla 12/42–1/43
Cdr *U 235* 20.1.43–20.5.43

Cdr *U 360* 5/43–2.4.44.
Lost 2.4.44 Arctic Ocean, NW of Hammerfest

BECKER, KLAUS [59]
b. 29.4.1920, Überlingen, Lake Constance
Class IX/1939; ObltzS 1.10.43
Officer and U-boat trg 9/39–2/42; *Baubelehrung* KLA U-North 2/42–3/42; 1WO *U 260* 3/42–11/43; U-Cdr's Course, 3.ULD, 23rd U-Flotilla and *Baubelehrung* 11/43–1/44
Cdr *U 367* 6.1.44–3/44
Tactical exercises 27th U-Flotilla 3/44–4/44
Cdr *U 260* 4/44–12.3.45
POW 12.3.45

BECKER, PHILIPP [60]
b. 21.10.1921, Rüsselsheim
Entry 1940; ObltzS (R) 1.3.44
Officer trg, courses 4/40–3/41; Comp. Leader 2nd Sperrbrecher Flotilla 3/41–10/41; U-boat trg and courses 10/41–7/42; *Baubelehrung* 7/42–8/42; 2WO *U 269* 8/42–9/43; 1WO *U 269* 9/43–5/44; various duties and U-Cdr's Course 6/44–8/44
Cdr *U 794* 1.9.44–5.5.45

BECKER, RICHARD [61]
b. 21.2.1911, Altona, Elbe
Class 1934; Kplt 1.3.42
1WO *U 43* 1/41–10/41; U-Cdr's Course and *Baubelehrung* 11/41–1/42
Cdr *U 218* from 24.1.42 until before 10.8.44 (Stock [1237] must have relieved Becker before 10.8.44 as he took the boat out from Brest that day on a transfer voyage to Norway.)
No information available 8/44–25.10.44 but probably *Baubelehrung* at 8.KLA/Hamburg
Cdr *U 2503* 26.10.44–11.11.44, command not taken up
No information available 12.11.44–1/45

Leader *K-Verband* base Heligoland 2/45–capitulation
Detained; freed 10.1.46

BECKMANN, HANS [62]
b. 6.1.1918, Rheine
Entry as rating (R) X/1939; ObltzS(R) 1.8.44
Basic military and shipboard trg, courses 10/39–2/42; Trg NCO, 4th Sperrbrecher Flotilla, *Sperrbrecher 120* 3/42–6/42; Naval physical education course, Helmsman's School 6/42–9/42; 1/NCO Trg Div 9/42–11/42; U-boat trg 11/42–5/43; WO *U 214* 5/43–5/44; U-Cdr's Course, 24th U-Flotilla 6/44–7/44 (U-Cdr's Torpedo Course 73); U-Cdr 4th and 32nd U-Flotillas, also *Baubelehrung* Type XXIII, 8.KLA 7/44–9/44
Cdr *U 2330* 7.9.44–3.5.45

BECKMANN, HEINZ [63]
b. 29.6.1913, Hamburg
Entry X/1939; ObltzS (R) 1.3.43
U-boat trg completed 4/42; 2WO *U 504* 4/42–3/43; U-Cdr's Course 4/43–5/43 (U-Cdr's Torpedo Course 45)
Cdr *U 159* 7.6.43–15.7.43
Lost 15.7.43 S of Haiti

BEDUHN, HEINZ [64]
b. 11.8.1907, Berlin
Class 1926; KKpt 1.8.40 (promoted at death)
U-boat trg 11/35–4/36; U-Cdr U-Flotilla *Weddigen*, *U 16* and *U 10* 1.5.36–29.9.37
Cdr *U 18* 30.9.37–31.10.37 (Per WASt and Beduhn's P/F. *U 18* was commissioned for the second time on 30.9.37. See Paukstadt [911].)
CO U-Boat School Flotilla (from 1.7.40 21st U-Flotilla), U-Boat School, Neustadt, Holstein 11/37–4/40
Cdr *U 23* 8.4.40–19.5.40 (per WASt and P/F)
Cdr *U 25* 20.5.40–3.8.40
Lost 3.8.40 North Sea, N of Terschelling

BEHNISCH, GÜNTER [65]
b. 12.6.1922, Dresden
Class XII/1939; ObltzS 1.12.43
U-boat trg completed 3/44; 1WO *U 952* 4/44–8/44; U-Cdr's Course and *Baubelehrung* Type XXIII, 8.KLA 8/44–10/44
Cdr *U 2337* 4.10.44–capitulation

BEHRENS, UDO [66]
b. 9.4.1911, Krotoschin, Posen
Class 1930; KKpt 1.6.43
WO *U 16*, *U 15*, *U 33*, *U 21* and *U 30* 1936–37 (WO *U 30* according to the rankings list at 1.11.36)
Cdr *U 16* and *U 24* 8.10.37–17.10.39 (had the same crew members on both boats)
Cdr *U 17* from 18.10.39 (but did not assume command until 6.1.40) to 7.7.40.
U-advisory capacity OKM/SKL 8/40–3/43; *Baubelehrung U 845* 3/43–4/43
Cdr *U 845* 1.5.43–9.7.43
1/Adm. Staff Officer, Staff FdU East 8/43–8/44; Liaison Officer with X Flotilla, Naval Gunnery School 8/44–12/44; 1/Adm. Staff Officer, Staff FdU East 12/44–capitulation
Detained; freed 11.11.45

BENDER, WERNER [67]
b. 28.10.1916, Stuttgart
Class 1936; Kplt 1.4.43
3/NCO Trg Div 6/39–2/40; UAA 2/40–4/40; Cadets' Trg Officer trg ship *Schlesien* 4/40–7/40; Secretarial/Signals Officer battleship *Bismarck* 8/40–1/41; U-boat trg 1/41–5/41; *Baubelehrung* 5/41–7/41; 1WO *U 161* 7/41–5/42; U-Cdr's Course, 24th U-Flotilla, courses, 1.UAA and 2 UAA, *Baubelehrung* 6.KLA 5/42–2/43
Cdr *U 841* 6.2.43–17.10.43

Lost 17.10.43 E of Cape Farewell

BENKER, HANS [68]
b. 21.2.1917, Bochum
Class 1936; Kplt 1.2.43
2WO *U 75* 12/40–5/41; U-Cdr's Course 5/41–7/41
Cdr *U 152* 22.7.41–30.9.41
Cdr *U 80* 6.10.41–4.5.42
Baubelehrung 8.KLA 5/42–6/42
Cdr *U 625* 4.6.42–2.1.44
Lost 2.1.44 North Atlantic, washed overboard and drowned

BENSEL, ROLF RÜDIGER [69]
b. 12.6.1923, Ratibor, Upper Silesia
Class X/1940; ObltzS 1.10.44
14th Minesweeping Flotilla 12/40–5/41; U-boat trg and Naval College Flensburg-Mürwik 6/41–9/41; WO sea trg *U 129* 10/41–4/42; U-boat courses 4/42–12/42; WO *U 101* and *U 34* 12/42–5/43; 2WO *U 667* 5/43–5/44; U-Cdr's Course 6/44–9/44
Cdr *U 120* 15.9.44–2.5.45
Detained; freed 26.10.45

BENTHIN, KARL-DIETRICH [70]
b. 25.9.1921, Königsberg, East Prussia
Class X/1940; ObltzS 1.10.44
Officer trg, courses and U-boat trg 10/40–4/43; WO *U 518* 4/43–5/44; U-Cdr's Course, 3.ULD 6/44–8/44 (U-Cdr's Torpedo Course 74); *Baubelehrung* Type XXIII, 8.KLA 9/44
Cdr *U 2335* 27.9.44–capitulation

BENTZIEN, HEINZ [71]
b. 28.1.1917, Fischhausen, East Prussia
Class X/1937; Kplt 1.1.45
Officer trg, courses 3/39–1/40; seconded to Luftwaffe 2/40–2/42; U-boat trg 2/42–8/42; *Baubelehrung* 8/42–9/42; 1WO *U 73* 9/42–1/43; U-Cdr's Course (U-Cdr's Torpedo Course 42) and *Baubelehrung* 1/43–4/43
Cdr *U 425* 21.4.43–17.2.45
Lost 17.2.45 Barents Sea, off Murmansk

BERENDS, FRITZ [72]
b. 23.9.1906, Wilhelmshaven
Entry 1933; ObltzS (R) 1.4.43
VP-Cdr 59th VP-Boat Flotilla 8/40–6/41; VP-Cdr 61st VP-Boat Flotilla 6/41–9/42; VP-Cdr Coastal Defence Flotilla *Ostland* 9/42–6/43; Instructor and trg ship cdr, Naval/Aerial Minelaying School 6/43–8/43; U-boat trg, courses (U-Cdr's Torpedo Course 72) and *Baubelehrung* 8/43–8/44
Cdr *U 321* 8/44–2.4.45
Lost 2.4.45 SW of Ireland

BERGEMANN, WILHELM [73]
b. 6.4.1920, Hannover
Class IX/1939; ObltzS 1.12.43
2WO *U 375* 10/41–5/43; 2.UAA and U-Cdr's Course, 24th U-Flotilla 5/43–7/43 (U-Cdr's Torpedo Course 48)
Cdr *U 152* 25.7.43–15.10.44
21st U-Flotilla 10/44–3/45; U-Cdr sea trg (supernumerary) *U 3030* 8.3.45–9.5.45

BERGER, JOACHIM [74]
b. 23.6.1913, Berlin
Class 1934; Kplt 1.11.1941
Trg Officer 2nd Torpedo-Boat Flotilla 10/39–11/39; ADC 2/NCO Trg Div. 11/39–4/40; Staff, Naval Commander Molde 5/40–3/41; relief instructor Naval Gunnery School 3/41–4/41; 24th U-Flotilla 4/41–5/41; 7th U-Flotilla, U-Cdr's Course and *Baubelehrung* 5/41–8/41
Cdr *U 87* 19.8.41–4.3.43
Lost 4.3.43 W of Leixoes, Portugal

BERKEMANN, PAUL [75]
b. 20.1.1913, Südkamen, Hamm
Enlisted VII/1933; ObltzS 1.7.44
Service as rating in U-boat arm 1/40–3/44; course 23rd U-Flotilla 3/44–5/44; WO *U 530* 5/44–12/44; *K-Verband* 12/44–1/45; *Baubelehrung* Type XXIII, 1.KLA 1/45–3/45
Cdr *U 4709* 3.3.45–3.5.45
5th U-Flotilla 5/45–capitulation

BERNADELLI, RICHARD [76]
b. 22.11.1908, Rüstringen
Class 1932; KKpt 1.11.44
WO heavy cruiser *Admiral Hipper* 8/39–3/43; U-boat trg 3/43–10/43; U-Cdr under instrn, 23rd U-Flotilla 11/43–12/43; *Baubelehrung* 6.KLA 12/43–2/44
Cdr *U 805* 12.2.44–capitulation
Detained; freed 7.3.46

BERNECK, HINRICH-OSCAR [77]
b. 5.7.1914, Roding, Oberpfalz
Class 1934; Kplt 1.4.42
U-boat depot ship *Saar* 5/38–3/40; U-boat trg 4/40–7/40; 1WO *U 43* 8/40–2/41
Cdr *U 4* 3.2.41–8.12.41
Baubelehrung 1.KLA 12/41–1/42
Cdr *U 461* (Type XIV U-tanker) 30.1.42–21.4.42
Cdr *UD 4* 30.4.42–8.12.42 but course 24th U-Flotilla 5/42–6/42
Cdr *U 638* 9.12.42–31.3.43
9th U-Flotilla 4/43–5/43; Leader torpedo attack exercises, 25th U-Flotilla 5/43–12/44; seconded Higher Command of Torpedo Schools 12/44–3/45; Senior Officer, Torpedo Trg Staff, Northern Norway 3/45–capitulation

BERTELSMANN, HANS-JOACHIM [78]
b. 29.4.1916, Cuxhaven
Class 1936; Kplt 1.9.43
Div. Officer heavy cruiser *Blücher* 9/39–4/40; Harbour Defence Flotilla Oslo 4/40–9/40; Group Leader 7th VP-Boat Flotilla 9/40–1/41; U-boat trg and courses 1/41–6/41; Navigating Officer U-boat tender *Waldemar Kophamel* 6/41–7/41; course, 24th U-Flotilla 8/41–9/41; 1WO *U 71* 10/41–1/42; U-Cdr's Torpedo Course 1/42–3/42
Cdr *U 142* 18.3.42–12.9.42
Cdr *U 603* 13.9.42–2.5.43 (relieved on grounds of sickness)
1st U-Flotilla 5/43–8/43 (hospital); Comp CO 2.ULD 8/43–1/44
Resumed as Cdr *U 603* 29.1.44–1.3.44
Lost 1.3.44 North Atlantic

BESOLD, HEINRICH [79]
b. 18.10.1920, Nürnberg
Class IX/1939; ObltzS 1.10.43
Officer trg, courses 9/39–8/40; clerical duties, Naval Ordnance Office, Boulogne 8/40–11/40; trg and courses 11/40–4/42; ADC and Comp. CO, Naval Ordnance Office, The Hague 4/42–3/43; navigation course, Helmsman's School 3/43–6/43 (transferred from Ordnance to Seaman Branch); U-boat trg 6/43–3/44; U-Cdr sea trg, *U 981* 3/44–5/44; 2nd U-Flotilla 5/44–7/44; U-Cdr sea trg and WO *U 518* 7/44–11/44; *Baubelehrung* 12/44–1/45
Cdr *U 1308* 17.1.45–2.5.45

BEUCKE, HEINZ-EHLER [80]
b. 12.1.1904, Berlin
Class 1922; KptzS 1.6.43
Adviser OKM/SKL-U 9/39–4/40; 1/Adm. Staff Officer, Adm. Norwegian West Coast 4/40–8/40; 3/Adm. Staff Officer, Naval Group West 8/40–2/41; U-boat trg and *Baubelehrung* 3/41–11/41
Cdr *U 173* 15.11.41–10/42
Staff, 2/Adm. U-Boats 11/42–2/43; Chief of Staff, Commanding Adm. U-Boats 2/43–5/43;

31

CO Command Div. U-Boats (SKL/Qu A U) at OKM 6/43–8/44; Planning Staff Officer, Naval High Command North Sea 8/44–capitulation
Detained; freed 18.4.47

BIELFELD, HEINZ [81]
b. 30.8.1916, Tientsin, China
Class 1934; Kplt 1.4.42
Group Trg Leader Aircraft Weapons School, Parow 11/38–4/40; *Küstenfliegergruppe 506* 5/4–9/40; U-boat trg and supernumerary WO *U 97* 10/41–2/41; U-Cdr sea trg aboard *U 151* as WO 2/41–8/41; 7th U-Flotilla, U-Cdr's Course and *Baubelehrung* 8/41–10/41
Cdr *U 703* 16.10.41–5.7.43
Baubelehrung 8.KLA 7/4–8/43
Cdr *U 1222* 1.9.43–11.7.44
Lost 11.7.44 Bay of Biscay, W of La Rochelle

BIGALK, GERHARD [82]
b. 26.11.1908, Berlin-Niederschönhausen
Class 1933; KKpt 5.4.45 effective 1.7.42
U-boat trg 11/39–3/40; U-Cdr under instrn, 1st U-Trg Flotilla 3/40–5/40
Cdr *U 14* 2.6.40–8/40
24th U-Flotilla 8/40–10/40; 7th U-Flotilla (supernumerary) 11/40–12/40; 6/Basic Trg Est. Stralsund and *Baubelehrung* for U-boats 12/40–1/41
Cdr *U 751* 31.1.41–17.7.42
Lost 17.7.42 NW Cape Ortegal (NW Spain)
Knight's Cross 26.12.41 (93rd KM, 41st U-boat holder)

BISCHOFF, GUSTAV [83]
b. 11.5.1916, Käseburg, Oldenburg
Class X/1939; ObltzS 1.3.44
Officer trg, courses 10/39–12/40; 4th VP-Boat Flotilla 12/40–1/42; U-boat trg and various courses 1/42–9/42; WO (supernumerary) *U 710* 9/42–11/42; *Baubelehrung* 8.KLA 11/42–12/42; 1WO *U 953* 12/42–3/44; course, 23rd U-Flotilla and *Baubelehrung* Type XXIII 4/44–1/45
Cdr *U 2359* 16.1.45–2.5.45
Lost 2.5.45 Kattegat

BITTER, OTTO [84]
b. 12.10.1918, Rüstringen
Class 1937b; Kplt 1.1.45
Officer trg and courses 3/39–7/41; 1WO 4th Minesweeping Flotilla 7/41–1/43; ADC 4th Minesweeping Flotilla 1/43–3/43; U-boat trg 3/43–9/43; courses 9/43–1/44 (U-Cdr's Torpedo Course 59); *Baubelehrung* 8.KLA 1/44–2/44
Cdr *U 1010* 22.2.44–16.7.44
Courses and *Baubelehrung* Type XXI, 8.KLA 7/44–1/45
Cdr *U 2535* 28.1.45–2.5.45
Seconded to Adm. Commanding U-Boats 5/45–capitulation

VON BITTER, GEORG [85]
b. 23.3.1921, Hötensleben, Helmstedt
Class IX/1939; ObltzS 1.10.43
WO trg *U 38* 9/41–12/41; 2WO *U 160* 2/41–5/43; U-Cdr's Course, 24th U-Flotilla 5/43–6/43 (U-Cdr's Torpedo Course 48), *Baubelehrung* 6/43–8/43
Cdr *U 750* 9/43–31.8.44
Flag Lt, Commanding Adm. U-Boats 9/44–1/45
Lost 13.1.45, fire aboard accommodation ship *Daressalem* at Kiel

BLAICH, FERDINAND [86]
b. 8.2.1912, Bietigheim
Entry 1/1940; ObltzS (R) 1.10.43
WO auxiliary warship *Ammerland* 2/40–9/40; WO and Div. Officer naval oiler *Spichern* 9/40–6/41; 1/NCO Trg Div. 6/41–8/41; WO, ADC and Navigation Officer naval oiler *Ermland*

8/41–9/42; First Officer auxiliary supply vessel *Passat* 9/42–11/42; *Baubelehrung* 11/42–5/43; U-boat trg 5/43–10/43; Secretarial Officer 6.KLA 10/43–2/44; course, 23rd and 27th U-Flotillas 2/44–4/44; courses and Type XXI, 6.KLA 4/44–1/45
Cdr *U 3024* 13.1.45–3.5.45

BLAUDOW, ERNST-ULRICH [87]
b. 9.11.1914, Stralsund
Entry 1935; Kplt (R) 1.11.44
13/Basic Trg Est. Stralsund 9/39–4/40; 1/NCO Trg Div. 4/40–6/40; WO 15th VP-Boat Flotilla 6/40–8/40; Coastal Defence Group, Norwegian West Coast 8/40–2/43; U-boat trg 3/43–8/43; course, 27th U-Flotilla and *Baubelehrung* 8.KLA 8/43–11/43 (U-Cdr's Torpedo Course 55)
Cdr *U 1001* 18.11.43–8.4.45
Lost 8.4.45 Atlantic, SW of Land's End

BLAUERT, HANS-JÖRG [88]
b. 21.3.1918, Prenzlau
Entry VIII/1939; ObltzS 1.4.42
Command Relay and No 2 Gunnery Officer destroyer *Z 23* 9/40–1/42; U-boat trg 1/42–7/42; 1WO *U 553* 7/42–10/42; *Baubelehrung* 7.KLA 10/42–12/42
Cdr *U 734* 5.12.42–9.2.44
Lost 9.2.44 SW of Ireland

BLEICHRODT, HEINRICH [89]
b. 21.10.1909, Berga, Kyffhäuser
Class 1933/31 (see Prien [947] Tr.) ; KKpt 1.7.43
WO/ADC sail trg ship *Gorch Fock* 4/37–7/39; Rangefinding/Wargames and Div. Officer heavy cruiser *Admiral Hipper* 7/39–10/39; assigned BdU, U-boat trg and courses 10/39–4/40; 1st U-Flotilla 4/40–6/40, incl WO *U 8* 11.4.40–29.4.40; 2nd U-Flotilla 6/40–8/40, inc. WO and U-Cdr sea trg *U 34* 18.6.40–22.7.40

Cdr *U 48* 4.9.40–16.12.40 (in command from 20.8.40 per P/F but see Rösing [1018])
Baubelehrung, U-Boats North/Deschimag Bremen 12/40–1/41
Cdr *U 67* 22.1.41–4.6.41
Cdr *U 109* from 5.6.41 to either 28.2.43 (per WASt) or 31.1.43 (per P/F)
27th U-Flotilla 2/43; Head of Trg in U-Boat Handling, AGRU-Front 2/43–6/43; tactical instructor for officers, 1 Div./2.ULD 7/43–2/44; CO 1 Div./2.ULD 2/44–6/44; CO 22nd U-Flotilla 7/44–capitulation
Detained; freed 25.9.45
Knight's Cross 24.10.40 (41st KM, 18th U-boat holder)
Oak Leaves 23.9.42 (125th WM, 17th KM, 15th U-boat holder)

BLISCHKE, HEINZ [90]
b. 1.9.1919, Schwiebus, Silesia
Class 1938; ObltzS 1.4.43
U-boat trg 2/41–9/41; *Baubelehrung* 9/41–11/41; 1WO *U 755* 11/41–3/43; U-Cdr's Course, 4th U-Flotilla (U-Cdr's Torpedo Course 44) 3/43–4/43; *Baubelehrung* 7.KLA 4/43–6/43
Cdr *U 744* 5.6.43–6.3.44
Lost 6.3.44 central North Atlantic

BLOCK, HELMUT [91]
b. 3.4.1915, Bremen
Entry 1938; ObltzS (R) 1.4.43
VP-Cdr Harbour Defence Flotilla, Molde, 8/40–2/43; U-boat trg, U-Cdr's Course and *Baubelehrung* 2/43–11/43 (U-Cdr's Torpedo Course 55)
Cdr *U 771* 18.11.43–11.11.44
Lost 11.11.44 Norwegian Sea, off Andfjord nr Harstad

BLUM, OTTO-ULRICH [92]
b. 4.2.1917, Kiel

Class 1936; Kplt 1.9.43
No 2 Radio Technical Officer light cruiser *Leipzig* 7/39–2/40; ADC and No 2 Radio Technical Officer heavy cruiser *Admiral Scheer* 3/40–6/41; U-boat trg 6/41–11/41; 2WO *U 373* 11/41–2/42; 1WO *U 373* 2/42–7/42; U-Cdr's Course and *Baubelehrung* 8/42–10/42
Cdr *U 760* 15.10.42–8.9.43
Interned in Spain 8.9.43–capitulation, freed 7.9.45

BODDENBERG, KARL [93]
b. 23.5.1914, Osenau, Odenthal
Enlisted 1933; ObltzS 1.4.43
Obstrm WO *U 201* 1/42–9/42; Torpedo School Mürwik, U-Cdr's Course, 24th U-Flotilla and *Baubelehrung* 9/42–2/43
Cdr *U 963* 17.2.43–12/44 (1WO Müller [846] had temporary command for a voyage Brest–La Pallice 13.8.44–21.8.44)
OKM/K/I/II 12/44–3/45, Comp. CO 4/Basic Trg Est. Stralsund 3/45–capitulation

BODE, THILO [94]
b. 19.2.1918, Bochum
Class 1936; Kplt 1.4.43
CO Battery, Naval Flak Detachment 222 8/39–6/40; Div. Officer destroyer *Z 6 Theodor Riedel* 7/40–3/42; U-boat trg 4/42–9/42; 1WO *U 505* 9/42–3/43; U-Cdr's Course, 24th U-Flotilla 4/43–5/43 (U-Cdr's Torpedo Course 45); 1WO *U 505* 5/43–8/43; *Baubelehrung* 6.KLA 8/43–9/43
Cdr *U 858* 30.9.43–capitulation

BÖHM, HERMANN [95]
b. 24.12.1910, Hamburg
Entry X/1937; ObltzS (R) 1.9.43
VP-Cdr 16th VP-Boat Flotilla 7/40–5/43; U-boat trg 5/43–9/43; WO (supernumerary) *U 1061* 9/43–10/43; 1WO *U 758* 11/43–2/44; U-Cdr's Course, 24th U-Flotilla 3/44–4/44; various duties, courses and *Baubelehrung* Type XXIII 4/44–10/44
Cdr *U 2341* 21.10.44–capitulation

BÖHME, KURT [96]
b. 21.1.1917, Elberfeld, Nordrhein-Westfalen
Class X/1937; Kplt 1.1.45
U-boat trg 10/40–3/41; Platoon Officer 2.UAA 3/41–5/41; *Baubelehrung* 5/41–6/41; 1WO *U 575* 6/41–3/42; 1WO *U 751* 3/42–6/42; U-Cdr's Course, 24th U-Flotilla 7/42–8/42; *Baubelehrung* 7.KLA 8/42–9/42
Cdr *U 450* 12.9.42–10.3.44
POW 10.3.44

BOEHMER, WOLFGANG [97]
b. 9.8.1920, Nordkirchen, Westphalia
Class XII/1939; ObltzS 1.12.43
Officer trg, courses 12/39–4/41; WO sea trg *U 431* 5/41–11/41; courses 11/41–5/42; supernumerary WO *U 263* 5/42–8/42; 2/Adm. U-Boats 8/42–11/42; 2WO *U 575* 11/42–3/43; 1WO *U 575* 3/43–7/43; U-Cdr's Course, 24th U-Flotilla (U-Cdr's Torpedo Course 53) 8/43–9/43
Cdr *U 575* 12.9.43–13.3.44 (U-Boat Archive per Boehmer; Heydemann [481] was first commander of *U 575* 19.6.41–29.7.43; no commander during St Nazaire overhaul 7/43–9/43; Boehmer was the second commander)
POW 13.3.44–12.11.46

BÖRNER, HANS-JOACHIM [98]
b. 24.7.1918, Oderau
Class X/1937; Kplt 1.1.45
WO and ADC 9th VP-Boat Flotilla 5/40–2/41; U-boat trg 2/41–10/41; 1WO *U 507* 10/41–10/42; U-Cdr's Course, 24th U-Flotilla 11/42–12/42; *Baubelehrung* 7.KLA 12/42
Cdr *U 735* 28.12.42–28.12.44

Lost 28.12.44 off Horten

BÖTTCHER, RICHARD [99]
b. 2.10.1906, Flensburg
Enlisted 1925; ObltzS 1.1.43
Flotilla helmsman 9th U-Flotilla 12/41–6/42; courses 6/42–9/42
Cdr *U 139* 1.10.42–6.9.43
Trg Officer 20th and 19th U-Flotillas 9/43–capitulation

BOHMANN, HEINO [100]
b. 11.3.1914, Holsse, Wesermünde
Class 1934; Kplt 1.9.41
Group Officer, Naval College Flensburg-Mürwik 3/39–9/39; 2ADC OKM 9/39–10/39; Cdr *Schiff 20* 10/39–3/40; VP-Cdr 18th VP-Group 3/40–11/40; U-boat trg 11/40–6/41; 1WO and U-Cdr under instrn *U 94* 6/41–8/41; *Baubelehrung* 9/41–10/41
Cdr *U 88* 15.10.41–12.9.42
Lost 12.9.42 Arctic Ocean, S of Spitzbergen

BOKELBERG, MAX [101]
b. 15.4.1919, Kiel
Class 1937a; Kplt 1.8.44
Heavy cruiser *Admiral Hipper* 4/39–10/39; 8/Basic Trg Est. Stralsund 10/39–1/40; heavy cruiser *Lützow* 1/40–5/40; 2/NCO Trg Div. 6/40–5/41; WO heavy cruiser *Admiral Hipper* 5/41–5/43; U-boat trg 5/43–11/43; U-Cdr's Course, 24th U-Flotilla 11/43–1/44 (U-Cdr's Torpedo Course 60); *Baubelehrung* 3.KLA 1/44–2/44
Cdr *U 323* 2.3.44–18.7.44
Baubelehrung Type XXI 8.KLA 7/44–12/44
Cdr *U 2530* 30.12.44–20.2.45 (per WASt).
(*U 2530* was commissioned on 30.12.44. The following day, during fitting out at Bay 4, Blohm & Voss, Hamburg, the boat sank as the result of a bomb hit astern. She was raised in January 1945, but received a direct hit while under repair in No 5 Dock on 17.1.45 and was condemned for scrap. Accordingly, it is doubtful whether Bokelberg was commander of the boat until 20.2.45, for as soon as it was obvious, on or shortly after 17.1.45, that the boat was irreparably damaged he would probably have been reassigned to 8.KLA as *Baubelehrung* Cdr for a new Blohm & Voss boat.)
Baubelehrung 8.KLA 2/45–capitulation

BOLDT, WALTER [102]
b. 5.12.1921, Elbing
Class XII/1939; ObltzS 1.12.43
1WO *U 415* 8/42–1/44; U-Cdr's Course, 3.ULD and 23rd U-Flotilla 1/44–3/44
Cdr *U 720* 1.4.44–22.11.44
21st U-Flotilla 11/44–1/45; instructor 1.ULD 1/45–2/45; service at 1.UAA 2/45–3/45; U-Cdr sea trg *U 3033* 8.3.45–4.5.45
14.6.45 accidental death at Flensburg

BOOS, HANS-HEINZ [103]
b. 14.2.1913, Kiel
Entry 1937; ObltzS (R) 1.7.43
Schiff 36 (merchant raider *Orion*) 12/39–11/41; Platoon Cdr, 1/Basic Trg Est. Stralsund 11/41–1/42; Helmsman's School, Gdynia 1/42–3/42; Signals Officer, destroyer *Z 6 Theodor Riedel* 3/42–5/43; U-boat trg 5/43–11/43; U-Cdr's Course, 24th U-Flotilla 11/43–2/44 (U-Cdr's Torpedo Course 61); *Baubelehrung* 8.KLA 2/44–3/44
Cdr *U 1015* 23.3.44–19.5.44
31st U-Flotilla 5/44–7/44
Cdr *U 1002* 3.7.44 (per WASt) or 6.7.44 (per *U 1102* WD; see Schubart [1138]) to capitulation

BOPST, EBERHARD [104]
b. 25.12.1913, Berlin-Charlottenburg

35

Class 1933; Kplt 1.4.41, posthumously KKpt with effect from 1.10.42
WO, Divisional and W/T Officer destroyer Z 11 *Bernd von Arnim* 12/38–4/40; land fighting for Narvik 4/40–5/40; Station Command North Sea 5/40–6/40; U-boat trg 7/40–1/41; U-Cdr's Course, 24th U-Flotilla, 1/41–2/41
Cdr *U 6* (21st U-Flotilla) 3/41–9/41
Baubelehrung 8.KLA 10/41–11/41
Cdr *U 597* 20.11.41–12.10.42
Lost 12.10.42 SW of Iceland

BORCHARDT, GUSTAV [105]
b. 25.12.1916, Berlin-Pankow
Class 1937b; ObltzS 1.4.42
Destroyer *Z 20 Karl Galster* 12/39–10/40; destroyer *Z 6 Theodor Riedel* 10/40–1/41; U-boat trg 1/41–6/41; 1WO U-boat tender *Saar* 6/41–1/42; 1WO *U 460* 1/42–10/42; WO (supernumerary) *U 135* 10/42–1/43; course, 26th U-Flotilla 1/43–2/43; 2.UAA 2/43–5/43; U-Cdr under instrn, 27th U-Flotilla 5/43
Cdr *U 563* 21.5.43–31.5.43
Lost 31.5.43 Bay of Biscay, SW of Brest

BORCHERDT, ULRICH [106]
b. 13.9.1909, Görlitz
Class 1931; Kplt 1.10.39, posthumously KKpt seniority to 1.3.42
Cdr *Schiff 26* 10/39–11/39; Cdr *Schiff 47* 11/39–3/40; Cdr *Schiff 111* 3/40–4/40; CO Harbour Defence Flotilla, Bergen 4/40–5/40; CO Harbour Defence Flotilla, Molde 5/40–10/40; U-boat trg 10/40–3/41; U-Cdr's Course, 24th U-Flotilla 30.3.41–25.4.41
Cdr *U 8* (22nd U-Flotilla) 29.4.41–22.5.41
7th U-Flotilla (supernumerary) and U-Cdr sea trg *U 553* 23.5.41–11.8.41; *Baubelehrung*, Kriegsmarine Depot, Hamburg, and 8.KLA 12.8.41–10.9.41
Cdr *U 587* 11.9.41–27.3.42

Lost 27.3.42 central North Atlantic (Translator's note: But see Lerchen [725] and Rollmann [1023]. Per Wolfgang Frank, *The Sea Wolves*, Borcherdt reported and shadowed a weakly defended convoy in 44°N 23°W for a few hours and was not heard from subsequently.)

BORCHERS, ROLF [107]
b. 1.11.1913, Stettin
Class 1933; Kplt 1.4.41
W/T and Signals Officer light cruiser *Emden* 3/39–3/41; U-boat trg 3/41–9/41; U-Cdr sea trg *U 206* 9/41–11/41
Cdr *U 149* 1.12.41–31.7.42
Cdr *U 226* 1.8.42–26.7.43 (per *U 226* WD)
Cdr *U 276* 20.10.43–18.7.44
Baubelehrung Type XXI 8.KLA for *U 2515* 7/44–9/44 (*U 2515* was commissioned by Linder [736] on 19.10.44; Borchers was *Baubelehrung* commander until relieved by Linder in September 1944.)
OKM/4SKL 9/44–capitulation

BORCHERT, DIETRICH [108]
b. 28.2.1909, Marnitz, Mecklenburg
Entry 1933/34; KKpt 1.4.45
Group Leader, Aircraft Weapons School (Sea) Parow 11/38–10/39; assigned BdU 11/39–3/40; U-Boat School and UAA, Plön 3/40–5/40; WO 2nd U-Flotilla 5/40–7/40; U-Cdr under instrn, 24th U-Flotilla 7/40
Cdr *U 24* 22.8.40–10.3.41
Baubelehrung 3/41–4/41
Cdr *U 566* 17.4.41–24.7.42
1st U-Flotilla 7/42–9/42; Company CO 2.ULD 10/42–7/43; Observation Officer 24th U-Flotilla 7/43–11/44; Group Leader U-Boat Acceptance Command (Danzig) 11/44–2/45, (Kiel) 2/45–capitulation
Detained; freed 27.11.45

BORGER, WOLFGANG [109]
b. 4.4.1913, Mainz
Class 1936; Kplt 1.8.43
U-boat trg 4/40–8/40; *Baubelehrung* 8/40; 2WO *U 94* 8/40–10/40; 2WO and 1WO *U 34* 10/40–9/41; 1WO U-boat depot ship *Isar* 9/41–7/42; 1WO *U 251* 7/42–5/43; U-Cdr's Course, 24th U-Flotilla 5/43–6/43 (U-Cdr's Torpedo Course 48); *Baubelehrung* 1.KLA 6/43–8/43
Cdr *U 394* 19.8.43–2.9.44
Lost 2.9.44 Norwegian Sea, W of Harstad

BORK, HELMUT [110]
b. 29.5.1910, Danzig
Entry VIII/1939; ObltzS (R) 1.4.43
2WO *U 134* 7/41–9/42; U-Cdr's Course, 24th U-Flotilla and *Baubelehrung* 9/42–11/42
Cdr *U 275* 25.11.42–7/44
3rd and 7th U-Flotillas 7/44–/44; Kplt on Staff, 8th and 5th U-Flotillas 9/44–capitulation

BORM, KARL [111]
b. 10.8.1911, Hamburg
Class 1934; Kplt 1.4.41
WO battleship *Scharnhorst* 4/39–9/39; Cdr torpedo-boat *T 146* (Mine Warfare School) 9/39–3/41; U-boat trg 4/41–9/41; U-Cdr's Course and *Baubelehrung* 9/41–10/41
Cdr *U 592* 16.10.41–24.7.43 (During overhaul at St Nazaire 7/43–9/43 *U 592* had no commander; former 1WO Jaschke [547] assumed command on 2.9.43.)
Heavy cruiser *Lützow* 7/43–9/43; Kplt on Staff, 7th U-Flotilla 10/43–7/44; 5th U-Flotilla 7/44–9/44; Kplt on Staff, 33rd U-Flotilla 9/44–12/44; Flotilla CO German warships in Holland 12/44–capitulation

BORNHAUPT, KONRAD [112]
b, 6.6.1920, Mediterranean Sea aboard steamer *Kowi*
Class 1937b; Kplt 1.1.45
Comp. Officer 1.ULD 3/41–9/41; *Baubelehrung* 9/41–10/41; 1WO *U 88* 10/41–5/42; 1WO U-boat depot ship *Wilhelm Bauer* 5/42–1/44; U-Cdr's Course, 3.ULD and 24th U-Flotilla 2/44–4/44 (U-Cdr's Torpedo Course 66)
Cdr *U 285* 17.4.44–15.4.45
Lost 15.4 45 SW of Ireland

BORNKESSEL, DIETER [113]
b. 7.8.1920, Dresden
Class XII/1939; ObltzS 1.12.43
Officer trg, courses, U-boat trg 12/39–2/41; WO sea trg *U 124* 3/41–9/41; courses 10/41–3/42; 3WO *U 178* 3/42–6/42; 2WO *U 616* 6/42–12/42; 1WO *U 29* 1/43–6/43; 1WO *U 354* 6/43–5/44; U-Cdr's Course, 24th U-Flotilla 5/44–7/44 (U-Cdr's Torpedo Course 73); *Baubelehrung* Type XXIII 8/44–10/44
Cdr *U 2332* 13.11.44 until mid-April 1945 (*U 2332* was taken over in mid-April 1945 by the crew originally intended for *U 2370*, commanded by Junker [567].)
Cdr *U 2370* mid-April 45–3.5.45. (*U 2370* was never commissioned and was in an unfinished condition when destroyed by a demolition party on 3.5.45 in bunker Fink II Box 3, Hamburg-Finkenwerder; information from U-Boat Archive per Bornkessel.)

BORTFELDT, KARL-HERMANN [114]
b. 12.4.1921, Hannover
Class IX/1939; ObltzS 1.10.43
Officer trg, courses and U-boat trg 9/39–9/41; WO 1st U-Flotilla 9/41–10/41; WO *U 71* 10/41–5/43; U-Cdr's Course, 24th U-Flotilla 5/43–6/43 (U-Cdr's Torpedo Course 48); U-Cdr 22nd U-Flotilla 6/43–7/43
Cdr *U 14* 21.7.43–1.7.44
Cdr *U 1167* 2.7.44–30.3.45
31st U-Flotilla 4/45–capitulation

BOSÜNER, HARALD [115]
b. 17.10.1913, Magdeburg
Entry 1934; Kplt 1.3.43
1WO *U 161* 9/42–6/43; U-Cdr's Course, 24th U-Flotilla 6/43–8/43 (U-Cdr's Torpedo Course 50); *Baubelehrung* 8.KLA 8/43–10/43
Cdr *U 1223* 6.10.43–3/44
Kplt on Staff 25th U-Flotilla 3/44–2/45
K-Verband 2/45–capitulation

BOTHE, FRIEDRICH [116]
b. 1.7.1917, Diemeringen, Alsace (when German province)
Class 1936; Kplt 1.5.43
U-boat trg 10/38–4/39; 2WO *U 30* 4/39–11/40; WO 24th U-Flotilla, *U 30* 11/40–3/41
Cdr *U 5* 28.3.41–6.1.42
21st U-Flotilla 1/42–2/42
Cdr *U 101* 4.2.42–31.3.42
Course, 24th U-Flotilla 4/42–6/42 and U-Cdr's Torpedo Course 6.5.42–2.6.42; *Baubelehrung* 7.KLA 6/42–7/42
Cdr *U 447* 11.7.42–7.5.43
Lost 7.5.43 W of Gibraltar

BRACHMANN, HANS-GÜNTHER [117]
b. 11.2.1904, Kiel
Class 1922; KptzS 1944
No 2 Gunnery Officer battleship *Gneisenau* 5/38–12/39; No 1 Gunnery Officer light cruiser *Köln* 12/39–4/41; U-boat trg 4/41–9/41; duties not recorded 9/41–3/42
Baubelehrung and Cdr *U 518* 3/42 or 25.4.42 to 18.8.42
Duties not recorded 9/42–12/42 (but according to Lohmann-Hildebrand specially assigned to Naval Commander 'R')
Adviser OKM 1/43–8/43; Cdr Naval Gunnery School I 8/43–capitulation
Detained; freed summer 1945

BRAEUCKER, FRIEDRICH [118]
b. 13.7.1919, Munich
Class 1937a; Kplt 1.7.44
9/Basic Trg Est. Stralsund and Torpedo School, Mürwik 11/39–3/40; 1st and 2nd Torpedo-Boat Flotillas 4/40–8/43; U-boat trg and U-Cdr's Torpedo Course 65 8/43–4/44; *Baubelehrung* 6.KLA 4/44–8/44
Cdr *U 889* 4.8.44–capitulation
Detained; freed 12/48

BRAMMER, HERBERT [119]
b. 24.4.1914, Rendsburg
Entry XI/1937; ObltzS 1.4.42
U-boat trg 11/40–10/41; *Baubelehrung* 10/41–12/41; 1WO *U 118* 12/41–12/42; U-Cdr's Course, 24th U-Flotilla 12/42–2/43; acting CO 5th U-Flotilla 2/43–3/43; Comp. Officer 2.UAA 3/43–4/43; *Baubelehrung* 4/43–5/43
Cdr *U 1060* 15.5.43–27.10.44
Lost 27.10.44 Norwegian Sea, S of Brönnöysund

BRAND, WILHELM [120]
b. 18.11.1915, Delmenhorst
Entry X/1939; ObltzS (R) 1.1.44
M/S-Cdr 42nd Minesweeping Flotilla 8/41–1/43; U-boat trg, U-Cdr's Course and *Baubelehrung* 7.KLA 1/43–11/43
Cdr *U 1196* 18.11.43–2/44
Naval Hospital Wesermünde 2/44–6/44
Courses, *Baubelehrung* and various duties 7/44–capitulation

BRANDENBURG, KARL [121]
b. 25.7.1906, Tribsees, Pomerania
Class 1934; FKpt, posthumously to 1.4.43
Cdr Naval Artillery Detachment 204 9/40–3/41; U-boat trg 3/41–10/41; *Baubelehrung* 10/41–11/41
Cdr *U 457* 5.11.41–16.9.42
Lost 16.9.42 Barents Sea, N of Murmansk

BRANDI, ALBRECHT [122]

b. 20.6.1914, Dortmund
Class 1935; FKpt appointed 9.5.44, seniority 1.12.44
WO minesweeper *M 1* 10/37–5/40; Cdr minesweeper *M 1* 5/40–4/41; U-boat trg 4/41–12/41; U-Cdr sea trg *U 552* 12/41–1/42; U-Cdr's Course and *Baubelehrung* 2/42–4/42
Cdr *U 617* 9.4.42–12.9.43
Interned at Cadiz 9/43–11/43
Cdr *U 380* 12/43–11.3.44
Cdr *U 967* 4/44–1.7.44
U/Adm. Staff Officer, Commanding Adm. Eastern Baltic (U-boat operations planner) 7/44–1/45; Officer Commanding *K-Verband* Forces in Holland 1/45–capitulation
Detained; freed 9/45
Knight's Cross 21.1.43 (148th KM, 79th U-boat holder)
Oak Leaves 11.4.43 (224th WM, 26th KM, 22nd U-boat holder)
Swords 9.5.44 (66th WM, 5th KM, 5th U-boat holder)
Diamonds 24.11.44 (22nd WM, 2nd KM, 2nd U-boat holder)

BRANS, HANS-JOACHIM [123]

b. 21.8.1915, Heidelberg
Class 1935; Kplt 1.11.42
Seconded to Luftwaffe until 3/42; U-boat trg 3/42–9/42; WO (supernumerary) *U 84* 9/42–12/42; U-Cdr's Course, 24th U-Flotilla 12/42–1/43; WO (supernumerary) *U 169* 1/43–2/43; *Baubelehrung* 6.KLA 2/43–3/43
Cdr *U 801* 24.3.43–17.3.44
Lost 17.3.44 nr Cape Verde Is

BRASACK, PAUL [124]

b. 9.5.1916, Stettin
Class 1937; Kplt 1.7.44
Navigator trg, Aircraft Weapons School (Sea) Parow 9/39–3/40; Navigator and Senior Flight Officer *1./Küstenfliegergruppe 706* 4/40–7/40; *KG 126*, later *1./KG 28*, 7/40–5/41; Staff *IX Fliegerkorps* 6/41–10/41; Reserve Group *KG 28*, Navigator Trg Officer *KG 4 General Wever* 10/41–2/42; U-boat trg 3/42–8/42; WO (supernumerary) *U 590* 8/42–11/42; trg, U-Cdr's Course and *Baubelehrung* 12/42–2/43
Cdr *U 737* 5.2.43–24.11.44 (originally listed to command *U 422*; see Poeschel [933])
Knight's Cross 30.10.44 (270th WM, 131st U-boat holder)

BRAUEL, WILHELM [125]

b. 17.9.1914, Hamburg
Class X/1937; Kplt 1.4.45
VP-Cdr with Harbour Defence Flotilla, Molde 5/40–7/42; U-boat trg 8/42–12/42; 1WO *U 103* 1/43–6/43; U-Cdr's Course 6/43–7/43 (U-Cdr's Torpedo Course 50)
Cdr *U 256* from either 16.8.43 (per *U 256* WD) or 1.9.43 (per WASt) until 27.6.44 (*U 256* had been decommissioned in November 1942 as a result of serious bomb damage received on 31.8.42. In the spring of 1943 it was decided that, in addition to the necessary repairs, the boat would be converted into a 'flak-trap', which delayed the recommissioning.)
Cdr *U 92* 28.6.44–12.10.44
Baubelehrung Type XXI 10/44–3/45
Cdr *U 3530* 23.3.45–23.4.45
Cdr *U 975* 24.4.45–capitulation
Detained; freed 27.10.47

BRAUN, KURT [126]

b. 27.8.1923, Braunschweig
Class V/1941; ObltzS 1.4.45
U-boat trg and courses 8/42–7/43; 2WO *U 763* 7/43–8/44
1WO and Acting Cdr *U 763* 8/44–10/44 (transfer voyage from La Pallice to Flensburg via Bergen)

Midshipmen's Trg Officer 3.ULD 10/44–1/45; 23rd U-Flotilla, FdU East and various duties 1/45–capitulation

BRECKWOLDT, FRIEDRICH [127]
b. 16.6.1912, Hamburg
Entry IX/1939; ObltzS (R) 1.4.44, seniority 1.8.43
WO VP-boat *V 1505* until 5/40; Kriegsmarine Yard, Horten, Norway 5/40–10/41; VP-Cdr 59th VP-Boat Flotilla 10/41–2/43; U-boat trg 2/43–9/43; U-Cdr's Course, 25th U-Flotilla 9/43–10/43; *Baubelehrung* 10/43–11/43
Cdr *U 679* 29.11.43–20.10.44
Flotilla Cdr *K-Verband* 11/44–capitulation

BREINLINGER, SIEGFRIED [128]
b. 24.4.1920, Radolfzell, Lake Constance
Class XII/1939; ObltzS 1.12.43
WO sea trg *U 108* 5/41–7/41; WO sea trg *U 38* 8/41–9/41; trg courses 10/41–3/42; supplementary WO *U 152* 3/42–6/42; *Baubelehrung* 6/42–7/42; 1WO *U 267* 7/42–9/43; U-Cdr's Course, 24th U-Flotilla 9/43–11/43 (U-Cdr's Torpedo Course 57); *Baubelehrung* 11/43–12/43
Cdr *U 320* 30.12.43–10.7.44 (per U-Boat Archive)
Baubelehrung Type XXI 9/44–1/45
Cdr *U 3018* 7.1.45–4.5.45

BREITHAUPT, WOLFGANG [129]
b. 19.9.1913, Hochheim, Erfurt
Class 1933; Kplt 1.2.41
Light cruiser *Köln* 10/38–3/41; U-boat trg 4/41–7/41; U-Cdr under instrn, 24th and 1st U-Flotillas, *Baubelehrung* 7/41–12/41
Cdr *U 599* 4.12.41–24.10.42
Lost 24.10.42 NE of Azores

VON BREMEN, HANSKURT [130]
b. 11.8.1918, Goslar, Lahn
Class 1938; ObltzS 1.4.43
WO 12th Minesweeping Flotilla 4/40–1/41; U-boat trg 2/41–6/41; Command Relay Officer, Staff BdU/Opns 7/41–8/41; *Baubelehrung* 9/41–11/41; 1WO *U 598* 12/41–1/43; U-Cdr's Course 2/43–3/43 (U-Cdr's Torpedo Course 43); *Baubelehrung* 3/43–5/43
Cdr *U 764* 6.5.43–capitulation

BREUN, GERHARD [131]
b. 7.4.1920, Nuremberg
Entry IV/1940; ObltzS (R) 1.3.44
38th Minesweeping Flotilla 6/40–11/40; Naval Gunnery School 11/40–12/40; 3/NCO Trg Div. 1/41–3/41; 34th Minesweeping Flotilla 4/41–4/42; 1.ULD 4/42–6/42; 2WO *U 266* 6/42–3/43; 2WO *U 410* 4/43–9/43; 1WO *U 410* 9/43–3/44; U-Cdr's Course, 24th U-Flotilla 4/44–6/44 (U-Cdr's Torpedo Course 72); Personnel Reserve and *Baubelehrung* Type XXIII, 22nd U-Flotilla 7/44–1/45
Cdr *U 2358* 16.1.45–5.5.45
Detained; freed 29.7.45

BROCKMANN, KARL [132]
b. 17.10.1914, Lehe-Wesermünde
Entry IV/1939; LtzS (R) 1.10.41
U-boat trg 1/41–6/41; 2WO *UD 1* 6/41–12/41; Acting Cdr *UC 1* 12/41–28.3.42
2WO *U 588* 3/42–7/42
Lost 31.7.1942 central North Atlantic (see Vogel [1305])

BRODDA, HEINRICH [133]
b. 9.5.1903, Altenessen, Essen
Class 1921; Kplt 1.1.1940
U-boat tender *Lech* 6/39–1/40; Cdr R-boat depot ship *Nettelbeck* 1/40–11/40; Cdr fleet escort *F 6* 11/40–3/41; U-boat trg 3/41–7/41; U-Cdr's

Course, 24th U-Flotilla 7/41–9/41;
Baubelehrung 9/41–10/41
Cdr *U 209* 11.10.41–7.5.43
Missing E of Newfoundland 7.5.43

BROSIN, HANS-GÜNTHER [134]
b.15.11.1916, Hannover
Class 1936; Kplt 1.7.43
Seconded to Luftwaffe 9/39–9/41; U-boat trg 9/41–1/42; 1WO *U 572* 1/42–6/42; U-Cdr's Course, 24th U-Flotilla 6.42–7/42; *Baubelehrung* 8.KLA 7/42–8/42
Cdr *U 634* 6.8.42–2.2.43
Cdr *U 134* 3.2.43–24.8.43
Lost 24.8.43 Bay of Biscay

BRÜCKNER, WERNER [135]
b. 13.10.1915, Hoyerswerda
Enlisted as rating 1934; ObltzS 1.1.45
ObStrm 2nd and 7th U-Flotillas, Personnel Reserve, *Baubelehrung* KLA Hamburg 11/40–6/43; 1.ULD and U-boat trg 6/43–2/44; 23rd U-Flotilla 2/44–3/44; U-Cdr's Course, 24th U-Flotilla 4/44–6/44 (U-Cdr's Torpedo Course 70); Cdr U-Holding Company 3, 21st U-Flotilla 6/44–11/44; *Baubelehrung* Type XXIII 8.KLA 11/44–12/44
Cdr *U 2351* 30.12.44–capitulation

BRÜLLAU, HEINZ [136]
b. 12.12.1917, Altona
Entry XII/1939; ObltzS (R) 1.3.44
WO and M/S-Cdr 10th VP-Boat Flotilla and 19th Minesweeping Flotilla 4/40–3/43; U-boat trg and courses 3/43–12/43 (U-Cdr's Torpedo Course 58); *Baubelehrung* 8.KLA 12/43–3/44
Cdr *U 905* 8.3.44–26.6.44
Duties 7/44–capitulation not recorded

BRÜLLER, ERNST-ULRICH [137]
b. 23.9.1917, Oppeln, Upper Silesia
Class 1936; Kplt 1.4.43
Platoon Cdr 7/Basic Trg Est. Stralsund 4/39–11/39; ADC U-Trg Flotilla 12/39–2/40; 1WO *U 4* 3/40–4/40; 2WO *U 28* 5/40–11/40; 1WO *U 28* 11/40–12/40
Cdr *U 7* 1/41–2/41
Cdr *U 23* 21.3.41–23.9.41
Baubelehrung 10/41–12/41
Cdr *U 407* 18.12.41 until 6.1.44 (per WASt) or 14.1.44 (per WD *U 407*, and see Korndörfer [581])
Comp. CO 1.ULD 2/44–3/45; Comp. CO (Special Purposes) Naval College Glücksberg 4/45–capitulation
Detained; freed 4/47

BRÜMMER-PATZIG, HELMUT [138]
b. 26.10 1890, Danzig
Class 1910; FKpt (zV) 1.2.44
WO pre-dreadnought *Pommern* until 11/15; U-Boat School, U-Boat Acceptance Command 11/15–1/16; WO *U A* (Scherb) 1/16–5/16; 1WO *U 55* (Werner) 6/16–9/17; hydroplanes instructor, U-Boat School, Eckernförde, 9/17–1/18; Cdr *U 86* 1/18–8/18; Cdr *U 90* 8/18–11/18 (Armistice)
BdU Staff 2/40–6/40; U-boat base Lorient 6/40–9/40; U-boat base Königsberg 9/40–10/40; *Baubelehrung UD 4* 11/40–1/41
Cdr *UD 4* 28.1.41–15.10.41
Senior torpedo attack instructor, 25th U-Flotilla 11/41–3/43; CO 26th U-Flotilla 4/43–3/45; retired 3.5.45

BRÜNIG, MATTHIAS [139]
b. 23.2.1920, Hamburg
Class 1938; ObltzS 1.4.43
Battleship *Gneisenau* 5/40–8/40; Cdr artillery transport *Gloria* 9/40–11/40; U-boat trg 11/40–2/41; Midshipmen's Trg Officer, Torpedo

School Mürwik 3/41–6/42; *Baubelehrung* 6/42–9/42; 1WO *U 195* 9/42–8/43; U-Cdr's Course 9/43–10/43

Cdr *U 108* from 17.10.43 until 12.6.44 (per WASt) or 11.4.44. *U 108* was bombed and sunk at Stettin 11.4.44 and salved and decommissioned 17.4.44. Brünig was relieved 11.4.44 and sent for *Baubelehrung* at 6.KLA for future command of *U 884*. (U-Boat Archive per Brünig.)

Baubelehrung Cdr *U 884* (never commissioned) 10/44–3/45

Cdr *U 3038* 4.3.45 to 27.4.45 or 3.5.45

BRÜNINGHAUS, HERBERT [140]

b. 11.10.1910, Siegen, Württemberg

Enlisted rating 1931; Kplt 1.4.45

ObStrm U-Flotilla *Hundius* (later 6th U-Flotilla) 10/38–6/41; courses 6/41–9/41

Cdr *U 6* 10/41–8/42 and 9/42–19.10.42

Cdr *U 148* 20.10.42–18.1.43

Courses and *Baubelehrung* 1/43–5/43

Cdr *U 1059* 1.5.43–30.9.43

Nautical specialist and Harbour Cdr, Hela, AGRU-Front 10/43–capitulation

BRÜNNER, JOACHIM [141]

b. 12.4.1919, Breslau

Class 1937b; ObltzS 1.4.42

Div. Officer and WO light cruiser *Leipzig* 12/40–10/41; U-boat trg 10/41–3/42; 27th U-Flotilla 3/42–6/42; Personnel Reserve, U-boat base, Narvik, 6/42–7/42; 1WO *U 703* 8/42–5/43; U-Cdr's Course, 2.UAA and 24th U-Flotilla 5/43–7/43 (U-Cdr's Torpedo Course 49)

Cdr *U 703* 6.7.43–9/44

Missing 9/44 E of Greenland

BRÜNNING, HERBERT [142]

b.13.9.1915, Hamburg

Class 1935; Kplt 1.9.42

Torpedo Officer/ADC light cruiser *Emden* 6/39–1/41; Torpedo Officer/ADC trg ship *Schlesien* 1/41–3/41; Torpedo Officer/ADC light cruiser *Emden* 3/41; U-boat trg 3/41–8/41; U-Cdr's Course, 24th U-Flotilla, U-Cdr sea trg *U 98* 9/41–12/41

Cdr *U 137* 8.12.41–1.9.42

Baubelehrung 8.KLA 9/42

Cdr *U 642* 1.10.42–5.7.44

29th U-Flotilla 7/44–8/44; *Baubelehrung* Type XXI 7.KLA 8/44–12/44

Cdr *U 3518* 29.12.44–3.5.45

Detained; freed 15.8.45

BRUDER, HERMANN [143]

b. 5.3.1921 place not recorded

Class XII/1939; ObltzS 1.12.43

Officer trg, courses 12/39–2/42; Platoon Cdr 1.ULD 3/42–2/43; 1WO *U 471* 3/43–1/44; U-Cdr's Course 2/44–4/44; *Baubelehrung* 4/44–6/44

Cdr *U 1058* 10.6.44–capitulation

Detained; freed 9.5.48

BRUNS, HEINRICH [144]

b. 3.4.1912, Castrop-Rauxel

Class 1931; Kplt 1.10.39, posthumously KKpt seniority 1.4.43

Signals Officer battleship *Scharnhorst* 8/39–9/39; Divisional Leader 1st Torpedo-Boat Flotilla Trg Div. 10/39–1/40; *Baubelehrung* 1/40–2/40; Cdr torpedo-boat *T 3* 2/40–9/40; hospitalised 10/40–12/40; Destroyer and Torpedo-Boat Crews' Holding Division 12/40–1/41; Navigating Officer trg ship *Schleswig-Holstein* 1/41–3/41; U-boat trg 3/41–7/41; WO (supernumerary) *U 75* 7/41–9/41; U-Cdr's Course, 26th U-Flotilla and *Baubelehrung* 10/41–12/41

Cdr *U 175* 5.12.41–17.4.43

Lost 17.4.43 SW of Ireland

BUCHHOLZ, HEINZ [145]
b. 3.8.1909, Goldap, East Prussia
Class 1929; KKpt 1.4.43
U-boat trg and courses 1/35–7/35; WO *U 8* 8/35–11/36; WO *U 34* 11/36–12/36; WO *U 22* 12/36–7/37; Cdr *U 24* 3.7.37–30.9.37; Cdr *U 15* 1.10.37–26.10.39 but relief instructor Torpedo School Flensburg-Mürwik 11/37–12/37; OKM/SKL-U 10/39–7/40; Senior Officer Trg and Torpedo Attack Instruction and Torpedo Adviser to 24th U-Flotilla 7/40–2/42; Acting CO 1st U-Flotilla 5/42–7/42; *Baubelehrung* KLA U-Nord 7/42–9/42
Cdr *U 195* 5.9.42–17.10.43
Cdr *U 177* 17.10.43–6.2.44
Lost 6.2.44 central Atlantic, W of Ascension Island

BUDZYN, SIGMUND [146]
b. 1.1.1916, Duisburg-Meiderich
Conscripted V/1941; ObltzS 1945
ObBtsMt *U 18* 1/41–5/41; Navigation School Gdynia 6/41–7/41; *Baubelehrung U 155* 7/41–8/41; ObStrm *U 155* 8/41–6/43; wounded and hospitalised 6/43–10/43; courses, WO and U-Cdr's trg 10/43–11/44 (U-Cdr's Torpedo Course 70); *Baubelehrung* Type XXIII 11/44–1/45
Cdr *U 2352* 11.1.45–5.5.45

BÜCHEL, PAUL [147]
b. 3.8.1907, Greifenberg, Pomerania
Class 1925; FKpt 1.10.43
U-boat trg 5/37–8/37; Cdr *U 32* 8/37 or 1.9.37 (see Lott [754]) to 11.2.40
CO U-Boat School Flotilla/21st U-Flotilla 3/40–6/43 and Cdr 1.Div./1.ULD 5/40–6/43; *Baubelehrung* 6.KLA 6/43–8/43
Cdr *U 860* 12.8.43–15.6.44
POW 15.6.44–4/46

BÜCHLER, RUDOLF [148]
b. 14.10.1915, Breslau
Class 1936; Kplt 1.7.43
U-boat trg 9/41–3/42; 1WO *U 161* 3/42–9/42; U-Cdr's Course, 24th U-Flotilla 10/42–11/42; *Baubelehrung* 1.KLA 11/42
Cdr *U 387* 24.11.42–9.12.44
Lost 9.12.44 Barents Sea, off Murmansk

BÜHRING, HANS-JÜRGEN [149]
b. 2.7.1920, Berlin
Class 1937b; ObltzS 1.4.42
WO *U 148* summer 1941–9/41; 1WO *U 657* 10/41–9/42; U-Cdr's Course, 24th U-Flotilla 9/42–10/42; *Baubelehrung* 1.KLA 10/42–11/42
Cdr *U 360* 12.11.42–5/43
5th U-Flotilla 5/43–10/43; instructor 2.ULD 10/43–10/44; Comp. CO 4.Naval Reserve Div. 10/44–4/45; CO 2.UAA 4/45–capitulation

VON BÜLOW, OTTO [150]
b. 16.10.1911, Wilhelmshaven
Class 1930; KKpt 1.4.43
Cdr Naval Flak Detachment 215 9/39–1/40; Naval Flak Detachment 221 2/40–3/40; U-boat trg 4/40–11/40
Cdr *U 3* 11.11.40–2.7.41
Baubelehrung 7/41–8/41
Cdr *U 404* 6.8.41–19.7.43
FdU/Trg 7/43–8/43; CO 23rd U-Flotilla 9/43–3/45
Cdr *U 2545* 29.3.45–18.4.45 (commissioning date 8.4.45 per U-Boat Archive, Aschmoneit-List)
Cdr Naval Assault Battalion No 1, Neustrelitz, Plön and Mürwik 4/45–5/45
Detained; freed 2.8.45
Knight's Cross 20.10.42 (129th KM, 65th U-boat holder)
Oak Leaves 26.4.43 (243rd WM, 29th KM, 23rd U-boat holder)

BÜRGEL, FRIEDRICH [151]
b. 24.10.1916, Düsseldorf
Class 1936; Kplt 1.5.43
Command Relay Officer heavy cruiser *Admiral Scheer* 4/38–1/40; Group Officer Naval College Mürwik 2/40–9/40; U-boat trg 10/40–3/41; 1WO *U 565* 4/41–1/42; U-Cdr's Course 2/42–4/42
Cdr *U 97* 5/42–15.10.42
Cdr *U 205* 19.10.42 (per *U 205* WD; see Reschke [996]) to 17.2.43
POW 17.2.43–3.12.47

BUGS, HANS-HELMUTH [152]
b. 11.3.1917, Angermünde
Class 1937a; ObltzS 1.3.41
WO gunnery trg ship *Brummer* 4/39–10/39; Platoon officer, Reserve Naval Artillery Div. 10/39–1/40; Platoon officer, Naval Flak Detachment 219 2/40–4/40; U-boat trg 4/40–9/40; Comp. Officer 1.ULD 9/40–6/41; *Baubelehrung* 7/41–8/41; 1WO *U 435* 8/41–5/42; U-Cdr's Course, 24th U-Flotilla and *Baubelehrung* 8.KLA 5/42–6/42
Cdr *U 629* 2.7.42–8.6.44
Lost 8.6.44 W of Brest

DE BUHR, JOHANN [153]
b. 23.3.1912, Ostrhanderfehn, Ostfriesland
Entry 1934/40; ObltzS (R) 1.3.43
Courses and U-boat trg 7/40–3/42; 1st U-Flotilla 3/42–5/42; 2WO and 1WO *U 86* 5/42–4/43; 2.UAA 4/43; U-Cdr's Course, 24th U-Flotilla 5/43–6/43 (U-Cdr's Torpedo Course 47); *Baubelehrung* 6.KLA 6/43–7/43
Cdr *U 347* 7.7.43–17.7.44
Lost 17.7.44 Norwegian Sea, W of Narvik

BUHSE, HEINZ [154]
3.1.1917, Heidelberg
Entry X/1939; ObltzS (R) 1.1.44
ADC Kriegsmarine Depot (Aalborg) 5/40–8/40, (Dunkirk) 8/40–1/41; Naval Transport Officer, Staff, Naval Commander Dunkirk 2/41–4/41; ADC and Comp. CO Naval Transport HQ Aegean 4/41–8/43; U-boat trg 8/43–2/44; U-Cdr under instrn, 19th U-Flotilla 2/44–5/44; U-Cdr's Course, 24th U-Flotilla 5/44–7/44 (U-Cdr's Torpedo Course 72)
Cdr *U 399* 3.7.44–26.3.45
Lost 26.3.45 English Channel, off Land's End

BUNGARDS, HANS [155]
b. 1.7.1917, Solingen, Ruhr
Class 1936; Kplt 1.8.43
Seconded to Luftwaffe 9/39–3/43; U-boat trg 4/43–9/43; WO 27th U-Flotilla 10/43; U-Cdr under instrn, 23rd U-Flotilla 10/43–12/43; *Baubelehrung* 6.KLA 12/43–1/44
Cdr *U 1103* 8.1.44–2.7.44
Baubelehrung Type XXI 8.KLA 7/44–10/44
Cdr *U 2512* 12.10.44–26.4.45
Cdr *U 3012* 27.4.45–28.4.45
(Following an accident aboard *U 3012* on 28.4.45, Bungards died the same day at the Reserve Hospital in Travemünde. Subsequently a Kplt Meyer presented himself as the new commander of *U 3012* on 1.5.45 and announced to the crew that he had always served previously on a torpedo boat or destroyer and had no U-boat experience. On 4.5.45 *U 3012* was sunk nr the lightship *Adlergrund* off the island of Fehmarn by rocket fire from British fighter-bombers. The identity of Kapitänleutnant Meyer has never been ascertained, and the spelling may be incorrect.)

BURGHAGEN, WALTER [156]
b. 21.9.1891, Dresden Class 1911; KKpt (zV) date not recorded
No 2 Wireless Telegraphy Technical Officer, battleship *Schlesien* until 3/16; U-boat trg, U-Boat School 3/16–8/16; WO *U 44*, *U 49* and

U 50 8/16–11/16; POW in England until 11/18 (Armistice)
Comp. CO 1.ULD 3/40–2/41; CO 2.ULD 2/41–10/42; *Baubelehrung* 10/42–12/42
Cdr *U 219* 12.12.42–capitulation
Interned and detained, freed 12/46

BURMEISTER, WALTER [157]
b. 9.2.1919, Aerzen, Hameln
Class 1937b; Kplt 1.1.45
Trg and courses until 5/40; Works Officer, Naval Ordnance Office, Kiel 5/40–6/40; Works Officer, Naval Ordnance Office, Wilhelmshaven 7/40–9/40; Comp. Officer, Naval Gunnery School 10/40–3/43; course, Helmsman's School 3/43–6/43 (transferred from Ordnance to Seaman Branch); U-boat trg 6/43–10/43; course 3.ULD 10/43–11/43; U-boat handling trg and U-Cdr's Torpedo Course, 23rd U-Flotilla 11/43–2/44; U-Cdr sea trg *U 267* 11.2.44–1.6.44
Cdr *U 1018* 2.6.44–27.2.45
Lost 27.2.45 English Channel, S of Penzance

BUSCHER, HANS [158]
b. 2.8.1918, Düsseldorf
Class 1938; ObltzS 1.9.43
Trg and courses, plus duties with 2nd and 36th Minesweeping Flotillas 8/39–9/41; WO 2nd Minesweeping Flotilla 9/41–9/43; U-boat trg 9/43–3/44; 19th, later 31st U-Flotilla 3/44–10/44; *Baubelehrung* 1.KLA 10/44–11/44
Cdr *U 1307* 1
7.11.44–capitulation

BUTTJER, JOHANN [159]
b. 26.5.1912, Norder, Ostfriesland
Rating entry 1931; Kplt 1.3.45
4/Basic Trg Est. Stralsund 5/39–8/40; Naval Harbour Detachment, Calais 8/40–3/41; light cruiser *Emden* 3/41–6/42; course, Helmsman's School 6/42–8/42; WO sea trg, 3rd Minesweeping Flotilla 9/42–1/43; U-boat trg 1/43–7/43; U-Cdr's Trg Course, 24th U-Flotilla 7/43–8/43 (U-Cdr's Torpedo Course 53); *Baubelehrung* 9/43–10/43
Cdr *U 768* 14.10.43–20.11.43
31st U-Flotilla 11/43–12/43; *Baubelehrung* 6.KLA 12/43–2/44
Cdr *U 774* 17.2.44–18.10.44
31st U-Flotilla 10/44
Duties until capitulation not recorded, died 12.8.45

C

CABOLET, SERVAIS [160]
b. 24.04.1908 Warstade, Lower Elbe
Date of entry not recorded; ObltzS (R) 1943
3rd Minesweeping Flotilla 4/40–6/40; VP-Cdr Harbour Defence Flotilla, Trondheim 7/40–6/41; VP-Cdr Harbour Defence Flotilla, Molde 6/41–11/41; VP-Cdr 59th VP-Boat Flotilla 11/41–12/42; hospitalised 12/42–3/43; U-boat trg, courses and *Baubelehrung* 3/43–5/44 (U-Cdr's Torpedo Course 60)
Cdr *U 907* 18.5.44–capitulation
Detained; freed 31.12.47

CALLSEN, PETER [161]
b. 28.10.1911, Sterup, Flensburg
Entry XI/1939; ObltzS (R) 1.10.43
WO 2nd VP-Boat Flotilla 4/40–6/41; WO 5th Minesweeping Flotilla 6/41–7/42; assigned BdU and U-boat trg 7/42–2/43; *Baubelehrung* 1.KLA 2/43–5/43; 1WO *U 1060* 5/43–5/44; course, 23rd U-Flotilla 5/44–6/44; U-Cdr under instrn, 31st U-Flotilla 7/44–11/44; *Baubelehrung* Type XXI 6.KLA 11/44–2/45
Cdr *U 3033* 27.2.45–4.5.45

VON CARLEWITZ, DIETRICH [162]
b. 11.7.1916, Bautzen; Class 1936
ObltzS 1.10.40
On Staff Naval Signals Officer, List 12/38–4/40, Thyborön 4/40–6/40 and Esbjerg within period when seconded Commanding Adm. France and Station Command Kiel 6/40–9/40; 3rd Radio Technical Officer heavy cruiser *Admiral Scheer* 9/40–6/41; U-boat trg 6/41–11/41; 7th U-Flotilla 11/41–12/41; WO *U 98* 12/41–6/42; U-Cdr's Course, 24th U-Flotilla 6/42–8/42; *Baubelehrung* 8.KLA 8/42–9/42
Cdr *U 710* 2.9.42–24.4.43
Lost 12.4.43 North Atlantic, S of Iceland

CARLSEN, CLAUS-PETER [163]
b. 7.10.1919, Berlin
Class 1937b; ObltzS 1.4.42
WO fleet escort vessel *F 7* 12/39–3/40; 1WO 13th Minesweeping Flotilla 4/40–2/41; U-boat trg 2/41–8/41; *Baubelehrung* 8/41–9/41; 1WO *U 251* 9/41–7/42; U-Cdr's Course and *Baubelehrung* 8/42–10/42
Cdr *U 732* 24.10.42–31.10.43
POW 31.10.43–1.11.47

CHRISTIANSEN, HELMUT [164]
b. 24.9.1918, Kollund, Flensburg
Entry 1938; ObltzS (R) 1.9.43
U-boat trg 5/43–10/43; various duties and courses 10/43–7/44; *Baubelehrung* 1.KLA 7/44–9/44
Cdr *U 1305* 13.9.44–capitulation

CHRISTIANSEN, UWE [165]
b. 25.1.1920, Flensburg
Class 1938; ObltzS 1.1.43
2WO and 1WO *U 572* 5/41–9/42; U-Cdr's Course, 24th U-Flotilla 9/42–11/42
Cdr *U 28* 1.12.42–7/43
Cdr *U 71* 7/43–7.6.44
Baubelehrung Type XXI 8.KLA 6/44–9/44
Cdr *U 2508* 26.9.44–3.5.45
Cdr *U 2365* 3.5.45–8.5.45

CHRISTOPHERSEN, ERWIN [166]
b. 13.4.1915, Sonderburg
Class 1936; Kplt 1.9.43
Seconded to Luftwaffe until 12/40; U-boat trg 1/41–6/41; 1WO *U 753* 6/41–6/42; U-Cdr's trg, 24th U-Flotilla 7/42–8/42; *Baubelehrung* 1.KLA 8/42–9/42
Cdr *U 228* 12.9.42–8/44 (see Engel [254])
Personnel Reserve 1.UAA 9/44–11/44; *Baubelehrung* Type XXI 11/44–1/45
Cdr *U 3028* 27.1.45–3.5.45 (see Curio [180])
Lost 4.5.45 Kleiner Belt, north coast Fynen, Denmark, aboard *U 2503* (see Wächter [1311])

CLAUSEN, HEINZ-EHLERT [167]
b. 12.7.1909, Rodewald, Neustad
Entry 1932; Kplt 1.7.41
Cdr UJ-*Warthe* (Anti-Submarine School) 9/39–10/40; U-boat trg 10/40–1/41; U-Cdr sea trg *U 101* 2/41–5/41; *Baubelehrung* 5/41–6/41
Cdr *U 403* 25.6.41–15.6.43
CO U-boat technical experimental group *Sultan* 6/43–capitulation
Detained; freed 3.8.45

CLAUSEN, ASMUS NICOLAI [168]
b. 2.6.1911, Flensburg
Entry 1929, Kplt 1.1.41, posthumously KKpt seniority 1.5.43
Cdr *M 134*, 4th Minesweeping Flotilla 9/39–11/39; 1WO *U 37* 11/39–7/40; U-Cdr's Course, 24th U-Flotilla 7/40–8/40; *Baubelehrung U 142* 8/40–9/40
Cdr *U 142* 4.9.40–13.10.40
Cdr *U 37* 26.10.40 (per WASt) or 14.10.40 (per P/F) or 12.10.40 (per *U 142* WD) to 2.5.41
Baubelehrung U-Boats North 5/41
Cdr *U 129* 21.5.41–13.5.42 (26.5.42 per P/F); also see Witt [1362]
Baubelehrung 6.KLA *U 182* 5/42–6/42
Cdr *U 182* 30.6.42–16.5.43
Lost 16.5.43 W of Madeira

Knight's Cross 13.3.42 (103rd KM, 46th U-boat holder)

CLAUSSEN, AUGUST-WILHELM [169]
b. 13.03.1919, Flensburg
Class X/37; Kplt 1.1.45
Light cruiser *Leipzig* 12/39–1/40; light cruiser *Köln* 1/4–4/40; acting VP-Cdr 13th VP-Boat Flotilla 5/40–7/40; ADC 7th VP-Boat Flotilla 7/40–9/41; VP-Cdr, 7th VP-Boat Flotilla 9/41–1/42; U-boat trg, courses and various duties 2/42–7/43; U-Cdr's trg, 24th U-Flotilla 8/43–9/43 (U-Cdr's Torpedo Course 53); *Baubelehrung* 8.KLA 9/43–11/43
Cdr *U 1226* 24.11.43–28.10.44
Missing North Atlantic 28.10.44

CLAUSSEN, EMIL [170]
b. 6.10.1917, Flensburg
Entry IV/1937; ObltzS 1.9.41
Aircraft Weapons School, Parow 10/39–5/40; 1WO 19th Minesweeping Flotilla 5/40–9/41; U-boat trg 9/41–3/42; WO *U 576* 3/42; 1WO *U 578* 4/42–7/42; U-Cdr's Course, 24th U-Flotilla 7/42–9/42; *Baubelehrung* 9/42–10/42
Cdr *U 469* 7.10.42–25.3.43
Lost, 25.3.43 North Atlantic, S of Iceland

CLEMENS, JOHANNES [171]
b. 21.5.1911, Gotha
Entry 1935, ObltzS (R) 1.3.43
VP-Cdr Harbour Defence Flotilla, Narvik 8/40–7/42; Cdr and Group Leader 10th VP-Boat Flotilla 7/42–3/43; U-boat trg 3/43–9/43; U-Cdr's trg, 24th U-Flotilla 9/43–11/43 (U-Cdr's Torpedo Course 56); *Baubelehrung* 5.KLA 11/43–2/43
Cdr *U 319* 4.12.43–15.7.44
Lost 15.7.44 SW of Lindesnes, Norway

COESTER, CHRISTIAN-BRANDT [172]
13.11.1919, Breslau
Class X/37; ObltzS 1.4.42
U-boat trg 7/40–10/40; ADC 22nd U-Flotilla 10/40–5/41; 2WO *U 124* 5/41–5/42; U-Cdr's Course, 24th U-Flotilla 5/42–6/42
Cdr *U 10* 23.6.42–2/43
Baubelehrung 8.KLA 2/43–4/43
Cdr *U 542* 7.4.43–28.11.43
Lost 28.11.43 N of Madeira

COHAUSZ, HANS [173]
b. 30.11.1907, Essen-Katernberg
Class 1926; FKpt 1.8.44
U-boat trg and courses 9/35–4/36; while assigned FdU 1.5.36–21.9.36 served as Cdr *U 15*, U-Flotilla *Weddigen* 16.5.36–2.8.36; *Baubelehrung* Deschimag AG Weser Bremen 22.9.36–7.10.36; Cdr *U 30*, U-Flotilla *Saltzwedel* 8.10.36–31.10.38; U-Cdr with U-Flotilla *Hundius* 1.11.38–3.1.39; Staff Officer at FdU 4.1.39–16.9.39
Cdr *U A* (7th U-Flotilla) 17.9.39–31.10.40
CO 1st U-Flotilla 1.11.40–14.2.42
Cdr *U A* (2nd U-Flotilla) 15.2.42–14.5.42
CO 11th U-Flotilla 15.5.42–19.12.44
U-Cdr Torpedo School Mürwik, 20.12.44–capitulation
Detained; freed 25.8.45

COLLMANN, HERWIG [174]
b. 1.9.1915 Posen
Class 1935; Kplt 1.4.42
1WO *U 56* 11/38–6/40
Cdr *U 17* 8.7.40–4.1.41
Baubelehrung 1/41–3/41
Cdr *U 562* 20.3.41–3.9.41
Senior Officer Trg, 24th U-Flotilla 11/41–9/44; CO 21st U-Flotilla 9/44–3/45; Staff Officer, Commanding Adm. U-Boats 3/45–capitulation

CONRAD, GERHARD [175]
b. 18.8.1922, Berlin-Karlshorst
Class XII/1939; ObltzS 1.12.43
Officer trg 12/39–4/41; U-boat trg 5/41–2/42; *Baubelehrung* 2/42–3/42; 2WO *U 260* 3/42–11/43; 1WO *U 260* 11/43–3/44; course 2.ULD 3/44–4/44; U-Cdr's Course, 23rd U-Flotilla 4/44–6/44
Cdr *U 214* 7/44–26.7.44
Lost 26.7.44 English Channel, SE of Eddystone

CORDES, ERNST [176]
b. 26.6.1913, Hagen-Haspe
Entry 1934; Kplt 1.9.43
2WO *U 123* 5/40–4/41; 2WO *U 103* 4/41–6/41; U-Cdr's Course, 24th U-Flotilla 7/41–8/41
Cdr *U 560* 25.8.41–15.7.42
Naval Liaison Officer/*Fliegerführer Atlantik* at BdU 8/42–2/43; *Baubelehrung* 2/43–3/43
Cdr *U 763* 13.3.43–31.10.44 (see Braun [126])
Cdr *U 1195* 1.11.44–7.4.45
Lost 6.4.45 English Channel, S of Spithead anchorage

CRANZ, WILHELM [177]
19.4.1915, Kiel
Entry X/1939; ObltzS (R) 1.2.44
Platoon Leader, Destroyer and Torpedo-Boat Crews' Holding Div. 1/42–7/42; U-boat trg 7/42–12/42; Personnel Reserve, 1st U-Flotilla 1/43; 2WO *U 653* 1/43–6/43; 1WO *U 653* 6/43–1/44; U-Cdr's Course, 24th U-Flotilla 2/44–3/44 (U-Cdr's Torpedo Course 66); Comp. Officer 15th Naval Reserve Division 4/44–11/44
Cdr *U 398* 9.11.44–4/45
Missing in English waters 17.4.45

CREMER, PETER-ERICH [178]
b. 25.03.1911, Metz, Lorraine (when German province)

Class 1932; KKpt 1.8.44
2WO destroyer *Z 6 Theodor Riedel* 10/39–7/40; U-boat trg 8/40–11/40; assigned BdU 11/40; U-Cdr's Course, 24th U-Flotilla 11/40–1/41; *Baubelehrung* 1/41
Cdr *U 152* 29.1.41–21.7.41
Baubelehrung U-Boats North Sea 7/41–8/41
Cdr *U 333* 25.8.41–9.10.42
Hospitalised 10/42–2/43; 2/Adm. Staff Officer (Chargé d'Affaires) OKM/2.SKL/BdU/Opns 2/43–5/43
Cdr *U 333* 18.5.43–19.7.44
1.UAA 7/44–10/44; *Baubelehrung* Type XXI 8.KLA 10/44–11/44
Cdr *U 2519* 15.11.44–2/45 (latter date per P/F)
Cdr Naval Anti-Tank Battalion 2/45–4/45 (This unit saw action south of Hamburg in April 1945 and was mentioned in Wehrmacht despatches on 25 April 1945 for the destruction of 24 enemy tanks. Cremer was not replaced as commander of *U 2519*, and the crew scuttled the boat at Kiel on 3 May 1945
Cdr Wachbatallion *Dönitz* 5/45
Detained; freed 6/45
Knight's Cross 5.6.42 (111th KM, 52nd U-boat holder)

CREUTZ, HORST [179]

b. 19.5.1915, Berlin-Pankow
Class 1935, Kplt 1.12.42
Heavy cruiser *Admiral Hipper* 12/39–3/43; U-boat trg 3/43–9/43; Platoon Leader 2.UAA 9/43–11/43; U-Cdr under instrn, 23rd U-Flotilla 11/43–12/43; *Baubelehrung* 1.KLA 12/43–3/44
Cdr *U 400* 18.3.44–17.12.44
Lost 17.12.44 North Atlantic, S of Cork

CURIO, OSKAR [180]

b. 28.2.1918, Klein-Algemissen, nr Hildesheim
Class 1937a; Kplt 1.1.44

1WO *U 373* 5/41–2/42; U-Cdr's Course, 2.UAA and 24th U-Flotilla 2/42–5/42
Cdr *U 80* 5.5.42–22.11.42
Baubelehrung 8.KLA 11/42–12/42
Cdr *U 952* 10.12.42–6.8.44
2.UAA 8/44–10/44; *Baubelehrung* Type XXI 8.KLA 10/44–12/44
Cdr *U 2528* 9.12.44 to 23.4.45, when the boat was taken out of commission for lack of fuel. A telex from the FdU ordered Curio's transfer to Norway to assume command of a boat ready to sail on patrol. He was instructed to travel aboard *U 1025* to Norway, but on 30 April 1945 this boat was taken out of service because of defective batteries. He received fresh orders to embark as a passenger for Norway on *U 2503* (commander Wächter [1311]); Christophersen [166] was also aboard for a similar purpose. Between 1720hrs and 1732hrs on 3 May the boat was bombed and severely damaged by Beaufighters of Nos 236 and 254 Squadrons RAF. Twelve men aboard *U 2503* were killed, including Chistophersen and Wächter; the latter was brought ashore alive but died later in a Danish hospital. Curio was below at the time of the attack and subsequently assumed command. The burning wreck of *U 2503* was towed to land by a passenger ferry and beached southwest of the Danish island of Omö. At 0512hrs the next morning explosive charges were used by Curio and Chief Engineer Gerhard Gneuss to destroy the submarine.

CZEKOWSKI, MARTIN [181]

b. 18.1.1922, Berlin
Class X/1940; ObltzS 1.10.44
Officer trg 10/40–9/42; 25th U-Flotilla 10/42–4/43; 2WO *U 608* 4/43–7/43; 1WO *U 608* 7/43–4/44; U-Cdr's Course 3.ULD 4/44–7/44; 22nd U-Flotilla 7/44–11/44; *Baubelehrung* Type XXIII 8.KLA 12/44–2/45
Cdr *U 2362* 5.2.45–5.5.45

CZYGAN, WERNER [182]

b. 25.11.1904, Mogilno, Posen

Class 1925, KKpt 1.4.40

Ship's company, working-up heavy cruiser *Blücher* 4/39–9/39; Wargames Officer *Blücher* 9/39–4/40; assisting Adm. Commanding Norwegian South Coast 4/40–6/40; 1/Adm. Staff Officer, Adm. Commanding Norwegian South Coast 6/40–8/40; 1/Adm. Staff Officer, Adm. Commanding Norwegian Polar Coast 8/40–3/41; U-boat trg and courses 3/41–10/41; *Baubelehrung* KLA U-East 10/41–12/41

Cdr *U 118* 6.12.41–12.6.43

Lost 12.6.43 W of Canary Is

D

DÄHNE, WOLFGANG [183]
b. 6.8.1921 Arnstadt, Thüringen
Class XII/1939; ObltzS 1.12.43
Officer trg 12/39–3/42; supernumerary WO *U 257* 3/43–7/43; 2WO *U 29* 7/42–12/42; *Baubelehrung* 12/42–1/43; 1WO *U 960* 1/43–10/43; U-Cdr's Course 11/43–12/43
Cdr *U 349* 5.1.44–5.5.45
Detained; freed 18.10.45

DAHLHAUS, EBERHARD [184]
b. 24.7.1920 Hagen
Class 1938; ObltzS 1.3.43
Trg and courses 7/39–5/41; *Baubelehrung* 5/41–6/41; 2WO *U 753* 6/41–12/42; U-Cdr's Course, 24th U-Flotilla 12/42–1/43
Cdr *U 634* 28.1.43 (per *U 634* WD and see Brosin [134]) or 3.2.43 (per WASt) to 30.8.43
Lost 30.8.43 Atlantic, E of Azores

DAHMS, HERMANN [185]
b. 31.8.1916 Stettin
Class 1936; Kplt 1.7.43
Seconded to Luftwaffe 9/39–8/41; U-boat trg 8/41–3/42; WO 2nd U-Flotilla 3/42–2/43; U-Cdr's Course, 2.UAA and 24th U-Flotilla 2/43–4/43 (U-Cdr's Torpedo Course 44); *Baubelehrung* 8.KLA 4/43–5/43
Cdr *U 980* 27.5.43–11.6.44
Lost 11.6.44 NW of Bergen

DAMEROW, WOLF-DIETRICH [186]
b. 28.5.1919, Schwedt, Oder
Class 1937b; ObltzS 1.4.42
WO 8th VP-Boat Flotilla 5/40–9/41; U-boat trg 9/41–3/42; *Baubelehrung* 8.KLA 3/42–6/42; 1WO *U 521* 6/42–3/43; U-Cdr's Course, 2.UAA and 24th U-Flotilla 3/43–6/43 (U-Cdr's Torpedo Course 45)
Cdr *U 106* 20.6.43–2.8.43
Military hospital and 2nd U-Flotilla 8/43–5/44
Died 21.5.44

DANGSCHAT, GÜNTHER [187]
b. 8.7.1915 Cranz, East Prussia
Class 1935; Kplt 1.10.42
M/S-Cdr 6th Minesweeping Flotilla 4/40–1/41; U-boat trg 1/41–6/41; 1WO *U 38* 7/41–12/41; U-Cdr's Course, 26th U-Flotilla 12/41–2/42; *Baubelehrung* 6.KLA 3/42–5/42
Cdr *U 184* 29.5.42–20.11.42
Lost 20.11.42 North Atlantic

DANKLEFF, WALTER (DIPL. ING.) [188]
b. 12.11.1906 Mulhouse, Alsace (when German province)
Entry II/1935; ObltzS (R) 1.3.43
WO and Cdr with School Flotilla, C-in-C Escort Forces Baltic 9/40–6/42; Cdr with 2nd Sperrbrecher Flotilla 6/42–1/43; U-boat trg 1/43–6/43; U-Cdr's Course, 24th U-Flotilla 7/43–8/43 (U-Cdr's Torpedo Course 51); *Baubelehrung* 6.KLA 8/43–9/43
Cdr *U 767* 11.9.43–18.6.44
Lost 18.6.44 English Channel, SW of Guernsey

DAU, ROLF [189]
b. 1.4.1906 Berlin-Charlottenburg

Class 1936; KKpt 1.4.41
U-boat trg, U-courses 10/34–8/35; Cdr Trg Group U-Boat School, *U 5* 31.8.35–27.9.36; U-Cdr U-Flotilla *Saltzwedel* 28.9.36–7.12.36; *Baubelehrung* Deschimag AG Weser Bremen 8.12.36–27.12.36; Cdr *U 31* 28.12.36–8.11.38; U-Flotilla *Hundius* 9.11.38–13.11.38 and Comp. CO 3/NCO Trg Div 9.11.38–14.12.38; U-Flotilla *Hundius* 15.12.38–6.6.39; *Baubelehrung* Deschimag AG Weser Bremen 7.6.39–14.7.39
Cdr *U 42* 15.7.39–13.10.39
POW 13.10.39

DAUBLEBSKY VON EICHHAIN, KARL [190]
b. 9.7.1909 Pola
Class 1929; KKpt 1.4.43
WO *U 7* 1935 and 1936 (per list rankings 1.11.1935 and 1.11.36).
Cdr *U 13* 1.10.37–5.11.39
Staff BdU/Ops 11/39–4/40; 2/Adm. Staff Officer BdU/Ops 4/40–2/43; 1/Adm. Staff Officer FdU West 3/43–capitulation
Detained; freed 6/46

DAUTER, HELMUT [191]
b. 9.8.1919 Danzig
Class 1937b; ObltzS 1.4.42
3WO torpedo-boat *Iltis* 12/39–2/40; seconded to Seeluftwaffe 2/40–12/40; U-boat trg 1/41–7/41; 1WO *U 454* 7/41–5/42; U-Cdr's Course, 24th U-Flotilla 6/42–7/42; *Baubelehrung* 7.KLA 7/42
Cdr *U 448* 1.8.42–14.4.44
POW 14.4.44–24.11.47

VON DAVIDSON, HEINZ [192]
b. 29.12.1918, Kiel
Class 1937a; Kplt 1.8.44
Torpedo-boat *T 110* 4/39–9/39; seconded to Luftwaffe, Flying School (Sea) 9/39–1/40; *Bordfliegerstaffel 1./196* (served on heavy cruiser *Admiral Hipper*, battleship *Tirpitz* and heavy cruiser *Lützow*) 1/40–1/42; U-boat trg 2/42–7/42; 1WO *U 135* 7/42–12/42; U-Cdr's Course and *Baubelehrung* 12/42–2/43
Cdr *U 281* 27.2.43–capitulation
Detained; freed 1.7.47

DECKERT, HORST [193]
b. 11.10.1918, Hannover
Class 1937a; Kplt 1.1.44
Platoon Leader 4/Reserve Naval Artillery Div. 10/39–3/40; U-boat trg 4/40–8/40; *Baubelehrung* 8/40–9/40; 2WO *U 73* 9/40–7/41
Cdr *U 8* 1.8.41–16.5.42
U-Cdr's Course, 24th U-Flotilla 5/42–7/42; 1WO *U 73* 7/42–9/42
Cdr *U 73* 1.10.42–16.12.43 (see Rosenbaum [1027])
POW 16.12.43

DEECKE, JOACHIM [194]
b. 29.6.1912, Lübeck
Class 1933; Kplt 1.4.41
U-boat trg and courses 11/39–5/40; ADC 2nd U-Flotilla 5/40–9/40; 1WO *U 37* 9/40–10/40
Cdr *U 9* 21.10.40–8.6.41
U-Cdr's Course, 24th U-Flotilla 6/41–7/41; *Baubelehrung* 7/41–8/41
Cdr *U 584* 21.8.41–31.10.43 (see Nölke [885])
Lost 31.10.43 central North Atlantic

DEECKE, JÜRGEN [195]
b. 28.4.1911, Lübeck
Class 1931; Kplt 1.10.39, posthumously KKpt seniority 1.4.40
Cdr *U 1* 29.10.38–4/40
Missing North Sea 6.4.40

DEETZ, FRIEDRICH [196]
b. 11.9.1916, Berlin
Class 1935; Kplt 1.6.42, posthumously Kkpt seniority 1.1.44
WO survey ship *Meteor* 1/39–9/39; WO fleet tender *F 2* 9/39–10/39; WO 6th Torpedo-Boat Flotilla 10/39–3/41; U-boat trg 3/41–8/41; U-Cdr under instrn, 24th U-Flotilla 9/41–10/41; U-Cdr sea trg and 1WO *U 205* 10/41–1/42; *Baubelehrung* KLA U-North 1/42–2/42
Cdr *U 757* 28.2.42–8.1.44
Lost 8.1.44 North Atlantic, SW of Ireland

DEGEN, HORST [197]
b. 19.7.1913, Münster, Westphalia
Class 1933; Kplt 1.3.41
2WO, Torpedo and Radio Technical Officer destroyer *Z 10 Hans Lody* 9/39–6/40; U-boat trg 7/40–12/40; U-Cdr's Course 1/41–3/41; U-Cdr sea trg *U 552* 3/41–5/41; *Baubelehrung* 5/41–7/41
Cdr *U 701* 16.7.41–7.7.42
POW 7/42–6/46

DEIRING, HUGO [198]
b. 25.7.1920, Grönenbach, Allgäu
Class 1938; ObltzS 1.4.43
Officer trg, trg ship *Schlesien* 7/39–9/39; courses 10/39–4/40; trg ship *Schleswig-Holstein* 5/40–7/40; 3rd E-Boat Flotilla 8/40–10/40; U-boat trg 11/40–3/41; WO *U 151* 4/41–9/41; *Baubelehrung* 9/41–11/41; 1WO *U 255* 10/41–10/42
Cdr *U 56* 15.11.42–27.2.44
Courses and *Baubelehrung* Type XXI 7.KLA 3/44–9/44
Cdr *U 3503* 9.9.44–8.5.45
Detained; freed 2/46

DICK, HANS-PETER [199]
b. 13.11.1920, Dresden
Class IX/1939; ObltzS 1.10.43
WO 5th U-Flotilla 10/42–11/42; *Baubelehrung* 11/42–12/42; 1WO *U 713* 12/42–11/43; U-Cdr's Course, 3.ULD and 24th U-Flotilla 11/43–2/44 (U-Cdr's Torpedo Course 61)
Cdr *U 612* 21.2.44–2.5.45

DIERKS, HANS-JOACHIM [200]
b. 16.7.1923, Georgsmarienhütte, Osnabrück
Class 1940; ObltzS 1945
WO sea trg *U 752*, *U 572* and *U 23* 1942; WO *U 978* 1943; 1WO *U 739* 1943–5/44; U-Cdr's Course 6/44–7/44
Cdr *U 14* 2.7.44–6.3.45
Cdr *U 137* 3/45–2.5.45
Detained; freed 26.7.1945

DIERKSEN, REINER [201]
b. 24.3.1908, Esenshausen, Baden-Württemberg
Class 1933; Kkpt 1.5.43
Cdr *M 5*, 1st Minesweeping Flotilla 10/38–6/40; CO 32nd Minesweeping Flotilla 7/40–3/41; U-boat trg, U-Cdr's Course, *Baubelehrung* 3/41–12/41
Cdr *U 176* 15.12.41–15.5.43
Lost 15.5.43 NE of Havana, Cuba

DIETERICH, MAX [202]
b. 6.9.1914, Mannheim
Class 1934; Kplt 1.4.42
Seconded to Luftwaffe 10/36–3/41; U-boat trg 3.41–7.41; 24th U-Flotilla 7/41–8/41; U-Cdr's Course and U-Cdr sea trg *U 572* 9/41–1/42
Cdr *U 78* 2/42–30.6.42
Baubelehrung 7/42–8/42
Cdr *U 637* 27.8.42–22.2.43
5th U-Flotilla 2/43–3/43; Kplt on Staff 30th U-Flotilla 4/43–8/43; Comp. Cdr 1.ULD 8/43–1/45
Cdr Naval Infantry Battalion 121 1/45–capitulation

DIETERICHS, HORST [203]
b. 1.3.1912, Naumburg, Saale
Class 1934; Kplt 1.4.42
U-boat trg 10/40–3/41; 1WO *U 46* 4/41–8/41;
  24th U-Flotilla and U-Cdr's Course 9/41–10/41;
  Baubelehrung 7.KLA 10/41
Cdr *U 406* 22.10.41–18.2.44
Lost 18.2.44 central North Atlantic

DIETRICH, WILLI [204]
b. 20.12.1909, Marburg
Enlisted 1928; ObltzS 1.4.43
Obstrm *U 35* 8/39–10/39; Obstrm *U 28* 1/40–1/41; *Baubelehrung* 1/41–3/41; Obstrm *U 125* 3/41–10/42; courses and U-Cdr's Torpedo Course 44 10/42–4/43; *Baubelehrung* 8.KLA 4/43–6/43
Cdr *U 286* 5.6.43–29.4.45
Lost 29.4.45 Barents Sea, off Murmansk

DIGGINS, KURT [205]
b. 17.10.1913, Gut Mohrberg, Eckernförde
Class 1934; Kplt 1.1.42
ADC heavy cruiser *Admiral Graf Spee* 4/39–12/39; interned Uruguay 12/39–6/40, returned to Germany; M/S-Cdr 6th Minesweeping Flotilla 9/40–12/40; M/S-Cdr 5th Minesweeping Flotilla 12/40–3/41; U-boat trg and U-Cdr's Course 4/41–11/41; *Baubelehrung* 11/41–12/41
Cdr *U 458* 12.12.41–22.8.43
POW 22.8.43–5.9.47

DINGLER, GOTTFRIED [206]
b. 16.2.1922, Holzen, Isartal
Class XII/1939; ObltzS 1.12.43
Officer trg and *Baubelehrung* 12/39–3/42; 2WO *U 92* 3/42–8/43; 1WO *U 92* 8/43–3/44; courses, 3.ULD and 23rd U-Flotilla 3/44–6/44; ADC 27th U-Flotilla 6/44–2/45; 1.UAA 2/45–4/45
Cdr *U 748* 21.4.45–5.5.45

DOBBERSTEIN, ERICH [207]
b. 15.12.1919, Landsberg, Warthe
Class 1938; ObltzS 1.4.43
U-boat trg completed 7/41; *Baubelehrung* KLA U-North 7/41–8/41; 2WO *U 155* 8/41–6/43; U-Cdr's Torpedo Course 48 and *Baubelehrung* 6/43–7/43
Cdr *U 988* 15.7.43–29.6.44
Lost 29.6.44 English Channel, W of Guernsey

DOBBERT, MAX [208]
b. 13.4.1910, place of birth not recorded
Entry date not recorded; ObltzS (R) 1.8.43
Prize Officer merchant raider *Komet* 7/40–8/41; Cdr prize *Kota Nopan* 8/41–11/41; courses and U-boat trg 12/41–9/42; supernumerary WO *U 593* 10/42–12/42; U-Cdr's Course 1/43–2/43; *Baubelehrung* 8.KLA 2/43–3/43
Cdr *U 969* 24.3.43–6.8.44
Duties not recorded 8/44–10/44; courses and *Baubelehrung* Cdr Type XXI 8.KLA for *U 2537* 10/44–3/45 (The boat was scheduled to enter service in February 1945 but was destroyed by bombing on Slipway 1, Blohm & Voss Yard, Hamburg, on 31.12.44. Dobbert was then given the *Baubelehrung* command of *U 2546*; this boat was commissioned at Blohm &Voss, Hamburg, on 21.3.45.)
Cdr *U 2546* 21.3.45–3.5.45

DOBENECKER, GÜNTER [209]
b. 9.2.1922, Berlin-Charlottenburg
Class 1940; ObltzS 1.10.44
Officer trg 7/Basic Trg Est. Stralsund 10/40–12/40; 16th Minesweeping Flotilla 1/41–4/41; Naval College Flensburg-Mürwik 4/41–10/41; WO sea trg *U 203* 11/41–3/42; courses 4/42–9/42; *Baubelehrung* 8.KLA 10/42–11/42; 2WO and 1WO *U 650* 11/42–3/44; U-Cdr's Course, 24th U-Flotilla 3/44–5/44 (U-Cdr's Torpedo Course 69); Loading Officer 27th U-Flotilla 5/44–7/44

Cdr *U 11* 14.7.44–15.12.44
Group Officer and instructor 2.ULD 12/44–3/45
Additional Cdr *U 2524* 4/45–5/45
Platoon Leader Wachbatallion Dönitz 5/45–capitulation
Detained; freed 12/47

DOBINSKY, HANS-JÜRGEN [210]
b. 24.7.1922, Rostock
Class XII/1939; ObltzS 1.12.43
WO *U 758* 5/42–10/42; *Baubelehrung* 8.KLA 10/42–12/42; 1WO *U 952* 12/42–8/43; 1WO *U 333* 9/43–7/44; courses 1.UAA, 3 ULD, 23rd and 27th U-Flotillas 7/44–1/45
Cdr *U 323* 27.2.45–3.5.45

DOBRATZ, KURT [211]
b. 9.4.1904, Stettin
Class 1922; KptzS 1.6.43
Seconded to Luftwaffe; Cdr *II.(K)/Lehrgeschwader 1* 7/39–8/40; IIa Staff *Luftflottenkommando 5* 8/40–3/43, also Cdr *1./KG 26*, 6/41–3/43; effective 1.4.43 reverted to OKM jurisdiction; U-boat trg 4/43–8/43; acting CO 24th U-Flotilla, U-Cdr's Torpedo Course 55 9/43–1/44; *Baubelehrung* 8.KLA 1/44–3/44
Cdr *U 1232* 8.3.44–31.3.45
Seconded to Commanding Adm. U-Boats aboard *Daressalem*; Chief of Staff Commanding Adm. U-Boats 4/45–5/45; Chargé d'Affaires Commanding Adm. U-Boats 5/45–capitulation
Detained; freed 26.2.46
Knight's Cross 23.1.1945 (290th KM, 136th U-boat holder)

DÖHLER, HANS-HEINRICH [212]
b. 5.12.1917, Bad Schwartau
Class 1937a; ObltzS 1.9.41
Heavy cruiser *Deutschland* (renamed *Lützow* 1/40) 7/39–4/40; U-boat trg 4/40–9/40; Comp. Officer 2.ULD 9/40–6/41; 2WO *U 751* 7/41–11/41; U-Cdr's Course, 26th U-Flotilla 11/41–12/41
Cdr *U 21* 4.1.42–24.9.42
Cdr *U 606* 2.10.42 (per P/F) or 6.10.42 (per *U 606* WD) to 22.2.43
Lost 22.2.43 central North Atlantic

DOHRN, ERWIN [213]
b. 18.3.1920, Kiel
Ordnance Branch entry 1938; ObltzS 1.4.43 (transferred Seaman Branch, 15.7.43)
Platoon leader Flak School Misdroy 2/41–10/42; Comp. Officer 2. Shipboard Flak Detachment 10/42–1/43; retrg with 1st Sperrbrecher Flotilla 1/43–3/43; U-boat trg and U-Cdr's Course 3/43–2/44 (U-Cdr's Torpedo Course 62); *Baubelehrung* 5.KLA 2/44–5/44
Cdr *U 325* 6.5.44–4/45
Missing in English waters 4/45

DOMMES, WILHELM [214]
b. 16.4.1907, Buchberg, West Prussia
Class 31/29, entry on 23.1.1933; FKpt 30.1.45
WO battleship *Scharnhorst* 1/39–3/40; U-boat trg 4/40–9/40; U-Cdr's Course, 24th U-Flotilla and sea trg *U 4* 9/40–1/41; U-Cdr sea trg *U 96* 1/41–2/41; *Baubelehrung* 2/41–4/41
Cdr *U 431* 5.4.41 to 31.12.42 (per P/F) or 6.1.43 (per *U 431* WD; also see Schöneboom [1110])
Seconded 2/Adm. U-Boats 1/43–2/43
Cdr *U 178* 22.2.43–25.11.43
12th U-Flotilla (shore command) 11/43–1/44; transferred to Naval Station Japan 1/44–2/44; Senior Officer Penang base 3/44–12/44; Senior Officer Singapore base and CO U-Boat Naval Bases South-East Asia 1/45–capitulation
Detained; freed 1.10.47
Knight's Cross 2.12.42 (135th KM, 71st U-boat holder)

DRESCHER, GÜNTHER [215]
b. 13.10.1919, Sprottau, Silesia
Class 1938; ObltzS 1.4.43
U-boat trg and courses completed 3/42; relief instructor Torpedo School Mürwik 3/42–7/42; *Baubelehrung* 8.KLA 7/42–9/42; 1WO *U 196* 9/42–1/44; U-Cdr's Course, 23rd U-Flotilla 1/44–3/44; courses and *Baubelehrung* Type XXI 6.KLA 3/44–1/45
Cdr *U 3026* 22.1.45–3.5.45

VON DRESKY, HANS-WILHELM [216]
b. 27.1.1908, Halle an der Saale
Class 1929; Kplt 1.8.38
WO *U 20* 2/36–9/37; Cdr *U 4* 30.9.37–28.10.38
Cdr *U 33* 29.10.38–12.2.40
Lost 12.2.40 Firth of Clyde

DREWITZ, HANS-JOACHIM [217]
b. 14.11.1907, Thorn
Class 1933; Kplt 1.4.40, posthumously KKpt seniority 1.8.43
M/S-Cdr 2nd Minesweeping Flotilla 5/39–9/41; U-boat trg 9/41–2/42; U-Cdr sea trg *U 203* 3/42–5/42; U-Cdr's Course, 24th U-Flotilla 5/42–6/42; *Baubelehrung* 8.KLA 6/42–7/42
Cdr *U 525* 30.7.42–11.8.43
Lost 11.8.43 North Atlantic, NW of Azores

DREWS, ULRICH [218]
b. 24.5.1916, Tilsit
Class 1936; Kplt 1.4.43
Seconded to Luftwaffe 9/39–3/43; U-boat trg 4/43–9/43; courses and U-Cdr under instrn, 23rd U-Flotilla 10/43–12/43; *Baubelehrung* 5.KLA 12/43–1/44
Cdr *U 321* 20.1.44–8/44
Baubelehrung Type XXI 8.KLA 9/44–1/45
Cdr *U 2534* 17.1.45–8.5.45

DRIVER, HEINRICH [219]
b. 10.7.1912, Sonderburg, Alsen
Class 1933; KKpt 1.4.45
1WO *U 13* 10/38–1/40; courses 1/40–3/40
Acting Cdr *U 20* 2.4.40–15.4.40
Cdr *U 23* 20.5.40–30.9.40
Cdr *U 145* 16.10.40–18.12.40
Baubelehrung 1/41–3/41
Cdr *U 371* 15.3.41 to 25.3.42 (per *U 371* WD) or 5.4.42 (per WASt)
Kplt on Staff 6th, 11th, 4th and 26th U-Flotillas 4/42–capitulation

DÜBLER, RUDOLF [220]
b. 12.10.1921, Greiz, Thüringen
Class XII/1939; ObltzS 1.12.43
Officer trg, 7/Basic Trg Est. Stralsund 12/39–2/40, sail trg ship *Albert Leo Schlageter* 2/40–6/40; light cruiser *Emden* 6/40–12/40; U-boat trg and courses Naval College Mürwik 12/40–4/41; WO sea trg *U 203* 5/41–9/41 and *U 83* 9/41–11/41; courses 1.ULD 11/41–2/42; Torpedo School Flensburg-Mürwik 2/42–3/42; 2.UAA Neustadt 3/42; Signals School 3/42–4/42; course Naval Gunnery School 4/42–5/42; supernumerary WO *U 464* 5/42–6/42; 2WO *U 81* 7/42–4/43; 1WO *U 81* 4/43–8/43; U-Cdr's Course, 2.UAA and *Baubelehrung* 8/43–11/43
Cdr *U 1101* 10.11.43–5.5.45
Station Officer and Patrol Leader Wehrmacht Police 5/45–8/45; Group Leader Naval Service Group Schleswig-Holstein (13th Landing Flotilla) 8/45–8/46; released 30.8.46

DÜLTGEN, GERT [221]
b. 1.9.1918, Kiel-Pries
Class X/1937; ObltzS 1.4.42
U-boat trg completed 6/42; 1WO *U 508* 7/42–2/43; course 2.UAA 2/43; U-Cdr's Course, 24th U-Flotilla 2/43–3/43 (U-Cdr's Torpedo Course 42); *Baubelehrung* 1.KLA 3/43–4/43
Cdr *U 391* 24.4.43–13.12.43

Lost 13.12.43 Bay of Biscay, NW of Cape Ortegal

DÜPPE, JOACHIM [222]
b. 23.1.1916, Schwerin
Entry 1/1940; ObltzS (R) 1.3.44
Officer and U-boat trg 5/40–3/41; *Baubelehrung* 3/41–4/41; 2WO *U 432* 4/41–8/42; courses 8/42–12/42
Cdr *U 4* 24.1.43–31.5.43
Navigation instructor 1.ULD 6/43–6/44; *Baubelehrung* Type XXI 8.KLA 7/44–11/44
Cdr *U 2505* 7.11.44–3.5.45

DUIS, HANS-DIEDERICH [223]
b. 6.2.1922, Saarbrücken
Class XII/1939; ObltzS 1.12.43
Officer and U-boat trg 12/39–5/41; WO sea trg *U 48* 5/41–11/41; courses 12/41–5/42; supernumerary WO *U 462* 6/42–7/42; WO *U 351* 7/42–4/43; *Baubelehrung* 5/43–6/43; 1WO *U 365* 6/43–6/44; U-Cdr's Course 6/44–8/44; courses 8/44–12/44
Cdr *U 792* 12/44–4.5.45
Detained; freed 9.9.45

DUMRESE, ADOLF [224]
b. 13.11.1909, Berlin
Class 1929; Kplt 1.11.38, posthumously KKpt seniority 1.3.42
Battery CO Naval Artillery Detachment 115 9/39; Kplt on Staff 5th Naval Artillery Regt 10/39–1/40; course Naval Gunnery School 1/40–4/40; U-boat trg 4/40–9/40; U-Cdr's Course, 24th U-Flotilla 9/40–12/40; *Baubelehrung* 12/40–12/41
Cdr *U 78* 15.2.41–7/41
Baubelehrung 7/41–8/41
Cdr *U 655* 11.8.41–24.3.42
Lost 24.3.42 Barents Sea

DUNKELBERG, HANS [225]
b. 7.8.1918, Mülheim, Ruhr
Class 1937b; ObltzS 1.4.42
WO destroyer *Z 10 Hans Lody* 12/40–6/42; U-boat trg 6/42–10/42; 1WO *U 406* 10/42–2/43; U-Cdr's Course, 2.UAA and 24th U-Flotilla 2/43–3/43 (U-Cdr's Torpedo Course 42)
Cdr *U 716* 15.4.43–24.1.45
Military hospital Narvik 1/45–3/45
13th U-Flotilla 3/45–capitulation

DUPPEL, MARTIN [226]
b. 9.2.1920, Böblingen, Württemberg
Class 1938, ObltzS 1.1.43
U-boat trg completed 6/41; ADC 1st U-Flotilla 6/41–10/41; 2WO *U 201* 11/41–1/42; 1WO *U 210* 1/42–10/42; U-Cdr's Course 10/42–12/42; *Baubelehrung* 8.KLA 12/42–1/43
Cdr *U 959* 21.1.43–25.7.43
F1a and Staff Officer (Planning), OKM/2.SKL/BdU/Opns 7/43–capitulation

E

EBERBACH, HEINZ-EUGEN [227]
b. 2.7.1921, Esslingen, Neckar
Class X/1939; ObltzS 1.10.43
Officer trg 10/39–2/41; U-boat trg 2/41–11/41; *Baubelehrung* 7.KLA 11/41–12/41; 2WO *U 407* 12/41–10/43; 1WO *U 407* 10/43–1/44; U-Cdr's Course, 3.ULD, 23rd and 27th U-Flotillas 1/44–5/44; Naval Trg Inspectorate, Induction Officer, Acceptance Centre for Officer Applicants 5/44–7/44
Cdr *U 967* 2.7.44–11.8.44 (*U 967* suffered minor damage on 5.7.44, and serious damage on 6.8.44, at Toulon from USAAF bombing, and was scuttled there on 19.8.44 as an alternative to extensive repair.)
Cdr *U 230* 12.8.44 or 17.8.44 (WASt) to 21.8.44
POW from 27.8.44

EBERLEIN, OTTO-EMIL [228]
b. 15.11.1913, Pirmasens, Pfalz
Entry 1/1938; ObltzS (R) 1.10.43
VP-Cdr Harbour Defence Flotilla Trondheim 8/40–11/41; VP-Cdr 59th VP-Boat Flotilla 12/41–7/43; U-boat trg 7/43–1/44; U-Cdr's Course, 23rd U-Flotilla 2/44–3/44; *Baubelehrung* 8.KLA 3/44–5/44
Cdr *U 1020* 17.5.44–3.1.45
Missing off Scottish coast from 12/44 (date of death officially 3.1.45)

EBERSBACH, HANS-JOACHIM [229]
b. 17.10.1918, Ehrenfriedensdorf, Saxony
Class 1937b; Kplt 1.10.45
U-boat trg 6/42–10/42; U-Cdr sea trg *U 618* 10/42–2/43; U-Cdr's Course, 2.ULD and 24th U-Flotilla 2/43–3/43 (U-Cdr's Torpedo Course 42); *Baubelehrung* 3/43–4/43
Cdr *U 975* 29.4.43–16.11.43
Induction Officer, No 2 Acceptance Centre for Officer Applicants 12/43–11/44; adviser in military section *SS-Reichssicherheitshauptamt* (RSHA) 11/45–2/45; Front Intelligence Command 140 3/45–capitulation

EBERT, EBERHARD [230]
b. 27.6.1907, Nagasaki, Japan
Entry date not recorded; ObltzS (R) 1.9.43
Aboard *M 1705*, 17th Minesweeping Flotilla 9/39–1/41 (course 9/40–10/40); course 2/41–3/41; navigation course 4/41–6/41; 2WO *V 901*, 9th VP-Boat Flotilla 7/41–8/41; 1WO *Reiher*, flagship Guard Vessel Flotilla 8/41–7/42; Cdr *V 908*, 9th VP-Boat Flotilla 7/42 2/43; U-boat trg 3/43–10/43; U-Cdr's Course, 24th U-Flotilla 10/43–11/43 (U-Cdr's Torpedo Course 58); *Baubelehrung* 7.KLA 11/43–1/44
Cdr *U 1201* 13.1.44–1.7.44
Baubelehrung Type XXI 6.KLA 7/44–11/44
Cdr *U 3010* 11.11.44–22.3.45
4th U-Flotilla (Cdr Personnel Reserve) 3/45–4/45; volunteered and trained for Naval Anti-Tank Regt *Gysae* 4/45–5/45; Comp. CO, Anti-Tank Battalion *von Hartmann* 3.5.45–capitulation
Detained; freed 20.8.45

EBERT, JÜRGEN [231]
b. 25.9.1916, Osterburg, Altmark
Class 1937a; Kplt 1.8.44

Seconded to Luftwaffe 9/39–6/43; U-boat trg and U-Cdr's Course 7/43–4/44 (U-Cdr's Torpedo Course 65) ; *Baubelehrung* 5.KLA 4/44–6/44
Cdr *U 927* 27.6.44–24.2.45
Lost 24.2.45 SE of Falmouth

ECK, HEINZ-WILHELM [232]
b. 27.3.1916, Hamburg
Class 1934, Kplt 1.12.41
M/S-Cdr 6th Minesweeping Flotilla 9/39–2/41; M/S-Cdr 8th Minesweeping Flotilla 3/41–6/42; U-boat trg 6/42–10/42; courses, U-Cdr under instrn and U-Cdr's Course, 2nd U-Flotilla, 2.UAA (U-Cdr's Torpedo Course 43) and 24th U-Flotilla 10/42–5/43 (between 11/42 and 2/43 spent time as U-Cdr sea trg aboard *U 124*); *Baubelehrung* 6.KLA 5/43–6/43
Cdr *U 852* 15.6.43–3.5.44
POW 3.5.44; condemned to death by British Military Tribunal and executed by firing squad (Translator's note: Together with two of his officers, Eck was convicted by a British Military Tribunal of the murder of survivors of the Greek steamer *Peleus* and shot by firing squad on 30.11.45. Eck did not deny the allegations and pleaded operational necessity. His hope for clemency lay in the argument that the British Admiralty would not have indicted him as a British submarine commander in similar circumstances. The defence sought to plead a parallel case (HM submarine *Rorqual*, 1941), where the deponents to the alleged atrocity were all pro-Allied Greek seamen and therefore not *a priori* anti-British. The British tribunal refused to hear this defence. Their ruling was a clear violation of Eck's right to a fair trial: all persons indicted under the War Crimes regulations were entitled to present a full defence of their own choosing. See Alfred M de Zayas, *The Wehrmacht War Crimes Bureau 1939–45*, University of Nebraska.)

ECKEL, KURT [233]
b. 16.5.1921, Vienna
Class XII/1939; ObltzS 1.12.43
1WO *U 979* 5/43–12/44; U-Cdr's Torpedo Course 79 12/44–1/45; Assistant to Planning Staff Officer, OKM/2SKL/BdU/Ops 2/45–4/45
Cdr *U 2325* 21.4.45–capitulation

ECKELMANN, HEINZ [234]
24.7.1916, Hamburg Class 1937a; ObltzS 1.9.41
Destroyer *Z 5 Paul Jakobi* 4/39–11/40; U-boat trg 11/40–5/41; 2WO *U 75* 5/41–12/41; U-Cdr's Course, 24th U-Flotilla 1/42–2/42; Midshipmen's Trg Officer, 10th U-Flotilla 2/42–7/42; *Baubelehrung* 8.KLA 7/42–8/42
Cdr *U 635* 13.8.42–6.4.43
Lost 6.4.43 North Atlantic, SW of Iceland

ECKERMANN, HANS [235]
b. 30.5.1905, Berlin-Schöneberg
Class 1925; FKpt 1.3.44
Cdr *U 20* 1.2.36–30.9.37; CO U-Flotilla *Lohs* 10/37–12/39 and senior officer responsible for U-Flotilla *Weddingen* 9/39–12/39; CO 1st U-Flotilla 1/40–10/40
Cdr *U A* 1.11.40–14.2.42
CO 8th U-Flotilla 2/42–1/43; A1 (Organisational), Staff, FdU Norway 1/43–11/44; Head of U-Boat Acceptance Command, Danzig Branch 11/44–4/45; General Adviser OKM/Mar-Wehrmacht Transport II 4/45–capitulation
Detained; freed 20.7.45

ECKHARDT, HERMANN [236]
b. 15.6.1916, Aachen
Class 1936; Kplt 1.3.43
U-boat trg 10/39–3/40; ADC U-Trg Flotilla 3/40–10/40; 2WO *U 94* 10/40–4/41; WO *U 28* 4/41–6/41
Cdr *U 28* 22.6.41–20.3.42
Naval Trg Command, Romania 3/42–1/43

Cdr *U 432* 16.1.43–11.3.43
Lost 1.3.43 central North Atlantic

EDELHOFF, ERNST [237]
b. 13.10.1917, Lübeck
Entry 1936; ObltzS (R) 1.7.43
WO 11th Minesweeping Flotilla 4/41–5/43; U-boat trg 5/43–10/43; U-Cdr's Course, 24th and 23rd U-Flotillas 10/43–1/44 (U-Cdr's Torpedo Course 61); *Baubelehrung* 5.KLA 1/44–4/44
Cdr *U 324* 5.4.44–capitulation (see Sauerbier [1053])

EHRHARDT, WALTHER [238]
b. 23.12.1919, Ravensburg, Württemberg
Class 1938; ObltzS 1.10.43
Command Relay Officer battleship *Scharnhorst* 5/40–4/43; U-boat trg courses and *Baubelehrung* 5/43–4/44
Cdr *U 1016* 4.4.44–9.5.45 (Probably towards the end of January 1945 Ehrhardt brought *U 637* from Danzig to Kiel as acting commander.)
Detained; freed 1.8.45 (In 1957 Ehrhardt commanded the West German Bundesmarine submarine *Hai*, ex-*U 2365*, in the rank of KKpt.)

EHRICH, HEINZ [239]
b. 15.9.1919, Wissen, Sieg
Class 1937b; ObltzS 1.4.42
Cdr *M 1109*, 11th Minesweeping Flotilla until 12/40; U-boat trg 1/41–9/41; *Baubelehrung* 9/41–12/41; 1WO *U 175* 12/41–2/43; U-Cdr's Course, 24th U-Flotilla 3/43
Cdr *U 334* 1.4.43–14.6.43
Lost 14.6.43 North Atlantic, SW of Iceland

EICHMANN, KURT [240]
b. 11.10.1917, Mülheim, Ruhr
Class 1937a; ObltzS 1.9.41
U-boat trg 4/40–11/40; *Baubelehrung* 11/40–12/40; 2WO *U 553* 12/40–9/41; U-Cdr trainee, 26th U-Flotilla 10/41–11/41
Cdr *U 151* 16.11.41–9/42
Cdr *U 98* before 22.10.42–19.11.42 (Schulze [1102] was relieved between the end of September and 22.10.42, the date when Eichmann sailed *U 98* from St Nazaire on his first voyage in command and the boat's ninth and last mission)
Lost 19.11.42 Atlantic, W of Gibraltar

EICK, ALFRED [241]
b. 9.3.1916, Essen
Class 1937; Kplt 1.4.44
Sea trg destroyer *Z 4 Richard Beitzen* 4/39–6/40; course Naval Gunnery School Kiel-Wik 6/40–7/40; IV WO (Secretarial Officer) and No 2 Gunnery Officer destroyer *Z 4 Richard Beitzen* 8/40–10/40; U-boat trg 10/40–3/41; ADC 1.ULD 3/41–10/41; *Baubelehrung* KLA U-Boats North Sea 10/41–12/41; 1WO *U 176* 12/41–3/43; course 2.UAA 3/43; U-Cdr's Torpedo Course 44 and U-Cdr under instrn., 24th, 5th and 27th U-Flotillas 3/43–5/43
Cdr *U 510* 22.5.43 (per P/F) or 1.6.43 (per WASt) until capitulation
Detained; freed 26.7.47
Knight's Cross 31.3.44 (209th KM, 115th U-boat holder)

VON EICKSTEDT, WOLFGANG [242]
b. 1.12.1915, Stettin
Class 1935; Kplt 1.4.43
Platoon Officer, Battery and Comp. CO Naval Artillery Detachment 122 9/38–7/40; heavy cruiser *Prinz Eugen* 8/40–3/41; U-boat trg 3/41–9/41; 1WO *U 553* 9/41–2/42; U-Cdr's Course, 24th U-Flotilla 3/42–5/42; courses and trg 5/42–11/42
Cdr *U 668* 16.11.42–4/45

Military hospital 4/45–capitulation
Detained; freed 1.10.45

EISELE, WILHELM [243]
b. 16.3.1907, Binau, Baden
Enlisted rating 1927; Kplt 1.1.45
StObStrm (Warrant Officer Coxswain) *U 4* and *U 10* 11/38–7/40; StObStrm *U 59* 7/40–10/40; courses 10/40–12/40
Cdr *U 57* 11.1.41–16.5.43
Cdr *U 78* 17.5.43–26.11.44
Senior Trg Officer 22nd U-Flotilla 11/44–2/45
Cdr *U 1103* 26.2.45–capitulation

ELFE, HORST [244]
b. 23.4.1917, Allenstein, East Prussia
Class 1936; Kplt 1.4.43
ADC U-Flotilla *Weddigen* 9/39–4/40; 2WO *U 99* 4/40–12/40
Cdr *U 139* 21.12.40–5.10.41
Cdr *U 93* 6.10.41–15.1.42
POW 15.1.42–1.4.47

ELLERLAGE, HERMANN [245]
b. 3.2.1913, Renslage über Bersenbrück, Hannover
Entry VIII/1940; ObltzS (R) 1.4.44
Flag Lt 23rd Landing Flotilla until 10/42; Group Leader 23rd Landing Flotilla 10/42–10/43; U-boat trg 10/43–5/44; U-Cdr's Course, 23rd and 31st U-Flotillas 5/44–10/44; *Baubelehrung* Type XXIII 8.KLA 10/44–11/44
Cdr *U 2344* 10.11.44–18.2.45
32nd U-Flotilla and 3.ULD 2/45–capitulation

ELLMENREICH, HELMUT [246]
b. 16.7.1913, Kassel
Class 1935; Kplt 1.7.42
WO merchant raider *Orion* (*Schiff 36*) 12/39–9/41; Naval High Command East 10/41–2/42; U-boat trg and U-Cdr sea trg *U 130* 2/42–11/42; *Baubelehrung* 8.KLA 11/42–12/42
Cdr *U 535* 23.12.42–5.7.43
Lost 5.7.43 North Atlantic, NE of Cape Finisterre

ELSINGHORST, JOSEF [247]
b. 26.8.1916, Bocholt, Westphalia
Entry IV/1939; ObltzS (R) 1.10.43
WO 18th Minesweeping Flotilla 10/41–12/42; M/S-Cdr 28th Minesweeping Flotilla 12/42–6/43; U-boat trg 6/43–12/43; course and U-Cdr trg, 23rd U-Flotilla 12/43–4/44; *Baubelehrung* 5.KLA 4/44–6/44
Cdr *U 822* 1.7.44–3.5.45

EMDE, BERNHARD [248]
b. 6.12.1917, Bremen
Class 1937; ObltzS 1.4.42
2WO 4th Minesweeping Flotilla 1/40–3/40; 1WO 19th Minesweeping Flotilla 4/40–3/41; M/S-Cdr 19th Minesweeping Flotilla 4/41–2/43; U-boat trg and U-Cdr's Course 3/43–10/43 (U-Cdr's Torpedo Course 55) ; *Baubelehrung* 10/43–11/43
Cdr *U 248* 6.11.43 31.10.44
Cdr *U 299* 1.11.44–capitulation
Detained; freed 1.3.47

EMMERMANN, CARL [249]
b. 6.3.1915, Hamburg
Class 1934; Kkpt 1.12.44
U-boat trg 3/39–6/40; courses Naval Gunnery School and 1.ULD 7/40–11/40; 1WO *U A* 11/40–8/41; U-Cdr's Course and *Baubelehrung* 9/41–11/41
Cdr *U 172* 5.11.41 to 31.10.43 (per P/F) or 1.11.43 (per WASt)
CO 6th U-Flotilla 11/43–8/44; Adviser, Experimental Group U-Boats (Leader Experimental Group Type XXIII), FdU/Trg 8/44–3/45
Cdr *U 3037* 3.3.45–22.4.45

CO 31st U-Flotilla, finally CO Naval Battalion *Emmermann* (involved in fighting for Hamburg) 4/45–capitulation
Detained; freed 2.9.45
Knight's Cross 27.11.42 (133rd KM, 70th U-boat holder)
Oak Leaves 4.7.43 (256th WM, 32nd KM, 25th U-boat holder)

EMMRICH, HEINZ [250]
b. 19.1.1913, Chemnitz
Entry 1941; ObltzS (R) 1.3.44
Merchant shipping adviser Naval Group South 6/41–8/43; U-boat trg 8/43–2/44; U-Cdr's pre-trg, 19th U-Flotilla 2/44–5/44; U-Cdr's Course, 24th U-Flotilla 6/44–7/44 (U-Cdr's Torpedo Course 73)
Cdr *U 320* 11.7.44 (per U-Boat Archive) or 1.8.44 (per WASt) to 8.5.45

ENDLER, SIEGFRIED [251]
b. 14.4.1915, Crossen, Brandenburg
Entry 1934; ObltzS (R) 1.9.43
1WO *U 748* 7/44–12/44; U-Cdr's Course 12/44–1/45 (U-Cdr's Torpedo Course 79); *Baubelehrung* 1.KLA 1/45–3/45
Cdr *U 4711* 21.3.45–4.5.45

ENDRASS, ENGELBERT [252]
b. 2.3.1911, Bamberg
Class 1935; Kplt 1.5.41
U-Boat School 10/37–6/38, 2WO *U 29* 10/37–1/38 and U-boat trg 1/38–4/38, plus various courses 4/38–6/38; Flag Lt FdU 6/38–9/38; U-Flotilla *Emsmann* 10/38–11/38; U-Flotilla *Wegener* and *Baubelehrung* Germaniawerft Kiel 11/38–12/38; 1WO *U 47* 12/38–1/40; trg as U-Cdr 1st U-Boat Trg Flotilla 1/40–5/40, rudder systems course U-Boat School 13.2.40–18.2.40 and course Mine Warfare School, Kiel 26.2.40–1.3.40

Cdr *U 46* 22.5.40–24.9.41 (per P/F)
Baubelehrung Kriegsmarine Depot, Hamburg 9/41–10/41
Cdr *U 567* 15.10.41–21.12.41
Lost 21.12.41 NE of Azores
Knight's Cross 5.9.40 (30th KM, 12th U-boat holder)
Oak Leaves 10.6.41 (14th WM, 5th KM, 5th U-boat holder)

ENGEL, HANS-ADOLF [253]
b. 16.8.1915, Rüstringen
Class 1936; Kplt 1.1.45
WO *U 83* 2/41–7/42; U-Cdr's Course, 24th U-Flotilla 7/42–9/42; *Baubelehrung* 6.KLA 9/42–10/42
Cdr *U 273* 21.10.42–31.3.43
Instructor 2.UAA 4/43–9/43; instructor ULD 10/43–4/44; Group Officer Naval College Mürwik 4/44–capitulation

ENGEL, HERBERT [254]
b. 29.6.1912, Hamburg
Conscripted (Translator's note: probably ex-Merchant Marine), VII/39; Kplt 1.9.43
ObStrm *U 48* 4/40–12/48; *Baubelehrung* 1/41–2/41; WO *U 559* 2/41–3/42; courses Torpedo School Mürwik and 24th U-Flotilla 3/42–7/42; *Baubelehrung* 8.KLA 7/42–8/42
Cdr *U 666* 26.8.42–9.12.43
Kplt on Staff 6th U-Flotilla 12/43–8/44
Cdr *U 228* from shortly before 12.8.44 (boat sailed from St Nazaire for Bergen, Norway, under his command on that day) to 4.10.44
Testing Adviser Staff FdU/Trg 10/44–2/45; Trg Officer 26th U-Flotilla 2/45–capitulation

ENGELMANN, KURT-EDUARD [255]
b. 8.4.1903, Neisse-Oberneuland, Upper Silesia
Class 1923; Kkpt 1.2.39, posthumously FKpt effective 15.3.43

No 1 Gunnery Officer heavy cruiser *Blücher* 9/39–/40; 1.Adm. Staff Officer, Adm. Norwegian North Coast 4/40–4/41; U-boat trg, U-Cdr's Course and *Baubelehrung* 4/41–10/41
Cdr *U 163* 21.10.41–13.3.43
Lost 13.3.43 Bay of Biscay

EPP, DIETRICH [256]
b. 9.8.1917, Leipzig
Class 1937a; ObltzS 1.9.41
Platoon Leader 12/Basic Trg Est. Stralsund 9/39–3/40; U-boat trg 4/40–9/40; ADC 2.ULD 9/40–4/41; *Baubelehrung* 4/41–5/41; 1WO *U 572* 5/41–2/42
Cdr *U 62* 14.4.42–15.9.42
Course 24th U-Flotilla 9/42–10/42; *Baubelehrung* 10/42–11/42
Cdr *U 341* 28.11.42–19.9.43
Lost 19.9.43 North Atlantic, SW of Iceland

EPPEN, GÜNTER [257]
b. 27.8.1912, Winsen, Luhe
Class 1933; Kplt 1.4.41
Instructor Naval Signals School, Aurich 9/39–3/40; Naval Signals Officer, Molde 3/40–6/41; U-boat trg 7/41–10/41; WO (supernumerary) *U 38* 10/41–12/41; courses 26th U-Flotilla, 2.UAA and *Baubelehrung* 12/41–5/42
Cdr *U 519* 7.5.42–10.2.43
Lost 10.2.43 North Atlantic, SW of Ireland

ERDMANN, DIETER [258]
b. 11.4.1920, Görlitz
Class 1938; ObltzS 1.1.43
WO 12th Anti-Submarine Flotilla 4/40–1/41; U-boat trg and *Baubelehrung* 1/41–10/41; 1WO *U 406* 10/41–10/42; U-Cdr's Course 10/42–12/42 with periods of command:
Cdr *U 555* 15.10.42–12/42 and 12/42–30.11.43
Cdr *U 904* 1.12.43–15.6.44

Duties not recorded 6/44–8/44; trg *K-Verband* Trg Command 250 8/44–9/44; CO *K-Verband* Flotilla 263 9/44–capitulation
Detained; freed 4.12.47

ERNST, HANS-JOACHIM [259]
b. 17.8.1918, Halle, Saale
Class 1937b; Kplt 1.1.45
No 2 Torpedo Officer destroyer *Z 22 Anton Schmitt* 12/39–3/40; naval aviation trg 4/40–10/40; *3./Küstenfliegergruppe 406* 10/40–3/43; Captain Trg Flight, Parow 4/43–6/43; U-boat trg 7/43–1/44; U-Cdr's Course and *Baubelehrung* 1/44–6/44
Cdr *U 1022* 7.6.44–capitulation
Detained; freed 1.11.47

VON DER ESCH, DIETRICH [260]
b. 31.1.1915, Berlin-Charlottenburg
Class 1934; Kplt 1.4.42
Seconded to Luftwaffe 10/36–9/40; U-boat trg 10/40–4/41; U-Cdr's Course, 24th U-Flotilla 4/41–6/41; WO *U 98* 6/41–8/41; *Baubelehrung* 8.KLA 8/41–9/41
Cdr *U 586* 4.9.41–30.9.43, also Acting Cdr *U 606* 14.9.42–26.9.42
Baubelehrung 6.KLA 10/43–11/43
Cdr *U 863* 3.11.43–29.4.44
Lost 29.9.44 South Atlantic, E of Recife

EULER, KLAUS [261]
b. 21.1.1919, Hannover
Class 1937b; Kplt 1.1.45
Light cruiser *Königsberg* 12/39–4/40; CO Torpedo Battery, Bergen 4/40–6/40; duties not recorded 6/40–8/40; Cdr VP-boat 8/40–12/40; WO 1st E-Boat Flotilla 1/41–3/41; No 2, later No 1 Torpedo Officer and ADC heavy cruiser *Lützow* 4/41–10/43; U-boat trg, WO and courses 10/43–12/44
Cdr *U 1162* 9.1.45–31.3.45

Duties until capitulation not recorded
Detained; freed 2.11.45

EWERTH, KLAUS [262]
b. 28.3.1907, Angerburg, East Prussia
Class 1925; FKpt 1.9.43, posthumously KptzS seniority 1.12.43
Cdr *U 1* 29.6.35–30.9.36; U-Cdr U-Flotilla *Saltzwedel* 1.10.36–11.10.36; *Baubelehrung*, Germaniawerft Kiel 12.10.36–2.11.36; U-Cdr U-Flotilla *Saltzwedel* 3.11.36–6.12.36; *Baubelehrung*, Germaniawerft Kiel 7.12.36–15.12.36; Cdr *U 36* 16.12.36–31.10.38; assigned Commanding Adm. Naval Station North Sea 11/38–7/39; instructor Torpedo School Mürwik 7/39–8/39
Cdr *U 26* 8/39–3.1.40
Adviser (A2) BdU/Organisational and 2/Adm. U-Boats 1/40–2/43; *Baubelehrung* 6.KLA 3/43–4/43
Cdr *U 850* 17.54.43–20.12.43
Lost 20.12.43 central Atlantic, W of Madeira

EY, HANS [263]
b. 19.6.1916, Hannover
Class 1935; Kplt 1.7.42
U-boat trg 10/39–3/40; Comp. CO 1.ULD 3/40–7/40; 1WO *U 94* 8/40–2/41; U-Cdr's Course 3/41–4/41; *Baubelehrung* 4/41–5/41
Cdr *U 433* 24.5.41–16.11.41
POW 16.11.41–24.6.47

F

FABER, ULRICH [264]
b. 10.10.1918, Stuttgart
Class 1937a; Kplt 1.4.44
Instructor Mine Warfare School, Kiel 2/42–3/43; courses and U-boat trg 3/43–11/43; U-boat handling instructor, 23rd U-Flotilla 12/43; U-Cdr's Torpedo Course 12/43–2/44; *Baubelehrung* 8.KLA 2/44–4/44
Cdr *U 1018* periodically at 31st U-Flotilla 24.4.44–15.1.45
U 1271 supernumerary (not Cdr) and Escort Liaison Officer, 3rd Escort Flotilla, periodically at Commanding Adm., U-boats (auxiliary warship *Daressalam*) 1/45–3/45; U-Cdr sea trg *U 3039* 4th U-Flotilla 17.3.45–3.5.45

FABRICIUS, FRITZ [265]
b. 18.5.1919, Fedderwarden-Groden, Frisia
Class 1937b; Kplt 1.1.45
Officer trg 10/37–3/40; Flying School, Bug 4/40–9/40; *Flieger-Ergänzungsgruppe (See)* 10/40–1/41; ship's aircrew *Bordfliegerstaffel 1./196* 1/41–6/43; U-boat trg 7/43–1/44; course 23rd U-Flotilla 1/44–4/44; Comp. Officer 7/(NCO) Trg Div. 4/44–7/44
Cdr *U 637* 21.7.44–30.9.44
1.UAA 10/44–12/44; duties not recorded 12/44–2/45; *Baubelehrung* Cdr *U–1028* (boat never commissioned) 2/45–capitulation
Detained; freed 17.8.45

FABRICIUS, LUDWIG [266]
b. 12.1.1921, Darmstadt
Class XII/1939; ObltzS 1.12.43
Officer and U-boat trg 12/39–4/41; WO sea trg *U 95* 5/41–10/41; supernumerary WO *U 210* 4/42–6/42; *Baubelehrung* 6/42–8/42; 1WO *U 666* 8/42–6/43; U-Cdr's Course, 24th U-Flotilla 7/43–8/43 (U-Cdr's Torpedo Course 52); *Baubelehrung* 9/43–10/43
Cdr *U 821* 11.10.43–1.12.43
Cdr *U 30* 2.12.43–14.12.44
Cdr *U 721* 18.12.44–4.5.45
Detained; freed 23.8.45

FAHR, THEODOR [267]
b. 30.11.1909, Zwötzen, Gera
Class 1930; KKpt 1.6.43
Divisional/No 1 Gunnery Technical Officer battleship *Gneisenau* 5/38–7/40; U-boat trg 7/40–1/41; U-Cdr sea trg *U 123* 1/41–3/41; *Baubelehrung* 8.KLA 3/41–4/41
Cdr *U 567* 24.4.41–14.10.41
Gunnery Officer heavy cruiser *Admiral Hipper* 10/41–11/41; AI/Ops Naval Group West 11/41–1/44; No 2 Gunnery Officer battleship *Tirpitz* 1/44–11/44
Lost 12.11.44 capsize of *Tirpitz*

FALKE, HANS [268]
b. 16.6.1920, Hamburg
Class 1939a; ObltzS 1.10.43
2WO *U 118* 12/41–12/42; 1WO *U 118* 12/42–5/43; U-Cdr's Course and *Baubelehrung* 5/43–8/43 (U-Cdr's Torpedo Course 48)
Cdr *U 992* 2.8.43–capitulation

FALKE, HANS [269]
b. 7.1.1920, Witten, Stockum
Ordnance Branch Entry XI/1937; ObltzS (R) 1.9.42

2/Mines Officer, 11th Minesweeping Flotilla 6/40–2/41; Mines Officer, minesweeper *Bali* 3/41–5/42; Mines Officer, Mine Warfare Command (La Pallice) 5/42–8/42, Mines Officer, Mine Warfare Command (Lorient), plus retrg from Ordnance to Seaman Branch, U-boat trg and courses 8/42–3/44 (U-Cdr's Torpedo Course 63); *Baubelehrung* 6.KLA 3/44–7/44
Cdr *U 1279* 5.7.44–3.2.45
Lost 3.2.45 North Sea, NW of Bergen

FAUST, ERICH [270]
b. 22.4.1921, Cuxhaven
Class XII/39; ObltzS 1.12.43
Officer and U-boat trg 12/39–5/42; WO (supernumerary) *U 412* 5/42–8/42; *Baubelehrung* 8.KLA 8/42–10/42; 1WO *U 667* 10/42–1/44; U-Cdr's Course, 27th U-Flotilla 2/44–4/44 (U-Cdr's Torpedo Course 66)
Cdr *U 618* 16.4.44–14.8.44
Lost 14.8.44 Bay of Biscay, W of St Nazaire

FECHNER, OTTO [271]
b. 15.11.1905, Kröben, Posen
Class 1924; KKpt 1.8.1939
Divisional/Radio Technical Officer battleship *Gneisenau* 5/38–8/40; Naval Signals School Mürwik 8/40–9/40; adviser Naval Orders Office *von Fischel* 9/40–11/40; Cdr Naval Signals Division North 11/40–3/41; U-boat trg and U-Cdr sea trg *U 108* 3/41–10/41; *Baubelehrung U 164* 11/4
Cdr *U 164* 28.11.41–6.1.43
Lost 6.1.43 off South America, NW of Pernambuco

FEHLER, JOHANN-HEINRICH [272]
b. 20.9.1910, Berlin-Charlottenburg
Entry 1936; Kplt 1.12.42
Merchant raider *Atlantis* 12/39–12/41; Naval High Command North 1/42–3/42; Group Officer Naval College Flensburg-Mürwik 3/42–3/43; U-boat trg 3/43–9/43; U-Cdr's Course, 2.UAA and 24th U-Flotilla 9/43–12/43 (U-Cdr's Torpedo Course 59); *Baubelehrung* 1.KLA 12/43–3/44
Cdr *U 234* 2.3.44–capitulation; POW 19.5.45

FEILER, GERHARD [273]
b. 6.9.1909, Breslau
Class 1934; KKpt 1.1.45
WO destroyer *Z 20 Karl Galster* 10/38–6/40; U-boat trg 7/40–1/41; U-Cdr under instrn, 24th and 7th U-Flotillas 1/41–4/41; *Baubelehrung* 4/41–5/41
Cdr *U 653* 25.5.41–30.9.43
1st U-Flotilla 10/43–1/44; Trg Officer 20th U-Flotilla 1/44–3/44; Head of Trg 19th U-Flotilla 4/44–capitulation

FEINDT, HANS-AREND [274]
b. 29.10.1921, Bremen
Class XII/1939; ObltzS 1.12.43
WO *U 34* 1/42–6/42; *Baubelehrung* 7/42–9/42; 1WO *U 641* 9/42–11/43; U-Cdr's Course and *Baubelehrung* 12/43–3/44
Cdr *U 758* 4.4.44–16.3.45
CO Naval Anti-Tank Company 3/45–capitulation
Detained; freed 5/45

FENN, HEINZ-KONRAD [275]
b. 20.7.1918, Kiel-Holtenau
Class 1937a; Kplt 1.8.44
Senior instructor 19/Naval Artillery Detachment 2/40–3/40; U-boat trg 4/40–9/40; 2WO *U 108* 10/40–7/41; U-Cdr's Course 8/41–9/41
Cdr *U 139* 6.10.41–17.5.42
Cdr *U 445* 30.5.42 to 25.1.44 (per WASt) or 27.1.44 (per *U 445* WD, and see Fischler [291])
Hospitalised 2/44–4/44; adviser Staff FdU Centre 5/44–8/44; U/Adm. Staff Officer, Staff Naval High Command Baltic 8/44–capitulation

Detained; freed 27.2.46

FENSKI, HORST-ARNO [276]
b. 3.11.1918, Königsberg, East Prussia
Class X/1937; ObltzS 1.4.42
Battleship *Gneisenau* 12/39–4/40; U-boat trg 4/40–9/40; Comp. Officer 1.ULD 9/40–4/41; *Baubelehrung* U-Boats East 4/41–5/41; 1WO *U 752* 5/41–6/42; U-Cdr's Course and Cdr *U 34*, 24th U-Flotilla 16.6.42–1.2.43
Cdr *U 410* 5.2.43–11.3.44
Cdr *U 371* 5.4.44–4.5.44
POW 4.5.44–4.5.46
Knight's Cross 26.11.1943 (194th KM, 106th U-boat holder)

FERRO, OTTO [277]
b. 24.1.1911, Hamburg
Entry 1940; ObltzS (R) 1.4.43
WO *U 332* 6/41–8/42; U-Cdr's Course, 24th U-Flotilla 8/42–9/42; *Baubelehrung* 8.KLA 9/42–10/42
Cdr *U 645* 22.10.42–24.12.43
Lost 24.12.1943 North Atlantic, NE of Azores

FEUFEL, KARL-HEINRICH [278]
b. 9.9.1918, Ludwigsburg, Württemberg
Ordnance branch entry 1938; ObltzS 1.4.43
Transferred to Seaman Branch 1943; U-boat trg 6/43–11/43; U-Cdr's Course, 23rd and 24th U-Flotillas 11/43–1/44 (U-Cdr's Torpedo Course 62); *Baubelehrung* 1/44–2/44
Cdr *U 1301* 11.2.44–8/44
Courses and *Baubelehrung* Type XXI 8.KLA 8/44–2/45
Cdr *U 2529* 22.2.45–14.4.45
31st U-Flotilla 4/45–capitulation

FIEBIG, GÜNTHER [279]
b. 6.3.1920, Kiel
Class 1938; ObltzS 1.4.43
Officer trg 10/38–4/40; WO fleet escort *F 7* 5/40–10/40; light cruiser *Emden* 11/40–3/41; Divisional Officer, Flak Director and ADC heavy cruiser *Lützow* 3/41–4/43; U-boat and U-Cdr trg 5/43–1/44 (U-Cdr's Torpedo Course 61); *Baubelehrung* 2/44–5/44
Cdr *U 1131* 20.5.44–1.4.45
Anti-Tank Command *Cremer*/Wachbatallion *Dönitz* 4/45–capitulation
Detained; freed 8/45

FIEDLER, HANS [280]
b. 14.10.1914, Wolmirsleben, Saxony-Anhalt
Class 1936; Kplt 1.9.43
Comp. Officer 7/Basic Trg Est. Stralsund 9/39–3/40; Trg Officer sail trg ship *Horst Wessel* and trg ship *Schleswig-Holstein* 3/40–8/40; Kriegsmarine Depot, Dunkirk 8/40–10/40; U-boat trg and *Baubelehrung* 10/40–3/41; 1WO *U 562* 3/41–10/41; U-Cdr's Course, 1st and 24th U-Flotillas 10/41–1/42; U-Cdr sea trg *U 120* 1/42–2/42
Cdr *U 120* 25.2.42–30.9.42
Cdr *U 564* 1.10.42–14.6.43 (see Suhren [1259])
1st U-Flotilla and *Baubelehrung* 8.KLA 6/43–10/43
Cdr *U 998* 7.10.43–27.6.44
Cdr *U 333* 20.7.44–31.7.44
Lost 31.7.44 North Atlantic, W of the Scilly Is

FIEHN, HELMUT [281]
b. 19.2.1916, Königsberg, Neumark, Brandenburg
Class 1935; Kplt 1.7.42
Seconded to Luftwaffe 11/37–8/41; U-boat trg 8/41–12/41; 1WO *U 67* 1/42–8/42; U-Cdr's Course, 24th U-Flotilla 9/42; *Baubelehrung* 6.KLA 9/42–10/42
Cdr *U 191* 20.10.42–23.4.43
Lost 23.4.43 North Atlantic, SE of Cape Farewell

FINDEISEN, EBERHARD [282]
b. 25.5.1916, Leipzig
Class 1936; Kplt 1.4.43
Group Officer Naval College Flensburg-Mürwik 9/41–3/43; Naval Liaison Officer, German Naval Command Italy 3/43–5/43; U-boat trg 5/43–11/43; U-Cdr's Course, 23rd and 24th U-Flotillas 11/43–1/44; *Baubelehrung* 6.KLA 1/44–3/44
Cdr *U 877* 24.3.44–27.12.44
POW 27.12.44

FINKE, OTTO [283]
b. 24.9.1915, Padang, Sumatra
Class 1936; Kplt 1.10.43
12th Minesweeping Flotilla 1/40–8/40; M/S-Cdr and Group Leader 42nd Minesweeping Flotilla 8/40–9/41; U-boat trg 9/41–3/42; 3rd U-Flotilla 3/42–5/42; 1WO 3rd U-Flotilla 5/42–11/42; U-Cdr's Course, 24th U-Flotilla and *Baubelehrung* 11/42–2/43
Cdr *U 279* 3.2.43–4.10.43
Lost 4.10.43 North Atlantic, SW of Iceland

VON FISCHEL, UNNO [284]
b. 5.11.1915, Kiel
Class 1934; ObltzS 1.4.39
Sea trg, trg ship *Schleswig-Holstein* and course Naval Gunnery School 4/39–3/40; U-boat trg 4/40–8/40; *Baubelehrung* 8/40–9/40; 1WO *U 97* 9/40–5/41; U-Cdr's Course, 24th U-Flotilla and *Baubelehrung* 5/41–6/41
Cdr U-374, 21.6.41–12.1.42
Lost 12.1.42 Western Mediterranean, E of Catania

FISCHER, ERICH [285]
b. 27.1.1922, Kappel, nr Marburg
Class X/1940; ObltzS 1.10.44
Officer and U-boat trg 10/40–9/42; WO 5th U-Flotilla 9/42–2/43; 1WO *U 363* 3/43–5/44; WO 11th U-Flotilla 6/44–11/44; U-Cdr's Course, 24th U-Flotilla 11/44–1/45
Cdr *U 137* 25.1.45–28.2.45
22nd U-Flotilla 3/45–capitulation

FISCHER, ERNST [286]
b. 20.2.1921, Oberdorla, Thüringen
Class X/1939; ObltzS 1.10.43
Officer and U-boat trg, *Baubelehrung* 10/39–11/41; 2WO *U 596* 11/41–3/43; U-Cdr's Course, 24th U-Flotilla 3/43–4/43 (U-Cdr's Torpedo Course 45)
Cdr *U 30* 5/43–1.12.43
Cdr *U 821* 2.12.43–31.12.43
Cdr *U 749* 1.1.44–11/44
Baubelehrung Type XXI 11/44–1/45
Cdr *U 3006* 16.1.45–1.5.45
Detained; freed 12/45

FISCHER, HANS-GEORG [287]
b. 3.2.1908, Rostock
Class 1926; FKpt 1.1.45
Cdr Naval Artillery Detachment 116 8/39–4/40; U-boat trg 4/40–7/40; U-Cdr's Course, 24th U-Flotilla 8/40–9/40; U-Cdr sea trg *U 38* 9/40–10/40; *Baubelehrung* 10/40–12/40
Cdr *U 109* 5.12.40–4.6.41
Wargames Officer heavy cruiser *Admiral Scheer* 6/41–1/43; First Lt *Schiff 5* (proposed merchant raider *Hansa*) 1/43–2/43; Senior Officer Personnel Div. 2/Adm. North Sea 4/43–4/45

FISCHER, HEINZ [288]
b. 18.4.1904, Schneidemühl, Posen, West Prussia
Class 1925; FKpt 1.4.44
U-Flotilla *Weddigen*, Cdr *T 23* 9/35–12/35; Flag Lt U-Flotilla *Weddigen* 12/35–3/36; student U-Boat school 3/36–6/36; Comp. Leader 2/U-Boat School 6/36–9/36; assigned CO 2nd U-Flotilla *Saltzwedel* 10/36; course Naval Physical Education School Mürwik and U-Flotilla

Saltzwedel 10/36; *Baubelehrung* Deschimag AG Weser Bremen 1.11.36–15.11.36; Cdr *U 29* 16.11.36–31.10.38; Senior Officer Crew Trg for U-Boats 11/38–6/39; OKM (Marinewehr 1) 6/39–10/39; Comp. CO U-Boat School 10/39; assigned BdU and acting CO U-Flotilla *Hundius* (6th U-Flotilla) 10/39–12/39; acting CO 2nd U-Flotilla 1/40–5/40; CO 2nd U-Flotilla 5/40–7/41 and acting Cdrt *U 26* 12.5.40–8.6.40; CO 4th U-Flotilla 8/41–capitulation
Detained; freed 9/45

FISCHER, KLAUS [289]
b. 7.10.1919, Berlin-Charlottenburg
Class 1938; ObltzS 1.4.43
Trg and courses 10/38–10/40; 2WO torpedo-boat *Iltis* 10/40–1/41; U-boat trg 1/41–8/41; WO *U 148* 9/41–10/41; *Baubelehrung* 11/41–12/41; 1WO *U 659* 12/41–11/42; U-Cdr's Course, 24th U-Flotilla and *Baubelehrung* 8.KLA 11/42–2/43
Cdr *U 961* 4.2.43–29.3.44
Lost 29.3.44 North Atlantic, E of Iceland

FISCHER, RUPRECHT [290]
b. 17.11.1916, Rüstringen
Class 1937a; Kplt 1.9.44
Comp. Officer 14/Basic Trg Est. Stralsund 9/39–7/40; M/S-Cdr 14th Minesweeping Flotilla 7/40–12/41; M/S-Cdr 22nd Minesweeping Flotilla 12/41–1/43; U-boat trg 2/43–7/43; U-Cdr's Course, 24th U-Flotilla 7/43–9/43; *Baubelehrung* 1.KLA 9/43–10/43
Cdr *U 244* 9.10.43–9.4.45
Lost 9.4.45 Kattegat, en route Norway as passenger aboard *U 804*

FISCHLER, GRAF VON TREUBERG, RUPPRECHT [291]
b. 20.2.1920, Murnau
Class 1939; ObltzS 1.10.43
Officer trg 9/39–10/40; Naval Signals Officer Souverin Moulin 10/40–11/40; course Mine Warfare School Kiel 11/40–1/41; 22nd U-Flotilla 2/41–4/41; U-boat trg 4/41–9/41; *Baubelehrung* KLA U-East 9/41–10/41; 2WO *U 214* 11/41–5/43; 1WO *U 214* 5/43–7/43; U-Cdr's Course, 2.UAA and 24th U-Flotilla 7/43–9/43 (U-Cdr's Torpedo Course 52)
Cdr *U 749* 29.9.43–31.12.43
Cdr *U 445* 26.1.44 or 27.1.44 (see mention under Fenn [275]) to 24.8.44
Lost 24.8.44 Bay of Biscay, W of St Nazaire

FITTING, HANS-HERMANN [292]
b. 27.5.1920, Stargard, Pomerania
Class 1939; ObltzS 1.10.43
Officer trg 9/39–8/40; Naval Harbour Section Antwerp 8/40–1/41; 8/Reserve Naval Artillery Division 1/41–5/41; 1st, 23rd and 25th U-Flotillas 5/41–3/43; course Helmsman's School 3/43–8/43; Torpedo School Mürwik, Signals School Mürwik and Naval Flak School VII 8/43–1/44; Platoon Leader 3.UAA 2/44; U-Cdr's trg, 19th and 24th U-Flotillas 2/44–4/44 (U-Cdr's Torpedo Course 70); U-Cdr sea trg *U 1056* 6/44–7/44
Cdr *U 1274* 7/44–16.4.45
Lost 16.4.45 North Sea, off Newcastle-upon-Tyne

FLACHSENBERG, WALTER [293]
b. 26.10.1908, Mönchen-Gladbach
Class 1929; KKpt 1.7.42
Cdr Naval Flak Detachment 264 9/39–10/39; Cdr Naval Flak Detachment 204 10/39–3/40; U-boat trg 4/40–12/40 inc. U-Cdr sea trg *U 100* 9/40
Cdr *U 71* 14.12.40 to 29.6.42 (per WASt) or 3.7.42 (*U 71* WD) (See Rodler von Roithberg [1015].)
Group Leader Underwater Experimentation, Torpedo Testing Command 8/42–8/44; Cdr Torpedo Testing Command 9/44–capitulation,

also CO Development Div., Torpedo Weapons Office II, OKM/Naval Armaments 4/45–capitulation

FLEIGE, KARL [294]
b. 5.9.1905, Hildesheim
Enlisted 1924; Kplt 20.4.45
StObStrm WO *U 20* 5/38–4/40; *Baubelehrung* 4/40–5/40; StObStrm WO *U 123* 5/40–8/41; Flotilla Coxswain 5th U-Flotilla aboard *St Louis* 8/41–4/42; assigned BdU 4/42; courses and U-Cdr's Torpedo Course, 2.UAA and 24th U-Flotilla 4/42–9/42; course 1.UAA 9/42–10/42; course Naval Signals School Flensburg-Mürwik 10/42–11/42; Platoon Officer 1.UAA 11/42–12/42
Cdr *U 18* 3.12.42 or 6.5.43 until 25.8.44 (*U 18* was transferred to the Black Sea in August 1942 and recommissioned at Constanza, Romania, on 6.5.43.)
Instructor 24th U-Flotilla 8/44 or 12/44 to 1/45; instructor 1.ULD 1/45–5/45
Cdr *U 4712* 4.5.45 (date per P/F, but must be incorrect as boat was destroyed in the Germaniawerft dockyard at Kiel the previous day)
Detained; freed 1.8.45
Knight's Cross 18.7.44 (238th KM, 123rd U-boat holder)

FÖRSTER, HANS-JOACHIM [295]
b. 20.2.1920, Gross-Köris, Teltow, nr Potsdam
Class 1938; ObltzS 1.4.43
Officer trg 10/38–4/40; Mine Clearance Ship 11 5/40–9/40 (working Baltic and North Sea); observer's course Naval Air Signals School Dievenow/Wollin 9/40–10/40; observer flight trg Aircraft Weapons School (Sea) Parow 10/40–11/40; Platoon Leader Destroyer and Torpedo-Boat Crews' Holding Div., Swinemünde 12/40–1/41; course Flak School Misdroy 1.41–2.41; Destroyer and Torpedo-Boat Crews' Holding Div., Swinemünde 2/41–4/41 and Platoon Officer Swinemünde 4/41–6/41; *Baubelehrung* destroyer *Z 29* 6/41; 3WO destroyer *Z 29* 6/41–10/41; course Torpedo School Flensburg-Mürwik 10/41–11/41; 2WO and Torpedo Officer destroyer *Z 29* 12/41–6/42; U-boat trg 7/42–12/42; 1WO *U 380* 12/42–5/43; U-Cdr's Torpedo Course, 2.UAA and 24th U-Flotilla 5/43–7/43 (U-Cdr's Torpedo Course 49); assigned Commanding Adm. U-Boats 7/43; *Baubelehrung* Nordseewerke, Emden, *U 348* 7/43–8/43; *Baubelehrung* 1.KLA/5th U-Flotilla for *U 479* 8/43; *Baubelehrung* 1.KLA (*U 480*) 8/43–10/43
Cdr *U 480* 6.10.43–24.2.45
Lost 24.2.45 English Channel, SW of Land's End
Knight's Cross 18.10.44 (266th KM, 130th U-boat holder)

FÖRSTER, HEINZ [296]
b. 25.6.1909, Berlin
Entry 1940; ObltzS (R) 1.2.43
Instruction and courses 1/40–9/41; sea trg 7th U-Flotilla (*U 553*), U-Cdr's Course and *Baubelehrung* 9/41–10/42
Cdr *U 359* 5.10.42–28.7.43
Lost 28.7.43 Caribbean Sea, S of San Domingo

FÖRSTER, HUGO [297]
b. 21.1.1905, place not known
Class 1923; KKpt 1.2.39
Navigation Officer heavy cruiser *Blücher* 1/40–4/40; Harbour Cdr Oslo 4/40; U-boat trg, U-Cdr's Course and *Baubelehrung* 5/40–4/41
Cdr *U 501* 30.4.41–10.9.41
POW 9/41–1/45, repatriated in exchange 1/45; suicide 27.2.45

FOLKERS, ULRICH [298]
b. 6.3.1915, Kiel
Class 1934; Kplt 1.11.41

WO destroyer *Z 8 Bruno Heinemann* 11/39 4/40; U-boat trg and assigned BdU 4/40–11/40; WO 27th U-Flotilla 11/40–12/40; WO 2nd U-Flotilla 12/40–1/41; 1WO *U 37* 1/41–3/41; U-Cdr's Torpedo Course, 24th U-Flotilla 3/41–4/41; Cdr (caretaker) *U 37* 3.5.41 to 15.11.41 (per WASt) or 31.10.41 (per P/F)

Cdr *U 125* (P/F states 1.11.41 but on that date the boat was at sea under the command of Kuhnke [679]; Folkers probably took over 15.12.41 as per Kuhnke's P/F and *U 125* WD) to 6.5.43

Lost 6.5.43 S of Greenland/E of Newfoundland

FORSTER, LUDWIG [299]

b. 9.10.1915, Lauingen, nr Dillingen
Class 1936; ObltzS 1.10.40
2WO *U 29* 4/39–12/40; 1WO *U 62* 12/40–5/41; Cdr (caretaker) *U 62* 20.5.41–9/41; U-Cdr's Course, 26th U-Flotilla 10/41–11/41
Cdr *U 654* from 25.11.41 (per P/F) or 2.12.41 (per *U 654* WD, and see Hesse [473]) to 22.8.42
Lost 22.8.42 off US coast, N of Columbia

VON FORSTNER, BARON SIEGFRIED [300]

b. 19.9.1910, Hannover
Class 1930; KKpt 1.4.43
Gunnery Technical Officer light cruiser *Nürnberg* 8/37–1/40, except 8/38–9/38 heavy cruiser *Deutschland*; course Naval Gunnery School Wik/light cruiser *Nürnberg* 1/40–3/40; U-boat trg 4/40–7/40; U-Cdr's Torpedo Course, 24th U-Flotilla 8/40–9/40; 7th U-Flotilla 9/40–11/40
Cdr *U 59* 11.11.40–16.4.41
Baubelehrung U-Boats Danzig 4/41–5/41
Cdr *U 402* 21.5.41–13.10.43
Lost 13.10.43 central North Atlantic (various assertions to the effect that Baron Siegfried von Forstner died aboard the escort carrier USS *Card* on 22.10.43 are incorrect)

VON FORSTNER, BARON WOLFGANG-FRIEDRICH [301]

b. 3.10.1916, Karlsruhe
Class 1937a; Kplt 1.4.44
Trg Aircraft Weapons School Bug 9/39–3/40; observer *2./Küstenfliegergruppe 606* 4/40–2/42; U-boat trg 3/42–9/42; 1WO *U 572* 9/42–3/43; U-Cdr's Course 3/43–5/43 (U-Cdr's Torpedo Course 43)
Cdr *U 472* 26.5.43–4.3.44
POW 4.3.44–29.11.47

FRAATZ, GEORG-WERNER [302]

b. 30.3.1917, Hamelin
Class 1935; Kplt 1.9.42, posthumously KKpt seniority 1.3.43
2WO *U 3* 8/39–10/39; Comp. Officer U-Boat School Neustadt 10/39–2/40; *Baubelehrung* 2/40–3/40; 1WO *U 101* 3/40–1/41; U-Cdr's Course, 24th U-Flotilla and *Baubelehrung* 1/41–4/41
Cdr *U 652* 3.4.41–2.6.42
Secretarial Officer 1st U-Flotilla 6/42–9/42; *Baubelehrung* 8.KLA 9/42
Cdr *U 529* 30.9.42–12.2.43
Missing central North Atlantic 2/43, official date of death 15.2.43 (Translator's note: U-Boat List 1956 states that *U 529* was sunk with all hands on 15.2.43 in 55°45'N 31°09'W, SW of Cape Farewell, by Liberator 'S' of No 120 Squadron RAF.)

FRÄNZEL, OTTO [303]

b. 29.4.1921, Eschenbach, Oberpfalz
Class 1939a; ObltzS 1.10.43
Officer and U-boat trg, *Baubelehrung* 9/39–11/41; 2WO *U 510* 11/41–4/43; 1WO *U 510* 4/43–8/43; courses and U-Cdr trg 9/43–12/43
Cdr *U 903* 15.12.43–24.4.45
Cdr *U 3011* 25.4.45–3.5.45
Detained; freed 7/45

FRAHM, KARL [304]
b. 3.8.1913, Alt-Meteln, Mecklenburg-Vorpommern
Enlisted rating 1931; ObltzS 1.10.44
ObStrm WO *U 6* 10/41–8/42; *Baubelehrung* 8/42–9/42; ObStrm 3WO *U 190* 9/42–4/44; courses 4/44–9/44; 21st U-Flotilla 9/44–11/44; *Baubelehrung* Type XXIII 8.KLA 12/44–2/45
Cdr *U 2363* 5.2.45–capitulation

FRAHM, PETER [305]
b. 14.6.1912, Oldenburg
Class 1932; Kplt 1.11.39, posthumously KKpt seniority 1.2.40
WO *U 15* 10/37–10/39
Cdr *U 15* 27.10.39–30.1.40
Lost 30.1.40 off Hoofden

FRANCESCHI, GERHARD [306]
b. 1.10.1921, Augsdorf
Class 1/41; ObltzS 1.4.45
WO sea trg *U 156* 1942; courses and *Baubelehrung* until 5/43; WO *U 764* 5/43–10/44; courses 10/44–1/45; *Baubelehrung* 1.KLA 1/45–3/45
Cdr *U 4704* 14.3.45–5.5.45

FRANKE, HANS-HEINO [307]
b. 27.5.1921, Berlin-Charlottenburg
Class 1940; ObltzS 1.10.44
Officer and U-boat trg 10/40–11/42; 2WO and 1WO *U 373* 11/42–4/44; U-Cdr's Course, 24th U-Flotilla 4/44–7/44 (U-Cdr's Torpedo Course 71); Personnel Reserve 21st U-Flotilla and *Baubelehrung* Type XXIII 8.KLA 7/44–1/45
Cdr *U 2355* 12.1.45–3.5.45

FRANKE, HEINZ [308]
b. 30.11.1915, Berlin-Steglitz
Class 1936, Kplt 1.4.43
Div. Lt and Flak Officer battleship *Gneisenau* 12/38–10/40; U-boat trg and *Baubelehrung* 10/40–4/41; 1WO *U 84* 4/41–12/41; U-Cdr's Torpedo Course, 26th U-Flotilla 12/41–1/42
Cdr *U 148* 16.1.42–19.10.42 (per P/F; see Mohr [834])
Cdr *U 262* (Period in some doubt: assumed command 20.10.42 per P/F or 26.10.42 per *U 262* WD. Relieved 25.1.44 per *U 262* WD or 4.2.44 per P/F, but latter entry cannot be correct as *U 262* put to sea from La Pallice on a North Atlantic mission under Wieduwilt [1349] on 3.2.44.)
Adviser 2.SKL/BdU/Opns 2/44–4/44; OKM Shipbuilding Commission 4/44–5/44; Staff Naval Group West 5/44–7/44; CO Instrn and Trg Units 350/400 (*K-Verband*) Surendorf 7/44–3/45
Cdr *U 3509* 15.3.45 to 3.4.45 or 9.4.45 (Per P/F. The bows of *U 3509* struck the bottom at Kiel on 3.4.45 following a bomb hit. This caused damage to the torpedo tube outer doors. Franke received orders to assume command of *U 3516* lying at Travemünde, but on arrival there was recalled to Kiel, where he was appointed commander of *U 2502* on 12.4.45. U-Boat Archive per Franke.)
Cdr *U 2502* 10.4.45 or 12.4.45 to capitulation. Detained; freed 17.11.45
Knight's Cross 30.11.43 (195th KM, 107th U-boat holder)

FRANKEN, WILHELM [309]
b. 11.9.1914, Schildesche, Bielefeld
Class 1935; KKpt 1.1.45
Platoon and Div. Officer battleship *Scharnhorst* 11/39–10/40; U-boat trg 10/40–3/41; *Baubelehrung* U-Boats North Sea 3/41; 1WO *U 331* 3/41–1/42; U-Cdr's Course, 24th U-Flotilla 1/42–3/42
Cdr *U 565* 17.3.42–7.10.43 per P/F (WASt gives the first date as 20.4.42 but this cannot be correct as *U 565* left La Spezia for a Mediterra-

nean patrol on 11.4.42 under Franken's command.)
29th U-Flotilla 10/43–12/43; personnel adviser (PII ordinary ratings), Staff, Commanding Adm. U-Boats 12/43–1/45
Accidental death 13.1.45, fire on board accommodation ship *Daressalam* at Kiel

FRANZ, JOHANNES [310]
b. 18.5.1907, Rhein
Class 1926, ObltzS 1.4.41
Cdr *U 27* 5.10.37–5.6.39, also 8.7.39–20.9.39
POW 20.9.39

FRANZ, LUDWIG [311]
b. 30.1.1918, Rüstringen
Class 1937a; ObltzS 1.4.42
Trg and courses until 11/39; WO sea trg destroyer *Z 11 Bernd von Arnim* 12/39–4/40; Naval Regiment *Berger* 4/40–7/40; Cdr Coastal Escort Group 7/40–6/41; Group Leader 51st VP-Boat Flotilla 7/41; U-boat trg 7/41–1/42; *Baubelehrung* KLA U-Boats East 1/42–3/42; 1WO *U 463* 4/42–12/42; U-Cdr's Course, 24th U-Flotilla 12/42–1/43; *Baubelehrung* 1/43–2/43
Cdr *U 362* 4.2.43–6.9.44
Lost 6.9.44 off Kravkov I, Kara Sea

FRANZE, JOACHIM [312]
b. 19.1.1918, Leipzig
Class 1937a, Kplt 1.4.44
Comp. Officer 10/Basic Trg Est. Stralsund 8/39–1/40; Comp. CO 10/Reserve Naval Artillery Div. 1/40–12/40; Battery Cdr Naval Artillery Detachment 286 12/40–7/41; Comp. CO Destroyer and Torpedo-Boat Div. 7/41–9/41; U-boat trg 9/41–5/42; 1WO *U 575* 5/42–11/42; U-Cdr's Course, 24th U-Flotilla 11/42–12/42; *Baubelehrung* 12/42–1/43.
Cdr *U 278* 16.1.43–capitulation

FRANZIUS, RUDOLF [313]
b. 5.6.1911, Hamburg
Class 1932; KKpt 1.10.44
Comp. CO VI/Naval Artillery Div. 2/39–9/39; No 2 Gunnery Officer and WO light cruiser *Karlsruhe* 9/39–4/40; No 3 Gunnery Officer and WO battleship *Gneisenau* 4/40–6/40; U-boat trg and 24th U-Flotilla (U-Cdr's Course) 7/40–12/40
Cdr *U 145* 19.12.40–21.10.41
Baubelehrung 7.KLA 10/41–11/41
Cdr *U 438* 22.11.41–29.3.43
Hospitalised 4/43–9/43; Induction Officer at Acceptance Centre for Officer Applicants, Naval Trg Inspectorate 9/43–6/44; Kplt on Staff, 24th U-Flotilla 6/44–1/45; CO 18th U-Flotilla 1/45–3/45; Head of Trg, 25th U-Flotilla 3/45–capitulation
Detained; freed 2.8.45

FRANZKE, HELMUT [314]
b. 2.12.1907, Berlin-Tempelhof
Class 1927; Kplt 1.4.40
1WO *U 26* 1/40–6/40
Cdr *U 3* 29.7.40–10.11.40; court-martialled, reduced to the ranks and expelled from U-Boat Arm 1/40–4/42; Ordinary Seaman 4/Basic Trg Est. Stralsund and 1st Flak Holding Regiment 4/42–5/44
Lost 28.5.44 as *Gefreiter* (Leading Seaman) aboard VP-boat

FRAUENHEIM, FRITZ [315]
b. 9.3.1912, Berlin
Class 1930; FKpt 1.12.44
U-boat trg 1/36–4/36; 1WO *U 25* 5/36–9/37
Cdr *U 21* 1.10.37 to 30.12.39 (per P/F) or 6.1.40 (per *U 21* WD, and see Stiebler [1234]) or 7.1.40 (per WASt)
U-Flotilla *Weddigen* and 1st U-Flotilla 1/40–2/40; *Baubelehrung* U-Boats Baltic 2/40–3/40

Cdr *U 101* 11.3.40–18.11.40

Officer instructor Section 1/2.ULD 12/40–4/41; U-Adm. Staff Officer, Liaison Officer *Fliegerführer Atlantik* 4/41–6/41; Acting CO 4th U-Flotilla 7/41; CO 6th U-Flotilla (command not taken up) 8/41–9/41; CO 23rd U-Flotilla (Eastern Mediterranean) 9/41–5/42; CO 29th U-Flotilla 5/42–7/43; assigned Commanding Adm. U-Boats (Military Hospital), then aboard U-boat depot ship *Erwin Wassner* and operational leader *K-Verband* units Nettuno, Italy 8/43–2/44; U-Adm. Staff Officer Naval High Command Baltic 2/44–4/44; Chief of Staff, Staff of Adm. *K-Verband* units 4/44–capitulation

Detained; freed, 9.1.46

Knight's Cross 29.8.40 (29th KM, 11th U-boat holder)

FREIWALD, KURT [316]

b. 29.10.1906, Berlin-Schöneberg

Class 1925; KptzS 1.4.45

U-Boat School 1.7.35–17.7.35; Cdr *U 7* and *U 21* 18.7.35–3.10.37, also Cdr *U 33* 22.11.36–20.12.36 and 3.6.37–25.7.37; ADC to C-in-C Kriegsmarine/Naval Command Office (A), Operations Division (A1), Reichs War Ministry 10/37–8/43; 24th U-Flotilla (U-Cdr's Torpedo Course 55) 1.9.43–30.9.43; U-Cdr's boat handling trg, AGRU-Front 1.10.43–31.10.43

Cdr *U 181* 1.11.43–capitulation

Detained; freed 23.11.47

FRERKS, PAUL [317]

b. 25.6.1908, place not recorded

Date of entry not known; ObltzS (R) 1.1.43

WO *U 117* to 8/43; acting Cdr *U 66* 6.8.43–1.9.43 (*U 66* was damaged by aircraft from the escort carrier USS *Card* on 3.8.43. 2WO Kurt Schütze was killed and Markworth [789], 1WO Klaus-Joachim Herbig and seven crew members were wounded. On 6.8.43 *U 117* arrived to assist, and Naval Asst. Surgeon Dr Schenk transferred to *U 66* to attend to the wounded. Frerks, who was WO aboard *U 117*, transferred to *U 66* as WO. During an attempt to refuel and re-provision *U 66* the following day, *Card*'s aircraft returned and *U 117* was sunk. *U 66* returned to Lorient with Frerks as acting commander.)

U-Cdr's Course and *Baubelehrung* 9/43–10/43

Cdr *U 975* 17.11.43–16.3.44 but relieved of command following disciplinary hearing

1.UAA 6/44–7/44; subsequent activities unknown

FRESDORF, WERNER [318]

b. 9.11.1908, Magdeburg

Class 1927; Kplt 1.10.36

U-boat trg 7/35–9/35; trg U-Flotilla *Weddigen* and *Baubelehrung U 17* 10/35–12/35

Cdr *U 17* 3.12.35–1.11.37, also torpedo adviser U-Flotilla *Weddigen* 22.11.36–25.9.37; Naval Academy Kiel 11/37–8/38; adviser on U-boat operations OKM/1.SKL 8/38–10/39

Killed in air crash nr Munsterlager 9.10.39

VON FREYBERG-EISENBERG-ALLMENDINGEN, BARON WALTER [319]

b. 5.11.1915, Geisenheim, Rheingau

Class 1935; Kplt 1.6.42

ADC heavy cruiser *Blücher* 9/39–4/40; U-boat trg 4/40–11/40; *Baubelehrung* KLA U-Boats North 11/40–12/40; 1WO *U 552* 12/40–6/41; U-Cdr's Course, 24th U-Flotilla 6/41–7/41

Cdr *U 52* 7.7.41–13.1.42

Baubelehrung 8.KLA 1/42–2/42

Cdr *U 610* 19.2.42–8.10.43

Lost 8.10.43 North Atlantic

VON FRIEDEBURG, HANS-GEORG [320]
b. 15.7.1895, Strasbourg (when German city)
Class IV/1914; GenAdm 1.5.45 seniority 1.2.44
On-board trg cruiser *Hansa* 4/14–8/14; Staff Officer Adm. Naval Staff (Cipher Service) 8/14–12/14; battleship *Kronprinz* 12/14–12/17; trg and courses U-Boat School 12/17–6/18; WO *U 114* 6/18–11/18; U-Boat Inspectorate 11/18–12/18; assisted CO Naval Station Baltic, also served aboard light cruiser *Regensburg* 12/18–10/19; WO cruiser *Königsberg* 10/19–5/20; ADC Basic Trg Est. North Sea 6/20–9/20; ADC cruiser *Hamburg* 9/20–2/22; Platoon Officer Coastal Defence Div. II 2/22–9/22; Divisional ADC Coastal Defence Div. II 9/22–6/24; assigned CO Naval Station North Sea and courses 6/24–12/24; WO and Torpedo Officer cruiser *Hamburg* 12/24–3/25 and 5/25–6/27, also instructor Torpedo School 4/25–5/25; assigned CO Naval Station North Sea 7/27–8/27; Naval School Mürwik 8/27–9/27; trg as ADC 10/27–4/29; Naval Administration Officer, Military District (*Wehrkreis*) Command 1 (Königsberg), on Staff, 1. Div 4/29–6/32; adviser Wehrmacht Office, Reichswehr Ministry 6/32–1/33; ADC to Reichs War Minister, Reichswehr Ministry 2/33–9/36; First Officer light cruiser *Karlsruhe* 9/36–3/38; Adm. Staff Officer, Staff of C-in-C Naval Forces Spain 3/38–11/38; Adm. Staff Officer, Staff of Commander Escort Forces North Sea 11/38–2/39; assigned FdU 2/39–6/39; Cdr *U 27* 6.6.39–8.7.39; Staff Officer (Special Purposes), Staff FdU, Chargé d'Affaires FdU 7/39–9/39; CO Organisation Div., Staff BdU 9/39–9/41; 2/Adm. U-Boats 9/41–1/43; Commanding Adm. U-Boats 2/43–4/45; Commander-in-Chief Kriegsmarine 5/45–capitulation
Committed suicide 23.5.45 (Translator's note: Following notification by the Allied Control Commission at Flensburg that he was to be arrested as a war criminal.)
Awarded Knight's Cross of the War Service Cross with Swords 17.1.45

VON FRIEDEBURG, LUDWIG-FERDINAND [321]
b. 21.5.1924, Wilhelmshaven-Rüstringen
Class V/41; ObltzS 1945
Officer and U-boat trg 5/41–6/43; 2WO *U 548* 6/43–6/44; 1WO *U 548* 7/44–8/44
Cdr *U 155* 15.8.44–11/44
U-Cdr's Course, 3.ULD and 24th U-Flotilla 11/44–1/45 (U-Cdr's Torpedo Course 79); *Baubelehrung* Type XXIII 1.KLA for *U 4710* 2/45–4/45
Cdr *U 4710* 1.5.45–5.5.45
Detained; freed 12.9.47 (Translator's note: On assuming command of *U 155* on 15.8.44, von Friedeburg was aged 20 years and 86 days and was the youngest officer to command a Second World War U-boat.)

FRIEDERICH, KARL [322]
b. 12.6.1914, Grootfontein, South-West Africa
Class 1937a; ObltzS 1.9.41
Platoon Leader, 8/Basic Trg Est. Stralsund 8/39–3/40; U-boat trg 4/40–9/40; *Baubelehrung* 9/40–10/40; 2WO *U 74* 10/40–11/41; U-Cdr's Course, 24th U-Flotilla 11/41–12/41
Cdr *U 5* 7.1.42–23.3.42
Cdr *U 74* 24.3.42–2.5.42
Lost 2.5.42 Mediterranean, off Cartagena, Spain

FRIEDLAND, KLAUS [323]
b. 28.6.1920, Erfurt
Class 1938; ObltzS 1.4.43
Officer and U-boat trg 10/38–5/41; *Baubelehrung* 5/41–6/41; WO *U 332* 6/41–1/43; U-Cdr's Course and *Baubelehrung* 3.KLA 1/43–2/43
Cdr *U 310* 24.2.43–26.9.43

Trg Officer 1.ULD 9/43–2/45; WO, Divisional and No 2 Torpedo Officer light cruiser *Emden* 2/45–capitulation

FRIEDRICH, RUDOLF [324]
b. 15.6.1914, Strehlen, Silesia
Class 1935; Kplt 1.9.42
Seconded to Luftwaffe 9/39–7/41; U-boat trg 8/41–3/42; 1WO *U 558* 3/42–6/42; U-Cdr's Course and *Baubelehrung* KLA U-Boats North 7/42–8/42
Cdr *U 759* 15.8.42–26.7.43
Lost 26.7.43 E of Jamaica

FRIEDRICHS, ADOLF [325]
b. 4.3.1914, Göttingen
Class 1935; Kplt 1.6.42
Seconded to Luftwaffe, inc. *1 /Küstenfliegergruppe 706*, until 12/40; U-boat trg 1/41–6/41; 2WO *U 98* 6/41–8/41; U-Cdr's Course, 24th U-Flotilla 9/41–10/41; *Baubelehrung* 10/41
Cdr *U 253* 21.10.41–25.9.42
Lost 25.9.42 W of Ireland

FRISCHKE, KARL-HEINZ, DR (LAW) [326]
b. 25.11.1912, Berlin-Charlottenburg
Entry 1936; Kplt (R) 1.4.45
1WO 1st VP-Boat Flotilla 1/40–1/41; Staff, Commander Escort Forces Baltic 2/41–3/43, inc. WO HQ ship *Reiher* 8/42–3/43; U-boat trg 3/43–9/43; U-Cdr sea trg *U 970* 9/43–1/44; U-Cdr's Course, 24th U-Flotilla 1/44–3/44 (U-Cdr's Torpedo Course 64); *Baubelehrung* 6.KLA 3/44–5/44
Cdr *U 881* 27.5.44–6.5.45
Lost 6.5.45 SE of Newfoundland

FRITZ, DETLEV [327]
b. 10.6.1921, Darmstadt
Class X/1939; ObltzS 1.10.43
2WO *U 73* 12/41–1/43; 1WO *U 73* 1/43–5/43; U-Cdr's Course and *Baubelehrung* 6/43–9/43 (U-Cdr's Torpedo Course 52)
Cdr *U 904* 25.9.43–30.11.43
Cdr *U 555* 1.12.44–3/45
Subsequent duties not recorded
Detained; freed 8/45

FRITZ, KARL-HEINZ [328]
b. 20.2.1921, Hamburg
Entry 1/41; LtzS (R)
WO *U 103* 6/43–8/44; Cdr *U 107* 8/44–18.8.44
Lost 18.8.44 Bay of Biscay, W of la Rochelle

FRITZE, GÜNTHER [329]
b. 12.6.1922, Burg, nr Magdeburg
Ordnance Branch entry XII/1939; ObltzS 1.12.43 (1.3.43 transferred into Seaman Branch)
U-boat trg and courses 6/43–2/44 (U-Cdr's Torpedo Course 63); *Baubelehrung* 2/44–3/44
Cdr *U 1206* 16.3.44–7/44
Courses and *Baubelehrung* Type XXI 7.KLA 8/44–12/44
Cdr *U 3514* 9.12.44–5.5.45

FRÖHLICH, WILHELM [330]
b. 10.3.1910, Zeitz
Class 1929; Kplt 1.7.38, posthumously KKpt seniority 1.12.39
U-boat trg, U-Boat School Neustadt/Holstein 5/37–8/37; course Torpedo School Flensburg-Mürwik 10/37–12/37; Torpedo School 12/37–1/38; supplementary course Torpedo School Mürwik 5.1.38–29.1.38; details absent 30.1.38–30.8.38; Cdr with Trg Group U-Boat School/U-School Flotilla 31.8.38–15.9.39, also Cdr *U 36* 1.2.39–15.9.39

Cdr *U 36* (U-Flotilla *Saltzwedel*) 16.9.39–4.12.39
Lost 4.12.39 North Sea, SW Kristiansand South

FRÖMMER, HEINZ [331]
b. 21.4.1921, Plauen, Vogtland
Class XII/1939; ObltzS 1.12.43
U-boat trg completed 8/42; *Baubelehrung* 1.KLA 8/42–9/42; 1WO *U 228* 9/42–8/43; U-Cdr's Course, 2.UAA and 24th U-Flotilla 8/43–9/43 (U-Cdr's Torpedo Course 54); *Baubelehrung* 5.KLA 9/43–10/43
Cdr *U 923* 4.10.43–9.2.45
Lost 9.2.45 Kiel Bay, off Kiel Lightvessel

FRÖMSDORF, HELMUT [332]
b. 26.3.1921, Schimmelwitz, Silesia
Class IX/1939; ObltzS 1.12.43
Officer trg 9/39–10/41; 1st and 22nd U-Flotillas 10/41–5/43; *Baubelehrung* 6.KLA 5/43–6/43; 1WO *U 853* 6/43–8/44, inc. period acting Cdr *U 853* 17.6.44–9.7.44; U-Cdr's Course 7/44–8/44
Cdr *U 853* 1.9.44–6.5.45
Lost 6.5.45 off US coast, SE of New London

FROHBERG, GÜNTHER [333]
b. 6.2.1921, Dresden
Class IX/1939; ObltzS 1.10.43
Officer trg 9/39–1/41; heavy cruiser *Prinz Eugen* 2/41–3/43; U-boat trg 4/43–9/43; supernumerary WO *U 980* 9/43–11/43; WO *U 952* 11/43–5/44; U-Cdr's Course, 24th U-Flotilla 6/44–7/44 (U-Cdr's Torpedo Course 73)
Cdr *U 1275* 18.7.44–capitulation
Detained; freed 7/45

FUCHS, KARL-HEINZ [334]
b. 18.1.1915, Haiger, Dillkreis, Hesse
Class 1935; Kplt 1.8.42
Rangefinding Officer battleship *Scharnhorst* 1/39–8/40; Kriegsmarine Depot Dunkirk 8/40–10/40; U-boat trg 10/40–5/41; courses and *Baubelehrung* 6/41–8/41; 1WO *U 154* 8/41–6/42; U-Cdr's Course, 24th U-Flotilla 6/42–8/42; *Baubelehrung* 8.KLA 8/42–9/42
Cdr *U 528* until 16.12.42 (per WASt) or 19.12.42 (per *U 528* WD)
Trg Adviser Higher Command of U-Boats 1/43–capitulation

FUHLENDORF, HARALD [335]
b. 11.5.1919, Hamburg
Entry XI/1939; ObltzS (R) 1.6.44
U-boat trg 8/43–2/44; U-Cdr's Course (U-Cdr's Torpedo Course 71), courses and *Baubelehrung* Type XXIII 2/44–11/44
Cdr *U 2343* 6.11.44–30.4.45

G

GABERT, PAUL [336]
b. 13.4.1913, Zangenberg, Zeitz
Entry 1933; Kplt 1.4.45
Instructor trg ship *Schlesien* 7/39–8/40; Instructor Automobile Div. Wilhelmshaven 8/40–9/40; Platoon Leader 6/Basic Trg Est. Stralsund 9/40–7/41; light cruiser *Emden* 7/41–3/43; U-boat trg 3/43–9/43; U-Cdr sea trg *U 965* 9/43–10/43; course 23rd U-Flotilla 10/43–1/44; *Baubelehrung* 7.KLA 2/44–4/44
Cdr *U 1210* 22.4.45–3.5.45

GÄNGE, ALBRECHT [337]
b. 1.6.1919, Naumburg, Saale
Class 1937b; ObltzS 1.4.42
Trg and courses to 3/41; 2WO mine clearance ship *Bali* 3/41–12/41; U-boat trg 1/42–6/42; 1WO *U 378* 6/42–6/43; U-Cdr's Course, 2.UAA and 24th U-Flotilla 6/43–7/43 (U-Cdr's Torpedo Course 50)
Cdr *U 226* 26.7.43–6.11.43
Lost 6.11.43 E of Newfoundland

GANZER, ERWIN [338]
b. 8.12.1912, Cologne
Entry 1935; Kplt 1.11.43
1st and 3rd VP-Boat Flotillas 9/39-6/40; naval oiler *Ermland* 6/40–9/40; naval oiler *Neumark* 9/40–12/40; aboard prize ships 12/40–5/41; naval supply ship *Kärnten* 5/41–7/41; Supply Ship Command (*Trossschiffsverband*) 8/41–4/42; sail trg ship *Horst Wessel* 5/42–11/42; U-boat trg and assigned Commanding Adm. U-Boats, also 27th and 10th U-Flotillas 11/42–11/43; *Baubelehrung* 6.KLA 11/43–1/44

Cdr *U 871* 15.1.44–26.9.44
Lost 26.9.44 NW of Azores

GAUDE, HANS-LUDWIG [339]
b. 23.1.1916. Stettin
Class 1936; Kplt 1.10.43
Platoon Leader 6/Naval Artillery Div. 4/39–3/40; *Baubelehrung M 18*, Oderwerke, Stettin 1/40–3/40; 1WO *M 18*, 3rd Minesweeping Flotilla 3/40–1/41; U-boat trg 1.ULD 1/41–6/41; 1WO *U 83* 7/41–9/41; 1WO *U 558* 9/41–11/41; U-Cdr's Course 11/41–12/41
Acting Cdr *U 19* 16.12.41–2/42; Cdr *U 19* 2/42–30.4.42 (*U 19* was decommissioned at Kiel on 30.4.42 preparatory to transfer to Black Sea)
Various courses and duties 5/42–9/42
Cdr *U 19* 1.10.42–2.12.43 (*U 19* was recommissioned at Constanza, Romania, on 28.12.42)
U-Adm. Staff Officer, Adm. Black Sea 3.12.43–31.1.44; Trg Officer 27th U-Flotilla 2/44–4/44; *Baubelehrung* Cdr *U 883* 1.5.44–1.10.44 (but *U 883* was not commissioned until 27.3.45, and then under Uebel [1286], at the Deschimag AG yard, Weser Bremen)
Trg Officer 27th U-Flotilla 10/44–12/44; *Baubelehrung* Type XXI 7.KLA 1.1.45–30.1.45
Cdr *U 3525* 31.1.45–30.4.45
Cdr *U 2343* 1.5.45–5.5.45
Interned at Flensburg-Mürwik, 5/45; Cdr 1/Naval Rifle Regiment 112 6/45–8/45; German Minesweeping Administration 8/45–12/47
Detained; freed 31.12.47

VON GAZA, JÜRGEN [340]
b. 7.9.1920, Magdeburg
Class 1939a; ObltzS 1.10.43

Officer trg 9/39–2/41; heavy cruiser *Admiral Hipper* 3/41–3/43; U-boat trg 4/43–10/43; *Baubelehrung* 10/43–11/43; 1WO *U 863* 11/43–6/44; 1WO *U 739* 6/44–10/44; courses, inc. U-Cdr's Course 10/44–1/45
Cdr *U 312* 1.2.45–capitulation
Detained; freed 3/47

GEBAUER, WERNER [341]
b. 10.9.1922, Bad Soden
Class XII/1939; ObltzS 1.12.43
Officer and U-boat trg 12/39–2/42; *Baubelehrung* 1.KLA 2/42–4/42; 2WO *U 212* 4/42–8/43; 1WO *U 212* 8/43–3/44; U-Cdr's Course, trg (courses), 3.ULD, 24th and 27th U-Flotillas 4/44–8/44 (U-Cdr's Torpedo Course 70)
Cdr *U 681* 2.8.44 or 8.8.44 (see Bach [25]) to 10.3.45
POW 10.3.45

GEHRKEN, HEINRICH [342]
b. 12.7.1911, Zwistringen, nr Bremen
Entry as NCO (R) III/1937; ObltzS (R) 1.4.43
1WO 2nd VP-Boat Flotilla 9/39–2/40; 1WO 12th Minesweeping Flotilla 4/40–7/40; 1/NCO Trg Div. 7/40–8/40; Senior Helmsman 56th Minesweeping Flotilla 9/40–2/43; U-boat trg 3/43–8/43; U-Cdr's Course, 24th U-Flotilla 8/43–10/43 (U-Cdr's Torpedo Course 55)
Cdr *UF 2* 10/43–5.7.44
Cdr *U 298* 18.7.44–capitulation

GEIDER, HORST [343]
b. 7.9.1918, Stuttgart
Class 1937a; ObltzS 1.9.41
Platoon Officer 16/Basic Trg Est. Stralsund 8/39–6/40; U-boat trg 6/40–9/40; Comp. Officer 1.ULD 9/40–7/41; 2WO *U 73* 8/41–12/41; U-Cdr's Course, 26th U-Flotilla 12/41–1/42
Cdr *U 61* 16.1.42–9.11.42

Baubelehrung 6.KLA 11/42–12/42
Cdr *U 761* 3.12.42–24.2.44
POW 24.2.44

GEISLER, HANS-FERDINAND [344]
b. 26.3.1921, Kiel
Class 1938; ObltzS 1.4.43
2WO *U 564* 4/41–6/42; U-Cdr's Course 6/42–7/42
Cdr *U 152* 1.8.42–20.9.42
Cdr *U 21* 25.9.42–28.1.43
Instructor 1.ULD 1/43–5/43; course Academy of Naval Warfare 6/43–8/43; instructor 1.ULD 8.43–5/44; *Baubelehrung* Type XXI 6.KLA 7/44–10/44
Cdr *U 3006* 6.10.44–3.12.44
Naval Military Hospital, Kiel and Malente 12/44–1/45; 4th U-Flotilla 1/45–2/45; *Baubelehrung* 6.KLA for *U 3049* (boat never commissioned) 15.2.45–capitulation

GEISSLER, HANS [345]
b. 1.10.1916, Rüdesheim
Class 1935; Kplt 1.9.42
M/S-Cdr 5th Minesweeping Flotilla 2/41–3/41; U-boat trg 3/41–8/41; U-Cdr's Course, 24th U-Flotilla 9/41–10/41; U-Cdr sea trg *U 561* 10/41–12/41; *Baubelehrung* 7.KLA 12/41–1/42
Cdr *U 440* 24.1.42–19.5.43
Induction Officer, Acceptance Centre for Officer Applicants 6/43–4/44; Navigation Officer light cruiser *Leipzig* 4/44–11/44 and trg ship *Nordland* 11/44–capitulation

GEISSLER, HEINZ [346]
b. 29.8 1917, Zeulenroda, Thüringen
Entry X/1938; ObltzS (R) 1.4.43
U-boat trg to 8/41; 2WO *U 376* 8/41–7/42; 1WO *U 376* 7/42–12/42; U-Cdr's Course, 24th U-Flotilla 12/42–2/43; *Baubelehrung* 1.KLA 2/43–3/43

Cdr *U 390* 3.3.43–5.7.44
Lost 5.7.44 Seine estuary

GELHAAR, ALEXANDER [347]
b. 24.11.1908, Frankfur
Class 1937; Kplt 1.10.36
U-boat trg, U-Boat School 9/35–9/36; Cdr *U 1* 1.10.36–2.2.38; Midshipmen's Instruction Group Leader, Naval Gunnery School 2/38–4/38; ADC, New Warships Trials Branch 4/38–5/38; *Baubelehrung* Germaniawerft, Kiel 5/38–6/38
Cdr *U 45* 25.6.38–14.10.39
Lost 14.10.39 E of Ireland

GELHAUS, HARALD [348]
b. 24.7.1915, Göttingen
Class 1935, Kplt 1.4.42
ADC, Signals and Platoon Officer battleship *Gneisenau* 5/38–10/39; U-boat trg 10/39–3/40; *Baubelehrung* U-Boats North Sea and WO 2nd U-Flotilla 3/40–7/40; 1WO *U 103* 7/40–3/41; U-Cdr's Torpedo Course, 24th U-Flotilla 3/41
Cdr *U 143* (22nd U-Flotilla) 31.3.41–30.4.41, (3rd U-Flotilla) 1.5.41–12.9.41, (22nd U-Flotilla) 13.9.41–30.11.41 (per P/F: furlough 19.11.41–30.11.41)
Cdr *U 107* 1.12.41–6.6.43
Adviser (1.U), OKM/1.SKL 6/43–2/44; Trg Officer 22nd and 27th U-Flotillas 2/44–12/44; Cdr U-Boat Operations, Adm. Eastern Baltic and 9th Escort Div. 12/44–4/45; assigned Naval High Command North Sea 4/45–capitulation
Detained; freed 13.8.45.
Knight's Cross 26.3.43 (155th KM, 85th U-boat holder)

GEMEINER, GERTH [349]
b. 2.10.1918, Dresden
Class 1937b; ObltzS 1.4.42
Trg and courses 9/39–9/40; Comp. Officer 2.ULD 9/40–6/41; 2WO *U 38* 6/41–12/41; 1WO *U 160* 12/41–5/42; U-Cdr's Course, 24th U-Flotilla 5/42–6/42
Cdr *U 146* 6/42–8/42
Cdr *U 137* 2.9.42–27.12.43
Cdr *U 154* 22.1.44–3.7.44
Lost 3.7.44 W of Madeira

GENGELBACH, DIETRICH [350]
b. 7.10.1914, Salzwedel
Class 1934; ObltzS 1.4.39, posthumously Kplt seniority 1.1.42
1WO torpedo-boat *Jaguar* 12/37–10/39; 1WO torpedo-boat *Seeadler* 10/39–4/40; U-boat trg 4/40–10/40; instructor Torpedo School Mürwik 10/40–1/41; instructor 24th U-Flotilla 1/41–3/41; 1WO *U 52* 3/41–5/41; *Baubelehrung* 5/41–6/41
Cdr *U 574* 12.6.41–19.12.41
Lost 19.12.41 North Atlantic, off Punta Delgada

GERICKE, OTTO [351]
b. 29.12.1908, Haguenau, Alsace (when German province)
Entry 1933; KKpt (R) seniority 1.12.43
Destroyer *Z 17 Diether von Roeder* 8/38–4/40 or 5/40; Naval Station Command Baltic 5/40–7/40; U-boat trg 7/40–1/41; U-Cdr sea trg *U 17* 1/41–3/41; courses and *Baubelehrung* 5/41–7/41
Cdr *U 503* 10.7.41–15.3.42
Lost 15.3.42 SE of Newfoundland

GERKE, ERNST-AUGUST [352]
b. 9.5.1921, Osnabrück
Class 1939b; ObltzS 1.12.43
WO sea trg *U 62* and *U 202* 1941–42; 2WO *U 377* 8/42–5/43; 1WO *U 377* 5/43–12/43, inc. period acting Cdr *U 377* 22.9.43–10.10.43 (deputising for Kluth [618] when latter

wounded); U-Cdr's Course 1/44–3/44 (U-Cdr's Torpedo Course 64); Cdr (supernumerary) with 27th U-Flotilla 4/44–5/44; acting Cdr *U 382* 5/44–29.6.44 and acting Cdr *U 650* 30.6.44 or 16.7.44 to 20.7.44 (Gerke acted as temporary commander of *U 382* and *U 650* to assist Zorn [1408], who was incapacitated with a fracture)
Cdr *U 673* 1.8.44–24.10.44
6th U-Flotilla and *Baubelehrung* Type XXI 6.KLA 10/44–2/45
Cdr *U 3035* .3.45–capitulation

GERLACH, PETER [353]
b. 25.2.1922, Memel
Class XII/1939; ObltzS 1.12.43
Officer and U-boat trg to 2/42; WO *U 453* 2/42–8/43; U-Cdr's Course, 24th and 23rd U-Flotillas 8/43–10/43; further trg 7.KLA and 27th U-Flotilla 10/43–11/43
Cdr *U 37* 20.11.43–8.1.44
Cdr *U 223* 12.1.44–30.3.44 (per *U 223* WD)
Lost 30.3.44 Mediterranean, N of Palermo, Sicily

GERLACH, WILHELM [354]
b. 15.8.1905, Eisenach, Thüringen
Entry NCO (R) XI/1939; ObltzS (R) 1.3.43
ObStrm *U 124* 7/40–9/41; courses 1.UAA 9/41–1/42; WO *U 124* 1/42–8/42; U-Cdr's Course and *Baubelehrung* 1.KLA 9/42–3/43
Cdr *U 490* 27.3.43–11.6.44
POW 11.6.44

GESSNER, HANS [355]
b. 6.5.1919, Mannheim
Class 1938; ObltzS 1.4.43, seniority 1.1.43
WO and UJ-Cdr 11th Anti-Submarine Flotilla 8/40–1/44; U-boat trg 1/44–7/44; WO *U 1105* 7/44–8/44; U-Cdr's Course, 3.ULD and 24th U-Flotilla 8/44–10/44 (U-Cdr's Torpedo Course 77)
Cdr *U 1008* 18.11.44–6.5.45

GIERSBERG, DIETRICH [356]
b. 26.11.1917, Berlin-Dahlem
Class 1937a; Kplt 1.3.44
2WO *T 108* 8/39–9/39; Platoon Leader 9/Basic Trg Est. Stralsund 9/39–3/40; ADC 1st Torpedo-Boat Flotilla 3/40–8/41; Comp. CO, *Baubelehrung*-Comp., 3rd T-Flotilla 8/41–9/41; U-boat trg 9/41–3/42; 1WO *U 155* 3/42–9/42; U-Cdr's Course and *Baubelehrung* 9/42–11/42
Cdr *U 419* 18.11.42–8.10.43
POW 8.10.43–12/47

GIESEWETTER, HERBERT [357]
b. 9.9.1922, Emmerich, Rhineland
Class 1939b; ObltzS 1.12.43
U-boat trg completed 1/42; Platoon Leader 1.UAA 1/42–3/42; trg and 2WO 5th U-Flotilla aboard *U 618* 4/42–8/42; 2WO *U 618* 9/42–2/43; WO 7th U-Flotilla 2/43–12/43; U-Cdr's Course, 24th U-Flotilla 1/44–2/44 (U-Cdr's Torpedo Course 63)
Cdr *U 60* 16.2.44–28.2.45
Cdr *U 368* 1.3.45–27.4.45 (assumed command in 1/45 per WASt))

GIESSLER, HANS-HENRICH [358]
b. 12.1.1911, Berlin
Class 1931; KKpt 1.10.43
1WO destroyer *Z 16 Friedrich Eckholdt* 8/38–10/39; Torpedo Inspectorate and Torpedo Testing Branch 10/39–3/41; U-boat trg, U-Cdr's Course and *Baubelehrung* 3/41–8/41
Cdr *U 455* 21.8.41–22.11.42 (per *U 455* WD)
Torpedo Inspectorate 12/42–10/44; at Ministry of Armaments and War Production (Speer) 11/44–

2/45; First Officer destroyer *Z 20 Karl Galster* 2/45–capitulation
Detained; freed 3/46

GILARDONE, HANS [359]
b. 9.7.1912, Munich
Class 1932; Kplt 1.2.40
Div. and WO light cruiser *Köln* 3/38–3/41; U-boat trg 3/41–7/41; U-Cdr's Course, 24th U-Flotilla 7/41–9/41; U-Cdr sea trg *U 203* 9/41–10/41; *Baubelehrung* 10/41–11/41
Cdr *U 254* 8.11.41–8.12.42
Lost 8.12.42 SE Cape Farewell

GLASER, WOLFGANG [360]
b. 24.2.1919, Heidelberg
Class 1937b; ObltzS 1.4.42
2WO fleet escort *F 8* 12/39–3/40; WO 2nd Minesweeping Flotilla 5/40–7/40; M/S-Cdr and Group Leader 42nd Minesweeping Flotilla 7/40–10/41; R-Cdr 3rd R-Boat Flotilla 10/41–3/43; U-boat trg 3/43–11/43; U-Cdr's Course, 23rd U-Flotilla 11/43–1/44; *Baubelehrung* 8.KLA 1/44–3/44
Cdr *U 1014* 14.3.44–4.2.45
Lost 4.2.45 The Minch

GLATTES, GERHARD [361]
b. 6.2.1909, Bruchsal, Baden
Class 1927, KKpt 1.9.41
U-boat trg and U-Boat School 3/36–9/36; Cdr *U 5* (U-Boat School Trg Group) 1.10.36–2.2.38; details not available 2/38–6/38; assigned FdU 3.6.38–26.6.38; details not available 27.6.38–10.9.38; U-Flotilla *Saltzwedel* 11.9.38–17.9.38; details not available 18.9.38–26.9.38; assigned FdU 27.9.38–2.10.38; U-Flotilla *Hundius* 3.10.38–17.11.38; *Baubelehrung* Deschimag AG Weser Bremen 18.11.38–9.12.38
Cdr *U 39* (U-Flotilla *Hundius*) 10.12.38–14.9.39
POW 14.9.39–8.4.47

GODE, HEINRICH [362]
(Entered Kriegsmarine under family name Jedamski; changed to Gode 1941)
b. 24.1.1922, Karolinenhof, nr Ortelsberg, East Prussia
Class 1939b; ObltzS 1.12.43
WO sea trg *U 108* 5/41–11/41; various duties until 6/43; *Baubelehrung* 8.KLA 6/43–7/43; 1WO *U 549* 7/43–4/44; U-Cdr's Course 4/44–6/44 (U-Cdr's Torpedo Course 71); U-Cdr 5th and 33rd U-Flotillas 6/44–1/45; *Baubelehrung* Cdr 8th U-Flotilla for *U 3536* 15.1.45–4/45 (Was scheduled commander for *U 3536* but completion work on this boat was abandoned on the approach of the Red Army. The boat's officers and seaman branch complement brought the almost completed *U 3531* from Danzig to Hela and then to Kiel under tow at the beginning of March 1945. The technical complement of *U 3536* had already left for Kiel in January 1945 aboard *U 3520*; this boat was mined and sunk off Kiel-Bülk on 31.1.1945.)
Cdr and surviving *U 3536* crew fought in the defence of the OKM, Berlin, 4/45–5/45

GODT, EBERHARD [363]
b. 5.8.1900, Lübeck
Class VII/1918; KAdm 1.3.43
Naval College Flensburg-Mürwik 7/18–10/18; battleship *Schlesien* 10/18–11/18; furlough 12/18–2/19; Naval Assault Comp., No 1 Guard Reserve Regt 2/19–7/19; Study 1919–20; II. Naval Brigade 3/20; Infantry Div., Naval Basic Trg Div. Baltic 11/20–1/21; 11th Minesweeping Half-Flotilla 2/21–6/21; cruiser *Arcona* 6/21–3/22; Naval College Mürwik plus duties aboard survey ship *Panther* and tender *Drache* 3/22–3/23; battleship *Hannover* 4/23–1/24; courses 1/24–9/24; Platoon Officer, Ships' Company *Hessen* 9/24–1/25; Div. Lt battleship *Hessen* 1/25–9/25; course Torpedo and Signals School 10/25–12/25; ADC Coastal Div. V 12/25–9/26; ADC V/Naval Artillery Div. 10/26–9/27; WO and ADC 2nd Torpedo-Boat Half-Flotilla 9/27–

9/29; WO 1st Torpedo-Boat Flotilla 9/29–9/30; Assistant, Mine Warfare Experimental Branch 9/30–3/32 and Cdr torpedo-boat *T 155* 9/31–12/31; Cdr tender *Nordsee*, 1st E-Boat Flotilla 3/32–9/32; Cdr *G 10*, 1st Torpedo-Boat Flotilla 9/32–9/34; Torpedo Officer and ADC light cruiser *Emden* 9/34–9/35; U-boat trg 10/35–12/35; assigned FdU 12/35–3/36; *Baubelehrung U 25* 3/36–4/36; Cdr *U 25* (U-Flotilla *Weddigen*) 6.4.36–31.8.36; Cdr *U 25* and *U 23* (U-Flotilla *Saltzwedel*) 1.9.36–3.1.38; 1/Adm. Staff Officer, Staff FdU 1/38–9/39; CO Operations Div. Staff BdU 10/39–2/43; Div. CO OKM/2.SKL/BdU/Opns 3/43–capitulation (Translator's note: Godt was taken to the United States and interrogated as a possible prosecution witness, but he declined so to appear. At the request of the tribunal he was then lodged at Nuremberg prison as a material defence witness for Dönitz.)

GÖING, WALTER [364]

b. 2.8.1914, Wilhelmshaven
Class 1934; Kplt 1.1.42
Cadet Trg Officer trg ship *Schlesien* 6/39–4/40; U-boat trg 4/40–11/40; Trg Officer Naval Gunnery School 10/40–2/41; 1WO *U 38* 2/41–7/41; U-Cdr's Course, 24th U-Flotilla and Naval Gunnery School 7/41–11/41
Cdr *U 755* 3.11.41–28.5.43
Lost 28.5.43 Mediterranean, NW of Majorca

GÖLLNITZ, HEINRICH [365]

b. 30.8.1909, Grossenhain, Saxony
Class 1935; Kplt 1.3.42, posthumously KKpt seniority 1.5.43
Comp. CO Naval Flak Detachment 274 9/39–3/40; U-boat trg 4/40–9/40; Comp. Officer 1.UAA 9/40–11/40; 1WO *U 111* 12/40–8/41; 22nd U-Flotilla 8/41–11/41; U-Cdr's Course, 24th U-Flotilla 11/41–12/41
Cdr *U 657* 20.12.41–17.5.43
Lost 17.5.43 E of Cape Farewell

GÖRNER, FRIEDRICH-KARL [366]

b. 24.11.1921, Herzberg, Elster
Class 1939b; ObltzS 1.12.43
Trg and courses until 1/42; WO 24th U-Flotilla 1/42–1/43, inc. *Baubelehrung* for *U 958*; WO *U 958* 1/43–8/44; U-Cdr's Course, 24th U-Flotilla 9/44–10/44 (U-Cdr's Torpedo Course 77); U-Cdr sea trg *U 145* 10/44–11/44
Cdr *U 145* 27.11.44–capitulation

GÖTZE, HANS [367]

b. 12.1.1916, Belgaum, Goa
Entry X1/1939; ObltzS (R) 1.10.43
Officer and U-boat trg 11/39–7/41; *Baubelehrung* 7/41–9/41; 2WO *U 586* 9/41–12/42; 1WO *U 586* 12/42–9/43; U-Cdr's Torpedo Course 54 9/43–10/43
Cdr *U 586* 1.10.43–5.7.44
29th U-Flotilla and *Baubelehrung* Type XXI 8.KLA 8/44–12/44
Cdr *U 2527* 23.12.44–2.5.45

GOLDBECK, HEINZ [368]

b. 10.2.1914, Berlin
Entry 1936; ObltzS (R) 1.9.43
Div. Officer and WO auxiliary warship *Ammerland* 10/39–2/43, also Naval Special Command, Toulon 11/42–12/42; U-boat trg 3/43–9/43; WO and U-Cdr sea trg *U 288* 9/43–10/43; U-Cdr's Course, 3.ULD and 23rd U-Flotilla 10/43–12/43; *Baubelehrung* 7.KLA 12/43–2/44
Cdr *U 1169* 9.2.44–5.4.45
Lost 5.4.45 St George's Channel

GOSCHZIK, GEORG [369]

b. 6.1.1912, Brieg, Silesia
Enlisted rating 1931; ObltzS 1.11.43
U-boat trg 5/43–11/43; WO *U 367* 11/43–2/44; 1WO *U 642* 2/44–5/44; 1WO *U 586* 5/44–7/44; U-Cdr's Course, 3.ULD and 23rd U-Flotilla

7/44–10/44; *Baubelehrung* Type XXIII 8.KLA 10/44–12/44
Cdr *U 2348* 4.12.44–capitulation

GOSEJACOB, HENRI [370]
b. 14.12.1915, Rüstringen
Entry 1936; ObltzS (R)
2WO 15th VP-Boat Flotilla 9/39–8/40; VP-Cdr 11th VP-Boat Flotilla 8/40–9/40; U-boat trg, WO, courses and U-Cdr's Course 9/40–12/42; *Baubelehrung* 8.KLA 12/42
Cdr *U 713* 29.12.42–24.2.44
Lost 24.2.44 NW of Narvik

GOSSLER, JOHANN-EGBERT [371]
b. 16.11.1914, Hamburg
Class 1935, Kplt 1.9.42
Div. Officer light cruiser *Leipzig* 5/39–2/40; Div. Officer and WO heavy cruiser *Prinz Eugen* 2/40–6/41; U-boat trg 7/41–10/41; 1WO *U 125* 11/41–6/42; course, 2.ULD and U-Cdr's Course, 24th U-Flotilla 7/42–10/42; U-boat base Hamburg and *Baubelehrung* 10/42–2/43
Cdr *U 538* 10.2.43–21.11.43
Lost 21.11.43 SW of Ireland

VON GOSSLER, KURT [372]
b. 21.9.1905, Stendal
Class 1933; KKpt 1.4.43
U-boat trg 7/35–12/35; U-Flotilla *Weddigen* 12/35–1/36; WO *U 12* and *U 15* 1/36–9/37; WO *U 25* 10/37–7/38, inc. gunnery instruction Naval Gunnery School 22.11.37–11.12.37; Cdr *U 10* (U-Boat School Trg Group) 1.8.38–30.9.38; Cdr *U 10* and *U 12* (U-Flotilla *Lohs*) 1.10.38–4.1.39; assigned FdU 5.1.39–9.1.39, 25.3.39–3.4.39 and 1.7.39–16.7.39, details not available periods 10.1.39–24.3.39 and 4.4.39–30.6.39; *Baubelehrung* Germaniawerft Kiel 17.7.39–11.8.39

Cdr *U 49* 12.8.39–15.4.40
POW 15.4.40–22.6.47

GRAEF, ADOLF [373]
b. 22.4.1916, Flensburg
Class 1936; Kplt 1.10.43
WO minelayer *Cobra* 9/39–10/39; 1WO fleet tender *F 7* 10/39–3/40; course and trg C-in-C Minesweepers West 4/40–5/40; 1WO 3rd Minesweeping Flotilla 5/40–1/41; U-boat trg 1/41–9/41; 1WO *U 652* 9/41–5/42; U-Cdr's Course 5/42–6/42
Cdr *U 664* 17.6.42–9.8.43
POW 9.8.43–11.5.46

GRÄF, ULRICH [374]
b. 15.12.1915, Dresden
Class 1935; Kplt 1.1.43
Light cruiser *Nürnberg* 1/40–5/40; 2WO torpedo-boat *Iltis* 5/40–10/40; U-boat trg 11/40–4/41; 1WO *U 74* 4/41–8/41; U-Cdr's Course, 24th U-Flotilla 9/41
Cdr *U 23* 24.9.41–26.3.42
Cdr *U 69* 31.3.42–17.2.43
Lost 7.2.43 western North Atlantic

GRAFEN, KARL [375]
b. 9.5.1915, Essen-Altenessen
Entry 1935; ObltzS 1.11.43
Platoon Officer 1.UAA 8/42–9/42; 1WO *U 24* 10/42–8/43; U-Cdr's Course, 2.UAA and 23rd U-Flotilla 9/43–10/43
Cdr *U 20* 1.11.43–10.9.44
Interned 10.9.44 Turkey

GRAMITZKY, FRANZ [376]
b. 18.5.1916, Lyck, East Prussia
Class 1936; Kplt 1.8.43
Platoon Leader 8/Basic Trg Est. Stralsund 4/39–9/39; WO *U 17* 9/39–10/39; 2WO *U A* 10/39–

11/39; WO *U 9* 11/39–6/40; 1WO *U 138* 6/40–12/40
Cdr *U 138* 1.1.41–18.6.41
POW 18.6.41

GRANDEFELD, WOLFGANG [377]
b. 11.2.1917, Hamburg
Class 1936; ObltzS 1.10.40
1WO 2nd Minesweeping Flotilla 4/39–9/40; R-Cdr 7th R-Boat Flotilla 10/40–3/41; M/S-Cdr 5th Minesweeping Flotilla 3/41–9/41; U-boat trg 9/41–4/42; 1WO *U 108* 4/42–12/42; U-Cdr's Course, 24th U-Flotilla 12/42–1/43
Cdr *U 174* 9.3.43–27.4.43
Lost 27.4.43 S of Newfoundland

GRASSE, MARTIN [378]
b. 10.11.1912, Schlaubekammer
Entry 1936; ObltzS (R) 1.9.43
WO and VP-Cdr 16th VP-Boat Flotilla 7/41–3/43; U-boat trg, courses and *Baubelehrung* 3/43–1/44 (U-Cdr's Torpedo Course 58)
Cdr *U 1168* 19.1.44–7/44
Baubelehrung Type XXI 7.KLA 7/44–11/44
Cdr *U 3511* 18.11.44–28.1.45
Died natural causes 28.1.45

GRAU, PETER [379]
b. 8.3.1920, Elmshorn
Class X/1939; ObltzS 1.4.43
Officer trg 10/39–10/40; Secretarial Officer and 3WO destroyer *Z 20 Karl Galster* 10/40–6/42; U-boat trg 6/42–10/42; 2WO *U 601* 10/42–3/43; 1WO *U 601* 5/43–7/43; U-Cdr's Course, 2.UAA and 24th U-Flotilla 7/43–8/43 (U-Cdr's Torpedo Course 52); *Baubelehrung* 7.KLA 8/43–9/43
Cdr *U 1191* 9.9.43–25.6.44
Lost 25.6.44 English Channel, SE of Torquay

GRAU, PETER-OTTMAR [380]
b. 3.5.1914, Hamburg
Class 1934; Kplt 1.1.42
Cdr *Otto Braun* (Mine Warfare Experimental Group) 8/39–10/39; Cdr *M 1201* and *M 1204*, 12th Minesweeping Flotilla 10/39–1/41; U-boat trg 1/41–8/41; U-Cdr sea trg *U 210* 9/41–30.9.41
Cdr *U 46* 10/41–19.11.41
Baubelehrung 11/41–12/41
Cdr *U 601* 18.12.41 to 23.10.43 (per *U 601* WD) but most probably 28.11.43 (per Grau to U-Boat Archive, confirmed WASt)
Baubelehrung 6.KLA 12/43–2/44
Cdr *U 872* 10.2.44–29.7.44 (after serious damage from a direct hit during a USAAF air raid on Bremen on 29.7.44, *U 872* was decommissioned on 10.8.44 and scrapped)
Baubelehrung Type XXI 6.KLA 8/44–12/44
Cdr *U 3015* 17.12.44–5.5.45
Detained; freed 9/45

GRAVE, GÜNTHER-PAUL [381]
b. 13.7.1917, Magdeburg
Class 1937a; ObltzS 1.9.41
Battleship *Scharnhorst* 7/39–4/40; U-boat trg 4/40–11/40; *Baubelehrung* 11/40–12/40; 2WO *U 71* 12/40–11/41; U-Cdr's Course, 26th U-Flotilla 11/41–12/41
Cdr *U 56* 20.1.42–14.11.42
Baubelehrung 1.KLA 11/42–1/43
Cdr *U 470* 7.1.43–16.10.43
Lost 16.10.43 North Atlantic, SW of Iceland

GRAWERT, JUSTUS [382]
b. 13.1.1923, Neu-Trebbin, Ob. Barnim, Brandenburg
Entry X/1940; ObltzS 1.10.44
U-boat trg 1/42–8/42; WO *U 80* 8/42–2/43; WO *U 34* 2/43; WO *U 333* 2/43–5/44; U-Cdr's

Course, 3.ULD and 24th U-Flotilla 5/44–8/44 (U-Cdr's Torpedo Course 74)
Cdr *U 750* 1.9.44–5.5.45

GREGER, EBERHARD [383]
b. 15.9.1915, Lieberose, Netherlands
Class 1935; ObltzS 1.10.1939
2WO destroyer *Z 9 Wolfgang Zenker* 2/39–10/39; U-boat trg 10/39–1/40; 1WO *U 30* 1/40–10/40; *Baubelehrung* 10/40–11/40; 1WO *U 110* 11/40–4/41; U-Cdr's Course, 24th U-Flotilla and *Baubelehrung* 3.KLA 4/41–6/41
Cdr *U 85* 7.6.41–14.4.42
Lost 14.4.42 western North Atlantic

GRETSCHEL, GÜNTER [384]
b. 26.10.1914, Scheibe, Glatz, Silesia
Class 1936; ObltzS 1.10.40
ADC U-Boat School Flotilla 2/39–9/39; courses 10/39–3/40; WO *U 6* 3/40–6/40; *Baubelehrung* 6/40–7/40; 2WO *U 93* 7/40–4/41
Cdr *U 59* 17.4.41–12/41
Courses and *Baubelehrung* 8.KLA 1/42–6/42
Cdr *U 707* 1.7.42–9.11.43
Lost 9.11.43 E of Azores

GRÉUS, FRIEDRICH-AUGUST [385]
b. 27.4.1921, Puschkau, Silesia
Class 1939a; ObltzS 1.10.43
Officer trg 4/39–8/40; Situation Room Midshipman on Staff C-in-C Torpedo-Boats 8/40–10/40; U-boat trg and WO, accommodation ship, U-School Flotilla, Pillau 10/40–1/42; *Baubelehrung* 1/42–4/42; WO *U 217* 5/42–5/43; 1WO *U 214* 7/43–12/43; various duties, inc. U-Cdr under instrn, courses and *Baubelehrung* 12/43–11/44 (U-Cdr's Torpedo Course 62)
Cdr *U 737* 25.11.44–19.12.44
Acting Cdr *U 716* 22.1.45 (per *U 716* WD) or 27.1.45 to 12.2.45
Infantry Trg 3/45–capitulation
Detained; freed 24.8.45

GRIMME, WILHELM [386]
b. 12.5.1907, Osnabrück
Entry 1925; Kplt 1.3.43, promotion following death
2nd U-Flotilla 4/39–6/41; courses 6/41–10/41
Cdr *U 146* 10/41–6/42
Course 24th U-Flotilla 7/42–8/42
Cdr *U 116* 11.9.42–15.10.42 (official date of death)
Missing from 6.10.42 North Atlantic

GROCHOWIAK, EDMUND [387]
b. 24.10.1917, Wanne-Eickel
Class 1937a; Kplt 1.1.45
U-boat trg 9/41–3/42; WO *U 105* 5/42–3/43; U-Cdr's Course, 2.UAA and 24th U-Flotilla 3/43–4/43; *Baubelehrung* 8.KLA 4/43–6/43
Cdr *U 982* 10.6.43–11.4.44
Comp. CO 2.ULD 4/44–3/45; Naval Signals Officer, Kiel 3/45–capitulation

GROSSE, HARALD [388]
b. 17.11.1906, Mainz
Class 1925; KKpt 1.11.39, posthumously FKpt seniority 1.6.40
Anti-Submarine School 1.7.35–12.8.35
Cdr *U 8* 13.8.35–3.11.36; Cdr *U 34* 4.11.36–22.12.36; Cdr *U 22* 23.12.36–4.10.37; Reichs War Ministry 10/37–1/39; adviser OKM/K (Office for U-Boat Affairs) 2/39–1/40
Cdr *U 53* 15.1.40–23.2.40
Lost 23.2.40 W of Orkneys

GROTE, HEINRICH [389]
b. 9.11.1920, Lingen, Ems
Class 1938; ObltzS 1.4.43

WO and M/S-Cdr 2nd Minesweeping Flotilla 3/41–8/43; U-boat trg and courses 8/43–6/44; Cdr with 31st U-Flotilla 6/44–1/45; U-Cdr sea trg *U 3516* 1/45–3/45
Cdr *U 3516* 3/45–2.5.45

GROTH, GERHARD [390]

b. 20.8.1917, Mexico City
Class 1937a; Kplt 1.3.44
U-boat trg 4/40–9/40; Staff 2.ULD 9/40–6/41; 2WO *U 96* 6/41–10/41; 1WO *U 96* 10/41–1/42; course 2.UAA 1/42–3/42
Cdr *U 143* 8.4.42–14.12.42
Baubelehrung 8.KLA 12/42–1/43
Cdr *U 958* 14.1.43–25.4.45
Cdr *U 397* 26.4.45–5.5.45

VON GUDENUS, GRAF KARL-GABRIEL [391]

b. 10.10.1920, Baden, Vienna
Class 1938; ObltzS 1.4.43
Officer trg 7/Basic Trg Est. Stralsund until 2/39; sail trg ship *Albert Leo Schlageter* 3/39–6/39; trg ship *Schleswig-Holstein* 7/39–10/39; courses Naval College Flensburg-Mürwik 10/39–4/40; WO 3rd Minesweeping Flotilla 5/40–1/41; U-boat trg 2/41–6/41; ADC 7th U-Flotilla 6/41–2/42; 1WO *U 71* 2/42–2/43; U-Cdr's Course, 24th U-Flotilla 3/43–4/43 (U-Cdr's Torpedo Course 44); *Baubelehrung* 7.KLA 4/43–6/43
Cdr *U 427* 2.6.43–capitulation

GÜNTHER, HORST [392]

b. 29.1.1922, Magdeburg
Class 1939b; ObltzS 1.12.43
Officer trg to 1/42; instructor 1.ULD 1/42–9/42; *Baubelehrung* 9/42–11/42; 1WO *U 275* 11/42–1/44; U-Cdr's Course 2/44–4/44 (U-Cdr's Torpedo Course 66); *Baubelehrung* Cdr 6.KLA 4/44–6/44, for *U 1287* (per Lohmann-Hildebrand almanac, and U-Boat Archive per Günther. Orders for the construction of *U 1286* to *U 1291* inclusive were cancelled on 6.11.43.)
Baubelehrung Type XXI 8.KLA 6/44–8/44
Cdr *U 2504* 12.8.44–19.11.44. (As from 20.11.44 *U 2504* was used only as a shore-based training and demonstration boat. Chief Engineer Oblt (Ing.) (R) Karl-Heinz Trelle acted as commander with full disciplinary authority.)
Baubelehrung 8.KLA 11/44–1/45
Cdr *U 2533* 18.1.45–30.4.45 (after which only a five-man demolition squad remained aboard. The boat was scuttled on 3.5.45 at Travemünde.)
Detained; freed 8/45

GUGGENBERGER, FRIEDRICH [393]

b. 6.3.1915, Munich
Class 1934; Kplt 1.9.41, seniority 1.10.40
U-boat trg 10/39–1/40; 1WO *U 28* 1/40–11/40; U-Cdr's Course, 24th U-Flotilla and Cdr *U 28* 16.11.40–11.2.41 (P/F of Kuhnke [679] has him in command until 3.1.41, *U 28* WD until at least 15.11.40; Guggenberger must have taken over from Kuhnke around the middle of November 1940); *Baubelehrung* U-Boats North Sea 2/41–4/41
Cdr *U 81* 26.4.41–24.12.42
Baubelehrung 6.KLA 1/43
Cdr *U 847* 23.1.43 to 1.2.43 (per *U 847* WD, and see Metzler [816]) or 4.2.43 (P/F Guggenberger)
Staff Officer OKM/2.SKL/BdU/Opns 2/43–5/43
Cdr *U 513* 15.5.43–19.7.43
POW 19.7.43
Knight's Cross 10.12.41 (91st KM, 39th U-boat holder)
Oak Leaves 8.1.43 (171st WM, 22nd KM, 18th U-boat holder)

GUSE, JOACHIM [394]
b. 8.6.1921, Kiel
Class 1939a; ObltzS 1.10.43
Officer and U-boat trg 9/39–4/41; WO sea trg
  U 48 6/41–9/41; 2WO *U 77* 9/41–4/42; 1WO
  U 77 4/42–11/42; hospitalised 11/42–6/43; U-
  Cdr's Course and *Baubelehrung* 6/43–10/43
  (U-Cdr's Torpedo Course 54)
Cdr *U 1193* 7.10.43–5.5.45
Detained; freed 12/46

GUTTECK, HANS-JOACHIM [395]
b. 10.4.1914, Greifswald
Coastal Artillery entry 1935; Kplt (R) 1.11.43
3rd Sperrbrecher Flotilla 3/43–9/43; U-boat trg
  9/43–2/44; course 23rd U-Flotilla 2/44–5/44;
  Baubelehrung 8.KLA 5/44–6/44
Cdr *U 1024* 28.6.44–12.4.45
Lost 12.4.45 S of Isle of Man

GYSAE, ROBERT [396]
b. 14.1.1911, Berlin-Charlottenburg
Class 1931; KKpt 1.6.43
Cdr torpedo-boat *T 107* (ex *G 7*) 10/38–10/39;
  CO Torpedo-Boat Flotilla 10/39–3/40; U-boat
  trg 4/40–9/40; *Baubelehrung* U-Boats Baltic
  9/40–10/40
Cdr *U 98* 12.10.40 to 23.3.42 (per WASt, and see
  Schulze [1163]) or 29.3.42 (per P/F)
Cdr *U 177* 24.3.42 (see Schulze [1163]) or
  30.3.42 (per P/F; WAST has only 'March
  1942') to 16.10.43
12th U-Flotilla 10/43–1/44; CO 25th U-Flotilla
  1/44–4/45; Cdr Naval Anti-Tank Regt 1 4/45–
  capitulation; Head of Personnel Section German
  Minesweeping Service, Baltic (German
  Minesweeping Administration), Kiel-
  Friedrichsort 6/45–12/47; discharged 12/47
Knight's Cross 31.12.41 (99th KM, 43rd U-boat
  holder)
Oak Leaves 31.5.43 (250th WM, 31st KM, 24th
  U-boat holder)

H

HABEKOST, JOHANNES [397]
b. 13.2.1907, Berlin-Spandau
Class 1933; Kplt 1.8.38
Cdr *U 31* 8.11.38–11.3.40
Lost 11.3.40 Jade Bay, off Wilhelmshaven

HACKLÄNDER, BURKHARD [398]
b. 17.12.1914, Lüneburg
Class 1933; Kplt 1.11.40
WO, Divisional and Torpedo Officer destroyer *Z 13 Erich Koellner* 8/39–4/40; POW 4/40–6/40; CO Harbour Defence Flotilla Bergen 7/40–10/40; U-boat trg 10/40–3/41; U-Cdr's Course, 24th U-Flotilla 3/41–4/41; 7th U-Flotilla (supernumerary) and *Baubelehrung* 4/41–7/41
Cdr *U 454* 24.7.41–1.8.43
POW 1.4.43

HACKLÄNDER, KLAUS [399]
b. 26.7.1916, Göttingen
Class 1937b; ObltzS 1.4.42
Heavy cruiser *Admiral Hipper* 12/39–7/42; U-boat trg 7/42–12/42; 2WO *U 172* 12/42–9/43; U-Cdr's Course 9/43–10/43
Cdr *U 423* 10/43–17.6.44
Lost 17.6.44 NE of Faroes

HAELBICH, GERHARD [400]
b. 12.11.1916, Kiel
Class 1936; Kplt 1.6.43
Seconded to Luftwaffe 9/39–2/42; U-boat trg 3/42–9/42; 1WO *U 404* 10/42–2/43; U-Cdr's Course 3/43–4/43 (U-Cdr's Torpedo Course 43); *Baubelehrung* 4/43–5/43
Cdr *U 673* 8.5.43–14.8.43
Kplt on Staff 1st U-Flotilla 9/43–9/44
Taken POW at Brest 20.9.44–8.1.48

HÄNERT, KLAUS [401]
b. 1.2.1918, Hirschberg, Silesia
Class 1936; Kplt 1.2.43
WO destroyer *Z 6 Theodor Riedel* to 6/40; Personal ADC to Commanding Adm. Naval Station North Sea 7/40–1/41; Torpedo Officer and WO destroyer *Z 15 Erich Steinbrinck* 2/41–12/41; U-boat trg 1/42–4/42; 2WO *U 68* 5/42–7/42; 1WO *U 68* 7/42–12/42; instructor 2.ULD 1/43–4/43; U-Cdr's Course, 24th U-Flotilla 4/43–5/43 (U-Cdr's Torpedo Course 47); *Baubelehrung* 8.KLA 5/43–7/43
Cdr *U 550* 28.7.43–16.4.44
POW 16.4.44–31.12.47

HAGUENAU, KARL-HEINZ [402]
b. 31.8.1919, place not recorded Class 1937b; Kplt 1.1.45
Cdr *U 34* 2.2.43–11.6.43
Cdr *U 704* 12.6.43–4/44
No further details available

HAGENE, GEORG [403]
b. 24.7.1908 Niederschöneweide, Teltow, Brandenburg
Entry 1927; KKpt 1.4.44
Heavy cruiser Blücher 9/39–4/40; Comp. CO Naval Holding Division Oslo 4/40–3/41; heavy cruiser *Lützow* 3/41–8/41; Group Leader Naval Gunnery School 8/41–9/41; WO heavy cruiser *Lützow* 9/41–9/42; Flak Gunnery Officer heavy

cruiser *Admiral Scheer* 9/42–4/43; U-boat trg and courses 4/43–2/44; *Baubelehrung* 7.KLA 2/44–4/44
Cdr *U 1208* 6.4.44–2.3.45 (last radio transmission 2.3.45)
Missing 2.3.45 English Channel

HAMM, HORST [404]
b. 17.3.1916, Düsseldorf; Class 1935; Kplt 1.9.42
2WO *U 26* 8/39–5/40; ADC 1st U-Flotilla 6/40–8/40; *Baubelehrung* 8/40–9/40; 1WO *U 96* 9/40–3/41; U-Cdr's Torpedo Course, 24th U-Flotilla 3/41
Cdr *U 58* 7.4.41–3.9.41
Cdr *U 562* 4.9.41–19.2.43
Lost 19.2.43 Mediterranean, NE of Benghazi

HAMMER, ULRICH [405]
b. 26.3.1918, Werro, Estonia
Class IX/1939; ObltzS 1.10.43
Officer and U-boat trg 9/39–10/41; 26th U-Flotilla 10/41–3/42; *Baubelehrung* 8.KLA 3/42–5/42; 1WO *U 621* 7.5.42–10.6.43; U-Cdr's Course, 24th U-Flotilla 6/43–7/43 (U-Cdr's Torpedo Course 50); *Baubelehrung* 7/43–8/43
Cdr *U 367* 27.8.43–5.1.44
Cdr *U 430* 6.1.44–30.3.45
Cdr *U 733* 1.4.45–5.5.45

VON HAMMERSTEIN-EQUORD, BARON ADOLF-WILHELM [406]
b. 11.3.1918, Munich
Class 1937a; Kplt 1.9.44
U-boat trg 10/40–4/41; *Baubelehrung* 4/41–5/41; 1WO *U 402* 5/41–10/41; 1WO *U 71* 10/41–4/42; U-Cdr's Torpedo Course, 24th U-Flotilla and U-Cdr sea trg *U 149* 4/42–7/42
Cdr *U 149* 1.8.42–14.5.44
3/Adm. Staff Officer/Opns, Staffs FdU Norway and FdU Polar Sea 5/44–capitulation

HANITSCH, HANS-ULRICH [407]
b. 12.8.1922, Berlin-Treptow
Class XII/1939; ObltzS 1.4.44
Officer and U-boat trg 12/39–12/41; *Baubelehrung* 12/41–2/42; 2WO *U 441* 2/42–8/43; 1st U-Flotilla 8/43–2/44; course 3.ULD and 23rd U-Flotilla 3/44–5/44
Cdr *U 428* 2.5.44–3.5.45

HANSEN, HANS-JOHANN [408]
b. 15.6.1918, place not recorded
Entry 1937b; ObltzS 1.12.42 (transfer into Naval Officer Corps 1.3.43)
WO 7th VP-Boat Flotilla 10/40–2/41; Comp. CO Trg Comp. 7th VP-Boat Flotilla 2/41–7/41; VP-Cdr 7th VP-Boat Flotilla 7/41–11/43; U-boat trg and U-Cdr's Torpedo Course 76 11/43–2/45; *Baubelehrung*-Cdr *U 1026* (never commissioned) 20.2.45–capitulation

HANSEN, HERMANN [409]
b. 6.5.1918, Flensburg
Entry XI/1939; ObltzS (R)
Officer and U-boat trg 11/39–4/41; *Baubelehrung* KLA U-Boats North 4/41–5/41; 2WO *U 129* 5/41–9/41; course 1/NCO Trg Div 9/41–12/41; *Baubelehrung*, 4th U-Flotilla and 1.KLA 12/41–3/42; 2WO *U 462* 3/42–1/43; WO 4th U-Flotilla, U-Cdr's Course and *Baubelehrung* 8.KLA 1/43–10/43
Cdr *U 999* 21.10.43–15.7.44
Baubelehrung Type XXI 8.KLA 7/44–10/44
Cdr *U 2517* 31.10.44–5.5.45

HANSEN, OTTO [410]
23.4.1918, Kiel
Class 1937a; ObltzS 1.9.41
Light cruiser *Emden* 10/39–3/40; WO 12th Minesweeping Flotilla 3/40–7/40; WO 3rd Minesweeping Flotilla 7/40–9/41; U-boat trg 9/41–5/42; 1WO *U 435* 5/42–4/43; U-Cdr's

Course, 2.UAA and 24th U-Flotilla 4/43–6/43 (U-Cdr's Torpedo Course 47)
Acting Cdr *U 269* 6/43–4.9.43 (see Harflinger [414])
Cdr *U 601* 29.11.43–25.2.44 (see Grau [380])
Lost 25.2.44 NW of Narvik

HANSMANN, BRUNO [411]
b. 1.12.1907, Lankwitz, Berlin
Class 1933; Kplt 1.10.38, posthumously KKpt seniority 1.12.41
U-boat trg 4/40–9/40; U-Cdr's Course, 24th U-Flotilla 9/40–12/40; U-Cdr sea trg *U 95* 12/40–1/41; Kplt on Staff 2nd U-Flotilla 1/41–3/41; *Baubelehrung* 3/41–4/41
Cdr *U 127* 24.4.41–15.12.41
Lost 15.12.41 W of Gibraltar

HAPPE, WERNER [412]
b. 23.9.1915, Alfeld. Leine
Class 1936; ObltzS 1.10.40
Seconded to Luftwaffe 8/41; U-boat trg 8/41–12/41; 2WO *U 68* 12/41–4/42; 1WO *U 68* 4/42–7/42; U-Cdr's Course, 24th U-Flotilla and 2.UAA 8/42–10/42
Cdr *U 192* 16.11.42–6.5.43
Lost 6.5.43 S of Cape Farewell

HARDEGEN, REINHARD [413]
b. 18.3.1913, Bremen
Class 1933; KKpt 1.3.44
Signals Officer and Comp. CO naval airfield Kamp, Pomerania 10/37–10/39; U-boat trg 11/39–6/40; U-Cdr's Course, 25th U-Flotilla 7/40–8/40; 1WO and U-Cdr sea trg *U 124* 8/40–12/40
Cdr *U 147* 11.12.40–4.4.41
Cdr *U 123* 17.5.41 (per P/F) or 19.5.41 (per *U 123* WD, and see Moehle [829]) to 31.7.42

Trg Officer 27th U-Flotilla 8/42–2/43; Senior Officer U-Boat Trg, Torpedo School Mürwik 3/43–10/44; adviser Office of Torpedo Ordnance at OKM 10/44–2/45; Battalion Cdr 1/Naval Infantry Regt 6 of 2/Naval Infantry Div. 2/45–capitulation
Detained; freed 9.11.46
Knight's Cross 23.1.42 (101st KM, 44th U-boat holder)
Oak Leaves 23.4.42 (89th WM, 13th KM, 11th U-boat holder)

HARLFINGER, KARL-HEINRICH [414]
b. 2.8.1915, Jena
Class 1935; Kplt 1.10.43
WO heavy cruiser *Blücher* 9/39–4/40; VP-Cdr Harbour Defence Flotilla (Oslo) 4/40–3/41, (Trondheim) 3/41–6/41; U-boat trg 6/41–11/41; 1WO *U 84* 11/41–6/42; U-Cdr's Course and *Baubelehrung* 6/42–8/42
Cdr *U 269* 19.8.42–29.4.43 (Harflinger was hospitalised on 27.4.43, and *U 269* was laid up in Bergen dockyard. Hansen [410] assumed temporary command of the boat in June 1943 and completed two Arctic missions, 6.7.43–14.7.43 and 22.7.43–4.9.43.)
Suicide 21.3.44

HARMS, ERICH [415]
b. 20.1.1910, Bant, Rüstringen
Entry IX/1939; ObltzS (R) 1.4.43
WO 15th Minesweeping Flotilla 9/39–11/40; Helmsman's School and U-boat trg 11/40–5/41; WO Torpedo Retrieval Vessel 3 5/41–10/41; *Baubelehrung* 10/41–11/41; 2WO *U 255* 11/41–10/42; 1WO *U 255* 10/42–3/43; U-Cdr's Course 4/43–5/43 (U-Cdr's Torpedo Course 47)
Cdr *U 255* 7.6.43–8/44
Courses and *Baubelehrung* Type XXI 6.KLA 8/44–1/45
Cdr *U 3023* 22.1.45–3.5.45

HARMS, OTTO [416]
b. 22.4.1909, Stralsund
Class 1934; Kplt 1.1.41
WO U-Flotilla *Hundius* and U-Boat School Flotilla 4/39–10/39; course U-Boat Trg Flotilla 10/39–11/39
Cdr *U 6* 27.11.39–17.1.40
Cdr *U 56* 22.1.40–13.10.40 (see Schnee [1102])
Acting Cdr *U 121* 10/40–5.11.40
Instructor 2.ULD 11/40–3/42; *Baubelehrung* 3/42–4/42
Cdr *U 464* 30.4.42–20.8.42
POW 20.8.42

HARNEY, KLAUS [417]
b. 26.3.1917, Düsseldorf
Class 1935; Kplt 1.4.42
No 2 Cadet Trg Officer trg ship *Schleswig-Holstein* 5/39–10/39; courses Naval College Mürwik 10/39–3/40; destroyer *Z 5 Paul Jacobi* 3/40–3/41; U-boat trg 3/41–10/41; U-Cdr sea trg *U 84* 10/41–12/41; *Baubelehrung* KLA U-Boats North 12/41
Cdr *U 756* 30.12.41–1.9.42
Lost 1.9.42 SW of Iceland

VON HARPE, RICHARD [418]
b. 19.8.1917, Dorpat, Estonia
Class 1937b; Kplt 1.1.45
Trg and courses 3/39–3/40; WO 6th Minesweeping Flotilla 4/40–7/41; 1WO 1st Minesweeping Flotilla 7/41–6/42; U-boat trg 6/42–10/42; 1WO *U 108* 10/42–5/43; U-Cdr's Course, 2.UAA and 24th U-Flotilla 5/43–7/43 (U-Cdr's Torpedo Course 49)
Cdr *U 129* 12.7.43–19.7.44 (See Witt [1362]. *U 129* was scuttled at Lorient on 18.8.44. Up to that time von Harpe must have been her commander.)
2nd U-Flotilla 7/44–9/44; *Baubelehrung* Type XXI 7.KLA 9/44–1/45

Cdr *U 3519* 6.1.45 (commissioning date per U-Boat Archive, Aschmoneit List) to 2.3.45
Lost 2.3.45 Baltic, N of Warnemünde

HARTEL, FRIEDRICH [419]
b. 10.1.1923, Petersdorf
Entry 1940; ObltzS (R) 1.12.44
U-boat trg completed 6/43; *Baubelehrung* 8.KLA 6/43–7/43; 1WO *U 989* 7/43–7/44; 22nd U-Flotilla, U-Cdr's Course and *Baubelehrung* Type XXIII 8.KLA 7/44–1/45
Cdr *U 2356* 12.1.45–capitulation

HARTENSTEIN, WERNER [420]
b. 27.2.1908, Plauen, Vogtland
Class 1928; KKpt 1.6.42
Cdr torpedo-boat *Seeadler* 11/38–10/39; Cdr torpedo-boat *Jaguar* 10/39–3/41; also (caretaking) CO 6th Torpedo-Boat Flotilla 5/40; U-boat trg 3/41–6/41; U-Cdr's Torpedo Course, 24th U-Flotilla 7/41–8/41; *Baubelehrung* KLA U-Boats North 8/41–9/41
Cdr *U 156* 4.9.41–8.3.43
Lost 8.3.43 E of Barbados
Knight's Cross 17.9.42 (125th KM, 63rd U-boat holder)

HARTMANN, CURT [421]
b. 14.10.1920, Gommen, Jerichow, nr Magdeburg
Class 1939a; ObltzS 1.10.43
U-boat trg 2/41–9/41; 2WO *U 171* 10/41–10/42; *Baubelehrung* 11/42–1/43; 2WO *U 170* 1/43–7/43; U-Cdr's Course, 24th U-Flotilla 7/43–8/43 (U-Cdr's Torpedo Course 52); *Baubelehrung* 1.KLA 8/43–9/43
Cdr *U 236* 29.9.43–29.5.44 (until 15.7.44 per WASt)
Furlough 6/44
Cdr *U 982* 16.7.44–9.4.45
31st U-Flotilla 4/45–capitulation

HARTMANN, ERNST [422]
b. 8.4.1921, Hamburg-Wandsbek
Entry IX/1939; ObltzS 1.2.44
Officer trg 7/Basic Trg Est. Stralsund 9/39–11/39; trg ship *Schleswig-Holstein* 12/39–4/40; Naval College Flensburg-Mürwik 5/40–8/40; at Calais for Operation 'Sealion' 8/40–11/40; Torpedo School Flensburg-Mürwik 11/40–1/41; U-boat trg 2/41–10/41, inc. period U-Cdr sea trg *U 137* 2/41–3/41; *Baubelehrung* 10/41–11/41; 2WO *U 704* 11/41–4/43; U-Cdr's Course, 24th U-Flotilla 4/43–5/43 (U-Cdr's Torpedo Course 46)
Cdr *U 3* 19.5.43–9.6.44
21st U-Flotilla 6/44–7/44; 3rd U-Flotilla 7/44–10/44; detailed as caretaker Cdr *U 382* at La Rochelle 24.7.44–26.7.44; hospitalised 27.7.44–12/44; 1.UAA (Personnel Reserve) 10/44–1/45; ADC Section 3/1.ULD 1/45–2/45; *K-Verband* Neustadt, Holstein 2/45–3/45; ADC FdU Wes 3/45–capitulation
Detained; freed 11.8.45

HARTMANN, KLAUS [423]
b. 7.2.1912, Plön, Holstein
Class 1933; Kplt 1.4.41
Light cruiser *Nürnberg* 10/38–4/40; U-boat depot ship *Wilhelm Bauer* 4/40–7/41; U-boat trg 7/41–11/41; U-Cdr's Course, 26th U-Flotilla 11/41–1/42; *Baubelehrung* 7.KLA 1/42–2/42
Cdr *U 441* 21.2.42 to 15.5.43 or 17.5.43 (per *U 441* WD)
1st U-Flotilla 5/43–7/43; 2.UAA 7/43–8/43
Cdr *U 441* 6.8.43–18.6.44
Lost 18.6.44 Bay of Biscay, NW of Brest

HARTMANN, OTTO [424]
b. 18.4.1917, Stuttgart
Class 1936; ObltzS 1.10.40, posthumously Kplt seniority 1.4.43
Naval Signals Officer (Wilhelmshaven) 12/38–4/40, (Kristiansand-Süd) 4/40–1/41; U-boat trg 1/41–5/41; relief instructor Naval College Mürwik 5/41–8/41; 1WO *U 97* 8/41–3/42; U-Cdr's Course, 2.UAA and 24th U-Flotilla 3/42–6/42
Cdr *U 77* 2.9.42 (per *U 77* WD, and see Schonder [1119]) or 8.9.42 (per WASt) to 28.3.43
Lost 28.3.43 Mediterranean, E of Cartagena, Spain

HARTMANN, WERNER [425]
b. 11.12.1902, Silstedt, nr Wernigerode, Harz
Class 1921; KptzS 1.4.43
U-boat trg 10/35–3/36; *Baubelehrung* U-Flotilla *Saltzwedel* 4/36–5/36; Cdr *U 26* 11.5.36–30.9.38
CO 6th U-Flotilla *Hundius* 10/38–31.12.39, CO 2nd U-Flotilla 1/40–5/40, inc. Cdr *U 37* 25.9.39–6.5.40
1/Adm. Staff Officer BdU/Opns 5/40–10/40; Cdr 2.ULD Gdynia 11/40–11/41; CO 27th U-Flotilla 12/41–10/42
Cdr *U 198* 3.11.42 (Musenberg [862] acted for Hartmann at commissioning ceremony) to 15.1.44 (per P/F) or 20.1.44 (per WASt)
Appointed FdU (Mediterranean) 1/44–8/44; Operational Cdr *K-Verband* Kriegsmarine in Italy 8/44–10/44; military leader *Deutscher Volkssturm* Danzig, West Prussia 11/44–2/45; Cdr Naval-Grenadier Regt 6 2/45–capitulation
Detained; freed 1.12.46
Knight's Cross 9.5.40 (8th KM, 4th U-boat holder)
Oak Leaves 5.11.44 (645th WM, 47th KM, 27th U-boat holder)

VON HARTMANN, GÖTZ [426]
b. 30.10.1913, Danzig
Class 1934; Kplt 1.11.41
Course Naval Gunnery School ending 9/39; Assistant and ADC Experimental Gunnery Branch Warships 9/39–2/40; Group Officer

Naval Gunnery School 2/40–4/40; U-boat trg 5/40–11/40; 1WO *U 93* 12/40–6/41; U-Cdr's Course 7/41–8/41
Cdr *U 555* 26.8.41–4.2.42
Cdr *U 563* 1.4.42 (see Bargsten [38]) to 20.5.43 (but Borchardt [105] must have relieved von Hartmann before 17.5.43 because of straight exchange with Klaus Hartmann [423])
Cdr *U 441* 16.5.43–5.8.43
Hospitalised until 11/43; general adviser OKM/Office of Gunnery, Dept AIII 12/43–4/45; Battalion Cdr 1/Naval Anti-Tank Regt 1 4/45–capitulation
Detained; freed 12/47

HARTWIG, PAUL [427]
b. 14.9.1915, Stein, Vogtland
Class 1935; Kplt 1.4.42
U-boat trg 7/40–12/40; *Baubelehrung* U-Boats North 12/40–3/41; 1WO *U 125* 3/41–11/41; U-Cdr's Course, 24th U-Flotilla 11/41–1/42; *Baubelehrung* 8.KLA 1/42–3/42
Cdr *U 517* 21.3.42–21.11.42
POW 21.11.42

HASENSCHAR, HEINRICH [428]
b. 27.9.1916, Höringhausen, Sauerland
Class 1936; Kplt 1.3.43
U-boat trg 10/39–6/40; WO *U 59* 6/40–12/40; *Baubelehrung* 12/40–1/41; WO *U 751* 1/41–7/41; U-Cdr's Course, 24th U-Flotilla 7/41–9/41
Cdr *U 29* 15.9.41–5.5.42
Baubelehrung 8.KLA 5/42–3.7.43
Cdr *U 628* 25.6.42–3.7.43
Lost 3.7.43 NW of Cape Ortegal

HASHAGEN, BERTHOLD [429]
b. 26.8.1909, Bremerhaven
Entry 1937; ObltzS (R) 1.3.43

1WO and Torpedo Officer *Schiff 4* 1/40–4/40; WO 12th VP-Boat Flotilla 5/40–8/40; VP-Cdr 12th VP-Boat Flotilla 8/40–3/41; U-boat trg 3/41–1/42; *Baubelehrung* 1/42–2/42; 1WO *U 515* 2/42–2/43; U-Cdr's Course and *Baubelehrung* 6.KLA 2/43–5/43 (U-Cdr's Torpedo Course 42)
Cdr *U 846* 29.5.43–4.5.44
Lost 4.5.44 N of Cape Ortegal

HASS, HANS-HEINRICH [430]
b. 12.10.1922, Eckernförde
Class X/1940; ObltzS 1.10.44
Officer and U-boat trg 10/40–3/42, inc. WO sea trg *U 96* 9/41–3/42; WO instrn and various duties 4/42–10/42; 1WO *U 96* 11/42–3/43; *Baubelehrung* 8.KLA 3/43–4/43; 1WO *U 543* 4/43–2/44; U-Cdr's Course, 3.ULD and 24th U-Flotilla 2/44–5/44 (U-Cdr's Torpedo Course 67); *Baubelehrung* Type XXIII 8.KLA 5/44–7/44
Cdr *U 2324* 25.7.44–month end 2/45
11th U-Flotilla, month end 2/45–5/45

HAUBER, HANS-GEROLD [431]
b. 8.7.1913, Stuttgart
Entry date unknown; ObltzS (R) 1.4.43
WO 14th Minesweeping Flotilla 9/40–1/41; Trg Officer Naval Trg Inspectorate 4/41–11/41; WO 6th VP-Boat Flotilla 11/41–7/42; Trg Officer Naval Trg Inspectorate 7/42–11/42; VP-Cdr 14th VP-Boat Flotilla 11/42–3/43; 1WO *U 170* 12/43–5/44
Cdr *U 170* 7/44–capitulation
Detained; freed 5/47

HAUPT, HANS-JÜRGEN [432]
b. 19.2.1911, Berlin
Entry 1935; ObltzS (R) 1.3.43

Platoon Leader 1/Basic Trg Est. Stralsund 11/40–1/41; WO *U 203* 2/41–6/42; U-Cdr's Course and *Baubelehrung* 6/42–7/42
Cdr *U 665* 22.7.42–22.3.43
Missing Bay of Biscay 22.3.43 (Translator's note: Other Lists state that while heading for Lorient *U 665* was sunk in 46°47'N 09°58'W by Wellington 'G' of No 172 Squadron RAF.)

HAUSE, KARL [433]
b. 15.7.1916, Posen
Class 1935; Kplt 1.9.42, posthumously KKpt seniority 1.11.43
WO and ADC U-School Flotilla/1st U-Trg Flotilla 8/39–3/40; Staff BdU/Organisational 3/40–7/40; *Baubelehrung* 7/40–9/40; U-Cdr 7th U-Flotilla 9/40–6/41
Cdr *U 351* 20.6.41–14.12.41
Baubelehrung 1.KLA 1/42–3/42
Cdr *U 211* 7.3.42–19.11.43
Lost 19.11.43 E of Azores

HECHLER, ERNST [434]
b. 21.11.1907, Lauterbach, Oberhessen
Class 1929; KKpt 1.6.42
1a Staff, *9.Fliegerdivision* 8/39–10/39; Senior Officer, Trg, Aircraft Weapons School (Sea) Parow 11/39–8/40; flight leader *Küstenfliegergruppe 126* 9/40–12/40; course Blind Flying School 1, Neuburg, Danube 1/41–2/41; detailed to *1./KG 28*, Nantes 2/41; General Staff course Academy of Air Warfare, Berlin Gatow 3/41–6/41; 1a Staff, Luftwaffe General with OKM Berlin 6/41–9/41; 1a Staff, Higher Command for Bomber Trg, Zoppot 10/41–5/42; 1a Staff, Aerial Minelaying Directorate, Reichs Air Ministry 5/42–6/43; reverted to Kriegsmarine 1.7.43; U-boat trg 7/43–1/44 (U-Cdr's Torpedo Course 60); *Baubelehrung* 6.KLA 1/44–2/44
Cdr *U 870* 3.2.44–30.3.45

A1 Opns Staff BdU/2.SKL/BdU Opns 4/45–capitulation
Discharged from military hospital 15.8.45
Knight's Cross 21.1.45 (289th KM, 135th U-boat holder)

HECKEL, FRIDTJOF [435]
b. 25.10.1920, Vienenburg/Harz; Class 1939b; ObltzS 1.12.43
Officer trg, sail trg ship *Albert Leo Schlageter* 2/40–4/40; trg ship *Schleswig-Holstein* 4/40–8/40; minesweeper *M 4* 8/40–2/41; U-boat trg and courses 2/41–4/41; WO sea trg *U 652* 5/41–10/41; WO course and 4th U-Flotilla 10/41–3/42; WO *U 101* and *T 158* 5/42–2/43; *Baubelehrung* 8.KLA 2/43–3/43; 1WO *U 541* 3/43–6/44; U-Cdr's Course and *Baubelehrung* Type XXIII 6/44–7/44 (U-Cdr's Torpedo Course 65)
Cdr *U 2322* 1.7.44–capitulation
Detained; freed 15.8.45

HEGEWALD, WOLFGANG [436]
b. 5.7.1917, Chemnitz
Class 1937a; Kplt 1.8.44
Div. Officer light cruiser *Königsberg* 4/39–10/39; 1WO 12th Anti-Submarine Flotilla 10/39–6/40; Group Leader Harbour Defence Flotilla Calais 8/40–8/41; acting CO Harbour Defence Flotilla Boulogne 9/41–11/41; Group Leader Harbour Defence Flotilla Boulogne 11/41–1/42; U-boat trg 1/42–6/42; 3rd U-Flotilla 6/42–8/42; 1WO *U 332* 8/42–3/43; course 2.UAA and 24th U-Flotilla 3/43–5/43 (U-Cdr's Torpedo Course 45)
Cdr *U 671* 7.5.43–5.8.44.
Lost 5.8.44 English Channel, S of Brighton

HEIBGES, WOLFGANG [437]
b. 1.7.1922, Lippstadt, Westphalia
Entry IV/1940; ObltzS (R) 1.4.44

Officer trg 4/40–2/42; WO and M/S-Cdr 38th Minesweeping Flotilla 2/42–6/42; U-boat trg 6/42–12/42; *Baubelehrung* 12/42–1/43; WO *U 278* 1/43–5/44; U-Cdr's Course, 3.ULD and 24th U-Flotilla 6/44–11/44 (U-Cdr's Torpedo Course 74)
Cdr *U 999* 11/44–5.5.45
Detained; freed 9.7.45

HEIDEL, WERNER [438]
b. 24.6.1909, Chemnitz
Class 1933; Kplt 1.11.39
U-boat trg 9/35–1/36; WO *U 14* 1/36–9/37; Cdr *U 6* 1.10.37–17.12.38, inc. course B for Torpedo Officers, Torpedo School 9/38–12/38
Cdr *U 7* 18.12.38–13.10.39
Baubelehrung Germaniawerft Kiel 10/39–11/39
Cdr *U 55* 21.11.39–30.1.40
Lost 30.1.40 SW of Scilly Is

HEIDTMANN, HANS [439]
b. 8.8.1914, Bahnhof Gleschendorf, Pönitz, Lübeck
Class 1934; Kplt 1.10.41
1WO *U 33* 9/38–1/40; U-Cdr sea trg and 1WO *U 14* (1st U-Boat Trg Flotilla) 1/40–6/40; U-Cdr's Course, 24th U-Flotilla 6/40–7/40
Acting Cdr *U 2* 7.7.40–5.8.40
Acting Cdr *U 14* 8/40–29.9.40
Cdr *U 21* 1.8.40–20.12.40 (from 1.8.40 per P/F, but this has the annotation 'from 9/40'. As *U 21* was in the yards during August and September 1940 she had no need of a commander. This would explain Heidtmann's appointments as acting commander of *U 2* and *U 14*.)
No 1 U-Flotilla 12/40–1/41; *Baubelehrung* Blohm & Voss 1/41–2/41
Cdr *U 559* 27.2.41–30.10.42
POW 30.10.42–5/47
Knight's Cross 12.4.43 (160th KM, 89th U-boat holder)

HEILMANN, SIEGFRIED [440]
b. 8.6.1917, Kiel
Class 1936; Kplt 1.4.43
1WO 1st Minesweeping Flotilla 4/39–7/40; Group Leader and M/S-Cdr 26th Minesweeping Flotilla 7/40–8/41; M/S-Cdr 7th Minesweeping Flotilla 9/41–11/41; M/S-Cdr 2nd Minesweeping Flotilla 11/41–7/42; U-boat trg and U-Cdr's Course 7/42–12/42; U-Cdr sea trg *U 659* 12/42–1/43; *Baubelehrung* 1.KLA 1/43–2/43
Cdr *U 389* 6.2.43–5.10.43
Lost 5.10.43 Denmark Strait, SE of Argmagsalik

HEILMANN, UDO [441]
b. 4.3.1913, Kiel
Class 1933; KKpt 1.4.45
1WO *U 18* 6/37–10/39
Cdr *U 24* 30.11.39 (29.10.39 per *U 24* WD, and see Jeppener-Haltenhoff [553]) to 21.8.40
Baubelehrung 8/40–9/40
Cdr *U 97* 28.9.40–5/42; torpedo attack instructor 26th U-Flotilla 6/42–3/43; adviser FdU/Trg 3/43–capitulation
Detained; freed autumn 1945

HEIN, FRITZ [442]
b. 25.12.1919, Gumbinnen, East Prussia
Class 1938; ObltzS 1.4.43
Officer trg 11/38–4/40; battleship *Scharnhorst* 4/40–10/40; battleship *Gneisenau* 10/40–6/42; U-boat trg 6/42–10/42; 2WO *U 333* 10/42–2/43; 1WO *U 333* 2/43–9/43; course 2.UAA 9/43 (U-Cdr's Torpedo Course 57); *Baubelehrung* 6.KLA 10/43–12/43
Cdr *U 300* 29.12.43–22.2.45
Lost 22.2.45 W of Cadiz

HEINE, KARL-FRANZ [443]
b. 30.10.1915, Kiel
Class 1934; Kplt 1.3.42

Cdr *U 303* 7.7.42–21.5.43
Cdr *U 403* 16.6.43–17.8.43
Lost 17.8.43 central Atlantic, off Dakar

HEINICKE, ERNST-GÜNTER [444]
b. 24.9.1908, Gera/Thüringen
Class 1927; KKpt 1.3.42
Cdr *U 3* 30.9.37–7/38; Cdr *U 51* 6.8.38–8/39; Cdr *U 53* 8/39–14.1.40
1st Officer merchant raider *Widder* 1/40–2/41; Senior Officer Underwater Testing Group, Torpedo Testing Branch 2/41–6/41; Senior Officer U-boat trg, Torpedo School Mürwik 6/41–4/43; Cdr Section 1, Torpedo School 4/43–1/44; Cdr Torpedo School 1 2/44–7/44; Cdr Torpedo School III 7/44–3/45; *Baubelehrung*-Cdr Type XXI 8.KLA for *U 2561* (boat never commissioned) 3/45–4/45
Detained; freed 6.10.45

HEINICKE, HANS-DIETER [445]
b. 18.5.1913, Gera, Thüringen
Class 1933; Kplt 1.4.41
1WO U-boat tender *Weichsel* 4/39–3/40; U-boat trg 4/40–8/40; *Baubelehrung* 8/40–9/40; 1WO *U 73* 9/40–4/41; U-Cdr's Course, 24th U-Flotilla 4/41–6/41; *Baubelehrung* 6/41
Cdr *U 576* 26.6.41–15.7.42
Lost 15.7.42 off Cape Hatteras, US coast

HEINRICH, ERWIN [446]
b. 27.3.1923, Karzin, Pomerania
Entry 1940; ObltzS 1944
WO sea trg *U 75* 10/41–4/42; trg, courses and *Baubelehrung* 4/42–2/43; WO *U 963* 2/43–3/44; courses, U-Cdr's Course (U-Cdr's Torpedo Course 71) and *Baubelehrung* Type XXIII 3/44–1/45
Cdr *U 2357* 13.1.45–5.5.45
Detained; freed 5.8.45

HEINRICH, GÜNTHER [447]
b. 20.1.1920, Schildau, Torgau
Class 1938; ObltzS 1.1.43
12th Anti-Submarine Flotilla 4/40–9/40; Flying School, Dievenow, and Aircraft Weapons School (Sea), Parow 9/40–12/40; U-boat trg 12/40–3/41; 1.ULD 4/41–10/41; *Baubelehrung* 10/41–11/41; 1WO *U 596* 11/41–11/42; U-Cdr's Course 11/42–12/42; *Baubelehrung* 8.KLA 12/42–1/43
Cdr *U 960* 28.1.43 19.5.44
POW 19.5.44–1.3.46

HEINRICH, HELMUTH [448]
b. 4.10.1913, Grünendeich, Stade
Entry date not known; ObltzS (R) 1.3.43
WO 11th VP-Boat Flotilla 5/40–7/40; WO and M/S-Cdr 56th Minesweeping Flotilla 8/40–2/43; U-boat trg 3/43–10/43 (U-Cdr's Torpedo Course 56); *Baubelehrung* 11/43–12/43
Cdr *U 299* 15.12.43–9.8.44 and 3.9.44–31.10.44 (per *U 299* WD)
Naval High Command Baltic 11/44–3/45
Cdr *U 255* 2.3.45 (per WASt) to capitulation

HEINSOHN, HEINRICH [449]
b. 12.2.1910, Lune (probably Luhne Rotenburg a.d. Wümme)
Class 1933; Kplt 1.4.40, posthumously KKpt seniority 1.5.43
WO/Wargames Officer trg ship *Schlesien* 6/39–6/40; U-boat trg 7/40–12/40
Cdr *U 8* 18.12.40–25.4.41
Baubelehrung 5/41–6/41
Cdr *U 573* 5.6.41–2.5.42
Interned Spain 5/42–3/43
Cdr *U 438* 30.3.43–6.5.43
Lost 6.5.43 NE of Newfoundland

HEINTZE, WERNER [450]
b. 16.3.1916, Berlin-Zehlendorf
Class 1935; Kplt 1.10.43

Cdr *U 708* 24.7.42–6/43
Group Officer Naval College Mürwik 6/43–4/44; seconded C-in-C Destroyers 4/44–5/44; 1st Officer destroyer *Z 15 Erich Steinbrinck* 5/44–12/44; 1st Officer destroyer *Z 25* 12/44–capitulation

HEITZ, HORST [451]
b. 9.4.1922, Mannheim
Class XII/1939; ObltzS 1.12.43
U-boat trg 5/41–5/42; *Baubelehrung* 5/42–6/42; 1WO *U 664* 6/42–6/43; U-Cdr's Course, 2.UAA 6/43–8/43 (U-Cdr's Torpedo Course 51)
Acting Cdr *U 6* 8/43–10/43
Baubelehrung 10/43–11/43
Cdr *U 792* 16.11.43–12/44
Baubelehrung 8.KLA 12/44–3/45
Cdr *U 1407* 29.3.45–7.5.45

HELLER, WOLFGANG [452]
b. 16.6.1910, Berlin; Class 1930; KKpt 1.7.43
Rangefinding Officer heavy cruiser *Deutschland* 9/37–2/40; guard detachment heavy cruiser *Lützow* 2/40–11/41; Adm. Staff Officer C-in-C Battleships/Cruisers 11/41–3/42; Station Command Baltic 3/42–4/42; U-boat trg 4/42–9/42; U-Cdr's Course, 24th U-Flotilla 9/42–10/42; U-Cdr under instrn, *U 155* 10/42–1/43; *Baubelehrung* 6.KLA 1/43–2/43
Cdr *U 842* 1.3.43–6.11.43
Lost 6.11.43 western North Atlantic

HELLMANN, HANS [453]
b. 8.3.1921, Primkenau, Silesia
Class IX/1939; ObltzS 1.10.43
WO trg, 26th U-Flotilla 9/41–3/42; *Baubelehrung* 3/42–4/42; 1WO *U 262* 4/42–6/43; U-Cdr's Course, 24th U-Flotilla and *Baubelehrung* 3.KLA 6/43–9/43 (U-Cdr's Torpedo Course 50)
Cdr *U 903* 4.9.43–14.12.43

Cdr *U 733* 15.12.43–3.3.45
Accidental death 3.3.45

HELLRIEGEL, HANS-JÜRGEN [454]
b. 16.6.1917, Berlin-Wilmersdorf
Class 1936; Kplt 1.4.43
U-boat trg 10/38–4/39; Comp. Officer 7/Basic Trg Est. Stralsund 4/39–12/39; 2WO *U 46* 12/39–3/41; U-Cdr's Torpedo Course, 24th U-Flotilla 3/41
Cdr *U 140* 7.4.41 to 27.3.42 (per P/F) or 9.12.41 (per WASt; date reported to U-Boat Archive by his successor, Popp [936], was 12/41)
Cdr *U 96* 28.3.42–15.3.43
Baubelehrung 8.KLA 3/43–4/43
Cdr *U 543* 21.4.43–2.7.44
Lost 2.7.44 SW of Tenerife
Knight's Cross 3.2.44 (204th KM, 110th U-boat holder)

HELLWIG, ALEXANDER [455]
b. 5.3.1916, Kirchberg, Saxony
Class 1935; Kplt 1.9.42
Seconded to Luftwaffe 10/37–4/42 with *Bordfliegerstaffel 5./196* (aboard light cruiser *Nürnberg* and under C-in-C Air West, Cherbourg); U-boat trg 4/42–9/42; 1WO *U 405* 9/42–4/43; U-Cdr's Course, 24th U-Flotilla 4/43–5/43 (U-Cdr's Torpedo Course 46); *Baubelehrung* 2.KLA 6/43–7/43
Cdr *U 289* 10.7.43–31.5.44
Lost 31.5.44 Barents Sea, SW of Bear I

HENGEN, DIETER [456]
b. 19.10.1922, Würzburg
Class X/1940; ObltzS 1.10.44
Officer trg 10/40–4/43, inc. WO sea trg *U 109* until 6/42; 2WO *U 255* 4/43–10/43; 1WO *U 255* 11/43–7/44; course 3.ULD 7/44–9/44; U-Cdr 22nd U-Flotilla, U-Holding Comp.16 9/44–

12/44; *Baubelehrung* Type XXIII 8.KLA 12/44–2/45
Cdr *U 2364* 14.2.45–end 4/45

HENKE, WERNER [457]
b. 13.5.1909, Rudak, Thorn
Class 1934; KKpt (zV) 1.6.44
Div. and Flak Gunnery Officer, trg ship *Schleswig-Holstein* 3/39–4/40; U-boat trg 4/40–5/40; 1WO U-boat tender *Lech* 5/40–11/40; 2WO *U 124* 11/40–5/41; 1WO *U 124* 6/41–10/41; U-Cdr's Torpedo Course, 24th U-Flotilla 11/41; Group Leader Torpedo Testing Group Gdynia 12/41–1/42; *Baubelehrung* 8.KLA 1/42–2/42
Cdr *U 515* 21.2.42–9.4.44 (POW)
Shot dead 15.6.44 while attempting to escape from US POW camp
Knight's Cross 17.12.42 (140th KM, 72nd U-boat holder)
Oak Leaves 4.7.43 (252nd WM, 33rd KM, 26th U-boat holder)

HENNE, WOLF [458]
b. 7.8.1905, Futschau, China
Class 1924; KKpt 1.7.39
Comp. CO Naval College Flensburg-Mürwik 4/38–1/40; CO 5th Torpedo-Boat Flotilla 1/40–12/40; at OKM 12/40–3/41 and BdU 3/41–6/41; U-Cdr's Course, 24th U-Flotilla 6/41–8/41; *Baubelehrung* KLA U-Boats North 8/41–9/41
Cdr *U 157* 15.9.41–13.6.42
Lost 13.6.42 N of Havana, Cuba

HENNIG, HELMUT [459]
b. 30.4.1914, Kahl, Main
Class 1934/36; Kplt 1.6.43
Platoon Officer 12/Basic Trg Est. Stralsund 4/39–2/41; 2WO *U 52* 11/39–2/41; U-Cdr's Course, 24th U-Flotilla 2/41–3/41

Cdr *U 24* 11.3.41–31.7.41
Instructor 1.ULD 9/41–10/42; *Baubelehrung* 8.KLA 10/42–11/42
Cdr *U 533* 25.11.42–16.10.43
Lost 16.10.43 Gulf of Oman, Indian Ocean

VON HENNIG, HEINZ [460]
b. 17.3.1922, Berlin-Friedenau
Class IX/1940; ObltzS 1.10.44
Officer trg 9/40–12/42; *Baubelehrung* 12/42–1/43; 2WO *U 421* 1/43–1/44; 1WO *U 421* 2/44–4/44; 29th U-Flotilla 4/44–6/44; U-Cdr's Course, 3.ULD and 23rd U-Flotilla 6/44–8/44; U-Cdr 21st U-Flotilla, U-Holding Comp.13 8/44–11/44; *Baubelehrung* Type XXIII 8.KLA 12/44–2/45
Cdr *U 2361* 3.2.45–capitulation

HENNING, FRITZ [461]
b. 10.4.1917, Schmira, Erfurt
Class 1937a; Kplt 1.4.44
Seconded to Luftwaffe 10/39–2/42; U-boat trg 3/42–10/42; 1WO *U 561* 10/42–4/43; U-Cdr's Course, 2.UAA and 24th U-Flotilla 4/43–6/43 (U-Cdr's Torpedo Course 46)
Cdr *U 561* 19.6.43–12.7.43 (U-Boat Archive per Henning)
29th U-Flotilla 7/43–10/43
Cdr *U 565* 8.10.43–24.9.44 (U-Boat Archive per Henning)
Details not available 9/44–4/45
Cdr *U 668* after 17.4.45–capitulation (U-Boat Archive per Henning, Ordered to Narvik to take command of *U 668*, replacing von Eickstedt [242], who had broken a leg while skiing. Henning assumed command at the beginning of May 1945.)

HEPP, HORST [462]
b. 10.10.1917, Kempen
Class 1936; Kplt 1.11.43

Baubelehrung U 162 8/41–9/41; 1WO *U 162* 9/41–6/42; U-Cdr's Course, 24th U-Flotilla 7/42–8/42; *Baubelehrung* KLA U-Boats East 8/42–10/42
Cdr *U 272* 7.10.42–12.11.42
8th U-Flotilla 11/42–1/43
Baubelehrung 1.KLA 1/43–2/43
Cdr *U 238* 20.2.43–9.2.44
Lost 9.2.44 SW of Ireland

HERBSCHLEB, KARL-HEINZ [463]
b. 19.10.1910, Eisenach, Thüringen
Class 1935; Kplt 1.3.42
Uboat trg 10/40–4/41; U-Cdr's Course, 24th U-Flotilla 4/41–5/41
Cdr *U 21* 19.5.41–3.1.42
U-Cdr sea trg *U 85* 1/42–3/42; *Baubelehrung* 3/42–4/42
Cdr *U 354* 22.4.42–20.2.44 (per WASt; 22.2.44 per *U 354* WD, and see Sthamer [1233])
13th U-Flotilla 2/44–4/44; Comp. CO Naval College Mürwik 4/44–capitulation

HERGLOTZ, HELMUT [464]
b. 15.3.1918, Berndorf, Wiener Neustadt
Class 1938; ObltzS 1.4.43
U-boat trg completed 4/41; WO *U 143* 4/41–10/41; *Baubelehrung* 7.KLA 10/41–11/41; 1WO *U 408* 11/41–10/42; U-Cdr's Course, 2.UAA and 24th U-Flotilla 10/42–11/42
Cdr *U 2* 20.11.42–12.12.43
Cdr *U 290* 27.12.43–4/45
Cdr *U 1303* 4/45–4.5.45

HERMANN, WOLFGANG [465]
b. 13.12.1908, Kiel
Class 1928, KKpt 1.8.42
Naval Signals Office (Elbe Weser Radio) 8/39–1/40, (Central) 1/40–3/41; U-boat trg 3/41–7/41; 24th, 1st and 2nd U-Flotillas 7/41–1/42; *Baubelehrung* 8.KLA 1/42–4/42

Cdr *U 662* 9.4.42–14.2.43
Adviser OKM/CO Naval Signals Service 2/43–1/44; Sperrbrecher Cdr No 2 Sperrbrecher Flotilla 1/44–12/44; Cdr *Sperrbrecher 11* 12/44–capitulation

HERRLE, FRIEDRICH-GEORG [466]
b. 13.8.1910, Neustadt an der Hardt, Rhineland-Pfalz
Entry XII/1939; ObltzS (R) 1.2.43
Further officer trg 12/39–8/40; trg 1st U-Flotilla 8/40–1/41; *Baubelehrung* 2/41–4/41; 2WO *U 84* 4/41–7/42; U-Cdr's Course and *Baubelehrung* 8/42–11/42
Cdr *U 307* 18.11.42–1.12.44
Cdr *U 312* 2.12.44–31.1.45
Cdr *U 393* 4/45–4.5.45
Lost 4.5.45 Baltic Sea, Little Belt

HERRMANN, WERNER [467]
b. 14.1.1920, Völklingen, Saar
Class 1938; ObltzS 1.4.43
2WO *U 96* 9/41–3/42; WO 1.KLA and 5th U-Flotilla 3/42–2/43; U-Cdr's Course, 24th U-Flotilla 3/43 (U-Cdr's Torpedo Course 43); instructor 2.ULD 4/43–7/44; *Baubelehrung* Type XXI 8.KLA 7/44–9/44
Cdr *U 2510* 27.9.44–2.5.45

HERTIN, WILLI [468]
b. 11.9.1914, Balve, Westphalia
Class 1935; Kplt 1.10.42
Seconded to Luftwaffe 8/39–5/41; Naval College Mürwik 6/41–1/42; U-boat trg 2/42–6/42; WO (supernumerary) and U-Cdr sea trg *U 552* 6/42–8/42; U-Cdr's Course, 24th U-Flotilla 9/42–10/42; *Baubelehrung* 8.KLA 10/42–11/42
Cdr *U 647* 5.11.42–3.8.43
Missing 3.8.43 E of Shetlands

HERWARTZ, OSKAR [469]
b. 1.1.1915, Hildesheim
Class 1935; Kplt 1.12.42
Seconded to Luftwaffe until 2/42; U-boat trg 3/42–8/42; 1WO *U 67* 8/42–12/42; U-Cdr's Course, 24th U-Flotilla 1/43–2/43; *Baubelehrung* 6.KLA 2/43–3/43
Cdr *U 843* 24.3.43–9.4.45
(Herwartz is said to have taken *U 181* from Batavia to Singapore as acting commander in 9/44 because Freiwald [316] was held up in Tokyo. U-Boat Archive states that this is dubious as it is not corroborated by the *U 181* War Diary.)

HERWARTZ, WOLFGANG [470]
b. 25.6.1917, Hildesheim
Class 1937, Kplt 1.8.44
Seconded to Luftwaffe 10/39–6/43; U-boat trg 7/43–12/43; U-Cdr's Course, 23rd U-Flotilla 12/43–3/44; *Baubelehrung* 1.KLA 4/44–5/44
Cdr *U 1302* 25.5.44–7.3.45
Lost 7.3.45 St George's Channel

HESEMANN, SIEGFRIED [471]
b. 7.7.1912, Dortmund-Dorsfelde
Class 1935; Kplt 1.12.41 posthumously KKpt seniority 1.5.43
2WO and Torpedo Officer destroyer Z 4 *Richard Beitzen* 10/38–6/40; U-boat trg 7/40–12/40; instructor, Torpedo School Mürwik 12/40–3/41; 1WO *U 95* 3/41–8/41; U-Cdr's Course, 7th and 24th U-Flotillas 8/41–9/41; torpedo trg leader 26th U-Flotilla 10/41–5/42; *Baubelehrung* KLA U-Boats North 5/42–7/42
Cdr *U 186* 10/7/42–12.5.43
Lost 12.5.43 N of Azores

HESS, HANS-GEORG [472]
b. 6.5.1923, Berlin
Entry 1940; ObltzS (R) 1.3.44
WO under instrn and U-boat trg 1.ULD 4/42–6/42; at BdU 6/42; WO *U 466* 6/42–5/44; U-Cdr's Torpedo Course 5/44–7/44; pre-tactical trg 20th U-Flotilla 7/44–9/44
Cdr *U 995* 10.10.44–capitulation
Norwegian captivity, freed 6/46
Knight's Cross 11.2.45 (292nd KM, 138th U-boat holder)

HESSE, HANS-JOACHIM [473]
b. 18.1.1906, Norden, Ostfriesland
Class 1925; KKpt 1.2.40, posthumously FKpt seniority 1.2.43
1st Gunnery Officer light cruiser *Königsberg* 7/39–4/40; Cdr Naval Artillery Detachment 504 4/40–10/40; at BdU and U-boat trg 10/40–3/41; courses and *Baubelehrung* 8.KLA 3/41–7/41
Cdr *U 654* 5.7.41–24.11.41 (see Forster [299])
1st U-Flotilla 11/41–2/42; *Baubelehrung* 7.KLA 2/42–3/42
Cdr *U 442* 21.3.42–12.2.43
Lost 12.2.43 W of Cape St Vincent, Portugal

HESSE, HERMANN [474]
b. 10.3.1909, Cologne
Class 1935; Kplt 1.2.42
Seconded to Luftwaffe, *Bordfliegerstaffel 1./196* (aboard naval oiler *Westerwald* and light cruiser *Karlsruhe*), also Course Leader Aircraft Weapons School (Sea) Bug/Rügen until 10/40; U-boat trg 10/40–2/41; U-Cdr sea trg *U 46* 2/41–4/41; U-Cdr's Course, 24th U-Flotilla and *Baubelehrung* 4/41–7/41
Cdr *U 133* 5.7.41–1.3.42
At 2/Adm. U-Boats 3/42–4/42; Comp. CO 2.ULD 4/42–11/42; *Baubelehrung* 8.KLA 11/42–1/43
Cdr *U 194* 8.1.43–24.6.43
Lost 24.6.43 S of Iceland

HESSLER, GÜNTER [475]

b. 14.6.1909, Beerfelde, Lebus, Frankfurt a.d. Oder

Class 1927; FKpt 1.12.44

Cdr torpedo-boat *Falke* (5th Torpedo-Boat Flotilla) 3/39–3/40, inc. course Naval Gunnery School 1/40–2/40; U-boat trg 4/40–7/40; U-Cdr's Course, 24th U-Flotilla 8/40–9/40; *Baubelehrung* U-Boats North Sea 9/40–10/40

Cdr *U 107* 8.10.40 to 1.12.41 (per *U 107* WD) or 23.11.41 (per P/F; see Gelhaus [348])

1/Adm. Staff Officer, Staff BdU/Opns and 2/SKL/BdU/Opns 11/41–capitulation (then British captivity. Technically freed 15.10.45 but taken directly to Nuremberg prison and held in custody in a segregated wing there for six months as a material witness for Dönitz's defence. Five more months in various camps ensued before his release from Hersbruck camp on 17.9.46.)

Knight's Cross 24.6.41 (76th KM, 34th U-boat holder)

HETSCHKO, GERT [476]

b. 6.8.1913, Wilhelmshaven

Class 1933; Kplt 1.4.41, posthumously KKpt seniority 1.5.43

ADC 2nd U-Flotilla 6/40–10/40; WO 7th U-Flotilla 12/40–5/41; U-Cdr's Course, 24th U-Flotilla 5/41–6/41

Cdr *U 453* 26.6.41–8.7.41

Cdr *U 121* 9.7.41–25.3.42

Torpedo Testing Branch 3/42–4/43; U-Cdr sea trg *U 89* 20.4.43–12.5.43

Lost 12.5.43 North Atlantic (see Lohmann [747])

HEUSINGER VON WALDEGG, BURKHARD [477]

b. 27.5.1920, Berlin-Schöneberg

Class 1938; ObltzS 1.4.43

Officer trg 7/Basic Trg Est. Stralsund 10/38–2/39, sail trg ship *Albert Leo Schlageter* 3/39–6/39; light cruiser *Emden* 7/39–9/39; courses and trg 9/39–6/41; WO sea trg 5th U-Flotilla 6/41–2/42; *Baubelehrung* 6.KLA 2/42–3/42; 1WO *U 177* 3/42–10/43; U-Cdr's Course, 24th U-Flotilla 11/43–1/44 (U-Cdr's Torpedo Course 61)

Cdr *U 198* 21.1.44 (20.1.44 per WASt; see Hartmann [425]) to 12.8.44

Lost 12.8.44 Indian Ocean, off Seychelles

HEWICKER, AUGUST-WILHELM [478]

b. 30.7.1918, Hamburg

Class 1937a; ObltzS 1.9.41

M/S-Cdr 42nd Minesweeping Flotilla 8/40–9/41; U-boat trg 9/41–3/42; WO under instrn, 26th U-Flotilla 3/42–6/42; 1WO *U 566* 7/42–12/42; U-Cdr's Course, 2.UAA and 24th U-Flotilla 12/42–1/43; *Baubelehrung* 8.KLA 1/43–3/43

Cdr *U 671* 3.3.43–4.5.43

Released from Officer Corps 4.5.43

HEYDA, WOLFGANG [479]

b. 14.11.1913, Arys, East Prussia

Class 1932; KKpt 1.8.44

Heavy cruiser *Admiral Scheer* 10/38–3/40; U-boat trg and courses 4/40–11/40

Cdr *U 120* 26.11.40–19.5.41

Baubelehrung 5/41–6/41

Cdr *U 434* 21.6.41–18.12.41

POW 18.12.41–6.5.47

HEYDEMANN, ERNST [480]

b. 20.6.1916, Güstrow, Mecklenburg

Class 1936; ObltzS 1.10.40

WO U-boat depot ship *Donau* 5/39–1/40; Div. Officer 7th U-Flotilla 1/40–3/40; U-boat trg 4/40–8/40; 1WO *U 142* 9/40–10/40; Sports Officer and acting ADC 2nd U-Flotilla 10/40–5/41; 1WO *U 141* 5/41–10/41

Cdr *U 17* 16.10.41–31.5.42

U-Cdr's Course, 24th U-Flotilla 6/42–7/42

Cdr *U 268* 29.7.42–19.2.43
Lost 19.2.43 Bay of Biscay, W of Nantes

HEYDEMANN, GÜNTHER [481]
b. 11.1.1914, Greifswald
Class 1933; Kplt 1.4.41
Trg ship *Schleswig-Holstein* 3/39–3/40, inc. course Naval Gunnery School 12/39–1/40; U-boat trg 4/40–9/40; *Baubelehrung* U-Boats 9/40–11/40; 1WO *U 69* 11/40–4/41; U-Cdr's Torpedo Course, 24th U-Flotilla 4/41–5/41; *Baubelehrung* 5/41–6/41
Cdr *U 575* 19.6.41–29.7.43
Leader torpedo attack trg, 23rd U-Flotilla 7/43–2/45; instructor 25th U-Flotilla 2/45–5/45; Office of Naval Intelligence, Neustadt 5/45; 4th Naval Escort Flotilla 6/45–9/45
Released from 4th Escort Flotilla 1.10.45
Knight's Cross 3.7.43 (175th KM, 94th U-boat holder)

HEYSE, ULRICH [482]
b. 27.9.1906, Berlin-Friedenau
Class 1933; KKpt 1.4.43
1WO destroyer *Z 6 Theodor Riedel* 10/38–6/40; U-boat trg and courses 7/40–2/41; Kplt on Staff 2nd U-Flotilla 2/41–3/41; *Baubelehrung* 6.KLA 3/41–5/41
Cdr *U 128* 12.5.41–28.2.43
Instructor and Comp. CO 2.ULD 3/43–12/43
Officer instructor 1.ULD 12/43–1/44; Cdr Section 1/1.ULD 1/44–3/45, inc. caretaking Cdr 1.ULD 2/45–3/45; CO 32nd U-Flotilla, 3/45–capitulation
Knight's Cross 21.1.43 (143rd KM, 78th U-boat holder)

HILBIG, HANS [483]
b. 5.7.1917, Rüstringen
Class 1936; Kplt 1.3.43
Seconded to Luftwaffe until 3/43; U-boat trg 4/43–10/43; 27th U-Flotilla 10/43; U-Cdr's Course, 23rd U-Flotilla 10/43–12/43; *Baubelehrung* 8.KLA 12/43–1/44
Cdr *U 1230* 26.1.44–capitulation

HILBIG, KURT [484]
b. 18.5.1919, Rüstringen
Class 1938; ObltzS 1.4.43
Officer trg 10/38–4/40; WO sea trg battleship *Scharnhorst* 4/40–8/40; Platoon Leader 2/Basic Trg Est. Stralsund 8/40–10/40; U-boat trg 10/40–3/41; 27th U-Flotilla 3/41–11/41; *Baubelehrung* 8.KLA 11/41–12/41; 1WO *U 601* 12/41–5/43; U-Cdr's Course, 24th U-Flotilla 6/43–7/43 (U-Cdr's Torpedo Course 49); *Baubelehrung* 8.KLA 7/43–8/43
Cdr *U 993* 19.8.43 to before 17.8.44 (Steinmetz [1227] had orders to transfer boat and crew to Norway and sailed *U 993* from Brest that day)
Comp. Officer 1.UAA 9/44–11/44; *Baubelehrung* Type XXI 7.KLA 11/44–3/45
Cdr *U 3526* 22.3.45–5.5.45
5th U-Flotilla 5/45–capitulation

HILDEBRANDT, HANS [485]
b. 24.12.1911, Bremen
Class 1936; Kplt 1.9.42
1st R-Boat Flotilla 5/38–3/40; course Mine Warfare School 3/40–5/40; Group Leader Harbour Defence Flotilla Trondheim 5/40–4/41; U-boat trg 4/41–9/41
Cdr *U 152* 1.10.41–31.7.42
Baubelehrung 8.KLA 8/42
Cdr *U 636* 20.8.42–14.2.44 (per *U 636* WD)
24th U-Flotilla 2/44–5/44; Testing Group Leader, Torpedo Testing Branch 5/44–8/44; Leader Gdynia Office, Torpedo Testing Branch 8/44–capitulation.

HILGENDORF, KLAUS [486]
b. 29.2.1912, Hamburg
Entry X/1939; ObltzS (R) 1.4.43

Further officer trg 10/39–9/40; WO 12th Minesweeping Flotilla 9/40–3/41; M/S-Cdr 12th Minesweeping Flotilla 4/41–11/42; M/S-Cdr 24th Minesweeping Flotilla 12/42–3/43; U-boat trg and U-Cdr sea trg 5/43–12/43 (U-Cdr's Torpedo Course 59); *Baubelehrung* 8.KLA 12/43–2/44

Cdr *U 1009* 10.2.44–capitulation

HILLE, WOLFGANG [487]
b. 12.3.1918, Ebstorf bei Ülzen
Class 1936; Kplt 1.9.43
ADC and WO 4th Minesweeping Flotilla 7/39–12/40; M/S-Cdr 4th Minesweeping Flotilla 12/40–9/41; U-boat trg 9/41–2/42; WO *U 202* 3/42–10/42; U-Cdr's Course, 2.UAA and 24th U-Flotilla 10/42–12/42; *Baubelehrung* 6.KLA 12/42–1/43

Cdr *U 762* 30.1.43–14.12.43

Comp. CO 2.ULD 12/43–10/44; U-Boat Trg Group South and Torpedo Inspectorate 10/44–capitulation

HILLMANN, JÜRGEN [488]
b. 21.9.1920, Gubkow, Mecklenburg
Class X/1940; ObltzS 1.10.44
WO sea trg *U 2* 8/42–1/43; WO *U 371* 2/43–2/44; U-Cdr's Course, 3.ULD and 24th U-Flotilla 3/44–6/44 (U-Cdr's Torpedo Course 68); 21st U-Flotilla 6/44–11/44; *Baubelehrung* Type XXIII 8.KLA 11/44–1/45

Cdr *U 2353* 9.1.45–capitulation

HILSENITZ, ERICH [489]
b. 28.9.1916, Hamburg
Class 1936; Kplt 1.9.43
U-boat trg 1/41–9/41; WO *U 108* 9/41–6/42; U-Cdr's Course, 24th U-Flotilla 6/42–8/42; U-Cdr under instrn, 10th U-Flotilla 8/42–10/42

Cdr *U 108* 10/42

Cdr *U 146* 2.11.42–11.7.43

Instructor 2.ULD 7/43–7/44; Staff, 19th and 13th U-Flotillas 7/44–capitulation

HINRICHS, JOHANNES [490]
b. 29.5.1913, Heide
Entry VII/1933; Kplt 1.4.45
Cdr *M 551*, 27th U-Flotilla 7/42–1/44; U-boat trg and courses 1/44–11/44; WO sea trg *U 2518* 11/44–1/45

Cdr *U 3005* 11.1.45–5.5.45

HINRICHS, OTTO [491]
b. 30.11.1913, Brake, Oberwald, Bremen
Entry 1936; ObltzS (R) 1.7.43
U-boat trg 1/41–8/41; WO *U 105* 9/41–8/42; WO *U 154* 9/42–2/43; U-Cdr's Course, 24th U-Flotilla 2/43–3/43 (U-Cdr's Torpedo Course 42); U-Cdr under instrn, 22nd U-Flotilla 3/43–5/43; *Baubelehrung* 1.KLA 5/43–8/43

Cdr *U 1061* 25.8.43–19.3.45

5th U-Flotilla 3/45–capitulation

HINSCH, HANS-PETER [492]
b. 30.7.1914, Hamburg
Class 1934; Kplt 1.4.42
WO *U 16* 1937 (per rank listings of 1.11.37); 1WO *U 30* 10/38–1/40

Cdr *U 4* 17.1.40–7.6.40

Baubelehrung 6/40–8/40

Cdr *U 140* 7.8.40–6.4.41

Baubelehrung 4/41–5/41

Cdr *U 569* 8.5.41–2.2.43 (per WASt; 6.2.43 per *U 569* WD, and see Johannsen [561])

Instructor and Torpedo Instructor 26th U-Flotilla 2/43–capitulation

Detained; freed 20.1.46

HINZ, RUDOLF [493]
b. 22.2.1920, Berlin-Neukölln
Class IX/1939; ObltzS 1.10.43

1WO *U 30* 9/41–3/42; *Baubelehrung* 8.KLA 3/42–4/42; 1WO *U 618* 4/42–9/43; U-Cdr's Course, 23rd U-Flotilla 10/43–11/43; Torpedo Instructor Trg Unit, Higher Command of Torpedo Schools 11/43–12/44; 11th U-Flotilla 12/44–1/45
Cdr *U 1004* 1/45–capitulation

VON HIPPEL, FRIEDRICH [494]
b. 2.1.1915, Düsseldorf
Class 1934; Kplt 1.12.41
2WO *U 26* 1937–38; ADC U-Flotilla *Hundius* 10/38–12/39; *Baubelehrung* 12/39–2/40; 1WO *U 65* 2/40–8/40; U-Cdr's Course, 24th U-Flotilla 8/40–9/40
Cdr *U 144* 2.10.40–16.11.40
Baubelehrung 11/40–12/40
Cdr *U 76* 3.12.40–5.4.41
POW 5.4.41

HIRSACKER, HEINZ [495]
b. 14.8.1914, Lübeck
Class 1934; Kplt 1.9.41
2WO *U 36* 8/37–12/37; details not available 1/38–12/39; 1WO *U 64* 12/39–4/40; 1WO *U 124* 6/40–8/40; details not available 9/40–5/41
Cdr *U 572* 29.5.41 to 15.12.42 (per WASt) or 18.12.42 (per *U 572* WD, and see Kummetat [681])
1st Officer destroyer *Z 10 Hans Lody* 1/43; 1st Officer destroyer *Z 33* 1/43; assigned C-in-C Destroyers 1/43–4/43
Condemned to death by court-martial for cowardice in the face of the enemy, executed by firing squad 24.4.43 (Translator's note: As commander of *U 572*, Hirsacker failed to make a resolute attempt to comply with orders to transit the Strait of Gibraltar and was denounced by his officers.)

HOECKNER, FRITZ [496]
b. 22.12.1912, Berlin-Schöneberg
Class 1933; Kplt 1.11.41, posthumously KKpt seniority 1.7.42
1WO fleet escort *F 7* 4/39–10/39; M/S-Cdr 12th Minesweeping Flotilla 10/39–10/40; M/S-Cdr 5th Minesweeping Flotilla 10/40–3/41; U-boat trg 3/41–6/41; U-Cdr's Course, 24th U-Flotilla 6/41–8/41; 1st U-Flotilla 9/41–10/41; *Baubelehrung* 10/41–11/41
Cdr *U 215* 22.11.41–3.7.42
Lost 3.7.42 off US coast, E of Boston

VON DER HÖH, HERMANN [497]
b. 23.4.1920, Neviges, Rhineland
NCO (R) entry IV/40; ObltzS (R)
2WO 15th Minesweeping Flotilla 3/41–9/41; 3WO and senior boatswain 12th and 13th Minesweeping Flotillas 1/41–4/42; U-boat trg 4/42–6/42; 2WO *U 445* 6/42–10/43; 1WO *U 445* 10/43–3/44; courses 3/44–10/44; *Baubelehrung* Type XXIII 10/44–11/44
Cdr *U 2346* 20.11.44–5.5.45

HÖLTRING, HORST [498]
b. 30.6.1913, Altona
Class 1933; Kplt 1.3.41
U-boat trg, 1st U-Trg Flotilla, UAA Plön, 2nd U-Trg Flotilla and *Baubelehrung* 3/40–10/40
Cdr *U 149* 13.11.40–30.11.41
Baubelehrung 8.KLA 12/41–1/42
Cdr *U 604* 8.1.42–11.8.43
Lost 24.8.43 central Atlantic aboard *U 185*

HOFFMANN, DIETRICH [499]
b. 17.6.1912, Bromberg
Entry 1932; KKpt 1.7.44
WO light cruiser *Emden* 5/38–9/39; WO light cruiser *Leipzig* 9/39–2/40; adviser OKM 2/40–3/41; U-boat trg 3/41–9/41; *Baubelehrung* 9/41–10/41

Cdr *U 594* 30.10.41 to 24.7.42 (per WASt) or 26.7.42 (per *U 594* WD, and see Mumm [859])
1st Officer destroyer *Z 30* 10/42–3/45, inc. caretaker Cdr *Z 30* 12/44–4/45

HOFFMANN, EBERHARD [500]
b. 16.5.1907, Diedenhofen
Class 1925; KKpt 1.11.39, posthumously FKpt seniority 1.9.42
OKM/1.SKL 6/39–11/40; heavy cruiser *Admiral Hipper* 11/40–12/40; OKM/1.SKL 12/40–3/41; 1.ULD 4/41–5/41; Torpedo School Mürwik 5/41–7/41; U-Cdr sea trg *U 109* 7/41–11/41; *Baubelehrung* 12/41–2/42
Cdr *U 165* 3.2.42–27.9.42
Lost 27.9.42 Bay of Biscay, off Lorient

HOFFMANN, EBERHARD [501]
b. 24.10.1912, Kletzko, Gnesen
Class 1933; KKpt 1.12.41
U-boat trg 11/39–4/40; Torpedo Testing Branch 4/40–6/40; WO and U-Cdr sea trg *U 51* 6/40–7/40; U-Cdr's Course, 24th U-Flotilla 7/40–8/40; 7th U-Flotilla 8/40–10/40
Cdr *U 146* 30.10.40–6.4.41
Baubelehrung 4/41–5/41
Cdr *U 451* 3.5.41–21.12.41
Lost 21.12.41 Moroccan coast, off Tangier

HOFFMANN, ERICH-MICHAEL [502]
b. 14.6.1919, Saarlautern
Class 1938; ObltzS 1.4.43
Officer trg, trg ship *Schleswig-Holstein* 7/39–10/39; courses 10/39–4/40; light cruiser *Nürnberg* 5/40–7/40; seconded to Luftwaffe 7/40–2/41; U-boat trg 2/41–9/41; *Baubelehrung* 9/41–10/41; 1WO *U 437* 10/41–11/42; U-Cdr's Course, 24th U-Flotilla 11/42–1/43; *Baubelehrung* 7.KLA 1/43–2/43
Cdr *U 738* 20.2.43–14.2.44
Lost 14.2.44 Baltic Sea, off Gdynia

HOFFMANN, HEINRICH-DIETRICH [503]
b. 19.8.1921, Wilhelmshaven
Class 1940; ObltzS 1.10.44
Officer and U-boat trg until 9/41; WO sea trg *U 86* 10/41–3/42; U-Boat School and WO course 3/42–10/42; supernumerary WO (for trg purposes) *U 711* 10/42–2/43; WO *U 238* 2/43–3/43; 2WO *U 957* 3/43–2/44; WO *Hugo Zeye* 2/44–9/44; course and 21st U-Flotilla 9/44–11/44
Cdr *U 141* 7.11.44–2.5.45

HOFFMANN, HERMANN [504]
b. 27.4.1921, Hannover
Class X/1939; ObltzS 1.10.43
Officer and U-boat trg and *Baubelehrung* 10/39–11/41; 2WO *U 172* 11/41–12/42; 1WO *U 172* 1/43–9/43; U-Cdr's Course 9/43–10/43
Cdr *U 172* 1.11.43–13.12.43
POW 13.12.43–8.5.46

HOFFMANN, RUDOLF [505]
b. 28.4.1917, Kolberg
Class 1936; Kplt 1.8.43
Course Flak School 6/39–9/39; 8/Basic Trg Est. Stralsund 9/39–4/40; Trg Officer 2nd Torpedo-Boat Flotilla 4/40–6/40; WO torpedo-boat *T 12* 6/40–3/41; course Naval Signals School 3/41–4/41; 1WO U-boat tender *Lech*, Flotilla Radio Technical Officer of 1st and 5th U-Flotillas 4/41–6/41; courses and trg 2.ULD, Torpedo and Signals Schools 6/41–11/41; 1WO *U 123* 12/41–3/42; U-Cdr's Course 3/42–5/42
Cdr *U 8* 1.6.42 (per WASt) or 17.5.42 (per P/F) to 15.3.43
Trg Officer 22nd U-Flotilla 3/43–7/43
Cdr *U 845* 10.7.43 (from 3.7.43 per P/F) to 7.10.43
Base Officer, Stettin, 4th U-Flotilla 10/43–2/44; Comp. CO 1.ULD Pillau 2/44–3/45; 1WO yacht *Grille* 3/45–capitulation
Detained; freed 19.3.1947

HOHMANN, OTTO [506]
b. 1.4.1910 Altenburg, Thüringen
Entry as Rating (R) 1937; ObltzS (R) 1.12.42
Boatswain WO *Schiff 7* 5/40–4/41; Cdr *Schiff 7* 5/41–2/43; U-boat trg 3/43–9/43; U-Cdr's Course and *Baubelehrung* 9/43–11/43 (U-Cdr's Torpedo Course 56)
Cdr *U 298* 1.12.43–17.7.44
Course and *Baubelehrung* Type XXI 8.KLA 7/44–12/44
Cdr *U 2526* 15.12.44–2.5.45

VON HOLLEBEN, HEINRICH [507]
b. 13.3.1919, Viña del Mar, Chile
Class 1938; ObltzS 1.4.43
UJ Cdr 17th Anti-Submarine Flotilla 1/42–3/43; U-boat trg and U-Cdr's Torpedo Course 59 4/43–9/43; Platoon Officer 3.ULD 10/43–1/44; *Baubelehrung* 1.KLA 1/44–3/44
Cdr *U 1051* 4.3.44–26.1.45
Lost 26.1.45 S of Isle of Man

HOLPERT, WILLIAM [508]
b. 11.6.1914, London, England
Enlisted rating 1934; ObltzS 1.10.43
Signal-ObMt (Yeoman of Signals) light cruiser *Karlsruhe* 10/39–4/40; Senior Watch NCO Naval Signals Office Kiel 4/40–6/40; courses, various duties, U-boat trg and WO until 1/44; U-Cdr's Course, 23rd U-Flotilla 1/44–3/44 (U-Cdr's Torpedo Course 65); *Baubelehrung* 8.KLA 4/44–5/44
Cdr *U 1021* 25.5.44–30.3.45
Lost 30.3.1945 The Minches

HOLTORF, GOTTFRIED [509]
b. 21.5.1912, Selfingen
Class 1936; Kplt 1.9.42, posthumously KKpt seniority 1.7.43
Cdr MMS *R 21* 4/39–12/39; Instructor Mine Warfare School 12/39–9/40; Cdr R-boat *R 57* 10/40; Instructor Mine Warfare School 10/40–3/41; U-boat trg 3/41–8/41; U-Cdr's Course, 24th U-Flotilla 9/41–10/41; 1st U-Flotilla 10/41–11/41; *Baubelehrung* 8.KLA 11/41
Cdr *U 598* 27.11.41–23.7.43
Lost 23.7.43 off Natal, Brazil

HOMANN, HANS [510]
b. 4.3.1918, Warnemünde
Entry as rating (R) 1938; ObltzS (R) 1.7.43
1st Minesweeping Flotilla 4/39–6/40; 1/NCO Trg Div. 7/40–8/40; bridge petty officer aboard *M 1*, Coastal Defence Group Norwegian West Coast 9/40–4/41; instructor 1/NCO Trg Div., Yachting School Chiemsee 4/41–11/41; WO 17th VP-Boat Flotilla 11/41–1/42; navigation course Helmsman's School Gdynia 1/42–3/42; Group Officer Yachting School (Glücksberg) 3/42–5/42, (Chiemsee) 5/42–11/42; WO 17th VP-Boat Flotilla 11/42–2/43; course 2.ULD 2/43–4/43; U-boat trg and courses 4/43–8/43; U-Cdr's Course, 27th and 24th U-Flotillas 8/43–10/43 (U-Cdr's Torpedo Course 55); *Baubelehrung* 10/43–11/43
Cdr *U 1165* 17.11.43–capitulation

HOPMANN, ROLF-HEINRICH [511]
b. 26.3.1906, Kiel
Class 1926; KKpt 1.11.40, posthumously FKpt seniority 1.11.43
1st Officer destroyer *Z 19 Hermann Künne* 1/39–4/40; land fighting for Narvik 4/40–7/40; 1/Adm. Staff Officer, Staff Naval Group (East) 7/40–8/40, (North) 8/40–3/41; U-boat trg 4/41–6/41; U-Cdr's Course, 24th U-Flotilla 6/41–8/41; *Baubelehrung* 7.KLA 8/41–9/41
Cdr *U 405* 17.9.41–1.11.43
Lost 1.11.43 central North Atlantic

HOPPE, JOACHIM [512]
b. 20.3.1915, Sehnde, Hannover
Class 1933; Kplt 1.4.41, posthumously KKpt seniority 1.5.41
U-Boat School 11/39–1/40; Torpedo School Mürwik 1/40–3/40; Naval Gunnery School 3/40; 1st U-Boat Trg Flotilla 3/40; U-boat depot ship *Erwin Wassner* 3/40–8/40; 1WO *U 65* 8/40–1/41; U-Cdr's Course 1/41–3/41
Cdr *U 65* 25.3.41–28.4.41
Lost 28.4.41 SE of Iceland

HORN, KARL-HORST [513]
b. 16.12.1916, Neusalz, Oder
Class 1935; Kplt 1.6.42
U-boat trg 4/40–12/40; *Baubelehrung* 12/40–1/41; 1WO *U 210* 1/41–8/41; U-Cdr's Course, 26th U-Flotilla 10/41–11/41; *Baubelehrung* 11/41–12/41
Cdr *U 705* 30.12.41–3.9.42
Lost 3.9.42 Bay of Biscay, W of Brest

HORNBOSTEL, KLAUS [514]
b. 4.6.1916, Cuxhaven
Class 1934; Kplt 1.9.41
Gunnery Technical Officer and WO heavy cruiser *Admiral Scheer* 9/39–2/43; U-boat trg 3/43–12/43; U-Cdr's trg 12/43–2/44; *Baubelehrung* 5.KLA 2/44–4/44
Cdr *U 806* 29.4.44–capitulation
Detained; freed 3/47

HORNKOHL, HANS [515]
b. 7.4.1917, Hamburg, Altona
Class 1936; Kplt 1.4.43
Seconded to Luftwaffe (See), long-range naval reconnaissance 9/39–8/41; U-boat trg 8/41–1/42; 3rd U-Flotilla 1/42–4/42; U-Cdr sea trg *U 753* 4/42–12/42; U-Cdr's Torpedo Course 12/42–1/43

Cdr *U 566* 25.1.43–24.10.43
Baubelehrung 8.KLA 12/43–1/44
Cdr *U 1007* 18.1.44–9.7.44
Baubelehrung Type XXI 7.KLA for *U 3509* 8/44–11/44 (*U 3509* received bomb damage on 6.9.44 whilst on the slip at Schichau Danzig and was subsequently mined while running trials in the Bay of Danzig in 11/44. The complement, under Hornkohl, transferred to *U 3512*, this boat being commissioned on 27.11.44. *U 3509* was repaired and eventually commissioned under Voswinkel [1309] on 29.1.45.)
Cdr *U 3512* 27.11.44–8.4.45
Cdr *U 2502* 9.4.45–12.4.45 (voyage Hamburg–Kiel)
Cdr *U 3041* 27.4.45–capitulation
Detained; freed 8/45

HORRER, HANS-JOACHIM [516]
b. 6.2.1908, Dortmund
Class 1933; Kplt 1.2.40, posthumously KKpt seniority 1.9.42
Div. Officer, Gunnery Officer and WO destroyer *Z 9 Wolfgang Zenker* 7/38–4/40; Naval Regiment *Berger* 4/40–6/40; U-boat trg 7/40–11/40; U-Cdr's Course, 24th U-Flotilla 11/40–1/41; *Baubelehrung* for *U 555* 18.1.41–29.1.41
Cdr *U 555* 30.1.41–25.8.41
Baubelehrung 8.KLA 26.8.41–24.9.41
Cdr *U 589* 25.9.41–14.9.42
Lost 14.9.42 SW of Spitzbergen

HORST, FRIEDRICH [517]
b. 12.4.1917, Rio Grande, Brazil
Entry XI/1939; ObltzS (R) 1.4.44
U-boat trg 1/41–6/41; WO *U 11* 6/41–8/42; 2WO *U 565* 8/42–8/43; 1WO *U 565* 8/43–12/43; U-Cdr's Course, 24th U-Flotilla 12/43–1/44 (U-Cdr's Torpedo Course 62)
Cdr *U 121* 23.2.44–2.5.45

HOSCHATT, ALFRED [518]
b. 10.2.1909, Görlitz
Entry 1927; KKpt 1.4.44
M/S-Cdr 1st Minesweeping Flotilla 4/39–3/41; U-boat trg 4/41–9/41; *Baubelehrung* KLA U-Boats East 9/41–10/41
Cdr *U 378* 30.10.41–11.10.42 (per WASt) (Hoschatt informed the U-Boat Archive that 1WO Schrewe [1127] was acting commander of *U 378* from 18.6.42 and Zetzsche [1398] from 12.9.42 to 11.10.42, during which period the latter completed an Arctic patrol 12.9.42–26.9.42. The *U 378* War Diary indicates that Mäder [770] relieved Hoschatt on 12.10.42.)
11th U-Flotilla 10/42–4/43; 2/Adm. Staff Officer, OKM/2.SKL/BdU/Opn 4/43–capitulation

HOSSENFELDER, ALBERT [519]
b. 5.3.1908, Sprottau, Lower Silesia
Entry 1935; ObltzS (R) 1.2.43
Cdr *V 109* 9/39–5/40; WO *Reiher* (Patrol Group East) 7/40–2/41; VP Cdr 17th VP-Boat Flotilla 2/41–9/41; U-boat trg 9/41–4/42; 2WO *U 371* 4/42–10/42; U-Cdr's Course, 24th U-Flotilla 11/42–12/42; *Baubelehrung* 6.KLA 12/42–1/43
Cdr *U 342* 12.1.43–17.4.44
Lost 17.4.44 SW of Iceland

HÜBSCH, HORST [520]
b. 31.12.1921, Kettwig, Ruhr
Class XII/1939; ObltzS 1.12.43
U-boat trg completed 5/42; 2WO *U 262* 5/42–5/43; 1WO *U 262* 6/43–1/44; U-Cdr's Course 1/44–3/44
Cdr *U 145* 13.3.44–26.11.44
Cdr *U 78* 27.11.44–16.4.45

HÜBSCHEN, OTTO [521]
b. 6.12.1919, Coesfeld, Westphalia
Class 1938; ObltzS 1.4.43
U-boat trg 3/40–3/41; *Baubelehrung* 4/41–5/41; WO *U 402* 5/41–8/42; WO and Acting Cdr *U 7*, *U 60* and *U 121* 9/42–12/42
Cdr *U 145* 15.12.42–12.3.44
Courses and *Baubelehrung* Type XXI 3/44–6/44
Cdr *U 2501* 27.6.44–20.11.44 (From 12/44 *U 2501* served as a shore trg boat under Chief Engineer (LI) Lt (Ing) Hans Noack, a former enlisted man, from 20.1.45 to 3.5.45. Noack was acting commander with full disciplinary authority.)
Baubelehrung 8.KLA 11/44–3/45
Cdr *U 2542* 5.3.45–3.4.45

HÜLSENBECK, EWALD [522]
b. 21.12.1919, Milspe, Ruhr
Class 1938; ObltzS 1.4.42
U-boat trg 3/41; Comp. Officer 2.UAA 3/41–5/41; 1WO *U 146* 6/41–8/41
Cdr *U 146* 27.8.41–10/41
Baubelehrung 8.KLA 10/41–11/41; 1WO *U 704* 11/41–11/42; U-Cdr's Course, 24th U-Flotilla 11/42–12/42; WO (supernumerary) *U 121* 12/42–2/43
Cdr *U 121* 9.2.43–22.2.44
Baubelehrung 7.KLA 2/44–4/44
Cdr *U 1209* 13.4.44–18.12.44
Lost 18.12.44 English Channel, nr Scilly Is

HÜTTEMANN, EBERHARD [523]
b. 25.6.1919, Sagan, Silesia
Class X/1937; ObltzS 1.4.42
U-boat trg completed 8/41; *Baubelehrung* 8.KLA 8/41–10/41; 1WO *U 590* 10/41–12/42; U-Cdr's Course, 24th U-Flotilla 12/42–1/43
Cdr *U 332* 27.1.43 (per *U 332* WD) or 12.2.43 (per WASt, but as *U 332* sailed from La Pallice on 28.1.43 the WASt note cannot be correct; and see Liebe [731]) to 29.4.43
Lost 29.4.43 Atlantic, E of Cape Finisterre

HUISGEN, FRIEDRICH [524]
b. 1.3.1915, Cologne
Entry 1936; Kplt (R) 1.4.45
Comp. CO Naval Flak Detachment 803 6/40–3/43; 2nd VP-Boat Flotilla 3/43–6/43; courses and U-Boat trg 6/43–2/44; WO *U 1162* 2/44–6/44; courses, 19th and 24th U-Flotillas 6/44–12/44 (U-Cdr's Torpedo Course 78)
Cdr *U 749* 12/44–4.4.45 (*U 749* was at Site 14, Germaniawerft, for fitment of a snorkel when destroyed in an American air raid on 4.4.45.)
Cdr *U 235* 5.4.45 or 2.4.45 (per WASt) until 14.4.45
Lost 14.4.45 NW of Skagens Horn, Denmark (Translator's note: Other Lists state that the boat was depth-charged and sunk in error by the German torpedo-boat *T 17* in 57°44'N 10°39'E.)

HUMMERJOHANN, EMMO [525]
b. 15.4.1916, Mellendorf, Sagan, Silesia
Class 1937a; ObltzS 1.9.41
ADC C-in-C Minesweepers 9/39–10/39; WO Escort Flotilla 10/39–3/40; WO 4th Minesweeping Flotilla 3/40–9/40; M/S-Cdr 44th Minesweeping Flotilla 11/40–11/41; U-boat trg 11/41–3/42; 27th U-Flotilla 3/42–5/42; 1WO *U 205* 6/42–12/42; U-Cdr's Course, 24th U-Flotilla and *Baubelehrung* 8.KLA 12/42–2/43
Cdr *U 964* 18.2.43–16.10.43
Lost 16.10.43 SW of Iceland

HUNCK, WILHELM [526]
b. 15.12.1914, Essen
Entry XI/1937; Kplt 1.11.43 (reactivated 1943)
WO and VP-Cdr Harbour Defence Flotilla Sandnesjöen 3/41–7/43; U-boat trg 7/43–12/43; U-Cdr's Course, 23rd U-Flotilla and 3.ULD 12/43–3/44; *Baubelehrung* 7.KLA 4/44–5/44
Cdr *U 827* 25.5.44–3/45
5th U-Flotilla 3/45–capitulation

HUNGER, HANS [527]
b. 16.3.1915, Finkenwalde
Class 1935; Kplt 1.8.42
Seconded to Luftwaffe 8/38–1/41, inc. *1./Küstenfliegergruppe 806*; U-boat trg 1/41–6/41; 1WO *U 75* 7/41–11/41; U-Cdr's Course, 26th U-Flotilla 11/41–1/42; *Baubelehrung* 1/42–2/42
Cdr *U 336* 14.2.42–4.10.43
Lost 4.10.43 SW of Iceland

HUNGERSHAUSEN, HEINZ [528]
b. 5.12.1916, Marburg, Lahn
Class 1936; Kplt 1.10.43
Platoon Leader 5/Basic Trg Est. Stralsund 4/39–1/40; WO and Cdr *M 15* 2/40–9/41; U-boat trg 9/41–3/42; WO *U 128* 3/42–2/43; U-Cdr's Course, 24th U-Flotilla 2/43–3/43 (U-Cdr's Torpedo Course 42); instructor Naval Gunnery School 3/43–4/43
Cdr *U 91* 20.4.43–25.2.44
POW 25.2.44

HUNGERSHAUSEN, WALTER [529]
b. 22.3.1919, Marburg, Lahn
Class 1938; ObltzS 1.4.43
Officer trg 11/38–9/40; seconded to Luftwaffe 9/40–2/41; U-boat trg 2/41–7/41; 24th U-Flotilla and *Baubelehrung* 7/41–1/42; 1WO *U 218* 1/42–12/42; U-Cdr's Course, 24th U-Flotilla 12/42–1/43; *Baubelehrung* 1/43–2/43
Cdr *U 280* 13.2.43–16.11.43
Lost 16.11.43 SW of Iceland

HUTH, WALTHER [530]
b. 14.4.1918, Wilhelmshaven
Class 1937a; ObltzS 1.9.41
Trg ship *Schleswig-Holstein* 4/39–3/40; U-boat trg and various duties 4/40–7/41; 1st U-Flotilla 7/41–10/41; 1WO *U 562* 10/41–5/42; U-Cdr's

Course, 24th U-Flotilla 5/42–6/42; *Baubelehrung* 7.KLA 6/42–7/42
Cdr *U 414* 1.7.42–25.5.43
Lost 25.5.43 western Mediterranean, NW of Ténès

VON HYMMEN, REINHARD [531]
b. 5.11.1914, Berlin
Class 1933; Kplt 1.12.40, posthumously KKpt seniority 1.11.42
Gunnery Officer and 1WO destroyer *Z 4 Richard Beitzen* 5/39–4/41; U-boat trg 4/41–7/41; U-Cdr's Course, 24th U-Flotilla 7/41–9/41; U-Cdr sea trg (supernumerary WO) *U 97* 9/41 and *U 564* 9/41–11/41; *Baubelehrung* 7.KLA 11/41
Cdr *U 408* 19.11.41–5.11.42
Lost 5.11.42 Arctic, N of Iceland

HYRONIMUS, GUIDO [532]
b. 17.11.1918, Augsburg
Class X/1937; ObltzS 1.4.42
Trg and courses 9/39–8/40; Platoon Officer Navy Basic Trg Depot Munsterlager 8/40–9/40; Platoon Officer Kriegsmarine Depot Boulogne 9/40–10/40; U-boat trg 10/41–3/41; *Baubelehrung* 3/41–6/41; 2WO *U 351* 6/41–12/41; *Baubelehrung* 12/41–1/42; 1WO *U 461* 1/42–12/42; *Baubelehrung* 8.KLA 12/42–1/43
Cdr *U 670* 27.1.43–20.8.43
5th U-Flotilla and *Baubelehrung* 8/43–10/43
Cdr *U 678* 25.10.43–7.7.44
Lost 7.7.44 English Channel, SW of Brighton

I

IBBEKEN, HANS [533]
b. 20.9.1899, Schleswig
Entry IV/1918; KptzS 1.6.42
Infantry trg Rifle Battalion 9 12/17–4/18; infantry and nautical trg Naval College 4/18–7/18; naval cadet trg ship *Freya* 7/18–9/18; naval cadet battleship *König Albert* 9/18–11/18; Company *Schleswig-Holstein* (Kurland), Iron Div. 12/18–5/19; Bight (Frisches Haff) and River Flotilla Tilsit 5/19–11/19; naval cadet cruiser *Regensburg* 16.11.19–20.11.19; II Naval Brigade (*Ehrhardt*) 11/19–9/20; Naval College 9/20–3/21; sail trg ship *Niobe* 4/21–5/21; aboard *M 90* 6/21–9/21 with period at Naval College 10.6.21–23.8.21; Naval College Mürwik 9/21–3/22; infantry course Coastal Defence Div. II 3/22–4/22; platoon cdr trg Coastal Defence Div. IV 4/22–5/22; course Naval Gunnery School 6/22–8/22; signals course for Naval Officer Aspirants, Signals School Mürwik 8/22–9/22; mining course Mine Warfare Experimental Branch 9/22–10/22; Torpedo School Mürwik 10/22–12/22; Platoon Officer 3. Coastal Defence Div. I 1/23–9/23; 2WO and Gunnery Officer torpedo-boat *G 8* 10/23–9/26 (during this period course at Naval Gunnery School 13.9.24–29.11.24 and ships' flak gunnery course Coastal Gunnery School 3.3.25–9.4.25); Command Naval Station Baltic 1.10.26–31.10.26; Comp. Officer Naval School Friedrichsort 11/26–9/29; ADC from 29.9.27 (during this period various revision courses at coastal and ships' gunnery establishments, and officers' Flak-MG course 19.4.29–3.5.29; Cdr gunnery trg boat *Hay* 9/29–9/31, navigation instruction voyage survey ship *Meteor* 22.10.29–2.11.29; Anti-Poison Gas Course A, Mine Warfare Experimental Branch 7.1.30–16.1.30; Comp. Cdr V. Naval Gunnery Div. 9/31–9/33; adviser Basic Trg Est. Stralsund 9/33–1/34; adviser II/Adm. Baltic 2/34–10/35; trg U-Boat School, seconded FdU 5/36–8/36; *Baubelehrung* Deschimag AG Weser Bremen 3.8.36–11.8.36; Cdr *U 27* 12.8.36–4.10.37; Cdr U-Flotilla *Saltzwedel* 10/37–9/39 (at FdU West 8/39); CO U-Boat School 9/39–6/40; CO 1.ULD 6/40–11/41; *Baubelehrung* 1.KLA U-North 12/41–2/42)
Cdr *U 178* 14.2.42–21.2.43
CO Torpedo School Mürwik 2/43–2/44; Higher Command of Torpedo Schools 2/44–3/45; Wehrmacht Cdr Kiel 3/45–4/45; Naval Cdr, Naval Defence Schleswig-Holstein, Kappeln 4/45–capitulation

ISERMEYER, HANS-ADOLF [534]
b. 1.1.1920, Jetzsch, Luckau
Class 1938; ObltzS 1.4.43
U-boat trg completed 3/41; *Baubelehrung* 3/41–5/41; 2WO *U 752* 5/41–6/42; 1WO *U 752* 6/42–9/42; U-Cdr's Course, 24th U-Flotilla 9/42–11/42
Cdr *U 80* 23.11.42 to 30.9.43 (or 31.10.43 per WASt; see Keerl [587] and Stege [1217])
Trg Officer 23rd U-Flotilla 10/43–4/45; 8.KLA *Baubelehrung*-Cdr *U 2562* (boat never commissioned) 4/45–capitulation

ITES, OTTO [535]
b. 5.2.1918, Norden, Ostfriesland
Class 1936; Kplt 1.3.43
U-boat trg 10/38–4/39; 2WO *U 51* 4/39; 2WO *U 48* 4/39–11/40; 1WO *U 48* 11/40–3/41; U-Cdr's KSL, 24th U-Flotilla 3/41

Cdr *U 146* 7.4.41–26.8.41
Cdr *U 94* 27.8.41 (per P/F) or 29.8.41 (per *U 94* WD, and see Kuppisch [684]) to 27.8.42
POW 27.8.42–1.5.46
Knight's Cross 28.3.42 (108th KM, 49th U-boat holder)

ITES, RUDOLF [536]
b. 5.2.1918, Norden, Ostfriesland
Entry 1936; ObltzS (R) 1.12.43
Naval Flak Detachment 216 8/39–2/41; Detachment 806 2/41–9/41; Detachment 808 9/41–12/41; retrg Seaman Branch officer, 2nd VP-Boat Flotilla 12/41–3/42; 1/NCO Trg Div. 3/42–6/42; Helmsman's School 6/42–9/42; U-boat trg 9/42–3/43; 2WO *U 709* 3/43–7/43; 1WO *U 709* 7/43–11/43; U-Cdr's Course, 3.ULD and 24th U-Flotilla 11/43–12/43
Cdr *U 709* 3.12.43–1.3.44
Lost 1.3.44 N of Azores

IVERSEN, JÜRGEN [537]
b. 24.2.1921, Neuenbrook, Holstein
Class X/1939; ObltzS 1.10.43
Officer trg 10/39–10/41; 2WO *U 355* 10/41–7/43; 1WO *U 355* 7/43–11/43; Comp. Officer 3.ULD 12/43–1/44; Comp. Officer 1.UAA 2/44; U-Cdr trg, 27th U-Flotilla 3/44–5/44
Cdr *U 8* 13.5.44–24.11.44
Cdr *U 1103* 25.11.44–25.2.45
Cdr 6th U-Flotilla 2/45–capitulation (per Lohmann-Hildebrand almanac. However, the 6th Flotilla was disbanded at St Nazaire in 8/44.)

J

JACOBS, PAUL [538]
b. 23.3.1915, Lübeck
Enlisted as rating 1934; ObltzS 1.7.44
ObStrm and 3WO *U 332* 6/41–4/43; courses 4/43–9/43; WO *U 738* 9/43–10/43; U-Cdr's Course, 3.ULD and 23rd U-Flotilla 10/43–12/43
Cdr *U 560* 13.12.43–3.5.45

VON JACOBS, NIKOLAUS [539]
b. 5.1.1913, St Petersburg, Russia
Class 1933; Kplt 1.4.41, posthumously KKpt seniority 1.12.43
Gunnery and 1st Officer, acting Cdr gunnery trg ship *Bremse* 5/38–6/41; U-boat trg 6/41–10/41; U-Cdr sea trg (supernumerary WO) *U 751* 10/41–11/41; U-Cdr's Course, 24th U-Flotilla 11/41–1/42; *Baubelehrung* 8.KLA 1/42–2/42
Cdr *U 611* 26.2.42–10.12.42
Lost 10.12.42 S of Iceland

JÄCKEL, KURT [540]
6.12.1919, Lozzöhnen, East Prussia
Entry VIII/1939; ObltzS 1.10.44
WO *U 529* 11/42–1/43; WO *U 714* 2/43–7/44; U-Cdr's Course, 3.ULD and 24th U-Flotilla 8/44–10/44 (U-Cdr's Torpedo Course 76); U-Cdr 22nd U-Flotilla 10/44–12/44; *Baubelehrung* Type XXIII 8.KLA 12/44–3/45
Cdr *U 2366* 10.3.45–5.5.45

JÄGER, WALTER [541]
b. 27.5.1897, Zeulenroda, Thüringen
NCO (R) entry 1943; ObltzS (R) 1.7.44
Trg 2/Adm. Baltic 1/43–2/43; recruited to 5/Trg Div. for new warships 2/43–4/43; officer's course Naval College Flensburg-Mürwik 4/43–6/43; demobilised 7/43–3/44; U-boat trg 4/44–11/44; U-Cdr sea trg (supernumerary WO) *U 1061* 11/44–3/45
Cdr *U 1061* 20.3.45–capitulation

JAEK, BERNHARD [542]
b. 14.10.1918, Zlotnitz, Posen
Class X/1937; Kplt 1.1.45
Naval Gunnery Ordnance Office Kiel-Dietrichsdorf 5/40–9/42 and Depot Officer Naval Gunnery Ordnance Office St Nazaire 10/42–3/43; transferred from Ordnance to Seaman Branch 3/43; navigation course Helmsman's School 3/43–5/43; U-boat trg 5/43–12/43; 1WO *U 218* 12/43–6/44; course 23rd U-Flotilla 6/44–8/44; U-Cdr sea trg 27th U-Flotilla 8/44–10/44; U-Cdr 31st U-Flotilla 10/44–12/44; *Baubelehrung* Type XXI 6.KLA 12/44–3/45
Cdr *U 3044* 27.3.45–25.4.45

JAENICKE, KARL [543]
b. 14.7.1915, Hamburg
Entry XI/1939; ObltzS 1.1.44
Officer trg 11/39–4/40; interpreter, Staff, Adm. Norwegian South Coast 4/40–9/40; 1WO and Prize Officer *Schiff 47* 9/40–2/41; 1WO and acting VP-Cdr 59th VP-Boat Flotilla 2/41–6/41; Cdr escort ship *Polarnacht* 7/41–2/42; VP-Cdr Harbour Defence Flotilla Kirkenes 2/42–8/42; U-boat trg 8/42–1/43; *Baubelehrung* 6.KLA 2/43–3/43; 1WO *U 801* 3/43–2/44; U-Cdr's Course, 23rd U-Flotilla 3/44–6/44; 3.ULD 6/44–1/45; *Baubelehrung* Cdr 7.KLA for

U 3533 6.1.45–2/45 (as completion not anticipated before expected arrival of Red Army at Danzig, boat towed to Kiel and demolished 3.5.45)
U-Cdr 5th U-Flotilla 2/45–capitulation

JAHN, GUNTER [544]
b. 27.9.1910, Hamburg
Class 1931; KKpt 1.11.43
WO light cruiser *Nürnberg* 8/38–1/40; course Mine Warfare School Kiel-Wik 1/40–2/40; WO light cruiser *Leipzig* 2/40–3/41; U-boat trg 3/41–6/41; U-Cdr's Course, 24th U-Flotilla 6/41–8/41; U-Cdr sea trg (supernumerary WO) *U 98* 8/41–10/41; *Baubelehrung* 8.KLA 10/41–11/41
Cdr *U 596* 13.11.41 to 27.7.43 (per P/F) or 31.7.43 (per WASt)
29th U-Flotilla 7/43; CO 29th U-Flotilla 8/43–9/44
POW 15.9.44–10.7.46
Knight's Cross 30.4.43 (163rd KM, 91st U-boat holder)

JAHRMÄRKER, WALTHER [545]
b. 23.9.1917, Marburg
Class 1935; Kplt 1.6.42
1WO and Torpedo Officer torpedo-boat *Möwe* 10/38–6/40; 1WO torpedo-boat *Panther* 6/40–12/40; Cdr torpedo-boat *Panther* 12/40–6/41; U-boat trg, U-Cdr sea trg and *Baubelehrung* 7.KLA 6/41–4/42
Cdr *U 412* 29.4.42–22.10.42
Lost 22.10.42 NE of Faroes

JANSSEN, GUSTAV-ADOLF [546]
b. 9.4.1915, Blankenese, Hamburg
Class 1936; Kplt 1.4.43
Command Relay Officer Staff FdU Wilhelmshaven 9/39–12/39; *Baubelehrung* 12/39–2/40; 2WO *U 65* 2/40–3/41; U-Cdr trg 4/41–7/41
Cdr *U 151* 22.7.41–15.11.41
Cdr *U 37* 16.11.41–30.6.42
Cdr *U 103* 15.7.42 (per P/F) or 14.7.42 (*U 103* WD) to 13.3.44
Trg Officer (20th U-Flotilla) 3/44–1/45, (25th U-Flotilla) 1/45–4/45
Cdr *U 3037* 23.4.45–3.5.45
Detained; freed 29.8.45

JASCHKE, HEINZ [547]
b. 16.7.20, Landau
Class IX/1939; ObltzS 1.9.43
U-boat trg completed 9/41; *Baubelehrung* 8.KLA 9/41–10/41; 2WO *U 592* 10/41–1/43; 1WO *U 592* 1/43–5/43; U-Cdr's Course, 2.UAA and 24th U-Flotilla 5/43–6/43 (U-Cdr's Torpedo Course 48); Trg Officer 24th U-Flotilla 6/43–9/43
Cdr *U 592* 2.9.43 (see Borm [111]) to 31.1.44
Lost 31.1.44 SE of Ireland

JEBSEN, JOHANN [548]
b. 21.4.1916, Pellworm
Class 1935; Kplt 1.7.42
2WO *U 39* 10/38–7/39; 1WO *U 20* 7/39–4/40; *Baubelehrung* 4/40–5/40; 1WO *U 123* 5/40–12/40; U-Cdr's Course, 24th U-Flotilla 1/41–3/41; *Baubelehrung* 3/41–4/41
Cdr *U 565* 10.4.41 to 17.3.42 or 19.4.42 (per WASt, and see Franken [309])
25th U-Flotilla 4/42–10/42; Tactical Instructor AGRU-Front 10/42–6/43; *Baubelehrung* 6.KLA 6/43–7/43
Cdr *U 859* 8.7.43–23.9.44
Lost 23.9.44 Indian Ocean, Strait of Malacca, off Penang

JENISCH, HANS [549]
b. 19.10.1913, Gerdauen, East Prussia
Class 1933; Kplt 1.11.40

U-boat trg 5/37–1/38; 1WO *U 32* 1/38–2/40
Cdr *U 32* 12.2.40–30.10.40
POW 30.10.40–20.6.47
Knight's Cross 7.10.40 (36th KM, 15th U-boat holder)

JENISCH, KARL-HEINRICH [550]

b. 20.4.1910, Gerdauen, East Prussia
Class 1929; Kplt 1.7.38
Torpedo School Mürwik 10/38–10/39
Cdr *U 22* 4.10.39–25.4.40 (official date of death)
Missing since 23.3.40 Skagerrak

JENSEN, KURT [551]

b. 23.2.1918, Flensburg
Class 1937a; ObltzS 1.9.41
Seconded to Luftwaffe 10/39–12/40; U-boat trg 1/41–7/41; *Baubelehrung* 7/41–8/41; 1WO *U 376* 8/41–7/42; U-Cdr's Course, 24th U-Flotilla 8/42–9/42; *Baubelehrung* 8.KLA 9/42–10/42
Cdr *U 644* 15.10.42–7.4.43
Lost 7.4.43 Norwegian Sea, NW of Narvik

JENSSEN, KARL-JOACHIM [552]

b. 31.7.1920, Waren, Müritz
Class 1938; ObltzS 1.4.43
U-boat trg completed 4/41; WO *U 141* 4/41–5/41; 3rd and 26th U-Flotillas 5/41–11/41; *Baubelehrung* 11/41–12/41; 1WO *U 705* 12/41–2/42; 1WO *U 563* 3/42–12/42; 1st U-Flotilla 12/42–2/43; 2.UAA 2/43–5/43; U-Cdr's Course, 24th U-Flotilla 6/43–7/43; *Baubelehrung* 7/43–8/43
Cdr *U 477* 18.8.43–3.6.44
Lost 3.6.44 W of Trondheim

JEPPENER-HALTENHOFF, HARALD [553]

b. 20.9.1907, Schaalhof, Mecklenburg
Class 33/31 (see Prien [947]); KKpt 1.9.43
2WO *U 36* 5/37–9/37; 1WO *U 17* 10/37–9/39
Cdr *U 17* 11.9.39–17.10.39 (change of commander 19.10.39 per *U 17* WD)
Cdr *U 24* 18.10.39–29.11.39 (per WASt, but relieved Behrens [66] 19.10.39 per *U 24* WD and was then replaced by Heilmann [441] 29.10.39)
At BdU 12/39–2/40; adviser (PI) for personal particulars of officers and NCOs and CO Personnel Section (Officers), Staff BdU/Organisational, also Staff Officer 2/Adm. U-Boats, Staff Officer Commanding Adm. U-Boats 2/40–capitulation
Detained; freed 15.10.45

JESCHKE, HUBERT [554]

b. 24.4.1921, Neustettin
Class IX/1939; ObltzS 1.10.43
2WO *U 437* 10/41–8/43; 1WO *U 437* 8/43–12/43; U-Cdr's Course, 3.ULD and 23rd U-Flotilla 12/43–1/44; 27th U-Flotilla 1/44–3/44
Cdr *U 975* 17.3.44–16.7.44
Baubelehrung 6.KLA and period hospitalised 7/44–2/45; Torpedo Testing Branch 3/45–capitulation
Detained; freed 22.11.45

JESCHONNEK, WOLF [555]

b. 13.7.1919, Liegnitz
Class 1938; ObltzS 1.1.43
WO 11th Minesweeping Flotilla 5/40–2/41; U-boat trg 2/41–6/41; Platoon Officer 2.ULD 6/41–1/42; 1WO *U 607* 1/42–3/43; U-Cdr's Torpedo Course 3/43–4/43
Cdr *U 607* 18.4.43 (relieved Mengersen [811] 18.4.43 per *U 607* WD; on 24.4.43 *U 607* sailed from St Nazaire under Jeschonnek for her fifth war patrol; WASt has the take-over date as 1.6.43) to 13.7.43
POW 13.7.43–6.5.46

VON JESSEN, RALF [556]
b. 25.2.1917, Kandy, Ceylon
Class 1935; Kplt 1.6.42
Comp. Officer 4/Basic Trg Est. Stralsund 10/38–9/39; WO, Div. and Torpedo Officer merchant raider *Thor* 3/40–6/41; U-boat trg 6/41–4/42; U-Cdr's Course, 24th U-Flotilla 4/42–5/42
Cdr *U 222* 23.5.42–2.9.42
Cdr *U 266* 12.9.42–15.5.43
Lost 15.5.43 North Atlantic

JESTEL, ERWIN [557]
b. 31.3.1923, Peuker, Habelschwerdt
Class 1940; ObltzS 1.10.44
U-boat trg completed 8/42; *Baubelehrung* 8.KLA 8/42–9/42; 2WO *U 642* 10/42–7/43; 1WO *U 642* 7/43–2/44; U-Cdr's Course, 3.ULD and 23rd U-Flotilla 2/44–4/44
Cdr *U 6* 17.4.44–9.7.44
Cdr *U 1204* 8/44–5.5.45

JEWINSKI, ERICH [558]
b. 10.3.1920, Friedrichsort, Kiel
Class 1938; ObltzS 1.4.43
Officer trg 10/38–10/40; battleship *Scharnhorst* 10/40–1/41; U-boat trg 1/41–4/41; U-boat course 2.ULD 4/41–6/41; 22nd U-Flotilla 6/41–9/41; *Baubelehrung* Kriegsmarine Depot Hamburg 9/41–10/41; 1WO *U 594* 10/41–3/43; radar course 2.UAA 8.3.43–14.3.43; U-Cdr's Course, 24th U-Flotilla 3/43–4/43 (U-Cdr's Torpedo Course 44)
Cdr *U 46* 1.5.43–10/43
Cdr *U 747* 10/43–5/44
Cdr *U 1192* 7/44–21.12.44
Baubelehrung Type XXI 8.KLA 12/44–2/45
Cdr *U 2539* 21.2.45–21.4.45
Killed 21.4.45 by bomb during air raid on U-boat basin, Kiel

JOBST, KARL [559]
b. 24.4.1913, Stralsund
NCO (R) entry 1936; ObltzS (R) 1.6.44
Platoon Leader 18th Landing Flotilla 3/42–6/42; course Helmsman's School 6/42–9/42; U-boat trg 9/42–4/43; *Baubelehrung* 7.KLA 4/43–6/43; 1WO *U 744* 6/43–2/44; U-Cdr's Course, 23rd U-Flotilla 3/44–5/44; *Baubelehrung* Type XXIII 8.KLA 5/44–8/44
Cdr *U 2326* 11.8.44–capitulation

JOHANN, JOHANN [560]
b. 4.9.1909, Düsseldorf
Entry 1927/1939; ObltzS (R) 1.7.43
Naval Flak Detachment 226 8/39–3/43; navigation course, trg/courses and U-Boat trg (retrg from Coastal Artillery to Seaman Branch) 3/43–2/45; U-Cdr sea trg *U 2539* 2/45–4/45
Acting Cdr *U 2539* 22.4.45–3.5.45

JOHANNSEN, HANS [561]
b. 3.6.1910, Hamburg-Bergedorf
Entry 1935; ObltzS (R) 1.11.42
VP-Cdr 2nd VP-Boat Flotilla 5/40–7/40; VP-Cdr Harbour Defence Flotilla Boulogne 8/4–9/41; U-boat trg 9/41–3/42; 2WO *U 566* 3/42–12/42; U-Cdr's Course, 2.UAA and 24th U-Flotilla 12/42–1/43
Cdr *U 569* 3.2.43 (see Hinsch [492]) to 22.5.43
POW 22.5.43

JOHN, ALFRED [562]
b. 5.5.1920, Altenkirchen, Westerwald
Class 1938; ObltzS 1.4.43
2/Admin. Officer 5th Torpedo-Boat Flotilla 6/40–12/41; Admin. Officer U-boat depot ship *Waldemar Kophamel* 12/41–9/42; 2. ADC Fleet Command 9/42–2/443; U-boat trg 3/43–2/44 (U-Cdr's Torpedo Course 63); U-Cdr sea trg *U 415* 3/44–4/44; *Baubelehrung* 7.KLA 5/44–6/44

Cdr *U 828* 17.6.44–3.5.45
Detained; freed 7/45

JORDAN, GÜNTHER [563]
b. 12.2.1919, Bremen
Class X/1937; ObltzS 1.4.42, posthumously Kplt seniority 1.4.44
U-boat trg completed 9/40; Comp. Officer 1.ULD 9/40–4/41; *Baubelehrung* 4/41–5/41; 1WO *U 132* 5/41–8/42; U-Cdr's Course, 24th U-Flotilla, 9/42–10/42; *Baubelehrung* 10/42–11/42
Cdr *U 274* 7.11.42–23.10.43
Lost 23.10.43 SW of Iceland

JÜRS, RALF [564]
b. 7.9.1919, place not reported
Class 1937a; Kplt 1.8.44
Battleship *Gneisenau* 9/39–3/40; trg Luftwaffe (See) 4/40–9/40; naval reconnaissance *2./Seeaufklärergruppe 125* 10/40–4/42; 1a *Seeaufklärergruppe 125* 5/42–6/43; U-boat trg /43–5/44; *Baubelehrung* 5/44–7/44
Cdr *U 778* 7.7.44–capitulation
Detained; freed 5.3.47

JÜRST, HARALD [565]
b. 18.3.1913, Wilhelmshaven
Class 1932; Kplt 1.1.40
1WO *U 36* from 12/36 (scheduled per rank listings 1.11.36) or 1937 (per rank listings 1.11.37)
Cdr *U 59* 4.3.39–17.7.40
Baubelehrung 7/40–8/40
Cdr *U 104* 19.8.40–28.11.40
Missing from 28.11.40 NW of Ireland

JULI, HERBERT [566]
b. 8.6.1916, Tientsin, China
Class 1935; Kplt 1.6.42
1WO *U 83* 2/41–11/41; course 26th U-Flotilla 11/41–12/41; 1st U-Flotilla and 2.UAA 12/41–3/42
Cdr *U 382* 25.4.42–1.4.43 (per *U 382* WD)
Instructor 1. and 2.ULD 5/43–3/45; at BdU 3/45–5/45; 3.ULD 5/45–capitulation

JUNKER, HANNS-JOACHIM [567]
b. 19.8.1923, Wilhelmshaven
Class 1940; ObltzS 1.10.44
Officer trg 7/Basic Trg Est. Stralsund 10/40–12/40; aboard destroyer *Z 25* 12/40–5/41; Naval College Flensburg-Mürwik 5/41–9/41; 21st U-Flotilla 9/41–1/42; U-boat trg 1/42–8/42; WO *U 121* 8/42–9/42; WO *U 5* 10/42–11/42; WO *U 72* 12/42–3/43; *Baubelehrung* 3/43–4/43; 2WO *U 716* 4/43–2/44; 1WO *U 716* 2/44–8/44; U-Cdr's Course 8/44–11/44; 22nd U-Flotilla (supernumerary) 11/44–12/44; *Baubelehrung* Type XXIII 8.KLA for *U 2370* 12/44–mid 4/45 (U-Boat Archive per Junker; before *U 2370* was commissioned Bornkessel [113] and Junker exchanged boats)
Cdr *U 2332* mid 4/45–3.5.45

JUNKER, OTTOHEINRICH [568]
b. 12.7.1905, Freiburg, Breisgau
Class 1924; FKpt 1.6.43
Cdr *U 33* 25.7.36–28.10.38; Group Leader Torpedo Testing Branch 11/38–8/42; at BdU 8/42–11/42
Cdr *U 532* 11.11.42–capitulation
Detained; freed 5.2.48

JUST, PAUL [569]
b. 24.12.1915, Hamburg
Class 1936; Kplt 1.8.43
Officer trg 4/36–30.9.38, inc. trg ship *Schlesien* winter 1936–37; seconded to Luftwaffe 10/38–12/40, inc. Aircraft Weapons School Bug/Rügen 1.10.38; observer

1./Küstenfliegergruppe 306 9/39–7/40; *Küstenfliegergruppe 806/Luftflotte 3* Nantes and Caen 7/40–12/40; awarded *Deutsches Kreuz* in Gold; U-boat trg, WO learner and *Baubelehrung* 1/41–9/41; 1WO *U 156* 9/41–7/42; U-Cdr's Course 7/42–8/42
Acting Cdr *U 6* 8/42–9/42 (trg boat, 7th U-Flotilla, Pillau)
Cdr *U 151* 9/42–5/43
Baubelehrung 8.KLA 5/43–6/43
Cdr *U 546* 2.6.43–24.4.45
POW 24.4.45–12.3.46

JUSTI, FRIEDRICH [570]
b. 10.4.1919, Karlsruhe
Class 1937b; Kplt 1.1.45
2WO 3rd Torpedo-Boat Flotilla 5/41–5/43; U-boat trg 5/43–10/43; courses 3.ULD, 23rd and 24th U-Flotillas 10/43–1/44 (U-Cdr's Torpedo Course 60); *Baubelehrung* 7.KLA 1/44–2/44
Cdr *U 1170* 1.3.44–3.5.45

K

KAEDING, WALTER [571]
b. 14.9.1915, Berlin
Enlisted 1935; LtzS 1.10.44
U-boat trg 9/39–4/40; *Baubelehrung* U-Boats Bremen 4/40–5/40; No 2 and No 1 Boatswain *U 123* 5/40–5/42; ObStrm (Coxswain's) course, Helmsman's School Gdynia 5/42–11/42; UAA Plön, 11/42; ObStrm *U 123* 12/42–6/44; 2nd U-Flotilla (lecture tour) 6/44–8/44; U-Officers' torpedo course, Torpedo School Mürwik 8/44–10/44; flak and radar courses Naval Signals School Flensburg-Mürwik 10/44–12/44; U-Cdr pre-trg, 19th U-Flotilla 12/44–1/45
Acting Cdr *U 56* 9.1.45–5.2.45 (28.1.45–31.1.45 for voyage Pillau–Kiel)
Baubelehrung U-boats Germaniawerft Kiel, *Baubelehrung U 4713* 6.2.45–3.5.45 (*U 4713* was destroyed with demolition charges at Kiel 3.5.45 shortly before commissioning)
Knight's Cross 15.5.44 (214th KM, 117th U-boat holder)

KÄSELAU, ERICH [572]
b. 25.3.1922, Kiel
Class 1940/41; ObltzS 1.1.45
U-boat trg completed 12/42; 2WO *U 237* 1/43–5/43; 2WO *U 990* 7/43–5/44; U-Cdr's Course, 23rd U-Flotilla, 6/44–7/44; supernumerary Cdr *U 922* 7/44–10/44
Cdr *U 922* 21.10.44–3.5.45

KAISER, HANS-DIETRICH [573]
b. 6.10.1921, Schwarzkollm, Silesia
Entry IV/1940; ObltzS (R) 1.3.44
2WO *U 267* 7/42–9/43; 1WO *U 267*, 9/43–7/44; U-Cdr's Course 7/44–9/44; *Baubelehrung* 8.KLA 9/44–10/44
Cdr *U 2338*, 9.10.44–4.5.45
Lost 4.5.45 Baltic, ENE of Frederica

KAISER, HERMANN [574]
b. 9.3.1907, Berlin
Class 1925; Obstlt (Luftwaffe) 1.8.42, FKpt seniority 1.11.43
Flight Leader *1./Küstenfliegergruppe 706* 10/38–6/40; 1a *Küstenfliegergruppe* Norderney 6/40–12/40; ADC *IX. Fliegerkorps* 12/40–2/42; Group Cdr *Seefliegergruppe* Athens 2/42–10/42 and Naval Trg Group Parow 10/42–8/43; Luftwaffe Liaison Officer Fleet Command 8/43–1/44; U-boat trg 1/44–5/44; courses and *Baubelehrung* Type XXI 6/44–9/44
Cdr *U 3002* 25.9.44–2.5.45

KAISER, KARL-ERNST [575]
b. 21.4.1920, Hannover-Waldheim
Class 1938; ObltzS 1.4.43
U-boat trg completed 7/41; 2WO and 1WO *U 555* 7/41–1/42; *Baubelehrung* 1/42–2/42; 1WO *U 608*, 2/42–4/43; U-Cdr's Course, 24th U-Flotilla 4/43–5/43; *Baubelehrung* 8.KLA 5/43–6/43
Cdr *U 986* 1.7.43–17.4.44
Lost 17.4.44 SW of Ireland

KALLIPKE, FRITZ [576]
b. 28.11.1909, Preussisch-Holland, East Prussia
Entry XI/1937; ObltzS (R) 1.9.43

VP-Cdr 16th VP-Boat Flotilla 7/41–2/43; U-boat trg 3/43–10/43; *Baubelehrung* 10/43–11/43
Cdr *U 397* 20.11.43–16.7.44
Baubelehrung Type XXI 8.KLA 7/44–10/44
Cdr *U 2516* 24.10.44–9.4.45
Cdr *U 2529* 15.4.45–capitulation (U-Boat Archive per Kallipke)

KALS, ERNST [577]
b. 2.8.1905, Glauchau, Saxony
Class 1924; KptzS 1.9.44
No 1 Gunnery and Midshipmen's Trg Officer light cruiser *Leipzig*, 4/39–1/40; instructor Naval Gunnery School Kiel-Wik 1/40–8/40; Naval Liaison Officer Army High Command 16 8/40–10/40; U-boat trg 10/40–2/41; U-Cdr sea trg *U 37* 2/41–3/41; U-Cdr's Torpedo Course, 24th U-Flotilla 3/41–4/41; *Baubelehrung* KLA U-Boats North Sea, 4/41–6/41
Cdr *U 130* 11.6.41 to 1.1.43 (per P/F) or 6.2.43 (per WASt)
CO 2nd U-Flotilla 2.1.43–capitulation, inc. CO U-boat base Lorient, CO Naval Escort Group Lorient and from 11/44 additionally Chief of Staff to Naval Commander Lorient (severely injured by landmine explosion 11/44)
Detained 10.5.45–20.1.48
Knight's Cross 1.9.42 (124th KM, 62nd U-boat holder)

VON KAMEKE, HORST-TESSEN [578]
b. 21.2.1916, Kiel
Class 1935; Kplt 1.11.42
Heavy cruiser *Admiral Hipper* 4/39–10/40; U-boat trg 10/40–3/41; *Baubelehrung* 3/41–7/41; 1WO *U 116* 7/41–9/42; 1WO *U 84* 9/42–12/42; U-Cdr's Course, 24th U-Flotilla 12/42–1/43
Cdr *UD 5* 13.1.43–22.2.43 (per WASt and U-Boat Archive per Scheltz [1073], his successor as Cdr)
Details not available 23.2.43–14.4.43 (but Cdr *UD 5* 13.1.43–14.4.43 per P/F)
Cdr *U 119* 15.4.43 or 16.4.43 (date when relieved Zech [1392] per *U 119* WD) to 24.6.43
Lost 24.6.43 NW of Cape Ortegal

KANDLER, HANS-ALBRECHT [579]
b. 31.10.1917, Jena
Class 1937a; ObltzS 1.9.41
1WO R-boat depot ship *Brommy* 4/39–10/39; Cdr *R 27* 12/39–9/41; U-boat trg 9/41–3/42; 1WO *U 565* 4/42–8/42; U-Cdr's Course, 24th U-Flotilla 8/42–9/42; *Baubelehrung* 9/42–10/42
Cdr *U 386* 10.10.42 to 9.6.43 or 10.6.43 (per *U 386* WD, and see Albrecht [8])
6th U-Flotilla 6/43–9/43
Cdr *U 653* 1.10.43–15.3.44
Lost 15.3.44 North Atlantic

KANDZIOR, HELMUT [580]
b. 25.9.1919, Krumhübel, Riesengebirge
Class 1938; ObltzS 1.4.43
U-boat trg completed 7/41; *Baubelehrung* 7/41–8/41; 2WO *U 333* 8/41–10/42, inc. acting Cdr 6.10.42–9.10.42; 1WO *U 333* 10/42–2/43; U-Cdr's Course, 24th U-Flotilla 2/43–4/43 (U-Cdr's Torpedo Course 43); *Baubelehrung* 7.KLA 4/43–5/43
Cdr *U 743* 15.5.43–9.9.44
Lost 9.9.44 NW of Ireland

KAPITZKY, RALPH [581]
b. 28.6.1916, Dresden
Class 1935; Kplt 1.6.42
Seconded to Luftwaffe 10/37–12/40, inc. IIa *Küstenfliegergruppe 806*; U-boat trg 1/41–6/41; 1WO *U 93* 6/41–11/41, inc. acting Cdr *U 93* 8/41–9/41
U-Cdr's Course 12/41–1/42; 2.UAA and *Baubelehrung* 8.KLA 1/42–3/42
Cdr *U 615* 26.3.42–6.8.43

Lost 6.8.43 Caribbean Sea, SE of Curaçao
(Translator's note: Eulogised by the Trinidadian naval historian Kelshall—see *The Caribbean U-Boat War*, USNIP/Airlife Books—as 'the bravest of all the U-boat commanders'. His boat being unable to dive following an aerial attack at dawn on 6.8.43, Kapitzky, mortally wounded, had all the flak ammunition piled around the gun platform and ordered a fight to the finish. When *U 615* eventually sank early on 7.8.43, taking the commander and two crewmen with it, under Kapitsky's direction his gunners had come under attack by aircraft on nine occasions. Little further damage had been sustained by the boat, but one of the aircraft had been shot down and two others and a small airship seriously damaged.)

KARPF, HANS [582]
b. 14.5.1916, Saarbrücken
Class 1935; Kplt 1.11.42, posthumously KKpt seniority 1.4.43
Platoon Officer battleship *Gneisenau* 3/39–8/40; Group Officer Kriegsmarine Depot Calais 8/40–10/40; U-boat trg 10/40–3/41; *Baubelehrung* 3/41–4/41; 1WO *U 566* 4/41–10/41; U-Cdr's Course, 24th U-Flotilla, 11/41
Cdr *U 10* 30.11.41–22.6.42
Baubelehrung 8.KLA 6/42–7/42
Cdr *U 632* 23.7.42–6.4.43
Lost 6.4.43 SW of Ireland

KASCH, LORENZ [583]
b. 20.8.1914, Hamburg
Class 1933; Kplt 1.12.40
Gunnery Officer merchant raider *Atlantis* (*Schiff 16*) 12/39–1/42; Station Command North Sea 1/42–3/42; U-boat trg 3/42–8/42; U-Cdr sea trg *U 107* 8/42–11/42, inc. period as acting Cdr *U 333* 9.10.42–22.11.42 (per *U 333* WD); U-Cdr's Course, 2.UAA and 24th U-Flotilla 11/42–1/43; *Baubelehrung* 8.KLA 1/43–3/43
Cdr *U 540* 10.3.43–17.10.43
Lost 17.10.43 E of Cape Farewell

KASCHKE, HERBERT [584]
b. 9.9.1911, Hamburg
Entry XI/1939; ObltzS (R) 1.5.44
WO and VP-Cdr 12th VP-Boat Flotilla 1/40–3/42; 1/NCO Trg Div. 3/42–6/42; WO 12th Minesweeping Flotilla 6/42–7/42; WO 11th VP-Boat Flotilla 7/42–2/43; U-boat trg 2/43–7/43; WO 27th U-Flotilla 7/43–8/43; U-Cdr's Course, 24th U-Flotilla 8/43–9/43 (U-Cdr's Torpedo Course 54)
Cdr *U 746* 16.9.43–4.1.44
Details not available 1/44–3/44; 1WO U-boat depot ship *Saar* 4/44–capitulation

KASPAREK, WALTER [585]
b. 13.12.1921, Nuremberg
Class XII/1939; ObltzS 1.12.43
Officer and U-boat trg 12/39–3/42; 5th U-Flotilla and *Baubelehrung* 1.KLA 3/42–6/42; 1WO *U 466* 6/42–8/43; courses 3rd U-Flotilla (supernumerary), 3.ULD and 23rd U-Flotilla 8/43–3/44; U-Cdr sea trg *U 143* 3/44–5/44
Cdr *U 143* 30.5.44–capitulation

KAUFMANN, WOLFGANG [586]
b. 23.6.1912, Würzburg
Class 1933; Kplt 1.12.40
Gunnery Technical and No 2 Gunnery Officer light cruiser *Leipzig* until 9/39; U-boat trg 9/39–4/40; WO *U 7* 4/40–6/40
Cdr *U 9* 11.6.40–20.10.40
Cdr *U 19* 21.10.40–8.11.40
Kplt on Staff 2nd U-Flotilla 11/40–1/41; *Baubelehrung* 1/41–3/41
Cdr *U 79* 13.3.41–23.12.41
POW 23.12.41–20.6.47

KEERL, HANS [587]
b. 5.1.1921, Freiburg
Entry IX/1939; Kplt 1.11.44
2WO *U 598* 12/41–2/43; 1WO *U 598* 2/43–4/43; U-Cdr's Course and *Baubelehrung* 5/43–8/43 (U-Cdr's Torpedo Course 49)
Cdr *U 291* 4.8.43–30.9.43 (Stege [1217] commanded *U 291* from 1.10.43 per his P/F and U-Boat Archive per Stege). Presumably Keerl would then have taken over *U 80* straightaway. See Isermeyer [534].)
Cdr *U 80* 1.10.43–28.11.44
Lost 28.11.44 Baltic Sea, W of Pillau

KELBLING, GERD [588]
b. 12.6.1915, Salzbrunn, Silesia
Class 1934; Kplt 1.9.41, seniority to 1.4.41
Cdr *M 89*, 4th Minesweeping Flotilla 11/39–7/40; Cdr *M 6*, 2nd Minesweeping Flotilla 8/40–1/41; U-boat trg 1/41–6/41; U-Cdr's Course, 24th U-Flotilla 6/41–8/41; U-Cdr sea trg *U 557* 8/41–9/41; *Baubelehrung* 8.KLA 10/41
Cdr *U 593* 23.10.41–13.12.43
POW 13.12.43–20.9.47
Knight's Cross 19.8.43 (182nd KM, 97th U-boat holder)

KELL, WALTER [589]
b. 4.12.1913, Altenwald, Saarland
Class 1933; Kplt 1.4.41
Seconded to Luftwaffe 10/35–12/39 inc. *Bordfliegerstaffel 1./196* aboard heavy cruiser *Deutschland* 8/39–12/39; U-boat trg 12/39–3/40; WO U-School Flotilla 3/40–4/40; 1.UAA and 1st U-Trg Flotilla 4/40–9/40, inc. period acting Cdr *U 8* 10.6.40–6.7.40
Cdr *U 8* 13.9.40–17.12.40
1st U-Flotilla 12/40–2/41; *Baubelehrung* 2/41–3/41
Cdr *U 204* 8.3.41–19.10.41
Lost 19.10.41 off Tangier

KELLER, GÜNTER [590]
b. 18.2.1917, Berlin
Class 1937a; Kplt 1.9.44
Seconded to Luftwaffe 10/39–7/43; U-boat trg 7/43–12/43; courses 23rd U-Flotilla, 3.ULD and 24th U-Flotilla 12/43–3/44; *Baubelehrung* 8.KLA 4/44–5/44
Cdr *U 683* 30.5.44–12.3.45
Missing English Channel 12.3.45 (Translator's note: Other Lists state sunk 12.3.45 with all hands in 49°52'N 05°52'W by HM ships *Loch Ruthven* and *Wild Goose*.)

KELLER, GÜNTHER [591]
b. 25.8.1921, Allmendshofen-Donaueschingen
Class XII/1939; ObltzS 1.12.43
Officer and U-boat trg 12/39–4/41; WO sea trg *U 372* 5/41–11/41; WO trg and courses 11/41–5/42; 3WO *U 336* 5/42–11/42; *Baubelehrung* 11/42–12/42; 1WO *U 277* 12/42–2/44; U-Cdr's Course 3/44–6/44
Cdr *U 981* 28.6.44–12.8.44
Baubelehrung 7.KLA 10/44–1/45
Cdr *U 3521* 14.1.45–2.5.45
Detained; freed 28.7.45

KELLER, SIEGFRIED [592]
b. 30.10.1917, Gotha
Class 1937a; ObltzS 1.9.1941
U-boat trg 10/39–3/40; Comp. Officer U-boat School 3/40–10/40; *Baubelehrung* 10/40–12/40; 2WO *U 109* 12/40–6/42; U-Cdr's Course details not recorded
Cdr *U 130* 7.2.43 (per WASt; see Kals [577])
Lost 12.3.43 W of Azores

VON KELLER, GRAF ALEXANDER [593]
b. 12.3.1919, Reval, Estonia
Class 1938; ObltzS 1.4.43

Officer trg 10/38–9/40; seconded to Luftwaffe 9/40–2/41; WO destroyer Z 7 *Hermann Schoemann* 2/41–12/41; Naval Trg Command Romania 12/41–7/42; U-boat trg 7/42–12/42; 1st U-Flotilla 12/42–1/43; 1WO *U 564* 1/43–6/43; U-Cdr's Course, 2.UAA and 24th U-Flotilla 7/43–10/43 (U-Cdr's Torpedo Course 53); Observation Officer 23rd U-Flotilla 10/43–11/43

Cdr *U 731* 1.12.43–15.5.44

Lost 15.5.44 Atlantic, off Tangier

KELLERSTRASS, GERHARD [594]

b. 8.7.1906, Duisburg-Ruhrort

Entry 1925; Kplt 1.10.44

Gunnery trg boats *Drache* 4/36–6/40 and *Edward* 6/40–1/41; 25th U-Flotilla, aboard fleet escort *F 10* 1/41–3/41; 27th U-Flotilla 3/41–6/43, inc. Cdr torpedo-boat *Löwe* 5/41–6/43; at BdU 7/43–12/43; U-boat handling and U-Cdr's Course, 23rd U-Flotilla and 3.ULD 12/43–3/44 (U-Cdr's Torpedo Course 65); *Baubelehrung* 1.KLA and 8.KLA 4/44–9/44, *Baubelehrung* Cdr for Type XIV U-tanker *U 491* (on which work was halted when boat was 80 per cent complete; contract rescinded 23.9.44)

1.UAA 9/44; U-Cdr 31st U-Flotilla 9/44–1/45; *Baubelehrung* and service with Staff, Adm. German Bight 1/45–capitulation

KELLING, HINRICH [595]

b. 20.12.1904, Büdelsdorf, Rendsburg

Enlisted rating 1925; Kplt 1.4.44

ObStrm *U 28* 10/38–3/40; courses and *Baubelehrung* 3/40–11/40

Cdr *U 150* 27.11.40–31.8.42

Course 24th U-Flotilla 9/42; U-Cdr 22nd U-Flotilla 10/42–1/43

Cdr *U 37* 4.1.43–19.11.43 and acting Cdr *U 423* 27.9.43–10/43

Cdr U-boat depot ship *Wilhelm Bauer* 11/43–4/45; 26th U-Flotilla 4/45–capitulation

KELLNER, ADOLF [596]

b. 28.4.1910, Schlewecke, Bad Harzburg

Class 1936; Kplt 1.9.42

Radio Technical Officer battleship *Gneisenau* 10/38–2/40; Platoon Officer 3/Basic Trg Est. Stralsund 3/40–4/40; Group Officer Naval College Mürwik 4/40–8/40; 2/Naval Signals Officer Fleet Command 8/40–10/40; Group Officer Naval College Mürwik 11/40–3/41; U-boat trg 4/41–10/41; 24th U-Flotilla 11/41; 1WO *U 592* 12/41–5/42; U-Cdr's Course and *Baubelehrung* 5/42–6/42

Cdr *U 357* 18.6.42–26.12.42

Lost 26.12.42 NW of Ireland

KENTRAT, EITEL-FRIEDRICH [597]

b. 11.9.1906, Stahlheim, Metz (when German province of Lorraine)

Class 1928; KKpt 1.1.43

Comp. CO 1/Basic Trg Est. Stralsund 5/38–9/39; *Baubelehrung* Kriegsmarine Depot Hamburg, merchant raider *Pinguin* 9/39; WO battleship *Scharnhorst* 9/39–10/39; U-boat trg 10/39–1/40; 1WO *U 25* 1/40–3/40; U-Cdr under instrn 1st U-Trg Flotilla 3/40–5/40

Cdr *U 8* 5.5.40–4.6.40, nominally to 12.9.40

Seriously wounded, hospitalised Esbjerg 6/40–9/40; *Baubelehrung* U-Boats North Sea 9/40–10/40

Cdr *U 74* 31.10.40–23.3.42

Adviser 2.Adm. U-boats 3/42–7/42; *Baubelehrung* KLA U-Boats North 7/42–9/42

Cdr *U 196* 11.9.42 to 21.9.44 (per P/F) or 30.9.44 (per WASt; see Striegler [1249])

German Naval Station (*Etappe*) Japan 22.9.44–27.3.45; Senior Officer naval base Kobe and Assistant to German Naval Attaché Tokyo 28.3.45–capitulation

Interned (by Japan) then detained (by Allied forces); freed 1.10.47

Knight's Cross 31.12.41 (98th KM, 42nd U-boat holder)

KESSLER, HORST [598]
b. 15.8.1914, Bromberg
Class 1934; Kplt 1.4.42
1WO *U 75* 12/40–7/41; U-Cdr's Course and *Baubelehrung* 7/41–11/41
Cdr *U 704* 18.11.41–4/43
Baubelehrung 8.KLA 5/43–6/43
Cdr *U 985* 24.6.43–19.4.44
CO Trg Command, 350 and 400/*K-Verband* Command 3/45–capitulation

VON KETELHODT, FREIHERR EBERHARD [599]
b. 30.1.1920, Berlin
Class X/1940; ObltzS 1.10.44
Officer and U-boat trg 10/40–11/42; 2WO *U 307* 11/42–1/44; 1WO *U 307* 1/44–5/44; U-Cdr's Course, 24th U-Flotilla, 5/44–7/44 (U-Cdr's Torpedo Course 72)
Cdr *U 712* 3.7.44–capitulation

KETELS, HANS-HEINRICH [600]
b. 11.3.1918, Heiligenhafen, Holstein
Class 1937a; Kplt 1.3.44
Platoon Leader 3/Reserve Naval Artillery Division 11/39–4/40; VP-Cdr Coastal Defence Group Norwegian West Coast 4/40–12/41; U-boat trg 1/42–5/42; WO *U 571* 5/42–11/42; U-Cdr's Course and *Baubelehrung* 8.KLA 12/42–3/43
Cdr *U 970* 25.3.43–7.6.44
Courses, various duties and *Baubelehrung* Type XXI 8.KLA 8/44–12/44
Cdr *U 2523* 26.12.44–28.1.45 (*U 2523* was badly damaged during an air raid while lying at Site 4, Blohm & Voss, Hamburg and was later decommissioned and scrapped.)
Cdr *U 3511* 29.1.45–31.3.45
Cdr *U 1162* 1.4.45–5.5.45
Detained; freed 12/45

KETELSEN, WOLFGANG [601]
b. 14.8.1911, Lüne/Lüneburg
Class 1935; Kplt 1.2.42
WO U-boat tender *Lech* 1/40–12/40; courses 3.ULD 12/40–6/41; WO torpedo retrieval boat *TF 157* 6/41–7/41; U-boat trg 7/41–1/42; 1WO *U 130* 2/42–9/42; U-Cdr's Course, 24th U-Flotilla 10/42–12/42
Cdr *UD 1* 15.12.42–17.5.43
M/S-Cdr 24th Minesweeping Flotilla 5/43–1/44 and 28th Minesweeping Flotilla 1/44–8/44; Staff 2/Adm. North Sea 10/44–4/45; Naval (Refugee) Reception Command, Husum 4/45–capitulation

KETTNER, PAUL-HUGO [602]
b. 20.7.1912, Alt-Rahlstedt
Class 1933; Kplt 1.4.41, posthumously KKpt seniority 1.8.42
U-boat trg and U-Cdr under instrn 10/39–10/40
Cdr *U 142* 14.10.40 to 20.10.41 or 12.10.41 (per *U 142* WD, and see Clausen [168])
Baubelehrung 1.KLA 10/41–11/41
Cdr *U 379* 29.11.41–9.8.42
Lost 9.8.42 SE of Cape Farewell

KIESEWETTER, WILHELM [603]
b. 28.10.1878, Leipzig
Class 1900; FKpt (R)(zV) 1.1.45
Navigation/First Officer, fishery and coastal protection boat *Ziethen* until 5/15; trg U-Boat School 6/15–9/15; trg U-Boat School Kiel, *U 2* and *U 1* 9/15; WO *U 45* (3rd U-Flotilla, Wilhelmshaven) 10/15–2/17; Cdr *UC 56* (1st U-Flotilla, Flanders) 3/17–5/18; interned in Spain 5/18–11/18; left naval service 21.1.1920; adviser (harbours/minefields) to Staff, Cdr Nordfriesland Coast 9/39–9/40; U-boat trg 9/40–11/40
Cdr *UC 1* 20.11.40–5/41
Group Leader U-Boat Acceptance Branch 6/41–6/44; Target Ship Officer, Trg Unit, Higher

Command of Torpedo Schools 6/44–10/44; Cdr gunnery trg ship *Hektor*, ex-merchant raider *Orion* 10/44–12/44; Naval High Command East 12/44–2/45; demobilised 28.2.45 (Translator's note: On relinquishing command of *UC 1* in 1941, Kiesewetter was, at 62 years of age, the oldest man to command a Second World War U-boat in commission.)

KIESSLING, ULRICH [604]
b. 17.2.1918, Hamburg
Entry X/1939; ObltzS (R) 1.1.44
WO 2nd Sperrbrecher Flotilla 9/41–11/41; WO 16th Minesweeping Flotilla 11/41–12/42; ADC and Cdr with 26th Minesweeping Flotilla 1/43–9/43; U-boat trg and U-Cdr's Course 9/43–7/44; WO 4th U-Flotilla 8/44–10/44; *Baubelehrung* 1.KLA 10/44–12/44
Cdr *U 1306* 20.12.44–5.5.45

KIETZ, SIEGFRIED [605]
b. 14.1.1917, Kassel
Entry V/1937; ObltzS 1.9.41
WO 2nd Minesweeping Flotilla 4/39–12/40; WO 5th Minesweeping Flotilla 12/40–9/41; U-boat trg 9/41–3/42; WO sea trg 26th U-Flotilla 3/42–6/42; 2WO *U 130* 6/42–1/43; U-Cdr's Course, 2.UAA and 26th U-Flotilla 1/43–2/43
Cdr *U 126* 1.3.43–3.7.43
Lost 3.7.43 NW of Cape Ortegal

KIMMELMANN, WALTER [606]
b. 23.8.1922; Bruck a.d. Leitha, Lower Austria
Class X/1940; ObltzS 1.10.44
Officer trg 10/40–8/42, inc. WO sea trg *U 552* 8/41–2/42; 2WO *U 431* 8/42–7/43; 1WO *U 431* 8/43–9/43; U-Cdr's Course, 2.UAA and 24th U-Flotilla 9/43–11/43 (U-Cdr's Torpedo Course 57); instructor torpedo attack Torpedo Trg Unit 11/43–7/44
Cdr *U 139* 4.7.44–2.5.45

KINDELBACHER, ROBERT [607]
b. 18.5.1915, Augsburg
Class 1935; Kplt 1.4.42
Seconded to Luftwaffe 10/37–8/41; U-boat trg 9/41–12/41; 1WO *U 96* 1/42–5/42; U-Cdr's Course, 24th U-Flotilla 5/42–6/42; *Baubelehrung* 8.KLA,6/42
Cdr *U 627* 18.6.42–27.10.42
Lost 27.10.42 S of Iceland

KINZEL, MANFRED [608]
b. 27.3.1915, Waldheim
Class 1935; Kplt 1.8.42
Seconded to Luftwaffe 10/37–8/41; U-boat trg 9/41–12/41; 3rd U-Flotilla 12/41–2/42; 2WO *U 404* 2/42–5/42; U-Cdr's Course, 24th U-Flotilla 5/42–6/42; *Baubelehrung* 6/42
Cdr *U 338* 25.6.42–20.9.43
Lost 20.9.43 SW of Iceland

KLAPDOR, HEINRICH [609]
b. 6.7.1914, Westen, Düsseldorf
Entry 1936; ObltzS 1.9.43
Platoon Officer 1.UAA, 8/42–10/42; 1WO *U 9* 10/42–7/43; U-Cdr's Course 2.UAA and 24th U-Flotilla, 7/43–8/43 (U-Cdr's Torpedo Course 52)
Cdr *U 9* 16.9.43–20.8.44 (Per *U 9* WD, after Klapdor was injured by a bomb splinter at Feodosia on 31.3.44 1WO Wolf-Dietrich Dehrmann assumed command and sailed the boat that evening for Yalta and Sevastopol, berthing at the latter port early on 2.4.44 for urgent repairs to the port diesel. Landt-Hayen [691] took over the boat on 5.4.44. See also Petersen [919].)

1.UAA and *Baubelehrung* 8.KLA 9/44–2/45
Cdr *U 2538* 16.2.45–8.5.45

KLATT, HANS [610]
b. 2.6.1914, Kiel
Class 1935, Kplt 1.11.42
1WO *U 557* 2/41–10/41; U-Cdr's Course, 24th U-Flotilla 11/41–12/41; *Baubelehrung* 8.KLA 12/41–1/42
Cdr *U 606* 22.1.42–1.10.42. (Von der Esch [260] assumed temporary command of *U 606* on 14.9.42 and completed an Arctic patrol 14.9.42–26.9.42 when Klatt was hospitalised.)
11th U-Flotilla 10/42–12/42 and 2.Adm. U-Boats 12/42–1/43; Base Officer 3rd U-Flotilla La Rochelle 1/43–8/44; Comp. CO Regt *Zapp* 8/44–capitulation

KLAUS, HANS-JOACHIM [611]
b. 17.5.1918, Berlin-Charlottenburg
Class 1937a; Kplt 1.4.44
Platoon Leader 7/Basic Trg Est. Stralsund 9/39–6/40; U-boat trg 6/40–10/40; ADC 25th U-Flotilla 10/40–2/41; *Baubelehrung* 2/41–3/41; 1WO *U 560* 3/41–10/41; 1WO *U 566* 10/41–7/42; U-Cdr's Course 7/42–8/42; *Baubelehrung* 9/42–10/42
Cdr *U 340* 16.10.42–2.11.43
POW 2.11.43–18.9.47

KLEINSCHMIDT, WILHELM [612]
b. 27.1.1907, Oldenburg
Class 1933; Kplt 1.4.39
Torpedo Officer light cruiser *Nürnberg* until 4/40; U-boat trg 4/40–8/40; U-Cdr sea trg *U 124* 8/40–9/40; U-Cdr's Course, 24th U-Flotilla 9/40–10/40; *Baubelehrung* 11/40–12/40
Cdr *U 111* 19.12.40–4.10.41
Lost 4.10.41 SW of Tenerife

KLINGSPOR, LEONHARD [613]
b. 17.6.1917, Siegen, Westphalia
Class 1937b; Kplt 1.1.45
Trg, Aircraft Weapons School (Sea) Parow 12/39–5/40; observer *3./Küstenfliegergruppe 906*, Air–Sea Rescue Command, Norderney and Brest 5/40–12/40 and observer same unit 12/40–2/42; U-boat trg 3/42–8/42; WO *U 129* 9/42–5/43; U-Cdr's Course 6/43–8/43 (U-Cdr's Torpedo Course 50); *Baubelehrung* 6.KLA 8/43–9/43
Cdr *U 293* 8.9.43–capitulation, inc. period acting Cdr *U 1007* 3.7.44–7.7.44 (for change of base from Kristiansand-Marvik via Egersund and Haugesund to Bergen to discharge torpedoes and provisions and return via Stavanger to Kristiansand, where Hornkohl [515] resumed command of *U 1007* on 7.7.44 and sailed that day for Kiel, arriving on 9.7.44)
Detained; freed 12.5.48

KLOEVEKORN, FRIEDRICH [614]
b. 19.2.1918, Saarbrücken
Class 1937a; Kplt 1.6.44
WO U-boat depot ship *Erwin Wassner* 3/42–6/42; U-Cdr sea trg *U 84* 6/42–8/42 and WO 1st U-Flotilla 8/42–2/43; U-Cdr's Course, 2.UAA and 24th U-Flotilla 2/43–3/43; *Baubelehrung* 1.KLA 3/43–5/43
Cdr *U 471* 5.5.43–6.8.44
1.UAA 8/44–9/44
Baubelehrung Type XXI 6.KLA 10/44–12/44
Cdr *U 3012* 4.12.44–24.4.45; scheduled to take over *U 1101* from Dübler [220] but had not done so by time of capitulation

VON KLOT-HEYDENFELDT, HARRO [615]
b. 25.4.1911, Riga, Lithuania
Class 1931; Kplt 1.10.1939

U-boat trg and U-Cdr under instrn U-Boat School Kiel 12/36–5/37; variously to FdU, U-Flotilla *Saltzwedel* and 2.WO *U 26* 5/37–6/37; Platoon Officer 1/NCO Trg Div. 6/37–5/38, and per bulletin of 30.9.37 U-Flotilla *Weddingen*; WO U-Flotilla *Saltzwedel* on *U 36*, *U 29* and *U 34* 5/38–10/38; Cdr *U 4* (Trg Group of U-Boat School) 29.10.38–16.1.40
Cdr *U 20* 17.1.40–15.4.40
Baubelehrung, Group U-Boats Baltic 15.4.40–26.4.40
Cdr *U 102* 27.4.40–1.7.40
Lost 1.7.40 Bay of Biscay

KLUG, WERNER [616]
b. 15.1.1920, Stettin
Class 1939a; ObltzS 1.10.43
Officer trg 7/Basic Trg Est. Stralsund, 9/39–2/40, trg ship *Schlesien* 2/40–5/40; Naval and Torpedo School Mürwik 5/40–11/40; Harbour Cdr HQ Boulogne 12/40–1/41; WO sea trg *U 69* 2/41–4/41; U-boat courses 4/41–10/41; WO *U 552* 10/41–6/43; U-Cdr's Course 6/43–8/43 (U-Cdr's Torpedo Course 51); *Baubelehrung* 8/43–11/43
Cdr *U 794* 14.11.43–31.8.44
Courses and *Baubelehrung* 9/44–2/45
Cdr *U 1406* 8.2.45–7.5.45
Detained; freed 31.12.45

KLUSMEIER, EMIL [617]
b. 27.7.1912, Bochum
Entry (as rating) 1930; Kplt 1.4.45
ObStrm and WO on U-boats 10/37–9/40, inc. *U 5* 1938–39; Staff BdU Operations 10/40–12/43; specialised courses 1/44–4/44; U-Cdr sea trg *U 963* 5/44–7/44; *Baubelehrung* Type XXIII 8.KLA 7/44–10/44
Cdr *U 2340* 16.10.44–30.3.45
Cdr *U 2336* 1.4.45–capitulation
Detained; freed 7/45

KLUTH, GERHARD [618]
b. 31.8.1918, Dresden
Class 1937b; ObltzS 1.4.42
Trg and courses 3/39–7/40; minelayer *Roland* 7/40–7/42; U-boat trg 7/42–12/42; 1WO *U 91* 1/43–6/43; U-Cdr's Course, 24th U-Flotilla 6/43–8/43
Cdr *U 377* 3.8.43–15.1.44
Lost 15.1.44 North Atlantic

KNACKFUSS, ULRICH [619]
b. 18.6.1920, Wilhelmshaven
Class 1938; ObltzS 1.1.43
Officer and U-boat trg 10/38–5/41; WO *U 48* 5/41–12/41; *Baubelehrung* 12/41–1/42; WO *U 257* 1/42–2/43; U-Cdr's Course, 24th U-Flotilla and *Baubelehrung* 2/43–5/43 (U-Cdr's Torpedo Course 43)
Cdr *U 345* 4.5.43–23.12.43
Cdr *U 821* 1.1.44–10.6.44
Lost 10.6.44 Bay of Biscay, off Brest

KNECHT, JOACHIM [620]
b. 13.8.1918, Wittenberg
Class 1937b; Kplt 1.1.45
Light cruiser *Emden* 12/39–5/40; Staff BdU Operations 5/40–10/40, inc. period WO *U 137*; U-boat trg 11/40–4/41; *Baubelehrung* 4/41–5/41; 1WO *U 653* 5/41–7/42; U-Cdr's Course, 24th U-Flotilla 7/42–8/42
Cdr *U 46* 8/42–30.4.43
Comp. Officer 8.KLA UAA Neustadt and Plön 5/43–9/44
Cdr *U 748* 18.9.44–29.11.44
Baubelehrung Type XXI 6.KLA for *U 3036* (never commissioned) 30.11.44–4/45 and for *U 3059* (also never commissioned) 4/45–capitulation

KNEIP, ALBERT [621]
b. 9.7.1921, Blankenese, Hamburg
Class IX/1939; ObltzS 1.10.43

Officer and U-boat trg 9/39–10/41; *Baubelehrung* 10/41–11/41; 2WO *U 174* 11/41–12/41; 1WO *U 171* 1/42–10/42; *Baubelehrung* 11/42–1/43; 1WO *U 170* 1/43–12/43; U-Cdr's Course 1/44–3/44 (U-Cdr's Torpedo Course 64)
Cdr *U 1223* 3/44–28.4.45
Detained; freed 31.8.45

KNIEPER, BERNHARD [622]
b. 1.3.1911, Bremen
NCO (S) entry 1/1941; ObltzS (R) 1.3.44
Strm (S) netlayer *1* 1/41–12/41; netlayer *Rau VIII* 3/42–5/42; details not available 5/42–8/43; U-boat trg 8/43–2/44; courses 19th and 23rd U-Flotillas 2/44–7/44
Cdr *U 267* 7.7.44–5.5.45

KNIPPING, ERWIN [623]
b. 22.11.1910, Kiel
Entry 1934/39; ObltzS (R) 1.11.43, seniority from 1.9.43
WO 17th VP-Boat Flotilla 6/41–2/43; U-boat trg 3/43–9/43; 1/Radar Trg Branch and U-Cdr's Course, 24th U-Flotilla 9/43–11/43 (U-Cdr's Torpedo Course 58); *Baubelehrung* 6.KLA 11/43–1/44
Cdr *U 1271* 12.1.44–mid 4/45

KNOKE, HELMUTH [624]
b. 11.8.1906, Trier
Entry III/1941; ObltzS (R) 1.11.43
U-boat trg 3/42–9/42; WO *U 462* 9/42–6/43; courses 12th U-Flotilla, 2.UAA and 23rd U-Flotilla 6/43–11/43; *Baubelehrung* 5.KLA 11/43–12/43
Cdr *U 925* 30.12.43–18.9.44
Missing from 18.9.44 Iceland/Faroes area

KNOLLMANN, HELMUT [625]
b. 9.8.1918, Meinerzhagen, Bergisch Land
Class 1937a; Kplt 1.4.44
Comp. Officer 4/Basic Trg Est. Stralsund 8/39–9/39; seconded to Luftwaffe 10/39–6/43; U-boat trg 7/43–12/43; U-Cdr's Course, 3.ULD and 24th U-Flotilla 1/44–3/44 (U-Cdr's Torpedo Course 65); *Baubelehrung* 7.KLA 4/44–7/44
Cdr *U 1273* 7.7.44–17.2.45
Lost 17.2.45 Oslofjord, off Horton

KNORR, DIETRICH [626]
b. 13.2.1912, Dessau
Class 1931; Kplt 1.10.1939
WO *U 10* 1937 (1.11.37 per rankings list); WO *U 16* 1938–39; Cdr *U 53* 24.6.39–8/39
Cdr *U 51* 8/39 and 15.1.40–20.8.40
Lost 20.8.40 Bay of Biscay, W of Nantes

KOCH, HEINZ [627]
b. 10.7.1914, Erfde, Schleswig-Holstein
Entry IV/1939; ObltzS 1.3.43
Officer trg 4/39–4/40; 2/Harbour Defence Flotilla 4/40–11/40; U-boat trg 11/40–4/41; WO *U 331* 4/41–6/42; U-Cdr's Course, 24th U-Flotilla, 6/42–7/42; *Baubelehrung* 7/42–8/42
Cdr *U 304* 5.8.42–28.5.43
Lost 28.5.43 SE of Cape Farewell

KOCH, LEOPOLD [628]
b. 15.9.1918, Sohlbach, Siegerland
Class 1937b; ObltzS 1.4.42
Acting Cdr *U 258* 12/42–3/43 (patrol 10.1.43–4.3.43)
Cdr *U 382* 1.4.43–14.11.43 (per WASt; 15.11.43 per *U 382* WD)
Killed 20.4.45 land-mine explosion

KOCH, WALTER-BRUNO [629]
b. 5.6.1919, Memel
Class 1938; ObltzS 1.10.42
Officer trg 10/38–11/40; WO minelayer *Roland* 11/40; battleship *Gneisenau* 11/40–1/41; various courses and U-boat trg 1/41–12/41; WO 5th U-Flotilla 12/41–9/42; courses and *Baubelehrung* 9/42–1/43; WO *U 309* 1/43–4/43; WO *U 601* 4/43–2/44; U-Cdr's Course, 3.ULD and 23rd U-Flotilla 3/44–5/44; *Baubelehrung* 5/44–6/44
Cdr *U 1132* 24.6.44–4.5.45
Detained; released autumn 1945

KOCH, WALTER-ERNST [630]
b. 30.9.1919, place not recorded
Class 1938; ObltzS 1.6.43
Officer trg until 4/40; light cruiser *Köln* 5/40–10/40; U-boat trg 10/40–4/41; WO *U 563* 4/41–7/42; course 24th U-Flotilla and 7.KLA 7/42–2/43; 1WO *U 737* 2/43–11/43; 3.ULD 11/43–12/43
Cdr *U 712* 15.12.43–2.7.44
Cdr *U 975* 17.7.44–23.4.45
Cdr *U 3530* 24.4.45–3.5.45 (U-Boat Archive per Koch)
3.ULD 5/45–capitulation

KOCK, UWE [631]
b. 25.11.1911, Kiel
Entry 1936; ObltzS (R) 1.4.45
WO and No 2 Radio Technical Officer trg ship *Schlesien* 1/40–7/40; WO/Cdr Mine Warfare Experimental Branch 7/40–8/43; U-boat trg 8/43–2/44; WO 19th U-Flotilla 2/44–5/44; U-Cdr's Course, 24th U-Flotilla 6/44–7/44 (U-Cdr's Torpedo Course 73)
Cdr *U 249* 17.7.44–capitulation

KÖHL, KURT [632]
b. 4.2.1912, Constance
Entry XI/1939; ObltzS (R)
2WO *U 562* 3/41–8/42; U-Cdr's Course, 24th U-Flotilla 8/42–9/42; *Baubelehrung* 8.KLA 10/42–12/42
Cdr *U 669* 16.12.42–7.9.43
Lost 7.9.43, NW of Cape Ortegal

KÖHLER, OTTO [633]
b. 17.11.1909, Dresden
Class 1931; KKpt 1.10.43
WO and Navigation Officer light cruiser *Königsberg* 2/38–3/40; M/S-Cdr 3rd Minesweeping Flotilla 3/40–3/41; U-boat trg 4/41–7/41; *Baubelehrung* 8/41–9/41
Cdr *U 377* 2.10.41–2.8.43
Adviser Torpedo Experimental Branch, Eckernförde 7/43–8/43; Head of Trg Est., Torpedo Arsenal East 8/43–capitulation

KÖHNTOPP, WALTER [634]
b. 19.4.1911, Marienthal
Entry 1/1937; Kplt 1.10.43
WO U-boat tender *Isar* 6/39–7/40; 3rd VP-Boat Flotilla 7/40–2/41; CO 59th VP-Boat Flotilla 2/41–6/41; U-boat trg 6/41–11/41; WO *U 77* 12/41–4/42; 29th U-Flotilla and course 24th U-Flotilla 4/42–6/42
Cdr *U 14* 1.7.42–20.7.43
Baubelehrung 8.KLA 7/43–9/43
Cdr *U 995* 16.9.43–9.10.44
13th U-Flotilla 10/44–capitulation

KÖLLE, WALTHER [635]
b. 3.8.1907, Ulm
Class 1926; FKpt 1.3.45
Heavy cruiser *Admiral Graf Spee* until 8/39; Comp. CO Naval College Mürwik 9/39–8/40; Senior Officer naval base Flushing 9/40–10/40; U-boat trg 11/40–7/41; *Baubelehrung* 7/41–8/41
Cdr *U 154* 2.8.41–30.9.42 (per WASt; relieved by Schuch [1139] 7.10.42 per *U 154* WD)

Cdr Section 1/Naval College Mürwik 10/42–8/43; Special Commando (Occupation of Genoa) 9/43–11/43; advance guard Naval College Schleswig 12/43; 1st Officer proposed merchant raider *Hansa* 1/44–9/44; OKW/Staff of Wehrmacht Command/Organisational 10/44–capitulation
Detained; freed 14.6.45

KÖLZER, KARL [636]
b. 13.3.1912, Opladen
Rating entry 1931; Kplt 1.4.45, seniority 1.1.45
ObStrm *U 21* 1939; ObStrm *U 101* 1940–41
Cdr *U 2* 10/41–15.5.42
Course, 24th U-Flotilla 6/42–7/42; ADC 21st U-Flotilla 7/42–8/42; instructor 1.ULD 8/42–6/43; *Baubelehrung* 8.KLA 6/43–8/43
Cdr *U 1221* 11.8.43–19.1.44
Trg Officer 1.UAA 2/44–4/44, instructor 3.ULD 4/44–capitulation

KÖLZER, KURT [637]
b. 14.3.1910, Gelsenkirchen
Class 1929; KKpt 1.4.43
Cdr *U 603* 2.1.42–12.9.42 (Kölzer was hospitalised 10.9.42; nothing further known)

KÖNENKAMP, JÜRGEN [638]
b. 14.8.1913, Danzig
Entry VIII/1932; Kplt 1.4.40
Trg ship *Schlesien* 5/38–3/40; U-boat trg 4/40–9/40
Cdr *U 14* 30.9.40–19.5.41
Baubelehrung 6/41–7/41
Cdr *U 375* 19.7.41–30.7.43
Lost 30.7.43 NW of Malta

KÖNIG, ALOIS [639]
b. 5.7.1920, Brochterbeck, Osnabrück
Class IX/1939; ObltzS 1.10.43

1WO *U 410* 2/42–4/43; U-Cdr's Course, 2.UAA and 24th U-Flotilla 4/43–5/43 (U-Cdr's Torpedo Course 47)
Cdr *U 6* 6/43–16.4.44
Instructor 1.ULD 5/44–11/44
Lost 28.11.44 on *U 80* (see Keerl [587])

KÖNIG, GOTTFRIED [640]
b. 24.10.1921, Bayreuth
Class XII/1939; ObltzS 1.12.43
Officer and U-boat trg 12/39–5/41; WO sea trg *U 43* 5/41–10/41; courses 10/41–3/42; *Baubelehrung* for *U 181* 3/42–5/42; 2WO *U 181* 5/42–2/43; 1WO *U 181* 2/43–1/44; U-Cdr's Course and *Baubelehrung* 1/44–5/44
Cdr *U 316* 5.5.44–2.5.45 (see Stuckmann [1252])
Detained; freed 7/45

KÖNIG, KLAUS-DIETRICH [641]
b. 14.11.1915, Kiel
Class 1937b; ObltzS 1.4.42
U-boat trg 10/40–3/41; 1WO *U B* 3/41–8/41; 1WO *UD 5* 11/41–1/43 (acting Cdr 16.12.42–9.1.43); U-Cdr's Course, 2.UAA and 24th U-Flotilla 1/43–3/43 (U-Cdr's Torpedo Course 42); *Baubelehrung* 8.KLA 3/43–4/43
Cdr *U 972* 8.4.43–15.12.43 (last radio signal)
Missing North Atlantic from 1/44

KÖNIG, LOTHAR [642]
b. 14.3.1921, Königsberg
Class XII/1939; ObltzS 1.12.43
U-boat trg completed 1/42; 2WO *U 440* 1/42–1/43; WO 1st U-Flotilla 2/43–7/43; U-Cdr's Course, 24th U-Flotilla 7/43–8/43 (U-Cdr's Torpedo Course 52); *Baubelehrung* 1.KLA 8/43–10/43
Cdr *U 237* 8.10.43–9/44
Cdr 23rd U-Flotilla 9/44–3/45; Comp. Officer 3.ULD 3/34–capitulation

KÖPKE, KLAUS [643]
b. 5.1.1915, Hannover
Class 1935; Kplt 1.7.42
Command Relay/Secretarial Officer heavy cruiser *Admiral Hipper* 4/39–4/40; U-boat trg 10/40–3/41; *Baubelehrung* 3/41–5/41; 1WO *U 569* 5/41–12/41; U-Cdr's Course and *Baubelehrung* 8th U-Flotilla and 6.KLA 12/41–2/42
Cdr *U 259* 18.2.42–15.11.42
Lost 15.11.42 Mediterranean, N of Algiers

KÖPPE, HELMUT [644]
b. 1.4.1909, Schleuningen
Class 1933; Kplt 1.10.1939, posthumously KKpt seniority 1.7.43
Div. Officer battleship *Gneisenau* 5/38–6/41; U-boat trg 7/41–10/41; U-Cdr's Course, 26th U-Flotilla 10/41–12/41; U-Cdr sea trg *U 751* 12/41–2/42; *Baubelehrung* 8.KLA 2/42–3/42
Cdr *U 613* 12.3.42–23.7.43
Lost 23.7.43 S of Azores

KÖRNER, WILLY-RODERICH [645]
b. 26.12.1914, Berlin-Wilmersdorf
Class 1935; Kplt 1.8.42
ADC and Radio Technical Officer Danube Flotilla 12/38–10/39; Flag Lt, Staff C-in-C Torpedo-Boats 12/39–10/40; U-boat trg 10/40–4/41; U-Cdr's Course, 24th U-Flotilla 4/41–5/41
Cdr *U 120* 20.5.41–24.2.42
Baubelehrung 3.KLA 2/42–5/42
Cdr *U 301* 9.5.42–21.1.43
Lost 21.1.43 Mediterranean, W of Bonifacio

KÖSTER, HELMUT [646]
b. 25.4.1914, Geestemünde
Class 1934; Kplt 1.12.41
Seconded to Luftwaffe 10/36–11/39; ADC and WO 6th Torpedo-Boat Flotilla 11/39–5/40; 1WO torpedo-boat *Leopard* 6/40–10/40; U-boat trg 10/40–4/41; U-Cdr's and various courses 5/41–8/41
Cdr *U 72* 9/41–1.12.41
U-Cdr (supernumerary WO) sea trg *U 567* 12.12.41–21.12.41
Lost 21.12.41 on board *U 567*

KOITSCHKA, SIEGFRIED [647]
b. 6.8.1917, Siebitz, Bautzen
Class 1937a; Kplt 1.6.44
Trg heavy cruiser *Admiral Hipper* 4/39–9/39; ADC 6/Basic Trg Est. Stralsund 9/39–6/40; U-boat trg 6/40–11/40; *Baubelehrung* U-Boats North Sea 11/40–12/40; 2WO *U 552* 12/40–12/41; U-Cdr's Torpedo Course, 26th U-Flotilla 12/41–1/42
Cdr *U 7* 16.1.42–7.10.42
Cdr *U 616* 8.10.42 (per P/F) or 20.10.42 (per WASt) to 17.5.44
POW 17.5.44–1.6.46
Knight's Cross 27.1.44 (203rd KM, 109th U-boat holder)

KOLBUS, HANS [648]
b. 5.10.1919, Löhne, Westphalia
Class 1938; ObltzS 1.4.43
Seconded to Luftwaffe 9/40–1/41; U-boat trg 1/41–6/41; courses and *Baubelehrung* 7/41–1/42; 1WO *U 409* 1/42–11/42; U-Cdr's Course, 24th U-Flotilla and *Baubelehrung* 7.KLA 11/42–1/43
Cdr *U 421* 13.1.43–29.4.44
29th U-Flotilla (*U 596*) 4/44–7/44; Cdr *U 596*, 7/44–8.9.44
Cdr *U 407* 9.9.44–19.9.44
POW 19.9.44

KOOPMANN, HERMANN [649]
b. 4.2.1910, Hohenhorst, Pinneberg
NCO (R) entry 1/1940; ObltzS (R) 1.7.43

Strm and WO *Schiff 11* 1/40–7/40; WO auxiliary minelayer *Togo* 8/40–3/42; WO proposed merchant raider *Coronel* 3/42–3/43; seconded to Naval Cdr Caucasus 4/43–5/43; 9th VP-Boat Flotilla 6/43–8/43; U-boat trg 8/43–2/44; WO 19th U-Flotilla 2/44–5/44; course 3.ULD and 24th U-Flotilla 5/44–7/44 (U-Cdr's Torpedo Course 73)
Cdr *U 1171* 17.7.44–capitulation

KORFMANN, FRITZ-OTTO [650]
b. 24.4.1923, Witten, Ruhr
Class 1940; ObltzS 1.10.44
2nd VP-Boat Flotilla 12/40–4/41; Naval College Flensburg-Mürwik 4/41–9/41; WO sea trg *U 375* 9/41–4/42; courses 4/42–9/42; WO trg and *Baubelehrung* 10/42–2/43; 1WO *U 362* 2/43–6/44; U-Cdr's Course 6/44–9/44 (U-Cdr's Torpedo Course 75); U-Holding Camp Pillau and *Baubelehrung* Type XXIII 8.KLA 9/44–2/45
Cdr *U 2365* 2.3.45–2.5.45
Detained; freed 20.7.45

KORNDÖRFER, HUBERTUS [651]
b. 20.11.1919, Altona
Class X/1939; ObltzS 1.10.43
2WO *U 593* 10/41–1/43; 1WO *U 593* 1/43–7/43; U-Cdr's Course, 24th U-Flotilla 8/43–9/43 (U-Cdr's Torpedo Course 53)
Cdr *U 139* 7.9.43–27.12.43
Cdr *U 407* 7.1.44–8.9.44 (see Brüller [137])
Details not available 10/44–12/44; *Baubelehrung* Cdr for *U 3537* from 22.1.45 (but presumably only until 3/45, as boat never commissioned)
Detained; freed 4.6.45

KORTH, CLAUS [652]
b. 7.11.1911, Berlin
Class 1932; KKpt 1.1.44

U-boat trg 3/36–12/36; U-Flotilla *Saltzwedel* and U-Torpedo Officers' course Torpedo School Mürwik 12/36–1/37, inc. period WO *U 21*; 1WO *U 31* 1/37–11/37; gunnery course, Gunnery School Kiel-Wik 11/37–12/37; 1WO *U 31* 12/37–7/38; mining course Mine Warfare School Kiel-Wik 7/38–9/38; 2nd U-Flotilla *Saltzwedel* 9/38–11/38; *Baubelehrung* U-Boat Arsenal Kiel 11/38–12/38
Cdr *U 57* 29.12.38–4.6.40
1st U-Flotilla 6/40; *Baubelehrung* U-Boats Baltic 7/40
Cdr *U 93* 30.7.40–30.9.41
3/Adm. Staff Officer, 2/Adm. U-boats 10/41–5/42; No 1 Trg Officer 27th U-Flotilla 6/42–3/44; adviser Torpedo Experimental Branch North, Eckernförde 3/44–capitulation
Detained; freed 15.11.45
Knight's Cross 29.5.41 (74th KM, 32nd U-boat holder)

KOSBADT, HANS-KARL [653]
b. 15.12.1917, Warnemünde
Class 1937a; ObltzS 1.9.41
No 2 Torpedo Officer destroyer *Z 9 Wolfgang Zenker* 4/39–10/39; Comp. Officer 2/NCO Trg Div. 10/39–8/40; Basic Trg Depot (Kriegsmarine) Munsterlager and Kriegsmarine Depot Boulogne 8/40–10/40; U-boat trg 10/40–3/41; Platoon Officer 2.UAA 3/41–6/41; 1WO *U 94* 6/41–5/42; U-Cdr's Course, 24th U-Flotilla and *Baubelehrung* 5/42–6/42
Cdr *U 224* 20.6.42–13.1.43
Lost 13.1.43 Mediterranean, W of Algiers

KOSNICK, FRITZ [654]
b. 4.3.1911, Elbing
Entry 1936; ObltzS (R) 1.6.44
Coastal artillery duty 9/39–4/43; retrg Seaman Branch officer 4/43–10/43; U-boat trg 10/43–4/44; AGRU-Front 4/44–7/44; U-Cdr's Course,

3.ULD and 24th U-Flotilla 8/44–10/44; WO 13th U-Flotilla 11/44–2/45
Cdr *U 739* 2/45–capitulation

KOTTMANN, HERMANN [655]

b. 4.12.1915, Hannover; Class 1936; Kplt 1.4.43
No 3 Flak Gunnery Officer heavy cruiser *Admiral Graf Spee* 5/39–12/39; interned Uruguay 12/39–7/40, returned Germany; Station Command North Sea 7/40–8/40; *Schiff 11* 8/40–9/40; Kriegsmarine Depot Dunkirk 9/40–11/40; pre-commissioning trg, ships' company battleship *Tirpitz* 11/40–1/41; battleship *Tirpitz* 1/41–6/41; U-boat trg 6/41–11/41; WO 8th and 1st U-Flotillas 11/41–8/42; U-Cdr's Course, 24th U-Flotilla, 8/42–9/42
Cdr *U 203* 21.9.42–25.4.43
POW 25.4.43

KRANICH, FRANZ [656]

b. 29.8.1913, Ballenstedt, Harz
Enlisted rating VII/1933; Kplt 1.12.44
No 1 Boatswain destroyer *Z 10 Hans Lody* 1/39–10/40; WO minelayer *Brummer* 10/40–11/40; WO 12th Anti-Submarine Flotilla 11/40–6/41; UJ-Cdr 14th Anti-Submarine Flotilla 6/41–4/44; U-boat trg 4/44–10/44; WO and U-Cdr trg 19th and 5th U-Flotillas (*U 3525*), 10/44–4/45
Cdr *U 3525* 1.5.45–3.5.45

KRANKENHAGEN, DETLEV [657]

b. 3.7.1917, Danzig
Class 1936; Kplt 1.6.43
3WO destroyer *Z 11 Bernd von Arnim* 12/38–4/40; Naval Regiment *Berger* 4/40–8/40; WO 2nd Minesweeping Flotilla 9/40–2/41; M/S-Cdr 2nd Minesweeping Flotilla 3/41–7/42; U-boat trg 7/42–11/42; U-Cdr's Course, 24th U-Flotilla and 2.UAA 11/42–5/43; *Baubelehrung* 8.KLA 6/43–7/43

Cdr *U 549* 14.7.43–29.5.44
Lost 29.5.44 SW of Madeira

KRAUS, HANS-WERNER [658]

b. 1.7.1915, Beulwitz, Saalfeld
Class 1934; Kplt 1.11.41
Comp. Officer Coastal Artillery School Wilhelmshaven 3/38–10/39; U-boat trg 10/39–1/40; 1WO *U 47* 1/40–11/40; U-Cdr's Course, 24th U-Flotilla 11/40–1/41; *Baubelehrung* U-Boats Baltic 1/41–2/41
Cdr *U 83* 8.2.41 to 19.10.42 (per P/F) or 21.9.42 (per *U 83* WD, and see Wörisshoffer [1368])
29th U-Flotilla 20.10.42–1.11.42 (per P/F); *Baubelehrung* 6.KLA 11/42
Cdr *U 199* 28.11.42–31.7.43
POW 31.7.43–22.5.46
Knight's Cross 19.6.42 (114th KM, 54th U-boat holder)

KRECH, GÜNTHER [659]

b. 21.9.1914, Wilhelmshaven
Class 1933; Kplt 1.4.41
3./*Küstenfliegergruppe 506* 11/38–10/39, inc. course, Torpedo School Flensburg-Mürwik 2/39–3/39; U-boat trg 11/39–3/40; WO *U 5* 3/40–4/40; *Baubelehrung* U-Boats East 4/40–5/40; 1WO *U 100* 5/40–11/40; U-Cdr's Course, 24th U-Flotilla 11/40–1/41; *Baubelehrung* for *U 558* 1/41–2/41
Cdr *U 558* 20.2.41–20.7.43
POW 20.7.43
Knight's Cross 17.9.42 (126th KM, 64th U-boat holder)

KREGELIN, LUDO [660]

b. 20.10.1919, Mönkebude, Pomerania
Class 1938; ObltzS 1.4.43
U-boat trg, 2/41–6/41; 3rd U-Flotilla, 6/41–11/41; 1WO *U 432*, 11/41–10/42; U-Cdr's Course, 24th U-Flotilla 10/42–11/42

Cdr *U 60*, 7.12.42–15.2.44 (inc. period as acting Cdr *U 38* in 1943)
Furlough, and *Ortung* course (see Meckel [800]) 2/44–5/44
Acting Cdr *U 236* 30.5.44–4.6.44
Baubelehrung Type XXI 6.KLA 6/44–8/44
Cdr *U 3003* 22.8.44–4.4.45
4th Flotilla 4/45–capitulation
Detained; freed 8.8.45

KREMPL, ERICH [661]
b. 15.5.1921, Wels, Danube
Class IX/1939; ObltzS 1.10.43
Officer and U-boat trg 9/39–1/42; WO *U 108* 1/42–5/43; U-Cdr's Course, 2.UAA and 24th U-Flotilla 5/43–6/43 (U-Cdr's Torpedo Course 49)
Cdr *U 71* 1.7.43–7/43
Cdr *U 28* 7/43–1.12.43
Cdr *U 1162* 2.12.43–8.1.45
Cdr *U 548* 9.2.45–19.4.45
Lost 19.4.45 off US coast, E of Boston

KREMSER, HORST [662]
b. 5.9.1917, Neusalz a.d. Oder, Lower Silesia
Class 1936; Kplt 1.2.43
Trg Officer light cruiser *Emden* 10/38–10/39; Group Officer Naval College Flensburg-Mürwik 10/39–8/40; Kriegsmarine Depot Dunkirk 8/40–10/40; U-boat trg, WO and U-Cdr's Course 10/40–5/42 (U-Cdr's Torpedo Course 15.4.42–15.5.42); *Baubelehrung* 5/42–6/42
Cdr *U 383* 6.6.42–1.8.43
Lost 1.8.43 Bay of Biscay, W of Brest

KRETSCHMER, OTTO [663]
b. 1.5.1912, Heidau, Liegnitz
Class 1930; FKpt 1.9.44
U-boat trg 1/36–4/36; at FdU, also Comp. Officer 2/Comp. U-boat School 1.5.36–2.10.36; WO U-Flotilla *Saltzwedel* 3.10.36–18.10.36; *Baubelehrung* Germaniawerft Kiel 19.10.36–3.11.36; 1WO *U 35* 3.11.36–30.9.37, inc. period acting Cdr *U 35* 8/37 following death of Michahelles [824] on 30.7.37 and until relieved by Lott [754])
Cdr *U 23* 1.10.37 to 1.4.40 (per P/F) or 28.2.40 (per *U 23* WD, and see Beduhn [64])
Baubelehrung U-Boats East 2.4.40–17.4.40
Cdr *U 99* 18.4.40–17.3.41
POW 17.3.41–31.12.47
Knight's Cross 4.8.40 (23rd KM, 7th U-boat holder)
Oak Leaves 4.11.40 (6th WM, 2nd KM, 2nd U-boat holder)
Swords 26.12.41 (5th WM, 1st KM, 1st U-boat holder)

KRIEG, JOHANN-OTTO [664]
b. 14.3.1919, Somnitz, Riesengebirge
Class X/1937; ObltzS 1.4.42
2WO *U 81* 4/41–7/42; U-Cdr's Course 7/42–9/42
Cdr *U 142* 13.9.42–24.12.42
Cdr *U 81* 25.12.42–9.1.44
CO *K-Verband* Flotilla 361 3/44–7/44; Senior Officer Trg and Staff Officer *K-Verband* 7/44–capitulation
Knight's Cross 8.7.44 (*K-Verband*)

KRIEGSHAMMER, JÜRGEN [665]
b. 4.8.1922, Kolberg
Class X/1940; ObltzS 1.10.44
WO *U 286* 6/43–7/44; WO 11th U-Flotilla 8/44; U-Cdr's Course 9/44–11/44
Cdr *U 8* 25.11.44–31.3.45
Cdr *U 150* 1.4.45–capitulation

KRÖNING, ERNST [666]
b. 13.1.1905, Elbing
Class 1925; Kplt 1.10.39, posthumously KKpt seniority 1.3.42

M/S-Cdr 2nd Minesweeping Flotilla 10/38–3/41; U-boat trg 4/41–6/41; U-Cdr's Course, 24th U-Flotilla 6/41–8/41; *Baubelehrung* 8.KLA 8/41–9/41
Cdr *U 656* 17.9.41–1.3.42
Lost 1.3.42 Atlantic, S of Cape Race

KRONENBITTER, WILLY [667]
b. 28.8.1908, Freiburg, Breisgau
Enlisted rating 1928; Kplt 1.4.45
Flotilla Strm 3rd U-Flotilla 7/41–1/42; nautical instructor 2.ULD 1/42–5/43; U-boat trg 5/43–11/43 (U-Cdr's Torpedo Course 57); nautical instructor 2.ULD 11/43–7/44; courses and *Baubelehrung* Type XXI 7.KLA 7/44–3/45
Cdr *U 3527* 10.3.45–1.5.45

KRÜER, WERNER [668]
b. 23.11.1914, Bassum, Bremen
Date of entry not recorded; ObltzS (R) 1.6.43
U-boat trg 3/42–9/42; 2WO *U 591* 9/42–4/43; U-Cdr's Course, 2.UAA and 24th U-Flotilla 4/43–5/43 (U-Cdr's Torpedo Course 46)
Cdr *U 590* from shortly before 8.6.43 (WASt has 20.6.43, but this cannot be correct as on 8.6.43 Krüer had already relieved Müller-Edzards [850] and left St Nazaire in command of *U 590* on her last voyage) to 9.7.43
Lost 9.7.43 off Amazon Delta

KRÜGER, ERICH [669]
b. 21.4.1918, Modlin, Warsaw
Entry X/1939; Obltzs (R) 1.1.44
VP-Cdr Harbour Defence Flotilla Trondheim 5/40–2/43; U-boat trg 3/43–8/43; 1WO *U 382* 8/43–3/44; details not available 4/44–10/44; course 23rd U-Flotilla 10/44–11/44
Cdr *U 307* 2.12.44–29.4.45

KRÜGER, JÜRGEN [670]
b. 16.7.1918, Berlin
Class 1937a; ObltzS 1.9.41
U-boat trg 10/40–5/41; WO *U 141* 5/41–11/41
Cdr *U 141* 30.11.41–15.6.42
Baubelehrung 8.KLA 6/42–7/42
Cdr *U 631* 16.7.42–17.10.43
Lost 17.10.43 SE of Cape Farewell

KRUSCHKA, MAX [671]
b. 7.5.1919, Schleswig
Class 1937b; Kplt 1.1.45
Destroyer *Z 4 Richard Beitzen* 12/39–10/40; U-boat trg 10/40–3/41; 2WO *U 554* 3/41–6/41; 1WO *U 554* 6/41–11/41; *Baubelehrung* 12/41–1/42; 1WO *U 217* 1/42–10/42; U-Cdr's Course, 2.UAA and 24th U-Flotilla 11/42–12/42
Cdr *U 621* 2.12.42 (per WASt) or 4.12.42 (per *U 621* WD, and see Schünemann [1143]) to 7.5.44 or 15.5.44 (per *U 621* WD, and see Stuckmann [1252])
Group Officer Naval College Mürwik 5/44–capitulation

KÜHL, PETER [672]
b. 19.10.1922, Lunden, Dithmarschen
Class 1/1941; ObltzS 1.1.45
WO sea trg *U 552* 1942; 2WO *U 565* 8/43–12/43; 1WO *U 565* 12/43–3/44; U-Cdr's Course, 3.ULD and 24th U-Flotilla 4/44–7/44 (U-Cdr's Torpedo Course 75)
Cdr *U 57* 1.8.44–5/45

KÜHN, HERBERT [673]
b. 24.4.1919, Wuppertal-Vowinckel
Class IX/1939; ObltzS 1.10.43
U-boat trg 3/41–11/41; 2WO *U 331* 11/41–4/42; WO 29th U-Flotilla 4/42–2/43; 2WO *U 73* 2/43–5/43; 2WO *U 81* 5/43–8/43; 1WO *U 81* 8/43–11/43; course 3.ULD 11/43–1/44

Cdr *U 38* 1/44 (1.2.44 per WASt, but definitely erroneous) to 14.4.44
Cdr *U 708* 15.4.44–3.5.45

KÜHNE, JOHANNES [674]
b. 1.1.1922, Kotzschka, Elsterwerda, Brandenburg
Class X/1940; ObltzS 1.10.44
Naval cadet 18th VP-Boat Flotilla *VP 1805* 12/40–6/41; courses 6/41–9/41; FzS (junior midshipman) 20th VP-Boat Flotilla 9/41–1/42; U-boat trg 1/42–9/42; WO 5th U-Flotilla 9/42–10/42; *Baubelehrung* 10/42–11/42; 2WO *U 387* 11/42–10/43; 1WO *U 387* 10/43–8/44; U-Cdr's Course, 3.ULD and 23rd U-Flotilla 9/44–11/44; Cdr U-Holding Company 2, 21st U-Flotilla 11/44–12/44; *Baubelehrung* Type XXIII 12/44–4/45
Cdr *U 2371* 24.4.45–3.5.45 (date of commissioning uncertain)

KUGELBERG, RUDOLF [675]
b. 15.11.1917, Rostock
Entry XI/1939; ObltzS (R) 1.1.44
2WO *U 565* 4/41–8/42; U-Cdr's Course, 24th U-Flotilla 8/42–10/42; U-Cdr, 21st U-Flotilla 11/42–1/43
Cdr *U 21* 29.1.43–11.5.44
Instructor 1.ULD 5/44–capitulation

KUHLMANN, HANS-GÜNTHER [676]
b. 12.11.1913, Cologne-Sülz
Entry 1/1937; ObltzS 1.10.40
No 2 Torpedo Officer heavy cruiser *Blücher* 9/39–1/40; 3WO *U 37* 1/40–6/40; 2WO *U 37* 6/40–10/40; 1WO *U 37* 11/40–2/41; U-Cdr's Course, 24th U-Flotilla 2/41–3/41
Cdr *U 7* 30.3.41–16.6.41
Baubelehrung 6/41–7/41
Cdr *U 580* 24.7.41–11.11.41

5th U-Flotilla 11/41–1/42; *Baubelehrung* KLA U-North 1/42–3/42
Cdr *U 166* 23.3.42–1.8.42
Lost 1.8.42 Gulf of Mexico

KUHLMANN, JÜRGEN [677]
b. 3.3.1920, Weissenfels
Class 1938; ObltzS 1.1.43
WO destroyer *Z 4 Richard Beitzen* 11/41–5/43; U-boat trg 5/43–11/43; U-Cdr's Course, 24th U-Flotilla 12/43–2/44 (U-Cdr's Torpedo Course 61); *Baubelehrung* 7.KLA 2/44–4/44
Cdr *U 1172* 20.4.44–27.1.45
Lost 27.1.45 St George's Channel

KUHN, HANS-JOACHIM [678]
b. 7.4.1910, Neisse, Upper Silesia
Class 1931; KKpt 1.12.43
1WO heavy cruiser *Admiral Graf Spee* 8/39–12/39; interned 12/39–7/40; returned to Germany 7/40–12/40; Station Command North 12/40–1/41; Trg Officer and Comp. CO Naval Flak School No 1 2/41–9/42; Trg Officer Naval Gunnery School 10/42–5/43; U-boat trg 5/43–1/44; *Baubelehrung* 8.KLA 1/44–3/44
Cdr *U 1233* 22.3.44–14.4.45

KUHNKE, GÜNTER [679]
b. 7.9.1912, Elbing
Class 1931; KKpt 1.9.43
U-boat trg and various courses 1/36–8/36; 1WO *U 27* 8/36–6/38, inc. torpedo attack course for WOs 11/36; courses while at U-Flotilla *Saltzwedel* 6/38–10/38; Cdr *U 28* 28.10.38–31.8.39, inc. gunnery course for WOs at Naval Gunnery School Kiel-Wik 13.3.39–31.3.39
Cdr *U 28* 1.9.39 to 3.1.41 (per P/F) or only until 16.11.40 (per *U 28* WD, WASt and P/F of Guggenberger [393])
2nd U-Flotilla 1/41–2/41; *Baubelehrung* U-Boats North 2/41–3/41

Cdr *U 125* 3.3.41–15.12.41 (per P/F and *U 125* WD, and see Folkers [298])

8th U-Flotilla 12/41–1/42; CO 10th U-Flotilla Lorient 1/42–9/44, with period as acting Cdr *U 853* 24.8.44–15.10.44 (per P/F, transfer voyage Lorient–Flensburg; sailed 27.8.44, arrived 14.10.44)

CO 33rd U-Flotilla 10/44–5/45; U-base Flensburg until 6/45; adviser Staff, German Minesweeping Administration Schleswig-Holstein 23.7.45–15.4.46 when demobilised

Knight's Cross 19.9.40 (31st KM, 13th U-boat holder)

KUMMER, HEINZ [680]

b. 25.5.1915, Dresden

Class 1936; Kplt 1.4.43

1WO *U 754* 8/41–4/42; 1st U-Flotilla 4/42–5/42; U-Cdr's Course, 24th U-Flotilla 5/42–6/42; *Baubelehrung* 1.KLA 6/42–7/42

Cdr *U 467* 15.7.42–25.5.43

Lost 25.5.43 SE of Iceland

KUMMETAT, HEINZ [681]

b. 19.11.1918, Tilsit

Class 1937a; ObltzS 1.9.41

No 2 Radio Technical Officer light cruiser *Köln* 3/40–8/40; 2WO and Signals Officer minelayer *Skagerrak* 8/40–3/41; U-boat trg 3/41–3/42; 7th U-Flotilla 3/42–4/42; WO (supernumerary) *U 455* 4/42–6/42; 1WO *U 455* 7/42–11/42; U-Cdr's Course, 2.UAA and 24th U-Flotilla 11/42–12/42

Cdr *U 572* 16.12.42 (per WASt) or 18.12.42 (per *U 572* WD, and see Hirsacker [495]) to 3.8.43

Lost 3.8.43 NE of Trinidad

KUMMETZ, HANS-ERICH [682]

b, 19.8.1922, Berlin-Schöneberg

Class XII/1939; ObltzS 1.12.43

Officer trg 7/Basic Trg Est. Stralsund 12/39–3/40; sail trg ship *Horst Wessel* 3/40–6/40; light cruiser *Emden* 6/40–12/40; Naval College Mürwik 12/40–5/41; WO sea trg *U 79* 5/41–9/41; trg and WO course 9/41–8/42; *Baubelehrung* 8/42–9/42; 1WO *U 642* 10/42–7/43; U-Cdr's Course and *Baubelehrung* 7/43–10/43 (U-Cdr's Torpedo Course 54)

Cdr *U 235* 29.10.43–1.4.45

5th U-Flotilla 4/45–capitulation

KUNTZE, JÜRGEN [683]

b. 12.9.1917, Berlin

Class 1936; Kplt 1.3.43

Command Relay Officer light cruiser *Nürnberg* 8/39–2/41; Group Officer Naval College Flensburg-Mürwik 2/41–4/41; Trg Officer Naval Gunnery School 4/41–7/41; U-boat trg 7/41–12/41; WO *U 46* 1/42–6/42; U-Cdr's Course, 24th U-Flotilla 6/42–7/42; *Baubelehrung* 1.KLA 7/42–8/42

Cdr *U 227* 22.8.42–30.4.43

Lost 30.4.43 N of Faroes

KUPPISCH, HERBERT [684]

b. 10.12.1909, Hamburg Class 1933; Kplt 1.11.1939

U-Boat School 9/35–12/35; Comp. Officer U-Boat School 1/36–9/36; U-boat trg and courses 9/36–4/37; WO *U 2* 5/37; 2WO *U 29* 5/37; Comp. Officer II/NCO Trg Div. 6/37–10/37; WO *U 9* and *U 23* 10/37–1/39; *Baubelehrung* Deutsche Werke Kiel 1/39–2/39; Cdr *U 58* 4.2.39–31.8.39

Cdr *U 58* 1.9.39 to 30.6.40 (per P/F) or 1.7.40 (per *U 58* WD, and see Schonder [1119])

1st U-Flotilla 7/40; *Baubelehrung* U-Boats Baltic 7/40–8/40

Cdr *U 94* 10.8.40 to 27.8.41 (per P/F of his successor Ites [535]) or 29.8.41 (per *U 94* WD) or 21.9.41 (per Kuppisch P/F) (*U 94* sailed from St Nazaire under Ites on 2.9.41.)

3/Adm. Staff Officer, Staff BdU/Opns 9/41–6/42; 6/Adm. Staff Officer, Staff BdU/Opns 6/42–12/42; adviser OKM/SKL 12/42–6/43
Cdr *U 516* 24.6.43–30.6.43 (per P/F)
Cdr *U 847* 30.6.43 (per *U 847* WD, and see Metzler [816]) or 1.7.43 (per P/F) to 27.8.43
Lost 27.8.43 Sargasso Sea
Knight's Cross 14.5.41 (69th KM, 29th U-boat holder)

KURRER, HELLMUT [685]
b. 16.2.1916, Eisleben
Class 1935; Kplt 1.6.42, posthumously KKpt seniority 1.4.43
1WO and Div. Officer torpedo-boat *T 6* 4/40–10/40; U-boat trg 10/40–3/41; *Baubelehrung* 4/41–5/41; 1WO *U 128* 5/41–6/42; U-Cdr's Course and *Baubelehrung* 1.KLA 6/42–8/42
Cdr *U 189* 15.8.42–23.4.43
Lost 23.4.43 E of Cape Farewell

KUSCH, OSKAR-HEINZ [686]
b. 6.4.1918, Berlin
Class 1937a; ObltzS 1.9.41
Light cruiser *Emden* 4/39–3/40; courses and U-boat trg 4/40–9/40; Comp. Officer 2.ULD 9/40–6/41; 2WO *U 103* 6/41–7/42; course 24th U-Flotilla 7/42–8/42; 1WO *U 103* 8/42–2/43
Cdr *U 154* 8.2.43–21.1.44
Executed by firing squad 12.5.44 (Translator's note: Kusch was denounced by 1WO Abel [1] for defeatist talk in the wardroom, court-martialled and condemned to death. For a full account of this affair see Vause, *Wolf; U-Boat Commanders in World War II*, USNIP/Airlife Books.)

KUSCHER, FEDOR [687]
b. 19.1.1919, Trebus
Entry XII/1939; ObltzS (R) 1.1.44

WO 34th Minesweeping Flotilla 5/40–9/41; WO 13th VP-Boat Flotilla 12/41–5/42; WO 22nd Minesweeping Flotilla 5/42–2/43; U-boat trg U-Cdr's Course, *Baubelehrung* and various duties 3/43–2/44 (U-Cdr's Torpedo Course 58)
Cdr *U 1274* 1.3.44–7/44
Courses and *Baubelehrung* Type XXI 7.KLA 7/44–12/44
Cdr *U 3515* 14.12.44–capitulation

KUTSCHMANN, GÜNTER [688]
b. 21.1.1911, Magdeburg
Class 1929; Kplt 1.7.38, posthumously KKpt seniority 1.2.40
Cdr *U 5* 3.2.38–4.12.39
Cdr *U 54* 5.12.39–20.2.40
Missing 20.2.40 North Sea

KUTTKAT, MARTIN [689]
b. 18.1.1922, Königsberg
Entry VI/1940; ObltzS 1.10.44
U-boat trg 1/42–9/42; supernumerary WO (for sea trg) *U 468* 9/42–2/43; *Baubelehrung* 2/43–3/43; 1WO *U 740* 3/43–5/44; course 3.ULD and 23rd U-Flotilla 5/44–10/44
Cdr *U 429* 16.10.44–30.3.45

L

LAMBY, HERMANN [690]
b. 30.12.1913, Bentheim
Class 1936; Kplt 1.10.43
Platoon Officer 10/Basic Trg Est. Stralsund 4/39–10/39; ADC and M/S-Cdr 12th Minesweeping Flotilla 9/39–9/41; U-boat trg 9/41–2/42; 1st U-Flotilla 3/42–4/42; 1WO *U 754* 4/42–5/42; 1WO *U 202* 5/42; 1WO *U 584* 5/42–10/42; U-Cdr's Course, 2.UAA and 24th U-Flotilla 10/42–12/42
Cdr *U 437* 21.12.42–4.10.44
Baubelehrung Type XXI 6.KLA 11/44–2/45
Cdr *U 3029* 5.2.45–3.5.45

LANDT-HAYEN, MARTIN [691]
b. 3.11.1920, Flensburg
Entry 1939; ObltzS (R) 1.1.44
WO sea trg then WO 1st Sperrbrecher Flotilla 12/41–8/42; U-boat trg 1.ULD 8/42–5/43; 1WO *U 20* 5/43–12/43; courses and U-Cdr's Course, 1/44–3/44 (U-Cdr's Torpedo Course 63); acting Cdr *U 9* 5.4.44–6.4.44 (per *U 9* WD, 24-hour voyage Sevastopol–Constanza; see Klapdor [609] and Petersen [919])
Cdr *U 24* 7.4.44–7/44 (relinquished command to Petersen [919] per *U 24* WD)
Courses and *Baubelehrung* Type XXIII 8/44–1/45
Cdr *U 4705* 2.2.45–3.5.45
Detained; freed 15.9.45

LANGE, GEORG [692]
b. 12.10.1892, Preussisch-Stargard
Class 1911; KKpt (zV) 1.4.42
Div. Lt battleship *Ostfriesland* until 2/15; trg and courses 3/15–9/15; WO light cruiser *Elbing* 9/15–6/16; WO and Wireless Technical Officer light cruiser *Danzig* 6/16–5/17; trg U-Boat School 5/17–8/17; WO trg *UB 60* 9/17–2/18; trg and course Torpedo School 2/18–4/18; WO *U 117* 4/18–11/18 (Armistice); demobilised 27.1.21 as Kplt (R)
Oberkommando der Wehrmacht, OKM/M.Wa.Wi 6/40–3/41; course ULD 3/41–5/41
Cdr *UC 1* 5/41–14.10.41 and 17.11.41–28.3.42 (per U-Boat Archive, *UC 1* was decommissioned as fire-damaged 4.1.42 and scrapped that year; Lange remained commander until March 1942 for the purpose of completing the boat's business, but what he did from then until September 1942 is not recorded); *Baubelehrung* 9/42–11/42
Cdr *UF 2* 5.11.42–10/43
Naval Cdr North Dalmatia 10/43–11/43; Harbour Cdr Leros 11/43–12/43; Harbour Cdr Milos and acting Cdr Island 1/44–6/44; Harbour Cdr Split 8/44–9/44; OKW/Wehmacht Patrol Trg Div. 10/44–capitulation
Detained; freed 9/45

LANGE, GERHARD [693]
b. 22.5.1920, Danzig
Class 1937b; ObltzS 1.4.42
Courses, U-boat trg completed 8/41; *Baubelehrung* 8/41–9/41; 1WO *U 436* 9/41–7/42; U-Cdr's Course, 24th U-Flotilla 8/42–9/42; *Baubelehrung* 7.KLA 9/42–10/42
Cdr *U 418* 21.10.42–1.6.43
Lost 1.6.43 NW of Cape Ortegal

LANGE, HANS [694]
b. 29.5.1915, Vegesack
Class 1935; Kplt 1.9.42

Trg Branch 5th Destroyer Division 3/38–10/40; U-boat trg 11/40–4/41; U-Cdr's Course, 24th U-Flotilla 4/41–5/41
Cdr *U 61* 5.5.41–15.1.42
Baubelehrung 1/42–3/42
Cdr *U 261* 28.3.42–15.9.42
Lost 15.9.42 W of Shetlands

LANGE, HANS-GÜNTHER [695]
b. 28.9.1916, Hannover
Class IV/1937; Kplt 1.8.44
Practical sea trg fishery protection vessel *Elbe* 4/39–10/39; Comp. Officer 14/Basic Trg Est. Stralsund 10/39–4/40; 2WO and 1WO torpedo-boat *Jaguar* 4/40–9/41; U-boat trg 9/41–12/41; 1WO *U 431* 12/41–6/42; U-Cdr's Course, 24th U-Flotilla 7/42–8/42; *Baubelehrung* 8.KLA 8/42–9/42
Cdr *U 711* 26.9.42–4.5.45
Detained; freed 8/45
Knight's Cross 26.8.44 (250th KM, 127th U-boat holder)
Oak Leaves 29.4.45 (846th WM, 52nd KM, 29th U-boat holder)

LANGE, HARALD [696]
b. 23.12.1903, Hamburg
Date of entry not recorded; ObltzS (R)
WO *Sperrbrecher II* 9/39–11/39; WO 9th VP-Boat Flotilla 2/40–5/40; VP-Cdr 9th VP-Boat Flotilla 6/40–10/41; U-boat trg and *Baubelehrung* 11/41–6/42; 1WO *U 180* 7/42–7/43; U-Cdr's Course 8/43–9/43; acting Cdr *U 180* 10/43–7.11.43
Cdr *U 505* 8.11.43–4.6.44
POW 4.6.44–5/46

LANGE, HELMUT [697]
b. 31.8.1916, Tilsit
Class 1937a; ObltzS 1.9.41

WO 1st Minesweeping Flotilla 4/39–9/41; U-boat trg 9/41–3/42; 1WO *U 375* 3/42–10/42; U-Cdr's Course, 2.UAA and 24th U-Flotilla 10/42–11/42
Cdr *U 72* 20.11.42–14.12.43
Baubelehrung 1.KLA 12/43–2/44
Cdr *U 1053* 12.2.44–15.2.45
Lost 15.2.45 Norwegian Sea, off Bergen

LANGE, KARL-HEINZ [698]
b. 10.2.1918, Stralsund
Class 1937a; Kplt 1944
WO 12th Minesweeping Flotilla 12/39–12/40; R-Cdr 7th R-Boat Flotilla 12/40–9/41; 1WO *Weser* (7th R-Boat Flotilla) 9/41–3/42; acting First Officer *Wachschiff 1* (Guard Group East) 3/42–5/42; acting First Officer survey ship *Meteor* 6/42–7/42; WO 2nd Minesweeping Flotilla 7/42–1/43; M/S-Cdr 26th Minesweeping Flotilla 3/43–8/43; U-boat trg and U-Cdr under instrn 8/43–4/44; 7th U-Flotilla 4/44–7/44
Cdr *U 667* 10.7.44–25.8.44
Lost 25.8.44 Bay of Biscay, off La Rochelle

LANGE, KURT [699]
b. 12.8.1903, Magdeburg
Entry 1922; Kplt 1.2.42
VP-Cdr 9th VP-Boat Flotilla 9/39–9/41; U-boat trg, various duties, U-Cdr's Course and *Baubelehrung* 9/41–10/42
Cdr *U 530* 14.10.42–1/45
Nautical adviser AGRU-Front, also Harbour Cdr Hela 1/45–capitulation

LANGE, RICHARD [700]
b. 14.11.1912, Heligoland
Entry VII/1940; ObltzS (R) 1.3.44
WO 17th VP-Boat Flotilla, 7/40–1/42; 1/NCO Trg Div 1/42–3/42; acting Group Leader to Cdr Minefields Western Baltic 3/42–6/42; Group

Leader Coastal Defence Flotilla Western Baltic 6/42–2/43; U-boat trg and U-Cdr under instrn 3/43–9/43 (U-Cdr's Torpedo Course 58); courses and *Baubelehrung* 6.KLA 9/43–1/44
Cdr *U 773* 20.1.44–17.4.44
31st U-Flotilla 4/44–7/44; U-boat base Wilhelmshaven 8/44–2/45; remustered to Army 2/45–capitulation

LANGENBERG, BRUNO [701]

b. 10.11.1920, Werbeln, Saarlautern
Entry 1938; ObltzS (R) 1.4.43
U-boat trg and *Baubelehrung* 5/41–10/41; 2WO *U 377* 10/41–7/42; 1WO *U 377* 8/42–2/43; U-Cdr's Course and *Baubelehrung* 3/43–7/43 (U-Cdr's Torpedo Course 45)
Cdr *U 366* 16.7.43–5.3.44
Lost 5.3.44 Arctic Ocean, NW of Hammerfest

LANGFELD, ALBERT [702]

b. 28.1.1918, Regensburg
Class 1937a; ObltzS 1.9.41
U-boat trg completed 3/41; *Baubelehrung* 8.KLA 3/41–5/41; 1WO *U 571* 5/41–3/42; U-Cdr's Course, 2.UAA, 24th U-Flotilla and *Baubelehrung* 7.KLA 3/42–5/42
Cdr *U 444* 9.5.42–11.3.43
Lost 11.3.43 central North Atlantic

LASSEN, GEORG [703]

b. 12.5.1915, Berlin-Steglitz
Class 1935; KKpt 1.4.45
U-boat trg 4/39–8/39; 1WO *U 29* 8/39–1/41
Cdr *U 29* 24th U-Flotilla 3.1.41–14.9.41
Baubelehrung 6.KLA in Bremen 9/41–10/41
Cdr *U 160* 16.10.41 to 14.6.43 (per P/F) or 9.6.43 (per *U 160* WD, and see Pommer-Esche [935])
Comp. CO and Tactical Instructor 1.ULD 6/43–5/45; Cdr Work Battalion *Lassen* 5/45–8/45
Detained; freed 31.8.45

Knight's Cross 10.8.42 (119th KM, 57th U-boat holder)
Oak Leaves 7.3.43 (208th WM, 24th KM, 20th U-boat holder)

LAU, KURT [704]

b. 4.3.1922, Hamburg
Class XII/1939; ObltzS 1.12.43
Supplementary WO *U 117* 12/41–10/42; *Baubelehrung* 11/42–12/42; WO *U 953* 12/42–12/43; U-Cdr's Course 1/44–3/44 (U-Cdr's Torpedo Course 64)
Cdr *U 1197* 20.3.44–25.4.45

LAUBERT, HELMUT [705]

b. 5.4.1919, Kassel
Class 1937b; Kplt 1.1.45
Light cruiser *Nürnberg* 12/39–4/40; U-boat trg 4/40–10/40; Secretarial and Base Officer 2nd U-Flotilla 10/40–1/41; *Baubelehrung* 1/41–3/41; 2WO *U 125* 3/41–11/42; U-Cdr's Course 11/42–12/42
Cdr *U 38* 5.1.43–22.8.43
Group Officer 1.ULD 8/43–3/44 and hospitalised 2/44–3/44; Comp. CO 4.Comp/Section 1/1.ULD 4/44–12/44; *Baubelehrung* Cdr Type XXI (*U 3048*, but boat never commissioned) 5.1.45–4.4.45; Airfield Cdr Bremen-Neuenlanderfeld 4/45
POW 25.4.45–10.5.46

LAUDAHN, KARL-HEINZ [706]

b. 5.9.1915, Melpt, Pomerania
Entry X/1939; Kplt 1.12.44
VP-Cdr 11th Harbour Defence Flotilla 4/40–7/40; U-boat trg UAA Plön 7/40–9/40; Strm *U 138* 9/40–3/41; *Baubelehrung* 3/41–4/41; 2WO *U 652* 4/41–11/41; courses 12/41–11/42; U-Cdr's Course, 24th U-Flotilla 11/42–12/42
Cdr *U 142* 25.12.42–4.3.44 (see Schauroth [1070])

22nd U-Flotilla 4/44–10/44; acting Cdr *U 1194* 12.10.44–19.11.44

Cdr *U 262* 25.11.44–capitulation (*U 262* was decommissioned at Kiel on 2.5.45)

LAUTERBACH-EMDEN, HANS-JÜRGEN [707]

b. 20.5.1919, Neubrandenburg

Class 1937a; Kplt 1.3.44

WO destroyer *Z 15 Erich Steinbrinck* 10/39–10/40; U-boat trg 11/40–4/41; Comp. Officer 1.ULD 4/41–10/41; *Baubelehrung* 10/41–11/41; 1WO *U 174* 11/41–9/42; U-Cdr's Course 9/42–10/42; 1WO *U 511* 10/42–12/42; *Baubelehrung* 8.KLA 1/43–2/43

Cdr *U 539* 24.2.43–capitulation

LAUTH, HERMANN [708]

b. 10.11.1920, Wellau, Wiesbaden

Class XII/1939; ObltzS 1.12.43

U-boat trg, courses and *Baubelehrung* completed 1/43; 1WO *U 959* 1/43–4/44; course 23rd U-Flotilla 5/44–7/44

Cdr *U 1005* 3.7.44–capitulation

LAUZEMIS, ALBERT [709]

b. 12.3.1918, Kairien, Memel

Class 1937a; Kplt 1.7.44

U-boat trg and *Baubelehrung* 6/40–2/41; 2WO *U 68* 2/41–1/42; 1WO *U 68* 1/42–4/42; U-Cdr's Course, 24th U-Flotilla 5/42

Cdr *U 139* 18.5.42–30.6.42

Cdr *U 37* 1.7.42–31.3.43

Cdr *U 68* 19.1.43 (per WASt) or 21.1.43 (per *U 68* WD, relieving Merten [813]) to 16.6.43 (Hospitalised 16.6.43–7/43 for treatment of wounds received when *U 68* was attacked at sea by aircraft on 14.6.43. 1WO Scherraus [1079] took over as acting commander and docked the boat at Lorient on 16.6.43. Seehausen [1183] was given temporary command of *U 68* in July until relieved by Lauzemis on his discharge from hospital towards the end of that month.)

Cdr *U 68* 30.7.43–10.4.44

Lost 10.4.44 NW of Madeira

LAWAETZ, ULF [710]

b. 5.11.1916, Copenhagen

Class 1937b; ObltzS 1.4.42

No 2 Gunnery Officer destroyer *Z 18 Hans Lüdemann* 11/39–4/40; land fighting for Narvik 4/40–7/40; Destroyer Crews' Holding Div. 7/40–9/40; ADC Naval Cdr Denmark 9/40–3/41; No 2 Gunnery Officer heavy cruiser *Lützow* 3/41–6/41; service of Naval Attaché Helsinki 6/41–9/41; U-boat trg 9/41–4/42; 1WO *U 564* 4/42–12/42; U-Cdr's Course and *Baubelehrung* 1/43–4/43

Cdr *U 672* 6.4.43–18.7.44

POW 18.7.44–12/45

LAWRENCE, PETER [711]

b. 4.8.1920, Kiel

Class 1938; ObltzS 1.1.43

WO 11th Anti-Submarine Flotilla 4/40–11/41, Cdr anti-submarine vessel *UJ 1112* 12/41–7/43; U-boat trg and courses 8/43–8/44 (U-Cdr's Torpedo Course 68); *Baubelehrung* 8/44–9/44

Cdr *U 328* 19.9.44–30.11.44

Cdr *U 2328* 1.12.44–capitulation

LEDER, JOACHIM [712]

b. 26.6.1918, Irrsingen, Liegnitz

Entry 1/1940; ObltzS (R) 1.3.44

U-boat trg and courses 10/43–11/44; WO 4th and 5th U-Flotillas 11/44–1/45; *Baubelehrung* Type XXIII 1/45–2/45

Cdr *U 4707* 20.2.45–5.5.45

5th U-Flotilla 5/45–capitulation

LEHMANN, HANS [713]
b. 24.9.1915, Brunsbüttelkoog
Entry 1938; ObltzS (R) 1.4.43
Heavy cruiser *Admiral Hipper* 2/40–3/40; 1/NCO Trg Div. 4/40–7/40; Cdr *V 402*, 4th VP-Boat Flotilla 7/40–10/41; course Naval Gunnery School Kiel-Wik 11/41; Cdr *V 407*, 4th VP-Boat Flotilla 11/41–6/42; U-boat trg, 2.ULD, supplementary WO *U 359* and U-Cdr's Course 8/42–6/43 (U-Cdr's Torpedo Course 50); 1WO *U 454* 6/43–7/43; *Baubelehrung* 8.KLA 7/43–9/43
Cdr *U 997* 23.9.43–capitulation
Knights Cross 8.5.45 on Dönitz's edict (317th KM, 145th U-boat holder)

LEHMANN-WILLENBROCK, HEINRICH [714]
b. 11.12.1911, Bremen
Class 1931; FKpt 1.12.44
WO sail trg ship *Horst Wessel* 10/37–3/39; U-boat trg 4/39–10/39
Cdr *U 8* 14.10.39–30.11.39
Cdr *U 5* 5.12.39–11.8.40
Baubelehrung U-Boats East 8/40–9/40
Cdr *U 96* 14.9.40 to 28.3.42 (per P/F Hellriegel [454]) or 1.4.42 (per Lehmann-Willenbrock to U-Boat Archive)
CO 9th U-Flotilla 4/42 or 5/42–9/44
Cdr *U 256* 2.9.44–18.10.44 (per P/F) (*U 256* was decommissioned at the end of June 1944 for the installation of a snorkel. 1WO Ernst-Günther Brischke had temporary command from the recommissioning on 16.8.44 until 1.9.44. The voyage transferring the boat from Brest to Bergen was effected between 4.9.44 and 17.10.44 under Lehmann-Willenbrock. Brischke was subsequently supplementary WO for *U 3524* 16.2.45–5.5.45.)
Detained; freed 7.5.46
Knight's Cross 26.2.41 (61st KM, 25th U-boat holder)
Oak Leaves 31.12.41 (51st WM, 10th KM, 8th U-boat holder)

VON LEHSTEN, DETLEF [715]
b. 14.8.1917, Hamburg
Class 1937b; Kplt 18.2.45
Seconded to Luftwaffe 3/42; U-boat trg 3/42–10/42; 1WO *U 584* 10/42–6/43; U-Cdr's Course, 24th U-Flotilla 6/43–7/43 (U-Cdr's Torpedo Course 50); *Baubelehrung* Cdr *U 996* 8.KLA 7/43–9/43 (boat damaged during bombing raid at Blohm & Voss Hamburg on 25.7.43 while fitting out; removed to Königsberg for repairs)
Cdr *U 373* 26.9.43–8.6.44
1.UAA 6/44–7/44; *Baubelehrung* Type XXI 7.KLA 7/44–11/44
Cdr *U 3508* 2.11.44–30.3.45
Cdr *U 3044* 26.4.45–5.5.45

LEILICH, HANS [716]
b. 12.2.1918, Pirmasens
Class 1937a; Kplt 1.9.44
Trg Officer trg ship *Schlesien* 11/39–8/40; Kriegsmarine Depot Boulogne 8/40–11/40; Group Leader and instructor Naval College Flensburg-Mürwik 11/40–9/41; U-boat trg 9/41–3/42; U-handling trg and WO 24th, 4th and 10th U-Flotillas 3/42–2/43; U-Cdr's Course, 24th U-Flotilla 3/43–4/43 (U-Cdr's Torpedo Course 43); *Baubelehrung* 8.KLA 4/43–5/43
Cdr *U 977* 6.5.43–3/45
Kplt, Staff, Harbour Cdr Swinemünde 4/45–capitulation

LEIMKÜHLER, WOLFGANG [717]
b. 10.8.1918, Wesermünde
Class 1937a; ObltzS 1.9.41
U-boat trg 4/40–8/40; WO sea trg *U 60* 8/40–10/40; 1st U-Flotilla 10/40–12/40; *Baubelehrung* 12/40–1/41; 2WO *U 201* 1/41–11/41; U-Cdr's Course, 24th U-Flotilla 11/41
Cdr *U 4* 9.12.41–15.6.42
Baubelehrung 6/42–7/42

Cdr *U 225* 11.7.42–15.2.43
Lost 15.2.43 central North Atlantic

LEINEMANN, HANNES [718]
b. 15.12.1908, Rüstringen
Entry 1928, Kplt 1.6.44
Staff BdU Operations 10/39–3/41; 2.UAA 3/41–4/41; WO *U 98* 4/41–5/42; U-Cdr's Course, 24th U-Flotilla 5/42–6/42
Cdr *U 266* 24.6.42–11.9.42
8th U-Flotilla 9/42–4/43, inc. period as Cdr *U 708*
2/Adm. Staff Officer, Staff FdU West 5/43–capitulation

LEISTEN, ARNO [719]
b. 24.12.1919, Düsseldorf
Class 1938; ObltzS 1.4.43
U-boat trg 2/41–6/41; Platoon Officer 2.ULD 6/41–1/42; *Baubelehrung* 1/42–2/42; 1WO *U 336* 2/42–4/43; U-Cdr's Course, 24th U-Flotilla 4/43–5/43 (U-Cdr's Torpedo Course 46); *Baubelehrung* 6.KLA 5/43–6/43
Cdr *U 346* 7.6.43–20.9.43
Lost 20.9.43 Baltic Sea, off Hela

LEMCKE, HANS [720]
b. 9.12.1918, Pragsdorf, Mecklenburg
Class 1937a; Kplt 1.7.44
Destroyer *Z 4 Richard Beitzen* 4/39–6/40; seconded to Luftwaffe 6/40–6/43; U-boat trg 7/43–1/44; U-Cdr's Course, 23rd and 24th U-Flotillas 1/44–5/44 (U-Cdr's Torpedo Course 67); *Baubelehrung* 5.KLA 5/44–7/44
Cdr *U 327* 18.7.44–27.2.45
Lost 27.2.45 Western Approaches

LEMCKE, RUDOLF [721]
b. 8.5.1914, Oppeln
Class 1933; KKpt 1.8.42

1WO, Div. and Gunnery Officer, destroyer *Z 22 Anton Schmitt* 9/39–4/40; land fighting for Narvik 4/40–7/40; Cdr with Destroyer Crews' Holding Div. 8/40–10/40; 2/Adm. North Sea 10/40; released from service 25.10.40
3rd R-Boat Flotilla 1/41–4/41; service reactivated 4/41; Naval Trg Command Romania 5/41–6/41; U-boat trg 7/41–10/41; U-Cdr sea trg (supernumerary WO) *U 568* 10/41–11/41; U-Cdr's Course, 24th U-Flotilla 12/41–1/42; *Baubelehrung* 1/42–2/42
Cdr *U 210* 21.2.42–6.8.42
Lost 6.8.42 S of Cape Farewell

LEMP, FRITZ-JULIUS [722]
b. 19.2.1913, Tsingtau, China
Class 1931; Kplt 1.10.39
U-boat trg and various duties 4/35–10/36; WO *U 28* from 9/36 (per rank listings 1.11.36); WO *U 28* 1937 (per rank listings 1.11.37); Cdr *U 28* 28.10.38–11/38 (per rank listings 1.11.38; P/F shows him taking over command of *U 30* from 11/38. See Kuhnke [679].)
Cdr *U 30* 11/38–9/40 (per P/F)
2nd U-Flotilla 10/40; *Baubelehrung* Group North Sea 10/40–11/40
Cdr *U 110* 21.11.40–9.5.41
Lost 9.5.41 E of Cape Farewell
Knight's Cross 14.8.40 (25th KM, 9th U-boat holder)

LENKEIT, PAUL EHRENFRIED [723]
b. 22.6.1915, Swinemünde
Class 1935, Kplt 1.12.42
Admin. Officer destroyer *Z 2 Georg Thiele* until 4/40; land fighting for Narvik 4/40–7/40; Staff Naval Cdr Narvik 7/40–1941; Comp. Leader 1/Basic Trg Est. Stralsund 1941–4/42; Flotilla Admin. Officer and Senior Officer, Base, 7th E-Boat Flotilla 4/42–3/43; retrg Admin. to Seaman Branch, U-boat trg and courses 3/43–5/44; *Baubelehrung* 6/44–7/44

Cdr *U 1301* 8/44–capitulation
Detained; freed 1947

LENZMANN, DIETER [724]
b. 14.9.1918, Hamburg
Entry X/1939; ObltzS (R)
WO *U 24* 7/44; Cdr *U 24* 7/44–25.8.44; 30th U-Flotilla 8/44–10/44; *Baubelehrung* Type XXI 7.KLA 10/44–1/45
Cdr *U 3522* 21.1.45–2.5.45

LERCHEN, KAI [725]
b. 27.4.1911, East London, South Africa
Class 1933; Kplt 1.4.41
3rd Gunnery Officer heavy cruiser *Admiral Hipper* 8/39–6/41; U-boat trg 6/41–10/41; supernumerary WO *U 85* 10/41–12/41; U-Cdr's Course, 24th U-Flotilla 12/41
Cdr *U 252* 21.12.41–14.4.42
Lost 14.4.42 SW of Ireland (Translator's note: However, see Hirschfeld, *Feindfahrten*, and Frank, *The Sea Wolves*. On 15.4.42, in his last signal, Lerchen reported the presence of a small, lightly defended convoy in grid square BE8371 in 44°N 23°W, suspected as U-boat trap by BdU. Lerchen was told to proceed with the utmost caution and attack only at night in most favourable conditions. He was not heard from subsequently. See Borcherdt [106] and Rollmann [1023].)

LESSING, HERMANN [726]
b. 20.10.1900, Florence, Italy
Class 1921; Oberst (Luftwaffe) 1.4.42, KptzS 1.7.43 with seniority 1.4.43
Flight leader *Bordfliegerstaffel 1./196* 10/37–9/39; Group Cdr *Küstenfliegergruppen 706* 10/39–6/40 and *906* 7/40–6/42; Liaison Officer Oberkommando der Luftwaffe to OKM/SKL 7/42–10/42; various duties 11/42–2/43; Cdr at Luftwaffe Navigation School Strausberg 3/43–6/43; U-boat trg and U-Cdr's Course 7/43–12/43 (U-Cdr's Torpedo Course 59); *Baubelehrung* 8.KLA 1/44–2/44
Cdr *U 1231* 9.2.44–3/45
Chief of Staff, Staff 2/Adm. Baltic and 2/Adm. Baltic/North Sea 3/45–capitulation
Detained; freed 10.10.45

LEU, WOLFGANG [727]
b. 6.7.1917, Kaltennordheim
Class 1937b; ObltzS 1.4.42
Seconded to Luftwaffe 2/40–3/42; U-boat trg 3/42–9/42; 1WO *U 456* 10/42–3/43; U-Cdr's Course, 2.UAA and 24th U-Flotilla 3/43–4/43 (U-Cdr's Torpedo Course 44); *Baubelehrung* 5.KLA 4/43–5/43
Cdr *U 921* 30.5.43–24.5.44
Lost 24/5/44 off Trondheim. (Proceeding to render aid to the sinking *U 476*, *U 921* came under repeated attack from enemy bombers. The boat escaped damage by manoeuvring at high speed, but after his flak guns had become unserviceable Leu was forced to dive. Last to leave the bridge, he became trapped by a sea boot in the conning-tower ladder, and once the lower hatch was closed the sea filled the tower and he was washed upwards. He had no choice but to secure the bridge hatch from outside, sacrificing himself to save boat and crew as *U 921* submerged beneath him. Despite the danger from the air, 1WO Neumann [873] surfaced at once, but in the heavy sea conditions Leu had had little chance of survival. Neumann took over temporary command (24.5.44–31.5.44) and berthed the boat safely at Trondheim with three wounded.)

LEUPOLD, GÜNTER [728]
b. 11.2.1921, Kittnau, Graudenz
Class 1938; ObltzS 1.4.43

1WO *U 355* 10/41–7/43; U-Cdr's Course, 2.UAA and 24th U-Flotilla 7/43–9/43 (U-Cdr's Torpedo Course 52)
Cdr *U 1059* 1.10.43–19.3.44
Detained; freed 19.3.44

LEY, WOLFGANG [729]
b. 21.6.1920, Krefeld
Class 1938; ObltzS 1.4.43
Officer trg 10/38–3/41; Platoon Officer 1.ULD 3/41–9/41; 1WO *U 591* 10/41–7/42; U-Cdr's Course 7/42–8/42
Cdr *U 61* 10.11.42–15.9.43
Cdr *U 310* 27.9.43–capitulation
Detained; freed 5.1.46

LIEBE, HEINRICH [730]
b. 29.1.1908, Gotha
Class 1927; FKpt 1.10.44
U-boat trg 9/35–9/36; Cdr *U 2* 1.10.36–31.1.38; FdU 2/38–4/38, with period as Cdr *U 10*; U-Cdr U-Boat School 4/38–8/38, with further period as Cdr *U 10*; *Baubelehrung* 8/38–10/38
Cdr *U 38* 24.10.38 to 14.7.41 (per P/F) or 22.7.41 (per *U 38* WD, and see Schuch [1139])
Adviser OKM/SKL 7/41–8/44; adviser W in Central Div., OKM/2.SKL/BdU/Opns 8/44–capitulation
Knight's Cross 14.8.40 (24th KM, 8th U-boat holder)
Oak Leaves 10.6.41 (13th WM, 4th KM, 4th U-boat holder)

LIEBE, JOHANNES [731]
b. 8.7.1913, Rosswein, Saxony
Class 1933; Kplt 1.4.41
Signals Officer Naval Airfield HQ 11/38–11/39; U-boat trg 11/39–7/40
Cdr *U 6* 11.7.40–3/41

WO (supernumerary) *U 48* 3/41–4/41; *Baubelehrung* 5/41–6/41
Cdr *U 332* 7.6.41–27.1.43 (see Hüttemann [523])
Kplt Staff 25th U-Flotilla 2/43–6/43; Comp. CO. 2.ULD 6/43–4/44; adviser Torpedo Experimental Branch Eckernförde 4/44–7/44; adviser OKM/Office of Torpedo Ordnance 8/44–capitulation
Detained; freed 29.7.45

LIESBERG, ERNST [732]
b. 15.6.1918, Wiesbaden
Class 1937b; ObltzS 1.4.42
U-boat trg 9/41–5/42; 1WO *U 454* 5/42–12/42; U-Cdr's Course, 24th U-Flotilla 12/42–1/43; *Baubelehrung* 8.KLA 1/43–2/43
Cdr *U 962* 11.2.43–8.4.44
Lost 8.4.44 NW of Cape Finisterre

VON LILIENFELD, ERICH [733]
b. 22.11.1915, Rittergur Rocht Wierland, Estonia
Class 1935; ObltzS 1.10.39
WO 1st Minesweeping Flotilla 1/40–8/40; M/S-Cdr, 14th Minesweeping Flotilla 8/40–1/41; U-boat trg 1/41–6/41; 7th U-Flotilla 7/41; 1WO *U 553* 8/41–11/41; U-Cdr's Course, 26th U-Flotilla 11/41–1/42; *Baubelehrung* 8.KLA 1/42–2/42
Cdr *U 661* 12.2.42–15.10.42
Lost 15.10.42 North Atlantic

LINCK, GERHARD [734]
b. 30.5.1919, Puppen, Ostfriesland
Class 1937b; ObltzS 1.4.42
ADC and 1WO torpedo-boat *T 19* 9/41–5/43; U-boat trg 5/43–10/43; courses 3.ULD, 23rd and 24th U-Flotillas 10/43–1/44 (U-Cdr's Torpedo Course 60); *Baubelehrung* 8.KLA 1/44–3/44
Cdr *U 1013* 2.3.44–17.3.44
Lost 17.3.44 Baltic Sea, E of Rügen I

LINDEMANN, KURT [735]
b. 31.7.1912, Hagen, Wesermünde
Entry VII/1940; ObltzS (R) 1.10.43
WO 17th VP-Boat Flotilla and Coastal Defence Flotilla *Ostland* 5/41–5/43; Group Leader Minefield Command Memel 5/43–6/43; U-boat trg 6/43–11/43; U-Cdr's Course, 23rd and 24th U-Flotillas (U-Cdr's Torpedo Course 62); *Baubelehrung* 7.KLA 2/44–3/44
Cdr *U 1207* 23.3.44–5.5.45

LINDER, GERHARD [736]
b. 21.3.1920, Münnerstad, Lower Franconia
Class 1938; ObltzS 1.4.43
2WO *U 571* 5/41–3/42; 1WO *U 571* 3/42–9/42; U-Cdr's Course 9/42–10/42
Cdr *U 579* 10/42–9/44
Baubelehrung Type XXI 8.KLA 9/44–10/44
Cdr *U 2515* 19.10.44–3.12.44
Cdr *U 3006* 4.12.44–15.1.45
Baubelehrung 8.KLA 2/45–4/45; Platoon Leader Naval Infantry Regt 6 4/45–capitulation

LINDER, HANS-HEINZ [737]
b. 11.2.1913, Otterberg, Kaiserslautern
Class 1933; Kplt 1.10.40, posthumously KKpt seniority to 1.9.44
U-boat trg 11/39–8/40
Cdr *U 18* 3.9.40–17.12.40
U-Cdr sea trg (supernumerary aboard *U 96*) 1/41–3/41; *Baubelehrung* 3/41
Cdr *U 202* 22.3.41–1.9.42
1st U-Flotilla 9/42–11/42; at 2/Adm. U-Boats 11/42–1/43; Trg Leader 25th U-Flotilla 1/43–9/44
Died 10.9.1944

LINDKE, SIEGFRIED [738]
b. 12.12.1900, Stettin
Rating entry V/1920; Kplt 1.3.45
StObStrm *U 62* 3/40–9/41

Cdr *U 142* 21.10.41–17.3.42
22nd U-Flotilla 4/42–4/43; Kplt Staff 22nd U-Flotilla 5/43–12/43; Cdr U-boat depot ship *Isar*, 20th and 25th U-Flotillas 12/43–capitulation

LINDSCHAU, ROLF [739]
b. 2.11.1914, Burg
Entry 1936; ObltzS (R) 1.9.43
WO and VP Cdr 16th VP-Boat Flotilla 11/40–2/43; U-boat trg, U-Cdr's Course and *Baubelehrung* 2/43–11/43
Cdr *U 249* 20.11.43–16.7.44
Courses and *Baubelehrung* Type XXI (*U 3017*) 6.KLA 8/44–1/45
Cdr *U 3017* 5.1.45–capitulation

LINK, GÜNTHER [740]
b. 4.3.1918, Klein-Koslau, East Prussia
Class 1937b; ObltzS 1.4.42
WO and M/S-Cdr Trg Flotilla C-in-C Escort Forces Baltic 5/40–11/41; U-boat trg 11/41–5/42; 1WO *U 86* 6/42–1/43; U-Cdr's Course, 2.UAA and 26th U-Flotilla 1/43–2/43; *Baubelehrung* 1.KLA 2/43–4/43
Cdr *U 240* 3.4.43–16.5.44
Lost 16.5.44 NE of Faroes

LITTERSCHEID, GERHARD [741]
b. 10.6.1914, Berlin
Class 1935; Kplt 1.11.42
WO E-boat depot ship *Carl Peters* 11/39–6/40; U-boat trg 7/40–11/40; *Baubelehrung* 12/40–1/41; 1WO *U 554* 1/41–5/41
Cdr *U 19* 1.6.41–2/42 (Gaude [339] took over as acting Cdr on 16.12.41 when Litterscheid was hospitalised)
Baubelehrung 2/42–3/42
Cdr *U 411* 18.3.42–19.10.42
6th U-Flotilla 10/42–12/42; Comp. CO Naval Flak School I 12/42–4/43; Comp. CO Naval Flak School VII 4/43–capitulation

LOEDER, HERBERT [742]
b. 3.4.1919, Hamburg
Class 1938; ObltzS 1.4.43
26th U-Flotilla 6/41–11/41; *Baubelehrung* 11/41–12/41; 1WO *U 380* 12/41–12/42; U-Cdr's Course, 24th U-Flotilla 1/43–2/43; *Baubelehrung* 8.KLA 2/43–3/43
Cdr *U 967* 11.3.43–4/44
At FdU West 4/44–6/44; U-Cdr sea trg *U 437* 6/44–7/44
Cdr *U 309* 8/44–16.2.45 (see Mahrholz [775])
Lost 16.2.45 E of Moray Firth

LOESCHKE, GÜNTHER [743]
b. 30.8.1921, Trier
Class IX/1939; ObltzS 1.10.43
Courses and U-boat trg 9/39–10/41; WO 5th and 8th U-Flotillas 10/41–4/42; *Baubelehrung* 4/42–5/42; 1WO *U 264* 5/42–11/43; U-Cdr's Course, 3.ULD and 23rd U-Flotilla 11/43–1/44
Cdr *U 7* 1/44–18.2.44
Lost 18.2.44 Baltic Sea, W of Pillau

LOESER, PAUL-KARL [744]
b. 26.4.1915, Berlin
Class 1935; Kplt 1.12.42
2WO *U 33* from 3/38; 2WO *U 40* 2/39–9/39; 1WO *U 43* 9/39–7/40; *Baubelehrung* 8/40–10/40; 1WO *U 108* 10/40–3/41; acting Cdr *U 30* 1.4.41–4/41; *Baubelehrung* 4/41–5/41
Cdr *U 373* 22.5.41–25.9.43
Trg Officer 20th U-Flotilla 10/43–10/44; anti-aircraft watch leader 19th U-Flotilla 11/44–2/45; nautical trg adviser 8.KLA 2/45–4/45; Guard Battalion *Dönitz* 4/45–capitulation
Detained; freed 16.8.45

LOEWE, AXEL-OLAF [745]
b. 3.1.1909, Kiel
Class 1928; KKpt 1.6.42

Naval Academy until 9/39; OKW/Wehrmacht Command Staff/L 10/39–10/40; U-boat trg 11/40–4/41; U-Cdr sea trg *U 74* 5/41–6/41; *Baubelehrung* 7/41–8/41
Cdr *U 505* 26.8.41–5.9.42
Adviser W-Staff BdU/Opns 12/42–7/44; Reichs Ministry for Armaments and War Production (Speer) 8/44–4/45; 1/Naval Anti-Tank Regt 4/45–capitulation
Detained; freed 30.12.45

LOEWE, ODO [746]
b. 12.9.1914, Ludwigslust
Class 1934; Kplt 1.4.42
1WO E-boat depot ship *Tanga* 3/39–12/39; pers. ADC Naval Group West 12/39–3/41; U-boat trg 3/41–7/41; WO (supernumerary) *U 71* 7/41–9/41; U-Cdr's Course, 26th U-Flotilla 10/41–11/41; *Baubelehrung* 11/41–12/41
Cdr *U 256* 18.12.41–30.11.42, inc. period as acting Cdr *U 254* 9/42–10/42
Baubelehrung 8.KLA 12/42
Cdr *U 954* 23.12.42–19.5.43
Lost 19.5.43 SE of Cape Farewell

LOHMANN, DIETRICH [747]
b. 12.10.1909, Hamelin
Class 1930; KKpt 1.4.43
WO, Div Officer and ADC sail trg ship *Horst Wessel* 1/38–9/39; Comp. CO 7/Basic Trg Est. Stralsund 9/39–3/40; U-boat trg 4/40–9/40; U-Cdr's Course, 24th U-Flotilla 9/40–11/40; WO (supernumerary) *U 99* 11/40–12/40; *Baubelehrung* 12/40–1/41
Cdr *U 554* 15.1.41–25.6.41
Cdr *U 579* 17.7.41–22.10.41
Cdr *U 89* 19.11.41–12.5.43
Lost 12.5.43 North Atlantic

LOHMEYER, PETER [748]
b. 2.1.1911, Zanzibar
Class 1932; KKpt 1.9.44

3./*Küstenmehrzweckstaffel 106* (Luftwaffe coastal multi-purpose squadron) until 10/39; WO *U 19* 11/39–6/40
Cdr *U 19* 26.6.40–20.10.40
Cdr *U 138* 21.10.40–31.12.40
Baubelehrung 1/41–2/41
Cdr *U 651* 12.2.41–29.6.41
POW 29.6.41–16.7.47

LOHSE, ERNST-BERNWARD [749]
b. 6.4.1913, Wurzen, Saxony
Class 1932; Kplt 1.11.39, posthumously KKpt seniority to 1.1.44
Gunnery Technical Officer heavy cruiser *Deutschland/Lützow* 9/38–6/40; U-boat trg 7/40–11/40; (caretaker) Cdr *U 21* 21.12.40–18.5.41; U-Cdr's Course, 24th U-Flotilla 5/41–6/41; U-Cdr sea trg *U 96* 6/41–7/41; *Baubelehrung* 7/41–8/41
Cdr *U 585* 28.8.41–30.3.42
Lost 30.3.42 Arctic Ocean, N of Murmansk

LOOFF, HANS-GÜNTHER [750]
b. 10.2.1906, Berlin
Class 1925; KKpt 1.1.40
Cdr *U 9* 21.8.35–1936/37 (per rankings of 1.11.36 Looff was still Cdr *U 9* at that time); Cdr *U 28* and *U 23* 1936/37–30.9.37 (U-Boat Archive per Kretschmer [663]); CO U-Flotilla *Weddigen* 10/37–9/39; 2/Adm. Staff Officer FdU West and FdU/SKL 9/39; 2/Adm Staff Officer, Staff BdU/Opns 9/39–3/40
Cdr *U 122* 30.3.40–22.6.40
Missing from 22.6.40 between North Sea and Bay of Biscay

LOOKS, HARTWIG [751]
b. 27.6.1917, Flensburg
Class 1936; Kplt 1.3.43
ADC 2nd Destroyer Flotilla 9/39–4/40; ADC Adm. Norwegian North Coast 4/40–12/40; U-boat trg 1/41–5/41; *Baubelehrung* 6/41–7/41; 1WO *U 375* 7/41–3/42; U-Cdr's Course 24th U-Flotilla 3/42–4/42; *Baubelehrung* 6.KLA 4/42–5/42
Cdr *U 264* 22.5.42–19.2.44
POW 19.2.44–20.9.47

LOOS, JOHANN-FRIEDRICH [752]
b. 20.4.1921, Ulsnis, Schleswig
Class XII/1939; ObltzS 1.12.43
U-boat trg completed 7/42; *Baubelehrung* 7/42–8/42; 2WO *U 636* 8/42–9/43; 1WO *U 636* 9/43–1/44; courses 13th U-Flotilla, 3.ULD and 24th U-Flotilla 1/44–4/44; Cadet Trg Officer U-boat depot ship *Lech* 5/44–10/44
Cdr *U 248* 1.11.44–16.1.45
Lost 16.1.45 central North Atlantic

LORENTZ, GÜNTHER [753]
b. 23.10.1913, Flensburg
Entry 1932; Kplt (zV) 1.3.42
U-Boat School 9/39–10/39; Cdr *U 10* 10/39–1/40
Cdr *U 63* 18.1.40–25.2.40
POW 25.2.40–20.9.47

LOTT, WERNER [754]
b. 3.12.1907, Willenberg, East Prussia
Class 1926; KKpt 1.11.40
Cdr *U 21* 9/36–31.3.37 (U-Boat Archive per Lott); *Baubelehrung* Germaniawerft Kiel 4/37; Cdr *U 32* 15.4.37–8/37 (Letter from Lott to U-Boat Archive states, 'I was named as commander of *U 35* by Dönitz personally on 15.8.37. Thereupon I gave up command of *U 32* to Paul Büchel [147].' The personal file of the latter shows him as commander of *U 32* as from 1.9.37. Presumably the changeover took place shortly before 15.8.37.)
Cdr *U 35* about 15.8.37 to 29.11.39
POW 29.11.39–13.10.46

LOTTNER, ERNST [755]
b. 15.8.1920, Lychen, Uckermark
Class IX/1939; ObltzS 1.10.43
Officer and U-boat trg 9/39–11/41; WO U-boat depot ship *Waldemar Kophamel* 11/41–1/42; *Baubelehrung* 1/42–3/42; 1WO *U 92* 3/42–7/43; U-Cdr's Course, 24th U-Flotilla 7/43–8/43; *Baubelehrung* 8/43–9/43
Cdr *U 349* 8.9.43–4.1.44
Cdr *U 746* 5.1.44–5.5.45
Detained; freed 25.7.45

LUBE, GÜNTHER [756]
b. 19.10.1920, Brunswick
Class IX/1939; ObltsS 1.10.43
Officer and U-boat trg 9/39–10/41; *Baubelehrung* 10/41–11/41; 1WO *U 254* 11/41–10/42; 1WO *U 407* 10/42–10/43; U-Cdr's Course, 23rd U-Flotilla 10/43–12/43
Cdr *U 139* 28.12.43–3.7.44
Cdr *U 552* 11.7.44–2.5.45

LÜBCKE, OLAF [757]
b. 27.8.1919, place not known
Class 1937b; Kplt 1.1.45
Seconded to Luftwaffe 9/39–6/43; U-boat trg, U-Cdr's Course and *Baubelehrung* 7/43–5/44
Cdr *U 826* 11.5.44–capitulation
Detained; freed 5/48

LÜBSEN, ROBERT [758]
b. 30.9.1916, Blexen, Oldenburg
Class 1937a; Kplt 1.1.44
Harbour Defence Flotilla Bergen 6/40–1/42; U-boat trg 1/42–6/42; 1WO *U 98* 6/42–10/42; U-Cdr's Course, 2.UAA and 24th U-Flotilla 10/42–11/42; *Baubelehrung* 6.KLA 11/42–12/42
Cdr *U 277* 21.12.42–1.5.44
Lost 1.5.44 Arctic Ocean, SW of Bear I

LÜDDEN, SIEGFRIED [759]
b. 20.5.1916, Neubrandenburg, Stargard
Class 1936; KKpt 1.1.45
At BdU and courses for U-boat trg 4/40–8/40; *Baubelehrung* U-Boats East 8/40; WO *U 141* 8/40–10/40; UAA Plön 10/40–11/40; 1WO 24th U-Flotilla 11/40–2/41; ADC 1st U-Flotilla 2/41–4/41; ADC 3rd U-Flotilla 5/41–7/41; ADC 5th U-Flotilla 7/41–9/41; 1WO *U 129* 9/41–5/42; U-Cdr's Course, 24th U-Flotilla, 5/42–6/42; *Baubelehrung* KLA U-Boats North 6/42–8/42
Cdr *U 188* 5.8.42 to 9.8.44 (P/F) or 20.8.44 (WASt)
12th U-Flotilla 10.8.44–8.9.44 (Italian P/F); 1.UAA 9/44–11/44; Depts F3 and A3 Commanding Adm. U-Boats 11/44–1/45
Killed 13.1.45 Kiel, fire aboard accommodation ship *Daressalam*
Knight's Cross 11.2.44 (205th KM, 111th U-boat holder)

LÜDERS, GÜNTER [760]
b. 18.7.1920, Kiel
Class 1938; ObltzS 1.4.43
U-boat trg completed 3/41; *Baubelehrung* 1.KLA 3/41–5/41; 2WO *U 653* 5/41–1/43; U-Cdr's Course, 2.UAA and 24th U-Flotilla 1/43–2/43; *Baubelehrung* 7.KLA 2/43–4/43
Cdr *U 424* 7.4.43–11.2.44
Lost 11.2.44 SW of Ireland

LÜHRS, DIERK [761]
b. 18.11.1919, Mannheim
Class 1938; ObltzS 1.1.43
Officer trg completed 4/40; WO and R-Cdr 3rd R-Boat Flotilla 5/40–2/42; U-boat trg 2/42–11/42; 1WO *U 596* 12/42–7/43; U-Cdr's Course, U-Cdr under instrn 7/43–11/43 (U-Cdr's Torpedo Course 52)
Cdr *U 453* 7.12.43–21.5.44
POW 21.5.44–3/46

LÜSSOW, GUSTAV [762]
b. 30.12.1917, Teterow, Mecklenburg
Class 1937a; ObltzS 1.9.41
Seconded to Luftwaffe 10/39–3/42; U-boat trg 3/42–9/42; WO (supernumerary) *U 566* 9/42–12/42; 1WO *U 566* 12/42–3/43; U-Cdr's Course, 2.UAA and 24th U-Flotilla 3/43–5/43 (U-Cdr's Torpedo Course 45)
Cdr *U 571* 31.5.43–28.1.44
Lost 28.1.44 W of Ireland

LÜTH, GÜNTHER [763]
b. 23.3.1917, Kiel
Entry III/1937; ObltzS (R) 1.9.43
WO and VP-Cdr Harbour Defence Flotilla Trondheim 6/41–12/41; VP-Cdr 59th and 61st VP-Boat Flotillas 1/42–2/43; U-boat trg 3/43–10/43; WO 5th U-Flotilla 10/43–1/44; U-Cdr's Course and *Baubelehrung* 1/44–5/44 (U-Cdr's Torpedo Course 64)
Cdr *U 1057* 20.5.44–capitulation

LÜTH, WOLFGANG [764]
b. 15.10.1913, Riga, Lithuania
Class 1933; KptzS 1.9.44
U-boat trg, courses and various duties 2/37–7/38; 2WO *U 27* 7/38–10/38; 1WO *U 38* 10/38–10/39; U-Boat School 10/39–11/39; 1st U-Boat Trg Flotilla 11/39–6/40, inc. periods as acting Cdr *U 13* 16.12.39–28.12.39 and Cdr *U 9* 30.12.39–10.6.40 (per P/F)
Baubelehrung U-Boats Baltic 6/40
Cdr *U 138* 27.6.40–20.10.40
Cdr *U 43* 21.10.40 (per P/F) or 1.11.40 (per WASt) to 11.4.42 (when boat sank in the harbour basin at Lorient; see Schwantke [1169])
Baubelehrung KLA U-Boats North 4/42–5/42
Cdr *U 181* 9.5.42–31.10.43
12th U-Flotilla 11/43–1/44; CO 22nd U-Flotilla 1/44–7/44; Cdr Section 1/Naval College Mürwik 7/44–9/44; Cdr Naval College Flensburg-Mürwik 9/44–5/45

Shot dead in error at Flensburg-Mürwik Naval College at 2300hrs on 13.5.45 (Translator's note: On the evidence the authors' conclusion 'in error' does not seem justified. The Court of Enquiry exonerated the German naval sentry involved, whose orders were to shoot to kill any person who had failed to respond to three challenges. He had no discretion for a warning shot. Lüth knew the sentry's orders, knew where he was patrolling and unaccountably ignored the three challenges. Jordan Vause's biography fully considers all the circumstances.) Lüth was interred with full military honours at Adelby Cemetery 15.5.45.
Knight's Cross 24.10.40 (42nd KM, 19th U-boat holder)
Oak Leaves 13.11.42 (142 WM, 18th KM, 16th U-boat holder)
Swords 15.4.43 (29th WM, 4th KM, 4th U-boat holder)
Diamonds 9.8.43 (7th WM, 1st KM, 1st U-boat holder)

LUIS, WILHELM [765]
b. 13.12.1915, Lübeck
Class 1935; Kplt 1.6.42, posthumously KKpt seniority to 1.7.43
Seconded to Luftwaffe 10/37–12/40, inc. *3./(M) Küstenfliegergruppe 806*; instructor Naval College Flensburg-Mürwik 12/40–1/42; U-boat trg 2/42–7/42; 1WO *U 504* 7/42–12/42; U-Cdr's Course, 24th U-Flotilla 12/42–1/43
Cdr *U 504* 6.1.43–30.7.43
Lost 30.7.43 NE of Cape Ortegal

LUTHER, OTTO [766]
b. 18.9.1918, Flensburg
Class 1937b; ObltzS 1.4.42
2.ADC Staff, Naval Cdr Stavanger 4/40–3/41; WO torpedo-boat *T 13* 6/41–7/42; U-boat trg 7/42–11/42; 6th U-Flotilla 11/42–4/43, inc. U-

Cdr sea trg *U 608* 1/43–3/43; U-Cdr's Course,
2.UAA and 24th U-Flotilla 4/43–6/43
Cdr *U 135* 4.6.43–15.7.43
POW 15.7.43

LUTTMANN, BERNHARD [767]
b. 17.4.1921, Wilhelmshaven
Class IX/1939; ObltzS 1.10.43
Officer trg 9/39–11/41; WO 25th U-Flotilla
11/41–4/42; *Baubelehrung* 4/42–5/42; 1WO
U 758 5/42–6/43; U-Cdr's Course, 24th U-
Flotilla 7/43 (U-Cdr's Torpedo Course 51)
Cdr *U 141* 29.7.43–6.11.44
Baubelehrung Type XXI 6.KLA 11/44–2/45
Cdr *U 3030* 14.2.45–9.5.45

LUTZ, FRIEDRICH [768]
b. 9.8.1911, Pfullendorf, Baden
Enlisted rating 1930; Kplt 1.4.45
R-Cdr 5th R-Boat Flotilla 9/39–3/43; U-boat trg
3/43–9/43; WO and U-Cdr trg 9/43–12/43 (U-
Cdr's Torpedo Course 59); *Baubelehrung*
1.KLA 12/43–2/44
Cdr *U 485* 23.2.44–capitulation

M

MACKEPRANG, HANS-PETER [769]
b. 3.12.1911, Kappeln, Schlei
Entry XI/1935; ObltzS (R) 1.10.43
VP-Cdr Coastal Defence Group Norwegian
  West Coast 8/40–7/43; U-boat trg 7/43–12/43;
  WO 23rd, 6th and 33rd U-Flotillas 12/43–
  12/44, inc. 2WO and 1WO *U 758* 3/44–12/44;
  U-Cdr's Course, 24th U-Flotilla 12/44–1/45
  (U-Cdr's Torpedo Course 79); 1WO *U 244*
  2/45–4/45
Acting Cdr *U 244* 10.4.45–capitulation

MÄDER, ERICH [770]
b. 3.10.1915, Beuchlitz, Halle, Saxony-Anhalt
Class 1936; Kplt 1.8.43
U-boat trg 10/40–2/41; *Baubelehrung* 2/41–4/41;
  1WO *U 80* 4/41–10/41; *Baubelehrung* 8.KLA
  10/41; 1WO *U 508* 10/41–9/42; U-Cdr's
  Course, 24th U-Flotilla 9/42–10/42
Cdr *U 378* 11.10.42 (per *U 378* WD) or 12.10.42
  (per WASt) to 20.10.43
Lost 20.10.43 central North Atlantic

MÄRTENS, HANS [771]
b. 30.1.1918, Bernburg, Saale
Class 1937a; Kplt 1.4.44
WO 12th Minesweeping Flotilla 2/40–8/40;
  M/S-Cdr and Group Leader 40th
  Minesweeping Flotilla 8/40–1/42; UJ Cdr 12th
  Anti-Submarine Flotilla 1/42–10/42; 21st
  Minesweeping Flotilla 11/42–1/43; WO 21st
  Minesweeping Flotilla 1/43; U-boat and U-
  Cdr trg 2/43–8/43; *Baubelehrung* 1.KLA
  9/43–10/43
Cdr *U 243* 2.10.43–8.7.44
Lost 8.7.44 Bay of Biscay, W of Nantes

VON MÄSSENHAUSEN, WILHELM [772]
b. 16.1.1915, Sydney, Australia Class 1935; Kplt
  1.9.42
Group Officer Naval College Flensburg-Mürwik
  3/30–3/40; U-boat trg 4/40–9/40; WO 24th U-
  Flotilla 9/40–1/41; *Baubelehrung* 1/41–3/41;
  1WO *U 79* 3/41–11/41; U-Cdr's Course, 26th
  U-Flotilla, 11/41–1/42; *Baubelehrung* 6.KLA
  1/42–2/42
Cdr *U 258* 4.2.42–20.5.43
Lost 20.5.43 North Atlantic

MÄUELER, HEINRICH [773]
b. 10.4.1920, Mittelirsen, Siegburg
Entry IV/1940; ObltzS (R)
U-boat trg completed 10/42; WO *U 302* 10/42–
  12/43; U-Cdr's Course and *Baubelehrung*
  7.KLA 12/43–2/44
Cdr *U 1204* 17.2.44–8/44
Courses and *Baubelehrung* Type XXI 6.KLA
  8/44–12/44
Cdr *U 3020* 23.12.44–2.5.45

MAHN, BRUNO [774]
b. 3.12.1887, Dorfilm, Leuthenberg, Thüringen
Entry 1911; KptzS 1.8.42
WO coastal defence vessel *Hildebrand* until
  1/16; U-Boat School, inc. WO *UB 25* until 4/16;
  WO *UB 33* 22.4.16–4/17; WO *UC 59* 12.5.17–
  6/18; Cdr *UB 21* until demobilised 23.11.18
  (final rank WW1 ObltzS (R) 16.11.17)
Naval Liaison Officer, General Command XIII
  Army Corps 10/37–4/40; U-boat trg and courses
  4/40–11/40
Cdr *U B* 30.11.40–31.7.41

Baubelehrung for *UD 5* 1.8.41–31.10.41
Cdr *UD 5* 1.11.41–12.1.43
Acting CO 8th U-Flotilla 1/43–3/43; Senior Officer U-boat base, Hamburg 4/43–8/43; CO 31st U-Flotilla 9/43–4/45; at FdU-Ost 4/45–capitulation

MAHRHOLZ, HANS-GERT [775]

b. 10.10.1918, Kiel
Class 1938; ObltzS 1.4.43
Baubelehrung 9/41–11/41; 1WO *U 89* 11/41–11/42; U-Cdr's Course 11/42–12/42; *Baubelehrung* 12/42–1/43
Cdr *U 309* 27.1.43 to between 12.8.44 (when Mahrholz docked at La Pallice) and 29.8.44 (when Loeder [742] sailed in command)
Course leader 1/Radar Trg Branch 10/44–capitulation
Detained; freed 15.10.45

MAKOWSKI, KURT [776]

b. 1.9.1915, Wiesbaden
Class 1936; ObltzS 1.10.40
WO *U 61* (1940 under Oesten [893]); *Baubelehrung* 12/40–1/41; 2WO *U 66* 1/41–5/41; U-Cdr's Course 6/41–7/41
Cdr *U 78* 7/41–2/42
Baubelehrung 8.KLA 3/42–4/42
Cdr *U 619* 23.4.42–5.10.42
Lost 5.10.42 W of Iceland

MANCHEN, ERWIN [777]

b. 18.6.1918, Königsberg, East Prussia
Class 1936; Kplt 1.2.43
Group Officer Naval College Flensburg-Mürwik 11/41–6/43; U-boat trg 6/43–10/43; U-Cdr's Course, 23rd and 24th U-Flotillas 11/43–2/44 (U-Cdr's Torpedo Course 61); *Baubelehrung* 6.KLA 2/44–4/44
Cdr *U 879* 19.4.44–30.4.45
Lost 30.4.45 off US coast, E of Cape Hatteras

MANGELS, HINRICH [778]

b. 24.8.1919, Grohn, Bremen
Class 1938; ObltzS 1.4.43
Officer trg 10/38–8/40; M/S-Cdr 44th Minesweeping Flotilla 8/40–11/40; U-boat trg 11/40–3/41; relief instructor Torpedo School Mürwik 3/41–7/42; *Baubelehrung* 7/42–8/42; 1WO *U 636* 8/42–9/43; U-Cdr's Course, 2.UAA and 24th U-Flotilla 9/43–11/43; *Baubelehrung* 7.KLA 11/43–1/44
Cdr *U 1200* 5.1.44–11.11.44
Lost 11.11.44 S of Ireland

MANGOLD, ERNST [779]

b. 15.11.1917, Bodenwerder, Hameln
Entry X/1935; ObltzS 1.12.43
2WO *U 553* 12/41–1/43; U-Cdr's Course and *Baubelehrung* 7.KLA 1/43–3/43
Cdr *U 739* 6.3.43–25.2.45
13th U-Flotilla 3/45–capitulation

MANHARDT VON MANNSTEIN, ALFRED [780]

b. 9.3.1908, Laurut, Galicia, Poland
Class 1925; KKpt 1.11.39, posthumously FKpt seniority to 1.5.43
Naval Signals Officer (South) 3/38–6/40, (South-West) 7/40–10/40; U-boat trg 10/40–5/41; *Baubelehrung* 5/41–6/41
Cdr *U 753* 18.6.41–13.5.43
Lost 13.5.43 Northern Atlantic

MANKE, ROLF [781]

b. 21.12.1915, Berlin-Lichterfelde
Class 1935; Kplt 1.1.43
Seconded to Luftwaffe 9/38–8/41; U-boat trg 8/41–1/42; 1WO *U 576* 1/42–5/42; U-Cdr's Course, 24th U-Flotilla 6/42–7/42; *Baubelehrung* 7/42–8/42
Cdr *U 358* 15.8.42–1.3.44
Lost 1.3.44 N of Azores

MANNESMANN, GERT [782]
b. 14.10.1910, Bonn
Date of entry not known; Kplt (R)
1WO 11th Minesweeping Flotilla 9/39–3/40; M/S Cd 13th Minesweeping Flotilla 3/40–8/40; Cdr and acting CO 56th Minesweeping Flotilla 8/40–5/41; U-boat trg 6/41–11/41; WO *U 563* 11/41–3/42; WO *U 156* 4/42–11/42; courses and U-Cdr's Course 12/42–3/43 (U-Cdr's Torpedo Course 43); *Baubelehrung* 8.KLA 4/43–5/43
Cdr *U 545* 19.5.43–10.2.44
2nd U-Flotilla 2/44–4/44; *Baubelehrung* Type XXI 8.KLA 4/44–7/44
Cdr *U 2502* 19.7.44–8.4.45
Killed 8.4.45 bombing raid (direct hit on Howaldt Bunker, Hamburg)

MANSECK, HELMUT [783]
b. 22.12.1914, Habelschwerdt, Silesia
Class 1934; Kplt 1.4.42
2WO destroyer *Z 15 Erich Steinbrinck* 8/39–10/39; *Baubelehrung* 11/39–12/39; 1WO torpedo-boat *T 2* 12/39–4/40; U-boat trg 4/40–11/40; *Baubelehrung* 11/40–12/40; 1WO *U 553* 12/40–8/41; U-Cdr's Course 9/41–10/41
Cdr *U 143* 1.12.41 (but presumably 11/41; see Gelhaus [348]) to 7.4.42
Baubelehrung 4/42–5/42
Cdr *U 758* 5.5.42–3.4.44
6th U-Flotilla and *Baubelehrung* Type XXI 6.KLA 4/44–8/44
Cdr *U 3002* 6.8.44–24.9.44
Baubelehrung Type XXI 6.KLA 9/44–10/44
Cdr *U 3007* 22.10.44–24.2.45
Cdr *U 3008* 3/45–capitulation
Detained; freed 2.3.47

MARBACH, KARL-HEINZ [784]
b. 5.7.1917, Kolberg
Class 1937a; Kplt 1.9.44
Light cruiser *Leipzig* 6/39–9/39; relief administrator Fleet Command 9/39–10/40; U-boat trg 10/40–3/41; 2.UAA 3/41–5/41; 2WO *U 101* 5/41–12/41; 1WO *U 101* 1/42–3/42, inc. period acting Cdr *U 101* 1.1.42–3.2.42 (per P/F); U-Cdr's Course, 24th U-Flotilla 4/42–5/42
Cdr *U 29* 6.5.42–30.6.42
Cdr *U 28* 1.7.42–30.11.42
Baubelehrung 8.KLA 30.11.42–16.12.42
Cdr *U 953* 17.12.42–8/44
Baubelehrung Type XXI 6.KLA 9/44–12/44
Cdr *U 3014* 17.12.44–3.5.45
Detained; freed 21.2.48
Knight's Cross 22.7.44 (239th KM, 124th U-boat holder)

MARCH, JÜRGEN [785]
b. 8.3.1914, Farm Treufels, South Africa
Class 1933; Kplt 1.10.40
2WO, Div. and Gunnery Officer destroyer *Z 15 Erich Steinbrinck* 4/40–10/40; U-boat trg, U-Cdr's Course and *Baubelehrung* 10/40–5/41
Cdr *U 452* 29.5.41–25.8.41
Lost 25.8.41 SE of Iceland

MARIENFELD, FRIEDRICH-WILHELM [786]
b. 1.3.1920, Hannover
Class 1938; ObltzS 1.4.43
Officer trg 10/38–4/40; destroyer *Z 7 Hermann Schoemann* 5/40–8/40; Cdr artillery lighter *Aventura* 8/40–10/40; U-boat trg 10/40–3/41; *Baubelehrung* 3/41–5/41; 2WO *U 205* 5/41–4/42; U-Cdr's Course 5/42–6/42
Cdr *U 4* 16.6.42–23.1.43
Instructor 1.ULD 1/43–9/43; *Baubelehrung* 8.KLA 10/43–12/43
Cdr *U 1228* 22.12.43–capitulation
Detained; freed 13.1.46

MARKERT, ALBRECHT [787]
b. 10.9.1919, Leipzig
Class 1938; ObltzS 1.1.43
U-boat trg completed 3/41; Secretarial Officer 2nd U-Flotilla 4/41–9/41; 2WO *U 107* 9/41–7/42; U-Cdr's Course 8/42
Cdr *U 140* 2.9.42–31.7.44
Comp. CO College of Naval Warfare Schleswig 8/44–5/45
Detained; freed 17.9.45

MARKS, FRIEDRICH-KARL [788]
b. 5.6.1914, Hannover; Class 1934; Kplt 1.3.42
WO, Div and 2nd Gunnery Officer, light cruiser *Königsberg*, 9/38–4/40; Battery CO Naval Artillery Detachment 504 4/40–8/40; Coastal Defence Group Norwegian West Coast 8/40–10/40; U-boat trg 10/40–4/41; WO *U 75* 4/41–7/41; U-Cdr's Course and *Baubelehrung* 7/41–8/41
Cdr *U 376* 21.8.41–10.4.43
Lost 10.4.43 Bay of Biscay, W of Nantes

MARKWORTH, FRIEDRICH [789]
b. 14.2.1915, Wolfenbüttel
Class 1934; Kplt 1.9.41
Heavy cruiser *Blücher* 9/39–4/40; duties on land 4/40–6/40; U-boat trg 7/40–1/41; 1WO *U 103* 2/41–11/41; U-Cdr's Course, 24th U-Flotilla 11/41–1/42; 2.UAA 1/42–4/42; 2nd U-Flotilla 4/42–5/42
Cdr *U 66* 1.6.42 (P/F, and see Frerks [317]) or 22.6.42 to 1.9.43
2nd U-Flotilla 9/43–10/43; Trg Officer 23rd U-Flotilla 10/43–2/45; 25th U-Flotilla 2/45–capitulation
Knight's Cross 8.7.43 (177th KM, 95th U-boat holder)

MARTIN, LOTHAR [790]
b. 19.6.1916, Engelsdorf, Saxony
Class 1937a; Kplt 1.6.44
Seconded to Luftwaffe 10/39–7/43; U-boat trg 7/43–1/44; U-Cdr's Course, 23rd U-Flotilla 1/44–3/44; *Baubelehrung* 6.KLA 4/44
Cdr *U 776* 13.4.44–capitulation

MASSMANN, HANNS-FERDINAND [791]
b. 25.6.1917, Kiel
Class 1936; Kplt 1.8.43
7/Basic Trg Est. Stralsund 4/39–1/40; ADC BdU/Organisational 1/40; WO *U 17* 1/40–5/40; *Baubelehrung* 5/40–6/40; 1WO *U 137* 6/40–12/40
Cdr *U 137* 15.12.40–7.12.41
Baubelehrung 7.KLA 12/41–1/42
Cdr *U 409* 21.1.42–12.7.43
POW 12.7.43–27.2.48

MATHES, LUDWIG [792]
b. 23.11.1908, Kaiserslautern
Class 1928; Kplt 1.6.37, posthumously KKpt seniority 1.3.40
U-Boat School Kiel (per bulletin 24.7.35), School U-Flotilla of U-Boat School Kiel (per bulletin 1.11.35) and variously Cdr *U 6* (bulletin 1.11.36), Cdr School U-Flotilla (bulletin 1.6.37) and Cdr *U 6* 7.9.35–30.9.37; U-Cdr U-Flotilla *Weddigen* (bulletin 1.11.37) and Cdr *U 9* 1.10.37–18.9.39; *Baubelehrung* 10/39–11/39
Cdr *U 44* 4.11.39–20.3.40
Lost 20.3.40 North Sea, SW of Narvik

MATSCHULAT, GERHARD [793]
b. 25.5.1920, Berlin
Entry XI/1938; ObltzS 1.4.43
U-boat trg completed 12/42; 1WO *U 458* 12/42–7/43; U-Cdr's Course, 2.UAA and 24th U-Flotilla 7/43–9/43 (U-Cdr's Torpedo Course 54); *Baubelehrung* 1.KLA 9/43–10/43
Cdr *U 247* 23.10.43–1.9.44
Lost 1.9.44 English Channel, off Land's End

MATTHES, PETER [794]
b. 9.1.1918, Probstheida, Saxony
Class 1937b; Kplt 1.1.45
Platoon Leader light cruiser *Königsberg* 1/40–4/40; assistant to Harbour Commander Bergen 4/40–12/40; VP-Cdr Harbour Defence Flotilla Bergen 12/40–6/41; WO 3rd Torpedo-Boat Flotilla 7/41–6/43; U-boat trg 6/43–12/43; course 23rd U-Flotilla and 3.ULD 12/43–4/44; *Baubelehrung* 5.KLA 4/44–6/44
Cdr *U 326* 6.6.44–4/45
Missing in British waters from 4/45; official date of death 15.6.45

MATTKE, WILLY [795]
b. 25.1.1909, Graudenz
Entry 1928; promoted KKpt 1.1.44, retroactive following death
1WO *U 62* 12/39–9/40
Cdr *U 61* 5.11.40–4.5.41; Personnel Examiner 2.UAA at BdU 7/41–11/42; instructor 2.UAA 12/42–4/43; *Baubelehrung* 8.KLA 4/43–5/43
Cdr *U 544* 5.5.43–16.1.44
Lost 16.1.44 NW of Azores

GRAF VON MATUSCHKA, FREIHERR VON TOPPOLCZAN UND SPAETGEN, HARTMUT [796]
b. 29.12.1914, Dresden-Blasewitz
Class 1934; Kplt 1.4.42
Course Naval Gunnery School 6/39–9/39; ADC 13/Basic Trg Div. Stralsund 9/39; 2.ADC Commandant's HQ Gdynia 9/39–11/39; ADC 9/Reserve Naval Artillery Div. 11/39–1/40; Comp. Officer ship's company, *Prinz Eugen* 1/40–7/40; WO and No 1 Rangefinding Officer heavy cruiser *Prinz Eugen* 8/40–2/43; U-boat trg and U-Cdr's Course 3/43–11/43 (U-Cdr's Torpedo Course 56); *Baubelehrung* 1.KLA 11/43
Cdr *U 482* 1.12.43–16.1.45
Lost 16.1.45 Northern Channel

MATZ, JOACHIM [797]
b. 1.10.1913, Magdeburg
Class 1932; KKpt 1.1.44
WO *U 14* 1937 (per rank listings 1.11.37); WO *U 30* 1937–38
Cdr *U 6* 17.12.38–26.11.39
Staff BdU/Organisational 11/39–6/40
Cdr *U 59* 18.7.40–10.11.40
Cdr *U 70* 23.11.40–7.3.41
POW 7.3.41–26.6.47

MAUS, AUGUST [798]
b. 7.2.1915, Wuppertal
Class 1934; Kplt 1.11.41
Cadet Trg Officer trg ship *Schleswig-Holstein* 6/39–4/40; U-boat trg 4/40–12/40; *Baubelehrung* U-Boats North 12/40–2/41; 1WO *U 68* 2/41–12/41; U-Cdr's Torpedo Course, 24th U-Flotilla 12/41–3/42; 1st U-Flotilla 3/42–4/42, inc. part of period as acting Kplt, Staff; U-Cdr's Course, 24th U-Flotilla 4/42–5/42; *Baubelehrung* U-Boats North 5/42–6/42
Cdr *U 185* 13.6.42–24.8.43
POW 24.8.43–1946
Knight's Cross 21.9.43 (187th KM, 101st U-boat holder)

MAYER, KARL-THEODOR [799]
b. 15.8.1921, St Veit a.d. Glan
Class XII/1939; ObltzS 1.12.43
Officer trg 7/Basic Trg Est. Stralsund 12/39–4/40; sail trg ship *Albert Leo Schlageter* 4/40; cadet trg ship *Schleswig-Holstein* 5/40–7/40; minesweeper *M 21* (Operation 'Sealion') 7/40–12/40; courses 12/40–5/41; torpedo-boat *Löwe* (27th U-Flotilla) and U-boat trg 2.ULD 6/41–3/42; *Baubelehrung* 3/42–4/42; 2WO *U 382* 4/42–2/44; U-Cdr's Course, 3.ULD and 21st U-Flotilla 3/44–5/44 (U-Cdr's Torpedo Course 68)
Cdr *U 72* 20.5.44–3/45
Torpedo Testing Officer for Type XXI U-boat 1.UAA 3/45–capitulation

MECKEL, HANS [800]
b. 15.2.1910, Moers-Asberg
Class 1928; FKpt 1.12.44
Cdr *U 3* 6.8.35–29.9.37; *U 19* 30.9.37–31.8.39
Cdr *U 19* 1.9.39–1.11.39
4/Adm. Staff Officer, Staff BdU 11/39–5/44; CO *Ortungsdienst* OKM/5.SKL 6/44–capitulation. (Translator's note: The *Ortungsdienst* was the scientific technical office dealing with all electronic methods of vessel location and position fixing by hydrophones, sonar, radar, etc., and the evaluation of enemy progress in the field.)
Demobilised 5/45 (Translator's note: However, Meckel was then appointed to assist Fleet Advocate FKpt Kranzbühler, Dönitz's Defence Counsel at Nuremberg.)

MEENEN, KARL-HEINZ [801]
b. 12.3.1921, Berlin-Steglitz
Class IX/1939; ObltzS 1.10.43
U-boat trg 2/41–12/41; 1WO *U 30* 1/42–7/42; *Baubelehrung* 7/42–8/42; 1WO *U 188* 8/42–8/44; 3.ULD and U-Cdr's Course 8/44–12/44 (U-Cdr's Torpedo Course 78)
Cdr *U 1192* 22.12.44–5.5.45
Detained; freed 4.8.45

MEENTZEN, BERNHARD [802]
b. 25.4.1915, Wesermünde
Entry 1938; ObltzS (R) 1.12.43
Naval Flak School 1 7/41–3/43; U-boat trg and U-Cdr's Course 3/43–12/43 (U-Cdr's Torpedo Course 58); *Baubelehrung* 6.KLA 12/43–1/44
Cdr *U 1272* 29.1.44–2.7.44
Courses and *Baubelehrung* Type XXI 6.KLA 8/44–1/45
Cdr *U 3016* 5.1.45–2.5.45

MEERMEIER, JOHANNES [803]
b. 14.11.1916, Sande, nr Paderborn
Class 1937a; Kplt 1.8.44
Seconded to Luftwaffe 10/39–2/42; U-boat trg 3/42–8/42; WO 7th U-Flotilla 8/42–3/43; U-Cdr's Course, 2.UAA and 24th U-Flotilla 3/43–4/43 (U-Cdr's Torpedo Course 44); *Baubelehrung* 8.KLA 4/43–5/43
Cdr *U 979* 20.5.43–capitulation

VAN METEREN, KURT [804]
b. 13.3.1908, Bremen
Entry X/1939; ObltzS (R) 1.2.44
Cdr VP-boat *Hornisse* 5/40–8/42; VP Cdr Harbour Defence Flotilla Bergen 9/42–2/43; U-boat trg 3/43–10/43; U-Cdr's Course, 24th U-Flotilla 10/43–12/43 (U-Cdr's Torpedo Course 58); *Baubelehrung* 1.KLA 12/43–1/44
Cdr *U 399* 22.1.44–2.7.44
32nd U-Flotilla and *Baubelehrung* Type XXI 6.KLA 7/44–1/45
Cdr *U 3021* 12.1.45–2.5.45

MEHL, WALDEMAR [805]
b. 7.9.1914, Grävenwiebach, Usingen, Taunus
Class 1933; KKpt 1.3.45
No 1 Radio Technical Officer trg ship *Schleswig-Holstein* 8/39–12/39; Comp. CO Naval Signals School Mürwik 12/39–4/40; Cdr Wesermünde Sector, (embarkation port for invasion Norway and Denmark) 4.4.40–10.4.40; Naval Signals Officer (Narvik) 4/40–1/41, (Bergen, Adm. Norwegian West Coast) 1/41–3/41; U-boat trg 4/41–7/41; U-Cdr sea trg *U 371* 28.7.41–1.11.41 (per P/F, further U-boat trg 2.11.41–4.11.41)
Cdr *U 62* 5.11.41–19.11.41
Cdr *U 72* 2.12.41–6.5.42
Cdr *U 371* 25.5.42–4.4.44 (U-Cdr's Torpedo Course 1.11.42–15.11.42)
4/Adm Staff Officer FdU Mediterranean 4/44–8/44; 1/Adm Staff Officer (A1U) Adm. Aegean 8/44–10/44; 4/Adm Staff Officer OKM/2.SKL, adviser BdU/Opns 10/44–capitulation
Knight's Cross 28.3.44 (208th KM, 114th U-boat holder)

MEHNE, KARL [806]
b. 14.7.1914, Bremen
Entry VIII/1937; Kplt 1.11.44
VP-Cdr 17th VP-Boat Flotilla 9/41–7/42; VP-Cdr Harbour Defence Flotilla Kirkenes 7/42–7/43; U-boat trg 7/43–12/43; U-Cdr's Course, 23rd U-Flotilla and 3.ULD 12/43–5/44; courses and *Baubelehrung* Type XXI 6.KLA 5/44–1/45 (*Baubelehrung* Cdr first for *U 891* then *U 3027*)
Cdr *U 3027* 25.1.45–3.5.45

MEIER, ALFRED [807]
b. 31.12.1907, Seesen, Gandersheim
NCO (R) entry VII/1939; ObltzS (R) 1.6.44
StrmMt and WO 11th Anti-Submarine Flotilla 3/40–11/42; U-boat trg 11/42–5/43; 1WO *U 183* 6/43–11/44
Cdr *UIT 25* 25.11.44 (per WASt; however, Schrein [1123] retained command of *UIT 25* until 2/45 according to a statement made by the latter to the U-Boat Archive) to capitulation

MEINLSCHMIDT, RUDOLF [808]
b. 1.7.1921, Ebenberg, Graslitz, Erzgebirge
Class XII/1939; ObltzS 1.12.43
U-boat trg completed 4/42; *Baubelehrung* 4/42–6/42; 2WO *U 223* 6/42–11/43; 1WO *U 223* 11/43–3/44; U-Cdr's Course, 3.ULD and 23rd U-Flotilla 3/44–6/44; U-Cdr trg 27th U-Flotilla 6/44–8/44; U-Cdr sea trg *U 235* 9/44–12/44; *Baubelehrung* Type XXI 8.KLA 12/44–3/45
Cdr *U 2544* 10.3.45–5.5.45

MELZER, VOLKER [809]
b. 9.1.1918, Gruiten, Düsseldorf
Entry X/1939; ObltzS (R) 1.1.44
WO 8th Minesweeping Flotilla 6/41–4/42; R-Cdr 12th R-Boat Flotilla 6/42–3/43; U-boat trg 4/43–10/43; 23rd U-Flotilla 10/43–12/43; WO *U 714* 12/43–3/44; course 27th U-Flotilla 3/44
Cdr *U 994* 1.4.44–capitulation

MENARD, KARL-HEINZ [810]
b. 18.10.1917, Danzig-Langfuhr
Class 1937a; Kplt 1.6.44
Seconded to Luftwaffe 10/39–6/43; U-boat trg 7/43–5/44; WO 27th U-Flotilla 5/44–9/44
Cdr *U 237* 10/44–4.4.45
No further details available

MENGERSEN, ERNST [811]
b. 30.6.1912, Bremke/Lippe
Class 1933; KKpt 1.12.44
U-boat trg 4/39–7/39; 2WO *U 33* 7/39; at FdU, and U-boat officer's torpedo course Torpedo School Mürwik 7/39–9/39; U-boat tender *Erwin Wassner* 9/39; 1WO *U 54* 9/39–10/39; U-Cdr trg, U-Boat Trg Flotilla 10/39–11/39
Cdr *U 18* 24.11.39–2.9.40
Baubelehrung KLA U-Boats East 3.9.40–17.9.40
Cdr *U 143* 18.9.40–2.11.40
Cdr *U 101* 3.11.40–31.12.41 (per P/F, supernumerary for period to 17.11.40)
Baubelehrung 8.KLA 1.1.42–28.1.42
Cdr *U 607* 29.1.42–18.4.43 (until 31.5.43 per P/F and WASt, and see Jeschonnek [555])
Senior Trg Officer U-boat handling, 27th U-Flotilla 6/43; CO 20th U-Flotilla 6/43–2/45; Tactical Instructor (Staff), 25th U-Flotilla 3/45–4/45; listed for CO 15th U-Flotilla 4/45–capitulation
Detained; freed 20.2.46
Knight's Cross 18.11.41 (88th KM, 38th U-boat holder)

MERKLE, REINHOLD [812]
b. 10.12.1921, Ulm
Class XII/1939; ObltzS 1.12.43
Officer and U-boat trg, inc. *Baubelehrung* 12/39–3/42; 2WO and 1WO *U 516* 3/42–3/44; course 3.ULD 3/44–5/44 (U-Cdr's Torpedo Course 69); 21st U-Flotilla 5/44–10/44
Cdr *U 1201* 14.10.44–capitulation

ObltzS Friedrich Altmeier
U 1227, U 155

Kplt Kurt Baberg
U 30, U 618, U 827

Kplt Fritz Bart
UD 4

Kplt Heinz Bielfeld
U 703, U 1222

Kplt Hans-Joachim Börner
U 735

Kplt Heino Bohmann
U 88

Kplt Carl Borm
U 592

Kplt Hans-Joachim Brans
U 801

ObltzS Hermann Bruder
U 1058

FKpt (zV) Helmut Brümmer-Patzig
UD 4

KKpt Heinz Buchholz
U 24, U 15, U 195, U 177

ObltzS Hans-Helmuth Bugs
U 629

ObltzS Hans Buscher
U 1307

ObltzS Uwe Christiansen
U 28, U 71, U 2508, U 2365

Kplt Ernst Cordes
U 560, U 763, U 1195

Kplt Hermann Dahms
U 980

Kplt Heinz von Davidson
U 281

KKpt Friedrich Deetz
U 757

KKpt Heinrich Driver
U 20, U 23, U 145, U 371

Kplt Jürgen Ebert
U 927

Kplt Heinz-Wilhelm Eck
U 852

Kplt Engelbert Endrass
U 46, U 567

Kplt Dietrich von der Esch
U 586, U 606, U 863

KptzS Klaus Ewerth
U 1, U 36, U 26, U 850

Kplt Johann-Heinrich Fehler
U 234

KKpt Walter Flachsenberg
U 71

ObltzS Ludwig Forster
U 62, U 654

KKpt Rudolf Franzius
U 145, U 438

KptzS Kurt Freiwald
U 7, U 21, U 33, U 181

Kplt Alexander Gelhaar
U 1, U 45

KKpt (R) Otto Gericke
U 503

KKpt Heinrich Göllnitz
U 657

Kplt Franz Gramitzky
U 138

ObltzS Günther-Paul Grave
U 56, U 470

ObltzS Friedrich-August Gréus
U 737, U 716

ObltzS Ernst Hartmann
U 3

Kplt Götz von Hartmann
U 555, U 563, U 441

Kplt Heinrich Hasenschar
U 29, U 628

ObltzS (R) Wolfgang Heibges
U 999

KKpt Udo Heilmann
U 24, U 97

Kplt Hans-Dieter Heinicke
U 576

Kplt Helmut Hennig
U 24, U 533

Kplt Fritz Henning
U 561, U 565, U 668

Kplt Horst Höltring
U 149, U 604

Kplt Hans Hornkohl
U 566, U 1007, U 3512, U 3041, U 2502

ObltzS Jürgen Iversen
U 8, U 1103

Kplt Gustav-Adolf Janssen
U 151, U 37, U 102, U 3037

Kplt Johann Jebsen
U 565, U 859

FKpt Ottoheinrich Junker
U 33, U 532

ObltzS Hans-Albrecht Kandler
U 386, U 653

ObltzS Günther Keller
U 981, U 3521

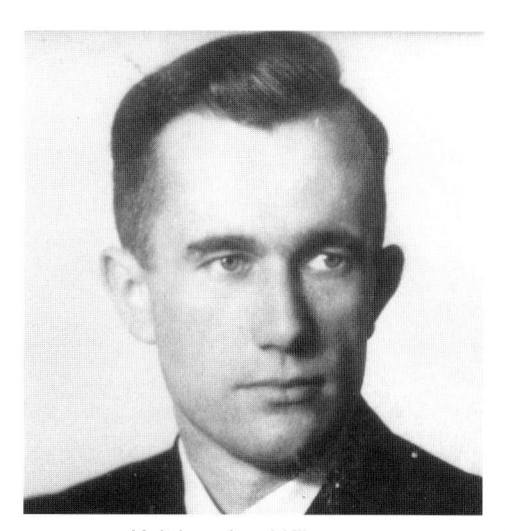

Kplt Leonhard Klingspor
U 1007

Kplt Walter Köhntopp
U 14, U 995

FKpt Walther Kölle
U 154

Kplt Helmut Köppe
U 613

ObltzS Erich Krempl
U 71, U 28, U 1162, U 548

ObltzS Johannes Kühne
U 2371

Kplt Hermann Lamby
U 437, U 3029

ObltzS (R) Martin Landt-Hayen
U 9, U 24, U 4705

Kplt Paul-Karl Löser
U 30, U 373

KKpt Axel-Olaf Loewe
U 505

Kplt Hartwig Looks
U 264

Kplt Robert Lübsen
U 277

ObltzS Gustav Lüssow
U 571

KptzS Wolfgang Lüth
U 13, U 9, U 138, U 43, U 181

ObltzS Hans-Gert Mahrholz
U 309

Kplt Helmut Manseck
U 143, U 758, U 3002, U 3007, U 3008

Kplt Hanns-Ferdinand Massmann
U 137, U 409

KptzS Karl-Friedrich Merten
U 68

ObltzS (R) Helmut Metz
U 487

ObltzS Willy Meyer
U 288

ObltzS Herbert Mumm
U 4, U 236

ObltzS Heinrich Niemeyer
U 547, U 1233

Kplt Herbert Opitz
U 206

Kplt Ulrich Pietsch
U 344

Kplt Klaus Popp
U 140, U 552, U 3006

Kplt Horst-Thilo Queck
U 622, U 92, U 2522

Kplt Gerhard Remus
U 34, U 566, U 2364

Kplt Hardo Rodler von Roithberg
U 24, U 71, U 989

KKpt Werner von Schmidt
U 9, U 12, U 15, U 25, U 40, U 116

Kplt Fritz Schneewind
U 511, U 183

Kplt Clemens Schöler
U 20, U 24

ObltzS Hermann Schulz
U 2369, U 2327

KKpt Friedrich Schuhmann-Hindenberg
U 245

Kplt Hans-Joachim Schwantke
U 43

ObltzS Hans-Adolf Schweichel
U 105, U 173

Kplt Wilhelm Spahr
U 178

Kplt Werner Techand
U 731

ObltzS Max Ulber
U 680

KptzS Jürgen Wattenberg
U 162

ObltzS Otto Wermuth
U 853, U 530

KKpt (zV) Georg von Wilamowitz-Moellendorf
U 2, U 459

ObltzS (R) Germanus Woermann
U 2339

KKpt (zV) Leo Wolfbauer
U 463

Kplt Joachim Zaubitzer
U 974

ObltzS Herbert Zoller
U 3, U 315

MERTEN, KARL-FRIEDRICH [813]
b. 15.8.1905, Posen
Class 1926; KptzS 1.5.45
Trg Officer trg ship *Schleswig-Holstein* 6/39–4/40; U-boat trg 4/40–9/40; U-Cdr's Course, 24th U-Flotilla 9/40–11/40; U-Cdr sea trg *U 38* 24.10.40–20.1.41 (U-Boat Archive per Merten; 30.11.40–23.1.41 per P/F); *Baubelehrung* U-Boats North 1/41–2/41
Cdr *U 68* 11.2.41–18.1.43 (per P/F; 21.1.43 per *U 68* WD, and see Lauzemis [709])
Acting CO 26th U-Flotilla 1/43–2/43; CO 24th U-Flotilla 3/43–5/44; FdU Central, Kiel 5/44–6/44; CO 24th U-Flotilla 6/44–3/45; Naval High Command East, Cdr Trg Formations and adviser at higher Staff levels 11.3.45–23.4.45; assigned for special duties Führer HQ Berlin 24.4.45; Naval High Command West, U-boat adviser A2, Special Missions, Alpine Region; 23.4.45 from Berlin to Alpine Fortress; Battalion Cdr 2/Naval Infantry Div. 5/45 (according to Merten, post not taken up); US detention at Biesenhofen, Bavaria 29.6.45–5.10.48 (Merten was detained in French custody on 8.3.49 in connection with the *Frimaire*, 15.6.42. The charges were dropped for lack of evidence on 10.9.49.)
Knight's Cross 13.6.42 (112th KM, 53rd U-boat holder)
Oak Leaves 16.11.42 (147th WM, 20th KM, 17th U-boat holder)

METHNER, JOACHIM [814]
b. 17.5.1918, Königsberg, East Prussia
Class 37a; ObltzS 1.9.41
Battleship *Tirpitz* 2/41–9/41; U-boat trg 9/41–5/42; 1WO *U 592* 5/42–1/43; U-Cdr's Course and *Baubelehrung* 7.KLA 1/43–3/43; Cdr *U 423* 3.3.43–26.9.43; 8th U-Flotilla and *Baubelehrung* 8.KLA 9/43–12/43
Cdr *U 1005* 30.12.43–2.7.44
Courses and *Baubelehrung* Type XXI 8.KLA 7/44–11/44

Cdr *U 2521* 21.11.44–4.5.45
Lost 4.5.45 Baltic Sea, SE of Flensburg Lightship

METZ, HELMUT [815]
b. 26.9.1906, Möllenbeck
Entry 1935; ObltzS (R) 1.10.42
WO *U A* 11/39–9/41; WO *U 129* 9/41–5/42; WO *U 373* 7/42–10/42; U-Cdr's Course, 24th U-Flotilla 10/42–11/42; *Baubelehrung* 1.KLA 11/42–12/42
Cdr *U 487* 21.12.42–13.7.43
Lost 13.7.43 central Atlantic

METZLER, JOST [816]
b. 26.2.1909, Altshausen, Württemberg
Class 1932; KKpt 1.10.43
1WO state yacht *Grille* 12/37–3/40; U-boat trg, 4/40–7/40; U-Cdr's Course, 24th U-Flotilla, 8/40–9/40; *Baubelehrung* U-Boats East 9/40–11/40
Cdr *U 69* 2.11.40–28.8.41
Hospitalised 8/41–10/41; Trg Leader Staff 25th U-Flotilla 11/41–5/42; Trg Leader 27th U-Flotilla 5/42–2/43
Cdr *U 847* 1.2.43 (per *U 847* WD, and see Guggenberger [393]) or 2.2.43 (per P/F) or 5.2.43 (per WASt) to 30.6.43 or 15.9.43 (per P/F)
No information (hospitalised) 1.7.43–15.9.43; acting CO 5th U-Flotilla 9/43–10/43; Leader U-Handling Trg 23rd U-Flotilla 10/43–3/44, also CO 19th U-Flotilla 10/43 and 4/44–capitulation
Knight's Cross 28.7.41 (78th KM, 35th U-boat holder)

MEYER, FRITZ [817]
b. 17.2.1916, Hannover
Class 1934; ObltzS 1.4.39
ADC U-Flotilla *Saltzwedel* 5/38–12/39; 1WO *U 34* 12/39–9/40
Cdr *U 34* 29.9.40–22.5.41
Baubelehrung 5/41–6/41

Cdr *U 507* 7.6.41–11.9.41
Lost 11.9.41 Denmark Strait, SE of Angmagsalik

MEYER, GERHARD [818]
b. 15.4.1915, Kiel
Entry 1935; ObltzS (R) 1.7.43
WO destroyer *Z 15 Erich Steinbrinck* 3/42–5/43; U-boat trg 5/43–1/44 (U-Cdr's Torpedo Course 61); *Baubelehrung* 1.KLA 1/44–3/44
Cdr *U 486* 22.3.44–12.4.45
Lost 12.4.45 Norwegian Sea, NW of Bergen

MEYER, HEINRICH [819]
b. 8.4.1922, Bäsdorf, Silesia
Class XII/1939; ObltzS 1.12.43
U-boat trg completed 12/41; 2WO *U 154* 12/41–7/43; U-Cdr's Course, 2.UAA and 24th U-Flotilla 7/43–8/43 (U-Cdr's Torpedo Course 53); *Baubelehrung* 6.KLA 9/43
Cdr *U 287* 22.9.43–capitulation

MEYER, HERBERT [820]
b. 30.11.1910, Gruppenbühren
Entry III/1937; ObltzS (R) 1.12.42
VP-Cdr School Flotilla, C-in-C Escort Forces 5/41–6/42; VP Cdr 9th VP-Boat Flotilla 7/42–2/43; U-boat trg 3/43–8/43; U-Cdr's Course, 24th U-Flotilla 9/43–10/43 (U-Cdr's Torpedo Course 56); *Baubelehrung* 6.KLA 10/43–12/43
Cdr *U 804* 4.12.43–9.4.45
Lost 9.4.45 Kattegat

MEYER, PAUL [821]
b. 27.8.1917, Zoppot
Entry 1936; ObltzS 1.4.43
WO destroyer *Z 30* 11/41–7/42; U-boat trg 7/42–12/42; 2WO *U 505* 12/42–7/43; 1WO *U 505* 7/43–6/44 acting Cdr *U 505* following suicide at sea of Zschech [1409] 24.10.43–7.11.43
POW 4.6.44

MEYER, RUDOLF [822]
b. 1.2.1920, Leipzig
Class 1938; ObltzS 1.4.43
Officer trg 10/38–10/40; battleship *Tirpitz* 11/40–5/43; U-boat trg 5/43–10/43; U-Cdr's Course, 3.ULD and 23rd U-Flotilla 10/43–2/44 (U-Cdr's Torpedo Course 63); *Baubelehrung* 1.KLA 2/44–4/44
Cdr *U 1055* 8.4.44–30.4.45
Lost 30.4.45 Bay of Biscay, W of Brest

MEYER, WILLY [823]
b. 2.10.1912, Gruppenbühren
Entry 1936; ObltzS (R) 1.2.43
8th VP-Boat Flotilla 9/39–9/41; U-boat trg 9/41–5/42; WO *U 657* 5/42–3/43; U-Cdr's Course, 24th U-Flotilla 3/43–5/43 (U-Cdr's Torpedo Course 45); *Baubelehrung* 6.KLA 5/43–6/43
Cdr *U 288* 26.6.43–3.4.44
Lost 3.4.44 Barents Sea, SE of Bear I

MICHAHELLES, HERMANN [824]
Details of birth not recorded
Class 1927; Kplt 1.10.36
Cdr *U 2* 25.7.35–30.9.36; U-Cdr 2nd U-Flotilla *Saltzwedel* 1.10.36–2.11.36; Cdr *U 35* 3.11.36–30.7.37. Per rank listings 1.11.36 Michahelles was scheduled to command *U 36* but he was still commanding *U 35* when *U 36* was commissioned on 3.11.36 (U-Boat Archive per Kretschmer [663])
Killed 30.7.37 in road traffic accident at Haunstetten, Augsburg

MICHAELOWSKI, HANS-BERNHARD [825]
b. 13.4.1912, Kiel
Class 1933; Kplt 1.1.41
2WO *U 35* 10/37–10/38; 1WO *U 35* 10/38–9/39; U-Boat School Neustadt 9/39–11/39
Acting Cdr *U 6* 11/39–12/39

Cdr *U 62* 21.12.39–20.5.41
Died 20.5.41

MICHEL, GEORG-HEINZ [826]
b. 19.9.1909, Hamm, Westphalia
Class 1931/33; KKpt 1.10.43
WO *U 33* 1937 (for 3 months); WO *U 12* 1937 (per rank listings 1.11.37); Cdr *U 29* 1.11.38–3.4.39; Cdr *U 25* 4.4.39–4.9.39; *Baubelehrung* 9/39
Cdr *U 54* 23.9.39–30.11.39
Cdr *U 8* 1.12.39 to 4.5.40 (per P/F) or 7.5.40 (per WASt) or 5.5.40 (per P/F Kentrat [597])
Group Leader Torpedo Testing Branch 6/40–3/42; Kplt Staff 1st U-Flotilla 4/42–10/43; Cdr II Section/1.ULD 11/43–2/45; Cdr 2.UAA 3/45–capitulation
Detained; freed 8/45

MIEDE, HEINRICH [827]
b. 4.3.1915, Dortmund
Enlistment as rating 1/35; LtzS 1.4.44
Course Torpedo School Mürwik 4/44–7/44; acting Cdr *U 56* 1.7.44–22.2.45; WO *U 1274* 3/45–4/45
Lost 16.4.45 North Sea, N of Newcastle

VON MITTELSTAEDT, GERT [828]
b. 14.1.1912, Niederlinxweiler, Saarland
Class 1932; Kplt 1.6.40
Div. Officer/WO heavy cruiser *Admiral Scheer* 9/38–3/40; U-boat trg 4/40–9/40; U-Cdr's Course, 24th U-Flotilla 10/40–11/40
Cdr *U 144* 17.11.40–9.8.41
Lost 9.8.41 Baltic Sea, N of Dagoe

MOEHLE, KARL-HEINZ [829]
b. 31.7.1910, Norden, Ostfriesland
Class 1930; KKpt 1.4.43
U-boat trg 3/36–12/36; WO *U-5* 12/36–1/37; WO U-Flotilla *Saltzwedel* 1/37–3/37; *Baubelehrung* U-Boats Deschimagwerft Bremen 4/37; 1WO *U 32* 4/37–9/37
Cdr *U 20* 1.10.37–17.1.40
1st U-Flotilla 1/40–2/40; *Baubelehrung* U-Boats North Sea 3/40–5/40
Cdr *U 123* 30.5.40–16.5.41 (per P/F) or 19.5.41 (per *U 123* WD, and see Hardegen [413])
At BdU 5/41–6/41; CO 5th U-Flotilla and Senior Officer U-boat base Kiel 6/41–capitulation
Sentenced to 5 years' imprisonment for handing down the *Laconia* order; released from British custody 9.11.49
Knight's Cross 26.2.41 (60th KM, 24th U-boat holder)

MÖGLICH, HANS [830]
b. 29.1.1916, Posen
Class 1935; Kplt 1.7.42
WO torpedo-boat *Albatros* 12/39–10/40; U-boat trg 10/40–3/41; *Baubelehrung* 4/41–6/41; 1WO *U 130* 6/41–4/42; U-Cdr's Course, 24th U-Flotilla 4/42–6/42; *Baubelehrung* 8.KLA 7/42–8/42
Cdr *U 526* 12.8.42–14.4.43
Lost 14.4.43 (mined in harbour approaches, Lorient)

MÖHLMANN, HELMUT [831]
b. 25.6.1913, Kiel
Class 1933; KKpt 1.4.45
1WO torpedo-boat *Luchs* 2/38–4/40; U-boat trg 5/40–10/40; 1st U-Flotilla 10/40–11/40; U-Cdr's Course, 24th U-Flotilla 15.11.40–18.12.40 (per P/F)
Cdr *U 143* 3.11.40 (per WASt) or 9.12.40 (per P/F) to 19.3.41
Cdr *U 52* 20.3.41–15.4.41 (per P/F, command not taken up); *Baubelehrung* 4/41–5/41
Cdr *U 571* 22.5.41–31.5.43 (per P/F)

Naval Academy Berlin 6/43–8/43; adviser A3 Staff, Commanding Adm. U-Boats 9/43–12/44; CO 14th U-Flotilla 12/44–capitulation
Detained; freed 30.9.45
Knight's Cross 16.4.43 (161st KM, 90th U-boat holder)

VON MÖLLENDORFF, GOSKE [832]
b. 12.3.1918, Krampfer, Westprignitz, Mecklenburg
Class 1937a; Kplt 1.8.44
WO and ADC Escort Flotilla 4/39–3/40; WO 3rd Minesweeping Flotilla 4/40–11/40; R-Cdr 7th R-Boat Flotilla 11/40–9/41; U-boat trg 10/41–4/42; 1WO *U 96* 4/42–10/42; U-Cdr's Course and *Baubelehrung* 1.KLA 10/42–12/42
Cdr *U 235* 19.12.42–19.1.43
Cdr *U 148* 19.1.43 to 29.11.43 (per WASt) or 15.12.43 (U-Boat Archive per von Möllendorff)
Cdr *U 38* 16.12.43 (for 'a few days': U-Boat Archive per von Möllendorff) then hospitalised 12/43–6/44; Comp. CO 2.ULD 6/44–capitulation (but Battalion Cdr in the last defence of Berlin from 4/45)
Detained; freed 2.7.45

MÖLLER, GÜNTHER [833]
b. 30.6.1918, Rostock
Class 1937b; ObltzS 1.4.42
U-boat trg 4/40–11/40; 24th U-Flotilla 11/40–12/40; at BdU/Opns 12/40–2/41; WO (*U ?*) 2/41–5/42; U-Cdr's Course, 24th U-Flotilla 5/42–6/42
Cdr *U 141* 16.6.42–15.2.43
Baubelehrung 6.KLA 16.2.43–6.4.43
Cdr *U 844* 7.4.43–16.10.43
Lost 16.10.43 SW of Iceland

MOHR, EBERHARD [834]
b. 12.10.1915, Düsseldorf
Class 1935; ObltzS 1.10.39, posthumously Kplt seniority 1.3.42
Battery Officer Naval Artillery Detachment 518 8/39–9/39; CO Vistula Flotilla 9/39–10/39; Battery Officer Naval Artillery Detachment 518 10/39; Battery Officer 9th Reserve Naval Artillery Div. 10/39–10/39; 2.ADC Commandant's HQ, Fortress Gdynia 11/39–3/40; U-boat trg 4/40–9/40; 24th U-Flotilla and UAA Plön 9/40–1/41; WO 2nd U-Flotilla 2/41–7/41; U-Cdr's Course, 24th U-Flotilla 7/41–9/41
Cdr *U 148* 15.9.41 to 15.1.42 or 1.3.42 (per WASt, and see Franke [308])
Cdr *U 133* 2.3.42–14.3.42
Lost 14.3.42 Mediterranean, off Salamis

MOHR, JOHANN [835]
b. 12.6.1916, Hannover
Class 1934; KKpt 1.4.43
Flag Lt to C-in-C *Deutschland* class heavy cruisers 2/38–3/40; U-boat trg 4/40–9/40; 2WO *U 124* 9/40–12/40; 1WO *U 124* 12/40–6/41; U-Cdr's Course, 24th U-Flotilla 6/41–7/41; 1.UAA 7/41; 2.UAA 7/41–9/41
Cdr *U 124* 8.9.41–3.4.43
Lost 3.4.43 W of Oporto
Knight's Cross 27.3.42 (107th KM, 48th U-boat holder)
Oak Leaves 13.1.43 (177th WM, 23rd KM, 19th U-boat holder)

MOHR, KURT [836]
b. 12.1.1922, Greifswald
Entry IV/1940; ObltzS (R) 1.3.44
WO 8th U-Flotilla 7/42–11/44; *Baubelehrung* 5.KLA 11/44–12/44
Cdr *U 930* 6.12.44–capitulation

MOHS, HANS-DIETER [837]
22.9.1919, Magdeburg
Class 1937b; Kplt 1.1.45

U-boat trg 4/40–10/40; *Baubelehrung* 10/40–2/41; 2WO *U 203* 2/41–10/41; 1WO *U 203* 11/41–3/42

Cdr *U 5* 26.2.43–5/42

U 60 5/42–6.12.42, inc. course 24th U-Flotilla 9/42–10/42; *Baubelehrung* 8.KLA 12/42–1/43

Cdr *U 956* 6.1.43–capitulation

VON MORSTEIN, HANS-JOACHIM [838]

b. 1.8.1909, Karlsruhe

Entry 1928; Kplt (zV) 1.12.41, seniority from 1.7.41

Courses 2.KLA and Naval Gunnery School 9/41–12/41; 1WO and Gunnery Officer gunboat *K 1* 12/41–4/42; First Officer *Minenräumschiff 12* 4/42–1/43; U-boat trg 1/43–8/43 (U-Cdr's Torpedo Course 55); WO 11th U-Flotilla 8/43–11/43; *Baubelehrung* 1.KLA 11/43–12/43

Cdr *U 483* 22.12.43–capitulation

VON MÜFFLING, BARON HANS-BRUNO [839]

b. 24.3.1919, Rohrbeck, Arnswalde

Class 1938; ObltzS 1.9.43

1WO *U 263* 5/42–9/43; 1WO *U 952* 9/43–3/44; U-Cdr's Course 3/44–6/44 (U-Cdr's Torpedo Course 70); no details recorded 6/44–1/45 (The assertion in the Lohmann-Hildebrand almanac that von Müffling was commander of *U 76* in this period is incorrect since *U 76* was sunk on 5.4.41. Similarly, the suggestion that the boat might have been *U 78* is incorrect: at the time in question *U 78* was commanded by Eisele [243].); *Baubelehrung* Type XXI 8.KLA 1/45–4/45

Cdr *U 2545* 19.4.45–3.5.45

VON MÜHLENDAHL, ARVED [840]

b. 1.11.1904, Reval

Class 1923; KptzS 1.9.43

Adm. Staff Officer, Staff, Station Command Baltic 11/38–3/40; 4/Adm. Staff Officer Commanding Adm. France 6/40–5/41 and Staff Naval Group South 8/41–2/43; U-boat trg 3/43–10/43 (U-Cdr's Torpedo Course 55); *Baubelehrung* 6.KLA 10/43–12/43

Cdr *U 867* 12.12.43–19.9.44

Lost 19.9.44, North Sea, NW of Bergen

MÜHLENPFORDT, KARL [841]

b. 27.6.1909, Wolfenbüttel

Entry VIII/1940; ObltzS (R) 1.5.43

Baubelehrung 6/41–7/41; 2WO *U 86* 7/41–9/42; U-Cdr's Course, 24th U-Flotilla 10/42–11/42; *Baubelehrung* 11/42–12/42

Cdr *U 308* 23.12.42–4.6.43

Lost 4.6.43 E of Faroes

MÜLLER, BERNHARD [842]

b. 10.10.1916, Kiel

Class 1937a; ObltzS 1.9.41

Seconded to Luftwaffe 9/39–12/40; U-boat trg 1/41–7/41; *Baubelehrung* 7/41–8/41; 1WO *U 584* 8/41–5/42; U-Cdr's Course, 24th U-Flotilla 6/42–7/42; *Baubelehrung* 8.KLA 7/42

Cdr *U 633* 30.7.42–7.3.43

Lost 7.3.43 North Atlantic

MÜLLER, HANS-GEORG [843]

b. 15.10.1922, Permauern, Labiau

Class X/1940; ObltzS 1.10.44

2WO *U 276* 12/42–2/43; 2WO *U 596* 3/43–7/43; 1WO *U 596* 7/43–3/44; U-Cdr's Course, 3.ULD and 24th U-Flotilla 4/44–6/44 (U-Cdr's Torpedo Course 70); U-Holding Company 1, 21st U-Flotilla 6/44–10/44; *Baubelehrung* Type XXIII 8.KLA 10/44–12/44

Cdr *U 2349* 11.12.44–5.5.45

MÜLLER, HEINZ-EBERHARD [844]
b. 14.3.1916, Stuttgart
Class 1936; Kplt 1.4.43
WO U-Flotilla *Emsmann* 5/39–12/39; U-Boat School Neustadt 12/39–10/40; *Baubelehrung* 10/40–11/40; 2WO *U 69* 11/40–1/41; instructor Torpedo School Mürwik 1/41–4/42; supplementary WO *U 145* and *U 60* 4/42–2/43; U-Cdr's Course, 1.UAA and 24th U-Flotilla 2/43–3/43
Cdr *U 662* 10.3.43–21.7.43
POW 21.7.43–2/44; repatriation exchange and hospitalised Glücksburg 2/44–6/44; relief administrator OKM/2.SKL/BdU/Opns 6/44–capitulation

MÜLLER, RUDOLF [845]
b. 17.6.1917, Lingen, Ems
Class 1937b; ObltzS 1.4.42
U-boat trg completed 9/41; *Baubelehrung* 8.KLA 9/41–11/41; 1WO *U 509* 11/41–11/42; 1WO *U 91* 12/42–1/43; U-Cdr's Course, 2.UAA and 26th U-Flotilla 1/43–2/43; *Baubelehrung* 6.KLA 2/43–3/43
Cdr *U 282* 13.3.43–29.10.43
Lost 29.10.43 SE of Greenland

MÜLLER, WERNER [846]
(Post-war adopted the surname Müller-Feldhammer)
b. 4.8.1920, Berlin
Class XII/1939; ObltzS 1.12.43
Supernumerary WO (sea trg) *U 232* 11/42–2/43; 1WO *U 239* 3/43–2/44; 1WO *U 953* 3/44–8/44 and acting Cdr *U 963* 13.8.44–21.8.44 (see Boddenberg [93]); U-Cdr's Course, 24th U-Flotilla 9/44–10/44 (U-Cdr's Torpedo Course 77); WO *U 1167* 10/44–12/44; various duties 12/44–capitulation, inc. acting Cdr *U 2327* 2/45–3/45 and WO *U 2327* until 5/45

MÜLLER, WILLI [847]
b. 25.4.1912, Wittenberge
Entry IX/1939; ObltzS (R) 1.9.43
WO 2nd Sperrbrecher Flotilla 1/41–7/42; R-Cdr 8th R-Boat Flotilla 7/42–1/43; U-boat trg 1/43–7/43; U-Cdr under instrn, 27th U-Flotilla 7/43–10/43 (U-Cdr's Torpedo Course 54); *Baubelehrung* 8.KLA 10/43–11/43
Cdr *U 1000* 4.11.43–29.9.44
Baubelehrung Type XXI 7.KLA 10/44–1/45
Cdr *U 3523* 29.1.45–5.5.45
Lost 5.5.45 Baltic Sea, E of Aarhus

MÜLLER-ARNECKE, WILHELM [848]
b. 30.10.1910, Bremen
Class 1933/31 (for explanation see Prien [947]; KKpt 1.9.43
1WO *U 19* 10/37–10/39
Cdr *U 19* 2.11.39–2.1.40
Adviser P.II (personal particulars, non-NCOs) Staff BdU/Organisational, also 2/Adm. U-Boats and Commanding Adm. U-Boats 1/40–11/44; Cdr Section 1/2.ULD 12/44–1/45; adviser P.II, Staff, Commanding Adm. U-Boats 1/45–capitulation
Detained; freed 15.9.45

MÜLLER-BETHKE, ERICH [849]
b. 23.7.1917, Wesermünde, Lehe
Class 1937b; Kplt 1.1.45
U-boat trg 3/43–11/43; U-Cdr's Course, 23rd U-Flotilla, 3.ULD and 24th U-Flotilla 11/43–2/44 (U-Cdr's Torpedo Course 63); *Baubelehrung* 6.KLA 3/44–5/44
Cdr *U 1278* 31.5.44–17.2.45
Lost 17.2.45 North Sea, NW of Bergen

MÜLLER-EDZARDS, HEINRICH [850]
b. 18.3.1910, Wesermünde-Geestemünde

Class 1933/32 (for explanation see Prien [947]); KKpt 1.9.44
ADC School Flotilla C-in-C Escort Forces North Sea 4/39–9/39; UJ-Cdr 12th Anti-Submarine Flotilla 9/39–7/40; CO Fast Anti-Submarine Group 7/40–3/41; U-boat trg 3/41–8/41; *Baubelehrung* 8.KLA 8/41–10/41
Cdr *U 590* 2.10.41–7.6.43 (See Krüer [668])
Tactical Instructor AGRU-Front 6/43–10/43; Tactical Instructor and Kplt Staff 20th U-Flotilla 10/43–5/44; Senior Officer Harbour Trg 19th U-Flotilla 5/44–6/44; Cdr Section 1/2.ULD 7/44–12/44; Navigation Officer trg ship *Schlesien* 12/44–capitulation
Detained; freed 7.8.45

MÜLLER-KOELBL, HARRO [851]
b. 17.10.1919, Bärwalde, Pomerania
Class 1938; ObltzS 1.4.43
1WO *U 183* 4/42–5/43; U-Cdr's Course, 2.UAA and 24th U-Flotilla 5/43–6/43 (U-Cdr's Torpedo Course 49); relief instructor 1.ULD 7/43–11/44; Group Officer Torpedo School Mürwik 11/44–2/45; *Baubelehrung* Cdr 6.KLA for *U 3051* (boat never commissioned, and see Beck [57]) 5.2.45–capitulation

MÜLLER-STÖCKHEIM, GÜNTHER [852]
b. 17.12.1913, Klein Stöckheim, Braunschweig
Class 1934; KKpt 1.7.43
Group Officer Naval College Flensburg-Mürwik 4/38–2/40, also Comp. Officer Section 4, 7/Basic Trg Est. Stralsund 4/39–2/40; 1/NCO Trg Div (for sail trg ship *Albert Leo Schlageter*) 2/40–4/40; U-boat trg 4/40–9/40; *Baubelehrung* U-Boats North Sea 9/40–10/40; UAA Plön 10/40–11/40; 1WO *U 123* 12/40–5/41; 2nd U-Flotilla 5/41–6/41; U-Cdr's Course, 24th U-Flotilla 6/41–7/41
Cdr *U 67* 3.7.41–16.7.43 (per P/F)
Lost 16.7.43 Sargasso Sea, SE of Lesser Antilles

Knight's Cross 27.11.42 (134th KM, 69th U-boat holder)

MÜNNICH, RALPH [853]
b. 11.2.1916, Chemnitz
Class 1935; Kplt 1.1.43
Seconded to Luftwaffe 10/37–12/40; U-boat trg 1/41–5/41; 1WO *U 106* 6/41–4/42; U-Cdr's Course, 2.UAA and 24th U-Flotilla 4/42–6/42; *Baubelehrung* 6.KLA 6/42–7/42
Cdr *U 187* 23.7.42–4.2.43
Lost 4.2.43 North Atlantic

MÜNSTER, HELMUT [854]
b. 14.9.1916, Magdeburg
Class 1937b; Kplt 1.1.45
Trg Flying School Parow 12/39–7/40; *Flieger-Ergänzungsgruppe (See)*, Kamp 8/40–9/40; observer *3./(See) Kampfgruppe 606* 9/40–12/40; U-boat trg 1/41–6/41; Platoon Officer 2.UAA 6/41–9/41; 2WO *U 43* 9/41–2/42; 1WO *U 43* 2/42–8/42; U-Cdr's Torpedo Course 8/42–9/42
Cdr *U 101* 15.9.42 or 26.10.42 to 22.10.43 (see von Witzendorff [1367])
Cdr *U 428* 26.10.43–1.5.44
Baubelehrung Type XXI 7.KLA 5/44–7/44
Cdr *U 3501* 29.7.44–4.10.44 8th U-Flotilla (As a KLA training boat, *U 3501* had only a fixed demonstration propellor. For the tow from Danzig to Bremen via Kiel an engineer officer had command, assisted by a boatswain as WO. At the Bremer Vulkan Yard, Vegesack, the interior of the boat was cleared for conversion to a fighting unit, but nothing came of this and the vessel was eventually employed as an electrical generator. Schmidt-Weichert [1099] took over command in 4/45. Bart [42], who had been promised *U 3060*, destroyed in an air raid, was appointed 1WO.)
Baubelehrung Type XXI 7.KLA 10/44–12/44
Cdr *U 3517* 22.12.44–2.5.45

MÜRL, HEINRICH [855]
b. 11.2.1912, Essen
Enlisted as rating 1932; ObltzS 1.7.44
BtsMt *U 19* 1936; ObStrm *U 98* 10/40–2/42; ObStrm *U 177* 3/42–10/43; courses 11/43–5/44 (U-Cdr's Torpedo Course 69); *Baubelehrung* Type XXIII 8.KLA 5/44–8/44
Cdr *U 2327* 19.8.44–2/45
1.UAA 2/45–3/45; Comp. CO, U-boat base Stavanger 3/45–capitulation

MÜTZELBURG, ROLF [856]
b. 23.6.1913, Kiel
Class 1932; Kplt 1.1.40
M/S-Cdr 12th Minesweeping Flotilla 9/39–10/39; U-boat trg 10/39–6/40
Cdr *U 10* 10.6.40–29.11.40
U-Cdr sea trg *U 100* 11/40–1/41; *Baubelehrung* U-Boats East 1/41–2/41
Cdr *U 203* 18.2.41–11.9.42
Lost in swimming accident Atlantic 11.9.42 (Translator's note: Drowned after striking his head against the hull of *U 203* while diving from deck.)
Knight's Cross 17.11.41 (87th KM, 37th U-boat holder)
Oak Leaves 15.7.42 (104th WM, 14th KM, 12th U-boat holder)

MUGLER, GUSTAV-ADOLF [857]
b. 10.10.1912, Danzig-Langfuhr
Class 1931; Kplt 1.10.39, posthumously KKpt seniority 1.3.40
WO *U 30* 1937 (per rank listings 1.11.37)
Cdr *U 41* 22.4.39–5.2.40
Lost 5.2.40 S of Ireland

MUHS, HARALD [858]
b. 1.10.1919, Hannover
Class 1938; ObltzS 1.1.43
No 2 Radio Technical Officer and WO destroyer *Z 15 Erich Steinbrinck* 10/40–6/42; U-boat trg 6/42–11/42; 1WO *U 409* 12/42–4/43; U-Cdr's Course, 24th U-Flotilla 4/43–5/43 (U-Cdr's Torpedo Course 46); *Baubelehrung* 8.KLA 5/43–6/43
Cdr *U 674* 15.6.43–2.5.44
Lost 2.5.44 Arctic Ocean, NW of Narvik

MUMM, FRIEDRICH [859]
b. 15.1.1915, Pahlen, Nord-Ditmarschen
Class 1936; Kplt 1.2.43
Platoon Leader heavy cruiser *Admiral Graf Spee* 4/38–12/39; interned 12/39–7/40; returned to Germany; Fleet Command 8/40–10/40; U-boat trg 10/40–3/41; 1WO *U 564* 4/41–11/41; U-Cdr under instrn 26th U-Flotilla 11/41–1/42
Cdr *U 52* 14.1.42–24.7.42
Cdr *U 594* 25.7.42–4.6.43
Lost 4.6.43 W of Gibraltar

MUMM, HERBERT [860]
b. 3.9.1920, Pahlen, Nord-Ditmarschen
Class X/1939; ObltzS 1.10.43
U-boat trg 4/41–9/41; Platoon Officer 1.ULD 10/41–2/42; *Baubelehrung* 3/42–4/42; 1WO *U 354* 4/42–6/43; U-Cdr's Course 6/43–8/43 (U-Cdr's Torpedo Course 51); instructor 1.ULD 8/43
Cdr *U 4* 23.8.43–5/44 (U-Boat Archive per Mumm)
Cdr *U 236* 5.6.44 (per U-Boat Archive) or 16.7.44 (per WASt) to 4.5.45

MURL, HEINZ [861]
b. 26.10.1919, Berlin
Class 1938; ObltzS 1.1.43
WO sea trg *U 24* 10/40–1/41; 1WO *U 72* 5/41–11/41; *Baubelehrung* 8.KLA 12/41–1/42; 1WO *U 513* 1/42–4/43; U-Cdr's Course 5/43–6/43; Trg Officer 2.ULD 6/43–1/45

Cdr *U 103* 23.1.45–18.2.45 (withdrawal, Gdynia–Hamburg; the boat had been decommissioned in 3/44 and was not recommissioned for the voyage); Trg Officer 2.ULD 2/45–4/45; Comp. CO Special Unit *Koralle* (BdU Escort and Protection Comp.), Camp *Koralle*, Berlin; thereafter protection of Reich Government until 23.5.45

MUSENBERG, WERNER [862]

b. 24.9.1904, Berlin

Class 1925; KptzS 1.4.45

Head of Personnel Branch Staff 2/Adm. Baltic 7/37–6/41; U-boat trg and *Baubelehrung* 6/41–5/42, inc. appointment within sphere of Commanding Adm. U-Boats

Cdr *U 180* 16.5.42–4.1.44 (see Hartmann [425]; Lange [696] was acting Cdr *U 180* 10/43–7.11.43)

Naval liaison officer/OKW 1/44–4/44; development leader Maritime Vocational Technical College Krumpendorf 4/44–8/44; leader Task Force *Musenberg* (*K-Verband* Holland) 8/44–capitulation

Detained; freed 15.3.45

N

NACHTIGALL, OTTO-HEINRICH [863]
b. 24.9.1914, Warmstadt
Entry VIII/1937; ObltzS (R) 1.3.44
12th and 38th Minesweeping Flotillas 3/42–1/43; U-boat trg 1/43–6/43; WO 27th U-Flotilla 6/43–8/43; U-Cdr under instrn 21st U-Flotilla 8/43–9/43 (U-Cdr's Torpedo Course 54)
Cdr *U 430* (ex-Italian *S-6*) 10.9.43 (date per Nachtigall but doubtful) to 5.1.44
Baubelehrung 7.KLA 1/44–3/44
Cdr *U 1171* 23.3.44–16.7.44
Courses and *Baubelehrung* 7.KLA Type XXI 8/44–12/44
Cdr *U 3513* 2.12.44–3.5.45

NAGEL, KARL-HEINZ [864]
b. 17.1.1917, Eisleben
Class 1937a; ObltzS 1.9.41
Destroyer *Z 15 Erich Steinbrinck* 4/39–10/39; WO and UJ Cdr 12th Anti-Submarine Flotilla 10/39–2/41; U-boat trg 2/41–7/41; *Baubelehrung* 8/41–9/41; 1WO *U 586* 9/41–6/42; U-Cdr's Course and *Baubelehrung* 8.KLA 6/42–9/42
Cdr *U 640* 17.9.42–14.5.43
Lost 14.5.43 off Cape Farewell

NECKEL, HERBERT [865]
b. 14.8.1916, Kiel
Class 1935; Kplt 1.12.42
U-boat trg 4/40–9/40; 1WO *U 30* 9/40–3/41; 1WO *U 108* 3/41–11/41; U-Cdr's Course, 26th U-Flotilla 11/41–12/41; Instructor 2.ULD 12/41–10/42; *Baubelehrung* 8.KLA 10/42

Cdr *U 531* 28.10.42–6.5.43
Lost 6.5.43, NE of Newfoundland

NEES, WERNER [866]
b. 8.2.1910, Hasbach, Rhineland
Entry 1928; Kplt 1.3.45
WO 2nd Minesweeping Flotilla 6/38–6/41; WO and VP Cdr 3rd VP-Boat Flotilla 7/41–1/43; U-boat trg 2/43–7/43; U-Cdr's Course, 27th and 24th U-Flotillas 7/43–8/43 (U-Cdr's Torpedo Course 53)
Cdr *U 363* 1.9.43–capitulation

NEIDE, KURT [867]
b 8.7.1916, Kiel
Class 1936; Kplt 1.7.43
Heavy cruiser *Lützow* until 8/40; LAT Cdr and Group Leader LAT (light artillery lighter) Group 8/40–10/40; course Naval Gunnery School 10/40–12/40; U-boat trg 12/40–5/41'; *Baubelehrung* 6/41–7/41; 1WO *U 134* 7/41–6/42; U-Cdr's Course, 24th U-Flotilla 6/42–7/42; *Baubelehrung* 7.KLA 7/42–8/42
Cdr *U 415* 5.8.1942–16.4.1944
Naval Academy 4/44–8/44; 6/Command Staff Officer OKM/2.SKL/BdU/Opns 9/44–capitulation
Detained; freed 15.8.45

NEITZEL, KARL [868]
b. 30.1.1901, Kolberg, Pomerania
Class 1923; KptzS 1.12.43
Naval Appointments Officer Staff 2/Adm. Baltic 2/38–11/39; CO 1st Minesweeping Flotilla

186

12/39–1/41; U-boat trg and *Baubelehrung* 2/41–11/41

Cdr *U 510* 25.11.41 to 21.5.43 (per P/F) or 31.5.43 (per WASt; see Eick [241])

Furlough 5/43–8/43; acting CO 25th U-Flotilla 8/43–1/44; Cdr 2.ULD 1/44–2/45; Cdr Naval Grenadier Regiment 7 2/45–capitulation

Detained; freed 23.1.46

Knight's Cross 27.3.43 (156th KM, 86th U-boat holder)

NEITZSCH, WILHELM [869]

b 14.5.1920, Langenzenn, nr Nuremberg

Class IX/1939; ObltzS 1.10.43

Torpedo-boat *Tiger* 6/41–6/43; U-boat trg 6/43–11/43; WO *U 518* 12/43–11/44; 3.ULD 12/44–2/45; 1WO *U 3509* 22.2.45–3.5.45, inc. acting Cdr *U 3509* 15.4.45–3.5.45

NEUBERT, KURT [870]

b. 24.3.1910 Bobrovnik, Upper Silesia

Class 1935; Kplt 1.7.42

WO and Div. Officer battleship *Scharnhorst* 8/39–6/40; U-boat trg 7/40–2/41; *Baubelehrung* 2/41–3/41; 1WO *U 126* 3/41–1/42; U-Cdr's Course, 24th U-Flotilla 1/42–4/42

Cdr *U 46* 4/42–5/42

Baubelehrung 6.KLA 6/42–7/42

Cdr *U 167* 4.7.42 to 4.2.43 (per WASt) or 8.2.43 (per *U 167* WD, and see Sturm, [1255]) (1WO Zahnow [1386] had command of *U 167* 8.1.43–16.1.43 when Neubert was wounded)

10th U-Flotilla 2/43–4/43; Base Officer U-boat base Hamburg 4/43–8/43; Kplt Staff 31st U-Flotilla 9/43–capitulation

NEUERBURG, HELLMUT [871]

b. 25.8.1917 Strasbourg (when German province)

Class 1936; Kplt 1.7.43

Seconded to Luftwaffe 10/38–3/43; U-boat trg 4/43–9/43; U-Cdr's Course, 2.UAA and 27th U-Flotilla 10/43–12/43 (U-Cdr's Torpedo Course 58); *Baubelehrung* 6.KLA 12/43–1/44

Cdr *U 869* 26.1.44–28.2.45

Lost 28.2.45 Atlantic Ocean, off Rabat, Morocco

NEUMANN, HANS-WERNER [872]

b 3.9.1906, Berlin-Charlottenburg

Entry 1925; KKpt 1.4.40, posthumously FKpt seniority to 1.8.43

Adviser 1c Naval Education Inspectorate 4/39–3/40; U-boat trg 4/40–9/40; U-Cdr's Course, 24th U-Flotilla and *Baubelehrung* 9/40–1/41

Cdr *U 72* 4.1.41–9/41

Baubelehrung 9/41–10/41

Cdr *U 117* 25.10.41–7.8.43

Lost 7.8.43 central North Atlantic

NEUMANN, HEINZ-JOACHIM [873]

b. 29.4.1909, Guben

Class 1930; KKpt 1.6.43

Battleship *Scharnhorst* 1/39–6/40; U-boat trg 7/40–11/40; U-Cdr's Course, 24th U-Flotilla 11/40–12/40; BdU/Staff Reserve 12/40–1/41; WO (supernumerary) *U 52* 1/41–3/41; *Baubelehrung* 3/41–4/41

Cdr *U 372* 19.4.41–4.8.42, inc. acting Cdr *U 371* 6.4.42–24.5.42

POW 4.8.42

NEUMANN, HERMANN [874]

b. 7.9.1919, Mombach, Mainz

Class 1938; ObltzS 1.4.43

Transferred to Seaman Branch from Ordnance 1.3.43; U-Cdr sea trg *U 228* 2/44–7/44; 33rd U-Flotilla and *Baubelehrung* Cdr *U 3057* (boat never commissioned) for 4th U-Flotilla, 6.KLA 9/44–capitulation

Detained; freed 2.4.47

NEUMEISTER, HERMANN [875]
b.. 4.1.23, Holzhausen, Ammersee
Class 1940; ObltzS 1.10.44
2WO *U 306* 11/42–1/43; 1WO *U 281* 2/43–3/44; U-Cdr's Course 4/44–6/44 (U-Cdr's Torpedo Course 69)
Cdr *U 3* 10.6.44 until 16.7.44 or 31.7.44 (*U 3* was decommissioned 1.8.44. Neumeister was probably commander of *U 291* from 7/44. See Stege [1217].)
Cdr *U 291* 17.7.44 or 1.8.44 to capitulation
Detained; freed 2.4.47

NEY, GÜNTER [876]
b. 27.3.1922, Berlin-Schöneberg
Class XII/1939; ObltzS 1.12.43
U-boat trg 11/41–8/42; WO 7.KLA and 8th U-Flotilla 8/42–12/42; 1WO *U 431* 1/43–7/43; U-Cdr's Course, 2.UAA and 24th U-Flotilla 7/43–8/43 (U-Cdr's Torpedo Course 52)
Cdr *U 283* 16.8.43–11.2.44
Lost 11.2.44 SW of Faroes

NEY, JOHANNES [877]
b. 16.6.1922, Munich
Class X/1940; ObltzS 1.10.44
WO *U 739* 2/44–3/45, acting Cdr *U 739* 26.2.45–3/45

NICOLAY, KURT-HEINZ [878]
b. 6.10.1917, Schleswig
Class 1937a; Kplt 1.2.44
U-boat trg 11/40–3/41; Comp. Officer 1.ULD 3/41–9/41; *Baubelehrung* 9/41–10/41; 1WO *U 163* 10/41–2/43; U-Cdr's Course, 2.UAA and 24th U-Flotilla 2/43–3/43 (U-Cdr's Torpedo Course 42); *Baubelehrung*, 3/43–4/43
Cdr *U 312* 21.4.43–1.12.44, also acting Cdr *U 348* 26.6.44–1.7.44 (delivery voyage Trondheim–Kiel)
Duties not recorded 12/44–2/45; adviser, Staff, C-in-C Escort Forces 2/45–capitulation

NIELSEN, KARL [879]
b. 30.9.1911, Hamburg
Entry 1935; ObltzS (R) 1.11.42
U-boat trg and U-Cdr's Course 3/43–10/43 (U-Cdr's Torpedo Course 56); *Baubelehrung* 10/43–11/43
Cdr *U 370* 19.11.43–5.5.45

NIEMEYER, HEINRICH [880]
b. 15.6.1910, Löbejün, Saalkreis, Saxony-Anhalt
Class X/1939; ObltzS 1.2.44
WO and acting VP Cdr 15th VP-Boat Flotilla 6/40–9/42; U-boat trg 9/42–2/43; 1WO *U 515* 2/43–3/44
Cdr *U 547* 16.4.44 (U-Boat Archive per Niemeyer) or 18.4.44 (per WD *U 547*, and see Sturm [1255]) to 6.1.45 (boat decommissioned Stettin 31.12.44)
Baubelehrung Type XXI 7.KLA for *U 3532* 7.1.45–14.4.45 (Neimeyer was the *Baubelehrung* Cdr for *U 3532*. This Schichau, Danzig, boat was never commissioned but made a voyage from Danzig to Hela 11.3.45–12.3.45 in company with the tug *Passat*; it left Hela on 16.3.45 and arrived at Kiel on 19.3.45 with refugees.)
Cdr *U 1233* 15.4.45–capitulation

NIESTER, ERICH [881]
b. 19.9.1921, Linz, Danube
Class IX/1939; ObltzS 1.10.43
Officer and U-boat trg 9/39–11/41; WO 26th U-Flotilla 11/41–3/42; *Baubelehrung* 3/42–4/42; 1WO *U 617* 4/42–8/43; U-Cdr's Course, 2.UAA and 24th U-Flotilla 8/43–9/43 (U-Cdr's Torpedo Course 54); *Baubelehrung* 6.KLA 9/43–10/43
Cdr *U 350* 7.10.43–30.3.45

NIETHMANN, OTTO [882]
b. 12.8.1919, Hamburg
Class 1938; ObltzS 1.4.43
U-boat trg 10/40–5/41; WO *U 30* 5/41–3/42; WO *U 373* 3/42–8/42
Cdr *U 6* 20.10.42–6/43
Baubelehrung 1.KLA 6/43–7/43
Cdr *U 476* 28.7.43–25.5.44
11th U-Flotilla 5/44–7/44; *Baubelehrung* Type XXI 7.KLA 7/44–10/44
Cdr *U 3507* 19.10.44–19.3.45
5th U-Flotilla 3/45–capitulation

NISS, HELLMUT [883]
b. 8.3.1906, Tönning/Holstein
Enlisted 1923; Kplt 1.4.45
Hauptfeldwebel (Staff Sgt) Ensign Comp. Danzig 1/40–3/41; course Navigation School 3/41–9/41; WO and M/S-Cdr 19th Minesweeping Flotilla 9/41–3/43; U-boat trg 4/43–10/43; U-Cdr's Course, 24th U-Flotilla 10/43–1/44 (U-Cdr's Torpedo Course 60); *Baubelehrung* 6.KLA 1/44–3/44
Cdr *U 1275* 22.3.44–17.7.44
32st U-Flotilla 7/44; *Baubelehrung* Type XXI 5. and 8.KLA 8/44–1/45
Cdr *U 2531* 10.1.45–2.5.45

NISSEN, JÜRGEN [884]
b. 28.5.1916, Sintrup
Class 1936; Kplt 1.4.43
WO and Gunnery Officer destroyer *Z 20 Karl Galster* 3/39–6/41; U-boat trg 6/41–12/41; WO 2nd U-Flotilla 12/41–7/42; U-Cdr's Course, 24th U-Flotilla 8/42–9/42
Cdr *U 146* 8.9.42 to 10/42 or 1.11.42 (perWASt)
Cdr *U 105* 25.10.42 (per WASt) or 29.10.42 (per *U 105* WD, and see Schuch [1139] and Schweichel [1178]) to 2.6.43
Lost 2.6.43 off Dakar

NÖLKE, KURT [885]
b. 5.9.1914, Hannover
Class 1935; KKpt 1.1.44
ADC Div. and Gunnery Officer minelayer *Königin Luise* 11/39–3/40; 1WO torpedo-boat *Jaguar* 3/40–10/40; U-boat trg and *Baubelehrung* 11/40–5/41; 1WO *U 82* 5/41–9/41; U-Cdr under instrn, 26th U-Flotilla 9/41–12/41
Cdr *U 20* 5.12.41–27.3.42 (boat decommissioned at Kiel 27.3.42 prior to transfer Black Sea)
Baubelehrung 6.KLA 4/42–5/42
Cdr *U 263* 6.5.42–20.1.44 (also acting Cdr *U 584* 20.12.42–11.2.43—completed one patrol. *U 263* was decommissioned 12/42 after receiving heavy damage in an air raid on 24.11.42. Nölke retained command during the boat's one-year lay-up under repair, per Lohmann-Hildebrand almanac and WASt. As the boat was unmanned and relatively well-protected, undoubtedly Nölke was engaged elsewhere during the period.)
Lost 20.1.44 Bay of Biscay, off La Rochelle

NOLLAU, HERBERT [886]
b. 23.3.1916, Wolfstein, Rhein-Pfalz
Class 1936; Kplt 1.10.43
Platoon Officer 13/Basic Trg Est. Stralsund 4/39–9/39; No 2 Radio Technical Officer heavy cruiser *Blücher* 9/39–4/40 and light cruiser *Emden* 4/40; ADC and Naval Signals Officer Horten, Harbour Defence Flotilla Oslo 4/40–1/41; U-boat trg 1/41–6/41; *Baubelehrung* 7/41–8/41; 1WO *U 505* 8/41–9/42; U-Cdr's Course and *Baubelehrung* 8.KLA 9/42–12/42
Cdr *U 534* 23.12.42–5.5.45
Detained; freed 20.8.45

NOLLMANN, ROLF [887]
b. 29.12.1914, Wollmeringen, Lorraine (when German province)
Class 1936, Kplt 1.11.43

ADC 1st E-Boat Flotilla 2/41–4/41; battleship *Gneisenau* 4/41–7/41; Naval Signals Officer (Ostende) 7/41–12/42, (Berlin) 12/42–3/43; course Helmsman's School Gdynia 3/43–6/43; U-boat trg 6/43–9/43; U-Cdr's Course, 24th U-Flotilla 10/43–11/43 (U-Cdr's Torpedo Course 57); *Baubelehrung* 7.KLA 11/43–12/43
Cdr *U 1199* 23.12.43–21.1.45
Lost 21.1.45 English Channel, between Wolf Rock and Scilly Is

NOLTE, GERHARD [888]
b. 23.1.1922, Tetschen, Elbe
Class XII/1939; ObltzS 1.12.43
U-boat trg 6/41–1/42; Platoon Officer 2.ULD 1/42–9/42; *Baubelehrung* 8.KLA 10/42–11/42; 1WO *U 648* 11/42–8/43; U-Cdr's Course, 2.UAA and 23rd U-Flotilla 8/43–9/43; *Baubelehrung* 7.KLA 9/43–10/43
Cdr *U 1194* 21.10.43–11.10.44
22nd U-Flotilla 10/44–12/44
Cdr *U 704* 19.12.44–24.3.45
1.UAA/ULD and 9/Naval Reserve Div. 3/45–4/45; illness
Missing Neubrandenburg area from 20.4.45

NONN, VICTOR-WILHELM [889]
b. 2.4.1917, Dresden
Class 1937a; Kplt 1.7.44
U-boat trg 10/40–3/41; UAA 3/41–6/41; 2WO *U 97* 6/41–5/42; 1WO *U 97* 5/42–7/42; U-Cdr's Torpedo Course 8/42–9/42
Cdr *U 152* 21.9.42–24.7.43
Cdr *U 596* 28.7.43–7/44
Trg Leader 19th U-Flotilla 8/44–capitulation
Detained; freed 7.11.47

NORDHEIMER, HUBERT [890]
b. 3.2.1917, Mirschkowitz, Silesia
Class 1936; Kplt 1.4.43

ADC 5/Basic Trg Est. Stralsund 12/38–11/39; Cadet Trg Officer light cruiser *Emden* 12/39–9/40; U-boat trg 10/40–3/41; *Baubelehrung* 4/41–5/41; 1WO *U 206* 5/41–10/41; course 11/41–12/41; Trg Officer 2.ULD 12/41–12/42; *Baubelehrung* 1.KLA 12/42–1/43
Cdr *U 237* 30.1.43–14.5.43
Baubelehrung 8.KLA 6/43–7/43
Cdr *U 990* 28.7.43–25.5.44
Baubelehrung Type XXI 8.KLA 7/44–10/44
Cdr *U 2512* 10.10.44–7.5.45

O

OEHRN, VICTOR [891]
b. 21.10.1907, Kedabeg, Caucasus, Russia
Class 1927; FKpt 1.8.44 with effect from 1.5.44
Cdr *U 14* 18.1.36–4.10.37; Comp. CO Naval College Flensburg-Mürwik 10/37–10/38; Naval Academy 11/38–8/39, inc. service light cruiser *Leipzig* for minefield exercises with C-in-C Reconnaissance Forces 19.6.39–23.6.39; Naval Academy, Adm. Staff Officer trg voyages aboard state yacht *Grille* 25.6.39–28.6.39 and 3.7.39–11.7.39; on board light cruiser *Leipzig* for Fleet torpedo exercises 19.8.39–21.8.39; Adm. Staff Officer, Staff FdU East 8/39–9/39; Adm. Staff Officer (special purposes), Staff FdU 9/39–10/39; 1/Adm. Staff Officer/BdU/Opns 10/39–5/40
Cdr *U 37* 6.5.40–26.10.40 (per P/F)
1/Adm. Staff Officer 10/40–11/41; FdU chargé d'affaires with C-in-C German Naval Command Italy 11/41–2/42, also 1/Adm. Staff Officer FdU Italy 11/41–2/42 and 2/42–5/42; Liaison Officer with C-in-C South (Kesselring) in Africa/El Alamein 5/42–7/42; seriously wounded while on special mission 13.7.42; POW 19th General Hospital, England; exchange repatriation 10/43; available for special missions at OKM/2.SKL/BdU/Opns 11/43–3/44 and at FdU Trg 4/44–6/44; FdU Central 6/44–8/44; Group Leader Operations Group 1a at OKM/Sec 1/SKL 8/44–capitulation
Detained; freed 8/45
Knight's Cross 21.10.40 (39th KM, 16th U-boat holder)

OELRICH, ADOLF [892]
b. 15.3.1916, Kiel
Class 1935; Kplt 1.12.42
Div. Officer battleship *Scharnhorst* 1/39–10/40; U-boat trg 10/40–3/41; *Baubelehrung* 4/41–5/41; 1WO *U 568* 5/41–1/42; U-Cdr's Course and *Baubelehrung* 3.KLA 1/42–3/42
Cdr *U 92* 3.3.42–8/43
Trg Officer 10th U-Flotilla 8/43–10/43; Sea Exercises Leader 20th U-Flotilla 11/43–2/45; Trg Officer 26th U-Flotilla 2/45–capitulation

OESTEN, JÜRGEN [893]
b. 24.10.1913, Berlin-Grunewald
Class 1933; KKpt 1.12.44
U-boat trg 5/37–8/37; WO gunnery trg boat *Jaguar* 8/37–10/37; WO *U 20* 10/37–1/38; U-Torpedo Officer's supplementary course Torpedo School Mürwik 1/38; WO *U 20* 1/38–10/38; radio signals course Naval Signals School Mürwik 10/38–12/38; 3rd U-Flotilla *Lohs* (WO *U 20*) 12/38–7/39; *Baubelehrung* 7/39–8/39
Cdr *U 61* 12.8.39 to 28.7.40 (per *U 61* WD, relieved by Stiebler [1234]) or 26.8.40 (per P/F)
Baubelehrung U-Boats North 8/40–9/40
Cdr *U 106* 24.9.40–19.10.41
CO 9th U-Flotilla 10/41–2/42; U-Adm. Staff Officer Adm. Polar Seas 3/42–1/43; Adm. Staff Officer (A op) FdU Norway 1/43–7/43; *Baubelehrung* 1.Comp/6.KLA Bremen 7/43–9/43
Cdr *U 861* 2.9.43–capitulation
Detained; freed 2.3.47
Knight's Cross 26.3.41 (64th KM, 26th U-boat holder)

OESTERMANN, HANS [894]
b. 19.5.1913, Bremervörde
Class 1933; Kplt 1.12.40

1WO destroyer *Z 7 Hermann Schoemann* 9/37–6/40; U-boat trg 7/40–11/40; U-Cdr's Course, 24th U-Flotilla 11/40–12/40; *Baubelehrung* 12/40–1/41
Cdr *U 151* 15.1.41–21.7.41
Baubelehrung, 7/41–8/41
Cdr *U 754* 28.8.41–31.7.42
Lost 31.7.42 NE of Boston, Massachusetts

OFFERMANN, HANS-WERNER [895]
b. 2.7.1921, Offingen, Danube
Class IX/1939; ObltzS 1.10.43
U-boat trg completed 10/41; WO *U 129* 10/41–9/43; U-Cdr's Course, 2.UAA and 23rd U-Flotilla 9/43–11/43; Trg Officer 20th U-Flotilla 11/43–1/44
Cdr *U 518* 8.1.44 (per WASt) or 13.1.44 (relieved Wissmann [1361] per *U 518* WD) to 22.4.45
Lost 22.4.45 NW of Azores

OHLENBURG, WILLY [896]
b. 12.3.1915, Stiddien, Braunschweig
Entry 1934; ObltzS 1.12.43
WO and VP Cdr 15th VP-Boat Flotilla 9/41–1/42; U-boat trg 1/42–8/42; Platoon Officer 1.UAA 8/42–9/42; 1WO *U 19* 10/42–8/43; U-Cdr's Course, 2.UAA and 23rd U-Flotilla 9/43–11/43
Cdr *U 19* 3.12.43–6.9.44 (On 6.9.44 Ohlenburg was shot in the knee as a result of a Schmeisser handling error. Verpoorten [1300] took over as acting Cdr until the boat was scuttled along with *U 20* and *U 23* in Turkish waters on 10.9.44)

OHLING, KLAUS [897]
b. 4.2.1918, Frankfurt/Main
Class 1937a; Kplt 1.4.44
Heavy cruiser *Admiral Scheer* 4/39–9/41; U-boat trg 9/41–3/42; 1WO *U 511* 3/42–12/42; U-Cdr's Course, 24th U-Flotilla 12/42–1/43; *Baubelehrung* 8.KLA 1/43–2/43
Cdr *U 965* 25.2.43–6.6.44
Course 24th U-Flotilla 8/44–12/44; Trg Leader *K-Verband*/Trg Command 300 12/44–5/45; 2nd R-Boat Flotilla 5/45–capitulation
Detained; freed 17.6.46

OHLSEN, PROSPER [898]
b. 16.1.1918, Lugano, Switzerland
Entry 1936; ObltzS 1.6.43
Platoon Leader 1.UAA 11/39–3/40; merchant raider *Thor* 3/40–10/41; 1st Sperrbrecher Flotilla 10/41–1/43; U-boat trg 1/43–8/43; 1WO *U 218* 8/43–1/44; U-Cdr's Course, 3.ULD and 27th U-Flotilla 1/44–4/44 (U-Cdr's Torpedo Course 64)
Cdr *U 855* 3.4.44–11.9.44
Missing W of Bergen from 11.9.44 (Translator's note: U-Boat List 1956 states sunk all hands 24.9.44 in 61°00'N 04°07'E by Liberator 'A' of No 224 Squadron RAF.)

OLDÖRP, HANS-JÜRGEN [899]
b. 23.6.1911, Lübeck
Class 1935; Kplt 1.7.42
Group Officer Naval College Flensburg-Mürwik 10/39–2/40; Trg Officer 1/NCO Trg Div. 2/40–4/40; course 24th U-Flotilla 9/40–1/41; *Baubelehrung* 8.KLA 1/41–2/41; 1WO *U 558* 2/41–10/41; *Baubelehrung* 11/41–12/41
Cdr *U 90* 20.12.41–24.7.42
Lost 24.7.42 E of Newfoundland

OPITZ, HERBERT [900]
b. 7.3.1915, Magdeburg
Class 1934; Kplt 1.9.41
Trg ship *Schleswig-Holstein* 9/36–6/38; Trg Officer light cruiser *Emden* 6/38–4/39; U-boat trg 4/39–9/39; 1WO *U 25* 9/39–1/40; U-Boat Trg Flotilla 8.1.40–14.1.40; WO *U 7* 15.1.40–

28.4.40; 1st U-Trg Flotilla 29.4.40–7.7.40; U-Cdr 21st U-Flotilla (inc. *U 5*) 8.7.40–6.4.41; *Baubelehrung* U-Boats East 4/41–5/41
Cdr *U 206* 17.5.41–30.11.41
Lost 30.11.41 Bay of Biscay, W of Nantes

OTTO, HERMANN [901]
b. 30.5.1914, Leising, Saxony
Class 1934; ObltzS 1.10.40, posthumously Kplt seniority 1.7.43
WO gunnery trg ship *Brummer* 5/39–1/41; U-boat trg 1/41–6/41; 1WO *U 403* 6/41–6/42; U-Cdr's Course 6/42–7/42; *Baubelehrung* 7.KLA 7/42–8/42
Cdr *U 449* 22.8.42–24.6.43
Lost 24.6.43 NW of Cape Ortegal

OTTO, PAUL-FRIEDRICH [902]
b. 3.4.1917, Waren, Müritz
Class 1937a; Kplt 1.6.44
U-boat trg 1/41–7/41; *Baubelehrung* 7/41–8/41; 1WO *U 136* 8/41–5/42; U-Cdr's Course, 24th U-Flotilla 6/42–8/42; *Baubelehrung* 6.KLA 8/42–9/42
Cdr *U 270* 5.9.42–15.7.44
UAA 7/44–10/44; *Baubelehrung* Type XXI 8.KLA 10/44–12/44
Cdr *U 2525* 12.12.44–5.5.45

OTTO, WALTER [903]
b. 11.3.1917, Erlangen
Class 1937a; Kplt 1.7.44
Platoon Officer Naval Artillery Detachment 116 8/39–9/39; seconded to Luftwaffe 10/39–2/42; U-boat trg 3/42–8/42; 1WO *U 436* 8/42–3/43; U-Cdr's Course, 2.UAA and 24th U-Flotilla 3/43–4/43 (U-Cdr's Torpedo Course 44); *Baubelehrung* 6.KLA 4/43–5/43
Cdr *U 285* 15.5.43–16.4.44

8th U-Flotilla (hospital) 4/44–7/44; Leader preliminary trg 31st U-Flotilla 7/44–1/45; Kplt on Staff 19th U-Flotilla 1/45–capitulation
Detained; freed 8/45

P

PAEPENMÖLLER, KLAUS [904]
b. 25.2.1918, Bielefeld
Class 1937a; ObltzS 1.9.41
1WO and Secretarial Officer Mine Warfare Experimental Branch 6/40–3/41; heavy cruiser *Lützow* 3/41–9/41; U-boat trg 9/41–4/42; 3rd U-Flotilla 5/42–6/42; 1WO *U 134* 6/42–2/43; U-Cdr's Course, 24th U-Flotilla 2/43–3/43 (U-Cdr's Torpedo Course 42); *Baubelehrung* 8.KLA 3/43–4/43
Cdr *U 973* 15.4.43–6.3.44
Lost 6.3.44 Arctic Ocean, NW of Narvik

PAHL, HANS-WALTER [905]
b. 16.8.1919, Cuxhaven
Entry 1938; ObltzS (transferred from Ordnance to Seaman Branch 1.4.43)
U-boat trg 6/43–11/43; WO under instrn 11/43–1/44; WO 29th U-Flotilla 1/44–5/44; U-Cdr's Course, 24th U-Flotilla 6/44–7/44 (U-Cdr's Torpedo Course 73); *Baubelehrung* Type XXIII 8.KLA 7/44–9/44
Cdr *U 2331* 12.9.44–10.10.44
32nd U-Flotilla 10/44–3/45
Cdr *U 2327* 3/45–2.5.45
Cdr *U 2369* 3.5.45–5.5.45

PAHLS, HEINRICH [906]
b. 13.12.1919, Langenfeld, Rhine-Wupper
Class IX/1939; ObltzS 1.10.43
Officer and U-boat trg, *Baubelehrung* 9/39–12/41
2WO *U 511* 12/41–12/43
Cdr *UIT 24* 6.12.43–capitulation

PALMGREN, GERHARD [907]
b. 11.11.1919, Kassel
Entry X/1938; ObltzS (R) 1.4.43
WO under instrn heavy cruiser *Admiral Hipper* 4/40–8/40; Platoon Leader 2/Basic Trg Est. Stralsund 8/40–10/40; U-boat trg 11/40–7/41; 24th U-Flotilla 7/41–1/42; *Baubelehrung* 7.KLA 1/42–2/42; 1WO *U 441* 2/42–2/43; U-Cdr's Course, 24th U-Flotilla 2/43–3/43 (U-Cdr's Torpedo Course 42); *Baubelehrung* 7.KLA 3/43–4/43
Cdr *U 741* 10.4.43–15.8.44
Lost 15.8.44 English Channel, NW of Le Havre

PANCKE, KARL-WILHELM [908]
b. 4.10.1915, Husum
Entry 1938; ObltzS (R) 1.8.43
VP Cdr 11th Harbour Defence Flotilla 5/40–10/40; courses 10/40–4/41; Minefield Cdr Gdynia 4/41–3/42; U-boat trg 3/42–9/42; 2WO *U 402* 9/42–3/43; 1WO *U 402* 4/43–6/43; U-Cdr's Course, 24th U-Flotilla 6/43–7/43 (U-Cdr's Torpedo Course 50); *Baubelehrung* 1.KLA 7/43–8/43
Cdr *U 242* 14.8.43–2/45
1.UAA 2/45–capitulation

PANITZ, JOHANNES [909]
b. 14.8.1913, Breslau
Entry VIII/1937; ObltzS (R) 1.3.43
2nd VP-Boat Flotilla (as WO) 5/40–6/41, (as VP-Cdr) 7/41–8/43; U-boat trg, WO and U-Cdr's Course 8/43–5/44 (U-Cdr's Torpedo Course 69); WO 5th U-Flotilla 5/44–7/44; *Baubelehrung* 1.KLA 7/44–9/44

Cdr *U 1065* 23.9.44–9.4.45
Lost 9.4.45, Kattegat, NW of Göteborg

PARDUHN, FRITZ [910]
b. 27.11.1918, Apen, Oldenburg
Class 1937b; Kplt 1.1.45
2nd R-Boat Flotilla 12/39–5/40; Ordnance Officer 12th Minesweeping Flotilla 5/40–8/41; no details available 8/41–3/43; 3rd Sperrbrecher Flotilla 3/43–5/43; Cdr Wesermünde District 5/43–8/43; U-boat trg 8/43–2/44 (conversion to Seaman Branch officer); U-Cdr's Course, 23rd and 24th U-Flotillas 2/44–5/44 (U-Cdr's Torpedo Course 69); U-Cdr sea trg *U 682* 5/44–7/44; *Baubelehrung* 6.KLA 7/44–8/44
Cdr *U 1107* 8.8.44–25.4.45
Lost 25.4.45 Bay of Biscay, W of Brest

PAUCKSTADT, HANS [911]
b. 27.9.1906, Grimnitz
Class 1926; FKpt 1.4.44
Studying at Anti-Submarine School 10/35–1/36; Cdr *U 18* 4.1.36–20.11.36 (*U 18* sank after collision with torpedo-boat *T 156* in Lübeck Bay 20.11.36); Cdr *U 12* 12/36–1.10.37; 4/U-Holding Comp./6th U-Flotilla, 1/Basic Trg Est. Stralsund 10/37; 4/U-Holding Comp./6th U-Flotilla 10/37–2/38; Cdr *U 34* and *U 30* 15.2.38–17.8.38; Adm. Staff Officer available to FdU 8/38–9/38; Cdr *U 34* 5.9.38–28.10.38; First Officer sail trg ship *Gorch Fock* 10/38–1/39; special course Bad Tölz 27.1.39–4.2.39; sail trg ship *Gorch Fock* 2/39–8/39; 1/Adm. Staff Officer, FdU East 8/39–9/39; 3/Adm. Staff Officer, Staff FdU 9/39–10/39; 3/Adm. Staff Officer, Staff BdU/Organisational 10/39–9/41; Staff 2/Adm. U-Boats 10/41–9/42, inc. acting Cdr *U 516* 11.5.42–27.5.42 (per *U 516* WD, deputizing for Wiebe [1346] during latter's sick leave); acting CO 5th U-Flotilla 9/42–11/42; *Baubelehrung* 1/6.KLA Bremen 11/42–12/42

Cdr *U 193* 10.12.42–31.3.44 (per P/F until 30.4.44)
CO 8th U-Flotilla 5/44–2/45; Cdr 1.UAA 2/45–capitulation

PAULSHEN, OTTOKAR [912]
b. 11.10.1915, Berlin-Charlottenburg
Class 1934; Kplt 1.10.41, posthumously KKpt seniority 1.12.41
1WO *U 26* 4/39–1/40; WO and U-Cdr sea trg *U 18* 1/40–6/40
Cdr *U 20* 8.6.40–5.1.41
Baubelehrung Kriegsmarine Depot Hamburg 1/41–2/41
Cdr *U 557* 13.2.41–16.12.41
Lost 16.12.41 Mediterranean, near Salamis

PELKNER, HANS-HERMANN [913]
b. 16.4.1909, Ober-Kauffung, nr Kassel
Class 1935; Kplt 1.11.41
WO fleet escort *F 5* 10/39–3/40; *Baubelehrung* 3/40–5/40; Cdr R-boat depot ship *Raule* 5/40–7/40; M/S-Cdr 4th Minesweeping Flotilla 7/40–1/41; U-boat trg 1/41–7/41; WO (supernumerary) *U 101* 7/41–9/41; U-Cdr's Course, 26th U-Flotilla 10/41–11/41; *Baubelehrung* 11/41–12/41
Cdr *U 335* 17.12.41–3.8.42
Lost 3.8.42 NE of Faroes

PERLEBERG, RÜDIGER [914]
b. 9.3.1913, Bremen
Enlisted rating 1933; ObltzS 1.1.43
VP Cdr Harbour Defence Flotilla Oslo 4/40–10/40; WO and No 2 Navigation Officer heavy cruiser *Admiral Hipper* 10/40–3/43; U-boat trg 3/43–9/43; U-Cdr's Course, 2.UAA and 24th U-Flotilla 9/43–1/44 (U-Cdr's Torpedo Course 59); *Baubelehrung* 6.KLA 2/44–3/44
Cdr *U 1104* 15.3.44–capitulation

PESCHEL, OTTO [915]
b. 28.8.1915, Kraupa/Torgau
Entry VII/1934; Kplt 1.12.44
WO and M/S-Cdr 18th Minesweeping Flotilla 10/40–11/42; M/S-Cdr 28th Minesweeping Flotilla 11/42–2/44; U-boat trg, WO and courses 2/44–10/44 (U-Cdr's Torpedo Course 77); 27th U-Flotilla 10/44–1/45; U-Cdr under instrn 8th and 31st U-Flotillas 1/45–3/45
Cdr *U 3004* 14.3.45–18.4.45
Cdr Battle Group *Peschel* 4/45–capitulation

PETERS, GEORG [916]
b. 3.3.1888, Greifswald
Enlisted 1904; KKpt (R)(zV) 1.7.43
Trg U-Boat Section 8/15–9/15; U-Boat Section 11/15; ObStrmMt *U 25* 11/15–1/16; ObStrm (Coxswain) course, Deck Officer School 1/16–9/16; U-Boat Section, 10/16–11/16; ObStrmMt *U 52* 11/16–2/17; U-Strm U-Boat Div. 2/17–4/17; U-Strm *U 96* 4/17–11/18; U-Boat Div. 11/18–1/19
WO U-Boat School 4/38–6/38; Cdr *U 8* 24.6.38–5.9.39
Cdr *U 11* 5.9.39–22.3.43, inc. acting Cdr *U 6* 6/40–7/40 (deputising for Schnee [1102])
Cdr *U A* 4th U-Flotilla 23.3.43–14.4.44
Cdr *U 38* 15.4.44–5.5.45. (Translator's note: On 5.5.45, the last effective date of the U-boat campaign, Peters had the unique distinction, at the age of 57, of having been the commander of a U-boat in commission on every day of the Second World War.)

PETERS, GERHARD [917]
b. 14.12.1921, Rendsburg
Class XII/1939; ObltzS 1.12.43
U-boat trg and *Baubelehrung* completed 2/42; 2WO *U 410* 2/42–4/43; 1WO *U 410* 4/43–9/43; U-Cdr's Course, 2.UAA and 24th U-Flotilla 9/43–11/43 (U-Cdr's Torpedo Course 57); *Baubelehrung* 7.KLA 11/43–12/43
Cdr *U 1198* 9.12.43–capitulation

PETERS, WILHELM [918]
b. 20.6.1916, Hannover
Class X/1937; Kplt 1.1.45
Officer trg 10/37–11/39; WO minesweepers *M 10* and *M 25* 12/39–9/41; U-boat course 1.ULD 9/41–11/41; U-boat trg 11/41–3/42; WO 26th U-Flotilla 3/42–5/42; WO *U 584* 5/42–2/43; radar course 2.UAA 17.2.43–28.2.43; U-Cdr's Course, 24th U-Flotilla 3/43
Cdr *U 96* 16.3.43 or 1.4.43 to 2/44 or 30.6.44
Cdr *U 999* 16.7.44 to 11/44 or 1.1.45
Baubelehrung Cdr 6.KLA for *U 3045* (never commissioned) 2.1.45–4/45
Cdr *U 3001* 4/45–3.5.45

PETERSEN, KLAUS [919]
b. 13.1.1917, Kiel
Class 1936; Kplt 1.6.43
WO light cruiser *Nürnberg* 12/38–10/40; U-boat trg and *Baubelehrung* 10/40–3/41; 1WO *U 563* 3/41–2/42
Cdr *U 14* 10.2.42–30.6.42
1.UAA and U-Cdr's Course 7/42–9/42
Cdr *U 24* 14.10.42–17.11.42
No details available 12/42–3/43
Cdr *U 24* 16.4.43–7.4.44
Acting Cdr *U 9* 7.4.44–6/44 (relieved Landt-Hayen [691] 7.4.44 and deputized for the wounded Klapdor [609])
30th U-Flotilla 6/44–7/44; CO 30th U-Flotilla and U-Adm. Staff Officer, Staff, Adm. Black Sea 7/44 to 8/44 or 10/44; Trg Leader 31st U-Flotilla 10/44–1/45; *Baubelehrung* Cdr 6.KLA for *U 3042* (never commissioned) 6.1.45–4/45; further details not known 4/45–capitulation

PETERSEN, KURT [920]
b. 20.9.1916, Sonderburg
Class 1936; Kplt 1.4.43
2nd Torpedo Officer heavy cruiser *Deutschland* 11/38–4/40; U-boat trg 5/40–9/40; 1WO *U 146* 10/40–12/40; 1WO *U B* 1/41–3/41; 1WO *U 371*

3/41–11/41; U-Cdr's Course 11/41–12/41; instructor 1.ULD 1/42–1/43; *Baubelehrung* 8.KLA 2/43–3/43
Cdr *U 541* 24.3.43–capitulation
Detained; freed 1/48

PETERSEN, THEODOR [921]
b. 14.1.1914, Flensburg
Enlisted rating 1/1934; ObltzS 1.1.43
ObStrm *U 138* 9/40–1/41; ObStrm and 3WO *U 43* 1/41–3/42; *Baubelehrung* 4/42–5/42; 1WO *U 181* 5/42–2/43; U-Cdr's Course, 2.UAA and 24th U-Flotilla 3/43 (U-Cdr's Torpedo Course 43); *Baubelehrung* 7.KLA 4/43–5/43
Cdr *U 612* 31.5.43–20.2.44
Baubelehrung 6.KLA 2/44–4/44
Cdr *U 874* 8.4.44–capitulation

PETRAN, FRIEDRICH [922]
b. 6.12.1919, Kassel
Class 1938; ObltzS 1.1.43
WO *Minenräumschiff 12* 5/40–10/40; WO light cruiser *Emden* 10/40–6/41; U-boat trg 7/41–12/41; *Baubelehrung* 6.KLA 12/41–2/42; 2WO *U 178* 2/42–7/44; U-Cdr's Course, 3.ULD and 27th U-Flotilla 7/44–12/44
Cdr *U 516* 12/44–capitulation

PFEFFER, GÜNTHER [923]
b. 23.10.1914, Berlin
Class 1934; Kplt 1.3.42
1WO *U 67* 1/41–5/41
Acting Cdr *U 67* 5.6.41–2.7.41
U-Cdr's Course, 24th U-Flotilla, 7th U-Flotilla and *Baubelehrung* KLA U-North 7/41–10/41
Cdr *U 171* 25.10.41–9.10.42
Baubelehrung 6.KLA 11/42–1/43
Cdr *U 170* 19.1.43–7/44

Acting Cdr *U 548* 8/44–11/44; boat evacuated Lorient 11.8.44 for Bergen (arrived 25.9.44) and later Flensburg (docked 12.10.44)
Trg Leader Higher Commander of Torpedo Schools and Wehrmacht Commandant's HQ Kiel 11/44–capitulation

PFEIFER, WERNER [924]
b. 2.5.1912, Dresden
Class 1933; Kplt 1.2.41
U-boat trg 11/39–3/40; Comp. Officer UAA Plön 4/40–6/40; U-Cdr's Course and WO aboard *U 138* 7/40–10/40
Cdr *U 56* 14.10.40–21.4.41
WO (supernumerary) *U 93* 4/41–6/41; *Baubelehrung* 6/41–7/41
Cdr *U 581* 31.7.41–2.2.42
POW 2.2.42–17.7.47

PICH, HELMUTH [925]
b. 26.6.1914, Babziens, Rastenburg
Class 1934; Kplt 1.2.42
Seconded to Luftwaffe 9/39–9/41, from 1.4.41 flight captain *2./Seeaufklärergruppe 126* (naval reconnaissance); U-boat trg 10/41–3/42; WO (supernumerary) *U 103* 3/42–6/42; *Baubelehrung* 6/42–9/42
Cdr *U 168* 10.9.42–6.10.44
POW 6.10.44–3/47

PICK, EWALD [926]
b. 27.5.1912, Fischbach, Dudweiler
Entry XII/1934; ObltzS (R) 1.7.43
Cdr *U 481* 10.11.43–29.2.44
Cdr *U 708* 1.3.44–14.4.44
Various duties 4/44–1/45; *Baubelehrung* 1.KLA 1/45–4/45
Cdr *U 1025* 12.4.45–24.4.45 (see Curio [180]); duties until capitulation not recorded

PIENING, ADOLF CORNELIUS [927]
b. 16.9.1910, Süderende (Föhr), Tondem
Class 1930; KKpt 1.4.43
2nd Minesweeping Flotilla (Cdr *M 72*) 1/38–
  3/39, (Cdr *M 2*) 3/39–10/40; U-boat trg 10/40–
  3/41; U-Cdr's Course, 24th U-Flotilla 4/41–
  5/41; U-Cdr sea trg (supernumerary) *U 48*
  22.5.41–21.6.41 (U-Boat Archive per Piening);
  Baubelehrung KLA U-North 7.41–8/41
Cdr *U 155* 23.8.41 to 2/44 (10.3.44 per WASt
  and P/F, but he must have been relieved before
  5.3.44, the date when Rudolph [1036] took
  U 155 out on patrol)
CO 7th U-Flotilla 3/44–capitulation
Detained; freed 1/48
Knight's Cross 13.8.42 (121st KM, 59th U-boat
  holder)

PIETSCH, ULRICH [928]
b. 5.12.1915, Laurahütte, UpperSilesia
Class 1936; Kplt 1.10.43
Ship's aircrew (*1./196*) battleship *Gneisenau*
  2/40–7/40 and heavy cruiser *Admiral Hipper*
  7/40–1/42 with period on light cruiser
  Nürnberg from 9/41; U-boat trg 2/42–7/42;
  1WO *U 373* 7/42–1/43; U-Cdr's Course,
  2.UAA and 26th U-Flotilla 1/43–2/43;
  Baubelehrung 6.KLA 2/43–3/43
Cdr *U 344* 26.3.43–22.8.44
Lost 22.8.44 Barents Sea, NW of Bear Island

PIETSCHMANN, WALTER [929]
b. 31.7.1919, Rauschwalde
Class 1937b; ObltzS 1.4.42
ADC and WO 17th Minesweeping Flotilla 5/40–
  1/41; U-boat trg 1/41–8/41; *Baubelehrung*
  9/41–10/41; 1WO *U 377* 10/41–8/42; U-Cdr's
  Course, 24th U-Flotilla 9/42–10/42;
  Baubelehrung 10/42–11/42
Cdr *U 712* 5.11.42–14.12.43
Cdr *U 762* 15.12.43–8.2.44
Lost 8.2.44 central North Atlantic

PIETZSCH, WERNER [930]
b. 30.4.1917, Potsdam
Class 1935; Kplt 1.7.42
ADC Reserve Naval Artillery Div. 9/39–12/39;
  WO 6th Torpedo-Boat Flotilla 1/40–5/40;
  adviser, Staff, C-in-C Torpedo-Boats 6/40–
  10/40; U-boat trg 10/40–3/41; relief instructor
  Naval Gunnery School 3/41–4/41;
  Baubelehrung Group U-North 5/41; 1WO
  U 129 5/41–3/42; 2.UAA 3/42–5/42;
  Baubelehrung 8.KLA 5/42–6/42
Cdr *U 523* 25.6.42–25.8.43
POW 25.8.43

PLOHR, HELMUT [931]
b. 2.12.1913, Schildesche
Enlisted rating 1933; ObltzS
ObStrm *U 145* 10/40–2/41; ObStrm *U 371* 3/41–
  5/43; Personnel Reserve, courses and trg 6/43–
  4/44; 22nd U-Flotilla 4/44–5/44
Cdr *U 149* 15.5.44–capitulation

POEL, GUSTAV [932]
b. 2.8.1917, Hamburg
Class 1936; Kplt 1.2.43
U-boat trg 10/38–4/39; 2WO *U 27* 4/39–5/39;
  WO 6th U-Flotilla *Hundius* and 2nd U-Flotilla
  5/39–6/40; BdU/Organisational 6/40–10/40;
  assistant to German Liaison Officer/Italian C-
  in-C Submarines 10/40–6/41; Tactical Instructor 25th U-Flotilla 6/41–12/41; U-Cdr's Torpedo Course, 26th U-Flotilla 12/41–1/42; Staff
  25th U-Flotilla 1/42–5/42; *Baubelehrung*
  7.KLA 5/42–6/42
Cdr *U 413* 3.6.42 to 19.4.44 (per WASt) or
  24.4.44 (per P/F)
Comp. CO 2 Section/Naval College Mürwik
  4/44–1/45; Staff Commanding Adm. U-Boats
  1/45–capitulation; Staff 13th Landing Flotilla
  6/45–10/45; released 6.10.45
Knight's Cross 21.3.44 (207th KM, 113 U-boat
  holder)

POESCHEL, WOLFGANG [933]
b. 25.3.1920, Berlin
Class 1938; ObltzS 1.4.43
WO *U 28* 4/41–12/41; *Baubelehrung* 12/41–1/42; 1WO *U 604* 1/42–11/42; U-Cdr's Course, 24th U-Flotilla 11/42–12/42; *Baubelehrung* 7.KLA 12/42–1/43
Cdr *U 737* 30.1.43–4.2.43
Cdr *U 422* 10.2.43–4.10.43
Lost 4.10.43 N of Azores

POMMEREHNE, WALTER [934]
b. 4.4.1908, Görlitz
Class 1931; KKpt 1.12.43
Staff C-in-C Escort Forces Baltic 8/39–9/39; Div. and No 1 Radio Technical Officer heavy cruiser *Blücher* 9/39–4/40; Harbour Cdr Horten 4/40–6/40; Station Command North Sea 6/40–7/40; 4/Adm. Staff Officer, Staff Naval C-in-C Northern France 7/40–10/40; Naval Signals Officer (Trouville) 10/40–6/41, (Kiel) 7/41–1/43, inc. period as signals adviser to Coastal Cdr Western Baltic 3/42–1/43; U-boat trg 1/43–9/43 (U-Cdr's Torpedo Course 53); *Baubelehrung* 6.KLA 10/43–11/43
Cdr *U 866* 17.11.43–12/44; seconded FdU Baltic 12/44–3/45; 4/Adml Staff Officer, Staff, Commanding Adm. Skagerrak 3/45–capitulation
Detained; freed 22.7.45

VON POMMER-ESCHE, GERD [935]
b. 22.1.1918, Nordhausen, Harz
Class 1937a; ObltzS 1.9.41
R-Cdr 1st R-Boat Flotilla 3/40–1/41; U-boat trg 1/41–7/41; *Baubelehrung* 6.KLA 7/41–10/41; 1WO *U 159* 10/41–2/43; U-Cdr's Course, 2.UAA and 24th U-Flotilla 2/43–6/43 (U-Cdr's Torpedo Course 42)
Cdr *U 160* 15.6.43–14.7.43 (see Lassen [703])
Lost 14.7.43 S of Azores

POPP, KLAUS [936]
b. 30.5.1917, Berlin
Class 1935; Kplt 1.8.42
Radio Technical Officer light cruiser *Königsberg* 3/30–4/40; Naval Signals Officer Trondheim 5/40–3/41; U-boat trg, U-Cdr's Course, 24th U-Flotilla and U-Cdr under instrn 4/41–12/41
Cdr *U 140* 10.12.41–1.9.42
Cdr *U 552* 2.9.42–10.7.44 (U-Boat Archive per Popp, but *U 53* WD gives 8.9.42 as the date when Popp relieved Topp [1280])
Baubelehrung 3.KLA 7/44–9/44; U-Cdr 4th U-Flotilla 9/44–11/44, inc. Cdr *U 3006* on 5.10.44 for commissioning only (U-Boat Archive per Popp); Comp. Officer Naval Signals School Mürwik 11/44–capitulation

POSER, GÜNTER [937]
b. 23.9.1916, Berlin
Class 1936; Kplt 1.2.43
Seconded to Luftwaffe 9/39–12/40; U-boat trg 1/41–7/41; 1WO *U 432* 7/41–11/41; U-Cdr under instrn 26th U-Flotilla 11/41–12/41
Cdr *U 59* 12/41–15.7.42
Cdr *U 202* 2.9.42–2.6.43
POW 2.6.43

POSKE, HANS-GEORG FRIEDRICH ('FRITZ') [938]
b. 23.10.1904, Berlin-Schöneberg
Class 1923; KptzS 1.10.43
Navigation Officer trg ship *Schlesien* 4/39–12/39; Navigation Officer, light cruiser *Nürnberg*, 12/39–4/40; Navigation Officer light cruiser *Königsberg* 4/40; Adm. Staff Officer, Staff, Adm. Norwegian West Coast 4/40–6/40; Cdr state yacht *Grille* 6/40–10/40; U-boat trg 10/40–3/41; U-Cdr's Course, 24th U-Flotilla 3/41–4/41; 3rd U-Flotilla 4/41–5/41; *Baubelehrung* U-Boats Kriegsmarine Depot Hamburg 5/41–7/41
Cdr *U 504* 30.7.41–5.1.43

Cdr 1.ULD 1/43–2/45; CO OKM/Special Staff
  Naval Infantry 2/45–capitulation
Detained; freed 5.3.46
Knight's Cross 6.11.42 (132nd KM, 68th U-boat
  holder)

PRAETORIUS, FRIEDRICH-HERMANN [939]
b. 28.2.1904, Kolberg
Class 1934; Kplt 1.1.42
U-boat trg 4/40–7/40; *Baubelehrung* 8/40–10/40;
  1WO *U 98* 10/40–6/41; *Baubelehrung* 7/41–
  8/41
Cdr *U 135* 16.8.41–11/42
Trg Officer (27th U-Flotilla) 2/43–2/45, (25th U-
  Flotilla) 2/45–capitulation

PREGEL, SIEGFRIED [940]
b. 2.2.1915, Leoben, Steiermark, Austria
Entry X/1933 Croatian Navy; XI/1942
  Kriegsmarine; Kplt seniority 1.2.43
11/Basic Trg Est. Stralsund and 1/NCO Trg Div.
  11/42–3/43; Div. Officer and WO heavy cruiser
  Prinz Eugen 3/43–8/43; U-boat trg and courses
  8/43–7/44
Cdr *U 323* 19.7.44–26.2.45
No further details available

PREHN, WILHELM [941]
b. 23.12.1914, Langen-Jarchow, Mecklenburg
Enlisted rating 1934; ObltzS 1.7.44
Rating U-Flotilla *Weddigen* 10/37–1/40; Helms-
  man's School and UAA Plön 1/40–8/40;
  ObStrm *U 97* 9/40–6/43; trg and courses, WO,
  U-Cdr's Course and *Baubelehrung* 6/43–3/45
Cdr *U 3034* 31.3.45 to mid 4/45, crew of *U 3505*
  (see Willner [1356]) manned *U 3034* 10.4.45–
  15.4.45

PRELLBERG, WILFRIED [942]
b. 18.10.1913, Hamelin
Class 1933; KKpt 1.1.44
WO *U 29* 1938; 1WO *U 34* 11/38–1/40; U-Cdr
  under instrn 1st U-Boat Trg Flotilla 1/40–5/40
Cdr *U 19* 1.5.40–19.6.40
Cdr *U 31* 8.7.40–2.11.40
POW 2.11.40

PREMAUER, RUDOLF [943]
b. 8.5.1919, Stuttgart
Class 1937b; Kplt 1.1.45
U-boat trg 2/41–11/41; 1WO *U 510* 11/41–4/43;
  U-Cdr's Course, 2.UAA and 24th U-Flotilla
  4/43–8/43 (U-Cdr's Torpedo Course 47);
  Baubelehrung 6.KLA 8/43–9/43
Cdr *U 857* 16.9.43–7.4.45
Lost 7.4.45 off Boston, US east coast

PRESSEL, KURT [944]
b. 1.4.1911, Wernigerode
Enlisted rating 1930; Kplt 1.7.43
ObStrm and WO *U 56* 4/39–6/41; WO *U 5* U-
  Cdr's Course, 24th U-Flotilla, 7/41–10/41
Cdr *U 60* 1.10.41–5/42
Cdr *U 5* 5/42–9.11.42
Baubelehrung, 8.KLA 11/42–12/42
Cdr *U 951* 3.12.42–7.7.43
Lost 7.7.43 NW of Cape Vincent

PREUSS, GEORG [945]
b. 30.12.1916, Andreasthal, Schwetz, Bromberg,
  West Prussia
Class 1936; Kplt 1.8.43
Seconded to Luftwaffe until 12/40; U-boat trg
  1/41–6/41; 1WO *U 433* 6/41–10/41; personnel
  adviser 7th U-Flotilla 10/41–3/42; Senior
  Testing Officer Torpedo Testing Branch 4/42–
  6/43; U-Cdr's Course and *Baubelehrung* 8.KLA
  6/43–10/43 (U-Cdr's Torpedo Course 52)
Cdr *U 1224* 20.10.43–15.2.44

Baubelehrung 6.KLA 3/44–4/44
Cdr *U 875* 21.4.44–capitulation
Detained; freed 21.3.47

PREUSS, JOACHIM [946]
b. 30.5.1914, Bremen
Class 1933; Kplt 1.12.40
1WO *U A* 9/39–10/39; Cdr *U 10* 1/40–9.6.40
Instructor ULD 6/40–4/41; *Baubelehrung* 4/41
Cdr *U 568* 1.5.41–29.5.42
POW 29.5.42–22.11.47

PRIEN, GÜNTHER [947]
b. 16.1.1908, Osterfeld, Thüringen
Class 1933/31; KKpt 1.3.41 (Translator's note: Class 1933/31 was a special induction of 15 junior officers from the mercantile marine to replace naval cadets of the small 1931 intake drowned in the *Niobe* sail training ship disaster of 1932. See also Bleichrodt [89].)
U-boat trg plus torpedo course on *U 3*, 10/35–4/36; at FdU 5/36–9/36; 2WO *U 26* 10/36–10/37; 1WO *U 26* 11/37–9/38; *Baubelehrung* Germaniawerft Kiel (*U 47*) 10/38–12/38
Cdr *U 47* 17.12.38–7.3.41
Missing S of Iceland 7.3.41
Knight's Cross 18.10.39 (2nd KM, 1st U-boat holder)
Oak Leaves 20.10.40 (5th WM, 1st KM, 1st U-boat holder)

PRÜTZMANN, ROBERT [948]
b. 4.5.1903, Dosmitten, Mohrungen, East Prussia
Class 1924; FKpt 1.8.43
Wargames Officer battleship *Scharnhorst* 1/39–3/40; U-boat trg 4/40–9/40
Cdr *U 30* 9/40–31.3.41
U-Cdr 2nd U-Flotilla 4/41–1/42; Station Command Baltic 1/42–3/42; Navigation Officer light cruiser *Leipzig* 3/42–2/43; Naval Liaison Officer *Luftflotte 5* 2/43–6/43; First Officer heavy cruiser *Admiral Scheer* 6/43–capitulation

VON PÜCKLER UND LIMPURG, GRAF WILHELM-HEINRICH [949]
b. 9.3.1913, Ludwigsburg
Class 1934; Kplt 1.4.42
WO 2nd Minesweeping Flotilla 3/39–5/40; R-Cdr 2nd R-Boat Flotilla 5/40–1/41; U-boat trg 1/41–6/41; 1WO *U 101* 6/41–11/41; U-Cdr's Course, 26th U-Flotilla 11/41–1/42; *Baubelehrung* 1.KLA 1/42–2/42
Cdr *U 381* 25.2.42–19.5.43
Lost 19.5.43 SE of Cape Farewell

PULST, GÜNTHER [950]
b. 26.3.1918, Braunschweig
Class X/1937; Kplt 1.1.45
Destroyer *Z 9 Wolfgang Zenker* 12/39–4/40; Comp. Leader Land Command Norway/Narvik 4/40–7/40; Cdr VP-boat *Rabe* (Coastal Defence Group Norwegian West Coast) 7/40–8/40; 2/Basic Trg Est. Stralsund 9/40–11/40; Group Officer Naval College Flensburg-Mürwik 11/40–4/42; U-boat trg 4/42–10/42; 1WO *U 752* 10/42–3/43; radar course 2.UAA 3/43; U-Cdr's Course, 24th U-Flotilla 3/43–4/43 (U-Cdr's Torpedo Course 44); *Baubelehrung* 1/Comp/8.KLA 4/43–5/43
Cdr *U 978* 12.5.43–capitulation
Detained; freed 26.3.48
Knight's Cross 21.12.44 (283rd KM, 133rd U-boat holder)

PURKHOLD, HUBERTUS [951]
b. 6.6.1916, Beuthen, Upper Silesia
Class 1935; Kplt 1.11.42
WO gunnery trg boat *Jaguar* 12/38–10/40; U-boat trg 10/40–1/41; U-Cdr's Course, 24th U-Flotilla and 1WO *U 30* until 5/41; period as acting Cdr *U 30* 4/41–22.4.41 (U-Boat Archive

per Baberg [24]; Loeser [744] and Purkold both had periods as acting Cdr of *U 30* before Baberg took command on 23.4.41)
Cdr *U 14* 20.5.41–9.2.42
Baubelehrung 6.KLA 2/42–3/42
Cdr *U 260* 14.3.42–4/44
Comp CO Naval College Mürwik 4/44–capitulation

PUSCHMANN, HANS-FRIEDRICH
[952]
b. 7.6.1922, Berlin
Class XII/1939; ObltzS 1.12.43
Supplementary WO (trg) *U 410* 3/42–7/42; *Baubelehrung* 7/42–8/42; 1WO *U 385* 8/42–6/44; course 3.ULD and U-Cdr's Course, 24th U-Flotilla 7/44–11/44 (U-Cdr's Torpedo Course 75)
Cdr *U 748* 30.11.44–20.4.45
3.ULD 4/45–capitulation

VON PUTTKAMER, KONSTANTIN
[953]
b. 31.7.1917, Swinemünde
Class 1936; ObltzS 1.10.40, posthumously Kplt seniority 1.2.43
Comp. Officer Naval Artillery Detachment 121 8/39–3/40; U-boat trg 4/40–10/40; WO *U 146* 11/40–12/40; *Baubelehrung* 12/40–3/41; 2WO *U 46* 3/41–8/41; 1WO *U 46* 8/41–10/41; U-Cdr's Course, 26th U-Flotilla 10/41–11/41
Cdr *U 46* 20.11.41–3/42
Baubelehrung 7.KLA 3/42–4/42
Cdr *U 443* 18.4.42–23.2.43
Lost 23.2.43 Mediterranean, off Algiers

Q

QUAET-FASLEM, JÜRGEN [954]
b. 25.5.1913, Göttingen
Class 1934; Kplt 1.3.42
Seconded to Luftwaffe 10/36–1/41; *Bordfliegerstaffel 1./196* (aircrew, battleship *Scharnhorst*), flight captain *3./Fliegerergänzungsgruppe (See)* until 1/41; U-boat trg 1/41–6/41; WO *U 98* 6/41–8/41; U-Cdr's Course, 24th U-Flotilla 9/41–10/41; *Baubelehrung* 8.KLA 10/41–11/41
Cdr *U 595* 6.11.41–14.11.42
POW 14.11.42

QUECK, HORST-THILO [955]
b. 9.1.1915, Braunschweig
Class 1935; Kplt 1.12.42
WO trg ship *Schleswig-Holstein* 7/39–8/40; WO minelayers *Deutschland* and *Skagerrak* 8/40–11/40; WO light cruiser *Leipzig* 11/40–6/41; U-boat trg 6/41–10/41; 1WO *U 372* 11/41–3/42; U-Cdr's trg course, 2.UAA and 24th Flotilla 3/42–5/42
Cdr *U 622* 14.5.42–24.7.43
Cdr *U 92* 8/43–27.6.44
1.UAA 6/44–9/44; *Baubelehrung* 8.KLA 9/44–11/44
Cdr *U 2522* 22.11.44–5.5.45

R

RAABE, ERNST [956]
b. 5.2.1907, Gross-Engelau, East Prussia
Entry 1926; Kplt 1.4.43
Heavy cruiser *Admiral Hipper* 12/39–3/43; U-boat trg 3/43–11/43 (U-Cdr's Torpedo Course 58); *Baubelehrung* 1.KLA 11/43–1/44
Cdr *U 246* 11.1.44–29.3.45
Lost 29.3.45 English Channel, off Land's End

RAABE, KARL-HEINZ [957]
b. 23.5.1920, Kiel-Russee
Class 1938; ObltzS 1.4.43
M/S-Cdr 44th Minesweeping Flotilla 8/40–10/41; M/S-Cdr 14th Minesweeping Flotilla 10/41–3/42; M/S-Cdr 44th Minesweeping Flotilla, 3/42–1/43; U-boat trg 1/43–9/43 (U-Cdr's Torpedo Course 54); *Baubelehrung* 7.KLA 9/43
Cdr *U 1161* 27.9.43–17.1.45
18th U-Flotilla 1/45–2/45
Cdr *U 1007* 2/45 to end 4/45

VON RABENAU, GEORG [958]
b. 3.7.1916, Stassfurt-Leopoldshall
Class 1936; Kplt 1.8.43
Observer trg Aircraft Weapons School Bug/Rügen Island 10/38–8/39; observer *1./Küstenfliegergruppe 506* 8/39–4/40; *Küstenfliegergruppe 806* 5/40–12/40; U-boat trg 1/41–5/41; *Baubelehrung* 6/41–7/41; 1WO *U 504* 7/41–7/42; U-Cdr's Course, 24th U-Flotilla 8/42; instructor 2.ULD 9/42–12/42
Cdr *U 528* 17.12.42 (per WASt) or 19.12.42 (relieved Fuchs [334] per *U 528* WD) to 11.5.43
POW 11.5.43–22.5.46

VON RABENAU, WOLF-RÜDIGER [959]
b. 7.1.1908, Spandau
Class 1933; Kplt 1.6.39, posthumously KKpt seniority 1.4.42
Div. Officer trg ship *Schlesien* 6/38–3/40; U-boat trg 4/40–11/40
Cdr *U 10* 30.11.40–9.6.41
Cdr *U 52* 10.6.41–6.7.41
Baubelehrung 7/41–9/41
Cdr *U 702* 3.9.41–4.4.42
Missing North Sea 4.4.42

RACKY, ERNST-AUGUST [960]
b. 1.9.1919, Schierstein, Wiesbaden
Class 1938; ObltzS 1.1.43
2WO *U 573* 5/41–5/42, interned Spain 2/43; U-Cdr's Course, 24th U-Flotilla 3/43 (U-Cdr's Torpedo Course 43)
Cdr *U 52* 1.4.43–22.10.43
Cdr *U 429* 27.10.43–15.10.44
Courses and *Baubelehrung* Type XXI 10/44–12/44
Cdr *U 3019* 23.12.44–2.5.45

RADEMACHER, EWALD [961]
b. 1.12.1917, Rheine, Steinfurt
Class 1937a; Kplt 1.10.44
Platoon Officer battleship *Gneisenau* 4/39–4/40; ADC 27th U-Flotilla 5/40–10/40; WO U-boat depot ship *Wilhelm Bauer* 10/40–2/43; U-boat trg 3/43–8/43; courses 27th and 24th U-Flotillas 8/43–11/43 (U-Cdr's Torpedo Course 56); *Baubelehrung* 11/43–12/43
Cdr *U 772* 23.12.43–30.12.44
Lost 30.12.44 S of Weymouth

RADEMACHER, RUDOLF [962]
b. 19.2.1919, Breslau
Class 1937b; ObltzS 1.4.42
Battleship *Tirpitz* 2/41–1/43; U-boat trg 1/43–6/43; U-Cdr's Course, 2.UAA and 24th U-Flotilla 6/43–8/43 (U-Cdr's Torpedo Course 51); *Baubelehrung* 1.KLA, 8/43–9/43
Cdr *U 478* 8.9.43–30.6.44
Lost 30.6.44 NE of Faroes

RADERMACHER, ALFRED [963]
b. 13.9.1913, Hilgert, Westerwald
Enlisted VII/1933; ObltzS 1.7.43
Battle-helmsman *U 5* 8/35–9/36; courses 10/36–9/37; No 2 and No 1 Boatswain *U 5* 10/37–4/39; Helmsman's School Flensburg 4/39–11/39; Basic Trg Establishment Kiel and 1st U-Flotilla (Personnel Reserve) 11/39–2/40; ObStrm *U 5* 2/40–8/40; *Baubelehrung* Germaniawerft Kiel 8/40–9/40; ObStrm *U 96* 9/40–4/42; courses 5/42–7/42; U-Cdr's Course, 24th U-Flotilla 8/42–9/42
Cdr *U 120* 15.9.42 to 24.5.43 (U-Boat Archive per Radermacher) or 1.10.42 to 25.7.43 (per WASt; this latter date cannot be correct as Radermacher commissioned *U 393* on 3.7.43 and would not also have been in command of *U 120*)
Acting Cdr *U 5* 3/43 (Whilst Radermacher was commanding *U 120* with the 21st U-Flotilla at Pillau he took temporary command of *U 5* for a few days at the beginning of 3/43 and thereby achieved the curious distinction of having served aboard *U 5* at every level from seaman to commander. He had previously served aboard the boat as helmsman, No 2 and No 1 boatswain and coxswain WO. *U 5* was lost a few days later—see Rahn [968].)
Baubelehrung 5/43–7/43
Cdr *U 393* 3.7.43–30.9.44
Head of *Unterwasserortung* (Underwater Systems of Ship Location) 24th U-Flotilla 10/44–2/45, 25th U-Flotilla 2/45–capitulation

RADKE, HANS-JÜRGEN [964]
b. 10.1.1916, Kiel
Class 1935; ObltzS 1.10.39
WO U-Flotilla *Wegener* 11/38–1/39; 1WO *U 52* 2/39–10/40; *Baubelehrung* 11/40–12/40
Cdr *U 148* 28.12.40–14.9.41
Baubelehrung 9/41–10/41
Accidental death 14.12.41 following inhalation of poisonous fumes aboard accommodation ship *Black Prince* at Danzig Neufahrwasser

RAHE, HEINZ [965]
b. 15.3.1916, Neumünster
Class 1936; Kplt 1.11.42
WO torpedo-boat *Wolf* 3/40–10/40; U-boat trg 11/40–4/41; 1WO *U 73* 4/41–9/41; U-Cdr's Course, 24th U-Flotilla 11/41–12/41; *Baubelehrung* 12/41–1/42
Cdr *U 257* 14.1.42–24.2.44
Lost 24.2.44 central North Atlantic

RAHLF, PETER [966]
b. 7.3.1909, Struckkamp, Fehmarn I
Entry IX/1939; ObltzS (R) 1.4.43
WO 2nd Sperrbrecher Flotilla 4/41–2/43; U-boat trg 2/43–7/43; U-Cdr's Course, 2.UAA and 24th U-Flotilla 7/43–9/43 (U-Cdr's Torpedo Course 54); *Baubelehrung* 9/43–10/43
Cdr *U 317* 23.10.43–26.6.44
Lost 26.6.44 NE of Shetlands

RAHMLOW, HANS-JOACHIM [967]
b. 18.10.1909, Striegau, Silesia
Class 1928; Kplt 1.6.37
Comp. CO Naval Artillery Detachment 134 9/39; Cdr 4th Reserve Naval Artillery Div. 9/39–1/40; Cdr 10th Reserve Naval Artillery Div. 1/40–3/40; U-boat trg 4/40–9/40; U-Cdr sea trg 7th U-Flotilla on *U 48* 10/40–11/40
Cdr *U 58* 25.11.40–6.4.41
Baubelehrung 4/41–5/41

Cdr *U 570* 15.5.41–27.8.41
POW 27.8.41

RAHN, HERMANN [968]
b. 14.10.1918, Worms
Class 1938; LtzS 1.4.41, posthumously ObltzS seniority 1.4.43
WO torpedo-boat *Jaguar* 5/40–1/41; U-boat trg 1/41–6/41; 1st U-Flotilla 6/41–11/41; 1WO *U 83* 11/41–9/42; U-Cdr's Course, 24th U-Flotilla 9/42–10/42
Cdr *U 5* 10.11.42–19.3.43
Lost 19.3.43 Baltic Sea, W of Pillau

RAHN, WOLFGANG [969]
b. 31.10.1920, Worms
Class 1938; ObltzS 1.4.43
U-boat trg 11/40–3/41; WO torpedo-boat *Tiger* (ex-Norwegian *Thor*) 3/41–10/41; *Baubelehrung* 10/41–12/41; 1WO *U 458* 12/41–11/42; U-Cdr's Course, 24th U-Flotilla 11/42–1/43; *Baubelehrung* 6.KLA 1/43–2/43
Cdr *U 343* 18.2.43–10.3.44
Lost 10.3.44 Mediterranean, S of Sardinia

RANZAU, EMIL [970]
b. 4.6.1908, Kiel
Entry 1/1939; ObltzS (R) 1.10.43
WO 61st VP-Boat Flotilla 9/41–8/42; U-boat trg 8/42–2/43; WO *U 107* 5/43–2/44; U-Cdr's Course 3/44–5/44
Cdr *U 150* 5/44–7.6.44
Cdr *U 71* 8.6.44–27.2.45
Comp. Officer 1.UAA 2/45–capitulation

VON RAPPARD, KONSTANTIN [971]
b. 13.6.1917, Wongrowitz, Posen
Class 1936; Kplt 1.8.43
WO 13th Minesweeping Flotilla 10/39–4/40; Gunnery Officer trg ship *Schlesien* 4/40–8/40; Group Officer Naval College Flensburg-Mürwik 8/40–9/40; Kriegsmarine Depot Boulogne 9/40–2/41; Div. Officer trg ship *Schleswig-Holstein* 2/41–6/41; U-boat trg 6/41–11/41; 1WO *U 103* 11/41–7/42
Cdr *U 560* 16.7.42–31.8.43
Leader torpedo attack trg, 23rd U-Flotilla 9/43–8/44; Leader U-boat base Kristiansand-South 8/44–3/45
Cdr *U 2324* 3/45–capitulation

RASCH, HERMANN [972]
b. 26.8.1914, Wilhelmshaven
Class 1934; Kplt 1.3.42
Sail trg ship *Albert Leo Schlageter* 7/39–8/39; ADC Staff, Station Command North Sea 8/39–4/40; U-boat trg and *Baubelehrung* 4/40–9/40; 1WO *U 106* 9/40–7/41; U-Cdr's Course 7/41–9/41
Cdr *U 106* 20.10.41–4/43
Adm. Staff Officer OKM/4.SKL 4/43–6/44; 4/Adm. Staff Officer OKM/2.SKL/BdU/Opns 6/44–10/44; Cdr Trg Command 300, later *K-Verband Rasch* (Cdr fleet two-man midget submarines) 10/44–capitulation; CO 1/Comp. 1/Minesweeping Reserve Div. 6/45–9/45; Staff HQ per order of KzS Dobratz [211], Naval High Command East 9/45–7/46
Released 7.7.46
Knight's Cross 29.12.42 (141th KM, 74th U-boat holder)

RASCH, KARL-HEINZ [973]
b. 6.4.1914, Bremerhaven
Entry 1/1934; Kplt 1.3.45
R-Cdr 1st R-Boat Flotilla 5/41–1/43; U-boat trg 2/43–8/43; U-Cdr's Course, 24th U-Flotilla 8/43–9/43 (U-Cdr's Torpedo Course 54); *Baubelehrung* 6.KLA 9/43–11/43
Cdr *U 296* 3.11.43–22.3.45
Lost 22.3.45 Northern Channel

RATHKE, HELLMUT [974]
b. 3.12.1910, Czychen, East Prussia
Class 1930; KKpt 1.6.43
Course Leader Torpedo School Mürwik 5/39–6/40; Staff Officer Naval Command Station Calais 6/40–10/40; Course Leader Torpedo School Mürwik 10/40–4/41; U-boat trg 4/41–7/41; *Baubelehrung* 7/41–8/41
Cdr *U 352* 28.8.41–9.5.42
POW 9.5.42–17.5.46

RATSCH, HEINRICH [975]
b. 18.10.1914, Berlin
Class 1934; Kplt 1.10.41
1WO *U 38* 1/40–11/40; 24th U-Flotilla 11/40–2/41
Cdr *U 28* 12.2.41–21.6.41
2.UAA 6/41–7/41
Baubelehrung 7/41–8/41
Cdr *U 583* 14.8.41–15.11.41
Lost 15.11.41 Baltic

RAUCH, DIETRICH [976]
b. 18.12.1916, Jena
Class 1936; Kplt 1.10.43
U-boat trg and U-courses 7/41–3/42; 1WO *U 107* 4/42–11/42; U-Cdr's Course 11/42–1/43
Cdr *U 141* 16.2.43–28.7.43
Officer instructor 1.ULD 8/43–11/43; *Baubelehrung* 6.KLA 11/43–12/43
Cdr *U 868* 23.12.43–21.7.44
4th U-Flotilla 7/44–11/44; Comp CO 2.ULD 11/44–4/45
Detained; freed 8.8.45

RAVE, ERNST-WOLFGANG [977]
b. 9.9.1917, Wuppertal-Elberfeld
Class 1937a; Kplt 1.12.44
Baubelehrung U 105 8/40–9/40; 2WO *U 105* 9/40–10/41; 2nd U-Flotilla 10/41–1/42; U-Cdr's Course, 24th U-Flotilla 1/42–3/42; Group Leader Torpedo Testing Branch 3/42–10/44; U-Cdr sea trg *U 554* 16.10.44–18.11.44
Cdr *U 554* 19.11.44–22.3.45
U-Cdr (supernumerary) *U 3002* 23.3.45–2.5.45

RECHE, REINHART [978]
b. 13.12.1915, Kreuzburg, Upper Silesia
Class 1934; Kplt 1.10.41
WO light cruiser *Emden* 6/39–10/39; Group Officer Naval College Flensburg-Mürwik 10/39–2/40; Trg Officer sail trg ship *Horst Wessel* 3/40–4/40; U-boat trg and *Baubelehrung* 4/40–1/41; 1WO *U 751* 1/41–9/41; U-Cdr's Course and *Baubelehrung* 6.KLA 10/41–11/41
Cdr *U 255* 29.11.41–6.6.43
A. Ops Staff, FdU Norway and FdU Polar Sea 6/43–capitulation
Detained until 1.11.45; 1/Helmsman aircraft catapult ship *Falke* 1/45–2/46; German Minesweeping Administration, Transport Flotilla Kiel 2/46–5/46; discharged 31.5.46
Knight's Cross 17.3.43 (153rd KM, 83rd U-boat holder)

RECKHOFF, JOHANN [979]
b. 15.1.1911, Duisburg-Ruhrort
Entry XI/1928, KKpt 1.8.43
Div. Officer and WO heavy cruiser *Admiral Graf Spee* 10/37–12/39; interned 12/39–11/40, returned to Germany; Wargames Officer heavy cruiser *Prinz Eugen* 12/40–3/43; U-boat trg 4/43–9/43; U-Cdr's Course 2.UAA and 23rd U-Flotilla 9/43–11/43; *Baubelehrung* 11/43–12/43
Cdr *U 398* 18.12.43–8.11.44
Various duties 11/44–4/45; Cdr sail trg ship *Albert Leo Schlageter* 4/45–capitulation

REEDER, GÜNTHER [980]
b. 2.11.1915, Berlin-Karlshorst
Class 1935; Kplt 1.6.42

1WO *U 58* 2/39–9/40; Cdr *U 7* 10/40–1/41 and 2/42–29.3.41; instructor 1.ULD 4/41–10/41; *Baubelehrung* 10/41
Cdr *U 214* 1.11.41–10.5.43 (per *U 214* WD)
9th U-Flotilla 5/43–9/43; instructor 3.ULD 10/43–capitulation

REESE, HANS-JÜRGEN [981]
b. 27.4.1918, Oldenburg
Class 1937a; ObltzS 1.9.41
ADC 13th Minesweeping Flotilla 12/39–8/40; M/S-Cdr 19th Minesweeping Flotilla 8/40–9/41; U-boat trg 9/41–3/42; 1WO *U 561* 4/42–10/42; U-Cdr's Course, 2.UAA and 24th U-Flotilla 10/42–11/42; *Baubelehrung* 7.KLA 11/42–12/42
Cdr *U 420* 16.12.42–26.10.43
Lost 26.10.43 North Atlantic

REFF, REINHARD [982]
b. 7.9.1913, Wollin, Pomerania
Entry XI/1937; ObltzS (R)
WO *U 453* 6/41–10/42; U-Cdr's Course, 24th U-Flotilla 11/42–12/42; *Baubelehrung* 7.KLA 12/42–1/43
Cdr *U 736* 16.1.43–6.8.44
POW 6.8.44

REHREN, HELLMUT [983]
b. 4.3.1922, Göttingen
Class XII/1939; ObltzS 1.12.43
WO sea trg *U 652* 5/41–9/41; courses 10/41–5/42; 2WO *U 652* 5/42–6/42; 29th U-Flotilla and *Baubelehrung* 8.KLA 6/42–9/42; supplementary WO *U 529* 9/42–10/42; courses 10/42–4/43; 2WO *U 564* 4/43–6/43; 1st U-Flotilla and *Baubelehrung* 8.KLA 6/43–10/43; 1WO *U 998* 10/43–6/44; 5th U-Flotilla, U-Cdr's Course, 3.ULD and 23rd U-Flotilla 7/44–9/44; Naval Reserve Div. 10/44–2/45

Cdr *U 926* 5.2.45–capitulation
Detained; freed 12.3.47

REHWINKEL, ERNST-AUGUST [984]
b. 30.10.1901, Hildesheim
Class year not known; KKpt 1.2.39, posthumously FKpt seniority 1.8.42
Instructor Group Leader Naval Gunnery School 5/37–10/40; U-boat trg 10/40–3/41; WO 24th U-Flotilla 3/41–5/41; *Baubelehrung* 5/41–7/41
Cdr *U 578* 10.7.41–10.8.42
Lost 10.8.42 N of Cape Ortegal

REICH, CHRISTIAN [985]
b. 21.11.1915, Bremen
Class 1936; Kplt 1.9.43
ADC minelayer *Tannenberg* 5/40–7/41; U-boat trg 7/41–3/42; 1WO *U A* 3/42–5/42; 1WO *U 202* 5/42–8/42; U-Cdr's Course, 24th U-Flotilla 8/42–9/42; *Baubelehrung* 7.KLA 9.42–11/42
Cdr *U 416* 4.11.42–30.3.43
Baubelehrung 7.KLA 4/43–5/43
Cdr *U 426* 12.5.43–8.1.44
Lost 8.1.44 Bay of Biscay, W of Nantes

VON REICHE, HEINZ [986]
b. 18.3.1908, Fürstenwalde
Class 1929; KKpt 1.4.43
WO *U 9* 1935 (per rank listing 1.11.35) and 1936 (per rank listing 1.11.36); Cdr *U 17* 2.11.37–11.9.39
Station Command Baltic 9/39–12/39; Comp. CO U-Boat School 12/39–3/41; BdU/Organisational 4/41–6/41; Kplt Staff 1st U-Flotilla 6/41–3/42; acting CO 3rd U-Flotilla 3/42–6/42; adviser Central Dept. (Z1) (Staff, 2/Adm. Baltic) 6/42–1/43, (Staff, Commanding Adm. U-Boats) 2/43–capitulation

REICHENBACH-KLINKE, KURT
[987]
b. 21.2.1917, Fürstenwalde, Lebus
Class 1935; Kplt 1.12.42
1WO *U 57* 12/38–9/40
Cdr *U 23* 1.10.40–20.3.41,
Course 1.ULD and 24th U-Flotilla 3/41–7/41; instructor 5.ULD 7/41–12/41; *Baubelehrung* 1.KLA 12/41–1/42
Cdr *U 217* 31.1.42–5.6.43
Lost 5.6.43 central North Atlantic

REICHMANN, WILFRIED [988]
b. 10.9.1905, Wittigwalde, Osterode
Class 1924; KKpt 1.7.39, posthumously FKpt seniority 1.7.42
3/Adm. Staff Officer, Staff Adm. Norwegian North Coast 6/40–10/40; U-boat trg, courses, *Baubelehrung* and various duties 10/40–7/41
Cdr *U 153* 19.7.41–13.7.42 (hospitalised 7.1.42–3.2.42)
Lost 13.7.42 off Columbia, US coast

REIMANN, ERNST [989]
b. 9.9.1920, Südernich
Class IX/1939; ObltzS 1.10.43
WO *U 953* 12/43–6/44; U-Cdr's Course, 3.ULD and 23rd U-Flotilla 7/44–9/44; Midshipmen's Trg Officer Torpedo and Signals School (1.ULD) 9/44–1/45; *Baubelehrung* Cdr Type XXI 6.KLA for *U 3050* (never commissioned) 2.2.45–capitulation

REIMERS, HANS-HEINRICH [990]
b. 19.10.1916, Neumünster
Entry 1939/40; ObltzS (R) 1.1.44
2WO *U 454* 7/41–3/43; U-Cdr's Course, 24th U-Flotilla 4/43–5/43 (U-Cdr's Torpedo Course 45); *Baubelehrung* 8.KLA 5/43–6/43
Cdr *U 983* 16.6.43–8.9.43
Baubelehrung 8.KLA 10/43–12/43

Cdr *U 722* 15.12.43–27.3.45
Lost 27.3.45 off Hebrides

REISENER, WOLFGANG [991]
b. 13.10.1918, Trelde, Harburg
Class 1938; ObltzS 1.4.43
Heavy cruiser *Admiral Hipper* 5/40–9/41; U-boat trg 10/41–4/42; *Baubelehrung* 4/42–6/42; 1WO *U 223* 6/42–11/43; U-Cdr's Course 11/43–12/43
Cdr *U 608* 4.1.44 (per WASt) or 21.1.44 (relieved Struckmeier [1251] per *U 608* WD) to 10.8.44
POW 10.8.44–3/46

REITH, HANS-ERWIN [992]
b. 17.1.1920, Lüneburg
Class 1939a; ObltzS 1.10.42
WO, inc. sea trg *U 105* 11/40–1/42; Command Relay Officer Staff BdU 1/42–10/42; 1WO *U 190* 10/42–12/43, incl U-Cdr's Torpedo Course 57 10/43–11/43; torpedo attack course Travemünde 1/44–5/44
Cdr *U 190* 6.7.44 (U-Boat Archive per Reith) or 1.10.44 (per WASt, but the former seems more likely since Reith sailed from Lorient for Germany in command of *U 190* on 17.8.44) to capitulation
Detained; freed 29.12.47

REMUS, GERHARD [993]
b. 10.5.1916, Schneidemühl
Class 1936; Kplt 1.4.43
Light cruiser *Emden* 6/38–10/40; U-boat trg 11/40–3/41; 1WO *U 652* 4/41–10/41; U-Cdr's Course 10/41–11/41
Cdr *U 34* 20.11.41–15.6.42
Cdr *U 566* 25.7.42–24.1.43
Head of torpedo attack trg 24th U-Flotilla 1/43–9/44; Trg Leader 24th U-Flotilla 10/44–2/45;

Head of torpedo attack trg 26th U-Flotilla 2/45–4/45

Cdr *U 2364* end 4/45–5.5.45; ADC and Signals adviser, Staff, Commanding Adm. U-Boats 5/45–capitulation

Detained; freed 3.8.45

REMUS, WERNER [994]

b. 26.9.1919, Schneidemühl

Class IX/1939; ObltzS 1.10.43

2WO *U 406* 10/41–4/43; U-Cdr's Course, 2.UAA and 24th U-Flotilla 4/43–5/43 (U-Cdr's Torpedo Course 46)

Cdr *U 339* 18.5.43–23.2.45

Cdr *U 554* 3/45–2.5.45

RENDTEL, HORST [995]

b. 27.11.1916, Lychen

Class 1936; Kplt 1.2.43

Command Relay Officer and ADC light cruiser *Köln* 4/38–11/39; Cadet Trg Officer trg ship *Schleswig-Holstein* 11/39–4/40; Group Officer Naval College Flensburg-Mürwik 4/40/–8/40; Kriegsmarine Depot Calais 8/40–10/40; U-boat trg 10/40–3/41; 1WO *U 202* 3/41–11/41; 1WO *U 555* 11/41–2/42

Cdr *U 555* 5.2.42–8/42

Baubelehrung 8.KLA 8/42–9/42

Cdr *U 641* 24.9.42–19.1.44

Lost 19.1.44 SW of Ireland

RESCHKE, FRANZ-GEORG [996]

b. 26.5.1908, Schnittken

Class 1929; KKpt 1.4.43

Comp. CO and instructor Signals School Mürwik 3/38–1/40; Comp. CO 3/NCO Trg Div. 1/40–2/40; U-boat trg 2/40–1/41; U-Cdr sea trg and WO *U 94* 7.1.41–19.2.41; instructor Torpedo School 3/41; *Baubelehrung* 3/41–5/41

Cdr *U 205* 3.5.41–19.10.42 (changeover date per *U 205* WD)

29th U-Flotilla 10/42–11/42; adviser U-boat questions OKM/SKL 11/42–capitulation

VON REVENTLOW-CRIMINIL, GRAF VIKTOR [997]

b. 5.5.1916, place not stated

Class 1936; Kplt 1.9.43

Cdr *U 1017* 13.4.44–16.6.44 (per WASt; relieved Riecken [1002] 6.9.44 per *U 1017* WD)

CO K-Flotilla 415 (*K-Verband*) 7/44–9/44; *K-Verband*, K-Staff North and various duties 9/44–capitulation

REX, HERBERT [998]

b. 27.8.1918, Köln-Riehl

Class 1937a; Kplt 1.3.44

U-boat trg 8/43–3/44; 26th and 19th U-Flotillas 3/44–10/44; course 24th U-Flotilla 11/44–12/44; *Baubelehrung* Cdr and instructor 4/Naval Reserve Div. 12/44–capitulation

REX, WILHELM [999]

b. 26.10.1910, Moenkebude

Entry 1935; ObltzS (R) 1.4.45

Baubelehrung U 680 11/43–12/43; WO and U-Cdr sea trg *U 680* 12/43–3/44; U-Cdr's Course, 3.ULD and 23rd U-Flotilla 3/44–5/44; 8th and 31st U-Flotillas 5/44–12/44

Cdr *U 1405* 21.12.44–3.5.45

RICHARD, HELLMUTH-BERT [1000]

b. 2.3.1917, Hildesheim

Class 1936; ObltzS 1.10.40

Seconded to Luftwaffe 10/38–12/40; U-boat trg 1/41–5/41; *Baubelehrung* 5/41–6/41; 1WO *U 453* 6/41–2/42; U-Cdr's Course, 2.UAA and 24th U-Flotilla 3/42–5/42; *Baubelehrung* 7.KLA 5/42–6/42

Cdr *U 446* 20.6.42–21.9.42
Lost 21.9.42 Bay of Danzig, nr Kallberg

RICHTER, FREIMUT [1001]
b. 29.11.1921, Darmstadt
Class XII/1939; ObltzS 1.12.43
WO sea trg *U 564* 5/41–11/41; U-boat course 1.ULD Pillau 11/41–2/42; torpedo course Torpedo School Mürwik 2/42–3/42; Platoon Leader 2.UAA 3/42; courses 3/42–5/42; supplementary WO *U 517* 5/42–8/42; *Baubelehrung* 8.KLA 8/42–9/42; 1WO *U 639* 9/42–5/43; 1WO *U 302* 5/43–2/44; electronic detection course (*F-Gerät*) 2/44–3/44; U-Cdr's Torpedo Course 67, 24th U-Flotilla 3/44–5/44; instructor 1/Basic Trg Est. Stralsund 5/44–1/45; *Baubelehrung* Cdr Type XXI 8.KLA for *U 2547* (never commissioned) 2.1.45–10.4.45; ADC Naval Anti-Tank Regt *Cremer* and Battle Group *Peschel* 4/45; Platoon Officer Guard Battalion *Dönitz* 4/45–5/45; 1WO *M 453*, Mine Protection, German Bight 5/45–8/45; Liaison officer (interpreter) with British minefield authority 8/45–11/45; demobilised 30.11.45

RIECKEN, WERNER [1002]
b. 8.6.1912, Neumünster
Entry 1934; ObltzS (R) 1.7.43
U-boat trg 8/43–1/44; course 3.ULD, 19th and 23rd U-Flotillas 1/44–6/44
Cdr *U 1017* 17.6.44–29.4.45 (see von Reventlow-Criminil [997])
Lost 29.4.45 NW of Ireland

RIEDEL, HEINZ [1003]
b. 30.12.1921, Rienberg, Moldau
Class XII/1939; ObltzS 1.12.43
U-boat trg 6/41–12/41; *Baubelehrung* 1/42–3/42; 2WO *U 612* 3/42–8/42; *Baubelehrung* 9/42–10/42; 2WO *U 230* 10/42–1/44; 1WO *U 230* 1/44–6/44; course 3.ULD and 27th U-Flotilla 7/44–2/45
Cdr *U 242* 2/45–30.4.45
Lost 30.4.45 Irish Sea, W of Blackpool

RIEGER, EBERHARD [1004]
b. 17.3.1923, Leipzig
Class X/1940; ObltzS 1.10.44
7/Basic Trg Est. Stralsund 10/40–12/40; 44th Minesweeping Flotilla 12/40–5/41; Naval College Flensburg-Mürwik 5/41–9/41; 1st U-Flotilla 9/41–10/41; WO sea trg (*U 201*) 10/41–1/42, (*U 564*) 1/42–3/42; trg and courses (inc. WO course) 1.ULD 3/42–8/42; U-boat courses 8/42–11/42; WO *U 272* 5.11.42–12.11.42; 8th U-Flotilla 11/42–1/43; *Baubelehrung* 1.KLA U-Boats East 1/43–3/43; 1WO *U 390* 3/43–2/44; electronic detection course (*F-Gerät*); U-Cdr's Course, 24th U-Flotilla 3/44–5/44 (U-Cdr's Torpedo Course 68)
Cdr *U 416* 16.5.44–12.12.44
Lost 12.12.44 Baltic Sea, NW of Pillau

RIEGER, HUBERT [1005]
b. 26.5.1920, Märing, Augsburg
Class XII/1939; ObltzS 1.12.43
Service with Luftwaffe, then U-boat trg, completed 5/44
Cdr *U 4* 5/44–9.7.44 (?)
1.ULD 8/44–12/44; 2.ULD 12/44–3/34; Naval Trg Battalion 313 3/45–capitulation

RIEKEBERG, WOLFGANG [1006]
b. 14.10.1918, Peine, Hannover
Class 1937a; Kplt 1.4.44
Gunnery Officer merchant raider *Stier* 3/42–12/42; Gunnery Officer proposed merchant raider *Hansa* 12/42–5/43; U-boat trg 5/43–10/43; course 23rd U-Flotilla 11/43–1/44; *Baubelehrung* 1.KLA 1/44–3/44
Cdr *U 1054* 25.3.44–19.9.44

Cdr *U 637* 1.10.44–26.4.45
Lost 26.4.45 off Norwegian coast (skirmish with British MTBs)

RIESEN, ROLF [1007]
b. 18.12.1919, Cologne
Class 1938; ObltzS 1.10.43
Div. Officer and WO heavy cruiser *Lützow* 3/41–12/41; Comp. Officer Destroyer and Torpedo-Boat Crews' Holding Div. 12/41–3/42; U-boat trg 4/42–9/42; *Baubelehrung* 6.KLA and 1WO (4th and 12th U-Flotillas) on *U 198* 9/42–2/44; course 23rd U-Flotilla 2/44–4/44
Cdr *U 180* 2.4.44–26.8.44
Missing 26.8.44 Bay of Biscay, W of Bordeaux (Translator's note: Sailed from Bordeaux for Japan with technical specialists and cargo; probably mined off Gironde estuary 22.8.44.)

VAN RIESEN, FRIEDRICH [1008]
b. 9.7.1911, Danzig
Entry 1938; ObltzS (R) 1.7.43
U-boat trg 7/43–11/43; WO, *Baubelehrung* and course U-Boat Arm 11/43–8/44; *Baubelehrung* 5.KLA 8/44–9/44
Cdr *U 1109* 10.9.44–capitulation

RIGELE, HERMANN [1009]
b. 16.9.1891, Sarajevo, Bosnia
Entry, Austro-Hungarian Navy (k.u.k) 1909; FKpt (zV) 1.9.42
2WO k.u.k. *U 11* (ex-*UB 15*) 5/15–12/16; Cdr k.u.k. *U 10* (ex-*UB 1*) 10.12.16–11.6.17; Cdr k.u.k. *U 17* 12.6.17–22.11.17; Cdr k.u.k. *U 20* 29.11.17–11.3.18; Cdr k.u.k. *U 31* 11.3.18–31.10.18
U-Cdr under instrn 21st U-Flotilla 8/40–9/40; *Baubelehrung* 9/40–11/40
Cdr *UD 1* 21.11.40–3.5.41
Baubelehrung 5/41–6/41
Cdr *UD 3* 8.6.41–23.10.43

Leader U-boat base Kiel 10/43–3/44; CO 32nd U-Flotilla 4/44–3/45; Port Commander Trieste 3/45–capitulation

RINCK, HANS [1010]
b. 2.6.1912, Hamburg-Finkenwerder
Class VII/1941; ObltzS (R) 1.4.44
WO 15th and 30th Minesweeping Flotillas 8/42–6/43; U-boat trg 6/43–11/43; WO, *Baubelehrung* and course U-Boat Arm 11/43–5/44
Cdr *U 1019* 4.5.44–capitulation

RINGELMANN, HELMUTH [1011]
b. 21.4.1912, Munich
Class 1931; Kplt 1.10.39, posthumously KKpt
U-Cdr under instrn 24th U-Flotilla 9/40–10/40; *Baubelehrung* 11/40–12/40
Cdr *U 75* 19.12.40–28.12.41
Lost 28.12.41 Mediterranean, off Mersa Matruh

RIX, ROBERT [1012]
b. 20.3.1907, Kiel
Entry XII/1939; ObltzS (R) 1.7.43
VP-Cdr 16th VP-Boat Flotilla 9/41–1/42 and 9th VP-Boat Flotilla 1/42–7/42; U-boat trg 7/42–2/43; no information available 2/43–12/43; U-Cdr's Course, 3.ULD and 23rd U-Flotilla 12/43–2/44
Cdr *U 58* 2/44–30.6.44
Cdr *U 96* 1.7.44–2/45
Harbour Cdr Helsingör 3/45–capitulation

ROBBERT, HEINZ [1013]
b. 20.8.1916, Hammersbeck
Entry X/1939, ObltzS (R) 1.11.44
WO *U 107* 5/43–4/44; course 23rd U-Flotilla 4/44–7/44; U-Cdr 31st U-Flotilla 7/44–12/44; *Baubelehrung* Type XXI 6.KLA 12/44–3/45
Cdr *U 3040* 8.3.45 to 25.4.45 or 3.5.45.1

RODIG, JOHANNES [1014]
b. 24.3.1917, Oschatz, Saxony
Class 1936; Kplt 1.7.43
WO merchant raider *Atlantis* 1/40–22.11.41 (Translator's note: survivors arrived at St Nazaire end 12/41); various shipboard duties under C-in-C Destroyers 1/42–6/42; WO destroyer *Z 37* 6/42–5/43; U-boat trg 5/43–10/43; courses 23rd, 24th and 25th U-Flotillas 11/43–1/44 (U-Cdr's Torpedo Course 60); *Baubelehrung* 6.KLA 2/44–4/44
Cdr *U 878* 14.4.44–10.4.45
Lost 10.4.45 Bay of Biscay, W of St Nazaire

RODLER VON ROITHBERG, HARDO [1015]
b. 14.2.1918, Vienna
Class 1937a; Kplt 1.1.44
WO destroyer *Z 20 Karl Galster* 4/39–10/39; Comp. Officer 4/Basic Trg Est. Stralsund 10/39–3/40; U-boat trg 4/40–8/40; *Baubelehrung* 8/40–9/40; 2WO *U 96* 9/40–7/41
Cdr *U 24* 1.8.41–5.5.42 (*U 24* was decommissioned 4/42 prior to transfer to the Black Sea)
Course 1.UAA 6/42
Cdr *U 71* 30.6.42 (per WASt) or 3.7.42 (per *U 71* WD, relieved Flachsenberg [293]) to 1.5.43
Baubelehrung 8.KLA 5/43–7/43
Cdr *U 989* 22.7.43–14.2.45
Lost 14.2.45 near Faroes

ROEDER-PESCH, HANS [1016]
b. 25.4.1914, Frankfurt/Main
Class 1937a; Kplt 1.11.43
Naval oiler *Dithmarschen* 1/40–4/40; course Signals School 4/40–6/40; Naval Signals Officer Esbjerg 6/40–8/40; WO (S) and Navigation Officer (S) naval oilers *Ermland* and *Uckermark* 9/40–3/42; U-boat trg 3/42–9/42; WO *U 86* 9/42–10/43; U-Cdr's Torpedo Course 57 10/43–11/43; *Baubelehrung* 7.KLA 11/43–12/43
Cdr *U 1167* 29.12.43–1.7.44
Head, Testing Group for Underwater Weapons (Torpedo Testing Branch) 8/44–capitulation

RÖMER, WOLFGANG [1017]
b. 22.10.1916, Rathenow, Havel
Class 1936; Kplt 1.7.43
2WO *U 52* 8/39–9/39; Trg Officer U-Boat School Neustadt 10/39–11/39; Trg Officer and ADC UAA Plön 11/39–6/40; *Baubelehrung* 6/40–7/40; 2WO *U 103* 7/40–4/41
Cdr *U 56* 22.4.41–19.1.42
Baubelehrung 1/42–3/42
Cdr *U 353* 31.3.42–16.10.42
POW 16.10.42–17.7.47

RÖSING, HANS RUDOLF [1018]
b. 28.9.1905, Wilhelmshaven
Class 1924; KptzS 1.3.43
Cdr *U 11* 21.9.35–1.10.37, inc. acting Cdr *U 35* spring/summer 1937, cruise to Punta Delgada (Rösing recruited his former *U 11* 1WO von der Ropp [1026] for the voyage—source U-Boat Archive per Kretschmer [663]); adviser Torpedo Testing Branch 10/37–8/38, with period as Cdr *U 10*; Group Commander East 8/38; Group Leader Torpedo Testing Branch 8/38–11/38; CO U-Flotilla *Emsmann* 12/38–12/39; Adm. Staff Officer/adviser BdU/Organisational 1/40; CO 7th U-Flotilla 1/40–5/40
Cdr *U 48* 21.5.40–3.9.40 (per P/F, and see Bleichrodt [89]); BdU Liaison Officer with Italian FdU Bordeaux 9/40–2/41; CO 3rd U-Flotilla 3/41–8/41; CO Central Div. Staff BdU 8/41–6/42; C-in-C U-Boats West (FdU West) 7/42–capitulation
Detained; freed 11/46
Knight's Cross 29.8.40 (28th KM, 10th U-boat holder)

RÖTHER, JOSEF [1019]
b. 7.10.1907, Iserlohn
Entry 1927; Kplt 1.7.41
First Officer netlayer *Genua* 9/39–6/40; VP-Cdr Harbour Defence Flotilla Oslo 6/40–3/41; U-boat trg and U-Cdr's Course 3/41–10/41; U-Cdr sea trg *U 552* 10/41–11/41; *Baubelehrung* 11/41–12/41
Cdr *U 380* 22.12.41–11/43
29th U-Flotilla 11/43–1/44; Kplt Staff 29th U-Flotilla 1/44–8/44; POW 21.8.44

RÖTTGER, HELMUT [1020]
b. 15.12.1918, Maltahöhe, German South-West Africa
Class 1937a; Kplt 1.4.44
Seconded to Luftwaffe 10/39–2/42; U-boat trg 3/42–9/42; 1WO *U 203* 9/42–1/43; courses 26th U-Flotilla and 8.KLA 1/43–3/43
Cdr *U 715* 17.3.43–13.6.44
Lost 13.6.44 NE of Faroes

ROGOWSKY, PETER [1021]
b. 10.6.1919, Berlin
Class 1938; ObltzS 1.6.43
U-boat trg 2/41–10/41; *Baubelehrung* 10/41–11/41; supplementary WO *U 595* 11/41–4/42; ADC 4th U-Flotilla 4/42–6/42; 2WO *U 185* 7/42–9/42; *Baubelehrung* 10/42–11/42; WO *UF 2* 11/42–3/43; WO *U 552* 3/43–5/44; courses 3.ULD, 23rd and 27th U-Flotillas 6/44–9/44; U-Cdr sea trg *U 866* 9/44–112/44
Cdr *U 866* 12/44–18.3.45
Lost 18.3.45 NE of Boston, Massachusetts

ROHLFING, KARL-HEINZ [1022]
b. 22.11.1910, Weener, Aurich
Entry 1/1935; ObltzS (R) 1.4.43
Battery CO Naval Flak Detachment 239 4/41–6/43 (nautical trg and conversion from Coastal Artillery to Seaman Branch Officer); U-boat trg 7/43–7/44; WO *U 1193* 7/44–1/45; *Baubelehrung* 1.KLA 2/45–4/45
Cdr *U 4712* 3.4.45–3.5.45

ROLLMANN, SIEGFRIED [1023]
b. 13.9.1914, Friedrichshafen, Lake Constance
Class 1934; Kplt 1.1.42
Light cruiser *Karlsruhe*, 11/39–3/40; U-boat trg 4/40–9/40; 1WO *U 52* 10/40–3/41; U-Cdr's Course, 24th U-Flotilla 3/41–4/41; *Baubelehrung* 4/41–5/41
Cdr *U 82* 14.5.41–7.2.42
Lost 7.2.42 NE of Azores (Translator's note: But see Hirschfeld, *Feindfahrten*, and Frank, *The Sea Wolves*. Rollmann was heading for Lorient when he reported a small, weakly defended convoy (two small warships and two freighters) in 44°N 23°W. The BdU ordered him to keep contact, but nothing further was ever heard from him. See also Borcherdt [106] and Lerchen [725].)

ROLLMANN, WILHELM [1024]
b. 5.8.1907, Wilhelmshaven
Class 1926; KKpt 1.12.40, posthumously FKpt seniority 1.11.43
Cdr *U 34* 26.10.38–28.9.40; 2nd U-Flotilla 9/40–10/40; Instructor and Comp. CO 2.ULD 10/40–1/43; *Baubelehrung* 1.Comp. 6.KLA 1/43–2/43 (on 26.1.43 Rollmann took *U 847* from Bremen to Kiel)
Cdr *U 848* 20.2.43–5.11.43
Lost 5.11.43 South Atlantic, SW of Ascension I
Knight's Cross 31.7.40 (19th KM, 6th U-boat holder)

ROOST, WERNER [1025]
Details from birth to naval entry not known
ObltzS (R)
U-boat trg and U-Cdr's Course (U-Cdr's Torpedo Course 73) until 8/44
Cdr *U 926* 1.8.44–4.2.45

VON DER ROPP, DIETRICH [1026]
b. 27.7.1909, Mitau, Lithuania
Class 1929; Kplt 1.8.38
WO *U 11* 1935 (per rank listings 1.11.35) and 1936 (per rank listings 1.11.36)
Cdr *U 12* 1.10.37–8.10.39
Lost 8.10.39 English Channel, off Dover

ROSENBAUM, HELMUT [1027]
b. 11.5.1913, Döbeln, Leipzig
Class 1932; Kplt 1.2.40, posthumously KKpt seniority 1.5.44
Trainee U-Boat School 2/37–4/37; 2WO *U 35* and *U 27* 4/37–9/37; II/Fleet Reserve Div. Baltic 10/37–3/38; Flag Lt FdU 3/38–6/38; 1WO *U 31* 6/38–10/38; course Naval Gunnery School Kiel-Wik 10/38–11/38; 1WO *U 26* 11/38–3/39; Cdr *U 2* 17.3.39–5.8.40; *Baubelehrung* U-Boats North 8/40–9/40
Cdr *U 73* 30.9.40–30.9.42 (per P/F) or 10.9.42 (when relieved by Deckert [193], per *U 73* WD)
CO 30th U-Flotilla and Adm. Staff Officer Adm. Black Sea 10/42–5/44
Killed 10.5.44 air crash at Constanza, Romania
Knight's Cross 12.8.42 (120th KM, 58th U-boat holder)

ROSENBERG, GÜNTHER [1028]
b. 19.1.1917, Hamburg
Class 1936; ObltzS 1.10.40
Div. Officer and WO light cruiser *Nürnberg* 12/38–11/39 and trg ship *Schlesien* 11/39–7/40; Kriegsmarine Depot Boulogne 8/40–10/40; U-boat trg 10/40–3/41; *Baubelehrung* 3/41–4/41; 1WO *U 372* 4/41–11/41; U-Cdr's Course, 26th U-Flotilla 11/41–12/41
Cdr *U 351* 15.12.41–24.8.42
Cdr *U 201* 15.7.42 (per WASt, but this cannot be correct: see Schnee [1102], who did not dock *U 201* at Brest until 8.8.42) or 25.8.42 to 17.2.43
Lost 17.2.43 E of Newfoundland

VON ROSENBERG-GRUSZCYNSKI, HANS-ACHIM [1029]
b. 4.6.1917, Wilhelmshaven
Class 1937a; ObltzS 1.9.41
FzS battleship *Scharnhorst* 4/39–8/39; Battery Officer Naval Flak Detachment 233 9/39–11/39; Comp. Officer and ADC 7/Basic Trg Est. Stralsund 11/39–6/40; U-boat trg 6/40–11/40; 2WO *U 37* 11/40–5/41
Cdr *U 18* 7.5.41–31.5.42
U-Cdr's Course, 24th U-Flotilla and *Baubelehrung* 1.KLA 5/42–7/42
Cdr *U 384* 18.7.42–19.3.43
Lost 19.3.43 SW of Iceland

VON ROSENSTIEL, JÜRGEN [1030]
b. 23.11.1912, Kiel
Class 1933; Kplt 1.4.41
Div. Officer, No 1 Radio Technical Officer and WO trg ship *Schlesien* 7/39–3/40; U-boat trg 4/40–8/40; 2nd U-Flotilla (supernumerary) 8/40–9/40; 2WO *U 38* 9/40–11/40; 1WO *U 38* 11/40–2/41; U-Cdr under instrn 24th U-Flotilla 2/41–3/41
Cdr *U 143* 20.3.41–30.3.41
Baubelehrung 4/41–5/41
Cdr *U 502* 31.1.41–5.7.42
Lost 5.7.42 Bay of Biscay, W of La Rochelle

ROSSMANN, HERMANN [1031]
b. 23.7.1918, Dürrenebersdorf, Gera
Class 1937b; ObltzS 1.4.42
Seconded to Luftwaffe 12/39–12/40; U-boat trg 1/41–6/41; *Baubelehrung* 7/41–8/41; 1WO *U 582* 8/41–5/42; U-Cdr's Course 6/42–7/42
Cdr *U 52* 25.7.42–31.3.43
Cdr *U 273* 1.4.43–19.5.43
Lost 19.5.43 SW of Iceland

ROSTIN, ERWIN [1032]
b. 8.10.1907, Güstrow, Mecklenburg
Class 1933; KKpt with effect from 1.7.42

M/S-Cdr 7th Minesweeping Flotilla 8/39–3/40; Cdr *M 98* 6th later 4th Minesweeping Flotilla 4/40–8/40; Cdr *M 21* 2nd Minesweeping Flotilla 8/40–3/41; U-boat trg 3/41–6/41; U-Cdr's Course, 24th U-Flotilla 6/41–8/41; *Baubelehrung* 1.Comp/U-Boats North 8/41–9/41
Cdr *U 158* 25.9.41–30.6.42
Lost 30.6.42 W of Bermuda
Knight's Cross 28.6.42 (115th KM, 55th U-boat holder)

ROTH, GÖTZ [1033]

b. 19.12.1919, Hessen, Braunschweig
Class 1938; ObltzS 1.1.43
2WO *U 161* 7/41–1/43; U-Cdr's Course 2/43–4/43 (U-Cdr's Torpedo Course 42)
Cdr *U 351* 26.5.43–5.10.43
Cdr *U 748* 6.10.43–17.9.44
Leader torpedo attack trg 24th U-Flotilla 9/44–1/45; Flag Lt on Staff Commanding Adm. U-Boats 1/45–3/45
Cdr *U 1232* 1.4.45–27.4.45 (U-Boat Archive per Roth)
Cdr *U 368* 28.4.45–capitulation
Detained; freed 23.3.47

VON ROTHKIRCH UND PANTHEN, SIEGRFIED [1034]

b. 23.10.1919, Breslau
Class 1938; ObltzS 1.4.43
WO *U 37* 6/41; WO *U 30* 7/41–11/41; *Baubelehrung* 11/41–12/41; 1WO *U 407* 12/41–11/42; 1WO *U 604* 12/42–3/43; U-Cdr's Course, 2.UAA and 24th U-Flotilla 3/43–4/43 (U-Cdr's Torpedo Course 45); *Baubelehrung* 4/43–5/43
Cdr *U 717* 19.5.43–2.5.45

RUDLOFF, KLAUS [1035]

b. 24.1.1916, Wilhelmshaven
Class 1935; Kplt 1.12.42

ADC to Sector Cdr Wilhelmshaven 8/39–4/40; Cdr torpedo-boat *Kjell* 4/40–7/40; U-boat trg 7/40–12/40; *Baubelehrung* 12/40–2/41; 1WO *U 559* 2/41–11/41; U-Cdr's Course, 26th U-Flotilla and *Baubelehrung* 11/41–2/42
Cdr *U 609* 12.2.42–7.2.43
Lost 7.2.43 central North Atlantic

RUDOLPH, JOHANNES [1036]

b. 24.4.1916, Kiel
Class 1937b; Kplt 1.3.45
U-boat trg 7/42–11/42; course 24th U-Flotilla 12/42–1/43; 1WO *U 155* 1/43–2/44
Cdr *U 155* 2/44–14.8.44 (see Piening [927])
Course 1.UAA 8/44–10/44
Cdr *U 155* 11/44–12/44
Baubelehrung Type XXI 8.KLA 1/45–5/45
Cdr *U 2552* 25.4.45–3.5.45

RÜGGEBERG, ROLF [1037]

b. 4.3.1907, Barcelona, Spain
Class 1926; FKpt 1.11.44
Trg Leader Naval Academy San Fernando (Cadiz) 1/39–6/40; Assistant to Naval Attaché Madrid 7/40–10/40; Acting Naval Attaché Lisbon 11/40–3/41; U-boat trg 4/41–8/41; U-Cdr sea trg *U 107* 8/41–11/41; *Baubelehrung* 12/41–1/42
Cdr *U 513* 10.1.42–14.5.43
CO 13th U-Flotilla 6/43–capitulation
Detained; freed 10/45

RUPERTI, GÜNTER [1038]

b. 7.7.1914, Rüstringen
Entry VIII/1939; Kplt 1.11.44
Group Leader Harbour Defence Flotilla Channel Islands 1/42–12/42, Marseilles 12/42–3/43; U-boat trg, courses and WO sea trg *U 955* 3/43–3/44; *Baubelehrung* 6.KLA 3/44–5/44
Cdr *U 777* 9.5.44–15.10.44

31st U-Flotilla 10/44–12/44; *Baubelehrung* Type XXI 6.KLA 12/44–3/45
Cdr *U 3039* 8.3.45–3.5.45

RUPPELT, GÜNTHER [1039]
b. 13.9.1919, Trostdorf, Breslau
Class 1937b; ObltzS 1.4.42
U-boat trg 10/40–5/41; 2WO *U 563* 5/41–4/42; U-Cdr's Course, 24th U-Flotilla 4/42–5/42
Cdr *U 579* 27.5.42–10/42
Cdr *U 356* 3.12.42–27.12.42
Lost 27.12.42 N of Azores

RUWIEDEL, KURT [1040]
b. 18.9.1917, Ehringhausen
Class 1936; ObltzS 1.10.40
Light cruiser *Köln* 12/38–1/41; U-boat trg 1/41–5/41; course 5/41–6/41
Cdr *U 10* 10.6.41–29.11.41
7th U-Flotilla 12/41–5/42
Cdr *U 337* 6.5.42–15.1.43
Lost 15.1.43 SW of Iceland

S

SAAR, FRANZ [1041]
b. 12.12.1919, Nürnberg
Class 1938; ObltzS 1.3.43
2WO *U 202* 3/41–5/42; acting Cdr *U 46* 5/42–7/42
Cdr *U 555* 8/42–4.10.42
Cdr *U 30* 5.10.42–16.12.42
Baubelehrung 8.KLA 12/42–1/43
Cdr *U 957* 7.1.43–20.3.43
Killed 20.3.43 in accident during diving exercises, AGRU-Front

SACH, HEINRICH [1042]
b. 28.4.1913, Thürk/Eutin
Entry 1938; ObltzS (R) 1.4.43
11th Harbour Defence Flotilla 8/39–7/40; 1/NCO Trg Div. 7/40–9/40; Helmsman's School 9/40–1/41; U-boat course 1/41–5/41; *Baubelehrung* 5/41–6/41; 2WO *U 374* 6/41–10/41; details not available 10/41–5/44; U-Cdr's Course, 24th U-Flotilla 5/44–7/44 (U-Cdr's Torpedo Course 72); 25th U-Flotilla 7/44–11/44; *Baubelehrung* Type XXI 6.KLA 11/44–2/45
Cdr *U 3031* 28.2.45–3.5.45 (per U-Boat Archive, *Aschmoneit List* commissioned 28.2.45, but former *U 3031* crew members state 18.2.45)

SACHS, ERWIN [1043]
b. 17.12.1887, Hohensalza, Posen
Class X/1916; KptzS 1.4.41
First Officer U-Flotilla *Weddigen* (per rank listings 1.11.35, bulletins of 1.1.36 and 2.10.36), additionally Senior Officer Reserve U-Boats; accommodation ship officer and Cdr *U 10* and *U 21* (per rank listings 1.11.36); per list of Kriegsmarine acceptances in the Acceptance Document, Sachs commissioned the following boats: *U 15* (7.3.36), *U 16* (16.5.36), *U 22* (21.8.36), *U 23* (24.9.36) and *U 24* (10.10.36); seconded FdU, accommodation ship officer (per rank listings 1.11.37); Comp. CO U-Boat School 6/39–9/39; seconded FdU 9/39–10/39; *Baubelehrung* E-boat depot ship *Carl Peters* 10/39–2/40; Group Leader then Leader Danzig Branch, U-Boat Acceptance Command 2/40–11/44; Naval High Command East 12/44–2/45
Died 28.2.45

SACHSE, DIETRICH [1044]
b. 22.8.1917, Gipstal
Class IX/1939; ObltzS 1.10.43
WO 27th U-Flotilla 3/42–4/42; *Baubelehrung* 5/42–6/42; 1WO *U 413* 6/42–6/43; U-Cdr's Course, 2.UAA and 24th U-Flotilla 6/43–8/43 (U-Cdr's Torpedo Course 51); *Baubelehrung* 8/43–9/43
Cdr *U 1162* 15.9.43–1.12.43
Cdr *U 28* 2.12.43–17.3.44 (*U 28* sank alongside the U-boat mole at Neustadt, Holstein, on 17.3.44 as the result of crew error. The boat was raised in 3/44 but only a caretaker crew remained aboard until final decommissioning on 4.8.44.)
Cdr *U 413* 20.4.44–20.8.44
Lost 20.8.44 English Channel, S of Brighton

SÄCK, FRANZ [1045]
b. 31.12.1909, Leithe, Gelsenkirchen
Enlisted rating 1928; ObltzS 1.1.43
ObStrm torpedo-boat *Greif* 11/38–1/40; U-boat trg and courses 1/40–4/40; ObStrm *U 120* 4/40–11/40; *Baubelehrung* 11/40–12/40; ObStrm

U 552 12/40–1/43; courses 2/43–6/43 (U-Cdr's Torpedo Course 49); relief trg instructor 1.ULD 7/43–11/43
Cdr *U 251* 23.11.43–19.4.45
31st U-Flotilla 4/45–capitulation

SALMAN, OTTO [1046]
b. 5.7.1908, Berlin-Schöneberg
Class 1932; KKpt 1.4.44
U-boat course Anti-Submarine School Kiel-Wik 5/35–7/35; nautical trg light cruiser *Köln* 8/35–9/35; U-boat trg 9/35–1/36; 1WO *U 19* 1/36–9/37; 1WO *U 32* 10/37–2/38; Cdr *U 7* 10.2.38–5.2.39; Gunnery Officer Course (B) Naval Gunnery School 2/39–5/39; Cdr *U 7* 31.5.39–2.7.39; instructor Naval Gunnery School 3.7.39–1.8.39; Cdr *U 7* 2.8.39–1.10.39; instructor Naval Gunnery School 2.10.39–24.10.39; Cdr *U 7* 25.10.39–13.11.39
Cdr *U 52* 14.11.39–9.6.41
5/Adm. Staff Officer BdU/Organisational 6/41–9/41; 5/Adm. Staff Officer at 2/Adm. U-Boats 10/41–1/43; adviser (A1) and CO Trg Div./Commanding Adm. U-Boats 2/43–4/45; Senior ADC and personal adviser to C-in-C Kriegsmarine 1.5.45–capitulation
Knight's Cross of the War Service Cross with Swords 2.5.45

SAMMLER, KARL-HEINZ [1047]
b. 15.1.1919, Altona
Class 1937b; ObltzS 1.4.42
U-boat trg 1/41–6/41; 2WO *U 66* 6/41–6/42; U-Cdr's Course, 24th U-Flotilla, 6/42–7/42
Cdr *U 59* 16.7.42–10.6.43
Baubelehrung 6/43–7/43
Cdr *U 675* 14.7.43–24.5.44
Lost 24.5.44 W of Aalesund

SANDER, PAUL [1048]
b. 5.10.1908, Primkenau, Schrottau, Silesia
Enlisted rating 1928; ObltzS 1.4.43
ObStrm *U 25* 4/36–5/40; *Baubelehrung* 6/40–7/40; ObStrm *U 103* 7/40–10/41; U-boat tender *Lech* 10/41–11/41; U-boat base Wilhelmshaven 11/41–4/42; 6th U-Flotilla 4/42–3/43; Cdr with 21st U-Flotilla 4/43–5/44, inc. Cdr *U 4* 1.6.43–22.8.43 (21st U-Flotilla)
Cdr *U 38* 23.8.43–14.12.43 (21st U-Flotilla)
Cdr *U 72* 15.12.43–19.5.44 (21st U-Flotilla)
Instructor 1.ULD 5/44–2/45; at *K-Verband* Command 2/45–capitulation

SASS, PAUL-HEINRICH [1049]
b. 3.10.1919, Cuxhaven
Class 1939; ObltzS 1.4.43
Flak Gunnery Officer light cruiser *Köln* 2/41–9/41; U-boat trg 9/41–3/42; 1WO *U 757* 3/42–4/43; U-Cdr's Course and *Baubelehrung* 4/43–5/43
Cdr *U 364* 3.5.43–30.1.44
Lost 30.1.44 Bay of Biscay, W of Bordeaux

SASS, WERNER [1050]
b. 16.1.1916, Okahandja, South-West Africa
Class 1937b; Kplt 1.1.45
WO 17th Minesweeping Flotilla 5/40–2/41; U-boat trg 2/41–9/41; *Baubelehrung* 9/41–10/41; 1WO *U 171* 10/41–3/42; 1WO *U 554* 3/42–6/42; *Baubelehrung* 6/42–7/42; 1WO *U 525* 7/42–5/43; U-Cdr's Course, 24th U-Flotilla 6/43–7/43 (U-Cdr's Torpedo Course 49); *Baubelehrung* 7/43–8/43
Cdr *U 676* 4.8.43–19.2.45
Lost 19.2.45 Gulf of Finland

SAUER, HEINZ-GERD [1051]
b. 7.4.1915, Eberswalde, Finow, Brandenburg
Entry XII/1939; ObltzS (R) 1.1.44
2WO *U 592* 1/43–5/43; 1WO *U 592* 5/43–7/43; U-Cdr's Course, 24th U-Flotilla 7/43–8/43 (U-Cdr's Torpedo Course 52)
Cdr *U 673* 15.8.43–31.7.44

Instructor 1.ULD 8/44–10/44; adviser FdU/Trg 10/44–4/45; service with Harbour Cdr Grenaa 4/45–capitulation

SAUERBERG, ERNST [1052]
b. 11.1.1914, Heide, Holstein
Entry 1934; ObltzS 1.12.42
U-boat trg 7/41–12/41; 26th U-Flotilla 12/41–1/42; *Baubelehrung* 1/42–2/42; 2WO *U 515* 2/42–6/43; U-Cdr's Course, 24th U-Flotilla 7/43–8/43; U-Cdr's Course and *Baubelehrung* 8/43–11/43 (U-Cdr's Torpedo Course 51)
Cdr *U 1225* 10.11.43–24.6.44
Lost 24.6.44 NW of Bergen

SAUERBIER, JOACHIM [1053]
b. 25.9.1919, Kempen, Posen
Class IX/1939; ObltzS 1.10.43
2WO *U 591* 10/41–7/42; 1WO *U 591* 7/42–6/43, inc. period as acting Cdr 15.5.43–17.5.43; U-Cdr's Course, 24th U-Flotilla 6/43–7/43 (U-Cdr's Torpedo Course 50)
Cdr *U 120* 26.7.43–14.9.44
Instructor 1.ULD 9/44–2/45
Cdr *U 56* 23.2.45–4/45
Lost 19.4.45 Kattegat, S of Göteborg (aboard *U 251* while travelling as a passenger to Norway, where he had orders to relieve Edelhoff [237] as Cdr of *U 324* lying at Bergen. As Sauerbier failed to arrive, Edelhoff remained Cdr of *U 324* until the capitulation.)

SAUSMIKAT, WERNER [1054]
b. 7.10.1917, Günthen
Class 1937b; Kplt 1.1.45
Seconded Luftwaffe 12/39–2/43; Naval High Command East and U-boat trg 2/43–8/43; WO *U 371* 8/43–2/44
Cdr *U 56* 28.2.44–30.6.44
Cdr *U 1103* 3.7.44–8.10.44
Cdr *U 774* 9.10.44–8.4.45
Lost 8.4.45 SW of Ireland

SCHAAFHAUSEN, LUDWIG [1055]
b. 30.11.1917, Kiel
Class 1937a; Kplt 1.9.44
Seconded Luftwaffe 9/39–1/42, inc. *Bordfliegerstaffel 5./196*; Naval High Command East 2/42; U-boat trg 3/42–3/43; 1WO *U 565* 3/43–8/43; U-Cdr's Course, 2.UAA and 24th U-Flotilla 8/43–9/43 (U-Cdr's Torpedo Course 54); *Baubelehrung* 1.KLA 9/43–10/43
Cdr *U 369* 15.10.43–15.4.45

SCHAAR, GERD [1056]
b. 5.3.1919, Berlin
Class 1937b; Kplt 1.1.45
Destroyer *Z 12 Erich Giese* 12/39–4/40; land fighting Narvik 4/40–7/40; VP-Cdr Harbour Defence Flotilla Molde 7/40–8/40; Destroyer Crews' Holding Div. 8/40–9/40; 2/Basic Trg Est. Stralsund and Group CO Artillery-Lighter Group Wilhelmshaven 9/40–10/40; Naval Gunnery School Kiel-Wik 10/40–12/40; Group Officer Naval College Flensburg-Mürwik 12/40–10/41; Naval Gunnery School Kiel-Wik 10/41–2/42; U-boat trg 2/42–9/42; U-Cdr sea trg *U 704* 9/42–11/42, afterwards WO *U 704* 11/42–2/43; 2.UAA 2/43; U-Cdr's Torpedo Course 43 and 24th U-Flotilla 3/43
Cdr *U 957* 1.4.43–21.10.44 (1WO Paul Tönshoff commanded the boat 17.10.44–21.10.44 voyage Trondheim–Narvik for decommissioning)
1.UAA and 13th U-Flotilla 10/44–1/45; *Baubelehrung* Type XXI for *U 2551* 23.1.45–4/45
Cdr *U 2551* 4/45–5.5.45 (decommissioning date uncertain but probably between 20.4.45 and 24.4.45)
CO Naval Police Troop Schleswig-Holstein 5/45–capitulation
Detained; freed 9/45

Knight's Cross 1.10.44 (261st KM, 129th U-boat holder)

SCHACHT, HARRO [1057]

b. 15.12.1907, Cuxhaven
Class 1926; KKpt 1.10.40, posthumously FKpt seniority 1.1.43 by edict of Adolf Hitler 21.3.44
Wireless telegraphy adviser C-in-C Naval Reconnaissance Forces at Reichs War Ministry/OKM 10/37–3/41; U-boat trg 3/41–6/41; U-Cdr's Torpedo Course and 24th U-Flotilla 6/41–8/41; U-Cdr sea trg *U 552* 8/41–9/41; *Baubelehrung* Kriegsmarine Depot Hamburg 9/41–10/41
Cdr *U 507* 8.10.41–13.1.43
Lost 31.3.43 NW of Natal, Brazil
Knight's Cross 9.1.43 (143rd KM, 75th U-boat holder)

SCHAD VON MITTELBIBERACH, BERCHTOLD [1058]

b. 1.9.1916, Bensheim, Hesse
Entry as rating 1936; ObltzS (R) 1.9.43
Hauptfeldwebel (= Staff Sergeant) Naval Recruiting Centre Hamburg 12/39–3/40; Hauptfw. 12/Basic Trg Est. Stralsund 3/40–6/40; financial auditor Kriegsmarine Reserve Div. Brake 6/40–3/41; ADC and Cdr with 44th Minesweeping Flotilla 4/41–9/43; U-boat trg and WO, plus *Baubelehrung* Type XXIII 9/43–10/44
Cdr *U 2342* 1.11.44–26.12.44
Lost 26.12.44 N of Swinemünde

SCHÄFER, FRIEDRICH [1059]

b. 28.2.1893, Hannover
Conscripted rating IV/1914; KKpt (R)(zV) 1.12.42
Battleship *Kaiser Wilhelm II* until 3/15; battleship *Kaiser Karl der Grosse* until 5/15; II/Ordinary Seamen's Div, until 7/15; battleship *Posen* until 9/15; coastal defence vessel *Siegfried* until 1/16 (as LtzS); WO torpedo-boat *S 23* until 4/16; trg at U-Boat School until 6/16; 2WO *U 55* 8.6.16–26.11.18; final rank LtzS (R); demobilised 30.11.18
Adviser Harbour Control Office Bremen 8/39–4/40; Counter-Intelligence Officer OKM/Foreign Office *Abwehr* 1M 4/40–1/41; 1WO *UD 4* 1/41–4/41
Cdr *UD 1* 4.5.41–2.11.41
Baubelehrung 11/41–12/41
Cdr *U 460* (Type XIV U-tanker) 24.12.41 to 1.8.42 (relieved by Schnoor [1107] per *U 460* WD) or 9.8.42 (per WASt)
Cdr *U A* 10.8.42–22.3.43
Cdr *UD 4* 23.3.43–22.11.44
Adviser and Group Leader U-Boat Acceptance Command Danzig 11/44–4/45; Naval High Command East 4/45–capitulation

SCHÄFER, HEINRICH [1060]

b. 30.1.1907, Wulsdorf, Bremerhaven
Entry VII/1925; FKpt 1.1.44
1WO gunnery trg ship *Mars* 11/40–6/41; U-boat trg 7/41–9/41; U-Cdr's Course, 26th U-Flotilla 10/41–11/41; U-Cdr under instrn 3rd U-Flotilla 11/41–3/42
Cdr *U 183* 1.4.42–19.11.43
2nd U-Flotilla 11/43–12/43
Cdr *UIT 23* 6.12.43–7.1.44
Died 8.1.44 Singapore

SCHAEFER, WOLF-AXEL [1061]

b. 3.3.1911, Kiel
Class 1930; KKpt 1.7.43
Naval Signals Officer on Staff of Cdr Pomeranian Coast 8/39–9/39; Comp. CO 7/Basic Trg Est. Stralsund 9/39–3/40; Naval Signals Officer (Swinemünde) 3/40–5/40, (Command Centre East) 5/40–6/40; 4/Adm. Staff Officer and Naval Signals Officer on Staff of Naval Cdr Northern France 6/40–8/40; Naval Signals Officer Boulogne 8/40–9/41; 4/Adm. Staff Officer German Naval Command Italy 9/41–

5/43; seconded Commanding Adm. U-Boats and U-boat trg 5/43–10/43; U-Cdr under instrn 23rd U-Flotilla 10/43–12/43; *Baubelehrung* 1.KLA 12/43–1/44
Cdr *U 484* 19.1.44–9.9.44
Lost 9.9.44 S of Hebrides

SCHÄFFER, HEINZ [1062]
b. 28.4.1921, Berlin
Class XII/1939; ObltzS 1.12.43
WO sea trg *U 561* and WO courses 1941–5/42; 1WO *U 445* 5/42–10/43; U-Cdr's Course, 2.UAA and 23rd U-Flotilla 10/43–12/43
Cdr *U 148* 30.11.43 (per WASt, and see von Möllendorf [832]) to 15.12.44
Cdr *U 977* 3/45–8/45 (Translator's note: Surrendered boat to Argentina.)

SCHAIPER (known as SCHÄFER), WOLFGANG [1063]
b. 4.4.1922, Rostock
Class XII/1939; ObltzS 1.12.43
1WO *U 269* 8/42–9/43; U-Cdr's Course, 2.UAA and 23rd U-Flotilla 9/43–11/43; *Baubelehrung* 1.KLA 11/43–1/44
Cdr *U 368* 7.1.44–1/45
Instructor 1.ULD 1/45–2/45; instructor 1.UAA 2/45–3/45; U-Cdr sea trg *U 3018* 8.3.45–4.5.45

SCHAMONG, KLEMENS [1064]
b. 15.4.1917, Cologne
Class 1937a; *Kplt 1.6.44*
1WO *U 333* 8/41–6/42; U-Cdr's Course, 24th U-Flotilla 6/42–8/42
Cdr *U 468* 12.8.42–11.8.43
POW 11.8.43

SCHATTEBURG, HANS [1065]
b. 16.5.1922, Kiel
Class XII/1939; ObltzS 1.12.43
WO sea trg *U 75* 5/41–7/41; trg and courses 8/41–7/42; 2WO *U 579* 8/42–2/43; *Baubelehrung* 2/43–3/43; 1WO *U 968* 3/43–4/44; U-Cdr's Course, 24th U-Flotilla 5/44–7/44 (U-Cdr's Torpedo Course 72)
Cdr *U 1272* 3.7.44–capitulation

SCHAUENBURG, GÜNTHER [1066]
b. 26.4.1920, Ludwigshafen
Class XII/1939; ObltzS 1.12.43
U-boat trg 6/41–3/42; *Baubelehrung* 3/42–5/42; 2WO *U 621* 5/42–6/43; 1WO *U 621* 6/43–10/43; 3.ULD 10/43–11/43; U-Cdr under instrn 23rd U-Flotilla 12/43; *Baubelehrung* 12/43–4/44
Cdr *U 793* 24.4.44–15.1.45
Baubelehrung Cdr 8.KLA for *U 1409* (never commissioned) 2/45–capitulation

SCHAUENBURG, HERBERT [1067]
b. 29.5.1912, Delmenhorst
Class 1931; Kplt 1.10.39, posthumously KKpt seniority 1.1.42
U-boat trg 4/40–9/40; U-Cdr's Course, 24th U-Flotilla 9/40–11/40; U-Cdr 21st U-Flotilla 11/40–1/41
Cdr *U 20* 6.1.41–19.5.41
Baubelehrung 5/41–7/41
Cdr *U 577* 3.7.41–9.1.42
Lost 9.1.42 Mediterranean, NW of Mersa Matruh

SCHAUENBURG, ROLF [1068]
b. 30.5.1913, Wintherthur, Switzerland
Class 1934; Kplt 1.2.42
No 2 Flak Gunnery Officer, heavy cruiser *Admiral Graf Spee* 8/39–12/39; interned, returned to Germany 12/39–12/40; *Baubelehrung* 12/40–2/41; *Schiff 31* 2/41–12/41; Destroyer and Torpedo-Boat Crews' Holding Div. 12/41–2/42; U-boat trg 2/42–8/42; WO and U-Cdr sea trg *U 432* 8/42–10/42; U-Cdr's Course, 24th U-

Flotilla 10/42–11/42; *Baubelehrung* 8.KLA 12/42–1/43
Cdr *U 536* 13.1.43–20.11.43
POW 20.11.43

SCHAUER, WERNER [1069]
b. 10.9.1922, Berlin-Steglitz
Class X/1940; ObltzS 1.10.44
WO *U 616* 12/42–3/43; U-Cdr's Torpedo Course 70 and course 3.ULD 4/44–6/44; 1WO and U-Cdr sea trg *U 369* 6/44–8/44; AGRU-Front, 22nd U-Flotilla and 8.KLA 8/44–12/44
Cdr *U 2350* 23.12.44–capitulation
Detained; freed 6/47

SCHAUROTH, CARL [1070]
b. 11.7.1921, Wolfenbüttel
Class X/1940; ObltzS 1.10.44
Baubelehrung for *U 228* 7/42–9/42; 2WO *U 228* 9/42–8/43; 1WO *U 228* 8/43–1/44; U-Cdr's Course, 3.ULD and 23rd U-Flotilla 2/44–3/44
Cdr *U 142* 5.3.44–6.2.45 (U-Boat Archive per Schauroth)
Cdr *U 146* 10.3.45–2.5.45. (U-Boat Archive per Schauroth)

SCHEER, WERNER [1071]
b. 6.6.1893, Vechta, Oldenburg
Class 1912; KAdm 1.9.41
Officer trg cruiser *Hansa* 4/12–3/13; courses Naval College Flensburg-Mürwik 4/13–7/14; battleship *Zähringen* 8/14–11/15; (Mobile) Telegraphy Station Kurland 11/15–12/16; U-boat trg 12/16–1/17; WO *U 30* 1/17–11/17; WO *UB 85* 11/17–4/18; POW 4/18–11/19
Command HQ Kiel 11/19–1/20; III. Naval Brigade 1/20–5/20; Naval Basic Trg Div. Baltic and on Staff Cdr Baltic Land Forces 6/20–1/21; battleship *Hannover* 1/21–2/21; Div. Officer and WO battleship *Hannover* 2/21–9/23; adviser Naval Basic Trg Div. Baltic 10/23–9/24; battleship *Hessen* 10/24–1/25; WO battleship *Hessen* 1/25–9/25; Cdr *M 113*, 1st Minesweeping Half-Flotilla 9/25–9/27; 4/Adm. Staff Officer Fleet Command 9/27–9/29; CO 1st Minesweeping Half-Flotilla 9/29–9/32; assisting Heads of Admiralty 10/32–9/33; adviser to Naval Trg Board and Naval Budgeting Div., Admiralty 9/33–9/35; at FdU 10/35–8/36, inc. Cdr *U 10* 21.12.35–1.5.36; CO U-Flotilla *Saltzwedel* 9/36–7/37; injured in accident 7/37–4/38; U-Cdr U-Boat School 4/38–9/39; CO Budgeting Div. OKM 10/39–2/41; Staff Officer Kriegsmarine Werft Wilhelmshaven 2/41–9/41; Chief of Staff Kriegsmarine Werft Wilhelmshaven 9/41–12/42; Cdr Kriegsmarine Arsenal Toulon and CO German Naval Command Toulon 12/42–9/43; CO Special Staff for Accommodation OKM 9/43–11/43; Group Departmental CO OKM/KIII 11/43–11/44; Cdr Military District Command Essen I 11/44–4/45
Detained; freed 10.3.47

SCHEIBE, HANS-MARTIN [1072]
b. 17.4.1918, Königsberg, East Prussia
Class 1936; Kplt 1.7.43
WO and Platoon Leader light cruiser *Königsberg* 9/39–4/40; Battery Officer Naval Artillery Detachment 504 4/40–1/41; U-boat trg 1/41–6/41; WO U-boat tender *Lech* 6/41–10/41; 1WO *U 431* 10/41–3/42; U-Cdr's Course, 2.UAA and 24th U-Flotilla 3/42–5/42
Cdr *U 72* 7.5.42–19.11.42
Cdr *U 455* 22.11.42–6.4.44 (per *U 455* WD)
Lost 6.4.44 Mediterranean, off La Spezia

SCHELTZ, HANS-ULRICH [1073]
b. 15.11.1909, Stettin
Entry 1934; Kplt (R) 1.11.43
WO *U 569* 12/41–10/42; courses 10/42–2/43

Cdr *UD 5* 23.2.43–capitulation (U-Boat Archive per Scheltz)

SCHENDEL, EBERHARD [1074]
b. 6.6.1920, Beutnitz, Jena, Thüringen
Class XII/1939; ObltzS 1.12.43
U-boat trg completed 4/42; *Baubelehrung* 4/42–5/42; 2WO *U 758* 5/42–6/43; 1WO *U 758* 6/43–11/43; U-Cdr's Course, 3.ULD and 24th U-Flotilla 11/43–2/44 (U-Cdr's Torpedo Course 61)
Cdr *U 636* 15.2.44 (relieved Hildebrandt [485] per *U 636* WD) to 21.4.45
Lost 21.4.45 W of Ireland

SCHENDEL, RUDOLF [1075]
b. 10.1.1914, Spandau
Class 1932; KKpt 1.11.44
WO light cruiser *Emden* 5/38–3/40; U-boat trg 4/40–10/40
Cdr *U 19* 8.11.40–31.5.41
Baubelehrung, 6/41–7/41
Cdr *U 134* 26.7.41–2.2.43 (WASt has latter date as 9.3.43. However, his successor Brosin [134] had already taken the boat to sea from La Pallice for an Atlantic patrol on 6.3.43.)
Comp. CO 1.ULD 3/43–4/44; *Baubelehrung* 8.KLA 4/44–6/44; acting CO 19th U-Flotilla 6/44–7/44; *Baubelehrung* Type XXI 8.KLA 7/44–9/44
Cdr *U 2509* 21.9.44–8.4.45 (After the destruction of *U 2509* by bombing at Blohm & Voss, Hamburg, on 8.4.45 the complement was remustered into an anti-tank unit at Hamburg-Harburg but disbanded on 17.4.45 to crew *U 2520* at Kiel on 20.4.45. *U 2520* was bombed and damaged on 25.4.45 and decommissioned and scuttled at Kiel on 3.5.45.)

SCHEPKE, JOACHIM [1076]
b. 8.3.1912, Flensburg
Class 1930; Kplt 1.6.39
U-boat trg 10/35–1/36; 1WO *U 13* 1/36–10/36; Comp. Officer III/Basic Trg Est. Stralsund 10/36–3/37; instructor Torpedo School Flensburg-Mürwik 3/37–10/38
Cdr *U 3* 29.10.38–2.1.40
Cdr *U 19* 3.1.40–30.4.40
1st U-Flotilla 1.5.40–18.5.40; *Baubelehrung* U-Boats Baltic 19.5.40–29.5.40
Cdr *U 100* 30.5.40–17.3.41
Lost 17.3.41 SE of Iceland
Knight's Cross 24.9.40 (32nd KM, 14th U-boat holder)
Oak Leaves 1.12.40 (7th WM, 3rd KM, 3rd U-boat holder)

SCHERFLING, WOLFGANG [1077]
b. 29.6.1923, Lychen
Class X/1940; ObltzS 1.10.44
WO *U 518* 6/43–3/44; 1WO *U 548* 4/44–7/44; U-Cdr's Course, 24th U-Flotilla 8/44–11/44 (U-Cdr's Torpedo Course 76)
Cdr *U 140* 20.11.44–2.5.45

SCHERINGER, HEINZ [1078]
b. 29.8.1907, Buenos Aires, Argentina
Class 1927; KKpt 1.1.42
Studying at Anti-Submarine School 7/35–9/35; Cdr *U 10* 11.9.35–21.12.35; at FdU 12/35–3/36; Platoon and Comp. Leader 1/Naval NCO Trg. Div. 3/36–4/37; WO, Wargames and III Deck Officer trg ship *Schleswig-Holstein* 4/37–3/39; Comp. CO 5/III Naval NCO Trg Div. 3/39–8/39; WO and No 4 Gunnery Officer battleship *Scharnhorst* 8/38–9/39; U-Cdr's Torpedo Course, seconded BdU and U-Boat School 9/39–11/39
Cdr *U 13* 6.11.39–2.1.40
Cdr *U 26* 3.1.40–11.5.40
2nd U-Flotilla 12.5.40–8.6.40
Cdr *U 26* 9.6.40–1.7.40
POW 2.7.40–13.5.47

SCHERRAUS, EKKEHARD [1079]
b. 1.10.1919, Danzig
Class 1938; ObltzS 1.1.43
2WO *U 507* 10/41–2/42; 11th U-Flotilla 3/42–11/42; 1WO *U 107* 11/42–12/42; 1WO *U 68* 12/42–1/44 and acting Cdr *U 68* 14.6.43–7/43; U-Cdr's Course, 3.ULD and 27th U-Flotilla 1/44–3/44 (U-Cdr's Torpedo Course 64); 3rd U-Flotilla 3/44–5/44; Cdr (supernumerary, acting) *U 1225* 15.5.44–12.6.44; 1.UAA and 2.ULD 6/44–capitulation

SCHETELIG, ROBERT [1080]
b. 6.10.1918, Lübeck
Class 1937a; ObltzS 1.9.41
Seconded Luftwaffe 10/39–12/40; U-boat trg 1/41–7/41; *Baubelehrung* 7/41–8/41; 1WO *U 87* 8/41–7/42; U-Cdr's Course, 24th U-Flotilla 7/42–8/42; *Baubelehrung* 1.KLA 9/42–10/42
Cdr *U 229* 3.10.42–22.9.43
Lost 22.9.43 SE of Cape Farewell

SCHEWE, GEORG [1081]
b. 24.11.1909, Ueckermünde/Pomerania
Entry 1928/30; KKpt 1.8.43
U-boat trg 10/36–4/37; WO *U 13* and *U 21* 4/37–1/39; instructor Torpedo School Flensburg-Mürwik 1/39–3/39; U-Flotilla *Weddigen* 3/39–7/39; *Baubelehrung* Deutsche Werke Kiel 7/39
Cdr *U 60* 22.7.39 to 19.7.40 or 12.8.40 (per WASt and P/F but unlikely—see Schnee [1102])
Baubelehrung U-Boats North 8/40–9/40
Cdr *U 105* 10.9.40–6.1.42
Staff FdU Mediterranean, 2/Adm. Staff Officer 2/42–5/42; 1/Adm. Staff Officer 5/42–9/44; 1.UAA 9/44; CO 33rd U-Flotilla 9/44–10/44; adviser OKM/5.SKL 10/44–capitulation
Detained; freed 25.4.46
Knight's Cross 23.5.41 (71st KM, 31st U-boat holder)

SCHIEBUSCH, GÜNTER [1082]
b. 26.10.1909, Posen
Class 1933; KKpt 1.1.44
WO and Div. Officer heavy cruiser *Admiral Graf Spee* 11/38–12/39; interned, returned to Germany 12/39–11/40; Naval High Command North 11/40–12/40; WO heavy cruiser *Prinz Eugen* 12/40; U-boat trg 12/40–9/41; *Baubelehrung* 9/41–10/41
Cdr *U 252* 4.10.41–20.12.41
Hospitalised 12/41–3/42; *Baubelehrung* 3/42–4/42
Cdr *U 262* 15.4.42 to 19.10.42 (per WASt and P/F Franke [308]) or 26.10.42 (per *U 262* WD, and see Atzinger [19])
5th U-Flotilla 10/42–11/42; First Officer destroyers *Z 10 Hans Lody* 11/42 and *Z 6 Theodor Riedel* 11/42–10/43; Comp. CO Naval College Flensburg-Mürwik 10/43–2/44; adviser OKM 2/44–5/44; adviser OKW 5/44–?

SCHILD, HANS-JÜRG [1083]
b. 13.5.1920, Johannisberg, Rheingau
Class 1938; ObltzS 1.4.43
Officer trg 10/38–4/40; heavy cruiser *Admiral Hipper* 5/40–5/41; Platoon Leader trg ship *Schleswig-Holstein* 5/41–5/42; Flag Lt Fleet Trg Group 5/42–12/42; Platoon Leader light cruiser *Köln* 12/42–3/43; U-boat trg 3/43–8/43; U-Cdr under instrn 27th U-Flotilla 8/43–10/43 (U-Cdr's Torpedo Course 56); *Baubelehrung* 10/43–11/43
Cdr *U 924* 20.11.43–3.5.45

SCHIMMEL, GÜNTHER [1084]
b. 13.8.1920, Neuhausen, Westerwald
Class XII/1939; ObltzS 1.12.43
U-boat trg completed 1/42; 1WO *U 59* 1/42–8/42; *Baubelehrung* 8/42–9/42; 1WO *U 711* 9/42–10/43; U-Cdr's Course, 23rd U-Flotilla, 10/43–12/43

Cdr *U 137* 28.12.43–24.1.45, inc. acting Cdr *U 30* 17.1.45–23.1.45 (U-Boat Archive per Schimmel)
Cdr *U 382* 15.1.45 (per WASt) or 24.1.45 (U-Boat Archive per Schimmel) to 20.3.45
Comp. CO land fighting 3/45–capitulation
Detained; freed 12.9.45

SCHIMMELPFENNIG, HARTMUTH [1085]

b. 4.10.1919, The Hague, Holland
Class 1937b; ObltzS 1.4.42
WO *U 586* 12/42–9/43; U-Cdr's Course, 2.UAA and 23rd U-Flotilla 9/43–11/43; *Baubelehrung* 8.KLA 11/43–12/43
Cdr *U 1004* 16.12.43–1/45
Reduced to the ranks; fell 27.4.45 in land fighting as ordinary seaman

SCHIMPF, KARL [1086]

b. 23.3.1914, place not stated
Class 1936; Kplt 1.10.43
WO 2nd Escort Flotilla 10/39–1/40; WO and Mining Officer merchant raider *Thor* 1/40–5/41; course Mine Warfare School 5/41–7/41; WO and M/S-Cdr 3rd Minesweeping Flotilla 7/41–7/42; U-boat trg 7/42–11/42; 1WO *U 514* 11/42–5/43; U-Cdr's Course 6/43–7/43 (U-Cdr's Torpedo Course 49); *Baubelehrung* 8/43–9/43
Cdr *U 803* 7.9.43–27.4.44
Specialist on Staff FdU East 5/44–7/44; *Baubelehrung* Type XXI 6.KLA 7/44–11/44
Cdr *U 3009* 10.11.44–1.5.45
Detained; freed 31.1.46

SCHLEY, HANS-JÜRGEN [1087]

b. 20.10.1920, Greifenberg, Pomerania
Class XII/1939; ObltzS 1.12.43
U-boat trg completed 2/42; 2WO *U 563* 3/42–12/42; 1WO *U 563* 12/42–4/43; U-Cdr's Course, 24th U-Flotilla 5/43 (U-Cdr's Torpedo Course 47)
Cdr *U 59* 11.6.43–30.6.44
Cdr *U 351* 1.7.44–19.3.45
Detained; released 7.8.45

SCHLIEPER, ALFRED [1088]

b. 15.1.1915, Cologne
Class 1934; ObltzS 1.4.39, posthumously Kplt seniority 1.1.42
WO torpedo-boat *Albatros* 11/38–12/39; instructor and lecturer Torpedo School Mürwik 12/39–4/40; U-boat trg 4/40–10/40; instructor Torpedo School Flensburg-Mürwik 10/40–1/41; course 24th U-Flotilla 1/41–3/41; 1WO *U 96* 3/41–6/41; *Baubelehrung* 6/41–7/41
Cdr *U 208* 5.7.41–7.12.41
Lost 7.12.41 W of Gibraltar

VON SCHLIPPENBACH, FREIHERR EGON REINER [1089]

b. 10.4.1914, Cologne-Lindenthal
Class 1934; KKpt 1.4.45
1WO *U 18* 11/39–4/40; U-boat courses 4/40–9/40; 1WO *U 3* 9/40–10/40; UAA Plön 10/40–11/40; 1WO *U 101* 11/40–3/41; U-Cdr's Torpedo Course, 24th U-Flotilla 3/41
Cdr *U 121* 31.3.41–8.7.41
Cdr *U 453* 9.7.41–6.12.43
29th U-Flotilla 12/43–1/44; Adm. Staff Officer and adviser OKM/1.SKL 1/44–7/44; Comp. CO and acting Cdr Section 1/School of Naval Warfare Schleswig 7/44–3/45; IIa Staff 1/Naval Infantry Div. 3/45–capitulation
Detained; freed 6.8.45
Knight's Cross 19.11.43 (192nd KM, 105th U-boat holder)

SCHLITT, KARL-ADOLF [1090]

b. 16.4.1918, Laboe
Class 1937a; Kplt 1.3.44

Seconded to Luftwaffe 10/39–7/43, served with *Bordfliegerstaffel 1./196* aboard battleships *Scharnhorst* and *Tirpitz* and heavy cruiser *Admiral Scheer*; U-boat trg and courses 8/43–6/44
Cdr *U 1206* 7/44–14.4.45
POW 14.4.45–29.2.48

SCHLÖMER, FOKKO [1091]
b. 25.8.1909, West-Grossefehn, Lower Saxony
Enlisted rating VII/1928; Kplt 1.7.42
U-boat trg and 27th U-Flotilla 2/43–9/43 (U-Cdr's Torpedo Course 54); *Baubelehrung* 7.KLA 9/43–10/43
Cdr *U 1164* 27.10.43–28.6.44
Baubelehrung Type XXI 6.KLA 7/44–10/44
Cdr *U 3008* 19.10.44–3/45
Later details not available

SCHLOTT, HEINRICH [1092]
b. 10.7.1922, Hamburg
Class X/1940; ObltzS 1.10.44
WO sea trg *U 572* 1942; WO torpedo retrieval vessel No 1/ 26th U-Flotilla 9/42–12/42; 2WO *U 703* 1/43–3/44; U-Cdr's Course 4/44–7/44 (U-Cdr's Torpedo Course 73); *Baubelehrung* Type XXIII 8.KLA 7/44–8/44
Cdr *U 2329* 1.9.44–capitulation

SCHMANDT, ADALBERT [1093]
b. 26.12.1909, Wustrow, Rostock
Entry 1/1940; ObltzS (R) 1.6.43
2WO and 1WO *U B* 2/41–11/41; 2WO *UD 5* 9/42–2/43; *Baubelehrung* 2/43–3/43
Cdr *U 489* (Type XIV U-tanker) 8.3.43–4.8.43
POW 4.8.43

SCHMID, HEINRICH [1094]
b. 22.5.1915, Bad Reichenhall
Class 1934; Kplt 1.4.42, posthumously KKpt seniority 1.5.43

WO 6th Torpedo-Boat Flotilla 9/38–4/40; U-boat trg 4/40–10/40; instructor Torpedo School Mürwik 10/40–12/40; *Baubelehrung* 12/40–1/41; 1WO *U 555* 1/41–5/41
Cdr *U 7* 17.6.41–15.1.42
Course and *Baubelehrung* 8.KLA 2.42–5/42
Cdr *U 663* 14.5.42–8.5.43
Lost 8.5.43 Bay of Biscay, W of Brest

SCHMIDT, FRIEDRICH [1095]
b. 11.6.1921, Oberhausen
Class XII/1939; ObltzS 1.12.43
WO *U 732* 10/42–3/43; 8th and 2nd U-Flotillas 3/43–2/44; WO *U 129* 2/44–7/44; WO *U 190* 7/44–10/44; U-Cdr's Course, 3.ULD and 23rd U-Flotilla 10/44–12/44
Cdr *U 793* 16.1.45–3.5.45

SCHMIDT, KARL-HEINZ [1096]
(Assumed surname Schmidt-Rösemann 16.7.1957)
b. 20.1.1911, place not recorded
Entry 1936; ObltzS (R) 1.4.43
Minelayer *Stralsund* 6/40–8/40; NCO Trg Div. Wesermünde 8/40–12/40; course ULD Pillau 12/40–4/41; *Baubelehrung* 5/41–6/41; 1WO *U 351* 6/41–3/42; 1WO *U 211* 3/42–12/42; U-Cdr's Course 1/43–2/43
Cdr *U 17* 23.2.43–25.5.44
Staff 22nd U-Flotilla 5/44–10/44
Cdr *U 1103* 9.10.44–24.11.44
Baubelehrung 1/7.KLA 1.1.45–21.3.45
Cdr *U 3529* 22.3.45–8.5.45

SCHMIDT, WERNER [1097]
b. 11.7.1920, Kiel-Friedrichsort
Class IX/1939; ObltzS 1.10.43
U-boat trg completed 2/42; 2WO *U 84* 2/42–12/42; 1WO *U 84* 1/43–5/43; U-Cdr's Course, 2.UAA and 24th U-Flotilla 5/43–6/43 (U-Cdr's

Torpedo Course 48); *Baubelehrung* 6.KLA 6/43–8/43
Cdr *U 292* 25.8.43–27.5.44
Lost 27.5.44 W of Trondheim

SCHMIDT, WERNER-KARL [1098]
b. 15.4.1915, Stettin
Class 1935; Kplt 1.9.42
Seconded to Luftwaffe 8/38–8/41; courses and U-boat trg 8/41–12/41; Kplt on Staff 29th U-Flotilla 1/42–4/42; Group Officer Naval College Flensburg-Mürwik 4/42–7/42; Trg Officer Naval Gunnery School 7/42–9/42; Group Officer Naval College Flensburg-Mürwik 10/42–3/43; U-boat courses 3/43–9/43; U-Cdr's Course, 24th U-Flotilla 9/43–11/43 (U-Cdr's Torpedo Course 56); *Baubelehrung* 1.KLA 11/43–12/43
Cdr *U 250* 12.12.43–30.7.44
POW 30.7.44–3/49

SCHMIDT-WEICHERT, HANS-JOACHIM [1099]
b. 7.5.1915, Altona
Class 1936; Kplt 1.8.43
U-boat trg 4/40–8/40; WO *U 95* 8/40–6/41
Cdr *U 9* 2.7.41–30.4.42
Comp. CO 1.UAA 5/42–9/42
Cdr *U 9* 28.10.42–15.9.43
Comp. CO 1.UAA 10/43–11/43
Kplt on Staff 22nd U-Flotilla 11/43–3/45; 4th U-Flotilla 3/45–4/45
Cdr *U 3501* 4/45–1.5.45 (one voyage Bremen–Vegesack to Wesermünde, where boat was scuttled in lower river 1.5.45)

VON SCHMIDT, WERNER [1100]
b. 17.4.1906, Görlitz
Class 1926; KKpt 1.4.41
Anti-Submarine School 9/33–9/34; 1WO U-boat depot ship *Isar* 12/34–9/35; U-Cdr U-Flotilla *Weddigen* (Cdr *U 9*, *U 12* and *U 15*) 30.9.35–1.10.37; U-Cdr U-Flotilla *Saltzwedel* (*U 25*) 3.1.38–12.12.38; U-Flotilla *Saltzwedel* 13.12.38–15.1.39; *Baubelehrung* Deschimag AG Weser Bremen for *U 40* 16.1.39–10.2.39; U-Cdr U-Flotilla *Hundius* (*U 40*) 11.2.39–20.9.39; U-Flotilla *Hundius* 21.9.39–24.10.39; U-Boat School Neustadt 25.10.39–30.11.39; U-Trg Leader 3/NCO Trg Div. Plön 1.12.39–4.2.40; U-Trg Leader UAA Plön 5.2.40–27.7.40; instructor and curriculum head 1.ULD Pillau 28.7.40–8.12.40; Senior Officer U-boat base Brest 9.12.40–2.4.41; Trg Leader for Italian Submarine Trg Group, 27th U-Flotilla 3.4.41–30.4.41; *Baubelehrung* Germaniawerft Kiel for *U 116* 1.5.41–25.7.41
Cdr *U 116* 26.7.41–10.9.42
1st U-Flotilla 11.9.42–1.11.42; CO 8th U-Flotilla and Senior Officer U-boat base Danzig 2.11.42–31.3.44; seconded FdU Baltic 1.4.44–5.9.44 and Higher Command U-Boats 6.9.44–15.10.44; Senior Officer U-Boat Acceptance Command Kiel 16.10.44–8.5.45
Detained; freed 6.2.46

SCHMOECKEL, HELMUT [1101]
b. 18.12.1917, Berlin
Class 1936; Kplt 1.3.43
Div. Officer, heavy cruiser *Admiral Hipper* 9/39–7/42; U-boat trg 7/42–11/42; 1WO *U 504* 12/42–6/43; U-Cdr's Course, 24th U-Flotilla 6/43–8/43 (U-Cdr's Torpedo Course 50); U-Cdr under instrn 4th U-Flotilla (*U 802*) 9/43–12/43
Cdr *U 802* 13.12.43–capitulation

SCHNEE, ADALBERT [1102]
b. 31.12.1913, Berlin
Class 1934; KKpt 1.12.44
U-boat trg 5/37–9/37; 1WO *U 23* 9/37–6/38; U-boat Torpedo Officer supplementary course Torpedo School Mürwik 6/38–7/38; 1WO *U 23*

7/38–9/38; torpedo course Torpedo School Mürwik 9/38–12/38; 1WO *U 23* 12/38–1/40; U-Cdr's Course 1/40

Cdr *U 6* 18.1.40–16.6.40 (per WASt) or 31.1.40–10.7.40 (per P/F; see also Harms [416] and Peters [916]); U-Cdr's Torpedo Course, 24th U-Flotilla 17.6.40–18.7.40

Cdr *U 60* 19.7.40 (per P/F; sailed to Kiel on patrol 30.7.40, and see Schewe [1081]) to 5.11.40

Acting Cdr *U 121* 6.11.40–27.11.40

Baubelehrung U-Boats East 12/40–1/41

Cdr *U 201* 25.1.41–24.8.42 (per P/F; see Rosenberg [1028])

1st U-Flotilla 8/42–10/42; Adm. Staff Officer (A1/Opns) Escorts, BdU, OKM/2.SKL 10/42–7/44; *Baubelehrung* Type XXI 8.KLA 7/44–9/44

Cdr *U 2511* 29.9.44–capitulation (Translator's note: This was the only Type XXI boat to reach the Atlantic on patrol.)

4.Comp/1. German Minesweeping Reserve Division 9/45–12/45

Released 6.12.45

Knight's Cross 30.8.41 (83rd KM, 36th U-boat holder)

Oak Leaves 15.7.42 (105th WM, 15th KM, 13th U-boat holder)

SCHNEEWIND, FRITZ [1103]

b. 10.4.1917, Padang, Sumatra

Class 1936; Kplt 1.3.43

Group Officer Naval College Flensburg-Mürwik 10/39–8/40, also Platoon Officer sail trg ship *Albert Leo Schlageter* 3/40–6/40; Kriegsmarine Depot Boulogne 8/40–10/40; U-boat trg 10/40–3/41; WO 1st and 3rd U-Flotillas 3/41–9/41; 1WO *U 506* 9/41–11/42; U-Cdr's Course, 24th U-Flotilla 11/42–12/42

Cdr *U 511* 18.12.42–20.11.43

Cdr *U 183* 20.11.43–23.4.45

Lost 23.4.45 Java Sea

SCHNEIDER, HERBERT [1104]

b. 25.6.1915, Nuremberg

Class 1934; Kplt 1.4.42

Group Officer, Specialist in Personnel Matters, later Group Trg Leader Aircraft Weapons School 2 (Sea) Bug/Rügen 7/39–7/40; observer *2./Küstenfliegergruppe 406* 8/40–9/40; U-boat trg 10/40–5/41; 1WO *U 123* 5/41–12/41; U-Cdr's Torpedo Course, 26th U-Flotilla 12/41–2/42; 2.UAA Neustadt/Holstein 2/42–4/42; *Baubelehrung* 8.KLA 4/42–6/42

Cdr *U 522* 11.6.42–23.2.43

Lost 23.2.43 S of Azores/SW of Madeira

Knight's Cross 16.1.43 (145th KM, 77th U-boat holder)

SCHNEIDER, MANFRED [1105]

b. 11.12.1920, Stettin

Class XII/1939; ObltzS 1.12.43

U-boat trg completed 7/42; *Baubelehrung* 8/42–10/42; 1WO *U 731* 10/42–3/44; courses 4/44–10/44 (U-Cdr's Torpedo Course 68); *Baubelehrung* Type XXIII 1.KLA 11/44–2/45

Cdr *U 4706* 7.2.45–capitulation

SCHNEIDEWIND, KARL-HERMANN [1106]

b. 7.3.1907, Hann-Münden

Class 1927; KKpt 1.9.43 seniority 1.3.42

U-boat trg 9/43–3/44; U-Cdr's Course, 3.ULD and 24th U-Flotilla 3/44–6/44 (U-Cdr's Torpedo Course 70); *Baubelehrung* 1.KLA 6/44–7/44

Cdr *U 1064* 29.7.44–capitulation. (Adalbert Schmitz was listed to take command of *U 1064* from Schneidewind at about the time of the capitulation but did not do so)

SCHNOOR, EBE [1107]

b. 22.6.1895, Emmelsbüll

Entry XII/1915; Kplt (R) 1.1.43

Student 1. and 2.ULD 1/41–2/41; U-courses 3/41–5/41; 2WO *U 143* 6/41–8/41; 2WO *U 108* 8/41–4/42
Cdr *U A* 15.5.42–9.8.42
Cdr *U 460* (Type XIV U-tanker) 1.8.42 or 10.8.42 (see Schäfer [1059]) to 4.10.43
Lost 4.10.43 N of Azores

SCHÖLER, CLEMENS [1108]
b. 30.5.1915, Selm, Westphalia
Class 1936; Kplt 1.8.43
Light cruiser *Königsberg* 12/38–4/40; Platoon Officer and Battery CO Naval Artillery Detachment 504 4/40–7/40; ADC Staff Naval Cdr Channel Coast 7/40–1/41; seconded BdU 1/41–6/41; 1WO U-boat depot ship *Wilhelm Bauer* 6/41–10/41; 1WO *U 564* 10/41–3/42; U-Cdr under instrn 24th U-Flotilla 4/42–5/42
Cdr *U 20* 7.5.42–26.9.42
1.UAA 9/42–11/42
Cdr *U 24* 18.11.42–15.4.43
Cdr *U 20* 27.5.43–31.10.43
Hospitalised 11/43–2/44; U-Adm. Staff Officer (A3)/Staff Adm. Black Sea 3/44–7/44, served simultaneously as CO 30th U-Flotilla 5/44–7/44; course Academy of Naval Warfare 10/44–2/45; Kplt on Staff 26th U-Flotilla 2/45–capitulation
Detained; freed 15.9.45

SCHÖNBERG, ADOLF [1109]
b. 7.8.1918, Babylon, New York
Class 1937b; ObltzS 1.4.42
Seconded to Luftwaffe 9/39–12/40; U-boat trg 1/41–6/41; *Baubelehrung* 7/41–8/41; 1WO *U 404* 8/41–7/42; U-Cdr's Course 8/42–9/42
Cdr *U 62* 16.9.42–19.7.43
Cdr *U 404* 20.7.43–28.7.43
Lost 28.7.43 NW of Cape Ortegal

SCHÖNEBOOM, DIETRICH [1110]
b. 4.12.1917, Amdorf, Leer
Class 1937; ObltzS 1.9.41
WO escort boat *F 10* 8/39–12/39; course Naval Gunnery School Kiel-Wik 12/39–2/40; 1WO escort boat *F 6* 2/40–6/40 and shooting course Naval Gunnery School 5/40–6/40; Cdr *R 152* and *R 7*, 11th and 7th R-Boat Flotillas 7/40–9/41; U-boat trg 9/41–3/42; 1WO *U 205* 3/42–6/42; U-Cdr under instrn 24th U-Flotilla 7/42–8/42
Cdr *U 58* 18.8.42 (per P/F) or 1.9.42 to 14.12.42 (per WASt)
Cdr *U 431* 15.12.42 (per P/F) or 1.1.43 (per WASt, and see Dommes [214]) to 21.10.43
Lost 21.10.43 Mediterranean, off Algiers
Knight's Cross 20.10.43 (188th KM, 102nd U-boat holder)

SCHÖTZAU, GERHARD [1111]
b. 16.4.1917, Fylitz, Neidenburg
Class 1936; Kplt 1.9.43
Ordnance Officer minelayer *Tannenberg* 9/39–5/40; Mine Warfare Officer gunnery trg ship *Brummer* 6/40–5/42; instructor Mine Warfare School 5/42–3/43; navigation course Helmsman's School and retrg to Seaman Branch officer 3/43–6/43; U-boat trg 6/43–12/43; U-Cdr's Course, 3.ULD, 24th and 27th U-Flotillas 12/43–3/44 (U-Cdr's Torpedo Course 63); *Baubelehrung* 6.KLA 3/44–5/44
Cdr *U 880* 11.5.44–16.4.45
Lost 16.4.45 N of Azores

SCHOLLE, HANS-ULRICH [1112]
b. 30.9.1909, Krögelin, Mecklenburg
Entry 1/1938; ObltzS (R) 1.6.44
U-boat trg 9/42–3/43; supernumerary WO (trg purposes) *U 388* 3/43–5/43; *Baubelehrung* 5/43–6/43; 1WO *U 985* 6/43–3/44; U-Cdr's Course, 23rd U-Flotilla 4/44–6/44; *Baubelehrung* Type XXIII 8.KLA 6/44–8/44

Cdr *U 2328* 25.8.44–30.11.44
Cdr *U 328* (4th U-Flotilla) 1.12.44–capitulation

SCHOLTZ, KLAUS [1113]
b. 22.3.1908, Magdeburg
Class 1927; FKpt 1.7.44
Comp. CO 7/Basic Trg Est. Stralsund 4/39–3/40; *Baubelehrung* Deschimag AG Weser Werft Bremen 7/40–10/40
Cdr *U 108* 22.10.40–14.10.42
CO 12th U-Flotilla 10/42–8/44; Cdr III Battalion/Naval Regt *Bademann* 8/44–9/44; POW 11.9.44–20.4.46
Knight's Cross 26.12.41 (92nd KM, 40th U-boat holder)
Oak Leaves 10.9.42 (123rd WM, 16th KM, 14th U-boat holder)

SCHOLZ, GÜNTHER [1114]
b. 27.2.1919, St Pölten, Austria
Class 1938; ObltzS 1.4.43 seniority 1.1.43
U-boat trg 10/40–3/41; Anti-Submarine School 3/41–10/41; 1WO *U 371* 10/41–2/43; U-Cdr's Course, 24th U-Flotilla 2/43–3/43 (U-Cdr's Torpedo Course 42); *Baubelehrung* 3/43–4/43
Cdr *U 284* 14.4.43–21.12.43
9th U-Flotilla 12/43–3/44
Cdr *UD 2* 2.4.44–4.7.44
Cdr *U 1052* 5.7.44–capitulation

SCHOLZ, HANS-ULRICH [1115]
b. 7.5.1911, Breslau
Entry 1/1940; ObltzS (R) 1.10.43
U-boat trg and courses 7/43–4/44; courses 24th U-Flotilla 5/44–7/44 (U-Cdr's Torpedo Course 71); U-Cdr sea trg *U 1017* 7/44–11/44; WO 27th U-Flotilla 11/44; *Baubelehrung* Type XXIII 1.KLA 11/44–1/45
Cdr *U 4703* 21.1.45–5.5.45

SCHOLZ, HEINZ-GÜNTHER [1116]
b. 12.1.1918, Dresden
Class 1937a; ObltzS 1.4.42
Seconded to Luftwaffe 4/40–1/41; U-boat trg 1/41–9/41; *Baubelehrung* 9/41–11/41; 1WO *U 172* 11/41–1/43; U-Cdr's Course, 2.UAA and 26th U-Flotilla 1/43–2/43; *Baubelehrung* 6.KLA 2/43–3/43
Cdr *U 283* 31.3.43–15.8.43
Died 15.8.43

SCHOMBURG, HEINZ [1117]
b. 28.9.1914, Barsighausen, Lower Saxony
Class 1935; Kplt 1.10.42
ADC, WO and Radio Officer merchant raider *Stier* 11/39–6/40; U-boat trg 7/40–12/40; *Baubelehrung* 12/40–2/41; 1WO *U 78* 2/41–8/41; Cdr *U 145* 22.10.41–25.11.41; 1WO *U 561* 12/41–5/42; U-Cdr's Course, 24th and 27th U-Flotillas 5/42–8/42
Cdr *U 561* 5.9.42 (per *U 561* WD) to 18.6.43
29th U-Flotilla 7/43–9/43; Induction Officer 1/Acceptance Centre for Officer Applicants to Kriegsmarine 9/43–1/44; CO Naval Induction Branch 1/44–10/44; Trg Officer and CO Special Task Force *Schomburg*, K-Verband/Trg Command 600 10/44–capitulation

SCHOMBURG, OSKAR [1118]
b. 19.8.1897 place not recorded
Entry X/1915; KptzS 1.1.40
Seconded FdU and Cdr *U 26* 1.10.38–8/39; at FdU East 8/39–9/39; Cdr Hela District 10/39; Chief of Staff, Staff of Cdr Escort Forces North Sea 11/39–4/40; Chief of Staff, Staff of Adm. Norwegian West Coast 4/40–4/41; Divisional CO OKM/SKL-U1 4/41–2/43; Chief of Staff Sea Mines Inspectorate 2/43–1/45; Naval Cdr Bergen 1/45–capitulation
Detained; freed 8.10.47

SCHONDER, HEINRICH [1119]
b. 23.7.1910, Erfurt
Class 1935; Kplt 1.9.41, posthumously KKpt seniority 1.6.43
U-boat trg 1/38–6/38; *Baubelehrung* Germaniawerft Kiel 6/38–8/38; 1WO *U 51* 8/38–10/38; WO course 10/38–11/38; 1WO *U 51* 11/38–8/39; 1WO *U 53* 8/39–1/40 and acting Cdr *U 53* 2/39–1/40; 1WO *U 9* 1/40–4/40; U-Cdr sea trg U-Trg Flotilla 5/40–6/40
Cdr *U 58* 1.7.40 (per WASt) to 24.11.40 (P/F has take-over date as 10.6.40, but this is improbable since Kuppisch [684] was commanding *U 58* at sea at the time)
Baubelehrung U-Boats North Sea 11/40–1/41
Cdr *U 77* 18.1.41 to 7.9.42 (P/F) or 2.9.42 (per *U 77* WD, relieved by Hartmann [424])
29th U-Flotilla 9/42–11/42; *Baubelehrung* 1/Comp/6.KLA 11/42–12/42
Cdr *U 200* 22.12.42–24.6.43
Lost 24.6.43 SW of Iceland
Knight's Cross 19.8.42 (122nd KM, 60th U-boat holder)

SCHRAMM, JOACHIM [1120]
b. 3.6.1916, Ruhla, Thüringen
Class 1936; ObltzS 1.10.40
Comp. Officer and instructor Torpedo School Mürwik 4/39–12/39; Torpedo Officer and WO destroyer *Z 18 Hans Lüdemann* 1/40–3/40; Platoon Leader 1st Torpedo-Boat Flotilla 3/40–5/40; WO torpedo-boat *T 4* 5/40–10/40; Liaison Officer C-in-C Torpedo-Boats/Opns 10/40–5/41; 1WO and Torpedo Officer torpedo-boat *Greif* 5/41–10/41; Torpedo School Mürwik 10/41–12/41; acting Cdr torpedo-boat *Greif* 12/41–1/42; U-boat trg 1/42–5/42; 1WO *U 109* 6/42–1/43; U-Cdr's Course, 26th U-Flotilla 2/43
Cdr *U 109* 1.3.43–4.5.43 or 7.5.43

SCHREIBER, GERD [1121]
b. 2.4.1912, Hirschberg, Silesia
Class 1931; KKpt 1.11.43
WO *U 34* 1936 (per rank listings 1.11.36) and 1937 (per rank listings 1.11.37); Torpedo Officer light cruiser *Königsberg* 6/39–11/39; U-Cdrs trg U-Trg Flotilla 11/39–1/40
Cdr *U 3* 3.1.40–28.7.40
Baubelehrung 7/40–8/40
Cdr *U 95* 31.8.40–28.11.41
POW 28.11.1941

SCHREIBER, HEINRICH [1122]
b. 30.4.1917, Magdeburg
Class 1937b; ObltzS 1.3.43
Platoon Leader Naval Flak Detachment 211 7/41–3/43; nautical trg 3rd Sperrbrecher Flotilla 3/43–5/43; course Naval School Wesermünde 5/43–8/43; U-boat trg 8/43–2/44; course 23rd U-Flotilla 2/44–3/44; 19th U-Flotilla 4/44–5/44; course 24th U-Flotilla 5/44–7/44
Cdr *U 270* 16.7.44–13.8.44
POW 13.8.44

SCHREIN, HERBERT [1123]
b. 30.5.1917, Kiel; Class 1937a; Kplt 1.10.44
WO gunnery trg ship *Brummer* 11/39–4/40; Cdr Harbour Defence Flotilla Horten 4/40–5/40; ADC to Naval Cdr Kristiansand South 5/40–3/41; WO torpedo-boat *T 13* 5/41–10/41; Torpedo Officer merchant raider *Thor* 10/41–11/42; Holding Regiment Japan 12/42–6/43; WO supply ship *Bogota* 6/43–7/43; WO naval oiler/supply ship *Brake* 7/43–9/43; 1WO *UIT 25* 9/43–2/45; acting Cdr *UIT 25* 1.9.44–24.11.44 (per WASt) or 10/44–2/45 (U-Boat Archive per Schrein, and see Meier [807])
WO and U-Cdr sea trg *U 183* 2/45–3/45; WO and U-Cdr sea trg *U 219* 4/45–capitulation
Detained; freed 15.4.47

SCHREINER, WOLFGANG [1124]
b. 20.4.1917, Frankfurt/Main

Class 1937a; ObltzS 1.9.41
Seconded to Luftwaffe 10/39–12/40; U-boat trg 9/41–10/41; 1WO *U 593* 10/41–6/42; U-Cdr's Course, 24th U-Flotilla 7/42–8/42; *Baubelehrung* 7.KLA 8/42–9/42
Cdr *U 417* 26.9.42–11.6.43
Lost 11.6.43 SE of Iceland

SCHRENK, HANS [1125]
b. 18.9.1917, Bad Frankenhausen
Class 1937a; Kplt 1.10.44
Light cruiser *Köln* 10/39–3/40; seconded Military Commandant Kiel 3/40–8/40; Kriegsmarine Depot Hamburg 8/40–10/40; WO state yacht *Hela* 10/40–9/41; U-boat trg 9/41–3/42; WO *U 593* 3/42–9/42; U-Cdr's Course, 24th U-Flotilla 9/42–10/42
Cdr *U 7* 8.10.42–1/44; *Baubelehrung* 5.KLA 1/44–4/44
Cdr *U 901* 29.4.44–capitulation

SCHRENK, HERMANN [1126]
b. 19.6.1918, Niedermeilingen, Hesse
Class 1937a; Kplt 1.9.44
WO 7th, 1st and 3rd Minesweeping Flotillas 12/39–7/41; Mining Officer merchant raider *Thor* 7/41–11/42; ADC Holding Regiment Japan 12/42–1/43; Cargo Officer motor ship *Rio Grande* 2/43–4/43; ADC Naval Attaché Tokyo 4/43–7/43; WO naval oiler/supply ship *Brake* 7/43–10/43; Special Command *Schneewind/ UIT 23* 10/43–11/43; 1WO *U 178* 11/43–7/44; courses Torpedo School 1, 3.ULD and 23rd U-Flotilla 7/44–1/45; WO 8th U-Flotilla 1/45–3/45
Cdr *U 3511* 1.4.45–3.5.45

SCHREWE, PETER [1127]
b. 3.12.1913, Grosshof, Tapiau, East Prussia
Class 1934; Kplt 1.1.43
Seconded to Luftwaffe 9/39–9/40, inc. duty with *Bordfliegerstaffel 1./196* (aboard battleship *Scharnhorst*); U-boat trg 10/40–3/41; 1WO *U 48* 3/41–7/41; 5th U-Flotilla 8/41–3/42; 1WO *U 378* 3/42–7/42, and whilst at 11th U-Flotilla 7/42–11/42 acting Cdr *U 378* 18.6.42–9.9.42 (deputy for Hoschatt [518] when latter hospitalised; boat was under overhaul at Trondheim at the time and did not sail) and acting Cdr *U 591* 9.9.42–12.11.42 (assumed responsibility for *U 591* while latter under overhaul at Trondheim); U-Cdr's Course, 2.UAA and 24th U-Flotilla 11/42–12/42; *Baubelehrung* 8.KLA 12/42–1/43
Cdr *U 537* 27.1.43–9.11.44
Lost 9.11.44 Java Sea, E of Surabaya

SCHREYER, HILMAR-KARL [1128]
b. 28.8.1914; Manebach, Thüringen
Enlisted rating 1933; ObltzS 1.4.43
VP-Cdr, 17th VP-Boat Flotilla 10/40–12/40; *Baubelehrung* 8.KLA 12/40–2/41; ObStrm and WO *U 558* 2/41–4/43; U-Cdr's Course, 2.UAA and 24th U-Flotilla 4/43–5/43 (U-Cdr's Torpedo Course 46); *Baubelehrung* 8.KLA 6/43–7/43
Cdr *U 987* 8.7.43–15.6.44
Lost 15.6.44 Norwegian Sea, W of Narvik

SCHROBACH, KURT [1129]
b. 11.9.1914, Kiel
Rating entry 1935; ObltzS 1.1.45
Leading telegraphist *U 5* and *U 96* (under Lehmann-Willenbrock [714]); WO sea trg *U 251* 1/42–10/42; courses 11/42–3/43; WO *U 596* 4/43–6/44; course 23rd U-Flotilla 6/44–8/44; U-Holding Company 12, 22nd U-Flotilla 9/44–11/44; *Baubelehrung* Type XXIII 8.KLA 11/44–1/45
Cdr *U 2360* 23.1.45–5.5.45

SCHRÖDER, GUSTAV [1130]
b. 6.7.1921, Schneidemühl
Class XII/1939; ObltzS 1.12.43
WO sea trg *U 184* 5/42–7/42; Comp. CO 4th U-Flotilla 7/42–2/43; *Baubelehrung* 2/43–3/43; 1WO *U 311* 3/43–2/44; U-Cdr's Course, 3.ULD and 24th U-Flotilla 2/44–5/44 (U-Cdr's Torpedo Course 67); Trg Officer 2/Basic Trg Est. Stralsund 5/44–12/44
Cdr *U 1056* 1/45–5.5.45

SCHRÖDER, HEINRICH [1131]
b. 25.1.1916, Byeloretzk
Entry 1936; ObltzS (R) 1.1.45
WO *U 358* 8/42–6/43; course 6/43–8/43; 2WO *U 155* 8/43–1/44; 1WO *U 155* 1/44–10/44; U-Holding Company 19 10/44–12/44; *Baubelehrung* Type XXIII 8.KLA 12/44–3/45
Cdr *U 2367* 17.3.45–9.5.45

SCHRÖDER, HERMANN [1132]
b. 3.12.1912, Hamburg
Entry 1/1937; ObltzS 1.10.40
U-boat trg 1/41–5/41; relief instructor Signals School Mürwik 5/41–7/41; 1WO *U 751* 8/41–2/42; 7th U-Flotilla 2/42–4/42; U-Cdr's Course, 2.UAA and 24th U-Flotilla 4/42–5/42; *Baubelehrung* 8.KLA 5/42
Cdr *U 623* 21.5.42–21.2.43
Missing 21.2.43 Atlantic

SCHROETELER, HEINRICH ANDREAS [1133]
b. 10.12.1915, Essen-Katernberg
Class 1936; Kplt 1.4.43
WO and M/S-Cdr 14th Minesweeping Flotilla 9/39–8/41; U-boat trg 9/41–3/42; 7th U-Flotilla 3/42–4/42; U-Cdr sea trg *U 96* 4/42–7/42; U-Cdr's Torpedo Course, 24th U-Flotilla 7/42–8/42; *Baubelehrung* 8.KLA 9/42–10/42
Cdr *U 667* 21.10.42 to 5/44 or 19.5.44 (P/F)

Service with OKM/2.SKL/BdU/Opns 5/44–7/44; relief administrator to 1/Adm. Staff Officer (A1/Opns) OKM/2.SKL/BdU/Opns 7/44–12/44; Trg Officer 27th U-Flotilla 1/45–2/45
Cdr *U 1023* 10.3.45–capitulation
Detained 11.5.45–20.5.48
Knight's Cross 2.5.45 (311th KM, 143rd U-boat holder)

SCHROETER, KARL-ERNST [1134]
b. 3.12.1912, Freystadt, Silesia
Class 1934; Kplt, posthumously KKpt seniority 1.5.43
1WO *U 9* 9/39–10/39; 1WO *U 38* 11/39–1/40; U-Trg Flotilla 1/40–4/40; *Baubelehrung* 5/40
Cdr *U 121* 28.5.40–30.3.41
Baubelehrung 4/41–5/41
Cdr *U 752* 24.5.41–23.5.43
Lost 23.5.43 central North Atlantic

VON SCHROETER, HORST [1135]
b. 10.6.1919, Bieberstein, Saxony
Class 1937b; Kplt 1.1.45
Shipboard trg battleship *Scharnhorst* 12/39–4/40; U-boat trg 4/40–10/40; ADC 1.ULD 10/40–4/41; 2WO *U 123* 4/41–2/42; 1WO *U 123* 2/42–6/42; U-Cdr's Torpedo Cours, 24th U-Flotilla 6/42–7/42
Cdr *U 123* 1.8.42–17.6.44
Baubelehrung Type XXI 8.KLA 6/44–8/44
Cdr *U 2506* 31.8.44–capitulation
Detained; freed 6/47
Knight's Cross 1.6.44 (219th KM, 120th U-boat holder)

SCHRÖTER, KARL-HEINZ [1136]
b. 13.3.1921, Apolda
Class IX/1939; ObltzS 1.10.43
WO *U 603* 1/42–8/43; U-Cdr's Course, 2.UAA and 24th U-Flotilla 8/43–9/43 (U-Cdr's Tor-

pedo Course 54); *Baubelehrung* 7.KLA 9/43–11/43
Cdr *U 1195* 4.11.43–31.10.44
Cdr *U 763* 1.11.44–24.1.45
24th U-Flotilla and *Baubelehrung* Cdr Type XXI 6.KLA for *U 3062* (never commissioned) 1/45–capitulation

SCHROTT, KARL [1137]
b. 25.3.1911, Viersen, Rhineland
Class 1932; Kplt 1.1.40
Courses 7/39–10/39
Cdr *U 7* 14.10.39 or 14.11.39 to 10/40
Baubelehrung, 10/40–11/40
Cdr *U 551* 7.11.40–23.3.41
Lost 23.3.41 SE of Iceland

SCHUBART, ALBRECHT [1138]
b. 19.7.1914, Hamburg
Entry 1936; ObltzS (R) 1.4.43
VP-Cdr 59th VP-Boat Flotilla and Harbour Defence Flotilla Kirkenes 10/40–8/42; VP-Cdr 16th VP-Boat Flotilla 8/42–2/43; U-boat trg 3/43–9/43; U-Cdr's Course, 23rd U-Flotilla 9/43–10/43; *Baubelehrung* 8.KLA 10/43–11/43
Cdr *U 1002* 30.11.43 to 2.7.44 or 6.7.44 (per *U 1002* WD, relieved by Boos [103])
Courses and *Baubelehrung* Type XXI 8.KLA 7/44–12/44
Cdr *U 2520* 25.12.44–19.4.45

SCHUCH, HEINRICH [1139]
b. 28.8.1906, Berlin
Class 1925; FKpt 1.9.43
Cdr *U 37* 4.8.38–24.9.39
Adviser to OKM/SKL-U 9/39–7/41
Cdr *U 38* 15.7.41–6.1.42 (see Liebe [730])
Cdr *U 105* 7.1.42–30.9.42
Cdr *U 154* 1.10.42 (WASt) or 7.10.42 (relieved Kölle [635], per *U 154* WD; either date may be correct as *U 154* sailed from Lorient on 12.10.42 under Schuch. See also Nissen [884] and Schweichel [1178] re *U 105*.) to 8.2.43 (per P/F Kusch [686] and *U 154* WD) or 18.2.43 (per WASt)
Head of Weapons Div. (A2), Staff Officer Commanding Adm. U-Boats 2/45–capitulation

SCHÜLER, PHILIPP [1140]
b. 17.10.1911, Frankfurt/Main
Class 1935; Kplt 1.2.42
Platoon Officer battleship *Gneisenau* 5/38–3/40; U-boat trg 4/40–10/40; 1WO *U 100* 10/40–2/41; U-Cdr's Course, 24th U-Flotilla 2/41–3/41
Cdr *U 141* 31.3.41–29.11.41
Baubelehrung 30.11.41–28.12.41
Cdr *U 602* 29.12.41–23.4.43
Missing 23.4.43 Western Mediterranean

SCHÜLER, WOLF-HARALD [1141]
b. 22.8.1921, Halle, Saxony-Anhalt
Class X/1939; ObltzS 1.10.43
WO *U 123* 3/42–6/43; U-Cdr's Course, 24th U-Flotilla 6/43–7/43 (U-Cdr's Torpedo Course 50); *Baubelehrung* 8.KLA 8/43–9/43
Cdr *U 720* 17.9.43–31.3.44
Courses and *Baubelehrung* Type XXIII 8.KLA 4/44–8/44
Cdr *U 2325* 3.8.44–20.4.45
Naval Anti-Tank Regiment 1 4/45–capitulation

SCHÜMANN, HENNING [1142]
b. 17.4.1919, Elmschenhagen, Schleswig-Holstein
Class 1937b; ObltzS 1.4.42
Radio Technical Officer and 3WO destroyer *Z 4 Richard Beitzen* 8/40–1/42; U-boat trg 1/42–7/42; 1WO *U 402* 8/42–3/43; U-Cdr's Course, 2.UAA and 24th U-Flotilla 3/43–4/43 (U-Cdr's Torpedo Course 44); *Baubelehrung* 4/43–5/43

Cdr *U 392* 29.5.43–17.3.44
Lost 17.3.44 Strait of Gibraltar

SCHÜNEMANN, HORST [1143]
b. 2.1.1914, Kiel
Class 1934; Kplt 1.4.42
WO 6th Torpedo-Boat Flotilla 8/39–3/40; U-boat trg 4/40–11/40; *Baubelehrung* 11/40–12/40; 1WO *U 71* 12/40–10/41
Cdr *U 62* 20.11.41–13.4.42
Baubelehrung 8.KLA 4/42–5/42
Cdr *U 621* 7.5.42–1.12.42 (per WASt) or 4.12.42 (relieved Krischka [671], per *U 621* WD)
9th U-Flotilla 1/43–9/43; Kplt on Staff 23rd U-Flotilla 9/43–2/45; Military hospital Reinfeld 2/45–capitulation
Detained; freed 11.4.46

SCHÜTT, HEINZ [1144]
b. 24.11.1915, Hamburg-Harburg
Entry 1936; ObltzS (R) 1.4.43
U-boat trg 1/41–5/41; *Baubelehrung* 3.KLA 6/41–8/41; 2WO *U 135* 8/41–10/42
Cdr *U 135* 11/42–3.6.43
5th U-Flotilla 6/43–10/43
Cdr *U 294* 6.10.43–capitulation

SCHÜTZE, HERBERT-VIKTOR [1145]
b. 24.2.1917, Hannover
Class 1935; Kplt 1.4.42
U-boat trg 4/40–9/40; WO 21st U-Flotilla 9/40–11/40; *Baubelehrung* 12/40–1/41; 1WO *U 77* 1/41–9/41; relief instructor Naval Gunnery School 9/41–11/41; U-Cdr's Course, 24th U-Flotilla 11/41–12/41; *Baubelehrung* 8.KLA 12/41–1/42
Cdr *U 605* 15.1.42–14.11.42
Lost 14.11.42 Mediterranean, off Algiers

SCHÜTZE, VIKTOR [1146]
b. 16.2.1906, Kiel
Class 1925; KptzS 1.3.44
U-boat trg 10/35–12/35; *Baubelehrung* 12/35–1/36; Cdr *U 19* 16.1.36–30.9.37; Leader 5th Destroyer Div. Crew Holding Company 10/37–5/38; Trg Section 3rd Destroyer Div. 5/38–6/38; First Officer destroyer *Z 15 Erich Steinbrinck*, 3rd Destroyer Div. 6/38–8/38; Cdr *U 11* 13.8.38–4.9.39, inc. mining course for Staff Officers, Mine Warfare School Kiel-Wik 1.12.38–7.12.38
Cdr *U 25* 5.9.39–19.5.40
Baubelehrung 5/40–7/40
Cdr *U 103* 5.7.40–12.8.41
CO 2nd U-Flotilla (Lorient) 8/41 to 1/43 or 2/43 (per Italian P/F); Head of U-boat trg FdU/Trg, 18th–20th and 23rd–27th U-Flotillas inclusive 2/43–5/45; Cdr Naval District Flensburg-Kappeln 5/45–capitulation
Detained; freed 3/46
Knight's Cross 11.12.40 (49th KM, 22nd U-boat holder)
Oak Leaves 14.7.41 (23rd WM, 7th KM, 7th U-boat holder)

SCHUG, WALTER [1147]
b. 22.10.1910, Cologne
Class 1934; Kplt 1.10.41
Comp. Leader 9/Reserve Naval Artillery Div. 9/39–2/40; Comp. CO Naval Assault Troop Div. 2/40–3/40; U-boat trg 4/40–10/40; 1WO *U 74* 10/40–4/41; U-Cdr's Course, 24th U-Flotilla 4/41–6/41; *Baubelehrung* 3.KLA 6/41–7/41
Cdr *U 86* 8.7.41–29.11.43
Lost 29.11.43 E of Azores

SCHUHART, OTTO [1148]
b. 1.4.1909, Hamburg
Class 1929; KKpt 1.4.43
U-boat trg 1/38–4/38; Senior Officer Naval Detachment research ship *Altau* 4/38–7/38;

1WO *U 25* 7/38–9/38; acting Cdr *U 8* 2.9.38–29.10.38; seconded FdU 10/38; U-Flotilla *Saltzwedel* 11/38–12/38
Cdr *U 25* 10.12.38–3.4.39
Cdr *U 29* 4.4.39–2.1.41
Instructor and Head of Officer Trg 1.ULD 1/41–6/43; Cdr Section 1/1.ULD and CO 21st U-Flotilla 6/43–1/44; CO 21st U-Flotilla 1/44–9/44; Cdr Section 1/Naval College Flensburg-Mürwik, then Cdr Naval Infantry Battalion *Schuhart* 9/44–8/45; Departmental Head German Minesweeping Service 8/45–12/45; demobilised 14.12.45
Knight's Cross 16.5.40 (9th KM, 5th U-boat holder)

SCHULTE, MAX [1149]
b. 24.9.1915, Wuppertal-Barmen
Class 1933; Kplt 1.10.40
WO *U 9* 10/38–9/39
Cdr *U 9* 19.9.39–29.12.39
Cdr *U 13* 3.1.40–31.5.40
POW 31.5.40–21.6.47

SCHULTE, WERNER [1150]
b. 7.11.1912, Kiel
Entry date not known; Kplt 1.10.39, posthumously KKpt seniority 1.10.42
WO Gunnery and Div. Officer light cruiser *Königsberg* 3/38–4/40; Staff Naval Cdr Bergen, 4/40–10/40; U-boat trg 10/40–3/41; U-Cdr's Course, 24th U-Flotilla 3/41–4/41; U-Cdr sea trg *U 98* 4/41–6/41; *Baubelehrung* 7/41–8/41
Cdr *U 582* 7.8.41–5.10.42
Lost 5.10.42 SW of Iceland

SCHULTZ, DIEDRICH [1151]
b. 5.11.1919, Bremen
Entry VIII/1940; ObltzS (R) 1.6.44
1WO *U 284* 4/43–12/43; 9th U-Flotilla 12/43–2/44; course 24th U-Flotilla 2/44–4/44 (U-Cdr's Torpedo Course 66); 1/Naval Reserve Div. 4/44–12/44; *Baubelehrung* Cdr 1.KLA for *U 4708* 10.12.44–9.4.45. (*U 4708* was destroyed by RAF bombing on 9.4.45, three days before the scheduled commissioning date, in Bunker Kilian South at Kiel. Schultz then received orders to take command of Angermann's [14] former charge, *U 2323*, which although having been sunk at Kieler Förde on 26.7.44 had been salved and was now almost serviceable. However, this boat was never commissioned.)
5th U-Flotilla 4/45–capitulation

SCHULTZ, HERMANN [1152]
b. 7.2.1920, Kiel
Class 1938; ObltzS 1.4.43
1WO *U 209* 10/41–9/42; U-Cdr's Course, 24th U-Flotilla and Cdr *U 150* 1.9.42 or 10/42–5/44 (U-Boat Archive per Schultz)
Baubelehrung Type XXI 7.KLA 5/44–8/44
Cdr *U 3502* 19.8.44–3.5.45

SCHULTZ, KARL-OTTO [1153]
b. 9.11.1914, Wesermünde-Lehe
Class 1934; Kplt 1.3.42
WO *U 22* 1937 (per rank listings 1.11.37); 1WO *U 22* 12/38–1/40; U-Boat School Neustadt 1/40–3/40; OKM 3/40–3/41; U-Cdr's Course, 24th U-Flotilla 3/41–5/41
Cdr *U 34* 23.5.41–19.11.41
Baubelehrung 11/41–12/41
Cdr *U 216* 15.12.41–20.10.42
Lost 20.10.42 SW of Ireland

SCHULTZE, HEINZ-OTTO [1154]
b. 13.9.1915, Kiel
Class 1934; Kplt 1.11.41
U-boat trg, various duties and courses 5/37–3/38; 2WO *U 31* 3/38–10/38; course Naval Gunnery School Kiel-Wik 10/38–11/38; 1WO *U 31*

11/38–1/40; U-Cdr under instrn 1st U-Boat Trg Flotilla 1/40–6/40 and trg Anti-Submarine School 13.2.40–17.2.40
Cdr *U 4* 8.6.40–28.7.40
Baubelehrung 7/40–8/40
Cdr *U 141* 21.8.40–30.3.41
Baubelehrung Schichauwerft Danzig 3/41–4/41
Cdr *U 432* 26.4.41–15.1.43
Baubelehrung 1/Comp./6.KLA 2/43–3/43
Cdr *U 849* 11.3.43–25.11.43
Lost 25.11.43 W of Congo Estuary
Knight's Cross 9.7.42 (116th KM, 56th U-boat holder)

SCHULTZE, HERBERT [1155]
b. 24.7.1909, Kiel
Class 1930; KKpt 1.4.43
U-boat trg 5/37–1/38 and acting Cdr *U 5* 8/37; Cdr *U 2* 30.1.38–16.3.39; *Baubelehrung* Germaniawerft Kiel 3/39–4/39
Cdr *U 48* 22.4.39–20.5.40 (per P/F)
Hospitalised 5/40–10/40; acting CO 7th U-Flotilla 10/40–12/40
Cdr *U 48* 16.12.40 (relieved Bleichrodt [89], per *U 48* WD) or 17.12.40 (per P/F) to 27.7.41 (per P/F)
CO 3rd U-Flotilla 7/41 or 8/41 to 3/42; U-Adm. Staff Officer at Staff, Naval Group North 3/42–12/42; 6/Adm. Staff Officer at OKM/2.SKL/BdU/Opns 12/42–3/44; Cdr Section II/Naval College Schleswig 3/44–5/45; Cdr of Wehrmacht Police Troop Battalion 5/45–8/45; Cdr Naval College Flensburg-Mürwik and Hans Krey Camp (appointed by Allies) 8/45–11/45
Knight's Cross 1.3.40 (3rd KM, 2nd U-boat holder)
Oak Leaves 12.6.41 (15th WM, 6th KM, 6th U-boat holder)

SCHULTZE, RUDOLF [1156]
b. 19.5.1922, Kronshagen, Rendsburg
Class XII/1939; ObltzS 1.12.43
2WO *U 608* 2/42–4/43; 1WO *U 608* 4/43–7/43; U-Cdr's Course 8/43–9/43
Cdr *U 61* 16.9.43–1.12.44
Baubelehrung Type XXI 12/41–2/45
Cdr *U 2540* 24.2.45–4.5.45
Detained; freed 10.10.45

SCHULTZE, WOLFGANG [1157]
b. 3.10.1910, Kiel
Class 1930; Kplt 1.6.39
Div. and Rangefinding Officer, battleship *Gneisenau* 5/38–4/40; U-boat trg 4/40–12/40
Cdr *U 17* 5.1.41–15.10.41
1st U-Flotilla 10/41–11/41
Baubelehrung 8.KLA 11/41–12/41
Cdr *U 512* 20.12.41–2.10.42
Lost 2.10.42 off US East Coast, N of Chayenne

SCHULZ, GEORG-WILHELM [1158]
b. 10.3.1906, Cologne
Entry 1932/30; KKpt 1.4.43
U-boat trg 9/35–12/35; WO *U 18* and *U 12* 12/35–9/37; 1WO *U 33* 10/37–1/39
Cdr *U 12* then *U 10* 5.1.39 to 15.10.39 (P/F has 9.10.39 but this cannot be correct as Schulz was patrolling the Orkneys from 26.9.39 to 15.10.39)
Cdr U-Flotilla *Hundius* 10/39–11/39; *Baubelehrung* Deschimag AG Weser Bremen 11/39–12/39
Cdr *U 64* 16.12.39–13.4.40
Cdr *U 124* 11.6.40–7.9.41
CO 6th U-Flotilla 9/41–10/43 and CO 8th U-Flotilla 10/41–1/42; Head (A1) New U-Boat Trials at FdU/Trg 10/43–4/45; CO 25th U-Flotilla 4/45–capitulation
Detained 6.5.45–15.7.45
Knight's Cross 4.4.41 (65th KM, 27th U-boat holder)

SCHULZ, HERMANN [1159]

b. 22.4.1913, Harsefeld, Lower Saxony

Enlisted XII/1934; ObltzS 1.4.45

ObStrm *U 255* 4/43–3/44; trg and courses 3/44–10/44 (U-Cdr's Torpedo Course 76); U-Holding Company 21 10/44–12/44; *Baubelehrung* Type XXIII 8.KLA 12/44–4/45

Cdr *U 2369* 18.4.45–2.5.45

Cdr *U 2327* 3.5.45–6.5.45

Detained; freed 7.8.45

SCHULZ, RICHARD [1160]

b. 20.9.1917, Bremen

Entry X/1939; ObltzS (R) 1.12.44

M/S-Cdr 34th Minesweeping Flotilla 6/41–9/42; courses and U-boat trg 9/42–6/43; acting Leader Holding Company 11th U-Flotilla 6/43–10/43; WO *U 636* 11/43–5/44; U-Cdr's Course 5/44–7/44

Cdr *U 58* 7/44–3.5.45

SCHULZ, WERNER [1161]

b. 28.9.1919, Berlin

Entry XI/1939; ObltzS (R) 1.4.44

Battery Officer Naval Flak Detachment 241 5/41–3/43; retrg for Seaman Branch, navigation course, U-boat trg, U-Cdr pre-trg, U-Cdr's Course and instruction 3/43–7/44 (U-Cdr's Torpedo Course 71); *Baubelehrung* 7.KLA 7/44–9/44

Cdr *U 929* 6.9.44–3.5.45

SCHULZ, WERNER-KARL [1162]

b. 25.10.10, Fürstenwalde

Entry 1928; KKpt 1.3.45

Cdr research boat *Störtebecker* 1/39–7/40; Cdr torpedo retrieval boat *TF 7*, 25th U-Flotilla 7/40–6/41; courses 6/41–10/41

Cdr *U 437* 25.10.41–20.12.42

6th U-Flotilla 12/42–2/43; Head of Torpedo Attack Trg 26th U-Flotilla 2/43–4/45; *K-Verband* 4/45–capitulation

SCHULZE, WILHELM [1163]

b. 27.7.1909, Dortmund

Class 1928; KKpt 1.9.42

No 1 Torpedo Officer heavy cruiser *Admiral Scheer* 8/38–6/41; U-boat trg 7/41–11/41; U-Cdr sea trg *U 71* 11/41–2/42; *Baubelehrung* 2/42–3/42

Cdr *U 177* 14.3.42–23.3.42 (per WASt, and see Gysae [396])

Cdr *U 98* 24.3.42 to 10/42 or 1.11.42 (per WASt, and see Eichmann [240])

Adviser OKM 11/42–10/44; adviser Torpedo Inspectorate 10/44–capitulation

Detained; freed 8/45

SCHUMANN-HINDENBERG, FRIEDRICH [1164]

b. 28.3.1913, Lübchow, Kolberg

Class 1932; KKpt 1.11.44

No 2 Gunnery/Wargames Officer trg ship *Schleswig-Holstein* 3/39–8/40; on Staff v.Fischel/Gadow for Operation 'Sealion' 8/40–11/40; Cdr control tower battleship *Tirpitz* 12/40–3/43; U-boat trg, U-Cdr's Course and *Baubelehrung* 1.KLA 3/43–12/43

Cdr *U 245* 18.12.43–capitulation

Detained; freed 26.3.47

SCHUNCK, HANS-NORBERT [1165]

b. 31.3.1920, Torgau

Class 1938; ObltzS 1.4.43

U-boat trg completed 6/41; 2WO *U 554* 7/41–9/41; 1WO *U 554* 9/41–11/41; *Baubelehrung* 12/41–1/42; 1WO *U 660* 1/42–10/42; 9th U-Flotilla 10/42–2/43; 1WO *U 377* 3/43–5/43; U-Cdr's Course, 24th U-Flotilla 6/43–7/43 (U-

Cdr's Torpedo Course 50); *Baubelehrung* 6.KLA 7/43–8/43
Cdr *U 348* 10.8.43–30.3.45
Cdr *U 103* 31.3.45–15.4.45 (After *U 348* had been destroyed by bombing at Hamburg on 30.3.45, Schunck took command of *U 103*, which had been out of commission since 3/44, for the voyage from Hamburg to Kiel—see Murl [861]—where it was proposed to use the boat as an electrical generator. On 15.4.45 *U 103* was wrecked by a bomb at Kiel. The transfer had taken only two days, and by then Schunck was already back in Hamburg, where his crew next took over *U 369*.)
Cdr *U 369* 16.4.45–capitulation
Detained; freed 3/47

SCHWAFF, WERNER [1166]

b. 3.3.1915, Peking, China
Class 1936; ObltzS 1.10.40, posthumously Kplt seniority 1.6.43
Seconded to Luftwaffe 10/38–12/40; U-boat trg 1/41–6/41; *Baubelehrung* 6/41–7/41; 1WO *U 654* 7/41–3/42; U-Cdr's Course, 24th U-Flotilla and *Baubelehrung* 3/42–5/42
Cdr *U 2* 16.5.42–19.11.42
Cdr *U 333* 22.11.42–17.5.43 (per *U 333* WD)
Cdr *U 440* 20.5.43–31.5.43
Lost 31.5.43 NW of Cape Ortegal

SCHWAGER, ERWIN [1167]

b. 9.1.1917, Santiago de Chile
Class 1937a; Kplt 1.4.44
1WO *U 573* 3/42–5/42; interned Spain 5/42–7/42; 1WO *U 404* 7/42–10/42; U-Cdr's Course and 24th U-Flotilla 10/42–12/42
Cdr *U 143* 15.12.42–8.2.43
22nd U-Flotilla 2/43–6/43; instructor 2.ULD 7/43–11/44; course 11/44–2/45; WO (supernumerary) 3rd Minesweeping Flotilla 2/45–capitulation

SCHWALBACH, BRUNO [1168]

b. 11.9.1917, Mannheim
Class 1937b; Kplt 1.1.45
Courses and trg 10/37–11/39; ADC, Divisional and Midshipmen's Trg Officer light cruiser *Nürnberg* 12/39–3/41; ADC heavy cruiser *Lützow* 3/41–4/42; WO and Cadet Trg Officer heavy cruiser *Lützow* 4/42–9/43; U-boat trg and *Baubelehrung* 10/43–10/44; U-Cdr sea trg *U 3508* 10/44–1/45
Cdr *U 1161* 18.1.45–4.5.45
Detained; freed 6/45

SCHWANTKE, HANS-JOACHIM [1169]

b. 30.8.1918, Hindenburg, Upper Silesia
Class 1936; ObltzS 1.10.40, posthumously Kplt seniority 1.8.43
11/Basic Trg Est. Stralsund 9/38–11/39; WO light cruiser *Karlsruhe* 11/39–4/40; U-boat trg 4/40–10/40; 1WO *U 143* 10/40–1/41; 2WO *U 43* 1/41–10/41; 1WO *U 43* 10/41–1/42; course 24th U-Flotilla 1/42–4/42
Cdr *U 43* 4/42 (per WASt) or 19.3.42 (per *U 43* WD, and see Lüth [764]) to 30.7.43
Lost 30.7.43 SW of Azores

SCHWARTING, BERNHARD [1170]

b. 30.1.1913, Brake
Rating entry 1936; ObltzS (R) 1.7.43
Flotilla Coxswain 3rd R-Boat Flotilla 4/41–1/42; UJ-Cdr 12th Anti-Submarine Flotilla 1/42–9/42; WO and VP-Cdr 13th VP-Boat Flotilla 9/42–1/43; U-boat trg 1/43–9/43; Platoon Officer 1.UAA 9/43–12/43, plus U-Cdr's Course 11/43 (U-Cdr's Torpedo Course 59); *Baubelehrung* 6.KLA 1/44–2/44
Cdr *U 1102* 22.2.44–12.5.44 (*U 1102* was decommissioned at Königsberg 12.5.44 after a diving mishap, later removed to Kiel and recommissioned by Sell [1188] 15.4.44 as a training boat for the Anti-Submarine School)

Cdr *U 905* 27.6.44–20.3.45
Lost 12.3.45 SE of Faroes

SCHWARTZKOPFF, VOLKMAR
[1171]
b. 25.4.1914, Halle, Saale
Class 1934; Kplt 1.2.42
Div. Officer destroyer *Karl Galster* 3/39–3/40; U-boat trg 4/40–10/40; *Baubelehrung* 11/40–12/40; 1WO *U 109* 12/40–9/41
2nd U-Flotilla 10/41–11/41; U-Cdr's Course, 24th U-Flotilla 11/41–12/41; Liaison Officer at BdU 12/41–3/42; *Baubelehrung* 8.KLA 3/42–5/42
Cdr *U 520* 19.5.42–30.10.42
Lost 30.10.42 E of Newfoundland

SCHWARZ, HANS-JOACHIM [1172]
b. 28.9.1919, Hannover
Entry 1938; ObltzS 1.1.43, transferred from Ordnance to Seaman Branch 1.3.43
21st U-Flotilla 7/40–4/42, as 2/Admin. Officer 4/41–4/42; 2/Admin. Officer 8th U-Flotilla 4/42–3/43; courses and U-boat trg 3/43–2/44 (U-Cdr's Torpedo Course 61); *Baubelehrung* 3/44–6/44
Cdr *U 1105* 3.6.44–capitulation
Detained; freed 22.4.48

SCHWARZ, RUDOLF [1173]
b. 19.7.1914, Brunsbüttelkoog
Entry 1936; ObltzS (R) 1.10.43
WO 3rd Sperrbrecher Flotilla 3/41–3/43; U-boat trg 3/43–10/43; WO *U 741* 10/43–2/44; *Baubelehrung* 1.KLA 2/44–4/44
Cdr *U 1056* 29.4.44–12/44
18th U-Flotilla, 1/45–2/45; navigation instructor *K-Verband* 2/45–capitulation

SCHWARZENBERG, HANS-DIETRICH [1174]
b. 23.5.1923, Dresden

Class X/1940; ObltzS 1.10.44
U-boat trg completed 8/42; *Baubelehrung* 8.KLA 8/42–9/42; 2WO *U 711* 9/42–10/43; 1WO *U 711* 10/43–5/44; U-Cdr's Course, 3.ULD and 23rd U-Flotilla 5/44–8/44
Cdr *U 579* 9/44–5.5.45
Lost 5.5.45 Baltic Sea, Little Belt

SCHWARZKOPF, WOLFGANG [1175]
b. 10.1.1921, Berlin
Class XII/1939; ObltzS 1.12.43
WO sea trg *U 202* 1941; courses until 3/42; supplementary WO *U 605* 3/42–8/42; *Baubelehrung* 8/42–10/42; 1WO *U 340* 10/42–9/43; 6th U-Flotilla and U-Cdr's Course 9/43–12/43
Cdr *U 2* 13.12.43–8.4.44
Cdr *U 21* 12.5.44–5.8.44
Cdr *U 704* 6.8.44–18.12.44
Details not available 1/45–2/45; 3.ULD and Naval Reception (Refugees) Command, Husum 3/45–capitulation

SCHWASSMANN, HEINZ [1176]
b. 3.2.1916, Potsdam
Class 1935; Kplt 1.1.43
Div. Officer trg ship *Schlesien* 4/39–8/40; Comp. CO Naval Holding Div. 8/40–11/40; *Baubelehrung* battleship *Tirpitz* 11/40–2/41; ADC and Signals Officer battleship *Tirpitz* 2/41–7/42; U-boat trg 7/42–10/42; course 2.UAA and 24th U-Flotilla 10/42–12/42; 1WO *U 753* 12/42–3/43; U-Cdr's Torpedo Course and *Baubelehrung* 3/43–4/43
Cdr *U 742* 1.5.43–18.7.44
Lost 18.7.44 Norwegian Sea, W of Narvik

SCHWEBCKE, HANS-JOACHIM
[1177]
b. 22.3.1918, Lübeck
Class 1937a; Kplt 1.6.44

Group Officer Naval College Flensburg-Mürwik 5/41–7/41; Flag Lt C-in-C E-Boats 7/41–1/42; U-boat trg 1/42–6/42; WO 6th U-Flotilla 6/42–11/42; U-Cdr's Course, 24th U-Flotilla 11/42–1/43; *Baubelehrung* 1/43–2/43
Cdr *U 714* 10.2.43–14.3.45
Lost 14.3.45 North Sea, off Firth of Forth

SCHWEICHEL, HANS-ADOLF [1178]
b. 26.5.1915, Bremen
Class 1936; ObltzS 1.10.40
ADC and Signals Officer light cruiser *Leipzig* 2/39–2/40; Flag Lt on Staff C-in-C Naval Reconnaissance Forces 2/40–6/41; U-boat trg 7/41–12/41; 1WO *U 126* 12/41–8/42; U-Cdr's Course, 2.UAA and 24th U-Flotilla 8/42–9/42
Cdr *U 105* 1.10.42–29.10.42 (Schweichel is only indicated as Cdr *U 105* by the boat's WD notes; WASt provides an unnamed commander for the period 1.10.42–24.10.42. See Schuch [1139] and Nissen [884].)
Cdr *U 173* 30.10.42–16.11.42 (Initially Schweichel was listed to command *U 105*, which was under repair at Lorient. As *U 173* was also at Lorient and in urgent need of a commander, at short notice Schweichel received orders to take command of *U 173*, which he did on or after 29.10.42.)
Lost 16.11.42 off Casablanca

SCHWEIGER, FRIEDHELM [1179]
b. 7.3.1917, Ziegenhals, Silesia
Class 1937a; Kplt 1.6.44
No 2 Torpedo Officer heavy cruiser *Blücher* 1/40–4/40; Comp. Leader Naval Artillery Detachment 301 4/40–5/40; ADC to Staff, Naval Cdr Kristiansand 5/40–6/40; torpedo adviser, Staff, Naval Cdr Molde 6/40–1/42; U-boat trg 1/42–6/42; 1WO *U 125* 6/42–3/43; U-Cdr's Course, 2.UAA and 24th U-Flotilla 3/43–4/43 (U-Cdr's Torpedo Course 44); *Baubelehrung* 4/43–5/43
Cdr *U 313* 20.5.43–capitulation

SCHWIRLEY, ERNST-WERNER [1180]
b. 7.6.1919, Bischofsburg, East Prussia
Class XII/1939; ObltzS 1.12.43
2WO *U 413* 6/42–6/43; 1WO *U 413* 6/43–12/43; U-Cdr's Course 3.ULD and 24th U-Flotilla 12/43–2/44; U-Cdr sea trg *U 982* 2/44–4/44
Cdr *U 982* 12.4.44–15.7.44
Baubelehrung Type XXI 7.KLA 7/44–11/44
Cdr *U 3510* 11.11.44–5.5.45

SEEGER, JOACHIM [1181]
b. 11.2.1912, Gut Nebelin, Prignitz, Wittenberge
Entry X/1939; ObltzS (R) 1.7.43
WO *U 218* 12/42–8/43; courses 8/43–10/43; Cdr *UD 3* (Anti-Submarine School) 24.10.43–13.10.44; 24th U-Flotilla 10/44–1/45
Cdr *U 393* 14.1.45–4/45

SEEGER, SIGURD [1182]
b. 6.7.1920, Züllichau, Brandenburg
Class IX/1939; ObltzS 1.10.43
WO sea trg *U 560* 6/42–9/42; 1WO *U 382* 9/42–9/43; U-Cdr's Course, 23rd U-Flotilla 10/43–11/43; instructor trg group Higher Command of Torpedo Schools 11/43–7/44
Acting Cdr *U 348* 18.6.44–21.6.44 (transfer voyage Bergen–Trondheim)
Cdr *U 1203* 17.7.44–capitulation

SEEHAUSEN, GERHARD [1183]
b. 29.7.1917, Borstel, Nienburg
Class 1937; Kplt 1.6.44
WO battleship *Gneisenau* 8/39–10/40; U-boat trg 10/40–3/41; instructor Torpedo School Mürwik 3/41–2/42; *Baubelehrung* and trg in U-boat

handling 2/42–4/42; 1WO *U 518* 4/42–5/43; U-Cdr's Course 5/43–7/43 (U-Cdr's Torpedo Course 48)
Acting Cdr *U 68* 7/43–29.7.43 (see Lauzemis [709])
Cdr *U 66* 2.9.43–6.5.44
Lost 6.5.1944 W of Cape Verde Is

SEELIGER, EDGAR [1184]
b. 26.7.1920, Wedel, Holstein
Entry IV/1940; ObltzS (R) 1.3.44
U-boat trg 6/42–12/42; *Baubelehrung* 8.KLA 12/42–1/43; 2WO *U 956* 1/43–2/44; 1WO *U 956* 2/44–8/44; courses 9/44–10/44; *Baubelehrung* Type XXIII 7.KLA 11/44–1/45
Cdr *U 4702* 12.1.45–5.5.45
Detained; freed 7/45

SEIBICKE, GÜNTHER [1185]
b. 30.8.1911, Eggersdorf, Lebus, Brandenburg
Class 1932; KKpt 1.6.43
Cdr *M 4*, 1st Minesweeping Flotilla 11/38–3/41; U-boat trg 4/41–9/41
Cdr *U 436* 27.9.41–26.5.43
Lost 26.5.43 W of Cape Ortegal
Knight's Cross 27.3.43 (157th KM, 87th U-boat holder)

SEIDEL, HANS [1186]
b. 15.5.1918, Oberweischlitz, Vogtland
Class 1937a; Kplt 1.4.44
Comp. Officer 1/Basic Trg Est. Stralsund 9/39–11/39; trg ship *Schlesien* 11/39–8/40; Naval Holding Div. and Kriegsmarine Depot Boulogne 8/40–11/40; Kriegsmarine Depot Ostende 11/40; courses and U-boat trg 11/40–3/42; 1WO *U 203* 3/42–9/42 and acting Cdr *U 203* 11.9.42–20.9.42 (see Mützelburg [856]); U-Cdr's Course, 24th U-Flotilla 10/42–11/42; *Baubelehrung* 11/42–12/42

Cdr *U 361* 18.12.42–17.7.44
Lost 17.7.44 Norwegian Sea, W of Narvik

SEILER, WOLFGANG [1187]
b. 4.8.1918, place not recorded
Class X/1939; ObltzS 1.10.43
1WO *U 616* 4/42–9/43; courses 10/43–1/44
Cdr *U 37* 9.1.44–21.12.44
Later details not available

SELL, ERWIN [1188]
b. 3.5.1915, Wesselburen, Dithmarschen
Entry 1940; ObltzS (R) 1.3.44
VP-Cdr 12th VP-Boat Flotilla 9/41–6/42; U-boat trg and *Baubelehrung* 6/42–1/43; 2WO *U 960* 1/43–10/43; 1WO *U 960* 10/43–2/44; courses 3/44–6/44; WO *U 4* 6/44–7/44
Cdr *U 1102* 15.8.44–capitulation (see Schwarting [1170])

SELLE, HORST [1189]
b. 14.2.1921, Lengerich, Westphalia
Class XII/1939; ObltzS 1.12.43
WO sea trg *U 125* 1941–42; courses until 5/42; 3WO *U 255* 5/42–10/42; 2WO *U 255* 10/42–3/43; 1WO *U 255* 3/43–11/43; course 3.ULD 11/43–1/44; *Baubelehrung* 1.KLA 1/44–4/44
Cdr *U 795* 22.4.44–3.5.45

SENKEL, HANS [1190]
b. 14.1.1910, Schönbrunn/Thüringen
Class 1933; Kplt 1.3.40, posthumously KKpt seniority 1.11.42
Destroyer *Z 14 Friedrich Ihn* 10/38–3/41; U-boat trg 3/41–7/41; 24th U-Flotilla 7/41–9/41; U-Cdr sea trg *U 74* 9/41–10/41
Cdr *U 658* 5.11.41–30.10.42
Lost 30.10.42 E of Newfoundland

SICKEL, HERBERT [1191]
b. 30.6.1914, Lüderitz Bay, German South-West Africa
Class 1935; Kplt 1.12.42
Seconded to Luftwaffe 11/37–12/40; U-boat trg 1/41–6/41; 1WO *U 73* 6/41–4/42; U-Cdr's Course, 24th U-Flotilla 4/42–5/42; *Baubelehrung* 5/42–6/42
Cdr *U 302* 16.6.42–6.4.44
Lost 6.4.44 SW of Azores

SIEBOLD, KARL-HARTWIG [1192]
b. 19.3.1917, Düneberg, Duchy of Lauenburg
Class 1936; Kplt 1.10.43
WO U-boat depot ship *Wilhelm Bauer* 3/40–6/41; U-boat trg 6/41–11/41; 1WO *U 66* 11/41–10/42; U-Cdr's Course, 2.UAA and 24th U-Flotilla 10/42–11/42
Cdr *U 554* 14.11.42–2.7.44
Baubelehrung Type XXI 7.KLA 7/44–9/44
Cdr *U 3504* 23.9.44–2.5.45

SIEDER, HEINZ [1193]
b. 28.6.1920, Munich; Class 1938; ObltzS 1.4.42
Officer trg, trg ship *Schlesien* 7/39–10/39; courses Naval College Mürwik and Naval Gunnery School 10/39–4/40; battleship *Scharnhorst* 4/40–2/41; U-boat trg 2/41–9/41; 1WO 26th U-Flotilla 9/41–12/41; *Baubelehrung* 7.KLA 12/41–1/42; 1WO *U 440* 1/42–4/43; U-Cdr's Course, 24th U-Flotilla 4/43–5/43 (U-Cdr's Torpedo Course 46); *Baubelehrung* 8.KLA 5/43–6/43
Cdr *U 984* 17.6.43–20.8.44
Lost 20.8.44 W of Brest, longitude of Land's End
Knight's Cross 8.7.44 (236th KM, 112th U-boat holder)

SIEGMANN, PAUL [1194]
b. 24.5.1913, Hamburg
Class 1935; Kplt 1.8.42
1WO torpedo-boat *Greif* 11/40–3/41; U-boat trg 3/41–7/41; WO 7th U-Flotilla 7/41–11/41; U-Cdr's Course, 24th U-Flotilla 11/41–1/42; *Baubelehrung* 8.KLA 1/42–3/42
Cdr *U 612* 5.3.42 to 6.8.42 (sank on this date after collision with *U 444*) or 30.9.42 (per WASt)
Baubelehrung 1.KLA for *U 230* from 1.10.42 (P/F) or 10/42
Cdr *U 230* 24.10.42–11.8.44 (dates not certain)
Baubelehrung Type XXI 8.KLA 8/44–9/44
Cdr *U 2507* 8.9.44–5.5.45

SIEMON, HILMAR [1195]
b. 29.3.1915, Apenrade
Class 1934; Kplt 1.4.42
U-boat trg 10/40–3/41; 1WO *U 97* 3/41–8/41; U-Cdr's Course, 24th U-Flotilla 9/41–10/41
Cdr *U 334* 9.10.41–31.3.43
Kplt on Staff 13th U-Flotilla and Comp. CO Naval College Flensburg-Mürwik 6/43–3/45
Cdr *U 396* 3/45 or 13.3.45 (per *U 396* WD) to 23.4.45
Lost 23.4.45 Atlantic, SW of Shetlands

SIMMERMACHER, VOLKER [1196]
b. 1.2.1919, Strasbourg
Class 1937a; Kplt 1.4.44
WO battleship *Scharnhorst* 10/40–5/41; U-boat trg 5/41–11/41; WO *U 107* 11/41–6/43; U-Cdr's Torpedo Course 50 6/43–7/43
Cdr *U 107* 7/43–8/44
Baubelehrung Type XXI 6.KLA 9/44–11/44
Cdr *U 3013* 22.11.44–3.5.45

VON SINGULE, RUDOLF [1197]
b. 8.4.1883, Pola, Austria-Hungary
Entry (Navy of Austria-Hungary k.u.k.) 1901; KKpt (zV) 1.2.42
2nd Officer k.u.k. *U 4* from 1908; Cdr k.u.k. *U 4* 21.9.12–7.7.13; Cdr torpedo-boat until 4/15;

Cdr k.u.k. *U 4* 9.4.15–30.11.17; instructor U-Boat School (U-Cdr's Course) 1.12.17–Armistice

Accommodation Ship Officer (3rd U-Flotilla) 6/41–8/41, (5th U-Flotilla) 8/41–11/41, inc. Cdr *UD 4* 16.10.41–29.4.42; 5th U-Flotilla 4/42–6/42; seconded FdU Italy 6/42–8/43; released from Kriegsmarine 31.8.43

Murdered by communists at Brünn, 2.5.45

SITEK, WALTER [1198]

b. 5.1.1913, Rendsburg

Entry VIII/1939; ObltzS (R) 1.4.43

2WO *U 581* 7/41–2/42; interned Spain 2/42–5/42

Cdr *U 17* 1.6.42–22.2.43

U-Cdr's Course, 24th U-Flotilla 3/43–4/43 (U-Cdr's Torpedo Course 44); *Baubelehrung* 8.KLA 4/43–6/43

Cdr *U 981* 3.6.43–27.6.44

6th U-Flotilla 6/44–9/44

Cdr *U 3005* 20.9.44–10.1.45

Further service with Harbour Cdr Fredericia 2/45–capitulation

SLEVOGT, HORST [1199]

b. 4.7.1922, Eckernförde

Class XII/1939; ObltzS 1.12.43

U-boat trg completed 10/41; *Baubelehrung* KLA East 10/41–1/42; 2WO *U 218* 1/42–12/42; 1WO *U 218* 12/42–6/43; 2.UAA and U-Cdr's Course 6/43–7/43 (U-Cdr's Torpedo Course 50)

Cdr *U 62* 20.7.43–31.10.44

Courses and *Baubelehrung* Type XXI 6.KLA 11/44–2/45

Cdr *U 3032* 12.2.45–3.5.45

SOBE, ERNST [1200]

b. 2.9.1904, Zschorna, Bautzen

Class 1924; FKpt 1.10.42

U-boat trg and student at U-Boat School 12/35–4/36; U-Flotilla *Weddigen* and at FdU 5/36–8/36; *Baubelehrung* Germaniawerft Kiel 8/36–9/36

Cdr *U 34* 12.9.36–14.2.38

U-Flotilla *Saltzwedel* and at FdU 2/38–4/38; Staff Officer FdU 5/38–6/38; CO U-Flotilla *Wegener* 6/38–12/39 and 7th U-Flotilla 1/40; CO AGRU-Front 1/40–11/41, inc. CO 27th U-Flotilla 1.7.41–23.11.41; at BdU and Naval Gunnery School Kiel 11/41–2/42; *Baubelehrung* 1.KLA U-Boats North Bremen 2/42–3/42

Cdr *U 179* 7.3.42–8.10.42

Lost 8.10.42 off Cape Town

VON SODEN-FRAUNHOFEN, GRAF ULRICH [1201]

b. 2.8.1913, Friedrichshafen

Class 1936; Kplt 1.1.43

ADC and WO 16th Minesweeping Flotilla 9/39–7/40; Group Leader and M/S-Cdr 40th Minesweeping Flotilla 7/40–11/40; M/S-Cdr 12th Minesweeping Flotilla 11/40–3/41; U-boat trg 4/41–10/41; 1WO *U 552* 10/41–3/42; U-Cdr's Course, 2.UAA and 24th U-Flotilla 3/42–5/42

Cdr *U 624* 28.5.42–7.2.43

Lost 7.2.43 central North Atlantic

SOHLER, HERBERT [1202]

b. 25.7.1908, Attendorn, Westphalia

Class 1928; KKpt 1.7.42

U-boat trg U-Boat School 5/37–4/38 inc. Trg Branch 3rd Destroyer Div. 17.8.37–4.1.38 and Midshipmen's Group Officer Naval Gunnery School 5.1.38–3.4.38; Cdr *U 10* 4.4.38–31.7.38; U-Flotilla *Wegener*, *Baubelehrung* 1.8.38–1.11.38; attached U-Flotilla *Saltzwedel* 21.8.38–2/9/39

Cdr *U 46* 2.11.38–21.5.40

Acting CO 7th U-Flotilla 5/40–7/40; BdU/Opns and acting CO 7th U-Flotilla 7/40–9/40; CO 7th U-Flotilla 9/40–2/44

Cdr Section 2/Naval College Flensburg-Mürwik 2/44–capitulation

SOMMER, HELMUT [1203]
b. 24.8.1914, Breslau
Class 1935; Kplt 1.8.42
Torpedo Officer destroyer *Z 2 Georg Thiele* 3/40–4/40; land fighting Narvik 4/40–7/40; WO destroyer *Z 15 Erich Steinbrinck* 7/40–3/41; U-boat trg, courses and U-Cdr's Course 4/41–6/42
Cdr *U 139* 1.7.42–30.9.42
Cdr *U 78* 11/42–16.5.43
Baubelehrung 6.KLA 5/43–6/43
Cdr *U 853* 25.6.43–9.7.44
10th U-Flotilla and 1.UAA 7/44–2/45; adviser 6.KLA 2/45–4/45; adviser Naval Trg Inspectorate, Induction Centre for Officer Applicants Stralsund 4/45–capitulation

SONS, FRIEDRICH-WILHELM [1204]
b. 14.8.1910, Wienmoos, Flensburg
Entry 1/1940; ObltzS (R) 1.7.43
M/S-Cdr 38th Minesweeping Flotilla 4/41–1/42, 46th Minesweeping Flotilla 1/42–2/43; U-boat trg 2/43–7/43; course 27th and 24th U-Flotillas 7/43–9/43 (U-Cdr's Torpedo Course 53); *Baubelehrung* 9/43–10/43
Cdr *U 479* 27.10.43–12.12.44
Lost 12.12.44 Gulf of Finland

SPAHR, WILHELM [1205]
b. 4.4.1904, Esingen, Schleswig
Enlisted 1921; Kplt 1.1.43
ObStrm *U 47* 12/38–2/40; instructor 1.ULD, Torpedo and Signals Schools, various duties and courses 2/40–12/41; *Baubelehrung* 1/42–2/42; 1WO *U 178* 2/42–11/43
Cdr *U 178* 25.11.43–25.8.44
Course 23rd U-Flotilla 9/44–10/44; 4/Naval Reserve Div. 10/44–2/45; Trg Leader 1.ULD 2/45–3/45; Trg Officer 19th U-Flotilla 3/45–capitulation

SPEIDEL, HANS HARALD [1206]
b. 20.5.1917, Danzig
Class 1936; Kplt 1.6.43
Seconded Luftwaffe; U-boat trg completed 12/41; 1WO *U 81* 1/42–7/42; U-Cdr's Course and *Baubelehrung* 8.KLA 8/42–10/42
Cdr *U 643* 8.10.42–8.10.43
POW 8.10.43

SPINDLEGGER, JOHANN [1207]
b. 31.7.1915, Aachen
Class 1935; Kplt 1.11.42
1WO *U 561* 3/41–12/41; course 26th U-Flotilla 12/41–2/42; course 2.UAA and *Baubelehrung* 8.KLA 2/42–4/42
Cdr *U 616* 2.4.42–7.10.42 (see Koitschka [647])
Cdr *U 411* 20.10.42–13.11.42
Lost 13.11.42 W of Gibraltar

SPORN, WOLFGANG [1208]
b. 12.9.1912, place not recorded
Class 1934; Kplt 1.3.42
Comp. Co and Head of Minelaying Operations, Coastal Defence Danzig 9/39–10/39; ADC and Comp. CO 9/Reserve Naval Artillery Div. 10/39–1/40; M/S-Cdr 4th Minesweeping Flotilla 1/40–8/40; A3a Staff Group West 8/40–3/41; U-boat trg and WO sea trg *U 569* 3/41–11/41; *Baubelehrung* 7.KLA 11/41–12/41
Cdr *U 439* 20.12.41–17.2.43
Staff Commanding Adm. U-boats 2/43–4/43; course leader and Comp. CO Mine Warfare School 4/43–capitulation
Detained; freed 15.8.45

STAATS, GEORG [1209]
b. 13.3.1916, Bremen

Class 1935; Kplt 1.4.42

Flak Officer battleship *Gneisenau* 11/38–4/39; U-boat trg 4/39–8/39; WO *U 5* 8/39–10/39; adviser to Staff BdU 10/39–1/40; 1WO *U A* 1/40–11/40; 7th U-Flotilla 11/40–1/41; U-Cdr's Course, 24th U-Flotilla 1/41–2/41; acting Cdr U-boat tender *Isar* 2/41–3/41; *Baubelehrung* U-Boats North 3/41–4/41

Cdr *U 80* 8.4.41–5.10.41

Baubelehrung 8.KLA 10/41

Cdr *U 508* 20.10.41–12.11.43

Lost 12.11.43 N of Cape Ortegal

Knight's Cross 14.7.43 (179th KM, 96th U-boat holder)

STÄHLER, HELLMUT [1210]

b. 8.9.1916, Horchheim, Worms

Class 1937a, Kplt 1.8.44

Seconded to Luftwaffe 9/39–1/43; Comp. Officer Naval College Flensburg-Mürwik 1/43–7/43; U-boat trg 7/43–12/43; courses 12/43–5/44; *Baubelehrung* 5.KLA 5/44–7/44

Cdr *U 928* 11.7.44–capitulation

STAHL, PETER-ARTHUR [1211]

b. 1.8.1913, Neuendeich, Holstein

Entry 1938; ObltzS (R) 1.4.43

U-boat trg 1/41–5/41; *Baubelehrung* 5/41–6/41; 2WO *U 575* 6/41–8/42; U-Cdr's Course, 24th U-Flotilla 9/42–10/42; *Baubelehrung* 8.KLA 10/42–11/42

Cdr *U 648* 12.11.42–23.11.43

Lost 23.11.43 NE of the Azores

STARK, GÜNTHER [1212]

b. 1.12.1917, Preussisch-Holland

Class 1936; Kplt 1.10.43

WO U-boat depot ship *Saar* 5/40–6/41; U-boat trg 7/41–12/41; 1st U-Flotilla 12/41–4/42; WO 1st U-Flotilla 4/42–1/43; U-Cdr's Course, 2.UAA and 26th U-Flotilla 1/43–2/43; *Baubelehrung* 7.KLA 2/43–3/43

Cdr *U 740* 27.3.43–9.6.44

Lost 9.6.44 SW of Scilly Is

STAUDINGER, OSKAR [1213]

b. 13.5.1917, Löbau, Saxony

Class 1936; Kplt 1.4.43

Seconded to Luftwaffe 10/38–8/41; U-boat trg 8/41–12/41; WO 1st U-Flotilla and course 24th U-Flotilla 12/41–8/42; *Baubelehrung* 8.KLA 8/42–9/42

Cdr *U 638* 3.9.42 to 8.12.42 (per WASt) or 10.12.42 (relieved by Bernbeck [77], per *U 638* WD)

Adviser Torpedo Experimental Branch Eckernförde 12/42–3/43

Cdr *U 638* 17.3.43 (per WASt, but this cannot be correct as Bernbeck commanded *U 638* at sea 4.2.43–31.3.43) or 1.4.43 to 5.5.43

Lost 5.5.43 NE of Newfoundland

STEEN, HANS [1214]

b. 28.9.1907, Kiel

Rating entry 1925; Kplt 1.3.44

ObBtsm battleship *Gneisenau* 4/38–2/40; instructor Naval College Flensburg-Mürwik 2/40–8/40; WO 11th Minesweeping Flotilla 8/40–1/41; U-boat trg 1/41–10/41; 1WO *U 117* 10/41–2/43; Torpedo School Mürwik and course 24th U-Flotilla 3/43–5/43 (U-Cdr's Torpedo Course 47); *Baubelehrung* 1.KLA 6/43–9/43

Cdr *U 233* 22.9.43–5.7.44

Lost 5.7.44 E of Halifax, Nova Scotia

STEFFEN, KARL [1215]

b. 16.10.1909, Stepenitz, Prignitz (Pritzwalk)

Entry VII/1940; ObltzS (R)

VP-Cdr Minefield Flotilla Western Baltic 5/41–8/43; U-boat trg 9/43–2/44; courses 19th U-

Flotilla, 3.ULD and 23rd U-Flotilla 2/44–7/44; WO sea trg *U 1132* 7/44–10/44; *Baubelehrung* 8.KLA 10/44–11/44
Cdr *U 2345* 15.11.44–capitulation

STEFFENS, KLAUS-DIETRICH [1216]

b. 17.6.1918, Danzig-Langfuhr
Class 1937a; ObltzS 1.9.41, posthumously Kplt seniority 1.8.44
Seconded to Luftwaffe 9/39–3/42; U-boat trg 3/42–10/42; WO *U 373* 10/42–4/43; U-Cdr's Course, 24th U-Flotilla 4/43–6/43 (KSL 47); *Baubelehrung* 8.KLA 6/43–7/43
Cdr *U 719* 27.7.43–26.6.44
Lost 26.6.44 W of Northern Ireland

STEGE, FRIEDRICH [1217]

b. 13.11.1920, Vehlen, Bückeburg
Class X/1939; ObltzS 1.10.43
U-boat trg completed 2/42; *Baubelehrung* for *U 212* 2/42–4/42; 1WO *U 212* 4/42–8/43; U-Cdr's Torpedo Course, 23rd U-Flotilla 9/43
Cdr *U 291* 1.10.43–16.7.44 (per P/F; see Keerl [587] and Isermeyer [534])
Cdr *U 397* 17.7.44–25.4.45
Cdr *U 958* 26.4.45–3.5.45
Detained; freed 9.9.45

STEGEMANN, HASSO [1218]

b. 30.7.1920, Kiel
Class IX/1939; ObltzS 1.10.43
U-boat trg from 10/41; 2WO *U 106* until 8/43; 27th U-Flotilla 8/43–11/43; *Baubelehrung* 11/43–12/43; 1WO *U 1227* 12/43; U-Cdr's Course, 3.ULD and 23rd U-Flotilla 12/43–2/44
Cdr *U 367* 3/44–15.3.45
Lost 15.3.45 Baltic Sea, off Hela

STEGMANN, JOHANN [1219]

b. 5.3.1912, Arnstadt, Thüringen
Entry 1935; ObltzS (R) 1.12.42 seniority 1.10.42
VP-Cdr Coastal Defence Group Bergen, Harbour Defence Flotilla Bergen and Coastal Defence Group Norwegian West Coast 5/40–7/43; U-boat trg 7/43–1/44; WO 23rd U-Flotilla 1/44–3/44; course 23rd U-Flotilla 3/44–5/44; *Baubelehrung* 6.KLA 5/44–8/44
Cdr *U 779* 24.8.44–capitulation

STEIN, HEINZ [1220]

b. 21.8.1913, Magdeburg
Entry I/1937; Kplt 1.2.43
2WO *U 24* 12/39–5/40; 1WO *U 8* 5/40–6/40, inc. acting Cdr *U 8* 5.6.40–9.6.40; 1WO *U 139* 7/40–10/40; 2WO *U 98* 10/40–4/41; WO sea trg *U 554* 4/41–6/41
Cdr *U 554* 26.6.41–3/42
Baubelehrung 8.KLA 3/42–4/42
Cdr *U 620* 30.4.42–13.2.43
Lost 13.2.43 NW of Lisbon

VON STEINAECKER, FREIHERR WALTER [1221]

b. 25.3.1917, Berlin
Class 1935; Kplt 1.4.42
Gunnery Technical Officer light cruiser *Leipzig* 9/39–2/40; WO, Divisional and Gunnery Officer destroyer Z 7 *Hermann Schoemann* 2/40–10/40; U-boat trg 10/40–3/41; *Baubelehrung* 3/41–5/41; 1WO *U 502* 5/41–4/42; U-Cdr's Course, 24th U-Flotilla 4/42–6/42; *Baubelehrung* 8.KLA,6/42–7/42
Cdr *U 524* 8.7.42–22.3.43
Lost 22.3.43 S of Madeira

STEINBRINK, ERICH [1222]

b. 13.3.1919, Ziegenort, Stettiner Haff
Class 1938; ObltzS 1.4.43

U-boat trg 3/43–9/43; course 2.UAA and 3.ULD 9/43–12/43 (U-Cdr's Torpedo Course 59); *Baubelehrung* 7.KLA 12/43–2/44

Cdr *U 1203* 10.2.44–16.7.44 (per *U 1203* WD)

Trg Officer 1.UAA 7/44–10/44; U-Cdr sea trg *U 296* 11/44–12/44

Acting Cdr *U 293* 12/44–3/45

Cdr *U 953* 4/45–capitulation

STEINERT, HERMANN [1223]

b. 10.12.1916, Traunstein

Class 1936; Kplt 1.5.43

Div. and No 2 Radio Officer light cruiser *Emden* 12/38–8/40; First Officer and Radio Officer minelayer *Schwerin* 8/40–11/40; Comp. Officer Destroyer Crews' Holding Div. 11/40–2/41; WO and Torpedo Officer destroyer *Z 27* 2/41–12/41; U-boat trg 12/41–5/42; courses 2.UAA and 26th U-Flotilla 5/42–9/42; 1WO and U-Cdr sea trg *U 155* 9/42–1/43

Cdr *U 128* 1.3.43–17.5.43

POW 17.5.43

STEINFELDT, FREIDRICH [1224]

b. 15.12.1914, Bad Doberan

Entry IV/1940; ObltzS (R) 1.3.44 seniority 1.10.43

M/S-Cdr 38th Minesweeping Flotilla 12/41–6/42; U-boat trg 6/42–11/42; 2WO *U 371* 11/42–2/43; WO *U 195* 2/43–8/43; U-Cdr's Course, 2.UAA and 23rd U-Flotilla 8/43–10/43

Cdr *UIT 21* 14.10.43–15.4.44. (*UIT 21*, ex-Italian *Guiseppe Finzi*, was seized by the German Navy at Bordeaux on 9.9.43 and decommissioned for conversion to a transport U-boat. Steinfeldt was marked down to command the vessel from 14.10.43—per WASt—but as a result of dockyard delays he took over *U 195* instead. Eventually *UIT 21* was scuttled at Bordeaux on 25.8.44 without having been commissioned.)

Cdr *U 195* 16.4.44–capitulation

STEINHAUS, ROLF [1225]

b. 1.4.1916, Hachenburg, Kaiserslautern

Class 1936; Kplt 1.6.43

14/Basic Trg Est. Stralsund 4/39–2/40; *Baubelehrung* 2/40–3/40; 2WO *U 101* 3/40–4/41; 24th U-Flotilla 4/41–5/41

Cdr *U 8* 23.5.41–31.7.41

Instructor 2.ULD 8/41–3/43; *Baubelehrung* 6.KLA 3/43–6/43

Cdr *U 802* 12.6.43–12.12.43

Adviser Trg Division, Staff of Commanding Adm. U-Boats 12/43–capitulation

STEINHOFF, FREIDRICH [1226]

b. 14.7.1909, Küllstadt, Thüringen

Class 1935; Kplt 1.12.41

M/S-Cdr 4th Minesweeping Flotilla 12/39–5/40; VP-Cdr Coastal Defence Group Bergen 5/40–3/41; U-boat trg 3/41–7/41; WO sea trg *U 96* 7/41–10/41; U-Cdr's Course, 26th U-Flotilla 10/41–11/41; *Baubelehrung* 8.KLA 11/41–12/41

Cdr *U 511* 8.12.41–17.12.42

Kplt on Staff 7th U-Flotilla 2/43–1/44; *Baubelehrung* 6.KLA 1/44–2/44

Cdr *U 873* 1.3.44–capitulation

Committed suicide in cell at Boston Jail as a result of alleged mistreatment 20.5.45

STEINMETZ, KARL-HEINZ [1227]

b. 19.2.1921, Kassel

Class XII/1939; ObltzS 1.12.43

WO 13th and 27th Minesweeping Flotillas 12/41–8/43; U-boat trg 8/43–2/44; WO 23rd U-Flotilla 2/44–4/44; 1WO *U 993* (3rd U-Flotilla) 2/44–8/44

Acting Cdr *U 993* 8/44–4.10.44 (boat evacuated Brest 17.8.44, arrived Bergen 18.9.44)

U-Cdr's Course, 3.ULD and 24th U-Flotilla 11/44–1/45 (U-Cdr's Torpedo Course 79); supplementary Cdr *U 714* 1/45–3/45

Lost 14.3.45 North Sea, off Firth of Forth

STELLMACHER, DIETRICH [1228]
b. 7.3.1915 Metz, Lorraine (when German province)
Entry IV/1939; ObltzS (R) 1.9.43 seniority 1.8.43
R-Cdr 2nd R-Boat Flotilla 12/40–1/43; U-boat trg 1/43–7/43; U-Cdr's Course, 27th and 24th U-Flotillas 7/43–9/43 (U-Cdr's Torpedo Course 53); *Baubelehrung* 6.KLA 9/43–10/43
Cdr *U 865* 25.10.43–9/44
Missing after putting to sea from Trondheim 8.9.44 (Translator's note: U-Boat List 1956 states sunk all hands 19.9.44 in 62°20'N 02°30'E NW of Bergen by Liberator 'S' of No 206 Squadron RAF.)

STELLMANN, ERNST-AUGUST [1229]
b. 19.4.1915, Düsseldorf
Entry 1935/39; ObltzS (R) 1.9.43
WO 19th Minesweeping Flotilla 6/41–7/42; U-boat trg and *Baubelehrung* 8.KLA 7/42–1/43; WO *U 956* 1/43–3/44; U-Cdr's Course, 3.ULD and 23rd U-Flotilla 4/44–6/44; various duties and *Baubelehrung* Type XXI 8.KLA 6/44–3/45
Cdr *U 2541* 1.3.45–8.4.45 (per WASt)
Cdr *R 226* (14th R-Boat Flotilla) 4/45–capitulation

STEPHAN, KARL-HEINZ [1230]
b. 18.9.1915, Posen
Entry 1936; Kplt (R) 1.4.43
Garrison Officer Naval Flak Detachment 262 9/39–7/40; Platoon and Comp. Leader 2/Reserve Naval Div. and Naval Artillery Detachment 201 7/40–3/41; Comp. CO Naval Flak Detachment 808 3/41–3/43; retrg as Seaman Branch officer and navigation course 34th Minesweeping Flotilla 3/43–8/43; U-boat trg 8/43–2/44; U-Cdr's Course, 23rd U-Flotilla 2/44–5/44; *Baubelehrung* 1.KLA 5/44–7/44
Cdr *U 1063* 8.7.44–15.4.45
Lost 15.4.45 English Channel, W of Land's End

STERNBERG, HEINZ [1231]
b. 16.2.1917, Freiburg, Breisgau
Class 1936; Kplt 1.2.43
ADC, Div./Platoon/Signals/Officer and Cdr control tower battleship *Gneisenau* 4/39–4/42; U-boat trg 4/42–11/42; 1WO *U 659* 11/42–3/43; U-Cdr's Course, 24th U-Flotilla 4/43–5/43 (U-Cdr's Torpedo Course 45); *Baubelehrung* 8.KLA 5/43–6/43
Cdr *U 473* 16.6.43–6.5.44
Lost 6.5.44 SW of Iceland

STEVER, EHRENREICH-PETER [1232]
b. 4.10.1918, Wilhelmshaven
Class 1937b; Kplt 1.1.45
WO and acting M/S-Cdr 15th, 7th, 6th and 21st Minesweeping Flotillas 5/40–10/42; M/S-Cdr 7th Minesweeping Flotilla 10/42–6/43; U-boat trg 6/43–11/43; courses 3.ULD and 23rd U-Flotilla 11/43–2/44; *Baubelehrung* 6.KLA 2/44–5/44
Cdr *U 1277* 3.5.44–capitulation

STHAMER, HANS-JÜRGEN [1233]
b. 26.7.1919, Lübeck
Class 1937b; ObltzS 1.4.42
OFzS heavy cruiser *Admiral Hipper* 12/39–3/40; trg at Aircraft Weapons School (Sea) Bug/Rügen 3/30–9/40;
Fliegerergänzungsgruppe (See) (= Aircrew Reserve Group) Kamp 10/40–11/40; II./KG 30 11/40–2/42; U-boat trg 3/42–9/42; 1WO *U 593* 9/42–1/43; 1WO *U 604* 1/43–6/43; 9th U-Flotilla 6/43–7/43; 1WO *U 91* 7/43–12/43; U-Cdr's Course, 3.ULD and 23rd U-Flotilla 12/43–2/44
Cdr *U 354* 20.2.44 (per P/F) or 22.2.44 (relieved Herbschleb [463], per *U 354* WD) to 24.8.44
Lost 24.8.44 Barents Sea, NW of North Cape

STIEBLER, WOLF-HARRO [1234]
b. 4.8.1907, Hann, Münden
Class 1932; KKpt 1.6.43
U-boat trg 4/39–9/39
Cdr *U 8* 6.9.39–13.10.39
Acting Cdr *U 17* 18.10.39–5.1.40
Cdr *U 21* 6.1.40–28.7.40
Cdr *U 61* 28.7.40–5.11.40 (see Oesten [893])
Torpedo Testing Branch 11/40–4/42
Cdr *U 461* (Type XIV U-tanker) 22.4.42–30.7.43
POW 30.7.43–30.10.47

VAN STIPRIAAN, JOHANNES [1235]
b. 9.12.1913, Norden, Ostfriesland
Entry IV/1940; ObltzS (R) 1.3.44
WO *U 539* 2/43–4/44; U-Cdr's Course, 3.ULD and 24th U-Flotilla 4/44–6/44 (U-Cdr's Torpedo Course 71); details not available 7/44–9/44
Cdr *U 237* 9/44–10/44; details not available 11/44–12/44
Baubelehrung Cdr 6.KLA for *U 3046* (never commissioned) 5.1.45–capitulation

STOCK, HANS [1236]
b. 2.8.1915, Lahr, Baden
Class 1935; Kplt 1.7.42, posthumously KKpt seniority 1.5.43
Seconded to Luftwaffe 11/37–1/41, inc. *Küstenfliegergruppe 606*; U-boat trg 1/41–6/41; 1WO *U 96* 6/41–10/41; U-Cdr's Course, 26th U-Flotilla 10/41–11/41; *Baubelehrung* 11/41–12/41
Cdr *U 659* 9.12.41–4.5.43
Lost 4.5.43 W of Cape Ortegal

STOCK, RUPPRECHT [1237]
b. 16.2.1916, Frankfurt/Main
Class 1937a; Kplt 1.6.44
Seconded to Luftwaffe 9/39–2/42; U-boat trg 2/42–8/42; 1WO *U 214* 8/42–5/43; acting Cdr *U 214* 7.5.43–10.5.43 (*U 214* Cdr Reeder [980] was wounded when boat was attacked by aircraft in Bay of Biscay on 7.5.43; on 10.5.43 Stock brought the boat into Brest, where Reeder was admitted to military hospital on arrival, Stock being given command next day. Per *U 214* WD.)
Cdr *U 214* 11.5.43–7/43
U-Cdr's Course, 24th U-Flotilla 7/43–28.7.43
Cdr *U 214* 29.7.43 (per *U 214* WD) to 7/44
Cdr *U 218* 8/44 (but before 10.8.44 since he sailed that day from Brest for Norway) to capitulation

VON STOCKHAUSEN, HANS-GERRIT [1238]
b. 11.8.1907, Kassel
Class 1926; KKpt 1.11.40
Student Anti-Submarine School Kiel 7/35–10/35; U-Flotilla *Weddigen* 10/35–11/35; Cdr *U 13* 30.11.35–30.9.37; courses 10/37–1/38; Adm. Staff Officer FdU 2/38–10/38; 2/Adm. Staff Officer FdU 10/38–8/39, inc. 2/Adm. Staff Officer, Staff FdU/SKL and FdU East 8/39; 4/Adm. Staff Officer, Staff FdU/BdU 9/39–11/39; *Baubelehrung* U-Boats North Sea 12/39–2/40
Cdr *U 65* 15.2.40–24.3.41
BdU/Organisational 3/41–4/41; CO 26th U-Flotilla 4/41–1/43
Killed 15.1.43 road traffic accident, Berlin
Knight's Cross 14.1.41 (53rd KM, 23rd U-boat holder)

STOEFFLER, OTTO [1239]
b. 12.3.1910, Düsseldorf
Entry X/1939; Kplt 1.11.43
U-boat trg 9/41–3/42; 1WO 10th U-Flotilla 3/42–10/42; U-Cdr sea trg *U 459* 12th U-Flotilla 11/42–3/43; U-Cdr's Course, 24th U-Flotilla

3/43–5/43 (U-Cdr's Torpedo Courses 44 and 46); *Baubelehrung* 1.KLA 5.43–7/43
Cdr *U 475* 7.7.43–3.5.45

STOELKER, GERHARD [1240]

b. 26.5.1910, Neenhusen, Ostfriesland
Rating entry XI/1939; ObltzS (R) 1.6.43
Strm and VP-Cdr Harbour Defence Flotillas (1) Channel Coast and (2) Brest 8/40–10/42; M/S-Cdr 46th Minesweeping Flotilla 10/42–6/43; U-boat trg 6/43–1/44; U-Cdr's Course. 24th U-Flotilla 1/44–3/44 (U-Cdr's Torpedo Course 64); *Baubelehrung* 7.KLA 3/44–5/44
Cdr *U 825* 4.5.44–capitulation

STOLZENBURG, GOTTFRIED [1241]

b. 8.12.1912, Uschütz
Entry 1/1938; ObltzS (R) 1.6.43
2WO *U 505* 1/42–1/43; U-Cdr's Course 2/43–3/43
Cdr *U 11* 23.3.43–13.7.44
Cdr *U 554* 7/44–18.11.44
Baubelehrung Type XXI 8.KLA 12/44–3/34
Cdr *U 2543* 7.3.45–3.5.45

STRÄTER, WOLFGANG [1242]

b. 21.5.1916, Cologne
Class 1935; Kplt 1.7.42
U-boat trg 1/41–4/41
Cdr *U 20* 20.5.41–4.12.41
2/Adm. Staff Officer/Adm. U-Boats and *Baubelehrung* 8.KLA 1/42–3/42
Cdr *U 614* 19.3.42–29.7.43
Lost 27.9.43 NW of Cape Finisterre

STRAUB, SIEGFRIED [1243]

b. 22.6.1918, Braunsberg
Class IX/1939; ObltzS 1.10.43
Seconded to Luftwaffe 12/40–4/41; U-boat trg 4/41–9/41; WO U-boat depot ship *Vega* 9/41–4/42; *Baubelehrung* 8.KLA 4/42–6/42; 1WO *U 625* 6/42–8/43; U-Cdr's Course, 2.UAA and 24th U-Flotilla 8/43–11/43 (U-Cdr's Torpedo Course 57); Leader torpedo attack trg Torpedo School Mürwik 11/43–1/44
Cdr *U 625* 26.1.44–10.3.44
Lost 10.3.44 W of Ireland

STRAUCH, GÜNTER [1244]

b. 5.12.1908, Elze-Gronau
Class 1934; Kplt 1.4.41
WO heavy cruiser *Admiral Hipper* 5/39–11/41; WO heavy cruiser *Lützow* 11/41–10/43; U-boat trg, courses and *Baubelehrung* 10/43–7/44
Cdr *U 1010* 17.7.44–capitulation

STREHL, HUGO [1245]

b. 5.10.1921, Munich
Class XII/1939; ObltzS 1.12.43
WO 5th Minesweeping Flotilla 6/41–9/43; U-boat trg 9/43–1/44; WO 23rd U-Flotilla 1/44–3/44; U-Cdr's Course, 3.ULD and 23rd U-Flotilla 4/44–6/44; Comp. Officer U-boat base Flensburg, also detailed to assemble a crew and work-up *U 2539* at Hamburg-Finkenwerder 6/44–11/44; U-Cdr sea trg *U 3507* 12/44–3/45
Cdr *U 351* 20.3.45–5.5.45

STRELOW, SIEGFRIED [1246]

b. 15.4.1911, Kiel
Class 1931; KKpt 1.7.43
Cdr *G 11*, Torpedo-Boat Trg Flotilla 10/38–12/39; Cdr torpedo-boat *Albatros* 12/39–4/40; Cdr minelayer *Brummer* 5/40; Cdr torpedo-boat *Löwe* 6/40–11/40; Wargames/Torpedo Officer light cruiser *Leipzig* 11/40–3/41; U-boat trg 4/41–5/41; U-Cdr's Torpedo Course, 24th U-Flotilla 5/41–7/41; *Baubelehrung* 7.KLA 7/41–8/41
Cdr *U 435* 30.8.41–9.7.43
Lost 9.7.43 W of Figueira da Foz, Portugal

Knight's Cross 27.10.42 (131st KM, 67th U-boat holder)

STRENGER, HARTMUT [1247]
b. 12.1.1917, Steinau, Oder
Class 1936; Kplt 1.8.43
Seconded to Luftwaffe 9/39–3/42; U-boat trg 4/42–9/42, inc. WO sea trg *U 593* 7/42–8/42; WO 7th U-Flotilla 9/42–4/43; U-Cdr's Torpedo Course 47 5/43–6/43; *Baubelehrung* 6.KLA 6/43–7/43
Cdr *U 290* 24.7.43–26.12.43
Comp. CO 2.ULD 1/44–1/45
Comp. CO 2.UAA 2/45–capitulation
Detained; freed 8/45

STRENGER, WOLFGANG [1248]
b. 9.2.1919, Steinau, Oder
Class X/1937; ObltzS 1.4.42
Seconded to Luftwaffe until 8/41; Naval High Command East 8/41–10/41; Destroyer and Torpedo-Boat Crews' Holding Div. 10/41–3/42; U-boat trg 3/42–9/42; 1WO *U 553* 9/42–12/42; U-Cdr's Course 1/43–2/43
Cdr *U 10* 2/43–2/44
Senior Officer R-boat fleet, 21st U-Flotilla 2/44–5/44; *Baubelehrung* 5/44–6/44
Cdr *U 1023* 15.6.44–9.3.45
5th U-Flotilla 3/45–capitulation

STRIEGLER, WERNER [1249]
b. 30.6.1918, Zittau, Saxony
Class 1937b; Kplt 1.1.45
U-boat trg 10/40–4/41; Staff Officer BdU/Opns 4/41–8/42; courses and trg 8/42–12/42; 1WO *U 511* 12/42–12/43
Cdr *UIT 25* 6.12.43–13.2.44
Cdr *UIT 23* 14.2.44–15.2.44 (Striegler had set out from Singapore for Penang and at 0850 on 15.2.44 was approaching his destination port from the south when *UIT 23* was torpedoed and sunk by HM submarine *Tally-Ho*. The pair of two-seater Arado 196 floatplanes based at Penang saved 15 crewmen, including Striegler.)
Cdr *UIT 25* 16.2.44 to 31.8.44 or 9/44 (U-Boat Archive per Schrein [1123])
Cdr *U 196* 22.9.44 or 1.10.44 (per P/F Kentrat [597] and WASt; *U 196* had been laid up under repair for about three months in the shipyard at Batavia, Jakarta) to 1.12.44
Missing 1.12.44 Sunda Strait, Indian Ocean, after setting out for Germany

STRÜBING, WERNER [1250]
b. 25.5.1907, Glückstadt
Entry 1/1942; ObltzS (R) 28.8.44
U-boat trg 3/43–8/43; U-Cdr's Course, 24th U-Flotilla 8/43–9/43 (U-Cdr's Torpedo Course 54); WO sea trg *UD 4* 9/43–10/43; *Baubelehrung* 8.KLA 10/43–12/43
Cdr *U 1003* 9.12.43–23.3.45
Lost 23.3.45 North Channel

STRUCKMEIER, ROLF [1251]
b. 27.7.1916, Obernkirchen, Schaumburg
Class 1935; Kplt 1.11.42
Rangefinder Officer heavy cruiser *Admiral Hipper* 9/39–4/40; 1st Torpedo-Boat Flotilla 5/40–10/40; U-boat trg 10/40–3/41; *Baubelehrung*, U-boats Group East, Germaniawerft Kiel 3/41–5/41; 1WO *U 205* 5/41–12/41; U-Cdr's Course, 24th U-Flotilla 11/41–12/41; *Baubelehrung* 8.KLA 12/41–2/42
Cdr *U 608* 5.2.42 to 3.1.44 (per WASt) or 12.1.44 (per *U 608* WD, and see Reisener [991])
Trg Officer (20th U-Flotilla) 1/44–10/44, (27th and 26th U-Flotillas) 10/44–capitulation

STUCKMANN, HERMANN [1252]
b. 2.1.1921, Wuppertal-Barmen
Class 1939; ObltzS 1.10.43

Officer trg 7/Basic Trg Est. Stralsund 9/39–11/39; trg ship *Schleswig-Holstein* 11/39–4/40; course Naval College Flensburg-Mürwik 5/40–8/40; seconded to Garrison Committee Neustadt 8/40–9/40; light artillery lighter *Memelland* 9/40–11/40; Radio Technical Officer course C, Signals School Mürwik 11/40–1/41; aboard U-boat tender *Saar*, 25th U-Flotilla 2/41–4/41; U-boat trg 4/41–12/41; 3WO *U 571* 12/41–3/42; 2WO *U 571* 3/42–10/42; 1WO *U 571* 10/42–5/43; U-Cdr's Course, 2.UAA and 24th U-Flotilla 5/43–6/43 (U-Cdr's Torpedo Course 48); *Baubelehrung* 3.KLA 6/43–8/43

Cdr *U 316* 5.8.43–4.5.44 (per P/F)

Cdr *U 621* 5.5.44 (P/F) or 15.5.44 (per *U 621* WD, and see Kruschka [671]) to 18.8.44

Lost 18.8.44 Bay of Biscay, off La Rochelle

Knight's Cross 11.8.44 (241st KM, 125th U-boat holder)

STUDT, BRUNO [1253]

b. 6.4.1918, Barmstedt, Holstein

Rating entry X/1939; ObltzS (R) 1.1.44

StrmMt *U 108* 10/40–7/41; courses 7/41–11/41; WO *U 459* (Type XIV U-tanker) 11/41–6/43; U-boat base officer 12th U-Flotilla (Bordeaux) 7/43–1/44

Cdr *U 488* (Type XIV U-tanker) 2/44–26.4.44

Lost 26.4.44 NW of Cape Verde Is

STÜHRMANN, GÜNTER [1254]

b. 11.3.1922, Bremen

Class X/1940; ObltzS 1.10.44

2WO *U 453* 11/42–8/43; 1WO *U 453* 8/43–3/44; U-Cdr's Course, 3.ULD and 24th U-Flotilla 4/44–6/44

Cdr *U 904* 16.6.44–4.5.45

STURM, KURT [1255]

b. 30.1.1906, Brandenburg, Havel

Class 1925; FKpt 1.10.43

CO 1st E-Boat Flotilla 6/38–11/39; Head of Personnel Div., Staff 2/Admiral North Sea 1/40–6/41; U-boat trg 6/41–1/42; *Baubelehrung* 7.KLA 1/42–2/42

Cdr *U 410* 23.2.42–4.2.43

Cdr *U 167* 5.2.43–6.4.43

Interned 4/43–5/43; *Baubelehrung* 8.KLA 5/43–6/43

Cdr *U 547* 16.6.43 to 15.4.44 (per WASt) or 18.4.44 (per *U 547* WD, and see Niemeyer [880])

General adviser OKM/Marinewehr/Transport I 5/44–capitulation

Detained; freed 1.10.45

SÜRENHAGEN, ALBERT [1256]

b. 25.3.1916; Dahl-Deipenbrink

Class 1936; Kplt 1.7.43

Heavy cruiser *Admiral Scheer* 12/38–4/40; Group Officer Naval School Flensburg-Mürwik 4/40–8/40; Comp. CO Naval Holding Div. 8/40–9/40; Group Leader and ADC Kriegsmarine Depot Boulogne 9/40–12/40; Group Officer Naval College Flensburg-Mürwik 12/40–4/42; Kplt on Staff 29th U-Flotilla 4/42–9/42; U-boat trg 9/42–1/43; WO *U 593* 1/43–4/43; U-Cdr's Course, 24th U-Flotilla 5/43–6/43 (U-Cdr's Torpedo Course 47); *Baubelehrung* 6.KLA 6/43–8/43

Cdr *U 855* 2.8.43–2.4.44

4th U-Flotilla 4/44–7/44; 2/Adm. Staff Officer (A.II), Staff FdU East 7/44–2/45; Senior Officer U-boat base Gdynia 2/45–3/45

Died 10.4.45

SUES, PETER [1257]

b. 26.9.1919, Lützow, Mecklenburg

Class 1938; ObltzS 1.4.43

U-boat trg 10/40–5/41; WO *U 204* 5/41–7/41; 1st U-Flotilla 7/41–10/41; WO *U 558* 11/41–10/42;

U-Cdr's Course, 2.UAA and 24th U-Flotilla 10/42–12/42
Cdr *U 388* 31.12.42–20.6.43
Lost 20.6.43 SE of Cape Farewell

SÜSS, WALTER [1258]
b. 27.10.1908, Plauen, Vogtland
Entry I/1940; ObltzS (R) 1.7.43
Platoon leader 7/Basic Trg Est. Stralsund 4/41–9/42; Comp. CO 1/NCO Trg Div. 9/42–4/43; retrg as Seaman Branch officer and navigation course 3rd Sperrbrecher Flotilla 4/43–8/43; U-boat trg 8/43–2/44; U-Cdr's Course, 24th U-Flotilla 2/44–5/44 (U-Cdr's Torpedo Course 69); U-Cdr sea trg *U 1210* 5/44–7/44; *Baubelehrung* 1.KLA 7/44–9/44
Cdr *U 1304* 6.9.44–5.5.45

SUHREN, REINHARD [1259]
b. 16.4.1916, Langenschwalbach, Taunus
Class 1935; FKpt 1.6.44
U-boat trg and U-boat courses (occasionally on *U 1*) 3/38–11/38; 2WO *U 51*, *U 46* and *U 47* 11/38–4/39; 1WO *U 48* 22.4.39–9.11.40; instructor and leader torpedo attack trg 24th U-Flotilla 10.11.40–2.3.41; *Baubelehrung U 564* 3.3.41–2.4.41
Cdr *U 564* 3.4.41–1.10.42 (per P/F)
1st U-Flotilla 1.10.42–25.10.42; instructor and Comp. CO 2.ULD 26.10.42–12.3.43; Group Leader and Chief of Staff 27th U-Flotilla 13.3.43–26.5.44; FdU Norway 27.5.44–9/44; FdU Polar Sea 9/44–capitulation
Detained; freed 16.5.46
Knight's Cross 3.11.40 (45th KM, 20th U-boat holder). (Translator's note: Suhren was the first non-Cdr to receive decoration for torpedo skill.)
Oak Leaves 31.12.41 (56th WM, 11th KM, 9th U-boat holder)
Swords 1.9.42 (18th WM, 3rd KM, 3rd U-boat holder)

SURETH, KURT [1260]
b. 8.7.1922, Hamburg
Class XII/1939; ObltzS 1.12.43
2WO *U 625* 6/42–8/43; 1WO *U 625* 6/42–8/43; 1WO *U 625* 8/43–1/44
Acting Cdr *U 625* 2.1.44–25.1.44
Courses and *Baubelehrung* 2/44–5/44 (U-Cdr's Torpedo Course 67); instructor 3/Basic Trg Est. Stralsund 5/44–1/45; *Baubelehrung* Cdr 8.KLA for *U 2549* (never commissioned) 8.1.45–4/45
Detained; freed 10/45

T

TAMMEN, RENKO [1261]
b. 21.12.22, Oldeborg, Aurich
Class I/1941; ObltzS 1.1.45
U-boat trg and courses 2/42–5/43; 2WO *U 380* 6/43–3/44; 2WO *U 967* 3/44–8/44; U-Cdr's Course, 3.ULD and 27th U-Flotilla 9/44–12/44
Cdr *U 148* 16.12.44–2.5.45

TASCHENMACHER, ERICH [1262]
b. 1.11.1919, Engerhafen, Aurich
Class 1938; ObltzS 1.4.43
WO battleship *Scharnhorst* 10/43–3/43; U-boat trg 3/43–10/43; courses 3.ULD and 23rd U-Flotilla 10/43–2/44; *Baubelehrung* 6.KLA 2/44–3/44
Cdr *U 775* 23.3.44–capitulation

TESCHAND, WERNER [1263]
b. 21.1.1919, Danzig
Class 1937b; Kplt 1.1.45
U-boat trg 1/41–6/41; *Baubelehrung* 7/41–8/41; 1WO *U 135* 8/41–7/42; U-Cdr's Course, 24th U-Flotilla 7/42–9/42; *Baubelehrung* 9/42–10/42
Cdr *U 731* 3.10.42–30.11.43
1st U-Flotilla 12/43–1/44; Trg Inspectorate 1/44–5/44; Commandant Naval Air Base Pillau 5/44–7/44; attached Staff Commanding Adm. U-Boats 8/44–capitulation

TEICHERT, MAX-MARTIN [1264]
b. 31.1.1915, Kiel
Class 1934; Kplt 1.12.41
Cdr auxiliary minesweeper *Wotan* 2/39–3/39; 2WO and Torpedo Officer destroyer *Z 14 Friedrich Ihn* 3/39–5/40; U-boat trg 6/40–12/40; UAA Plön 12/40–2/41; 1WO *U 94* 2/41–6/41; U-Cdr's Course, 24th U-Flotilla 7/41–8/41; *Baubelehrung* KLA U-East 8/41–9/41
Cdr *U 456* 18.9.41–12.5.43
Lost 12.5.43 North Atlantic
Knight's Cross 19.12.43 (198th KM, 108th U-boat holder)

THÄTER, GERHARD [1265]
b. 18.11.1916, Kiel
Class 1936; Kplt 1.10.43
Comp. Officer 6/Basic Trg Est. Stralsund 4/39–1/40; E-Boat Cdr 2nd and 6th E-Boat Flotillas 1/40–6/41; U-boat trg 7/41–12/41; 1WO *U 568* 12/41–4/42; U-Cdr's Course and *Baubelehrung* 4/42–6/42
Cdr *U 466* 17.6.42–19.8.44
Baubelehrung 7.KLA 9/44–10/44
Cdr *U 3506* 14.10.44–2.5.45

THIEL, GERNOT [1266]
b. 13.5.1922, Koblenz
Class X/1940; ObltzS 1.10.44
Courses and U-boat trg 9/41–11/42; WO sea trg *U 305* 11/42–2/43; *Baubelehrung* 6.KLA 2/43–3/43; WO *U 763* 3/43–8/44; U-Cdr's Course, 23rd U-Flotilla 9/44–10/44
Cdr *U 152* 16.10.44–2.5.45

THIENEMANN, SVEN [1267]
b. 4.12.1912, Münster, Westphalia
Entry X/1939; ObltzS (R) 1.5.44
WO 13th Anti-Submarine Flotilla 11/39–7/41; WO and acting UJ-Cdr 14th Anti-Submarine Flotilla 10/41–7/42; UJ-Cdr 14th Anti-Subma-

rine Flotilla 7/42–1/43; U-boat trg 1/43–10/43; U-Cdr's Course, 24th U-Flotilla 11/43–12/43 (U-Cdr's Torpedo Course 59); *Baubelehrung* 8.KLA 12/43–4/44

Cdr *U 682* 17.4.44–31.3.45

Cdr *U 1271* mid 4/45–capitulation (U-Boat Archive per Thienemann)

THILO, ULRICH [1268]

b. 4.1.1903, Münster

Class 1922; KptzS 1.7.43

CO Torpedo School Flotilla 11/38–11/39; general adviser OKM/Marinewehr 11/39–3/41; U-boat trg 4/41–10/41; *Baubelehrung* 10/41–11/41

Cdr *U 174* 26.11.41–8.3.43

Group CO, Torpedo School Flotilla, CO School Group, Higher Command of Torpedo Schools 3/43–12/44; Officer Commanding Naval Transport Gdynia and Swinemünde 12/44–capitulation

THIMME, JÜRGEN [1269]

b. 26.9.1917, Berlin

Class 1937a; ObltzS 1.9.41

WO fleet escort *F 3* 8/40–5/41; WO 3rd Minesweeping Flotilla 5/41–9/41; U-boat trg 9/41–4/42; 1WO *U 214* 4/42–10/42; U-Cdr's Course, 24th U-Flotilla 10/42–11/42; *Baubelehrung* 6.KLA 11/42–12/42

Cdr *U 276* 9.12.42–19.10.43

8th and 11th U-Flotillas 10/43–11/44; supernumerary WO *U 294* 11/44–2/45

Cdr *U 716* 25.1.45 (per WASt, but Gréus [385] was acting commander until 12.2.45) to capitulation.

THOMSEN, ROLF [1270]

b. 6.5.1915, Berlin

Class 1936; Kplt 1.3.43

Trg Aircraft Weapons School Bug/Rügen 10/38–8/39; observer *1./Küstenfliegergruppe 106* 8/39–9/40; 1/Adm. Staff Officer/Opns, Staff C-in-C Air (Naval Air Forces) 9/40–3/41; acting Cdr and 1/Adm. Staff Officer *Küstenfliegergruppe 125* 4/41–3/42; adviser to Plenipotentiary for the Aerial Torpedo, also ADC *KG 26* 4/42–4/43; U-boat trg 4/43–1/44

Cdr *U 1202* 27.1.44–capitulation, inc. Leader U-boat base Bergen, 11th U-Flotilla 26.4.45–2.6.45 (per P/F)

Detained 3.6.45–9.2.46

Knight's Cross 4.1.45 (287th KM, 134th U-boat holder)

Oak Leaves 29.4.45 (845th WM, 51st KM, 28th U-boat holder)

THURMANN, HELMUT [1271]

b. 5.1.1915, Lippstadt

Class 1935; Kplt 1.4.43 (transferred Ordnance Branch to Seaman Branch 1943)

Mines Officer minelayer *Preussen* 8/39–2/40; Cadet Trg Officer Naval School Flensburg-Mürwik, minelayer *Tannenberg* and with ship's company *Tannenberg* 2/40–11/41; Mines Officer minelayer *Ulm* 11/41–4/42; Mines Officer on Staff 1.Escort Div. 4/42–5/42; Mines Officer Naval Mine Ordnance Office Cuxhaven 6/42–2/43; courses and U-boat trg 3/43–2/44; *Baubelehrung* 8.KLA 2/44–4/44

Cdr *U 1234* 19.4.44–14.5.44

Baubelehrung 6.KLA 6/44–8/44

Cdr *U 3004* 30.8.44–13.3.45

Kplt Staff 1.Naval Assault Battalion, 3/45–capitulation

Detained; freed 28.12.46

THURMANN, KARL [1272]

b. 4.9.1909, Mülheim, Ruhr

Class 1928; KKpt 1.8.42

Cdr Naval Artillery Detachment 122 8/39–3/40; U-boat trg 4/40–10/40; U-Cdr sea trg *U 29*

26.10.40–5.12.40; *Baubelehrung* U-Boats North, Hamburg 12/40
Cdr *U 553* 23.12.40–20.1.43
Missing from 20.1.43 central North Atlantic (official date of death 28.1.43)
Knight's Cross 24.8.42 (123rd KM, 61st U-boat holder)

VON TIESENHAUSEN, FREIHERR HANS-DIEDRICH [1273]

b. 22.2.1913, Riga, Lithuania
Class 1934; Kplt 1.1.42
U-boat course 10/39–12/39; 2WO *U 23* 12/39–5/40; course Torpedo School Flensburg-Mürwik 5/40–6/40; 1st U-Flotilla 6/40; *Baubelehrung* U-Boats East 6/49–7/40; 1WO *U 93* 7/40–12/40; U-Cdr's Torpedo Course, 24th U-Flotilla 1/41–2/41; *Baubelehrung* Nordseewerke Yard Emden 2/41–3/41
Cdr *U 331* 31.1.41–17.11.42
POW 17.11.42
Knight's Cross 27.1.42 (102nd KM, 45th U-boat holder)

TIESLER, RAIMUND [1274]

b. 7.3.1919, Rastenburg, East Prussia
Class 1937; Kplt 1.1.45
WO destroyer *Z 7 Hermann Schoemann* 12/39–10/40; U-boat trg 10/40–6/41; *Baubelehrung* 6/41–7/41; 1WO *U 578* 7/41–3/42; hospitalised (pelvic fracture) 28.3.42–30.8.42; U-Cdr's Course and *Baubelehrung* 9/42–11/42; Cdr *U 649* 19.11.42–24.2.43; 5th U-Flotilla and *Baubelehrung* 2/43–5/43
Cdr *U 976* 5.5.43–25.3.44
7th U-Flotilla and *Baubelehrung* Type XXI 8.KLA 3/44–7/44
Cdr *U 2503* 1.8.44 to 25.10.44 or 11.11.44
31st U-Flotilla 10/44–2/45; advise U-boat Personnel Office 2/45–capitulation

TILLESSEN, HANS-RUTGER [1275]

b. 16.4.1913, Wilhelmshaven
Class 1934; Kplt 1.4.42
ADC heavy cruiser *Deutschland* 4/39–1/40; Div. Officer and WO heavy cruiser *Prinz Eugen* 8/40–7/42; U-boat trg 7/42–11/42; course 24th U-Flotilla 11/42–12/42; U-Cdr sea trg *U 506* 12/42–5/43; U-Cdr under instrn 27th and 26th U-Flotillas 6/43
Cdr *U 516* 1.7.43 or 6.7.43 (per WASt, and see Wiebe [1346] and Kuppisch [684]) to 12/44
CO *K-Verband* Flotilla and Base Leader 1/45–capitulation
Detained; freed 9.4.46

TIMM, HEINRICH [1276]

b. 30.4.1910, Bremen
Class 1933; KKpt 1.7.44
Cdr *M 7*, 1st Minesweeping Flotilla 7/39–3/41; U-boat trg 3/41–8/41; U-Cdr's Torpedo Course, 24th U-Flotilla 8/41–9/41
Cdr *U 251* 20.9.41–1.9.43
Cdr *U 862* 7.10.43–capitulation
Detained; freed 9.4.48
Knight's Cross 17.9.44 (256th KM, 128th U-boat holder)

TINSCHERT, OTTO [1277]

b. 2.3.1915, Otterndorf
Class 1935; Kplt 1.9.42
Seconded to Luftwaffe 11/38–8/41, inc. *1./Küstenfliegergruppe 906*; U-boat trg 8/41–1/42; WO *U 97* 1/42–5/42; U-Cdr's Course, 24th U-Flotilla 5/42–6/42; *Baubelehrung* 6.KLA 6/42–7/42
Cdr *U 267* 11.7.42–13.7.43
Cdr *U 650* 14.7.43–26.11.43 (Tinschert, who had a kidney complaint and was unable to carry out a full schedule of duties, took over *U 650*, which was laid up in the yards at St Nazaire and not battleworthy, from von Witzendorff [1367]. The respective commands of *U 267* and *U 650*

changed twice between Tinschert and von Witzendorff in the period July–November 1943)
Cdr *U 267* 27.11.43–6.7.44
1.UAA and *Baubelehrung* Type XXI 6.KLA 7/44–12/44
Cdr *U 3011* 21.12.44–24.4.45
Cdr *U 903* 25.4.45–3.5.45

VON TIPPELSKIRCH, HELMUT
[1278]
b. 7.12.1917, Cuxhaven
Class 1937a; ObltzS 1.9.41
WO 1st Minesweeping Flotilla 4/39–6/40; Attached C-in-C Minesweepers West and C-in-C Escorts West 7/40–3/41; R-Cdr 3rd R-Boat Flotilla 4/41–9/41; U-boat trg 10/41–4/42; 1WO *U 160* 4/42–12/42; U-Cdr's Course, 24th U-Flotilla 12/42–2/43
Cdr *U 439* 18.2.43–4.5.43
Lost 4.5.43 W of Cape Ortegal

TODENHAGEN, DIETHER [1279]
b. 22.7.1920, Hannover
Class 1937b; ObltzS 1.4.42
WO/Secretarial Officer 2nd Minesweeping Flotilla 12/39–1/41; U-boat trg 1/41–8/41; *Baubelehrung* 8.KLA 9/41–10/41; 1WO *U 703* 10/41–8/42; U-Cdr's Course, 24th U-Flotilla 8/42–9/42
Cdr *U 48* 26.9.42–10/43
Course 3.ULD 11/43–12/43; *Baubelehrung* 8.KLA 12/43–1/44
Cdr *U 1008* 1.2.44–17.11.44
Cdr *U 365* 18.11.44–13.12.44
Lost 13.12.44 Arctic Ocean, E of Jan Mayen

TOPP, ERICH [1280]
b. 2.7.1914, Hannover
Class 1934; FKpt 1.12.44
U-boat trg U-Boat School 10/37–6/38; Trg Officer NCO Trg Div. Kiel-Friedrichsort 6/38–9/38; U-Flotilla *Wegener* 9/38–11/38; 1WO *U 46* 11/38–4/40
Cdr *U 57* 5.6.40 (per P/F) or 12.7.40 (per WASt) to 15.9.40 (*U 57* sank near the Brunsbüttel lock 3.9.40 after a collision with the Norwegian freighter *Rona*)
1st U-Flotilla 9/40–11/40; *Baubelehrung* U-Boats North Sea 11/40–12/40
Cdr *U 552* 4.12.40 to 1.9.42 or 8.9.42 (when relieved by Popp [936], per *U 552* WD) or 18.9.42 (per P/F)
7th U-Flotilla 9/42–11/42; CO 27th U-Flotilla 11/42–8/44; Leader Testing Group U-Boats 8/44–1/45, after 1.12.44 solely for Type XXI boats
Cdr *U 3010* 23.3.45–25.4.45
Cdr *U 2513* 26.4.45–capitulation
Detained; freed 17.8.45
Knight's Cross 20.6.41 (75th KM, 33rd U-boat holder)
Oak Leaves 11.4.42 (87th WM, 12th KM, 10th U-boat holder)
Swords 17.8.42 (17th WM, 2nd KM, 2nd U-boat holder)

TROJER, HANS-HARTWIG [1281]
b. 22.1.1916, Birthähn, Siebenbürgen
Class 1936; Kplt 1.4.43
2WO *U 34* 8/39–9/40; 1WO *U 34* 9/40–11/40; *Baubelehrung* U-Boats North Sea 12/40–1/41; 2WO *U 67* 1/41–6/41; U-Cdr's Course, 24th U-Flotilla 6/41–7/41
Cdr *U 3* 3.7.41–2.3.42
Baubelehrung KLA U-Boats East 3/42–5/42
Cdr *U 221* 9.5.42–27.9.43
Lost 27.9.43 SW of Ireland
Knight's Cross 24.3.43 (154th KM, 84th U-boat holder)

VON TROTHA, CLAUS [1282]
b. 25.3.1914, Cologne
Class 1936; Kplt 1.4.43

3WO destroyer *Z 2 Georg Thiele* 5/39–2/40;
1WO torpedo-boat *T 151* 4/40–5/40; Group
Officer Naval College Flensburg-Mürwik 5/40–
10/40; U-boat trg, courses and *Baubelehrung*
10/40–4/41; 1WO *U 81* 4/41–1/42; U-Cdr's
Course 2/42–3/42
Cdr *U 554* 3/42–9/42
Baubelehrung 9/42–10/42
Cdr *U 306* 21.10.42–31.10.43
Lost 31.10.43 NE of Azores

VON TROTHA, WILHELM [1283]
b. 7.8.1916, Kiel
Class 1936; Kplt 1.9.43
WO/Platoon Officer light cruiser *Königsberg*
12/38–4/40; seconded Adm. Norwegian West
Coast 4/40–1/41; Trg Officer trg ship
Schleswig-Holstein 1/41–3/41; Destroyer and
Torpedo-Boat Crew Holding Div. 3/41–4/41;
instructor Torpedo School 4/41–6/41; U-boat
trg 7/41–10/41; 1st U-Flotilla 10/41–3/42; WO
sea trg *U 582* 3/42–5/42; 1WO *U 582* 5/42–
8/42; U-Cdr under instrn and *Baubelehrung*
7.KLA 9/42–11/42
Cdr *U 733* 14.11.42–11.5.43 (per WASt; *U 733*
sank 8.4.43 after collision off Gdynia)
Baubelehrung 7.KLA 5/43–6/43
Cdr *U 745* 19.6.43–4.2.45
Missing from 4.2.45 Gulf of Finland

TROX, HANS-GEORG [1284]
b. 21.1.1916, Schrotz, Deutsch Krone, Posen,
West Prussia
Class 1936; Kplt 1.6.43
Comp. Officer 12/Basic Trg Est. Stralsund
10/38–9/39; WO 6th Minesweeping Flotilla
9/39–1/41; M/S-Cdr 6th Minesweeping Flotilla
1/41–9/41; U-boat trg 9/41–4/42; WO under
instrn 29th U-Flotilla 5/42–6/42; 1WO *U 83*
6/42–12/42; U-Cdr's Course, 24th U-Flotilla
12/42–1/43

Cdr *U 97* 2.2.43–16.6.43
Lost 16.6.43 Mediterranean, W of Haifa

TURRE, EDUARD [1285]
b. 31.1.1920, Odenheim, Bruchsal, Baden
Class IX/1939; ObltzS 1.10.43
U-boat trg 4/41–9/41; WO 26th and 24th U-
Flotillas 9/41–8/42; *Baubelehrung* 8.KLA 8/42–
10/42; 1WO *U 530* 10/42–3/44; U-Cdr's
Course, 3.ULD and 24th U-Flotilla 3/44–5/44
(U-Cdr's Torpedo Course 69); 21st U-Flotilla
5/44–7/44
Cdr *U 868* 22.7.44–capitulation

U

UEBEL, JOHANNES [1286]
b. 15.4.1901, Munich
Entry date not known; ObltzS (R) 1.3.44 seniority 1.1.44
Cdr *U 883* 27.3.45–capitulation

UFERMANN, FRITZ [1287]
b. 6.10.1912, Mülheim
Enlisted rating 1938; ObltzS 1.4.45
ObStrm *U 410* 2/42–3/44; trg and courses 3/44–10/44 (U-Cdr's Torpedo Course 76); 22nd U-Flotilla 10/44–12/44; *Baubelehrung* 8.KLA 12/44–4/45
Cdr *U 2368* 11.4.45–5.5.45

UHL, GEORG [1288]
b. 4.1.1915, Frankfurt/Main
Class 1939; ObltzS 1.6.43
WO and VP-Cdr 10th VP-Boat Flotilla 6/40–11/42; U-boat trg 11/42–5/43; 1WO *U 592* 7/43–11/43; courses 3.ULD, 24th and 27th U-Flotillas 12/43–4/44 (U-Cdr's Torpedo Course 62)
Cdr *U 269* 6.4.44 (per *U 269* WD) to 25.6.44
Lost 25.6.44 English Channel, off Torquay

UHLIG, HERBERT [1289]
b. 27.2.1916, Chemnitz
Class 1935; Kplt 1.6.42
Seconded to Luftwaffe 9/39–12/40, inc. service with *Bordfliegerstaffel 5./196*; U-boat trg 1/41–5/41; 1WO *U 105* 6/41–5/42; U-Cdr's Course, 24th U-Flotilla 5/42; acting torpedo attack instructor 26th U-Flotilla 5/42–7/42; *Baubelehrung* 8.KLA 7/42–9/42

Cdr *U 527* 7/42–9/42
POW 23.7.43

ULBER, MAX [1290]
b. 12.10.1916, Fellhammer, Waldenburg, Silesia
Class XII/1939; ObltzS 1.12.43
U-boat trg and courses 5/41–7/42; *Baubelehrung* 7/42–8/42; WO *U 358* 8/42–9/43; U-Cdr's Course, 24th U-Flotilla 10/43–11/43 (U-Cdr's Torpedo Course 57); *Baubelehrung* 8.KLA 11/43–12/43
Cdr *U 680* 21.12.43–capitulation

ULBING, WILLIBALD [1291]
b. 19.8.1920, Vienna
Class XII/1939; ObltzS 1.12.43
U-boat trg 7/41–1/42; WO 26th and 24th U-Flotillas 1/42–9/43; WO *U 129* 9/43–8/44; course 3.ULD and 23rd U-Flotilla 8/44–10/44; *Baubelehrung* 8.KLA 10/44–12/44
Cdr *U 2347* 2.12.44–5.5.45

UMLAUF, HANS [1292]
b. 29.1.1918, Dilsburg, Saar
Class 1937a; Kplt 1.6.44
Ordnance Officer, Naval Heavy Gun Ordnance Offices Brest and St Nazaire 12/40–9/42; Ordnance Officer, Staff, 22nd Naval Flak Regiment and Naval Flak Detachment 703 9/42–3/43; converted to Seaman Branch Officer; navigation course Helmsman's School 3/43–5/43; U-boat trg 5/43–3/44; U-Cdr sea trg *U 270* 3/44–7/44
Cdr *U 1168* 7/44–4.5.45

UNTERHORST, ERNST-GÜNTHER
[1293]
b. 5.4.1919, Hadersleben
Class 1937b; Kplt 1.1.45
Seconded to Luftwaffe 11/39–4/42; U-boat trg 4/42–10/42; 1WO *U 403* 11/42–5/43; U-Cdr's Torpedo Course 50 6/43–7/43; *Baubelehrung* Cdr *U 395* (never commissioned) 7/43–8/43; acting Cdr *U 394* 7.8.43–18.8.43
Cdr *U 396* 16.10.43–3/45
Later details not available

UNVERZAGT, GÜNTER [1294]
b. 3.5.1921, Offenbach
Class XII/1939; ObltzS 1.12.43
U-boat trg 5/41–1/42; Platoon Leader 2.ULD 1/42–9/42; *Baubelehrung* 3.KLA 10/42–11/42; 1WO *U 307* 11/42–1/44; courses 3.ULD, 23rd and 27th U-Flotillas 1/44–6/44
Cdr *U 965* 7.6.44–27.3.45 (voyage Hammerfest–Narvik 1.9.44–3.9.44 under 1WO Gerhard Dabelow as acting Cdr)
Lost 27.3.45 N of Scotland

UPHOFF, HORST [1295]
b. 3.10.1916, Bad Oeynhausen
Class 1935; Kplt 1.7.42
Div. Officer and WO U-boat depot ship *Donau* 10/38–10/39; U-boat course 10/39–3/40; 1WO *U 46* 3/40–1/41; U-Cdr's Course, 24th U-Flotilla 1/41–3/41; *Baubelehrung* 3/41–4/41
Cdr *U 84* 29.4.41–24.8.43
Lost 24.8.43 central North Atlantic

UTISCHILL, KARL-ERICH [1296]
b. 25.2.1921, Gablonz, Neisse, Silesia
Class IX/1939; ObltzS 1.10.43
WO sea trg *U 37* 9/41–1/42; WO *U 565* 1/42–3/43; U-Cdr's Course 3/43–5/43 (U-Cdr's Torpedo Course 45)
Cdr *U 151* 5/43–31.8.44

Courses and *Baubelehrung* Type XXI 8.KLA 9/44–4/45
Cdr *U 2548* 9.4.45–3.5.45

V

VALENTINER, HANS-GUIDO [1297]
b. 12.1.1919, Wuppertal
Class 1937a; Kplt 1.7.44
U-boat trg and ULD 7/40–7/41; *Baubelehrung* 7/41–8/41; 1WO *U 455* 8/41–6/42; 7th U-Flotilla and *Baubelehrung* 7/42–8/42
Cdr *U 385* 29.8.42–11.8.44
POW 11.8.44

VON VARENDORFF, AMELUNG [1298]
b. 20.12.1913, Kiel
Class 1935; ObltzS 1.10.39
2WO *U 47* 9/39–11/40; 1WO *U 47* 11/40–1/41; U-Cdr's trg course, 24th U-Flotilla 1/41–2/41; nautical instructor 2.ULD 2/41–8/41
Cdr *U 213* 30.8.41–31.7.42
Lost 31.7.42 W of Punta Delgada, Azores

VENIER, FRANZ [1299]
b. 15.6.1893, Eger
Entry Austro-Hungarian (k.u.k.) Navy 1912; KKpt (zV) 1.9.43
3rd Officer k.u.k. *U 4* 1917; 2nd Officer k.u.k. *U 4* 1918
WO *UD 3* 6/41–11/41
Cdr *UD 1* 3.11.41–14.12.42
Baubelehrung UD 2 15.12.42–29.1.43
Cdr *UD 2* 30.1.43–1.4.44
Member U-Boat Acceptance Command 4/44–10/44
Lost 10.10.44 Baltic Sea, on board *U 2331* (see Pahl [905])

VERPOORTEN, HUBERT [1300]
b. 7.9.1922, Hamborn
Class X/1940; ObltzS 10.9.44
U-boat trg completed 1/43, inc. WO sea trg *U 558* 1/42–6/42; *Baubelehrung* 7.KLA 1/43–3/43; WO 8th, 9th and 13th U-Flotillas (*U 703*) 3/43–5/44; course 3.ULD and 23rd U-Flotilla 5/44–8/44; U-Cdr sea trg *U 23* 8/44–9/44; acting Cdr *U 19* 7.9.44–10.9.44 (see Ohlenburg [896])
Interned in Turkey 10.9.44

VIETH, JOACHIM [1301]
b. 10.1.1916, Marienburg, West Prussia
Entry 1936; ObltzS (R) 1.4.43
M/S-Cdr 42nd Minesweeping Flotilla 10/40–9/42; AL-Cdr 2nd Artillery Lighter Flotilla 9/42–8/43; U-boat trg 8/43–3/44; course 23rd U-Flotilla 3/44–5/44; U-Cdr under instrn 13th U-Flotilla 5/44–12/44; *Baubelehrung* Type XXI 6.KLA 12/44–3/45
Cdr *U 3041* 10.3.45–26.4.45
No further details available

VOCKEL, JÜRGEN [1302]
b. 19.9.1922, Berlin
Class X/1941; ObltzS 1.11.44
U-boat trg 3/42–11/42; supernumerary WO *U 198* 11/42–2/43; WO *U 969* 3/43–5/44; U-Cdr's Course, 3.ULD and 23rd U-Flotilla 5/44–7/44; *Baubelehrung* Type XXIII 8.KLA 7/44–9/44
Cdr *U 2336* 30.9.44–30.3.45
Killed 30.3.45 in air raid on Hamburg

VÖGE, ULRICH [1303]
b. 5.11.1919, Hamburg
Class 1938; ObltzS 1.4.43

Cdr *U 239* 13.3.43–24.7.44
Cdr *U 2536* 6.2.45–3.5.45
Detained; freed 11.10.45

VOGEL, HANS [1304]
b. 22.5.1918, Wiesbaden
Class 1937b; Kplt 30.1.45
Observer Luftwaffe (See) 2/40–2/42; U-boat trg 3/42–8/42; WO *U 453* 9/42–12/42; U-Cdr's Course 1/43–2/43
Cdr *U 143* 9.2.43–29.5.44
Baubelehrung Type XXI 6.KLA 6/44–7/44
Cdr *U 3001* 20.7.44–26.11.44
Baubelehrung 6.KLA 12/44–1/45
Cdr *U 3025* 20.1.45–3.5.45
Detained; freed 27.8.45

VOGEL, VICTOR [1305]
b. 22.11.1912, Tübingen
Class 1932; Kplt 1.2.40, posthumously KKpt seniority 1.8.42
UJ-Cdr 12th Anti-Submarine Flotilla 7/39–9/39; M/S-Cdr with 12th Minesweeping Flotilla 9/39–11/39, M/S-Cdr 2nd Minesweeping Flotilla 11/39–2/40; M/S-Cdr 1st and 3rd Minesweeping Flotillas 2/40–3/41; U-boat trg 3/41–6/41; U-Cdr's Course, 24th U-Flotilla 6/41–8/41; *Baubelehrung* KLA/Hamburg 8/41–9/41
Cdr *U 588* 18.9.41–31.7.42
Lost 31.7.42 central North Atlantic

VOGELSANG, ERNST [1306]
b. 31.8.1911, Frankfurt/Main
Class 1931; Kplt 1.10.39
WO and Gunnery Officer destroyer *Z 5 Paul Jacobi* 10/38–5/40; U-boat trg 6/40–11/40; U-Cdr's Course, 24th U-Flotilla 11/40–12/40
Cdr *U 18* 8.12.40–6.5.41
Cdr *U 132* 29.5.41–5.11.42
Lost 5.11.43 SE of Cape Farewell

VOGLER, HELMUT [1307]
b. 23.9.1916, Bad Oldesloe
Class 1935; Kplt 1.7.42
U-boat trg 10/40–3/41; *Baubelehrung* 3/41–4/41; 1WO *U 567* 4/41–12/41; U-Cdr's Course, 26th U-Flotilla and 2.UAA 12/41–2/42; *Baubelehrung* 1.KLA 2/42–4/42
Cdr *U 212* 25.4.42–21.7.44
Lost 21.7.44 English Channel, S of Brighton

VOIGT, HORST [1308]
b. 19.10.1919, Leipzig
Class 1938; ObltzS 1.4.43
R-Cdr 2nd R-Boat Flotilla until 9/41; R-Cdr 6th R-Boat Flotilla 9/41–11/42; AL-Cdr 2nd Artillery Lighter Flotilla 11/42–3/43; U-boat trg 3/43–10/43; course 23rd U-Flotilla 10/43–12/43; *Baubelehrung* 8 KLA 12/43–1/44
Cdr *U 1006* 11.1.44–16.10.44
POW 16.10.44

VOSWINKEL, KARL-HEINZ [1309]
b. 25.12.1915, Neuwied, Rhine
Class 1938; Kplt 1.3.45
VP-Cdr 3rd VP-Boat Flotilla 4/41–3/43; U-boat trg and U-Cdr's Course 3/43–12/43 (U-Cdr's Torpedo Course 59); *Baubelehrung* 6.KLA 12/43–2/44
Cdr *U 1273* 16.2.44–6.7.44
Courses and *Baubelehrung* 7.KLA 7/44–1/45
Cdr *U 3509* 29.1.45–14.3.45
5th U-Flotilla 3/45–4/45; Naval Command Aarhus 4/45–capitulation

VOWE, BRUNO [1310]
b. 10.7.1904, Fürstenwalde
Entry 1923; Kplt (R) 1.1.44
UAA Plön 5/40–12/40; WO *U 107* 12/40–3/41; Comp. Cdr 2.ULD 3/41–3/42
Cdr *U 462* 5.3.42–30.7.43
POW 30.7.43

W

WÄCHTER, KARL-JÜRG [1311]
b. 2.5.1916, Oberweissbach, Thüringen
Class 1936; Kplt 1.6.43
Seconded to Luftwaffe 9/39–1/41; U-boat trg 1/41–6/41; 1WO *U 576* 6/41–4/42; U-Cdr's Course, 2.UAA and 24th U-Flotilla 4/42–5/42; *Baubelehrung* 1.KLA 5/42–6/42
Cdr *U 233* 6.6.42–12.1.44 (per *U 223* WD)
29th U-Flotilla 1/44–3/44; Comp. CO 1.ULD 3/44–11/44
Cdr *U 2503* 12.11.44–4.5.45 (see Curio [180])
Lost 4.5.45 Baltic Sea, off N coast of Fynen, Denmark

WAGNER, HERBERT [1312]
b. 10.1.1917, Rüstringen
Class 1937a; Kplt 1.7.44
WO E-boat depot ship *Adolf Lüderitz*, 3rd E-Boat Flotilla 4/40–8/40; E-Boat Cdr 3rd E-Boat Flotilla 8/40–4/42; WO light cruiser *Emden* 4/42–5/42; Torpedo Officer light cruiser *Köln* 5/42–3/43; U-boat trg 3/43–8/43; course 27th U-Flotilla 8/43–11/43 (U-Cdr's Torpedo Course 56); *Baubelehrung* 7 KLA 11/43–12/43
Cdr *U 1166* 8.12.43–4/44
2.ULD 5/44–11/44; *K-Verband* 11/44–capitulation

WAHLEN, ROLF-BIRGER [1313]
b. 28.7.1915, Altona, Elbe
Class 1936; Kplt 1.10.43
WO gunnery trg ship *Bremse* 1/39–6/40; U-boat trg 6/40–3/41; 2WO *U A* 3/41–9/41; 1WO *U A* 9/41–12/41; U-Cdr's Course, 24th U-Flotilla 1/42–3/42
Cdr *U 23* 27.3.42–19.6.44 (per WASt; but boat decommissioned by Wahlen 10/42 prior transfer Black Sea)
30th U-Flotilla 6/44–9/44; *Baubelehrung* 8.KLA 9/44–10/44
Cdr *U 2514* 17.10.44–8.4.45
Land fighting anti-tank unit 9.4.45–19.4.45
Cdr *U 2541* 20.4.45–5.5.45

WALDSCHMIDT, HERBERT [1314]
b. 10.2.1922, Dortmund
Class XII/1939; ObltzS 1.12.43
U-boat trg and courses 5/41–3/42 inc. sea trg aboard *U 5* 5/41–6/41; WO *U 564* 3/42–4/43; U-Cdr's Course, 2.UAA and 24th U-Flotilla 4/43–5/43 (U-Cdr's Torpedo Course 47); relief instructor 2.ULD 6/43–7/43
Cdr *U 146* 31.5.43 to 30.12.44 (U-Boat Archive per Waldschmidt) or 12.7.43 to 21.12.44 (per WASt)
Baubelehrung Cdr *U 2374* (never commissioned) 8.KLA 31.12.44–28.3.45 (The building contract for the boat was originally placed with the Deutschewerft yard at Toulon, and then transferred to the yard at Hamburg. The contracts for *U 2372–U 2377* were next transferred to Germaniawerft on 23.11.44 but the order for *U 2374* was rescinded before the keel was laid.)
Baubelehrung Cdr for *U 4719* (never commissioned), 5th U-Flotilla 29.3.45–8.5.45

WALKERLING, HEINZ [1315]
b. 19.5.1915, Kiel
Class 1935; Kplt 1.6.42
WO minelayer *Hansestadt Danzig* 8/39–3/40; destroyer *Z 8 Bruno Heinemann* 3/40–10/40; U-

boat trg 10/40–3/41; 1WO *U 431* 4/41–11/41; U-Cdr's Course, 24th U-Flotilla 11/41–12/41; *Baubelehrung* 3.KLA 12/41–1/42
Cdr *U 91* 28.1.42–19.4.43
9th, 24th and 19th U-Flotillas 4/43–9/44; Torpedo School Flensburg-Mürwik 9/44–capitulation

WALLAS, GEORG [1316]
b. 11.2.1905, Dresden
Entry 1925; Kplt 1.11.42
U-boat trg 11/39–11/40
Cdr *U 60* 6.11.40–30.9.41; course 26th U-Flotilla and *Baubelehrung* 10/41–12/41
Cdr *U 356* 20.12.41–2.12.42
Relief Adm. Staff Officer, Staff FdU Italy 12/42–9/44; Comp. CO 33rd U-Flotilla 9/44–capitulation

WALTHER, HERBERT [1317]
b. 3.11.1912, Berlin
Enlisted 1933; LtzS 1.4.44
ObStrm and WO *U 331*, also ObStrm 29th U-Flotilla 4/41–1/44; courses 1/44–7/44
Cdr *U 59* 7/44–4/45

WATTENBERG, JÜRGEN [1318]
b. 28.12.1900, Lübeck
Class 1921; KptzS 1.4.43
Navigation Officer heavy cruiser *Admiral Graf Spee* 10/38–12/39; interned, fled to Germany 12/39–5/40; Station Command North Sea 5/40–7/40; Naval Liaison Officer to CO Wehrmacht Signals 7/40–10/40; U-boat trg 10/40–3/41; U-Cdr sea trg *U 103* 4/41–7/41; *Baubelehrung* 8/41–9/41
Cdr *U 162* 9.9.41–3.9.42
POW 3.9.42–17.5.46

WEBER, KARL-OTTO [1319]
b. 10.10.1914, Krempe, Holstein
Entry as rating 1936; Kplt 1.12.44 active 1.3.43
StrmMt *U 93* 7/40–3/41; 2WO and 1WO *U 371* 3/41–4/42, plus acting Cdr *U 371* (relieved Driver [219] on account of latter's illness) 26.3.42–6.4.42; U-Cdr's Course and *Baubelehrung* 5/42–8/42
Cdr *U 709* 12.8.42–2.12.43
9th U-Flotilla 12/43–1/44; instructor and Comp. CO 2.ULD 2/44–11/44; Kplt on Staff 11th U-Flotilla 12/44–capitulation

WEBER, KLAUS [1320]
b. 20.10.1922, Wuppertal-Elberfeld
Class I/1941; Oblt (Ing) 1.3.45
Chief Eng. *U 1054* 3/44–9/44; Chief Eng. *U 637* from 10/44 and acting Cdr *U 637* 27.4.45–capitulation

WEBER, PAUL [1321]
b. 30.3.1913, Bremen
Entry XI/1937; Kplt 1.10.44, Regular Officer Corps status 1.9.43
WO *U 257* 1/42–5/43; U-Cdr's Course, 2.UAA and 24th U-Flotilla 5/43–6/43; 5th U-Flotilla 7/43–8/43; *Baubelehrung* 8/43–9/43
Cdr *U 677* 20.9.43–16.7.44
1WO *U 3001* 20.7.44–26.11.44
Baubelehrung Type XXI 6.KLA 11/44–1/45
Cdr *U 3022* 25.1.45–5.5.45

WEBER, WERNER [1322]
b. 10.11.1907, Berlin
Entry 1925; KKpt 1.3.44
1WO Div. and Gunnery Officer U-boat depot ship *Saar* 6/39–5/40; Cdr U-boat depot ship *Donau* 5/40–12/40; Comp. CO BdU Staff Quarter 12/40–2/43; U-boat trg 3/43–8/43; course 2.UAA, 27th and 24th U-Flotillas 8/43–9/43 (U-Cdr's Torpedo Course 55)

Cdr *U 845* 8.10.43–10.3.44
Lost 10.3.44 central Atlantic

WEDEMEYER, HEIMAR [1323]
b. 22.9.1906, Marburg, Lahn
Entry 1934; Kplt 1.11.43
VP-Cdr and Group Leader 10th VP-Boat Flotilla 9/39–3/40; VP-Cdr 11th VP-Boat Flotilla 3/40–3/42; U-boat trg 3/42–9/42; 1WO *U 66* 10/42–4/43; U-Cdr's Course and *Baubelehrung* 4/43–6/43 (U-Cdr's Torpedo Course 45)
Cdr *U 365* 8.6.43–17.11.44
Kplt on Staff 14th U-Flotilla 12/44–capitulation

WEHRKAMP, HELMUT [1324]
b. 29.3.1921, Wilhelmshaven
Class XII/1939; ObltzS 1.1.44
U-boat trg completed 5/42; *Baubelehrung* 8.KLA 5/42–7/42; 1WO *U 629* 7/42–1/44; 1st U-Flotilla 1/44–3/44; course 3.ULD, 23rd and 27th U-Flotillas 3/44–6/44
Cdr *U 275* 7/44–10.3.45
Lost 10.3.45 English Channel, S of Newhaven

WEIDNER, FRIEDRICH [1325]
b. 2.10.1916, Eisenach
Class X/1937; Kplt 1.3.45
2WO *U 431* 4/41–7/42; 1WO *U 431* 8/42–2/43; U-Cdr's Course, 2.UAA and 24th U-Flotilla 2/43–4/43 (U-Cdr's Torpedo Course 43)
Cdr *UD 1* 18.5.43–28.11.43 (decommissioned 22.11.43 at Kiel Arsenal)
Baubelehrung 1.KLA 11/43–1/44
Cdr *U 1052* 20.1.44–4.7.44
Baubelehrung Type XXI 8.KLA 7/44–11/44
Cdr *U 2518* 4.11.44–capitulation

WEIHER, HORST [1326]
b. 5.5.1910, Gleiwitz
Class 1936; Kplt 1.7.43

ADC 7th U-Flotilla 8/39–3/40; WO 4th Minesweeping Flotilla 4/40–8/40; M/S-Cdr and Group Leader 42nd Minesweeping Flotilla 8/40–4/41; M/S-Cdr 8th Minesweeping Flotilla 4/41–9/41; U-boat trg 9/41–3/42; WO 29th U-Flotilla 3/42–7/42; 29th U-Flotilla 7/42–4/43; U-Cdr's Course, 2.UAA and 24th U-Flotilla 4/43–6/43 (U-Cdr's Torpedo Course 47); *Baubelehrung* 6.KLA 6/43–7/43
Cdr *U 854* 19.7.43–4.2.44
Lost 4.2.44 Baltic Sea, N of Swinemünde

WEINGÄRTNER, HANNES [1327]
b. 11.7.1908, Innsbruck, Austria
Class 1928; KKpt 1.6.42
Anti-Submarine School Kiel 7/35–8/35; Cdr *U 4* 17.8.35–29.9.37
Cdr *U 10* and *U 16* 30.9.37–11.10.39
CO 1st U-Trg Flotilla 10/39–6/40; CO 24th U-Flotilla 7/40–7/42; BdU/Organisational Staff with 24th U-Flotilla 7/42–2/43; seconded 2/Adm. U-Boats and Commanding Adm. U-Boats 3/43–4/43; *Baubelehrung* 1/6.KLA U-Boats North 4/43–5/43
Cdr *U 851* 21.5.43–27.3.44
Missing E of Newfoundland between 27.3.44 and 4/44 (official date of death 8.6.44)

WEITZ, FRIEDRICH [1328]
b. 18.4.1920, Essen
Class 1938; ObltzS 1.4.43 seniority 1.1.43
Light cruiser *Leipzig* 3/41–7/41; U-boat trg 7/41–1/42; *Baubelehrung* 1/42–2/42; 1WO *U 610* 2/42–5/43; U-Cdr's Course, 2.UAA and 24th U-Flotilla 5/43–7/43
Cdr *U 959* 26.7.43–2.5.44
Lost 2.5.44 Arctic Ocean, SE of Jan Mayen

WELLNER, HORST [1329]
b. 30.8.1908, Zwickau, Saxony
Class 1929; Kplt 1.10.38

WO *U 10* 1935 (per rank listings, 1.11.35); WO *U 16* 1936 (per rank listings, 1.11.36) and some service as WO *U 10* until 9/37
Cdr *U 14* 5.10.37 to 11.10.39 or 18.10.39 (per WASt)
Cdr *U 16* 12.10.39–25.10.39
Lost 25.10.39 English Channel, off Dover

WENDELBERGER, ERHARD [1330]
b. 19.10.1921, Klattau, Czechoslovakia
Class XII/1939; ObltzS 1.12.43
U-boat trg completed 5/42; supplementary WO *U 516* 5/42–8/42; *Baubelehrung* 8/42–9/42; 1WO *U 450* 9/42–4/43; 1WO *U 309* 4/43–2/44; U-Cdr's Course, 3.ULD and 24th U-Flotilla 3/44–5/44 (U-Cdr's Torpedo Course 69); WO 21st U-Flotilla 5/44–11/44
Cdr *U 720* 23.11.44–capitulation

VON WENDEN, EBERHARD [1331]
b. 3.12.1917, Berlin-Charlottenburg
Class 1937a; Kplt 1.10.44
Light cruiser *Köln* 10/39–5/40; 2WO and 1WO E-boat depot ship *Adolf Lüderitz* 6/40–5/43; U-boat trg and U-Cdr's Course 5/43–12/43 (U-Cdr's Torpedo Course 60); *Baubelehrung* 1/44–2/44
Cdr *U 926* 29.2.44–31.7.44
5th U-Flotilla 8/44–12/44
Cdr *U 37* 22.12.44–8.5.45
Detained; freed 17.12.45

WENDT, KARL-HEINZ [1332]
b. 22.2.1920, Stettin
Class 1938; ObltzS 1.4.43
Cadet Trg Officer, No 3 then No 2 Radio Technical Officer heavy cruiser *Admiral Hipper* 5/40–3/43; Special Staff Scheurlen 3/43–5/43; U-boat trg 5/43–10/43; course 3.ULD and 23rd U-Flotilla 10/43–2/44; *Baubelehrung* 6.KLA 2/44–4/44
Cdr *U 1276* 6.4.44–20.2.45
Lost 2.2.45 S of Waterford, Ireland

WENDT, WERNER [1333]
b. 6.2.1916, Költschen, Ost-Sternberg
Entry 1938; ObltzS (R) 1.4.43
U-boat trg 1/41–8/41; WO 6th U-Flotilla, U-Cdr's Course, 24th U-Flotilla 8/41–5/43 (U-Cdr's Torpedo Course 46); *Baubelehrung* 5/43–6/43
Cdr *U 765* 19.6.43–6.5.44
POW 6.5.44

WENGEL, HANS [1334]
b. 15.5.1914, Dresden
Class 1935; Kplt 1.1.43
VP-Cdr 3rd VP-Boat Flotilla 4/41–8/43; U-boat trg and U-Cdr's Course 8/43–5/44 (U-Cdr's Torpedo Course 68); *Baubelehrung* 8.KLA 6/44
Cdr *U 1164* 29.6.44–24.7.44
8th U-Flotilla 7/44–8/44; *Baubelehrung* 7.KLA 8/44–12/44
Cdr *U 3516* 18.12.44–3/45
Later details not available

WENTZ, ROLF-WERNER [1335]
b. 1.1.1920, Lübeck
Class X/1939; ObltzS 1.10.43
2WO *U 380* 12/41–5/43; 1WO *U 380* 5/43–9/43; courses 10/43–11/43; torpedo attack instructor Higher Command of Torpedo Schools 12/43–11/44
Cdr *U 963* 12/44–capitulation
Detained; freed 9.5.48

WENZEL, WOLFGANG [1336]
b. 29.3.1910, Dresden
Class 1934; Kplt 1.4.42

Navigation officer merchant raider *Atlantis* 9/39–12/41; U-boat trg and U-Cdr under instrn 1/42–8/42; *Baubelehrung* 1.KLA 8/42–11/42
Cdr *U 231* 14.11.42–13.1.44
POW 13.1.44–17.5.46

WERMUTH, OTTO [1337]
b. 28.7.1920, Aalen, Württemberg
Class IX/1939; ObltzS 1.10.43
Officer trg 11/Basic Trg Est. Stralsund 9/39–11/39; trg ship *Schleswig-Holstein* 11/39–4/40; Naval College Flensburg-Mürwik, 4/40–9/40; Motor Launch Section Emden 9/40–11/40; Torpedo School Mürwik, 11/40–1/41; Air Signals School Dievenow 2/41–3/41; destroyer *Z 23* 3/41–4/41
U-boat trg 4/41–9/41; WO *U 37* 9/41–6/42; 2WO *U 103* 7/42–6/43; 1WO *U 103* 6/43–2/44; course 3.ULD, 23rd and 27th U-Flotillas 3/44–7/44
Cdr *U 853* 10.7.44–31.8.44
1.UAA 9/44; supplementary WO *U 530* 14.9.44–1/45
Cdr *U 530* 1/45 (Translator's note: Surrendered to Argentina 7/45)

WERNER, ALFRED [1338]
b. 22.12.1918, Bad Ems
Entry 1938; ObltzS (R) 1.4.43
U-boat trg 1/41–8/41; *Baubelehrung* 9/41–10/41; 2WO *U 703* 10/41–1/43; U-Cdr's Course, 24th U-Flotilla 1/43–3/43 (U-Cdr's Torpedo Course 42)
Cdr *U 8* 16.3.43–12.5.44
Cdr *U 921* 1.6.44–30.9.44
Lost 30.9.44 Arctic Ocean, NW of Hammerfest

WERNER, HERBERT A. [1339]
b. 13.5.1920, Freiburg, Breisgau
Class XII/1939; ObltzS 1.12.43

WO sea trg *U 557* 4/41–11/41; courses 12/41–4/42; 1WO *U 612* 5/42–8/42 (see Siegmann [1194]); 1WO *U 230* 10/42–12/43; courses 3.ULD, 24th and 27th U-Flotillas 1/44–4/44
Cdr *U 415* 17.4.44–14.7.44
1st U-Flotilla 7/44–8/44
Cdr *U 953* 8/44–4/45
33rd U-Flotilla 4/45–capitulation
Detained until autumn 1945

WERR, ARNO [1340]
b. 8.12.1920, Berlin-Lichterfelde
Class IX/1939; ObltzS 1.10.43
U-boat trg completed 2/42; WO *U 572* 2/42–4/43; U-Cdr's Course, 2.UAA and 24th U-Flotilla 4/43–6/43 (U-Cdr's Torpedo Course 47); *Baubelehrung* 1.KLA 6/43–7/43
Cdr *U 241* 24.7.43–18.5.44
Lost 18.5.44 NE of Faroes

WESTPHALEN, OTTO [1341]
b. 12.3.1920, Hamburg
Class 1938; ObltzS 1.4.43
Officer trg 1/7.Basic Trg Est. Stralsund 10/38–2/39; sail trg ship *Gorch Fock* 2/39–6/39; trg ship *Schlesien* 7/39–10/39; Naval College Flensburg-Mürwik 10/39–2/40; Torpedo School Flensburg-Mürwik 3/40–4/40; torpedo-boat *Kondor*, 5th Torpedo-Boat Flotilla 5/40–10/40
U-boat trg 10/40–3/41; 2WO *U 566* 4/41–3/42; 1st U-Flotilla 3/42–4/42; U-Cdr's Torpedo Course, 24th U-Flotilla (*U 121*) 20.4.42–15.5.42
Cdr *U 121* 16.5.42–8.2.43
Baubelehrung 1.Comp/8.KLA 2/43–3/43
Cdr *U 968* 18.3.43–capitulation
Knight's Cross 23.3.45 (297th KM, 139th U-boat holder)

WETJEN, EBERHARD [1342]
b. 18.12.1914, Eldringen, Celle
Class 1936; ObltzS 1.10.39

WO torpedo-boat *Falke* 4/39–5/40; ADC 7th Torpedo-Boat Flotilla 6/40–7/40; U-boat trg 7/40–12/40; course 24th U-Flotilla 12/40–2/41; 1WO *U 147* 2/41–4/41
Cdr *U 147* 5.4.41–2.6.41
Lost 2.6.41 NW of Ireland

WEX, HANS-DIETER [1343]
b. 5.9.1920, Mönchen-Gladbach
Class XII/1939; ObltzS 1.12.43
WO under instrn *U 67* 5/41; WO sea trg *U 109* 6/41–3/42 (Translator's note: per Wolfgang Hirschfeld, *Feindfahrten*); WO (supernumerary) *U 515* 3/42–7/42; WO *U 30*, *U 554* and *U 80* 7/42–7/43; WO *U 380* 7/43–2/44; U-Cdr's Course, 3.ULD and 24th U-Flotilla 3/44–4/44 (U-Cdr's Torpedo Course 67); Eto (electric torpedo) Group Leader Torpedo Testing Branch 4/44–6/44; WO *U 1194* 6/44–11/44; *Baubelehrung* 11/44–1/45
Cdr *U 2354* 11.1.45–capitulation

WICHMANN, WALTER [1344]
b. 30.4.1919, Succase, Elbing
Class 1937b; ObltzS 1.4.42
U-boat trg 2/41–8/41; *Baubelehrung* 8/41–9/41; 1WO *U 588* 9/41–6/42; U-Cdr's Course, 24th U-Flotilla 7/42–8/42; *Baubelehrung* 8.KLA 8/42–9/42
Cdr *U 639* 10.9.42–30.8.43
Lost 30.8.43 Arctic Ocean, N of Mys Zelaniya

WICKE, HELMUT [1345]
b. 8.11.1920, Oberursel, Taunus
Class X/1939; ObltzS 1.10.43
Naval Command Centre Kleikamp 9/40–10/40; course Torpedo School Mürwik 11/40–1/41; 7th U-Flotilla 2/41–3/41; U-boat trg 4/41–9/41; 2WO *U 106* 10/41–4/43; U-Cdr's Course 4/43–5/43 (U-Cdr's Torpedo Course 46)
Cdr *U 560* 1.9.43–12.12.43

Cdr *U 351* 13.12.43–30.6.44
Cdr *U 1007* 10.7.44–2/45
Cdr *U 1231* 3/45–capitulation

WIEBE, GERHARD [1346]
b. 24.1.1907, Lautenburg
Class 1925; FKpt 1.11.43
Group Leader Torpedo Testing Branch 10/38–6/41; U-boat trg 6/41–1/42; U-Cdr's Course and *Baubelehrung* 1/42–3/42
Cdr *U 516* 10.3.42–23.6.43 (see Pauckstadt [911]. Kuppisch [684] commanded *U 516* from 24.6.43 per his P/F. Tillessen [1275] relieved Wiebe 6.7.43 per *U 516* WD. Presumably either Kuppisch did not take up command or Tillessen took over from Kuppisch and not Wiebe.)
No details available 7/43–10/43; Group Leader Torpedo Inspectorate 11/43–9/44; Cdr Section 1/Naval College Schleswig 10/44–capitulation
Detained; freed 8/47

WIEBOLDT, GÜNTER [1347]
b. 9.2.1919, Bremerhaven
Class 1937b; Kplt 1.1.45
Naval College Flensburg-Mürwik 4/39–9/39; Naval Signals School Mürwik and Mine Warfare School Kiel 10/39–11/39; WO 2nd R-Boat Flotilla 12/39–4/40; WO 2nd VP-Boat Flotilla 4/40–8/40; VP-Cdr 2nd VP-Boat Flotilla 8/40–1/43; U-boat trg, U-Cdr's Course and *Baubelehrung* 2/43–10/43
Cdr *U 295* 20.10.43–capitulation
Detained; freed 5/47

WIECHMANN, ARNOLD [1348]
b. 31.8.1909, Schwann, Karlsruhe
Entry IX/1939; ObltzS (R) 1.4.43
WO 6th Sperrbrecher Flotilla 6/42–7/43; U-boat trg, courses and WO 8/43–10/44 (U-Cdr's

Torpedo Course 68); *Baubelehrung* Type XXIII 1.KLA 10/44–1/45
Cdr *U 4701* 10.1.45–5.5.45

WIEDUWILT, HELMUT [1349]
b. 28.11.1919, Gera
Class 1938; ObltzS 1.3.43
U-boat trg 9/41–3/42; WO target ship *Vega* 3/42–4/42; 1WO *U 465* 5/42–3/43; U-Cdr's Course, 24th U-Flotilla 3/43–4/43 (U-Cdr's Torpedo Course 44); *Baubelehrung* 8.KLA 4/43–6/43
Cdr *U 718* 25.6.43–18.11.43
Cdr *U 262* 5.2.44 (per WASt and P/F Franke [308] but 25.1.44 per *U 262* WD, which is more likely since Wieduwilt left La Pallice for the North Atlantic in command of *U 262* on 3.2.44) to 24.11.44
Trg Command 300 *K-Verband* 11/44–capitulation

WIGAND, WOLF [1350]
b. 17.7.1920, Göttingen
Entry XII/1939; ObltzS (R) 1.1.44
Transferee from Medical Branch to Officer (Reserve)
U-boat trg 8/43–4/44; U-Cdr under instrn 23rd U-Flotilla 4/44–8/44; *Baubelehrung* 6.KLA 8/44–11/44
Cdr *U 1108* 18.11.44–capitulation

VON WILAMOWITZ-MOELLENDORF, GEORG [1351]
b. 7.11.1893, Weimar
Entry IV/1912; KKpt (zV) 1.6.42
FzS, Staff C-in-C Baltic Naval Forces until 10/14; serving officer torpedo-boat *S 122* 10/14–1/15; WO torpedo-boat *T 109* 1/15–5/16, inc. radio telegraphy course 7/15–8/15; WO torpedo-boat *V 159* 5/16–7/17; WO *U 46* until 8/17; WO *U 82* 8/17–10/17; WO *U 95* 10/17–7/18; WO *U 91* until 10/18; 3rd U-Flotilla 10/18–Armistice; demobilised 27.12.1919
Cdr Construction Battalion 100 8/39–5/40; 1.ULD 6/40–8/40
Cdr *U 2* 6.8.40–10/41
Baubelehrung 1.KLA 10/41–11/41
Cdr *U 459* (U-tanker) 15.11.41–24.7.43
Lost 24.7.43 NW of Cape Ortegal

WILBERG, ERNST-AUGUST [1352]
b. 1.9.1913, Dortmund-Aplerbeck
Entry I/1938; ObltzS (R) 1.7.43
U-boat trg 1/41–6/41; 2WO and 1WO *UD 3* 6/41–3/43; 1WO *U 757* 4/43–9/43; U-Cdr's Course, 2.UAA and 24th U-Flotilla 9/43–12/43 (U-Cdr's Torpedo Course 57)
Cdr *U 666* 10.12.43–10.2.44
Lost 10.2.44 W of Ireland

WILKE, HANS-DIETRICH [1353]
b. 11.6.1912, Wilhelmshaven
Entry 1932; ObltzS (R) 1.7.43
Baubelehrung U 579 6/41–7/41; 2WO *U 579* 7/41–10/41; 2WO *U 89* 11/41–4/43; U-Cdr's Course and *Baubelehrung* 5/43–7/43 (U-Cdr's Torpedo Course 47)
Cdr *U 766* 30.7.43–24.8.44 (per U-Boat Archive)
Cdr *U 382* 25.8.44–14.1.45
Baubelehrung Cdr for *U 2553* (never commissioned) 8.KLA 1/45–capitulation

WILL, JOSEF [1354]
b. 30.4.1906, Mülheim, Ruhr
Entry X/1939; ObltzS (R) 1.4.43
VP-Cdr 17th VP-Boat Flotilla 7/40–2/43; U-boat trg 3/43–9/43; U-Cdr's Course, 24th U-Flotilla 9/43–10/43 (U-Cdr's Torpedo Course 55); *Baubelehrung* 10/43–11/43
Cdr *U 318* 13.11.43–capitulation

WILLEKE, KLAUS [1355]
b. 16.2.1919, place not recorded
Class 1937b; Kplt 1.1.45
U-boat trg and courses 1/44–8/44; supernumerary WO (U-Cdr sea trg) *U 3004* 8/44–11/44; U-Cdr trg 19th U-Flotilla 11/44–3/45; U-Cdr sea trg (*U 3527*) 3/45 and (*U 2506*) 3/45–5/45
Cdr *U 3514* 6.5.45–capitulation (per U-Boat Archive)

WILLNER, HORST [1356]
b. 13.10.1919, Klotzsche
Class 1938; ObltzS 1.4.43
1WO *U 405* 7/42–10/42; U-Cdr's Course, 24th U-Flotilla, 10/42–11/42
Cdr *U 58* 15.12.42–2.7.44 but Cdr *U 96* 2/44–30.6.44 (intermediate period covering for Peters [918])
Baubelehrung Type XXI 8.KLA 7/44–10/44
Cdr *U 3505* 7.10.44–3.4.45
Cdr *U 3034* mid 4/45–5.5.45 (see Prehn [941])

WILZER, WOLF-WERNER [1357]
b. 23.9.1916, Shanghai, China
Class 1937a; Kplt 1.6.44
WO *U 573* 6/41–9/41; WO *U 37* 9/41–12/41; *Baubelehrung* 12/41–1/42; 1WO *U 91* 1/42–1/43; U-Cdr's Course, 2.UAA and 26th U-Flotilla 1/43–2/43; *Baubelehrung* 2/43–3/43
Cdr *U 363* 18.3.43–31.8.43
Instructor Torpedo School Flensburg-Mürwik 9/43–capitulation

WINKLER, WERNER [1358]
b. 14.5.1917, Wilhelmshaven
Class 1936; ObltzS 1.4.41
Sport/Div.Officer heavy cruiser *Admiral Scheer* 4/38–6/41; 1WO *U 569* 12/41–5/42; U-Cdr's Course, 24th U-Flotilla 5/42–6/42; *Baubelehrung* 8.KLA 6/42–7/42
Cdr *U 630* 9.7.42–6.5.43
Lost 6.5.43 S of Cape Farewell

WINTER, WERNER [1359]
b. 26.3.1912, Hamburg
Class 1930; KKpt 1.6.43
U-boat trg 7/35–1/36; 1WO *U 17* 1/36–9/37; Cdr *U 22* 1.10.37–3.10.39
Naval Station Baltic 10/39–11/39; 5/Adm. Staff Officer BdU/Opns 11/39–5/41; at BdU 5/41–7/41
Cdr *U 103* 13.8.41–14.7.42
CO 1st U-Flotilla 7/42–9/44; Staff Naval Cdr Brest 6.9.44–18.9.44
POW 18.9.44–21.11.47
Knight's Cross 5.6.42 (110th KM, 51st U-boat holder)

WINTERMEYER, MAX [1360]
b. 2.2.1914, Essen
Class 1934; Kplt 1.4.42
1WO *U 105* 9/40–7/41; U-Cdr's Course, 24th U-Flotilla 7/41–9/41
Cdr *U 62* 9/41–4.11.41
Instructor 1.ULD 11/41–8/42; *Baubelehrung* 6.KLA 8/42–9/42
Cdr *U 190* 24.9.42–5.7.44 (see Reith [992])
Staff FdU/Trg 9/44–2/45; Course Leader 25th U-Flotilla 2/45–capitulation

WISSMANN, FRIEDRICH-WILHELM [1361]
b. 16.12.1915, Kiel
Class 1935; Kplt 1.12.42
WO and M/S-Cdr 7th, 3rd and 32nd Minesweeping Flotillas 8/39–4/41; U-boat trg 4/41–9/41; 1WO *U 109* 9/41–2/42; U-Cdr's Course, 2.UAA and 24th U-Flotilla 3/42–5/42
Cdr *U 18* 1.6.42–18.8.42

Cdr *U 518* 17.8.42 (per WASt) or 19.8.42 (relieved Brachmann [117], per *U 518* WD) to 7.1.44 (per WASt) or 13.1.44 (relieved by Offermann [895], per *U 518* WD)

Trg Officer 2nd, 20th and 26th U-Flotillas 1/44–capitulation

WITT, HANS-LUDWIG [1362]

b. 25.12.1909, Bautzen, Saxony

Class 1929; KKpt 1.2.43

Wargames/Cadet Trg Officer trg ship *Schlesien* 5/38–10/39; Comp. CO Naval College Flensburg-Mürwik 10/39–2/40; Trg Leader sail trg ship *Gorch Fock* 3/40–4/40 and sail trg ship *Albert Leo Schlageter* 5/40–6/40; Cadet Trg Officer cadet trg ship *Tannenberg* 5/40–7/40; at Commanding Adm. Naval Station North 7/40; Group West 8/40–10/40; U-boat trg, U-Cdr's Course and *Baubelehrung* 10/40–7/41; WO and acting Cdr *U 161* 8.7.41–30.11.41

Cdr *U 161* 1.12.41–31.12.41, then U-Cdr sea trg *U 161* 31.12.41–13.5.42 (per P/F)

Cdr *U 129* 14.5.42 to 11.7.43 (per P/F) or 8.7.43 (relieved by von Harpe [418], per *U 129* WD)

Relief adviser at A1 OKM/2.SKL/BdU/Opns 7/43–3/44; 6/Adm. Staff Officer OKM/2.SKL/BdU/Opns 3/44–10/44; *Baubelehrung* Type XXI 8.KLA 10/44–11/44 and 7.KLA for *U 3524* 11/44–1/45

Cdr *U 3524* 26.1.45–5.5.45

Detained 8.5.45

Knight's Cross 17.12.42 (139th KM, 72nd U-boat holder)

WITTE, ERWIN [1363]

b. 17.2.1911, Karlsruhe

Class 1936; Kplt 1.2.43

2WO *U 47* 8/39–9/39; Comp. Officer U-Boat School 9/39–4/40; 2WO *U 43* 4/40–2/41; adviser 3rd U-Flotilla 3/41–8/41; adviser 5th U-Flotilla 8/41–12/42; Kplt on Staff 5th U-Flotilla 1/43–11/43; U-Cdr trg 11/43–6/44; 11th U-Flotilla 6/44–12/44

Cdr *U 155* 12/44–20.4.45

Later details not available

WITTE, HELMUT [1364]

b. 6.4.1915, Bojendorf, Holstein, Fehmarn

Class 1934; KKpt 20.4.45

2WO destroyer *Z 22 Anton Schmitt* 9/39–4/40; land fighting Naval Regiment Narvik 4/40–6/40; U-boat trg 7/40–12/40; 1WO *U 107* 12/40–7/41; U-Cdr's Course 9/41–10/41

Cdr *U 159* 4.10.41–6.6.43

Hospitalised, 6/43–11/43; course Naval Academy Bad Homburg 11/43–2/44; adviser and member Shipbuilding Commission 3/44–4/44; Adm. Staff Officer and permanent representative Admiral *K-Verband* groups with OKM/SKL, inc. CO Task Group *Panther* (Rhine-Weser), Naval High Command Baltic and finally Naval Liaison Officer to VIII British Corps in Schleswig-Holstein 4/44–capitulation

Detained; freed 14.7.45

Knight's Cross 22.10.42 (130th KM, 66th U-boat holder)

WITTE, WERNER [1365]

b. 5.1.1915, Berlin-Friedenau

Class 1935; Kplt 1.2.43, posthumously KKpt seniority 1.7.43

Flag Lt Staff FdU East 8/39–9/39; 13/Basic Trg Est. Stralsund 9/39–3/40; WO minelayer *Hansestadt Danzig* 3/40–7/40; M/S-Cdr 15th Minesweeping Flotilla 7/40–9/41; U-boat trg 9/41–2/42; 1WO *U 109* 3/42–6/42; U-Cdr's Course, 24th U-Flotilla 7/42–8/42

Cdr *U 509* 9/42 (U-Boat Archive per Ackermann [4], a former *U 509* WO, and see Wolff [1376]) to 15.7.43

Lost 15.7.43 NW of Madeira

WITTENBERG, FRIEDRICH [1366]
b. 28.10.1918, Wildeshausen, Oldenburg
Class 1937b; ObltzS 1.7.42
Course Naval College Flensburg-Mürwik 7/39–9/39; course Naval Gunnery School 10/39–11/39; Platoon and Secretarial Officer battleship *Gneisenau* 12/39–8/40; Kriegsmarine Basic Trg Est. Munsterlager and Group Officer Kriegsmarine Depot Calais 8/40–10/40; U-boat trg 10/40–3/41; WO *UD 1* 4/41–11/41; *Baubelehrung* KLA U-Boats East 11/41–12/41; 1WO *U 460* 12/41–1/42; 5th U-Flotilla 1/42–6/42; WO *U 506* 6/42–5/43; U-Cdr's Torpedo Course 48 and *Baubelehrung* 6.KLA 5/43–8/43
Cdr *U 856* 19.8.43–7.4.44
POW 7.4.44–20.5.46

VON WITZENDORFF, ERNST [1367]
b. 26.6.1916, Neustrelitz
Class 1937a; Kplt 1.1.45
Torpedo-boat *Luchs* 10/39–3/40; torpedo-boat *Jaguar* 3/40–4/40; U-boat trg 4/40–8/40; 1WO *U 62* 8/40–11/40; *Baubelehrung* 11/40–1/41; 2WO *U 77* 1/41–9/41; 1WO *U 77* 9/41–12/41; 23rd U-Flotilla 12/41–1/42
Cdr *U 121* 1/42 or 26.3.42 (per WASt) to 19.4.42
Cdr *U 46* 20.4.42–5/42 (boat into yards for refit)
Cdr *U 101* 5/42 to 14.9.42 (per WASt) or 25.10.42 (U-Boat Archive per von Witzendorff)
Baubelehrung 8.KLA 10/42–11/42
Cdr *U 650* 26.11.42–13.7.43
Cdr *U 267* 14.7.43–26.11.43 (*U 650* and *U 267* were exchanged between the two commanders von Witzendorff and Tinschert [1277] on account of the latter's kidney condition. Von Witzendorff completed a North Atlantic patrol commanding *U 267* 3.10.43–26.11.43.)
Cdr *U 650* 27.11.43 to 30.6.44 or 16.7.44 (relieved by Gerke [352] 30.6.44, per *U 650* WD, following which Zorn [1408] took command on 17.7.44)
7th U-Flotilla 7/44–9/44; *Baubelehrung* Type XXI 8.KLA 28.9.44–1/45
Cdr *U 2524* 16.1.45–3.5.45, also Cdr *U 1007* end 4/45–2.5.45. (U-Boat Archive per von Witzendorff. *U 2524* had completed all working-up exercises and after a short refit would have been combat-ready, but a shortage of fuel ruled out operations. At the end of April 1945 von Witzendorff was ordered to relieve Raabe [957] of *U 1007* and make for Norway, after having first shipped aboard an experienced fighting crew—including part of the complement of *U 2524*. On 2.5.45 *U 1007* had to be beached in the River Trave near the Flender Werft, Lübeck, after receiving serious damage in a rocket attack by four RAF fighter-bombers. The crew was removed by tugs and motor launches and took charge of the battle-worthy *U 2524* at Travemünde. The following day *U 2524* was wrecked east of Fehmarn by Beaufighters of No 16 Group Coastal Command (Nos 236 and 254 Squadrons RAF). The torpedo-boat *Löwe* put the survivors ashore at Flensburg. Chief Engineer ObltzS (Ing) (R) Werner Braun lost his life while scuttling *U 2524*.)
Comp CO Guard Battalion *Dönitz* 5/45–capitulation
Detained; freed 11/47

WÖRISSHOFFER, ULRICH [1368]
b. 21.3.1917, Maulbach, Hesse
Class 1936; ObltzS 1.10.40, posthumously Kplt seniority 1.3.43
Seconded to Luftwaffe 10/38–9/41; U-boat trg 9/41–12/41; 1WO *U 565* 1/42–4/42; U-Cdr's Course, 24th U-Flotilla, 5/42–7/42; 21st U-Flotilla 7/42–10/42
Cdr *U 83* 16.10.42 (per WASt) or 2.11.42 (see Kraus [658]) to 9.3.43
Lost 9.3.43 Mediterranean, SE of Cartagena, Spain

274

WOERMANN, GERMANUS [1369]
b. 16.12.1918, Windhoek, German South-West Africa
Entry VIII/1940; ObltzS (R) 1.6.44
U-boat trg 9/42–2/43; various duties and 11th U-Flotilla 2/43–5/44; courses and *Baubelehrung* 3.ULD and 8.KLA 6/44–11/44 (U-Cdr's Torpedo Course 74)
Cdr *U 2339* 16.11.44–5.5.45

WOHLFARTH, HERBERT [1370]
b. 5.6.1915, Kanazawa, Japan
Class 1933; Kplt 1.10.40
U-boat trg and various duties 5/37–9/38; WO *U 16* 9/38–10/39
Cdr *U 14* 19.10.39–1.6.40
1st U-Flotilla and *Baubelehrung* U-Boats Baltic 6/40
Cdr *U 137* 15.6.40–14.12.40
1st U-Flotilla 12/40–1/41; *Baubelehrung* 1/41–2/41
Cdr *U 556* 6.2.41–27.6.41
POW 27.6.41–14.7.47
Knight's Cross 15.5.41 (70th KM, 30th U-boat holder)

WOLF, ECKEHARD [1371]
b. 11.3.1918, Crossen
Class 1937b; Kplt 1.1.45
2WO *U 560* 3/41–10/41; 1WO *U 560* 10/41–7/42; courses and *Baubelehrung* 8.KLA 8/42–3/43 (first patrol aboard U-tanker *U 459*)
Cdr *U 966* 4.3.43–10.11.43
Interned in Spain 10.11.43–July 1945

WOLF, HEINZ [1372]
b. 2.8.1914, Emmerich, Rhine
Class 1934; Kplt 1.4.42
WO minelayer *Roland* 9/39–11/39; Cdr with Escort Flotilla 11/39–3/40; M/S-Cdr 2nd and 18th Minesweeping Flotillas 4/40–5/41; U-boat trg 5/41–10/41; WO 7th and 29th U-Flotillas 10/41–1/42; U-Cdr's Course, 2.UAA and 24th U-Flotilla 2/42–4/42; *Baubelehrung* 1.KLA 4/42–5/42
Cdr *U 465* 20.5.42 to 2.5.43
Lost 2.5.43

WOLFBAUER, LEO [1373]
b. 21.7.1895, Pernegg, Bruck a.d. Mur
Entry 1913 Austro-Hungarian (k.u.k.) Navy; KKpt (zV) 1.4.42
U-Officer's course and 3rd Officer k.u.k. *U 29* 1917; 2nd Officer k.u.k. *U 29* 1918–Armistice
24th U-Flotilla 3/40–2/42; *Baubelehrung* 2/42–4/42
Cdr *U 463* 2.4.42–16.5.43
Lost 16.5.43 SW of Scilly Is

WOLFF, GÜNTER [1374]
b. 31.1.1920, Stettin
Entry X/1939; ObltzS (R) 1.1.44
Mine clearance vessel *Bali* 9/41–2/43; U-boat trg 3/43–8/43; 1WO *U 441* 8/43–6/44; U-Cdr's Course, 24th U-Flotilla 6/44–7/44, U-Cdr 31st U-Flotilla 7/44–1/45; *Baubelehrung* Cdr 2.KLA and 8.KLA for *U 2550* (never commissioned) 1/45–8.4.45

WOLFF, HEINZ [1375]
b. 13.3.1918, Elberfeld
Class 1937a; Kplt 1.7.44
VP-Cdr 13th VP-Boat Flotilla 6/40–6/42; U-boat trg 6/42–10/42; 1WO *U 437* 10/42–8/43; U-Cdr trg, 2.UAA and 23rd U-Flotilla 8/43–10/43
Cdr *U 974* 9.11.43–19.4.44
Cdr *U 985* 20.4.44–15.11.44
1.UAA 11/44–1/45; *Baubelehrung* Cdr 7. KLA for *U 3534* (never commissioned) 6.1.45–3/45; later details not known

WOLFF, KARL-HEINZ [1376]
b. 16.10.1909, Danzig
Class 1928; FKpt 1.4.44
Seconded to Luftwaffe until 3/41; U-boat trg 3/41–6/41; U-Cdr sea trg *U 74* 7/41–8/41; course and *Baubelehrung* 9/41–11/41
Cdr *U 509* 4.11.41–9/42 (see Witte [1365])
Various duties 10/42–3/43; Comp. CO Naval College Flensburg-Mürwik 3/43–10/43; First Officer destroyer *Z 15 Erich Steinbrinck* 10/43–5/44; Naval High Command North 5/44–8/44; adviser OKM/1.SKL 8/44–1/45; Cdr Section II/Naval College Mürwik 1/45–capitulation

WOLFRAM, RALF-REIMAR [1377]
b. 31.3.1912, Wilhelmshaven
Class 1930; KKpt 1.6.43
ADC Staff Naval Group West 8/39–12/39; Leader Trg Div. 2nd Torpedo-Boat Flotilla 12/39–3/40; *Baubelehrung* torpedo-boats 3/40–4/40; Cdr torpedo-boat *T 6* 4/40–11/40; Trg Leader Destroyer Crews' Holding Div. 12/40–1/41; *Baubelehrung* destroyer *Z 27* 1/41–2/41; First Officer destroyer *Z 27* 2/41–10/41; adviser Torpedo Inspectorate 10/41–3/42; U-boat trg 3/42–7/42; U-Cdr under instrn 2nd U-Flotilla 7/42–9/42
Cdr *U 108* 15.10.42–16.10.43
Baubelehrung 6.KLA 10/43–12/43
Cdr *U 864* 9.12.43–9.2.45
Lost 9.2.45 Norwegian Sea, W of Bergen

WOLLSCHLÄGER, OTTO [1378]
b. 31.3.1902, Ditfurt, Quedlinburg
Rating entry 1922; Kplt 1.3.45
U-course U-Boat School 10/37–11/37; Staff U-Flotilla *Weddigen* 11/37–1/38; Reserve Group FdU on *U 3* 1.2.38–20.2.38; U-School Flotilla on *U 7* 21.2.38–12.12.38; 3./1 Basic Trg Est. Stralsund 12/38–2/39; ObStrm U-School Flotilla on *U 7* 11.2.39–18.1.40; ObStrm U-School Flotilla, 21st U-Flotilla on *U 3* 19.1.40–1.10.41; Anti-Submarine School, acting Cdr *U 17* 2.10.41–14.10.41
Cdr *UC 1* 15.10.41–16.11.41
Cdr *UC 2* 17.11.41–27.9.43
Baubelehrung 8.KLA 9/43–11/43
Cdr *U 721* 8.11.43–17.12.44
Trg Officer 22nd U-Flotilla 12/44–3/45; 1.UAA 3/45–capitulation

WREDE, HANS-CHRISTIAN [1379]
b. 9.8.1920, Kiel
Class IX/1939; ObltzS 1.10.43
Baubelehrung U 448 6/42–8/42; 1WO *U 448* 8/42–12/43; U-Cdr's Course, 3.ULD and 23rd U-Flotilla 12/43–2/44; Trg Officer 4th U-Flotilla 2/44–10/44
Cdr *U 1234* 17.10.44–5.5.45

WÜRDEMANN, ERICH [1380]
b. 15.1.1914, Hamburg
Class 1933; Kplt 1.11.40
ADC 2nd Destroyer Div. destroyer *Z 5 Paul Jacobi* 12/37–10/38; 3WO then 2WO and Torpedo Officer, then 1WO and Torpedo Officer, finally Radio Technical Officer destroyer *Z 5 Paul Jacobi* 11/38–10/40; U-boat trg 11/40–3/41; U-Cdr's Torpedo Course, 24th U-Flotilla 3/41–4/41; U-Cdr sea trg *U 43* 4/41–7/41; *Baubelehrung* 8.KLA 7/41–9/41
Cdr *U 506* 15.9.41–12.7.43
Lost 12.7.43 W of Vigo, Spain
Knight's Cross 14.3.43 (152nd KM, 82th U-boat holder)

WÜST, HELMUTH [1381]
b. 31.7.1920, Wiesbaden
Class IX/1939; ObltzS 1.10.43
Naval Gun Ordnance Office 4/42–3/43; converted from Ordnance to Seaman Branch officer 1.3.43; Navigation course Helmsman's School 3/43–6/43; U-boat trg 6/43–12/43; 1WO *U 307*

12/43–9/44; U-Cdr's Course, 3.ULD and 24th
U-Flotilla 9/44–12/44; 27th U-Flotilla 12/44
Cdr *U 146* 22.12.44–9.3.45 (see Schauroth
[1070])
Later details not available

WULFF, HEINRICH [1382]
b. 11.2.1908, Hamburg
Entry VIII/1940; ObltzS (R) 1.2.43
U-boat trg 1/41–7/41; 5th U-Flotilla 7/41–8/41;
2WO *U 584* 8/41–8/42; U-Cdr's Course, 24th
U-Flotilla, 8/42–9/42; *Baubelehrung* 8.KLA
9/42–10/42
Cdr *U 646* 29.10.42–17.5.43
Lost 17.5.43 SE of Iceland

WUNDERLICH, KARL [1383]
b. 28.5.1911, Gefell, Vogtland
Entry II/1941; ObltzS (R) 1.1.44
WO *U 106* 2/41–4/42; WO *U 29* 4/42–5/42;
courses 6/42–9/42; WO *U 628* 9/42–6/43;
courses 6/43–10/43
Cdr *UIT 22* 11.10.43–11.3.44
Lost 11.3.44 S of Cape of Good Hope

WYSK, GERHARD [1384]
b. 2.5.1920, Weilburg, Lahn
Class 1938; ObltzS 1.4.43
WO 1st, 38th, 7th and 5th Minesweeping Flotillas 7/40–3/43; U-boat trg 3/43–9/43; course 2.UAA 9/43–10/43; Comp. Officer 3.ULD 10/43–12/43; *Baubelehrung* 5.KLA 12/43–2/44
Cdr *U 322* 5.2.44–25.11.44
Lost 25.11.44 W of Shetlands

Z

ZAHN, WILHELM [1385]
b. 29.7.1910, Ebensfelde, Staffelstein
Class 1930; KKpt 1.4.43
1WO *U 33* 7/36–9/37; 1WO *U 35* 9/37–10/38
Cdr *U 56* 26.11.38–21.1.40
Instructor Torpedo School Flensburg-Mürwik 1/40–7/41 but Harbour Cdr Kristiansand South 4/40–5/40; at BdU, 8/41
Cdr *U 69* 28.8.41–31.3.42
3/Adm. Staff Officer (A3) on Staff 2/Adm. U-Boats and Staff Commanding Adm. U-Boats 4/42–9/43; Cdr Section II/2.ULD 10/43–12/44 and Section I/2.ULD 1/45–3/45; Group Leader A, Torpedo Inspectorate 3/45–capitulation
Detained; freed 12/45

ZAHNOW, GÜNTER [1386]
b. 5.6.1920, Altdamm, Randow, Pomerania
Class IX/1939; ObltzS 1.10.43
1WO *U 167* 7/42–4/43, inc. acting Cdr *U 167* 8.1.43–16.1.43 (see Neubert [870]); interned until 5/43; *Baubelehrung* 8.KLA 6/43; 1WO *U 547* 6/43–3/44; U-Cdr's Course and *Baubelehrung* 3/44–5/44 (U-Cdr's Torpedo Course 69)
Cdr *U 747* 5/44–9.4.45
Later details not available

ZANDER, HERMANN [1387]
b. 28.7.1910, Böhlitz-Ehrenburg, Leipzig
Entry 1929; Kplt 1.4.45
Torpedo Officer light cruiser *Nürnberg* 11/41–5/43; U-boat trg 5/43–10/43; courses 3.ULD, 23rd and 24th U-Flotillas 10/43–1/44 (U-Cdr's Torpedo Course 60); *Baubelehrung* 7.KLA 1/44–3/44
Cdr *U 1205* 2.3.44–3.5.45

ZANDER, JOACHIM [1388]
b. 20.4.1917, Berlin-Charlottenburg
Class 1936; Kplt 1.4.43
WO 7th and 6th Minesweeping Flotillas 8/39–1/41; U-boat trg 1/41–6/41; 1WO *U 201* 7/41–1/42; U-Cdr's Course, 24th U-Flotilla 1/42–3/42
Cdr *U 3* 3.3.42–30.9.42
Instructor 1.ULD 10/42–2/43; *Baubelehrung* 2/43–3/43
Cdr *U 311* 23.3.43–22.4.44
Lost 22.4.44 North Atlantic

ZAPF, WERNER [1389]
b. 23.7.1915, Schwarzenbrunn, Thüringen
Entry 1/1936; ObltzS 1.4.45
U-boat trg and courses 8/42–9/43; WO 11th U-Flotilla 9/43–2/44; WO *U 965* 2/44–8/44; U-Cdr's Course, 24th U-Flotilla 9/44–12/44
Cdr *U 61* 2.12.44–3/45
3.ULD and Naval Anti-Tank Brigade 3/45–5/45
Fell 3.5.45 in land defence of Germany

ZAPP, RICHARD [1390]
b. 3.4.1904, Germersheim, Pfalz
Class 1926; FKpt 1.1.45
Cdr Naval Flak Detachment 251 8/39–3/40; U-boat trg 4/40–10/40; U-Cdr (supernumerary) sea trg *U 46* 10/40–11/40; *Baubelehrung* U-Boats North Sea 11/40–1/41
Cdr *U 66* 21.1.41–21.6.42

CO 3rd U-Flotilla 6/42–10/44; Cdr Naval Regiment *Zapp* at La Rochelle 10/44–capitulation
Detained 9.5.45–5.7.47
Knight's Cross 23.4.42 (109th KM, 50th U-boat holder)

ZAUBITZER, JOACHIM [1391]

b. 28.4.1918, Göttingen
Class 1937a; Kplt 1.4.44
No 2 Torpedo Officer heavy cruiser *Admiral Scheer* 4/39–9/41; at BdU, U-boat trg and courses 9/41–3/42; 1WO *U 129* 3/42–2/43; U-Cdr's Course 1.UAA 2/43 (U-Cdr's Torpedo Course 42); *Baubelehrung* 1/8.KLA 3/43–4/43
Cdr *U 974* 22.4.43–8.11.43
Trg Leader and Comp. CO for prospective U-boat officers Torpedo School Flensburg-Mürwik 11/43–capitulation

ZECH, ALOIS [1392]

b. 14.9.1907, Langerringen, Landsberg am Lech
Entry 1925; KKpt 1.8.43
Instructor Mine Warfare School 10/37–5/40; M/S-Cdr 3rd Minesweeping Flotilla 5/40–5/41; U-boat trg and courses 5/41–12/41; Comp. CO 2.UAA 12/41–2/42; *Baubelehrung* 1.KLA 2/42–4/42
Cdr *U 119* 2.4.42 to 14.4.43 (per WASt) or until relieved by von Kameke [578] 16.4.43 (per *U 119* WD)
12th U-Flotilla 4/43–7/43; adviser Naval Mines Inspectorate 7/43–capitulation

ZEDELIUS, GÜNTHER [1393]

b. 19.5.1915, Othmarschen, Hamburg
Class 1935; Kplt 1.10.42
Seconded Luftwaffe 10/37–1/42; U-boat trg 2/42–9/42; 1WO *U 130* 9/42–1/43; U-Cdr's Course, 2.UAA and 26th U-Flotilla 1/43–2/43
Cdr *U 637* 23.2.43–20.7.44
Released from service 21.7.44

ZEHLE, DIETRICH [1394]

b. 17.9.1921, Hildesheim
Class XII/1939; ObltzS 1.12.43
WO sea trg 1st Minesweeping Flotilla 8/40–12/40; Naval College Flensburg-Mürwik 12/40–4/41; aboard *T 153* 5/41–6/41; U-boat trg 6/41–1/42; Platoon Officer 2.ULD 1/42–9/42; *Baubelehrung* 10/42–11/42; 1WO *U 360* 11/42–3/44; U-Cdr's Course, 3.ULD and 24th U-Flotilla 3/44–5/44 (U-Cdr's Torpedo Course 68); courses 27th U-Flotilla 5/44–7/44
Acting Cdr *U 299* 9.8.44–3.9.44
11th U-Flotilla 9/44–11/44
Acting Cdr *U 1009* 11/44–2/45
U-Cdr 11th U-Flotilla 2/45–4/45; attached Higher Command of Naval Flak 4/45–capitulation

ZEISSLER, HERBERT [1395]

b. 17.9.1920, Magdeburg
Class 1938; ObltzS 1.1.43
U-boat trg 10/40–4/41; *Baubelehrung* 4/41–5/41; WO *U 373* 5/41–8/41; WO *U 30* 8/41–9/41; Comp. Leader 1.UAA 9/41–5/42; *Baubelehrung* 5/42–6/42; 1WO *U 338* 6/42–7/43; U-Cdr's Course, 2.UAA and 24th U-Flotilla 7/43–8/43 (U-Cdr's Torpedo Course 52); *Baubelehrung* 7.KLA 8/43–9/43
Cdr *U 1192* 23.9.43–7/44
Cdr *U 140* 1/8.44–19.11.44
Cdr *U 1194* 20.11.44–capitulation
Detained; freed 21.8.45

ZENKER, WALTER [1396]

b. 2.1.1914, Holzminden
Enlisted rating 1931; ObltzS 1.10.43
ObStrm *U 17* 8/40–11/40; *Baubelehrung* 11/40–12/40; ObStrm *U 553* 12/40–9/42; courses 9/42–4/43 (U-Cdr's Torpedo Course 43)
Cdr *U 57* 17.5.43–31.7.44
22nd U-Flotilla 8/44–9/44

Cdr *U 393* 1.10.44–13.1.45
Baubelehrung Cdr *U 3535* (never commissioned)
  7.KLA 1.45–3/45; later details not available

ZEPLIEN, WALTER [1397]
b. 17.9.1918, Greifswald
Class 1937b; ObltzS 1.4.42
R-Cdr 7th R-Boat Flotilla 1/41–7/42; U-boat trg
  7/42–11/42; 1WO *U 575* 12/42–3/43
Cdr *U 971* 1.4.43–24.6.44
POW 24.6.44

ZETZSCHE, HANS-JÜRGEN [1398]
b. 5.10.1915, Annaberg, Erzgebirge
Class 1934; Kplt 1.1.42
1WO *U 28* 11/38–1/40; 1WO *U 10* 1/40–4/40
Cdr *U 20* 16.4.40–7.6.40
Course 6/40–7/40
Acting Cdr *U 8* 7.7.40–28.7.40
Cdr *U 4* 29.7.40–2.2.41
Baubelehrung 2/41–3/41
Cdr *U 560* 6.3.41–24.8.41
Baubelehrung 8/41–10/41
Cdr *U 591* 9.10.41–8.9.42
Acting Cdr *U 378* 10.9.42–11.10.42 (made Arctic
  patrol 12.9.42–26.9.42)
Naval Liaison Officer *Fliegerführer* (AOC)
  Lofotens 9/42–11/42
Cdr *U 591* 12.11.42–17.5.43 (Zetzsche was
  wounded during an attack on the boat by a
  Sunderland aircraft on 15.5.43 and was
  stretchered off on docking at St Nazaire on
  17.5.43. 1WO Sauerbier [1053] was acting Cdr
  for these two days. Per WASt, Zetzsche re-
  mained as commander until 10.6.43.)
Hospitalised 5/43–3/44 (U-Boat Archive per
  Zetzsche); with Staff FdU/Trg 3/44–9/44; 2/
  later 1/Command Staff Officer, Staff FdU/Polar
  Sea 9/44–capitulation and AOrg, Staff FdU
  Polar Sea 11/44–capitulation
Detained; freed 25.4.47

ZIEHM, ERNST [1399]
b. 20.7.1914, Kiel
Class 1933; Kplt 1.4.41
WO Escort Flotilla 10/38–10/39; M/S-Cdr 12th
  Minesweeping Flotilla 10/39–11/40; M/S-Cdr
  2nd Minesweeping Flotilla 11/40–9/41; U-boat
  trg 9/41–3/42; U-Cdr under instrn 1st U-Flotilla
  3/42–5/42; U-Cdr 24th U-Flotilla 6/42
Cdr *U 78* 1.7.42–11/42
Cdr *U 232* 28.11.42–8.7.43
Lost 8.7.43 W of Oporto

ZIESMER, REIMAR [1400]
b. 23.11.1917, Berlin
Class 1937a; Kplt 1.9.44
U-boat trg 4/40–8/40; *Baubelehrung* 9/40–10/40;
  2WO *U 98* 10/40; 2WO *U 38* 11/40–9/41; U-
  Cdr's Course 10/41–11/41
Cdr *U 145* 26.11.41–14.12.42
Baubelehrung 1.KLA 12/42–1/43
Cdr *U 236* 9.1.43 to 14.5.43 or 30.5.43 (U-Boat
  Archive per Ziesmer)
Cdr *U 591* 1.6.43 (U-Boat Archive per Ziesmer)
  or 11.6.43 (per WASt) to 30.7.43
POW 30.7.43

ZIMMERMANN, EBERHARD [1401]
b. 27.10.1916, Danzig-Langfuhr
Class 1937b; Kplt 1.1.45
WO destroyer *Z 20 Karl Galster* 11/39–10/40; U-
  boat trg 10/40–3/41; *Baubelehrung* 4/41–6/41;
  2WO *U 130* 6/41–6/42; U-Cdr's Course, 24th
  U-Flotilla 6/42–7/42
Cdr *U 351* 25.8.42–25.5.43
Baubelehrung 6.KLA 5/43–6/43
Cdr *U 548* 30.6.43–8.2.45; later details not available
Detained; freed 12/47

ZIMMERMANN, GERO [1402]
b. 28.6.1910, Berlin
Class 1929; Kplt 1.11.38

Radio Technical Officer to Naval Signals Officer Swinemünde 9/39–3/40; U-boat trg 4/40–9/40; U-Cdr's Course, 24th U-Flotilla 9/40–11/40; U-Cdr sea trg *U 124* 11/40–2/41; *Baubelehrung* 2/41–4/41
Cdr *U 410* 10.4.41–3.8.41
Lost 3.8.41 SW of Ireland

ZIMMERMANN, HEINRICH [1403]
b. 21.1.1907, Duisburg
Class 1933; Kplt 1.6.39
M/S-Cdr and acting CO 7th Minesweeping Flotilla 8/39–5/40; M/S-Cdr 3rd Minesweeping Flotilla 5/40–3/41; U-boat trg, U-Cdr's Course and *Baubelehrung* 3/41–8/41
Cdr *U 136* 30.8.41–11.7.42
Lost 11.7.42 W of Madeira

ZINKE, ARNIM [1404]
b. 30.7.1908, Ludwigshafen
Class 1933; KKpt 1.6.44
Staff 2/Adm. Baltic 11/38–12/39; Cdr fleet escort *F 5* 9/39–12/39 and 12/39–10/40; M/S-Cdr 3rd Minesweeping Flotilla 10/40–4/41; Course Leader (Nautical) Mine Warfare School 4/41–5/43; U-boat trg 5/43–10/43; courses and *Baubelehrung* 8.KLA 10/43–1/44
Cdr *U 1229* 13.1.44–20.8.44
Lost 20.8.44 SE of Newfoundland

ZIPFEL, RUDOLF [1405]
b. 12.9.1914, Irchwitz, Aubachtal
Entry 1936; ObltzS (R) 1.7.43
U-boat trg 8/43–2/44; 23rd VP-Boat Flotilla 2/44–3/44; 19th VP-Boat Flotilla 4/44; U-Cdr's Course, 23rd U-Flotilla 4/44–6/44; U-boat base Hamburg-Finkenwerder 6/44–11/44; U-Cdr 31st and 8th U-Flotillas 11/44–1/45, inc. *Baubelehrung* 8.KLA; U-Cdr 11th U-Flotilla 1/45–2/45; 2/Naval Infantry Div. Comp. Officer 2/45; *K-Verband*, U-Group *Brandi*, 5th (U) K-Flotilla 2/45–capitulation
Killed 4.6.45 in motorcycle accident while member of U-Group *Brandi* at Ijmuiden, Netherlands

VON ZITZEWITZ, ALEXANDER [1406]
b. 23.3.1916, Kassel
Class 1934; Kplt 1.10.41, posthumously KKpt seniority 1.8.43
Flag Lt Staff C-in-C Torpedo-Boats 6/39–11/39; Flag Lt Staff C-in-C Destroyers 11/39–3/40; Gunnery Officer destroyer *Z 16 Friedrich Eckholdt* 4/40; ADC 3rd Destroyer Flotilla 4/40–7/40; Station Command Baltic 7/40; Comp. Officer Destroyer Crews' Holding Div. 7/40–9/40; Gunnery Officer and 1WO destroyer *Z 23* 9/40–6/41; U-boat trg 6/41–10/41; 3rd U-Flotilla 10/41–11/41; U-Cdr's Course, 26th U-Flotilla 11/41–1/42; *Baubelehrung* 8.KLA 1/42–3/42
Cdr *U 706* 16.3.42–3.8.43
Lost 3.8.43 NW of Cape Ortegal

ZOLLER, HERBERT [1407]
b. 19.5.1919, Rottweil, Neckar
Class 1938; ObltzS 1.4.43
Officer trg sail trg ship *Gorch Fock* 3/39–6/39, light cruiser *Emden* 7/39–9/39; courses 9/39–4/40; Military Hospital Kiel 5/40–6/40; trg battleship *Gneisenau* 7/40–10/40; U-boat trg 10/40–3/41; *Baubelehrung* 8.KLA 3/41–5/41; WO *U 569* 5/41–7/42; U-Cdr's Course, 24th U-Flotilla 7/42–8/42; WO (supernumerary) *U 3* 8/42–9/42
Cdr *U 3* 1.10.42–18.5.43
Baubelehrung 3.KLA 5/43–7/43
Cdr *U 315* 10/7/43–capitulation

ZORN, RUDOLF [1408]

b. 20.7.1917, Ochsenfurt, Mainfranken

Class 1937b; ObltzS 1.4.42 and ObltzS (zV) 1.4.44

Heavy cruiser *Blücher* 12/39–4/40; ADC to CO Sea Defence Oslofjord 4/40–7/40; Group Leader Harbour Defence Flotilla Oslo 7.40–1/41; U-boat trg 1/41–8/41; *Baubelehrung* 8/41–9/41; 1WO *U 456* 9/41–10/42; U-Cdr's Course, 24th U-Flotilla 10/42–11/42

Cdr *U 29* 15.11.42–20.8.43

Baubelehrung 7.KLA 8/43–10/43

Cdr *U 416* 4.10.43–14.11.43

Cdr *U 382* 15.11.43–16.7.44

(On the termination of his military service contract on 31.3.44, Zorn was retained in the Kriegsmarine on the expiring terms and conditions on a conscription basis effective the following day.)

Cdr *U 650* 17.7.44 or 20.7.44 (relieved Gerke [352], per *U 650* WD) to 7.1.45

Missing North Atlantic from 12/44 or 1/45, official date of death 7.1.45

ZSCHECH, PETER [1409]

b. 1.10.1918, Constantinople, Turkey

Class 1936; Kplt 1.4.43

WO destroyer *Z 7 Hermann Schoemann* 7/39–4/40; WO destroyer *Z 14 Friedrich Ihn* 4/40–10/40; U-boat trg 10/40–3/41; relief instructor Torpedo School Mürwik 3/41–8/41; WO *U 124* 8/41–7/42; U-Cdr's Course, 24th U-Flotilla 8/42–9/42

Cdr *U 505* 6.9.42–24.10.43

Suicide 24.10.43 (Translator's note: At sea, in Control Room of *U 505*.)

ZURMÜHLEN, BERNHARD [1410]

b. 23.2.1909, Bielefeld

Class 1934; Kplt 1.4.40, posthumously KKpt seniority 1.11.43

Radio Technical Officer trg ship *Schleswig-Holstein* 8/39–8/40; Mobile Signals Troop, Naval Signals Officer Bruges 8/40–11/40; instructor Signals School Mürwik 11/40–3/41; U-boat trg 3/41–7/41; U-Cdr's Course, 24th U-Flotilla 7/41–9/41; WO (supernumerary) *U 331* 9/41–11/41; *Baubelehrung* 8.KLA 11/41–12/41

Cdr *U 600* 11.12.41–25.11.43

Lost 25.11.43 N of Punta Delgada, Azores

ZWARG, HEINZ [1411]

b. 22.11.1917, place not recorded

Class 1937a; Kplt 1.4.44

ADC Fleet Command 9/39–3/40; U-boat trg 3/40–9/40; 2WO *U 97* 9/40–6/41; Naval Liaison Officer on Staff Italian C-in-C Submarines Bordeaux 7/41–10/41; A Ia, Staff BdU/Opns 11/41–10/43

Cdr *U 416* 15.11.43–15.5.44

Cdr *U 276* 19.7.44–29.9.44

Baubelehrung Type XXI 7.KLA 11/44–3/45

Cdr *U 3528* 18.3.45–1.5.45

Detained; freed 22.11.45

Index

The German U boat fleet is listed in numerical order followed by fifteen foreign submarines confiscated and impressed into the Kriegsmarine. The commanders of each boat are listed by surname and identifying numeral in date sequence with effect from the date of commissioning and until when the boat was lost, scrapped or decommissioned. As explained by the authors in their Preface, in some cases it has not been possible to establish a full record of the commanders of boats pre-war. Intervening vacant periods are shown with dates.

U 1 Ewerth [262], Gelhaar [347], not known 3.2.38–28.10.38, Deecke [195],

U 2 Michahelles [824], Liebe [731], Schultze [1155], Rosenbaum [1027], Heidtmann [439], v. Wilamowitz [1351], Kölzer [636], Schwaff [1166], Herglotz [464], Schwarzkopf [1175],

U 3 Meckel [800], Heinicke [444], Schepke [1076], Schreiber [1121], Franzke [314], v. Bülow [150], Trojer [1281], Zander [1388], Zoller [1407], Hartmann [422], Neumeister [875]

U 4 Weingartner [1327], v. Dresky [216], v. Klot-Heydenfeldt [615], Hinsch [492], Schultze [1154], Zetzsche [1398], Bernbeck [77], Leimkühler [717], Marienfeld [786], Düppe [222], Sander [1048], Mumm [860], Rieger (?) [1004]

U 5 Dau [189], Glattes [361], Kutschmann [688], Lehmann-Willenbrock [714], Opitz [900], Bothe [116], Friederich [322], Mohs [837], Pressel [944], Radermacher [963], Rahn [968]

U 6 Mathes [792], Heidel [438], Matz [797], Michalowski [825], Harms [416], Schnee [1102], Peters [916], Liebe [731], Bopst [104], Brüninghaus [140], Just [569], Brüninghaus [140], Niethmann [882], König [639], Heitz [451], Jestel [557]

U 7 Freiwald [316], Salman [1046], Heidel [438], Salman [1046], Schrott [1137], Reeder [980], Brüller [137], Reeder [980], Kuhlmann [676], Schmid [1094], Koitschka [647], Schrenk [1125], Hübschen [521], Loeschcke [743]

U 8 Grosse [388], Peters [916], Schuhart [1148], Stiebler [1234], Lehmann-Willenbrock [714], Michel [826], Kentrat [597], Stein [1220], Kell [589], Zetzsche [1398], Kell [589], Heinsohn [449], Borcherdt [106], Steinhaus [1225], Deckert [193], Hoffmann [505], Werner [1338], Iversen [537], Kriegshammer [665]

U 9 Looff [750], v. Schmidt [1100], Mathes [792], Schulte [1149], Lüth [764], Kaufmann [786], Deecke [194], Schmidt-Weichert [1099], vacant 1.5.42–27.10.42, Schmidt-Weichert [1099], Klapdor [609], Landt-Hayen [691], Petersen [919]

U 10 Schulz [1158], Lorentz [753], Preuss [946], Mützelburg [856], v. Rabenau [959], Ruwiedel [1040], Karpf [582], Coester [172], Strenger [1284], Ahlers [7]

U 11 Rösing [1018], Schütze [1146], Peters [916], Stolzenburg [1241], Dobenecker [209]

U 12 v. Schmidt [1100], Pauckstadt [911], v. d. Ropp [1026]

U 13 v. Stockhausen [1238], Daublebsky [190], Scheringer [1078], Lüth [764], Schulte [1149]

U 14 Oehrn [891], Wellner [1329], Wohlfarth [1370], Bigalk [82], Heidtmann [439], Könenkamp [638], Purkhold [951], Petersen [919], Köhntopp [634], Bortfeldt [114], Dierks [200]

U 15 v. Schmidt [1100], Cohausz [173], Buchholz [149], Frahm [305]

INDEX

U 16 Beduhn [64], Weingärtner [1327], Behrens [66], Wellner [1329]

U 17 Fresdorf [318], v. Reiche [986], Jeppener-Haltenhoff [553], Behrens [66], Stiebler [1234], Behrens [66], Collmann [174], Schultze [1157], Wollschläger [1378], Heydemann [480], Sitek [1198], Schmidt [1096], Bartsch [46]

U 18 Baumgärtel [55], Pauckstadt [911], vacant 21.11.36–29.9.37, Beduhn [64], Bauer [50], Mengersen [811], Linder [737], Vogelsang [1306], Rosenberg-Gruszcynski [1029], Wissmann [1361], vacant 19.8.42–2.12.42, Fleige [294], Bartsch [46], Arendt [18], Fleige [294], Baumgärtel [55]

U 19 Schütze [1146], Meckel [800], Müller-Arnecke [848], Schepke [1076], Prellberg [942], Lohmeyer [748], Kaufmann [586], Schendel [1075], Litterscheid [741], Gaude [339], vacant 1.5.42–30.9.42, Gaude [339], Ohlenburg [896], Verpoorten [1300]

U 20 Eckermann [235], Moehle [829], v. Klot-Heydenfeldt [615], Driver [219], Zetzsche [1398], Paulshen [912], Schauenburg [1067], Sträter [1242], Nölke [885], vacant 28.3.42–6.5.42, Schöler [1108], vacant 27.9.42–26.5.43, Schöler [1108], Grafen [375]

U 21 Lott [754], Ambrosius [12], Freiwald [316], Sachs [1043], Frauenheim [315], Stiebler [1234], Heidtmann [439], Lohse [749], Herbschleb [463], Döhler [212], Geisler [344], Kugelberg [675], Schwarzkopf [1175]

U 22 Grosse [388], Winter [1359], Jenisch [550]

U 23 Godt [363], Looff [750], Kretschmer [663], Beduhn [64], Driver [219], Reichenbach-Klinke [987], Brüller [137], Gräf [374], Wahlen [1313], Arendt [18]

U 24 Buchholz [145], Behrens [66], Jeppener-Haltenhoff [553], Heilmann [441], Borchert [108], Hennig [459], Rodler v. Roithberg [1015], vacant 4/42–13.10.42, Petersen [919], Schöler [1108], Petersen [919], Landt-Hayen [691], Lenzmann [724]

U 25 Godt [363], v. Schmidt [1100], Schuhart [1148], Michel [826], Schütze [1146], Beduhn [64]

U 26 Hartmann [425], Schomburg [1118], Ewerth [262], Scheringer [1078], Fischer [288], Scheringer [1078]

U 27 Ibbeken [533], Franz [310]

U 28 Ambrosius [12], Looff [750], Kuhnke [679], Lemp [722], Guggenberger [393], Ratsch [975], Eckhardt [236], vacant 21.3.42–30.6.42, Marbach [784], Christiansen [165], Krempl [661], Sachse [1044], vacant 18.3.44–4.8.44

U 29 Fischer [288], Michel [826], Schuhart [1148], Lassen [703], Hasenschar [428], Marbach [784], vacant 1.7.42–14.11.42, Zorn [1408], Aust [23], Arco-Zinneberg [17]

U 30 Cohausz [173], Pauckstadt [911], Lemp [722], Prützmann [948], Loeser [744], Purkhold [951], Baberg [24], Bauer [49], Saar [1041], vacant 12/42–5/43, Fischer [286], Fabricius [266], Schimmel [1084]

U 31 Dau [189], Habekost [397], vacant 12.3.40–7.7.40, Prellberg [942]

U 32 Lott [754], Büchel [147], Jenisch [549]

U 33 Junker [568], Freiwald [316], v. Dresky [216]

U 34 Sobe [1200], Grosse [388], Pauckstadt [911], Rollmann [1024], Meyer [817], Schultz [1153], Remus [993], Fenski [276], Hagenau [402], Aust [23]

U 35 Michahelles [824], Rösing [1018], Kretschmer [663], Lott [754]

U 36 Ewerth [262], Fröhlich [330]

U 37 Schuch [1139], Hartmann [425], Oehrn [891], Clausen [168], Folkers [298], Janssen [546], Lauzemis [709], Kelling [595], Gerlach [353], Seiler [1187], v. Wenden [1331]

U 38 Liebe [730], Schuch [1139], uncertain 7.1.42–4.1.43, Laubert [705], Sander [1048], Kregelin [660], v. Möllendorff [832], Kühn [673], Peters [916]

U 39 Glattes [361]

U 40 v. Schmidt [1100], Barten [44]

U 41 Mugler [857]

U 42 Dau [189]

U 43 Ambrosius [12], Lüth [764], Schwantke [1169]
U 44 Mathes [792]
U 45 Gelhaar [347]
U 46 Sohler [1202], Endrass [252], Grau [380], v. Puttkammer [953], Neubert [870], v. Witzendorff [1367], Saar [1041], Knecht [620], Jewinski [558]
U 47 Prien [947]
U 48 Schultze [1152], Rösing [1018], Bleichrodt [89], Schultze [1152], Atzinger [19], Todenhagen [1279]
U 49 v. Gossler [372]
U 50 Bauer [50]
U 51 Heinicke [444], vacant 8/39–14.1.40, Knorr [626]
U 52 Barten [44], vacant 18.9.39–13.11.39, Salman [1046], Möhlmann [831], v. Rabenau [959], v. Freyberg [319], Mumm [859], Rossmann [1031], Racky [960]
U 53 Knorr [626], Heinicke [444], Schonder [1119], Grosse [388]
U 54 Michel [826], Kutschmann [688]
U 55 Heidel [438]
U 56 Zahn [1385], Harms [416], Pfeifer [924], Römer [1017], Grave [381], Deiring [198], Sausmikat [1054], Miede [827], Kaeding [571], Sauerbier [1053]
U 57 Korth [652], Topp [1280], vacant 3.9.40–10.1.41, Eisele [243], Zenker [1396], Kühl [672]
U 58 Kuppisch [684], Schonder [1119], Rahmlow [967], Hamm [404], Barber [37], Schöneboom [1110], Willner [1356], Rix [1012], Schulz [1160]
U 59 Jürst [565], Matz [797], v. Forstner [300], Gretschel [384], Poser [937], Sammler [1047], Schley [1087], Walther [1317]
U 60 Schewe [1081], Schnee [1102], Wallas [1316], Pressel [944], Mohs [837], Hübschen [521], Kregelin [660], Giesewetter [357]
U 61 Oesten [893], Stiebler [1234], Mattke [795], Lange [694], Geider [343], Ley [729], Schultze [1156], Zapf [1389]

U 62 Michalowski [825], Forster [299], Wintermeyer [62], Mehl [805], Schünemann [1143], Epp [256], Schönberg [1109], Slevogt [1199], Augustin [22]
U 63 Lorentz [753]
U 64 Schulz [1158]
U 65 v. Stockhausen [1238], Hoppe [512]
U 66 Zapp [1390], Markworth [789], Frerks [317], Seehausen [1183]
U 67 Bleichrodt [89], Pfeffer [923], Müller-Stockheim [852]
U 68 Merten [813], Lauzemis [709], Scherraus [1079], Seehausen [1183], Lauzemis [709]
U 69 Metzler [816], Auffermann [20], Zahn [1385], Gräf [374]
U 70 Matz [797]
U 71 Flachsenberg [293], v. Roithberg [1015], vacant 2.5.43–30.6.43, Krempl [661], Christiansen [165], Hartmann [421], Ranzau [970]
U 72 Neumann [872], Köster [646], Mehl [805], Scheibe [1072], Lange [694], Sander [1048], Mayer [799]
U 73 Rosenbaum [1027], Deckert [193]
U 74 Kentrat [597], Friederich [322]
U 75 Ringelmann [1011]
U 76 v. Hippel [494]
U 77 Schonder [1119], Hartmann [424]
U 78 Dumrese [224], Makowski [776], Dieterich [202], Ziehm [1399], Sommer [1203], Eisele [243], Hübsch [520]
U 79 Kaufmann [586]
U 80 Staats [1209], Benker [68], Curio [180], Isermeyer [534], Keerl [587]
U 81 Guggenberger [393], Krieg [664]
U 82 Rollmann [1023]
U 83 Kraus [658], Wörisshoffer [1368]
U 84 Uphoff [1295]
U 85 Greger [383]
U 86 Schug [1147]
U 87 Berger [74]
U 88 Bohmann [100]
U 89 Lohmann [747]
U 90 Oldörp [899]

INDEX

U 91 Walkerling [1315], Hungershausen [528]
U 92 Oelrich [892], Queck [955], Brauel [125]
U 93 Korth [652], Elfe [244]
U 94 Kuppisch [684], Ites [535]
U 95 Schreiber [1121]
U 96 Lehmann-Willenbrock [714], Hellriegel [454], Peters [918], Willner [1356], Rix [1012]
U 97 Heilmann [441], Bürgel [151], vacant 16.10.42–1.2.43, Trox [1284]
U 98 Gysae [396], Schulze [1163], Eichmann [240]
U 99 Kretschmer [663]
U 100 Schepke [1076]
U 101 Frauenheim [315], Mengersen [811], Marbach [784], Bothe [116], vacant 1.4.42–5/42, v. Witzendorff [1367], Münster [854]
U 102 v. Klot-Heydenfeldt [615]
U 103 Schütze [1146], Winter [1359], Janssen [546], vacant 14.3.44–22.1.45, Murl [861], Schunck [1165]
U 104 Jürst [565]
U 105 Schewe [1081], Schuch [1139], Schweichel [1178], Nissen [884]
U 106 Oesten [893], Rasch [972], vacant 4/43–19.6.43, Damerow [186]
U 107 Hessler [475], Gelhaus [348], vacant 7.6.43–7/43, Simmermacher [1196], Fritz [328]
U 108 Scholtz [1113], Hilsenitz [489], Wolfram [1377], Brünig [139],
U 109 Fischer [287], Bleichrodt [89], Schramm [1120]
U 110 Lemp [722],
U 111 Kleinschmidt [612]
U 112–115 numbers not allocated
U 116 v. Schmidt [1100], Grimme [386]
U 117 Neumann [872]
U 118 Czygan [182]
U 119 Zech [1392], v. Kameke [578]
U 120 Bauer [48], Heyda [479], Körner [645], Fiedler [280], Radermacher [963], not known 25.5.43–25.7.43, Sauerbier [1053], Bensel [69]
U 121 Schroeter [1134], Harms [416], Schnee [1102], v. Schlippenbach [1089], Hetschko [476], von Witzendorff [1367], Westphalen [1341], Hübschen [521], Hülsenbeck [522], Horst [517]
U 122 Looff
U 123 Moehle [829], Hardegen [413], v. Schroeter [1135]
U 124 Schulz [1158], Mohr [835]
U 125 Kuhnke [679], Folkers [298]
U 126 Bauer [48], Kietz [605]
U 127 Hansmann [411]
U 128 Heyse [482], Steinert [1223]
U 129 Clausen [168], Witt [1362], v. Harpe [418]
U 130 Kals [577], vacant 2.1.43–6.2.43, Keller [592]
U 131 Baumann [52]
U 132 Vogelsang [1306]
U 133 Hesse [474], Mohr [834]
U 134 Schendel [1075], Brosin [134]
U 135 Praetorius [939], Schütt [1144], Luther [766]
U 136 Zimmermann [1403]
U 137 Wohlfarth [1370], Massmann [791], Brünning [142], Gemeiner [349], Schimmel [1084], Fischer [285], Dierks [200]
U 138 Lüth [764], Lohmeyer [748], Gramitzky [376]
U 139 Bartels [43], Elfe [244], Fenn [275], Lauzemis [709], Sommer [1203], Böttcher [99], Korndörfer [651], Lube [756], Kimmelmann [606]
U 140 Hinsch [492], Hellriegel [454], Popp [936], Markert [787], Zeissler [1395], Scherfling [1077]
U 141 Schultze [1154], Schüler [1140], Krüger [670], Möller [833], Rauch [976], Luttmann [767], Hoffmann [503],
U 142 Clausen [168], Kettner [602], Lindke [738], Bertelsmann [78], Krieg [664], Laudahn [706], Schauroth [1070], Baumgärtel [55]
U 143 Mengersen [811], Möhlmann [831], v. Rosenstiel [1030], Gelhaus [348], Manseck [783], Groth [390], Schwager [1167], Vogel [1304], Kasparek [585]
U 144 v. Hippel [494], v. Mittelstaedt [828]
U 145 Driver [219], Franzius [313], Schomburg

[1117], Ziesmer [1400], Hübschen [521], Hübsch [520], Görner [366]

U 146 Hoffmann [501], Ites [535], Hülsenbeck [522], Grimme [386], Gemeiner [349], Nissen [884], Hilsenitz [489], Waldschmidt [1314], Wüst [1381], Schauroth [1070]

U 147 Hardegen [413], Wetjen [1342]

U 148 Radke [964], Mohr [834], Franke [308], Brüninghaus [140], v. Möllendorff [832], Schäffer [1062], Tammen [1261]

U 149 Höltring [498], Borchers [107], v. Hammerstein-Equord [406], Plohr [931]

U 150 Kelling [595], Schultz [1152], Ranzau [970], v. Ahlefeld [6], Anschütz [15], Kriegshammer [665]

U 151 Oestermann [894], Janssen [546], Eichmann [240], Just [569], Utischill [1296], v. Arco [16]

U 152 Cremer [178], Benker [68], Hildebrandt [485], Geisler [344], Nonn [889], Bergemann [73], Thiel [1266]

U 153 Reichmann [988]

U 154 Kölle [635], Schuch [1139], Kusch [686], Gemeiner [349]

U 155 Piening [927], Rudolph [1036], v. Friedeburg [321], Rudolph [1036], Witte [1363], Altmeier [11],

U 156 Hartenstein [420]

U 157 Henne [458]

U 158 Rostin [1032]

U 159 Witte [1364], Beckmann [63]

U 160 Lassen [703], v. Pommer-Esche [935]

U 161 Witt [1362], Achilles [2]

U 162 Wattenberg [1318]

U 163 Engelmann [255]

U 164 Fechner [271]

U 165 Hoffmann [500]

U 166 Kuhlmann [676]

U 167 Neubert [870], Zahnow [1386], Sturm [1255]

U 168 Pich [925]

U 169 Bauer [49]

U 170 Pfeffer [923], Hauber [431]

U 171 Pfeffer [923]

U 172 Emmermann [249], Hoffmann [504]

U 173 Beucke [80], Schweichel [1178]

U 174 Thilo [1268], Grandefeld [377]

U 175 Bruns [144]

U 176 Dierksen [201]

U 177 Schulze [1163], Gysae [396], Buchholz [145]

U 178 Ibbeken [533], Dommes [214], Spahr [1205]

U 179 Sobe [1200]

U 180 Musenberg [862], Lange [694], vacant 5.1.44–1.4.44, Riesen [1007]

U 181 Lüth [764], Freiwald [316]

U 182 Clausen [168]

U 183 Schäfer [1060], Schneewind [1103]

U 184 Dangschat [187]

U 185 Maus [798]

U 186 Hesemann [471]

U 187 Münnich [853]

U 188 Lüdden [759]

U 189 Kurrer [685]

U 190 Wintermeyer [1360], Reith [992]

U 191 Fiehn [281]

U 192 Happe [412]

U 193 Pauckstadt [911], Abel [1]

U 194 Hesse [474]

U 195 Buchholz [145], vacant 18.10.43–15.4.44, Steinfeldt [1224]

U 196 Kentrat [597], Striegler [1249]

U 197 Bartels [43]

U 198 Hartmann [425], Heusinger v. Waldegg [477]

U 199 Kraus [658]

U 200 Schonder [1119]

U 201 Schnee [1102], Rosenberg [1028]

U 202 Linder [737], Poser [937]

U 203 Mützelburg [856], Seidel [1186], Kottmann [655]

U 204 Kell [589]

U 205 Reschke [996], Bürgel [151]

U 206 Opitz [900]

U 207 Meyer [817]

U 208 Schlieper [1088]

U 209 Brodda [133]

INDEX

U 210 Lemcke [720]
U 211 Hause [433]
U 212 Vogler [1307]
U 213 v. Varendorff [1298]
U 214 Reeder [980], Stock [1237], Conrad [175]
U 215 Hoeckner [496]
U 216 Schultz [1153]
U 217 Reichenbach-Klinke [987]
U 218 Becker [61], Stock [1237]
U 219 Burghagen [156]
U 220 Barber [37]
U 221 Trojer [1281]
U 222 v. Jessen [556]
U 223 Wächter [1311], Gerlach [353]
U 224 Kosbadt [653]
U 225 Leimkühler [717], U226 Borchers [107] Gänge [337]
U 227 Kuntze [683]
U 228 Christophersen [166], Engel [254]
U 229 Schetelig [1080]
U 230 Siegmann [1194], Eberbach [227]
U 231 Wenzel [1336]
U 232 Ziehm [1399]
U 233 Steen [1214]
U 234 Fehler [272]
U 235 v. Möllendorff [832], Becker [58], vacant 21.5.43–28.10.43, Kummetz [682], Huisgen [524]
U 236 Ziesmer [1400], vacant 15.5.43–28.9.43, Hartmann [421], Kregelin [660], Mumm [860]
U 237 Nordheimer [890, vacant 15.5.43–9/44, König [642], van Stipriaan [1235], Menard [810]
U 238 Hepp [462]
U 239 Vöge [1303]
U 240 Link [740]
U 241 Werr [1340]
U 242 Pancke [908], Riedel [1003]
U 243 Märtens [771]
U 244 Fischer [290], Mackeprang [769]
U 245 Schumann-Hindenburg [1164]
U 246 Raabe [956]
U 247 Matschulat [793]
U 248 Emde [248], Loos [752]
U 249 Lindschau [739], Kock [631]
U 250 Schmidt [1098]
U 251 Timm [1276], vacant 2.9.43–22.11.43, Säck [1045]
U 252 Schiebusch [1082], Lerchen [725]
U 253 Friedrichs [325]
U 254 Gilardone [359], Loewe [746]
U 255 Reche [978], Harms [415], vacant 8/44–1.3.45, Heinrich [448]
U 256 Loewe [746], vacant 1.12.42–31.8.43, Brauel [125], vacant (snorkel installation) 28.6.44–1.9.44, Lehmann-Willenbrock [714]
U 257 Rahe [965]
U 258 v. Mässenhausen [772], Koch [628]
U 259 Köpke [643]
U 260 Purkhold [951], Becker [59]
U 261 Lange [694]
U 262 Schiebusch [1082], Atzinger [19], Franke [308], Wieduwilt [1349], Laudahn [706]
U 263 Nölke [885]
U 264 Looks [751]
U 265 Auffhammer [21]
U 266 Leinemann [718], v. Jessen [556]
U 267 Tinschert [1277], v. Witzendorff [1367], Tinschert [1277], Knieper [622]
U 268 Heydemann [480]
U 269 Harfinger [414], vacant 30.4.43–6/43, Hansen [410], Harfinger [414], vacant 22.3.44–5.4.44, Uhl [1288]
U 270 Otto [902], Schreiber [1122]
U 271 Barleben [39]
U 272 Hepp [462]
U 273 Engel [253], Rossmann [1031]
U 274 Jordan [563]
U 275 Bork [110], Wehrkamp [1324]
U 276 Thimme [1269], Borchers [107], Zwarg [1411]
U 277 Lübsen [758]
U 278 Franze [312]
U 279 Finke [283]
U 280 Hungershausen [529]
U 281 v. Davidson [192]
U 282 Müller [845]
U 283 Scholz [1116], Ney [876]

U 284 Scholz [1114]
U 285 Otto [903], Bornhaupt [112]
U 286 Dietrich [204]
U 287 Meyer [819]
U 288 Meyer [823]
U 289 Hellwig [455]
U 290 Strenger [1247], Herglotz [464], Baum [51]
U 291 Keerl [587], Stege [1217], Neumeister [875]
U 292 Schmidt [1097]
U 293 Klingspor [613], Steinbrink [1222]
U 294 Schütt [1144]
U 295 Wieboldt [1347]
U 296 Rasch [973]
U 297 Aldegarmann [10]
U 298 Hohmann [506], Gehrken [342]
U 299 Heinrich [448], Zehle [1394], Heinrich [448], Emde [248]
U 300 Hein [442]
U 301 Körner [645]
U 302 Sickel [1191]
U 303 Heine [443]
U 304 Koch [627]
U 305 Bahr [30]
U 306 v. Trotha [1282]
U 307 Herrle [466], Krüger [669]
U 308 Mühlenpfordt [841]
U 309 Mahrholz [775], Loeder [742]
U 310 Friedland [323], Ley [729]
U 311 Zander [1388]
U 312 Nicolay [878], Herrle [466], v. Gaza [340]
U 313 Schweiger [1179]
U 314 Basse [1147]
U 315 Zoller [1407]
U 316 Stuckmann [1252], König [640]
U 317 Rahlf [966]
U 318 Will [1354]
U 319 Clemens [171]
U 320 Breinlinger [128], Emmrich [250]
U 321 Drews [218], Berends [72]
U 322 Wysk [1384]
U 323 Bokelberg [101], Pregel [940], Dobinsky [210]

U 324 Edelhoff [237]
U 325 Dohrn [213]
U 326 Matthes [794]
U 327 Lemcke [720]
U 328 Lawrence [711], Scholle [1112]
U 329–330 numbers not allocated
U 331 v. Tiesenhausen [1273]
U 332 Liebe [729], Hüttemann [523]
U 333 Cremer [178], Kandzior [580], Kasch [583], Schwaff [1166], Cremer [178], Fiedler [280]
U 334 Siemon [1195], Ehrich [239]
U 335 Pelkner [913]
U 336 Hunger [527]
U 337 Ruwiedel [1040]
U 338 Kinzel [608]
U 339 Basse [47], Remus [994]
U 340 Klaus [611]
U 341 Epp [256]
U 342 Hossenfelder [519]
U 343 Rahn [969]
U 344 Pietsch [928]
U 345 Knackfuss [619]
U 346 Leisten [719]
U 347 de Buhr [153]
U 348 Förster [295], Schunck [1165], Seeger [1182], Nicolay [878]
U 349 Lottner [755], Dähne [183]
U 350 Niester [881]
U 351 Hause [433], Rosenberg [1028], Zimmermann [1401], Roth [1033], Wicke [1345], Schley [1087], Strehl [1245]
U 352 Rathke [974]
U 353 Römer [1017]
U 354 Herbschleb [463], Sthamer [1233]
U 355 La Baume [54]
U 356 Wallas [1316], Ruppelt [1039]
U 357 Kellner [596]
U 358 Manke [781]
U 359 Förster [296]
U 360 Bühring [149], Becker [58]
U 361 Seidel [1186]
U 362 Franz [311]
U 363 Wilzer [1357], Nees [866]

U 364 Sass [1049]
U 365 Wedemeyer [1323], Todenhagen [1279]
U 366 Langenberg [701]
U 367 Hammer [405], Becker [58], Stegemann [1218]
U 368 Schaiper/Schäfer [1063], Giesewetter [357], Roth [1033]
U 369 Schaafhausen [1055], Schunck [1165]
U 370 Nielsen [879]
U 371 Driver [219], Weber [1319], Neumann [873], Mehl [805], Fenski [276]
U 372 Neumann [873]
U 373 Loeser [744], v. Lehsten [715]
U 374 v. Fischel [284]
U 375 Könenkamp [638]
U 376 Marks [788]
U 377 Köhler [633], Kluth [618], Gerke [352]
U 378 Hoschatt [518], Schrewe [1127], Zetzsche [1398], Mäder [770]
U 379 Kettner [602]
U 380 Röther [1019], Brandi [122]
U 381 v. Pückler [949]
U 382 Juli [566], Koch [628], Zorn [1408], Gerke [352], vacant 30.6.44–24.8.44, Wilke [1353], Schimmel [1084]
U 383 Kremser [662]
U 384 v. Rosenberg-Gruszcynski [1029]
U 385 Valentiner [1297]
U 386 Kandler [579], Albrecht [8]
U 387 Büchler [148]
U 388 Sues [1257]
U 389 Heilmann [440]
U 390 Geissler [346]
U 391 Dültgen [221]
U 392 Schümann [1142]
U 393 Radermacher [963], Zenker [1396], Seeger [1181], Herrle [466]
U 394 Unterhorst [1293], Borger [109]
U 395 Unterhorst [1293]
U 396 Unterhorst [1293], Siemon [1195]
U 397 Kallipke [576], Stage [1217], Groth [390]
U 398 Reckhoff [979], Cranz [177]
U 399 van Meeteren [804], Buhse [154]
U 400 Creutz [179]
U 401 Zimmermann [1402]
U 402 v. Forstner [300]
U 403 Clausen [167], Heine [443]
U 404 v. Bülow [150], Schönberg [1109]
U 405 Hopmann [511]
U 406 Dieterichs [203]
U 407 Brüller [137], Korndörfer [651], Kolbus [648]
U 408 v. Hymmen [531]
U 409 Massmann [791]
U 410 Sturm [1255], Fenski [276]
U 411 Litterscheid [741], Spindlegger [1207]
U 412 Jahrmärker [545]
U 413 Poel [932], Sachse [1044]
U 414 Huth [430]
U 415 Neide [867], Werner [1339]
U 416 Reich [985], vacant 31.3.43–3.10.43, Zorn [1408], Zwarg [1411], Rieger [1004]
U 417 Schreiner [1124]
U 418 Lange [693]
U 419 Giersberg [356]
U 420 Reese [981]
U 421 Kolbus [648]
U 422 Brasack [124], Poeschel [933]
U 423 Methner [814], Kelling [595], Hackländer [399]
U 424 Lüders [760]
U 425 Bentzien [71]
U 426 Reich [985]
U 427 v. Gudenus [391]
U 428 (ex-Italian *S-1*) Münster [854], Hanitsch [407]
U 429 (ex-Italian *S-4*) Racky [960], Kuttkat [689]
U 430 (ex-Italian *S-6*) Nachtigall [863], Hammer [405]
U 431 Dommes [214], Schöneboom [1110]
U 432 Schultze [1154], Eckhardt [236]
U 433 Ey [263]
U 434 Heyda [479]
U 435 Strelow [1246]
U 436 Seibicke [1185]
U 437 Schulz [1162], Lamby [690]

U 438 Franzius [313], Heinsohn [449]
U 439 Sporn [1208], v. Tippelskirch [1278]
U 440 Geissler [345], Schwaff [1166]
U 441 Hartmann [423], v. Hartmann [426], Hartmann [423]
U 442 Hesse [473]
U 443 v. Puttkamer [953]
U 444 Langfeld [702]
U 445 Fenn [275], Fischler [291]
U 446 Richard [1000]
U 447 Bothe [116]
U 448 Dauter [191]
U 449 Otto [901]
U 450 Böhme [96]
U 451 Hoffmann [501]
U 452 March [785]
U 453 Hetschko [476], v. Schlippenbach [1089], Lührs [761]
U 454 [398]
U 455 Giessler [358], Scheibe [1072]
U 456 Teichert [1264]
U 457 Brandenburg [121]
U 458 Diggins [205]
U 459 v. Wilamowitz-Moellendorf [1351]
U 460 Schäfer [1059], Schnoor [1107]
U 461 Bernbeck [77], Stiebler [1234]
U 462 Vowe [1310]
U 463 Wolfbauer [1373]
U 464 Harms [416]
U 465 Wolf [1372]
U 466 Thäter [1265]
U 467 Kummer [680]
U 468 Schamong [1064]
U 469 Claussen [170]
U 470 Grave [381]
U 471 Kloevekorn [614]
U 472 v. Forstner [301]
U 473 Sternberg [1231]
U 474 number not allocated
U 475 Stoeffler [1239]
U 476 Niethmann [882]
U 477 Jenssen [552]
U 478 Rademacher [962]
U 479 Förster [295], Sons [1204]

U 480 Förster [295]
U 481 Pick [926], Andersen [13], Bischoff [83]
U 482 Graf v. Matuschka [796]
U 483 v. Morstein [838]
U 484 Schaefer [1061]
U 485 Lutz [768]
U 486 Meyer [818]
U 487 Metz [815]
U 488 Bartke [45], Studt [1253]
U 489 Schmandt [1093]
U 490 Gerlach [354]
U 491 Kellerstrass [594]
U 492–500 numbers not allocated
U 501 Förster [297]
U 502 v. Rosenstiel [1030]
U 503 Gericke [351]
U 504 Poske [938], Luis [765]
U 505 Lowew [745], Zscech [1409], Meyer [821], Lange [694]
U 506 Würdemann [1380]
U 507 Schacht [1057]
U 508 Staats [1209]
U 509 Wolff [1376], Witte [1365]
U 510 Neitzel [868], Eick [241]
U 511 Steinhoff [1226], Schneewind [1103]
U 512 Schultze [1157]
U 513 Rüggeberg [1037], Guggenberger [393]
U 514 Auffermann [20]
U 515 Henke [457]
U 516 Wiebe [1346], Pauckstadt [911], Kuppisch [684], Tillessen [1275], Petran [922]
U 517 Hartwig [427]
U 518 Brachmann [117], Wissmann [1361], Offermann [895]
U 519 Eppen [257]
U 520 Schwartzkopff [1171]
U 521 Bargsten [38]
U 522 Schneider [1104]
U 523 Pietzsch [930]
U 524 v. Steinaecker [1221]
U 525 Drewitz [217]
U 526 Möglich [830]
U 527 Uhlig [1289]
U 528 Fuchs [334], Rabenau [958]

INDEX

U 529 Fraatz [302]
U 530 Lange [699], Wermuth [1337]
U 531 Neckel [865]
U 532 Junker [568]
U 533 Hennig [459]
U 534 Nollau [886]
U 535 Ellmenreich [246],
U 536 Schauenburg [1068]
U 537 Schrewe [1127]
U 538 Gossler [371]
U 539 Lauterbach-Emden [707]
U 540 Kasch [583]
U 541 Petersen [920]
U 542 Coester [172]
U 543 Hellriegel [454]
U 544 Mattke [795]
U 545 Mannesmann [782]
U 546 Just [569]
U 547 Sturm [1255], Niemeyer [880]
U 548 Zimmermann [1401], Pfeffer [923], Krempl [661]
U 549 Krankenhagen [657]
U 550 Hänert [401]
U 551 Schrott [1137]
U 552 Topp [1280], Popp [936], Lube [756]
U 553 Thurmann [1272]
U 554 Lohmann [747], Stein [1220], v. Trotha [1282], Siebold [1192], Stolzenburg [1241], Rave [977], Remus [994]
U 555 Horrer [516], v. Hartmann [426], Rendtel [995], Saar [1041], Erdmann [258], Fritz [327]
U 556 Wohlfarth [1370]
U 557 Paulshen [912]
U 558 Krech [659]
U 559 Heidtmann [439]
U 560 Zetzsche [1398], Cordes [176], v. Rappard [971], Wicke [1345], Jacobs [538]
U 561 Bartels [43], Schomburg [1117], Henning [461]
U 562 Collmann [174], Hamm [404]
U 563 Bargsten [38], v. Hartmann [426], Borchardt [105]
U 564 Suhren [1259], Fiedler [280]
U 565 Jebsen [548], Franken [309], Henning [461]
U 566 Borchert [106], Remus [993], Hornkohl [515]
U 567 Fahr [267], Endrass [252]
U 568 Preuss [946]
U 569 Hinsch [492], Johannsen [561]
U 570 Rahmlow [967]
U 571 Möhlmann [831], Lüssow [762]
U 572 Hirsacker [495], Kummentat [681]
U 573 Heinsohn [449]
U 574 Gengelbach [350]
U 575 Heydemann [481], vacant 30.7.43–11.9.43, Boehmer [97]
U 576 Heinicke [445]
U 577 Schauenburg [1067]
U 578 Rehwinkel [984]
U 579 Lohmann [747], vacant 23.10.41–26.5.42, Ruppelt [1039], Linder [736], Schwarzenberg [1174]
U 580 Kuhlmann [676]
U 581 Pfeifer [924]
U 582 Schulte [1150]
U 583 Ratsch [975]
U 584 Deecke [194], Nölke [885]
U 585 Lohse [749]
U 586 v.d.Esch [260], Götze [367]
U 587 Borcherdt [106]
U 588 Vogel [1305]
U 589 Horrer [516]
U 590 Müller-Edzards [850], Krüer [668]
U 591 Zetzsche [1398], Schrewe [1127], Zetzsche [1398], Sauerbier [1053], Ziesmer [1400]
U 592 Borm [111], vacant 25.7.43–1.9.43, Jaschke [547]
U 593 Kelbling [588]
U 594 Hoffmann [499], Mumm [859]
U 595 Quaet-Faslem [954]
U 596 Jahn [544], Nonn [889], Kolbus [648]
U 597 Bopst [104]
U 598 Holtorf [509]
U 599 Breithaupt [129]
U 600 Zurmuhlen [1410]
U 601 Grau [380], Hansen [410]

U 602 Schüler [1140]
U 603 Kölzer [637], Bertelsmann [78], Baltz [36], Bertelsmann [78]
U 604 Höltring [498]
U 605 Schütze [1145]
U 606 Klatt [610], v. d. Esch [260], Döhler [212]
U 607 Mengersen [811], Jeschonnek [555]
U 608 Struckmeier [1251], Reisener [991]
U 609 Rudloff [1035]
U 610 v. Freyberg [319]
U 611 v. Jacobs [539]
U 612 Siegmann [1194], vacant 6.8.42–30.5.43, Petersen [921], Dick [199]
U 613 Köppe [644]
U 614 Sträter [1242]
U 615 Kapitzky [581]
U 616 Spindlegger [1207], Koitschka [647]
U 617 Brandi [122]
U 618 Baberg [24], Faust [270]
U 619 Makowski [776]
U 620 Stein [1220]
U 621 Schünemann [1143], Kruschka [671], Stuckmann [1252]
U 622 Queck [955]
U 623 Schröder [1132]
U 624 v. Soden-Fraunhofen [1201]
U 625 Benker [68], Sureth [1260], Straub [1243]
U 626 Bade [27]
U 627 Kindelbacher [607]
U 628 Hasenschar [428]
U 629 Bugs [152]
U 630 Winkler [1358]
U 631 Krüger [670]
U 632 Karpf [582]
U 633 Müller [842]
U 634 Brosin [134], Dahlhaus [184]
U 635 Eckelmann [234]
U 636 Hildebrandt [485], Schendel [1074]
U 637 Dieterich [202], Zedelius [1393], Fabricius [265], Riekeberg [1006], Ehrhardt [238], Weber [1320]
U 638 Staudinger [1213], Bernbeck [77], Staudinger [1213]

U 639 Wichmann [1344]
U 640 Nagel [864]
U 641 Rendtel [995]
U 642 Brünning [142]
U 643 Speidel [1206]
U 644 Jensen [551]
U 645 Ferro [277]
U 646 Wulff [1382]
U 647 Hertin [468]
U 648 Stahl [1211]
U 649 Tiesler [1274]
U 650 v. Witzendorff [1367], Tinschert [1277], v. Witzendorff [1367], Gerke [352], Zorn [1408]
U 651 Lohmeyer [748]
U 652 Fraatz [302]
U 653 Feiler [273], Kandler [579]
U 654 Hesse [473], Forster [299]
U 655 Dumrese [224]
U 656 Kröning [666]
U 657 Radke [964], Göllnitz [365]
U 658 Senkel [1190]
U 659 Stock [1236]
U 660 Baur [56]
U 661 v. Lilienfeld [733]
U 662 Hermann [465], vacant 15.2.43–9.3.43, Müller [844]
U 663 Schmid [1094]
U 664 Graef [373]
U 665 Haupt [432]
U 666 Engel [254], Wilberg [1352]
U 667 Schroeteler [1133], vacant 20.5.44–9.7.44, Lange [698]
U 668 v. Eickstedt [242], Henning [461]
U 669 Köhl [632]
U 670 Hyronimus [532]
U 671 Hewicker [478], Hegewald [436]
U 672 Lawaetz [710]
U 673 Haelbich [400], Sauer [1051], Gerke [352]
U 674 Muhs [858]
U 675 Sammler [1047]
U 676 Sass [1050]
U 677 Weber [1321], Ady [5]
U 678 Hyronimus [532]

U 679 Breckwoldt [127], Aust [23]
U 680 Ulber [1290]
U 681 Bach [25], Gebauer [341]
U 682 Thienemann [1267]
U 683 Keller [590]
U 684–700 numbers not allocated
U 701 Degen [197]
U 702 v. Rabenau [959]
U 703 Bielfeld [81], Brünner [141]
U 704 Kessler [598], vacant 4/43–11.6.43, Hagenau [402], Ady [5], Schwarzkopf [1175], Nolte [888]
U 705 Horn [513]
U 706 v. Zitzewitz [1406]
U 707 Gretschel [384]
U 708 Heintze [450], Andersen [13], Pick [926], Kühn [673]
U 709 Weber [1319], Ites [536]
U 710 v. Carlowitz [162]
U 711 Lange [695]
U 712 Pietschmann [929], Koch [630], v. Ketelhodt [599]
U 713 Gosejacob [370]
U 714 Schwebcke [1177]
U 715 Röttger [1020]
U 716 Dunkelberg [225], Gréus [385], Thimme [1269]
U 717 v. Rothkirch [1034]
U 718 Wiedulwilt [1349]
U 719 Steffens [1216]
U 720 Schüler [1141], Boldt [102], Wendelberger [1330]
U 721 Wollschläger [1378], Fabricius [266]
U 722 Reimers [990]
U 723–730 numbers not allocated
U 731 Techand [1263], v. Keller [593]
U 732 Carlsen [163]
U 733 v. Trotha [1283], vacant 12.5.43–14.12.43, Hellmann [453], Hammer [405]
U 734 Blauert [88]
U 735 Börner [98]
U 736 Reff [982]
U 737 Poeschel [933], Brasack [124], Gréus [385]

U 738 Hoffmann [502]
U 739 Mangold [779], Kosnick [654]
U 740 Stark [1212]
U 741 Palmgren [907]
U 742 Schwassmann [1176]
U 743 Kandzior [580]
U 744 Blischke [90]
U 745 v. Trotha [1283]
U 746 (ex-Italian *S-2*) Kaschke [584], Lottner [755]
U 747 (ex-Italian *S-3*) Jewinski [558], Zahnow [1386]
U 748 (ex-Italian *S-5*) Roth [1033], Knecht [620], Puschmann [952], Dingler [206]
U 749 (ex-Italian *S-7*) Fischler [291], Fischer [286], Huisgen [524]
U 750 (ex-Italian *S-9*) v. Bitter [85], Grawert [382]
U 751 Bigalk [82]
U 752 Schroeter [1134]
U 753 v. Mannstein [780]
U 754 Oestermann [894]
U 755 Göing [364]
U 756 Harney [417]
U 757 Deetz [196]
U 758 Manseck [783], Feindt [274]
U 759 Friedrich [324]
U 760 Blum [92]
U 761 Geider [343]
U 762 Hille [487], Pietschmann [929]
U 763 Cordes [176], Braun [126], Schröter [1136]
U 764 v. Bremen [130]
U 765 Wendt [1333]
U 766 Wilke [1353]
U 767 Dankleff [188]
U 768 Buttjer [159]
U 769–770 numbers not allocated
U 771 Block [91]
U 772 Rademacher [961]
U 773 Lange [700], Baldus [32]
U 774 Buttjer [159], Sausmikat [1054]
U 775 Taschenmacher [1262]
U 776 Martin [790]

U 777 Ruperti [1038]
U 778 Jürs [564]
U 779 Stegmann [1219]
U 780–91 numbers not allocated
U 792 Heitz [451], Duis [223]
U 793 Schauenburg [1066], Schmidt [1095]
U 794 Klug [616], Becker [60]
U 795 Selle [1189]
U 796–800 numbers not allocated
U 801 Brans [123]
U 802 Steinhaus [1225], Schmoeckel [1101]
U 803 Schimpf [1086]
U 804 Meyer [820]
U 805 Bernadelli [76]
U 806 Hornbostel [514]
U 807–820 numbers not allocated
U 821 Fabricius [266], Fischer [286], Knackfuss [619]
U 822 Elsinghorst [247]
U 823–824 numbers not allocated
U 825 Stoelker [1240]
U 826 Lübcke [757]
U 827 Hunck [526], Baberg [24]
U 828 John [562]
U 829–840 numbers not allocated
U 841 Bender [67]
U 842 Heller [452]
U 843 Herwartz [469]
U 844 Möller [833]
U 845 Behrens [66], Hoffmann [505], Weber [1322]
U 846 Hashagen [429]
U 847 Guggenberger [393], Rollmann [1024], Metzler [816], Kuppisch [684]
U 848 Rollmann [1024]
U 849 Schultze [1154]
U 850 Ewerth [262]
U 851 Weingärtner [1327]
U 852 Eck [232]
U 853 Sommer [1203], Frömsdorf [332], Wermuth [1337], Kuhnke [679], Frömsdorf [332]
U 854 Weiher [1326]
U 855 Sürenhagen [1256], Ohlsen [898]

U 856 Wittenberg [1366]
U 857 Premauer [943]
U 858 Bode [94]
U 859 Jebsen [548]
U 860 Büchel [147]
U 861 Oesten [893]
U 862 Timm [1276]
U 863 v. d. Esch [260]
U 864 Wolfram [1377]
U 865 Stellmacher [1228]
U 866 Pommerehne [934], Rogowsky [1021]
U 867 v. Mühlendahl [840]
U 868 Rauch [976], Turre [1295]
U 869 Neuerburg [871]
U 870 Hechler [434]
U 871 Ganzer [338]
U 872 Grau [380]
U 873 Steinhoff [1226]
U 874 Petersen [921]
U 875 Preuss [945]
U 876 Bahn [29]
U 877 Findeisen [282]
U 878 Rodig [1014]
U 879 Manchen [777]
U 880 Schötzau [1111]
U 881 Frischke [326]
U 882 number not allocated
U 883 Gaude [339], Uebel [1286]
U 884 Brünig [139]
U 885–888 numbers not allocated
U 889 Braeucker [118]
U 890 number not allocated
U 891 Mehne [806]
U 892–900 numbers not allocated
U 901 Schrenk [1125]
U 902 number not allocated
U 903 Hellmann [453], Fränzel [303], Tinschert [1277]
U 904 Fritz [327], Erdmann [258], Stührmann [1254]
U 905 Brüllau [136], Schwarting [1170]
U 906 number not allocated
U 907 Cabolet [160]
U 908–920 numbers not allocated

U 921 Leu [727], Neumann [873], Werner [1338]
U 922 v. und z. Arco-Zinneberg [17], Aust [23], Käselau [572]
U 923 Frömmer [331]
U 924 Schild [1083]
U 925 Knoke [624]
U 926 v. Wenden [1331], Roost [1025], Rehren [983]
U 927 Ebert [231]
U 928 Stähler [1210]
U 929 Schulz [1161]
U 930 Mohr [836]
U 931–950 numbers not allocated
U 951 Pressel [994]
U 952 Curio [180]
U 953 Marbach [784], Werner [1339], Steinbrink [1222]
U 954 Loewe [746]
U 955 Baden [28]
U 956 Mohs [837]
U 957 Saar [1041], Schaar [1056]
U 958 Groth [390], Stege [1217]
U 959 Duppel [226], Weitz [1328]
U 960 Heinrich [447]
U 961 Fischer [289]
U 962 Liesberg [732]
U 963 Boddenberg [93], Müller [846], Wentz [1335]
U 964 Hummerjohann [525]
U 965 Ohling [897], Unverzagt [1294]
U 966 Wolf [1371]
U 967 Loeder [742], Brandi [122], Eberbach [227]
U 968 Westphalen [1341]
U 969 Dobbert [208]
U 970 Ketels [600]
U 971 Zeplien [1397]
U 972 König [641]
U 973 Paepenmöller [904]
U 974 Zaubitzer [1391], Wolff [1375]
U 975 Ebersbach [229], Frerks [317], Jeschke [554], Koch [630], Brauel [125]
U 976 Tiesler [1274]
U 977 Leilich [716], Schäffer [1062]
U 978 Pulst [950]
U 979 Meermeier [803]
U 980 Dahms [185]
U 981 Sitek [1198], Keller [591]
U 982 Grochowiak [387], Schwirley [1180], Hartmann [421]
U 983 Reimers [990]
U 984 Sieder [1193]
U 985 Kessler [598], Wolff [1375]
U 986 Kaiser [575]
U 987 Schreyer [1128]
U 988 Dobberstein [207]
U 989 v. Roithberg [1015]
U 990 Nordheimer [890]
U 991 Balke [33]
U 992 Falke [268]
U 993 Hilbig [484], Steinmetz [1227]
U 994 Ackermann [4], Melzer [809]
U 995 Köhntopp [634], Hess [472]
U 996 v. Lehsten [715]
U 997 Lehmann [713]
U 998 Fiedler [280]
U 999 Hansen [409], Peters [918], Heibges [437]
U 1000 Müller [847]
U 1001 Blaudow [87]
U 1002 Schubart [1138], Boos [103]
U 1003 Strübing [1250]
U 1004 Schimmelpfennig [1085], Hinz [493]
U 1005 Methner [814], Lauth [708]
U 1006 Voigt [1308]
U 1007 Hornkohl [515 Klingspor [613], Wicke [1345], Raabe [957], v. Witzendorff [1367]
U 1008 Todenhagen [1279], Gessner [355]
U 1009 Hilgendorf [486], Zehle [1394]
U 1010 Bitter [84], Strauch [1244]
U 1011–1012 numbers not allocated
U 1013 Linck [734]
U 1014 Glaser [340]
U 1015 Boos [103]
U 1016 Ehrhardt [238],
U 1017 v. Reventlow-Criminil [997], Riecken [1002]
U 1018 Faber [264], Burmeister [157]

U 1019 Rinck [1010]
U 1020 Eberlein [228]
U 1021 Holpert [508]
U 1022 Ernst [259]
U 1023 Strenger [1248], Schroeteler [1133]
U 1024 Gutteck [395]
U 1025 Pick [925], Curio [180]
U 1026 Hansen [408]
U 1027 number not allocated
U 1028 Fabricius [265]
U 1029–1050 numbers not allocated
U 1051 v. Holleben [507]
U 1052 Weidner [1325], Scholz [1114]
U 1053 Lange [694]
U 1054 Riekeberg [1006]
U 1055 Meyer [822]
U 1056 Schwarz [1173], Schröder [1130]
U 1057 Lüth [763]
U 1058 Bruder [1143]
U 1059 Brüninghaus [140], Leupold [728]
U 1060 Brammer [119]
U 1061 Hinrichs [491], Jäger [541]
U 1062 Albrecht [9]
U 1063 Stephan [1230]
U 1064 Schneidewind [1106]
U 1065 Panitz [909]
U 1066–1100 numbers not allocated
U 1101 Dübler [220]
U 1102 Schwarting [1170], vacant 13.5.44–14.8.44, Sell [1188]
U 1103 Bungards [155], Sausmikat [1054], Schmidt [1096], Iversen [537], Eisele [243]
U 1104 Perleberg [914]
U 1105 Schwarz [1171]
U 1106 Bartke [45]
U 1107 Parduhn [910]
U 1108 Wigand [1350]
U 1109 caretaking engineer officer only 31.8.44–9.9.44, van Riesen [1008]
U 1110 Bach [26]
U 1111–1130 numbers not allocated
U 1131 Fiebig [279]
U 1132 Koch [629]
U 1133–1160 numbers not allocated

U 1161 (ex-Italian *S-8*) Raabe [957], Schwalbach [1168]
U 1162 (ex-Italian *S-10*) Sachse [1044], Krempl [661], Euler [261], Ketels [600]
U 1163 Balduhn [31]
U 1164 Schlömer [1091], Wengel [1334]
U 1165 Homann [510]
U 1166 Wagner [1312 Ballert [35]
U 1167 Roeder-Pesch [1016], Bortfeldt [114]
U 1168 Grasse [378], Umlauf [1292]
U 1169 Goldbeck [368]
U 1170 Justi [570]
U 1171 Nachtigall [863], Koopmann [649]
U 1172 Kuhlmann [677]
U 1173–1190 numbers not allocated
U 1191 Grau [379]
U 1192 Zeissler [1395], Jewinski [558], Meenen [801]
U 1193 Guse [394]
U 1194 Nolte [888], Laudahn [706], Zeissler [1395]
U 1195 Schröter [1136], Cordes [176]
U 1196 Brand [120], Ballert [34]
U 1197 Baum [51], Lau [704]
U 1198 Peters [917]
U 1199 Nollmann [887]
U 1200 Mangels [778]
U 1201 Ebert [230], Ahlers [7], Merkle [812]
U 1202 Thomsen [1270]
U 1203 Steinbrink [1222], Seeger [1182]
U 1204 Mäueler [773], Jestel [557]
U 1205 Zander [1387]
U 1206 Fritze [329], Schlitt [1090]
U 1207 Lindemann [735]
U 1208 Hagene [403]
U 1209 Hülsenbeck [522]
U 1210 Gabert [336]
U 1211–1220 numbers not allocated
U 1221 Kölzer [636], Ackermann [3]
U 1222 Bielfeld [81]
U 1223 Bosüner [115], Kneip [621]
U 1224 Preuss [945]
U 1225 Sauerberg [1052], Scherraus [1079]
U 1226 Claussen [169]

INDEX

U 1227 Altmeier [11]
U 1228 Marienfeld [786]
U 1229 Zinke [1404]
U 1230 Hilbig [483]
U 1231 Lessing [726], Wicke [1345]
U 1232 Dobratz [211], Roth [1033]
U 1233 Kuhn [678], Niemeyer [880]
U 1234 Thurmann [1271, vacant 15.5.44–16.10.44, Wrede [1379]
U 1235 Bahn [29], Barsch [40]
U 1236–1270 numbers not allocated
U 1271 Knipping [623], Thienemann [1267]
U 1272 Meentzen [802], Schattenburg [1065]
U 1273 Voswinkel [1309], Knollmann [625]
U 1274 Kuscher [687], Fitting [292]
U 1275 Niss [883], Frohberg [333]
U 1276 Wendt [1332]
U 1277 Stever [1232]
U 1278 Müller-Bethke [849]
U 1279 Falke [269]
U 1280–1300 numbers not allocated
U 1301 Feufel [278], Lenkeit [723]
U 1302 Herwartz [470]
U 1303 Baum [51], Herglotz [464]
U 1304 Süss [1258]
U 1305 Christiansen [164]
U 1306 Kiessling [604]
U 1307 Buscher [158]
U 1308 Besold [79]
U 1309–1404 numbers not allocated
U 1405 Rex [999]
U 1406 Klug [616]
U 1407 Heitz [451]
U 1408 number not allocated
U 1409 Schauenburg [1066]

New Series
U 2321 Barschkis [41]
U 2322 Heckel [435]
U 2323 Angermann [14], Schultz [1151]
U 2324 Hass [430], v. Rappard [971]
U 2325 Schüler [1141], Eckel [233]
U 2326 Jobst [559]
U 2327 Mürl [855], Müller [846], Pahl [905], Schulz [1159]
U 2328 Scholle [1112], Lawrence [711]
U 2329 Schlott [1092]
U 2330 Beckmann [62]
U 2331 Pahl [905]
U 2332 Bornkessel [113], Junker [567]
U 2333 Baumann [53]
U 2334 Angermann [14]
U 2335 Benthin [70]
U 2336 Vockel [1302], Klusmeier [617]
U 2337 Behnisch [65]
U 2338 Kaiser [573]
U 2339 Woermann [1369]
U 2340 Klusmeier [617]
U 2341 Böhm [95]
U 2342 v. Mittelbiberach [1058]
U 2343 Fuhlendorf [335], Gaude [339]
U 2344 Ellerlage [245]
U 2345 Steffen [1215]
U 2346 v.d.Höh [497]
U 2347 Ulbing [1291]
U 2348 Goschzik [369]
U 2349 Müller [843]
U 2350 Schauer [1069]
U 2351 Brückner [135]
U 2352 Budzyn [146]
U 2353 Hillmann [488]
U 2354 Wex [1343]
U 2355 Franke [307]
U 2356 [419]
U 2357 Heinrich [446]
U 2358 Breun [131]
U 2359 Bischoff [83]
U 2360 Schrobach [1129]
U 2361 v. Hennig [460]
U 2362 Czekowski [181]
U 2363 Frahm [304]
U 2364 Hengen [456], Remus [993]
U 2365 Korfmann [650], Christiansen [165]
U 2366 Jäckel [540]
U 2367 Schröder [1131]
U 2368 Ufermann [1287]
U 2369 Schulz [1152], Pahl [905]

U 2370 Junker [567], Bornkessel [113]
U 2371 Kühne [674]
U 2372–2373 numbers not allocated
U 2374 Waldschmidt [1314]
U 2375–2499 numbers not allocated
U 2501 Hübschen [521], caretaker engineer officer only 21.11.44–3.5.45
U 2502 Mannesmann [782], Hornkohl [515], Franke [308]
U 2503 Tiesler [1274], Wächter [1311]
U 2504 Günther [392], caretaker engineer officer only 20.11.44–2.5.45
U 2505 Düppe [222]
U 2506 v. Schroeter [1135]
U 2507 Siegmann [1194]
U 2508 Christiansen [165]
U 2509 Schendel [1075]
U 2510 Herrmann [467]
U 2511 Schnee [1102]
U 2512 Nordheimer [890]
U 2513 Bungards [155], Topp [1280]
U 2514 Wahlen [1313]
U 2515 Borchers [107], Linder [736]
U 2516 Kallipke [576]
U 2517 Hansen [409]
U 2518 Weidner [1325]
U 2519 Cremer [178]
U 2520 Schubart [1138], Schendel [1075]
U 2521 Methner [814]
U 2522 Queck [955]
U 2523 Ketels [600]
U 2524 v. Witzendorff [1367]
U 2525 Otto [902]
U 2526 Hohmann [506]
U 2527 Götze [367]
U 2528 Curio [180], caretaker engineer officer only 24.4.45–2.5.45
U 2529 Feufel [278], Kallipke [576]
U 2530 Bokelberg [101]
U 2531 Niss [883]
U 2532 number not allocated
U 2533 Günther [392]
U 2534 Drews [218]
U 2535 Bitter [84]

U 2536 Vöge [1303]
U 2537 Dobbert [208]
U 2538 Klapdor [609]
U 2539 Jewinski [558], Johann [560]
U 2540 Schultze [1156]
U 2541 Stellmann [1229], Wahlen [1313]
U 2542 Hübschen [521]
U 2543 Stolzenburg [1241]
U 2544 Meinlschmidt [808]
U 2545 v. Bülow [150], v. Müffling [839]
U 2546 Dobbert [208]
U 2547 Richter [1001]
U 2548 Utischill [1296]
U 2549 Sureth [1260]
U 2550 Wolff [1374]
U 2551 Schaar [1056]
U 2552 Rudolph [1036]
U 2553 Wilke [1353]
U 2554–2557 numbers not allocated
U 2558 no firm information; *Baubelehrung* Cdr thought to be Brunke (?), most of crew ex-*U 2523*
U 2559–2560 numbers not allocated
U 2561 Heinicke [444]
U 2562 Isermeyer [634]

New Series
U 3001 Vogel [1304], vacant 27.11.44–4/45, Peters [918]
U 3002 Manseck [783], Kaiser [574]
U 3003 Kregelin [660]
U 3004 Thurmann [1271], Peschel [915], vacant after 19.4.45
U 3005 Sitek [1198], Hinrichs [490]
U 3006 Popp [936], Geisler [344], Linder [736], Fischer [286]
U 3007 Manseck [783]
U 3008 Schlömer [1091], Manseck [783]
U 3009 Schimpf [1086]
U 3010 Ebert [230], Topp [1280], vacant from 26.4.45
U 3011 Tinschert [1277], Fränzel [303]
U 3012 Kloevekorn [614], Bungards [155]/Meier (?)

U 3013 Simmermacher [1196]
U 3014 Marbach [784]
U 3015 Grau [380]
U 3016 Meentzen [802]
U 3017 Lindschau [739]
U 3018 Breinlinger [128]
U 3019 Racky [960]
U 3020 Mäueler [773]
U 3021 van Meeteren [804]
U 3022 Weber [1321]
U 3023 Harms [415]
U 3024 Blaich [86]
U 3025 Vogel [1304]
U 3026 Drescher [215]
U 3027 Mehne [806]
U 3028 Christophersen [166]
U 3029 Lamby [690]
U 3030 Luttmann [767]
U 3031 Sach [1042]
U 3032 Slevogt [1199]
U 3033 Callsen [161]
U 3034 Prehn [941], Willner [1356]
U 3035 Gerke [352]
U 3036 Knecht [620]
U 3037 Emmermann [249], Janssen [546]
U 3038 Brünig [139]
U 3039 Ruperti [1038]
U 3040 Robbert [1013]
U 3041 Vieth [1301], Hornkohl [515]
U 3042 Petersen [919]
U 3043 number not allocated
U 3044 Jaek [542], v. Lehsten [715]
U 3045 Peters [918]
U 3046 van Stipriaan [1235]
U 3047 no details available
U 3048 Laubert [705]
U 3049 Geisler [344]
U 3050 Reimann [989]
U 3051 Müller-Koelbl [851]
U 3052 number not allocated
U 3053 Dr Carl Billich *Baubelehrung* Cdr but nothing further known
U 3054–3056 numbers not allocated
U 3057 Neumann [874]
U 3058 number not allocated
U 3059 Knecht [620]
U 3060 Bart [42]
U 3061 number not allocated
U 3062 Schröter [1136]

New Series
U 3501 Münster [854], vacant 5.10.44–4/45, Wunderlich [1383], Schmidt-Weichert [1099]
U 3502 Schultz [1152]
U 3503 Deiring [198]
U 3504 Siebold [1192]
U 3505 Willner [1356]
U 3506 Thäter [1265]
U 3507 Niethmann [882], Schley [1087]
U 3508 v. Lehsten [715]
U 3509 Hornkohl [515], Voswinkel [1309], Franke [308], Neitzsch [869]
U 3510 Schwirley [1180]
U 3511 Grasse [378], Ketels [600], Schrenk [1126]
U 3512 Hornkohl [515]
U 3513 Nachtigall [863]
U 3514 Fritze [329], Willeke [1355]
U 3515 Kuscher [687]
U 3516 Wengel [1334], Grote [389]
U 3517 Münster [854]
U 3518 Brünning [142]
U 3519 v. Harpe [418]
U 3520 Ballert [35]
U 3521 Keller [591]
U 3522 Lenzmann [724]
U 3523 Müller [847]
U 3524 Witt [1362]
U 3525 Gaude [339], Kranich [656]
U 3526 Hilbig [484]
U 3527 Kronenbitter [667]
U 3528 Zwarg [1411]
U 3529 Schmidt [1096]
U 3530 Brauel [125], Koch [630]
U 3531 Heinz (?) Bergner *Baubelehrung* Cdr 7.KLA to 18.12.44; nothing further known
U 3532 Niemeyer [880]

U 3533 Jaenicke [543]
U 3534 Wolff [1375]
U 3535 Zenker [1396]
U 3536 Gode [362]
U 3537 Korndörfer [651]

New Series
U 4701 Wiechmann [1348]
U 4702 Seeliger [1184]
U 4703 Scholz [1115]
U 4704 Franceschi [306]
U 4705 Landt-Hayen [691]
U 4706 Schneider [1105]
U 4707 Leder [712]
U 4708 Schultz [1151]
U 4709 Berkemann [75]
U 4710 v. Friedeburg [321]
U 4711 Endler [251]
U 4712 Rohlfing [1022], Fleige [294]
U 4713 Kaeding [571]
U 4714 v. Ahlefeld [6]
U 4715–4718 numbers not allocated
U 4719 Waldschmidt [1314]

Foreign Submarines Acquired
U A (ex-Turkish *Baltiray*) Cohausz [173], Eckermann [235], Cohausz [173], Schnoor [1107], Schäfer [1059], Peters [916], Arco-Zinneberg [17]
U B Mahn [774]
UC 1 Kiesewetter [603], Lange [692], Wollschläger [1378], Lange [692], Brockmann [132]
UC 2 Wollschläger [1378]
UD 1 Rigele [1009], Schäfer [1059], Venier [1299], Ketelsen [601], Weidner [1325]
UD 2 Venier [1299], Scholz [1114]
UD 3 Rigele [1009], Seeger [1181]
UD 4 Brümmer-Patzig [138], v. Singule [1197], Bernbeck [77], Schäfer [1059], Bart [42]
UD 5 Mahn [774], König [641], v. Kameke [578], Scheltz [1073]

UF 2 Lange [692], Gehrken [342]
UIT 21 Steinfeldt [1224]
UIT 22 Wunderlich [1383]
UIT 23 Schäfer [1059], vacant 8.1.44–13.2.44, Striegler [1249]
UIT 24 Pahls [906]
UIT 25 Striegler [1249], Schrein [1123], Meier [807]